**Exponential function:** $y = P_0 a^x$    **Logarithm function:** $y = \ln x$

**Periodic functions**

**Logistic function:** $y = \dfrac{L}{1 + Ce^{-kx}}$    **Surge function:** $y = axe^{-bx}$

# FORMULA SUMMARY: ALGEBRA

## Lines

Slope of line through $(x_1, y_1)$ and $(x_2, y_2)$:

$$m = \frac{y_2 - y_1}{x_2 - x_1}$$

Point-slope equation of line through $(x_1, y_1)$ with slope $m$:

$$y - y_1 = m(x - x_1)$$

Slope-intercept equation of line with slope $m$ and $y$-intercept $b$:

$$y = b + mx$$

## Definition of Zero, Negative, and Fractional Exponents

$$a^0 = 1, \quad a^{-1} = \frac{1}{a}, \quad \text{and, in general, } a^{-x} = \frac{1}{a^x}$$

$$a^{1/2} = \sqrt{a}, \quad a^{1/3} = \sqrt[3]{a}, \quad \text{and, in general, } a^{1/n} = \sqrt[n]{a}.$$

$$\text{Also, } a^{m/n} = \sqrt[n]{a^m} = (\sqrt[n]{a})^m.$$

## Rules of Exponents

1. $a^x \cdot a^t = a^{x+t}$     For example, $2^4 \cdot 2^3 = (2 \cdot 2 \cdot 2 \cdot 2) \cdot (2 \cdot 2 \cdot 2) = 2^7$.

2. $\dfrac{a^x}{a^t} = a^{x-t}$     For example, $\dfrac{2^4}{2^3} = \dfrac{2 \cdot 2 \cdot 2 \cdot 2}{2 \cdot 2 \cdot 2} = 2^1$.

3. $(a^x)^t = a^{xt}$     For example, $(2^3)^2 = 2^3 \cdot 2^3 = 2^6$.

## Definition of Natural Log

$y = \ln x$ means $e^y = x$; *for example:* $\ln 1 = 0$, since $e^0 = 1$.

## Rules of Natural Logarithms

$$\ln(AB) = \ln A + \ln B$$

$$\ln\left(\frac{A}{B}\right) = \ln A - \ln B$$

$$\ln A^p = p \ln A$$

## Identities

$$\ln e^x = x$$

$$e^{\ln x} = x$$

# APPLIED CALCULUS

## Fifth Edition

# APPLIED CALCULUS

## Fifth Edition

Produced by the Calculus Consortium and initially funded by a National Science Foundation Grant.

Deborah Hughes-Hallett
*University of Arizona*

Andrew M. Gleason
*Harvard University*

Eric Connally
*Harvard University Extension*

Selin Kalaycıoğlu
*New York University*

Brigitte Lahme
*Sonoma State University*

David O. Lomen
*University of Arizona*

Patti Frazer Lock
*St. Lawrence University*

David Lovelock
*University of Arizona*

Guadalupe I. Lozano
*University of Arizona*

William G. McCallum
*University of Arizona*

Brad G. Osgood
*Stanford University*

Cody L. Patterson
*University of Arizona*

Aaron D. Wootton
*University of Portland*

Daniel E. Flath
*Macalester College*

Douglas Quinney
*University of Keele*

Karen Rhea
*University of Michigan*

Adam H. Spiegler
*Loyola University Chicago*

Jeff Tecosky-Feldman
*Haverford College*

Thomas W. Tucker
*Colgate University*

with the assistance of
Otto K. Bretscher
*Colby College*

Coordinated by
Elliot J. Marks

# WILEY

| PUBLISHER | Laurie Rosatone |
| SENIOR ACQUISITIONS EDITOR | David Dietz |
| DEVELOPMENTAL EDITOR | Anne Scanlan-Rohrer/Two Ravens Editorial |
| SENIOR PRODUCT DESIGNER | Tom Kulesa |
| MARKETING MANAGER | Melanie Kurkjian |
| OPERATIONS MANAGER | Melissa Edwards |
| ASSISTANT CONTENT EDITOR | Jacqueline Sinacori |
| SENIOR PRODUCTION EDITOR | Ken Santor |
| CONTENT EDITORIAL ASSISTANT | Courtney Welsh |
| COVER DESIGNER | Madelyn Lesure |
| COVER AND CHAPTER OPENING PHOTO | © Patrick Zephyr/Patrick Zephyr Nature Photography |

Problems from Calculus: The Analysis of Functions, by Peter D. Taylor (Toronto: Wall & Emerson, Inc., 1992). Reprinted with permission of the publisher.

This book was set in Times Roman by the Consortium using TeX, Mathematica, and the package AsTeX, which was written by Alex Kasman. It was printed and bound by R.R. Donnelley / Willard. The cover was printed by R.R. Donnelley.

This material is based upon work supported by the National Science Foundation under Grant No. DUE-9352905. Opinions expressed are those of the authors and not necessarily those of the Foundation.

Library of Congress Cataloging-in-Publication Data

Hughes-Hallett, Deborah.
   Applied calculus / Deborah Hughes-Hallett, Patti Frazer Lock, Andrew M. Gleason. -- Fifth edition.
      pages cm
   Includes index.
   ISBN 978-1-118-17492-0 (paperback : alk. paper) -- ISBN 978-1-118-39368-0  1.  Calculus.  I. Lock, Patti Frazer. II. Gleason, Andrew M. III. Title.
   QA303.2.H843 2014
   515--dc23
                              2013033550

ISBN: 978-1-118-17492-0

Binder Ready Version ISBN: 978-1-118-39368-0

Printed in the United States of America

10 9 8 7 6 5 4 3 2 1

*We dedicate this book to Andrew M. Gleason.*

*His brilliance and the extraordinary kindness and dignity with which he treated others made an enormous difference to us, and to many, many people. Andy brought out the best in everyone.*

*Deb Hughes Hallett*
*for the Calculus Consortium*

# PREFACE

Calculus is one of the greatest achievements of the human intellect. Inspired by problems in astronomy, Newton and Leibniz developed the ideas of calculus 300 years ago. Since then, each century has demonstrated the power of calculus to illuminate questions in mathematics, the physical sciences, engineering, and the social and biological sciences.

Calculus has been so successful because of its extraordinary power to reduce complicated problems to simple rules and procedures. Therein lies the danger in teaching calculus: it is possible to teach the subject as nothing but the rules and procedures—thereby losing sight of both the mathematics and of its practical value. This edition of *Applied Calculus* continues our effort to promote courses in which understanding reinforces computation.

## Mathematical Concepts and Modeling

The first stage in the development of mathematical thinking is the acquisition of a clear intuitive picture of the central ideas. In the next stage, the student learns to reason with the intuitive ideas in plain English. After this foundation has been laid, there is a choice of direction. All students benefit from both mathematical concepts and modeling, but the balance may differ for different groups of students. For instructors wishing to emphasize the connection between calculus and other fields, the text includes:

- A variety of problems and examples from the **biological sciences** and **economics**.
- Models from the **health sciences** and of **population growth**.
- New problems on **sustainability**.
- New case studies on **medicine** by David E. Sloane, MD.

## Active Learning: Good Problems

As instructors ourselves, we know that interactive classrooms and well-crafted problems promote student learning. Since its inception, the hallmark of our text has been its innovative and engaging problems. These problems probe student understanding in ways often taken for granted. Praised for their creativity and variety, the influence of these problems has extended far beyond the users of our textbook.

The Fifth Edition continues this tradition. Under our approach, which we called the "Rule of Four," ideas are presented graphically, numerically, symbolically, and verbally, thereby encouraging students with a variety of learning styles to expand their knowledge. This edition expands the types of problems available:

- End of **Section Problems** reinforce the ideas of that section and make connections with earlier sections; **Chapter Review Problems** ask students to review ideas from the whole chapter.

- **ConcepTests** promote active learning in the classroom. These can be used with or without clickers (personal response systems), and have been shown to dramatically improve student learning. ConcepTests are particularly useful to instructors teaching in a "flipped classroom." Available in a book or on the web at www.wiley.com/college/hughes-hallett.

- **Projects** at the end of each chapter provide opportunities for a sustained investigation, often using skills from different parts of the course. These now include medical case studies based on clinical practice.

- True-False **Strengthen Your Understanding** questions at the end of every chapter enable students to check their progress.

- **Spreadsheet Projects** in the Appendix to the book provide the opportunity for students to develop their spreadsheet skills while deepening their understanding of functions and calculus.

- **Focus on Practice** exercises at the end of Chapter 3 and 6 (Differentives and Antiderivatives) build student skill and confidence.

- **Online Problems** available in WileyPLUS or WeBWorK, for example. Many problems are randomized, providing students with expanded opportunities for practice with immediate feedback.

## Origin of the Text: A Community of Instructors

This text, like others we write, draws on the experience of a diverse group of authors and users. We have benefitted enormously from input from a broad spectrum of instructors—at research universities, four-year colleges, community colleges, and secondary schools. For *Applied Calculus*, the contributions of colleagues in biology, economics, medicine, business, and other life and social sciences have been equally central to the development of the text. It is the collective wisdom of this community of mathematicians, teachers, natural and social scientists that forms the basis for the new edition.

## What Student Background is Expected?

This book is intended for students in business, the social sciences, and the life sciences. A background in trigonometry is *not* required; the sections involving trigonometry are optional.

We have found the material to be thought-provoking for well-prepared students while still accessible to students with limited algebra backgrounds. Providing numerical and graphical approaches as well as the algebraic gives students several ways of mastering the material. This approach encourages students to persist, thereby lowering failure rate; a pre-test over background material is available in the appendix to the book; An algebra refresher is avalable at the student book companion site at www.wiley.com/college/hughes-hallett.

## Mathematical Skills: A Balance Between Symbolic Manipulation and Technology

To use calculus effectively, students need familiarity with both symbolic manipulation and the use of technology. The balance between them may vary, depending on the needs of the students and the wishes of the instructor. The book is adaptable to many different combinations.

The book does not require any specific software or technology. It has been used with graphing calculators, many types of software, including computer algebra systems. Any technology with the ability to graph functions and perform numerical integration will suffice. Students are expected to use their own judgment to determine where technology is useful.

## The Fifth Edition

Because different users often choose very different topics to cover in a one-semester applied calculus course, we have designed this book for either a one-semester course (with much flexibility in choosing topics) or a two-semester course. Sample syllabi are provided in the Instructor's Manual.

The fifth edition has the same vision as previous editions. In preparing this edition, we solicited comments from a large number of mathematics instructors who had used the text. We continued to discuss with our colleagues in client disciplines the mathematical needs of their students. We were offered many valuable suggestions, which we have tried to incorporate, while maintaining our original commitment to a focused treatment of a limited number of topics. The changes we have made include:

- **Updated data** and **fresh applications** throughout the book, including
  - New problems on **sustainability**.
  - New case studies on **medicine** by David E. Sloane, MD.
- Many **new problems** have been added, designed to build student confidence with basic concepts and to reinforce skills.
- The material on **integration** has been **streamlined and reorganized**.
  - In **Chapter 5**, Sections 5.1-5.5 have been streamlined.
  - **Section 5.6** on Average Value is the former Section 6.1.
  - **Chapters 6,7** have been rearranged and combined, putting an introduction to antiderivatives before the applications to consumer surplus and present value. This gives instructors the choice of evaluating definite integrals numerically or using the Fundamental Theorem of Calculus.

- New **projects** have been added in Chapters 1, 2, 3, 4, 5, and 10.
- As in the previous edition, a **Pre-test** is included for students whose skills may need a refresher prior to taking the course.

## Content

This content represents our vision of how applied calculus can be taught. It is flexible enough to accommodate individual course needs and requirements. Topics can easily be added or deleted, or the order changed.

### Chapter 1: Functions and Change

Chapter 1 introduces the concept of a function and the idea of change, including the distinction between total change, rate of change, and relative change. All elementary functions are introduced here. Although the functions are probably familiar, the graphical, numerical, verbal, and modeling approach to them is likely to be new. We introduce exponential functions early, since they are fundamental to the understanding of real-world processes. The trigonometric functions are optional.

*A brief introduction to elasticity has been added to Section 1.3.*

### Chapter 2: Rate of Change: The Derivative

Chapter 2 presents the key concept of the derivative according to the Rule of Four. The purpose of this chapter is to give the student a practical understanding of the meaning of the derivative and its interpretation as an instantaneous rate of change. Students will learn how the derivative can be used to represent relative rates of change. After finishing this chapter, a student will be able to approximate derivatives numerically by taking difference quotients, visualize derivatives graphically as the slope of the graph, and interpret the meaning of first and second derivatives in various applications. The student will also understand the concept of marginality and recognize the derivative as a function in its own right.

*Focus on Theory:* This section discusses limits and continuity and presents the symbolic definition of the derivative.

### Chapter 3: Short-Cuts to Differentiation

The derivatives of all the functions in Chapter 1 are introduced, as well as the rules for differentiating products, quotients, and composite functions. Students learn how to find relative rates of change using logarithms.

*Focus on Theory:* This section uses the definition of the derivative to obtain the differentiation rules.

*Focus on Practice:* This section provides a collection of differentiation problems for skill-building.

### Chapter 4: Using the Derivative

The aim of this chapter is to enable the student to use the derivative in solving problems, including optimization and graphing. It is not necessary to cover all the sections.

### Chapter 5: Accumulated Change: The Definite Integral

Chapter 5 presents the key concept of the definite integral, in the same spirit as Chapter 2.

The purpose of this chapter is to give the student a practical understanding of the definite integral as a limit of Riemann sums, and to bring out the connection between the derivative and the definite integral in the Fundamental Theorem of Calculus. We use the same method as in Chapter 2, introducing the fundamental concept in depth without going into technique. The student will finish the chapter with a good grasp of the definite integral as a limit of Riemann sums, and the ability to approximate a definite integral numerically and interpret it graphically. The chapter includes applications of definite integrals in a variety of contexts, including the average value of a function.

Chapter 5 can be covered immediately after Chapter 2 without difficulty.

*The introduction to the definite integral has been streamlined. Average values, formerly in Section 6.1, are now in Section 5.6.*

*Focus on Theory:* This section presents the Second Fundamental Theorem of Calculus and the properties of the definite integral.

### Chapter 6: Antiderivatives and Applications

This chapter combines the former Chapter 6 and 7. It covers antiderivatives from a graphical, numerical, and algebraic point of view. The Fundamental Theorem of Calculus is used to evaluate definite integrals.

Optional application sections are included on consumer and producer surplus and on present and future value; the integrals in these sections can be evaluated numerically or using the Fundamental Theorem. The chapter concludes with optional sctions on integration by substitution and integration by parts.

*Section 6.1, on graphical and numerical antiderivatives, is based on the former Section 7.5. Section 6.2, on symbolic antiderivatives, is based on the former Section 7.1. Using the Fundamental Theorem to find definite integrals is in Section 6.3, formerly Section 7.3. Sections 6.4 and 6.5 are the former Sections 6.2 and 6.3. Sections 6.6 and 6.7 are the former Sections 7.2 and 7.4.*

*Focus on Practice:* This section provides a collection of integration problems for skill-building.

### Chapter 7: Probability

This chapter covers probability density functions, cumulative distribution functions, the median and the mean.
*Chapter 7 is the former Chapter 8.*

### Chapter 8: Functions of Several Variables

This chapter introduces functions of two variables from several points of view, using contour diagrams, formulas, and tables. It gives students the skills to read contour diagrams and think graphically, to read tables and think numerically, and to apply these skills, along with their algebraic skills, to modeling. The idea of the partial derivative is introduced from graphical, numerical, and symbolic viewpoints. Partial derivatives are then applied to optimization problems, ending with a discussion of constrained optimization using Lagrange multipliers.
*Chapter 8 is the former Chapter 9.*

*Focus on Theory:* This section uses optimization to derive the formula for the regression line.

### Chapter 9: Mathematical Modeling Using Differential Equations

This chapter introduces differential equations. The emphasis is on modeling, qualitative solutions, and interpretation. This chapter includes applications of systems of differential equations to population models, the spread of disease, and predator-prey interactions.
*Chapter 9 is the former Chapter 10.*

*Focus on Theory:* This section explains the technique of separation of variables.

### Chapter 10: Geometric Series

This chapter covers geometric series and their applications to business, economics, and the life sciences.
*Chpater 10 is the former Chapter 11.*

### Appendices

The first appendix introduces the student to fitting formulas to data; the second appendix provides further discussion of compound interest and the definition of the number $e$. The third appendix contains a selection of spreadsheet projects.

## Supplementary Materials

Supplements for the instructor can be obtained by sending a request on your institutional letterhead to Mathematics Marketing Manager, John Wiley & Sons Inc., 111 River Street, Hoboken, NJ 07030-5774, or by contacting your local Wiley representative. The following supplementary materials are available.

- **Instructor's Manual** (ISBN 978-1-118-71506-2) containing teaching tips, sample syllabii, calculator programs, and overhead transparency masters.

- **Instructor's Solution Manual** (ISBN 978-1-118-71498-0) with complete solutions to all problems.
- **Student's Solution Manual** (ISBN 978-1-118-71499-7) with complete solutions to half the odd-numbered problems.
- **Additional Material for Instructors**, elaborating specially marked points in the text, as well as password protected electronic versions of the instructor ancillaries, can be found on the web at www.wiley.com/college/hughes-hallett.
- **Additional Material for Students**, at the student book companion site at www.wiley.com/college/hughes-hallett, includes an algebra refresher and web quizzes.

Getting Started Technology Manual Series:

- **Getting Started with Mathematica**, $3^{rd}$ edn, by C-K. Cheung, G.E. Keough, Robert H. Gross, and Charles Landraitis of Boston College (ISBN 978-0-470-45687-3)
- **Getting Started with Maple**, $3^{rd}$ edn, by C-K. Cheung, G.E. Keough, both of Boston College, and Michael May of St. Louis University (ISBN 978-0-470-45554-8)

## ConcepTests

ConcepTests (ISBN 978-1-118-71494-2), or clicker questions, modeled on the pioneering work of Harvard physicist Eric Mazur, are questions designed to promote active learning during class, particularly (but not exclusively) in large lectures. Evaluation data shows that students taught with ConcepTests outperformed students taught by traditional lecture methods 73% versus 17% on conceptual questions, and 63% versus 54% on computational problems.[1] A supplement to *Applied Calculus*, $5^{th}$ edn, containing ConcepTests by section, is available from your Wiley representative.

## Wiley Faculty Network

The Wiley Faculty Network is a peer-to-peer network of academic faculty dedicated to the effective use of technology in the classroom. This group can help you apply innovative classroom techniques and implement specific software packages. Visit www.wherefacultyconnect.com or ask your Wiley representative for details.

## WileyPLUS

WileyPLUS, Wiley's digital learning environment, is loaded with all of the supplements above, and also features:

- E-book, which is an exact version of the print text, but also features hyperlinks to questions, definitions, and supplements for quicker and easier support.
- Homework management tools, which easily enable the instructor to assign and automatically grade questions, using a rich set of options and controls.
- QuickStart pre-designed reading and homework assignments. Use them as-is or customize them to fit the needs of your classroom.
- Guided Online (GO) Exercises, which prompt students to build solutions step-by-step. Rather than simply grading an exercise answer as wrong, GO problems show students precisely where they are making a mistake.
- Algebra & Trigonometry Refresher quizzes, which provide students with an opportunity to brush-up on material necessary to master calculus, as well as to determine areas that require further review.
- Graphing Calculator Manual, to help students get the most out of their graphing calculator, and to show how they can apply the numerical and graphing functions of their calculators to their study of calculus.

[1]"Peer Instruction in Physics and Mathematics" by Scott Pilzer in *Primus*, Vol XI, No 2, June 2001. At the start of Calculus II, students earned 73% on conceptual questions and 63% on computational questions if they were taught with ConcepTests in Calculus I; 17% and 54% otherwise.

## Acknowledgements

First and foremost, we want to express our appreciation to the National Science Foundation for their faith in our ability to produce a revitalized calculus curriculum and, in particular, to Louise Raphael, John Kenelly, John Bradley, Bill Haver, and James Lightbourne. We also want to thank the members of our Advisory Board, Benita Albert, Lida Barrett, Bob Davis, Lovenia DeConge-Watson, John Dossey, Ron Douglas, Don Lewis, Seymour Parter, John Prados, and Steve Rodi for their ongoing guidance and advice.

In addition, we want to thank all the people across the country who encouraged us to write this book and who offered so many helpful comments. We would like to thank the following people, for all that they have done to help our project succeed: Ruth Baruth, Graeme Bird, Jeanne Bowman, Lucille Buonocore, Scott Clark, Jeff Edmunds, Sunny Fawcett, Lynn Garner, Sheldon P. Gordon, Ole Hald, Jenny Harrison, Adrian Iovita, Thomas Judson, Christopher Kennedy, Donna Krawczyk, Suzanne Lenhart, Madelyn Lesure, Georgia Kamvosoulis Mederer, Nolan Miller, Andrew Pasquale, Richard D. Porter, Laurie Rosatone, Kenneth Santor, Anne Scanlan-Rohrer, Alfred Schipke, Virginia Stallings, "Suds" Sudholz, Ralph Teixeira, Joe B. Thrash, J. Jerry Uhl, Rachel Deyette Werkema, Hannah Winkler, and Hung-Hsi Wu.

Reports from the following reviewers were most helpful in shaping the fifth edition:

Anthony Barcellos, Catherine Benincasa, Bill Blubagh, Carol Demas, Darlene Diaz, Lauren Fern, Wesley Griffith, Juill Guerra, Molly Martin, Rebecca McKay, Barry Peratt, Karl Schaffer, Randy Scott, Paul Vicknair, Tracy Whelan, P. Jay Zeltner.

Reports from the following reviewers were most helpful in shaping the third edition:

Victor Akatsa, Carol Blumberg, Mary Ann Collier, Murray Eisenberg, Donna Fatheree, Dan Fuller, Ken Hannsgen, Marek Kossowski, Sheri Lehavi, Deborah Lurie, Jan Mays, Jeffery Meyer, Bobra Palmer, Barry Peratt, Russ Potter, Ken Price, Maijian Qian, Emily Roth, Lorenzo Traldi, Joan Weiss, Christos Xenophontos.

Reports from the following reviewers were most helpful in shaping the second edition:

Victor Akatsa, Carol Blumberg, Jennifer Fowler, Helen Hancock, Ken Hannsgen, John Haverhals, Mako E. Haruta, Linda Hill, Thom Kline, Jill Messer Lamping, Dennis Lewandowski, Lige Li, William O. Martin, Ted Marsden, Michael Mocciola, Maijian Qian, Joyce Quella, Peter Penner, Barry Peratt, Emily Roth, Jerry Schuur, Barbara Shabell, Peter Sternberg, Virginia Stover, Bruce Yoshiwara, Katherine Yoshiwara.

Deborah Hughes-Hallett        David O. Lomen          Douglas Quinney

Patti Frazer Lock             David Lovelock          Karen Rhea

Daniel E. Flath               Guadalupe I. Lozano     Adam Spiegler

Andrew M. Gleason             William G. McCallum     Jeff Tecosky-Feldman

Eric Connally                 Brad G. Osgood          Thomas W. Tucker

Selin Kalaycıoğlu             Cody L. Patterson       Aaron D. Wooton

Brigitte Lahme

# APPLICATIONS INDEX

## Life Sciences and Ecology

## To Students: How to Learn from this Book

- This book may be different from other math textbooks that you have used, so it may be helpful to know about some of the differences in advance. At every stage, this book emphasizes the *meaning* (in practical, graphical or numerical terms) of the symbols you are using. There is much less emphasis on "plug-and-chug" and using formulas, and much more emphasis on the interpretation of these formulas than you may expect. You will often be asked to explain your ideas in words or to explain an answer using graphs.

- The book contains the main ideas of calculus in plain English. Success in using this book will depend on reading, questioning, and thinking hard about the ideas presented. It will be helpful to read the text in detail, not just the worked examples.

- There are few examples in the text that are exactly like the homework problems, so homework problems can't be done by searching for similar–looking "worked out" examples. Success with the homework will come by grappling with the ideas of calculus.

- For many problems in the book, there is more than one correct approach and more than one correct solution. Sometimes, solving a problem relies on common sense ideas that are not stated in the problem explicitly but which you know from everyday life.

- Some problems in this book assume that you have access to a graphing calculator or computer. There are many situations where you may not be able to find an exact solution to a problem, but you can use a calculator or computer to get a reasonable approximation.

- This book attempts to give equal weight to four methods for describing functions: graphical (a picture), numerical (a table of values), algebraic (a formula), and verbal (words). Sometimes it's easier to translate a problem given in one form into another. For example, you might replace the graph of a parabola with its equation, or plot a table of values to see its behavior. It is important to be flexible about your approach: if one way of looking at a problem doesn't work, try another.

- Students using this book have found discussing these problems in small groups helpful. There are a great many problems which are not cut-and-dried; it can help to attack them with the other perspectives your colleagues can provide. If group work is not feasible, see if your instructor can organize a discussion session in which additional problems can be worked on.

- You are probably wondering what you'll get from the book. The answer is, if you put in a solid effort, you will get a real understanding of one of the crowning achievements of human creativity—calculus—as well as a real sense of the power of mathematics in the age of technology.

# CONTENTS

## Chapter One

# FUNCTIONS AND CHANGE

## Contents

# 1.1  WHAT IS A FUNCTION?

In mathematics, a *function* is used to represent the dependence of one quantity upon another.

Let's look at an example. Syracuse, New York has the highest annual snowfall of any US city because of the "lake-effect" snow coming from cold Northwest winds blowing over nearby Lake Ontario. Lake-effect snowfall has been heavier over the last few decades; some have suggested this is due to the warming of Lake Ontario by climate change. In December 2010, Syracuse got 66.9 inches of snow in one 12-day period, all of it from lake-effect snow. See Table 1.1.

**Table 1.1**   *Daily snowfall in Syracuse, December 5–16, 2010*

| Date (December 2010) | 5 | 6 | 7 | 8 | 9 | 10 | 11 | 12 | 13 | 14 | 15 | 16 |
|---|---|---|---|---|---|---|---|---|---|---|---|---|
| Snowfall in inches | 6.8 | 12.2 | 9.3 | 14.9 | 1.9 | 0.1 | 0.0 | 0.0 | 1.4 | 5.0 | 11.9 | 3.4 |

You may not have thought of something so unpredictable as daily snowfall as being a function, but it *is* a function of date, because each day gives rise to one snowfall total. There is no formula for the daily snowfall (otherwise we would not need a weather bureau), but nevertheless the daily snowfall in Syracuse does satisfy the definition of a function: Each date, $t$, has a unique snowfall, $S$, associated with it.

We define a function as follows:

> A **function** is a rule that takes certain numbers as inputs and assigns to each a definite output number. The set of all input numbers is called the **domain** of the function and the set of resulting output numbers is called the **range** of the function.

The input is called the *independent variable* and the output is called the *dependent variable*. In the snowfall example, the domain is the set of December dates $\{5, 6, 7, 8, 9, 10, 11, 12, 13, 14, 15, 16\}$ and the range is the set of daily snowfalls $\{0.0, 0.1, 1.4, 1.9, 3.4, 5.0, 6.8, 9.3, 11.9, 12.2, 14.9\}$. We call the function $f$ and write $S = f(t)$. Notice that a function may have identical outputs for different inputs (December 11 and 12, for example).

Some quantities, such as date, are *discrete*, meaning they take only certain isolated values (dates must be integers). Other quantities, such as time, are *continuous* as they can be any number. For a continuous variable, domains and ranges are often written using interval notation:

The set of numbers $t$ such that $a \le t \le b$ is called a *closed interval* and written $[a, b]$.

The set of numbers $t$ such that $a < t < b$ is called an *open interval* and written $(a, b)$.

## The Rule of Four: Tables, Graphs, Formulas, and Words

Functions can be represented by tables, graphs, formulas, and descriptions in words. For example, the function giving the daily snowfall in Syracuse can be represented by the graph in Figure 1.1, as well as by Table 1.1.

Figure 1.1: Syracuse snowfall, December, 2010

Other functions arise naturally as graphs. Figure 1.2 contains electrocardiogram (EKG) pictures showing the heartbeat patterns of two patients, one normal and one not. Although it is possible to construct a formula to approximate an EKG function, this is seldom done. The pattern of repetitions is what a doctor needs to know, and these are more easily seen from a graph than from a formula. However, each EKG gives electrical activity as a function of time.

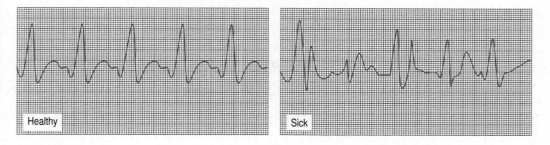

Figure 1.2: EKG readings on two patients

As another example of a function, consider the snow tree cricket. Surprisingly enough, all such crickets chirp at essentially the same rate if they are at the same temperature. That means that the chirp rate is a function of temperature. In other words, if we know the temperature, we can determine the chirp rate. Even more surprisingly, the chirp rate, $C$, in chirps per minute, increases steadily with the temperature, $T$, in degrees Fahrenheit, and can be computed, to a fair degree of accuracy, using the formula

$$C = f(T) = 4T - 160.$$

## Mathematical Modeling

A *mathematical model* is a mathematical description of a real situation. In this book we consider models that are functions, such as $C = f(T) = 4T - 160$.

Modeling almost always involves some simplification of reality. We choose which variables to include and which to ignore—for example, we consider the dependence of chirp rate on temperature, but not on other variables. The choice of variables is based on knowledge of the context (the biology of crickets, for example), not on mathematics. To test the model, we compare its predictions with observations.

In this book, we often model a situation that has a discrete domain with a continuous function whose domain is an interval of numbers. For example, the annual US gross domestic product (GDP) has a value for each year, $t = 0, 1, 2, 3, \ldots$. We may model it by a function of the form $G = f(t)$, with values for $t$ in a continuous interval. In doing this, we expect that the values of $f(t)$ match the values of the GDP at the points $t = 0, 1, 2, 3, \ldots$, and that information obtained from $f(t)$ closely matches observed values.

Used judiciously, a mathematical model captures trends in the data to enable us to analyze and make predictions. A common way of finding a model is described in Appendix A.

## Function Notation and Intercepts

We write $y = f(t)$ to express the fact that $y$ is a function of $t$. The independent variable is $t$, the dependent variable is $y$, and $f$ is the name of the function. The graph of a function has an *intercept* where it crosses the horizontal or vertical axis. Horizontal intercepts are also called the *zeros* of the function.

---

**Example 1**  (a) Graph the cricket chirp rate function, $C = f(T) = 4T - 160$.
(b) Solve $f(T) = 0$ and interpret the result.

Solution  (a) The graph is in Figure 1.3.

Figure 1.3: Cricket chirp rate as a function of temperature

(b) Solving $f(T) = 0$ gives the horizontal intercept:

$$4T - 160 = 0$$
$$T = \frac{160}{4} = 40.$$

Thus at a temperature of $40°F$, the chirp rate is zero.

For temperatures below $40°F$, the model would predict negative values of $C$, so we conclude that the model does not apply for such temperature values.

---

**Example 2**    The value of a car, $V$, is a function of the age of the car, $a$, so $V = g(a)$, where $g$ is the name we are giving to this function.

(a) Interpret the statement $g(5) = 9$ in terms of the value of a car if $V$ is in thousands of dollars and $a$ is in years.

(b) In the same units, the value of a Honda[1] is approximated by $g(a) = 13.78 - 0.8a$. Find and interpret the vertical and horizontal intercepts of the graph of this depreciation function $g$.

**Solution**    (a) Since $V = g(a)$, the statement $g(5) = 9$ means $V = 9$ when $a = 5$. This tells us that the car is worth $9000 when it is 5 years old.

(b) Since $V = g(a)$, a graph of the function $g$ has the value of the car on the vertical axis and the age of the car on the horizontal axis. The vertical intercept is the value of $V$ when $a = 0$. It is $V = g(0) = 13.78$, so the Honda was valued at $13,780 when new. The horizontal intercept is the value of $a$ such that $g(a) = 0$, so

$$13.78 - 0.8a = 0$$
$$a = \frac{13.78}{0.8} = 17.2.$$

At age 17 years, the Honda has no value.

---

## Increasing and Decreasing Functions

In the previous examples, the chirp rate increases with temperature, while the value of the Honda decreases with age. We express these facts saying that $f$ is an increasing function, while $g$ is decreasing. See Figure 1.4. In general:

> A function $f$ is **increasing** if the values of $f(x)$ increase as $x$ increases.
> A function $f$ is **decreasing** if the values of $f(x)$ decrease as $x$ increases.
>
> The graph of an *increasing* function *climbs* as we move from left to right.
> The graph of a *decreasing* function *descends* as we move from left to right.

---

[1] From data obtained from the Kelley Blue Book, www.kbb.com.

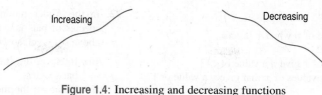

Figure 1.4: Increasing and decreasing functions

## Problems for Section 1.1

**1.** Which graph in Figure 1.5 best matches each of the following stories?[2] Write a story for the remaining graph.

   **(a)** I had just left home when I realized I had forgotten my books, so I went back to pick them up.

   **(b)** Things went fine until I had a flat tire.

   **(c)** I started out calmly but sped up when I realized I was going to be late.

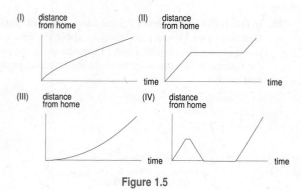

Figure 1.5

In Problems 2–5, use the description of the function to sketch a possible graph. Put a label on each axis and state whether the function is increasing or decreasing.

**2.** The height of a sand dune is a function of time, and the wind erodes away the sand dune over time.

**3.** The amount of carbon dioxide in the atmosphere is a function of time, and is going up over time.

**4.** The number of air conditioning units sold is a function of temperature, and goes up as the temperature goes up.

**5.** The noise level, in decibels, is a function of distance from the source of the noise, and the noise level goes down as the distance increases.

**6.** The population of Washington DC grew from 1900 to 1950, stayed approximately constant during the 1950s, and decreased from about 1960 to 2005. Graph the population as a function of years since 1900.

**7.** Let $W = f(t)$ represent wheat production in Argentina,[3] in millions of metric tons, where $t$ is years since 2006. Interpret the statement $f(4) = 14$ in terms of wheat production.

**8.** The concentration of carbon dioxide, $C = f(t)$, in the atmosphere, in parts per million (ppm), is a function of years, $t$, since 1960.

   **(a)** Interpret $f(40) = 370$ in terms of carbon dioxide.[4]

   **(b)** What is the meaning of $f(50)$?

**9. (a)** The graph of $r = f(p)$ is in Figure 1.6. What is the value of $r$ when $p$ is 0? When $p$ is 3?

   **(b)** What is $f(2)$?

Figure 1.6

For the functions in Problems 10–14, find $f(5)$.

**10.** $f(x) = 2x + 3$        **11.** $f(x) = 10x - x^2$

**12.**

**13.**

**14.**

| $x$ | 1 | 2 | 3 | 4 | 5 | 6 | 7 | 8 |
|---|---|---|---|---|---|---|---|---|
| $f(x)$ | 2.3 | 2.8 | 3.2 | 3.7 | 4.1 | 5.0 | 5.6 | 6.2 |

---

[2] Adapted from Jan Terwel, "Real Math in Cooperative Groups in Secondary Education." *Cooperative Learning in Mathematics*, ed. Neal Davidson, p. 234 (Reading: Addison Wesley, 1990).

[3] http://ageconsearch.umn.edu/bitstream/115558/2/AAE680.pdf, accessed September 2012.

[4] *Vital Signs 2007-2008*, The Worldwatch Institute, W.W. Norton & Company, 2007, p. 43.

**15.** Let $y = f(x) = x^2 + 2$.

    **(a)** Find the value of $y$ when $x$ is zero.
    **(b)** What is $f(3)$?
    **(c)** What values of $x$ give $y$ a value of 11?
    **(d)** Are there any values of $x$ that give $y$ a value of 1?

In Problems 16–19 the function $S = f(t)$ gives the average annual sea level, $S$, in meters, in Aberdeen, Scotland,[5] as a function of $t$, the number of years before 2008. Write a mathematical expression that represents the given statement.

**16.** In 1983 the average annual sea level in Aberdeen was 7.019 meters.

**17.** The average annual sea level in Aberdeen in 2008.

**18.** The average annual sea level in Aberdeen was the same in 1865 and 1911.

**19.** The average annual sea level in Aberdeen increased by 1 millimeter from 2007 to 2008.

**20.** **(a)** A potato is put in an oven to bake at time $t = 0$. Which of the graphs in Figure 1.7 could represent the potato's temperature as a function of time?
    **(b)** What does the vertical intercept represent in terms of the potato's temperature?

**Figure 1.7**

**21.** An object is put outside on a cold day at time $t = 0$. Its temperature, $H = f(t)$, in °C, is graphed in Figure 1.8.

    **(a)** What does the statement $f(30) = 10$ mean in terms of temperature? Include units for 30 and for 10 in your answer.
    **(b)** Explain what the vertical intercept, $a$, and the horizontal intercept, $b$, represent in terms of temperature of the object and time outside.

**Figure 1.8**

**22.** In the Andes mountains in Peru, the number, $N$, of species of bats is a function of the elevation, $h$, in feet above sea level, so $N = f(h)$.

    **(a)** Interpret the statement $f(500) = 100$ in terms of bat species.
    **(b)** What are the meanings of the vertical intercept, $k$, and horizontal intercept, $c$, in Figure 1.9?

**Figure 1.9**

**23.** In tide pools on the New England coast, snails eat algae. Describe what Figure 1.10 tells you about the effect of snails on the diversity of algae.[6] Does the graph support the statement that diversity peaks at intermediate predation levels?

**Figure 1.10**

**24.** Figure 1.11 shows the amount of nicotine, $N = f(t)$, in mg, in a person's bloodstream as a function of the time, $t$, in hours, since the person finished smoking a cigarette.

    **(a)** Estimate $f(3)$ and interpret it in terms of nicotine.
    **(b)** About how many hours have passed before the nicotine level is down to 0.1 mg?
    **(c)** What is the vertical intercept? What does it represent in terms of nicotine?
    **(d)** If this function had a horizontal intercept, what would it represent?

**Figure 1.11**

---

[5]www.decc.gov.uk, accessed June 2011
[6]Rosenzweig, M.L., *Species Diversity in Space and Time*, p. 343 (Cambridge: Cambridge University Press, 1995).

**25.** A deposit is made into an interest-bearing account. Figure 1.12 shows the balance, $B$, in the account $t$ years later.

   **(a)** What was the original deposit?
   **(b)** Estimate $f(10)$ and interpret it.
   **(c)** When does the balance reach $5000?

**Figure 1.12**

**26.** The use of CFCs (chlorofluorocarbons) has declined since the 1987 Montreal Protocol came into force to reduce the use of substances that deplete the ozone layer. World annual CFC consumption, $C = f(t)$, in million tons, is a function of time, $t$, in years since 1987. (CFCs are measured by the weight of ozone that they could destroy.)

   **(a)** Interpret $f(10) = 0.2$ in terms of CFCs.[7]
   **(b)** Interpret the vertical intercept of the graph of this function in terms of CFCs.
   **(c)** Interpret the horizontal intercept of the graph of this function in terms of CFCs.

**27.** When a patient with a rapid heart rate takes a drug, the heart rate plunges dramatically and then slowly rises again as the drug wears off. Sketch the heart rate against time from the moment the drug is administered.

**28.** The gas mileage of a car (in miles per gallon) is highest when the car is going about 45 miles per hour and is lower when the car is going faster or slower than 45 mph. Graph gas mileage as a function of speed of the car.

**29.** After an injection, the concentration of a drug in a patient's body increases rapidly to a peak and then slowly decreases. Graph the concentration of the drug in the body as a function of the time since the injection was given. Assume that the patient has none of the drug in the body before the injection. Label the peak concentration and the time it takes to reach that concentration.

**30.** Financial investors know that, in general, the higher the expected rate of return on an investment, the higher the corresponding risk.

   **(a)** Graph this relationship, showing expected return as a function of risk.
   **(b)** On the figure from part (a), mark a point with high expected return and low risk. (Investors hope to find such opportunities.)

**31.** The number of sales per month, $S$, is a function of the amount, $a$ (in dollars), spent on advertising that month, so $S = f(a)$.

   **(a)** Interpret the statement $f(1000) = 3500$.
   **(b)** Which of the graphs in Figure 1.13 is more likely to represent this function?
   **(c)** What does the vertical intercept of the graph of this function represent, in terms of sales and advertising?

**Figure 1.13**

**32.** Figure 1.14 shows fifty years of fertilizer use in the US, India, and the former Soviet Union.[8]

   **(a)** Estimate fertilizer use in 1970 in the US, India, and the former Soviet Union.
   **(b)** Write a sentence for each of the three graphs describing how fertilizer use has changed in each region over this 50-year period.

**Figure 1.14**

**33.** The six graphs in Figure 1.15 show frequently observed patterns of age-specific cancer incidence rates, in number of cases per 1000 people, as a function of age.[9] The scales on the vertical axes are equal.

   **(a)** For each of the six graphs, write a sentence explaining the effect of age on the cancer rate.
   **(b)** Which graph shows a relatively high incidence rate for children? Suggest a type of cancer that behaves this way.
   **(c)** Which graph shows a brief decrease in the incidence rate at around age 50? Suggest a type of cancer that might behave this way.

[7] *Vital Signs 2007-2008*, The Worldwatch Institute, W.W. Norton & Company, 2007, p. 47.
[8] The Worldwatch Institute, *Vital Signs 2001*, p. 32 (New York: W.W. Norton, 2001).
[9] Abraham M. Lilienfeld, *Foundations of Epidemiology*, p. 155 (New York: Oxford University Press, 1976).

**(d)** Which graph or graphs might represent a cancer that is caused by toxins which build up in the body over time? (For example, lung cancer.) Explain.

Figure 1.15

**34.** Table 1.2 shows the average annual sea level, $S$, in meters, in Aberdeen, Scotland,[10] as a function of time, $t$, measured in years before 2008.

Table 1.2

| $t$ | 0 | 25 | 50 | 75 | 100 | 125 |
|-----|-----|-----|-----|-----|-----|-----|
| $S$ | 7.094 | 7.019 | 6.992 | 6.965 | 6.938 | 6.957 |

**(a)** What was the average sea level in Aberdeen in 2008?

**(b)** In what year was the average sea level 7.019 meters? 6.957 meters?

**(c)** Table 1.3 gives the average sea level, $S$, in Aberdeen as a function of the year, $x$. Complete the missing values.

Table 1.3

| $x$ | 1883 | ? | 1933 | 1958 | 1983 | 2008 |
|-----|-----|-----|-----|-----|-----|-----|
| $S$ | ? | 6.938 | ? | 6.992 | ? | ? |

Problems 35–38 ask you to plot graphs based on the following story: "As I drove down the highway this morning, at first traffic was fast and uncongested, then it crept nearly bumper-to-bumper until we passed an accident, after which traffic flow went back to normal until I exited."

**35.** Driving speed against time on the highway

**36.** Distance driven against time on the highway

**37.** Distance from my exit vs time on the highway

**38.** Distance between cars vs distance driven on the highway

## 1.2  LINEAR FUNCTIONS

Probably the most commonly used functions are the *linear functions*, whose graphs are straight lines. The chirp-rate and the Honda depreciation functions in the previous section are both linear. We now look at more examples of linear functions.

### Olympic and World Records

During the early years of the Olympics, the height of the men's winning pole vault increased approximately 8 inches every four years. Table 1.4 shows that the height started at 130 inches in 1900, and increased by the equivalent of 2 inches a year between 1900 and 1912. So the height was a linear function of time.

Table 1.4  *Winning height (approximate) for Men's Olympic pole vault*

| Year | 1900 | 1904 | 1908 | 1912 |
|------|------|------|------|------|
| Height (inches) | 130 | 138 | 146 | 154 |

If $y$ is the winning height in inches and $t$ is the number of years since 1900, we can write

$$y = f(t) = 130 + 2t.$$

[10]www.decc.gov.uk, accessed June 2011.

Since $y = f(t)$ increases with $t$, we see that $f$ is an increasing function. The coefficient 2 tells us the rate, in inches per year, at which the height increases. This rate is the *slope* of the line in Figure 1.16. The slope is given by the ratio

$$\text{Slope} = \frac{\text{Rise}}{\text{Run}} = \frac{146 - 138}{8 - 4} = \frac{8}{4} = 2 \text{ inches/year.}$$

Calculating the slope (rise/run) using any other two points on the line gives the same value.

What about the constant 130? This represents the initial height in 1900, when $t = 0$. Geometrically, 130 is the intercept on the vertical axis.

You may wonder whether the linear trend continues beyond 1912. Not surprisingly, it does not exactly. The formula $y = 130 + 2t$ predicts that the height in the London 2012 Olympics would be 354 inches or 29 feet 6 inches, which is considerably higher than the actual value of 19 feet 7.04 inches.[11] There is clearly a danger in *extrapolating* too far from the given data. You should also observe that the data in Table 1.4 is discrete, because it is given only at specific points (every four years). However, we have treated the variable $t$ as though it were continuous, because the function $y = 130 + 2t$ makes sense for all values of $t$. The graph in Figure 1.16 is of the continuous function because it is a solid line, rather than four separate points representing the years in which the Olympics were held.

Figure 1.16: Olympic pole vault records        Figure 1.17: World record time to run the mile

**Example 1**    If $y$ is the world record time to run the mile, in seconds, and $t$ is the number of years since 1900, then records show that, approximately,

$$y = g(t) = 260 - 0.4t.$$

Explain the meaning of the intercept, 260, and the slope, $-0.4$, in terms of the world record time to run the mile and sketch the graph.

Solution    The intercept, 260, tells us that the world record was 260 seconds in 1900 (at $t = 0$). The slope, $-0.4$, tells us that the world record decreased at a rate of about 0.4 seconds per year. See Figure 1.17.

## Slope and Rate of Change

We use the symbol $\Delta$ (the Greek letter capital delta) to mean "change in," so $\Delta x$ means change in $x$ and $\Delta y$ means change in $y$.

[11] http://www.london2012.com/athletics/event=athletics-men-pole-vault/.

**Figure 1.18**: Difference quotient $= \dfrac{f(x_2) - f(x_1)}{x_2 - x_1}$

The slope of a linear function $y = f(x)$ can be calculated from values of the function at two points, given by $x_1$ and $x_2$, using the formula

$$\text{Slope } = \frac{\text{Rise}}{\text{Run}} = \frac{\Delta y}{\Delta x} = \frac{f(x_2) - f(x_1)}{x_2 - x_1}.$$

The quantity $(f(x_2) - f(x_1))/(x_2 - x_1)$ is called a *difference quotient* because it is the quotient of two differences. (See Figure 1.18.) Since slope $= \Delta y / \Delta x$, the slope represents the *rate of change* of $y$ with respect to $x$. The units of the slope are $y$-units over $x$-units.

## Linear Functions in General

A **linear function** has the form

$$y = f(x) = b + mx.$$

Its graph is a line such that
- $m$ is the **slope**, or rate of change of $y$ with respect to $x$.
- $b$ is the **vertical intercept** or value of $y$ when $x$ is zero.

If the slope, $m$, is positive, then $f$ is an increasing function. If $m$ is negative, then $f$ is decreasing.

Notice that if the slope, $m$, is zero, we have $y = b$, a horizontal line. For a line of slope $m$ through the point $(x_0, y_0)$, we have

$$\text{Slope } = m = \frac{y - y_0}{x - x_0}.$$

Therefore we can write the equation of the line in the *point-slope form*:

The equation of a line of slope $m$ through the point $(x_0, y_0)$ is

$$y - y_0 = m(x - x_0).$$

**Example 2**    The solid waste generated each year in the cities of the US is increasing. The solid waste generated,[12] in millions of tons, was 238.3 in 2000 and 251.3 in 2006.

(a)  Assuming that the amount of solid waste generated by US cities is a linear function of time, find a formula for this function by finding the equation of the line through these two points.

(b)  Use this formula to predict the amount of solid waste generated in the year 2020.

---

[12]*Statistical Abstracts of the US*, 2009, Table 361.

Solution

(a) We think of the amount of solid waste, $W$, as a function of year, $t$, and the two points are $(2000, 238.3)$ and $(2006, 251.3)$. The slope of the line is

$$m = \frac{\Delta W}{\Delta t} = \frac{251.3 - 238.3}{2006 - 2000} = \frac{13}{6} = 2.167 \text{ million tons/year.}$$

We use the point-slope form to find the equation of the line. We substitute the point $(2000, 238.3)$ and the slope $m = 2.167$ into the equation:

$$W - W_0 = m(t - t_0)$$
$$W - 238.3 = 2.167(t - 2000)$$
$$W - 238.3 = 2.167t - 4334$$
$$W = 2.167t - 4095.7.$$

The equation of the line is $W = 2.167t - 4095.7$. Alternatively, we could use the slope-intercept form of a line to find the vertical intercept.

(b) To calculate solid waste predicted for the year 2020, we substitute $t = 2020$ into the equation of the line, $W = -4095.7 + 2.167t$, and calculate $W$:

$$W = -4095.7 + 2.167(2020) = 281.64.$$

The formula predicts that in the year 2020, there will be 281.64 million tons of solid waste.

---

**Recognizing Data from a Linear Function:** Values of $x$ and $y$ in a table could come from a linear function $y = b + mx$ if differences in $y$-values are constant for equal differences in $x$.

---

**Example 3**    Which of the following tables of values could represent a linear function?

| $x$ | 0 | 1 | 2 | 3 |
|---|---|---|---|---|
| $f(x)$ | 25 | 30 | 35 | 40 |

| $x$ | 0 | 2 | 4 | 6 |
|---|---|---|---|---|
| $g(x)$ | 10 | 16 | 26 | 40 |

| $t$ | 20 | 30 | 40 | 50 |
|---|---|---|---|---|
| $h(t)$ | 2.4 | 2.2 | 2.0 | 1.8 |

Solution

Since $f(x)$ increases by 5 for every increase of 1 in $x$, the values of $f(x)$ could be from a linear function with slope $= 5/1 = 5$.

Between $x = 0$ and $x = 2$, the value of $g(x)$ increases by 6 as $x$ increases by 2. Between $x = 2$ and $x = 4$, the value of $y$ increases by 10 as $x$ increases by 2. Since the slope is not constant, $g(x)$ could not be a linear function.

Since $h(t)$ decreases by 0.2 for every increase of 10 in $t$, the values of $h(t)$ could be from a linear function with slope $= -0.2/10 = -0.02$.

---

**Example 4**    The data in the following table lie on a line. Find formulas for each of the following functions, and give units for the slope in each case:

(a) $q$ as a function of $p$

(b) $p$ as a function of $q$

| $p$ (dollars) | 5 | 10 | 15 | 20 |
|---|---|---|---|---|
| $q$ (tons) | 100 | 90 | 80 | 70 |

Solution

(a) If we think of $q$ as a linear function of $p$, then $q$ is the dependent variable and $p$ is the independent variable. We can use any two points to find the slope. The first two points give

$$\text{Slope} = m = \frac{\Delta q}{\Delta p} = \frac{90 - 100}{10 - 5} = \frac{-10}{5} = -2.$$

The units are the units of $q$ over the units of $p$, or tons per dollar.

To write $q$ as a linear function of $p$, we use the equation $q = b + mp$. We know that $m = -2$, and we can use any of the points in the table to find $b$. Substituting $p = 10$, $q = 90$ gives

$$q = b + mp$$
$$90 = b + (-2)(10)$$
$$90 = b - 20$$
$$110 = b.$$

Thus, the equation of the line is

$$q = 110 - 2p.$$

(b) If we now consider $p$ as a linear function of $q$, then $p$ is the dependent variable and $q$ is the independent variable. We have

$$\text{Slope} = m = \frac{\Delta p}{\Delta q} = \frac{10 - 5}{90 - 100} = \frac{5}{-10} = -0.5.$$

The units of the slope are dollars per ton.

Since $p$ is a linear function of $q$, we have $p = b + mq$ and $m = -0.5$. To find $b$, we substitute any point from the table, such as $p = 10$, $q = 90$, into this equation:

$$p = b + mq$$
$$10 = b + (-0.5)(90)$$
$$10 = b - 45$$
$$55 = b.$$

Thus, the equation of the line is

$$p = 55 - 0.5q.$$

Alternatively, we could take our answer to part (a), that is $q = 110 - 2p$, and solve for $p$.

Appendix A shows how to fit a linear function to data that is not exactly linear.

## Families of Linear Functions

Formulas such as $f(x) = b + mx$, in which the constants $m$ and $b$ can take on various values, represent a *family of functions*. All the functions in a family share certain properties—in this case, the graphs are lines. The constants $m$ and $b$ are called *parameters*. Figures 1.19 and 1.20 show graphs with several values of $m$ and $b$. Notice the greater the magnitude of $m$, the steeper the line.

Figure 1.19: The family $y = mx$ (with $b = 0$)          Figure 1.20: The family $y = b + x$ (with $m = 1$)

## Problems for Section 1.2

For Problems 1–4, find an equation for the line that passes through the given points.

For Problems 5–8, determine the slope and the $y$-intercept of the line whose equation is given.

**1.** $(0, 2)$ and $(2, 3)$

**2.** $(0, 0)$ and $(1, 1)$

**3.** $(-2, 1)$ and $(2, 3)$

**4.** $(4, 5)$ and $(2, -1)$

**5.** $7y + 12x - 2 = 0$

**6.** $3x + 2y = 8$

**7.** $12x = 6y + 4$

s  **8.** $-4y + 2x + 8 = 0$

**9.** Figure 1.21 shows four lines given by equation $y = b + mx$. Match the lines to the conditions on the parameters $m$ and $b$.

(a)  $m > 0, b > 0$        (b)  $m < 0, b > 0$

(c)  $m > 0, b < 0$        (d)  $m < 0, b < 0$

**Figure 1.21**

**10.** (a) Which two lines in Figure 1.22 have the same slope? Of these two lines, which has the larger $y$-intercept?
(b) Which two lines have the same $y$-intercept? Of these two lines, which has the larger slope?

**Figure 1.22**

**11.** A city's population was 30,700 in the year 2010 and is growing by 850 people a year.

(a) Give a formula for the city's population, $P$, as a function of the number of years, $t$, since 2010.
(b) What is the population predicted to be in 2020?
(c) When is the population expected to reach 45,000?

**12.** A company rents cars at $40 a day and 15 cents a mile. Its competitor's cars are $50 a day and 10 cents a mile.

(a) For each company, give a formula for the cost of renting a car for a day as a function of the distance traveled.
(b) On the same axes, graph both functions.
(c) How should you decide which company is cheaper?

**13.** Figure 1.23 shows the distance from home, in miles, of a person on a 5-hour trip.

(a) Estimate the vertical intercept. Give units and interpret it in terms of distance from home.
(b) Estimate the slope of this linear function. Give units, and interpret it in terms of distance from home.
(c) Give a formula for distance, $D$, from home as a function of time, $t$ in hours.

**Figure 1.23**

**14.** Which of the following tables could represent linear functions?

(a)

| $x$ | 0 | 1 | 2 | 3 |
|---|---|---|---|---|
| $y$ | 27 | 25 | 23 | 21 |

(b)

| $t$ | 15 | 20 | 25 | 30 |
|---|---|---|---|---|
| $s$ | 62 | 72 | 82 | 92 |

(c)

| $u$ | 1 | 2 | 3 | 4 |
|---|---|---|---|---|
| $w$ | 5 | 10 | 18 | 28 |

**15.** For each table in Problem 14 that could represent a linear function, find a formula for that function.

**16.** A cell phone company charges a monthly fee of $25 plus $0.05 per minute. Find a formula for the monthly charge, $C$, in dollars, as a function of the number of minutes, $m$, the phone is used during the month.

**17.** Annual revenue $R$ from McDonald's restaurants worldwide can be estimated by $R = 19.1 + 1.8t$, where $R$ is in billion dollars and $t$ is in years since January 1, 2005.[13]

(a) What is the slope of this function? Include units. Interpret the slope in terms of McDonald's revenue.
(b) What is the vertical intercept of this function? Include units. Interpret the vertical intercept in terms of McDonald's revenue.
(c) What annual revenue does the function predict for 2015?
(d) When is annual revenue predicted to hit 35 billion dollars?

---

[13]Based on McDonald's Annual Report 2007, accessed at www.mcdonalds.com, May 2012.

**18.** A company's pricing schedule in Table 1.5 is designed to encourage large orders. (A gross is 12 dozen.) Find a formula for:

   **(a)** $q$ as a linear function of $p$.
   **(b)** $p$ as a linear function of $q$.

Table 1.5

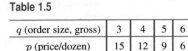

| $q$ (order size, gross) | 3 | 4 | 5 | 6 |
|---|---|---|---|---|
| $p$ (price/dozen) | 15 | 12 | 9 | 6 |

**19.** World milk production rose at an approximately constant rate between 2000 and 2012.[14] See Figure 1.24.

   **(a)** Estimate the vertical intercept and interpret it in terms of milk production.
   **(b)** Estimate the slope and interpret it in terms of milk production.
   **(c)** Give an approximate formula for milk production, $M$, as a function of $t$.

**Figure 1.24**

**20.** The percentage of people, $P$, below the poverty level in the US[15] is given in Table 1.6.

   **(a)** Find a formula for the percentage in poverty as a linear function of time in years since 2000.
   **(b)** Use the formula to predict the percentage in poverty in 2006.
   **(c)** What is the difference between the prediction and the actual percentage, 12.3%?

Table 1.6

| Year (since 2000) | 0 | 1 | 2 | 3 |
|---|---|---|---|---|
| $P$ (percentage) | 11.3 | 11.7 | 12.1 | 12.5 |

**21.** World grain production was 1241 million tons in 1975 and 2048 million tons in 2005, and has been increasing at an approximately constant rate.[16]

   **(a)** Find a linear function for world grain production, $P$, in million tons, as a function of $t$, the number of years since 1975.

   **(b)** Using units, interpret the slope in terms of grain production.
   **(c)** Using units, interpret the vertical intercept in terms of grain production.
   **(d)** According to the linear model, what is the predicted world grain production in 2015?
   **(e)** According to the linear model, when is grain production predicted to reach 2500 million tons?

**22.** Annual sales of music compact discs (CDs) have declined since 2000. Sales were 942.5 million in 2000 and 384.7 million in 2008.[17]

   **(a)** Find a formula for annual sales, $S$, in millions of music CDs, as a linear function of the number of years, $t$, since 2000.
   **(b)** Give units for and interpret the slope and the vertical intercept of this function.
   **(c)** Use the formula to predict music CD sales in 2012.

**23.** Search and rescue teams work to find lost hikers. Members of the search team separate and walk parallel to one another through the area to be searched. Table 1.7 shows the percent, $P$, of lost individuals found for various separation distances, $d$, of the searchers.[18]

Table 1.7

| Separation distance $d$ (ft) | 20 | 40 | 60 | 80 | 100 |
|---|---|---|---|---|---|
| Approximate percent found, $P$ | 90 | 80 | 70 | 60 | 50 |

   **(a)** Explain how you know that the percent found, $P$, could be a linear function of separation distance, $d$.
   **(b)** Find $P$ as a linear function of $d$.
   **(c)** What is the slope of the function? Give units and interpret the answer.
   **(d)** What are the vertical and horizontal intercepts of the function? Give units and interpret the answers.

**24.** In a California town, the monthly charge for waste collection is $8 for 32 gallons of waste and $12.32 for 68 gallons of waste.

   **(a)** Find a linear formula for the cost, $C$, of waste collection as a function of the number of gallons of waste, $w$.
   **(b)** What is the slope of the line found in part (a)? Give units and interpret your answer in terms of the cost of waste collection.
   **(c)** What is the vertical intercept of the line found in part (a)? Give units and interpret your answer in terms of the cost of waste collection.

---

[14]http://www.dairyco.org.uk/library/market-information/datum/world-milk-production.aspx, accessed May 2012.
[15]www.census.gov/hhes/www/poverty/histpov/hstpov2.html
[16]*Vital Signs 2007-2008*, The Worldwatch Institute, W.W. Norton & Company, 2007, p. 21.
[17]*The World Almanac and Book of Facts 2008* (New York).
[18]From *An Experimental Analysis of Grid Sweep Searching*, by J. Wartes (Explorer Search and Rescue, Western Region, 1974).

**25.** The number of species of coastal dune plants in Australia decreases as the latitude, in °S, increases. There are 34 species at 11°S and 26 species at 44°S.[19]

    **(a)** Find a formula for the number, $N$, of species of coastal dune plants in Australia as a linear function of the latitude, $l$, in °S.

    **(b)** Give units for and interpret the slope and the vertical intercept of this function.

    **(c)** Graph this function between $l = 11°$S and $l = 44°$S. (Australia lies entirely within these latitudes.)

**26.** Table 1.8 gives the average weight, $w$, in pounds, of American men in their sixties for height, $h$, in inches.[20]

    **(a)** How do you know that the data in this table could represent a linear function?

    **(b)** Find weight, $w$, as a linear function of height, $h$. What is the slope of the line? What are the units for the slope?

    **(c)** Find height, $h$, as a linear function of weight, $w$. What is the slope of the line? What are the units for the slope?

**Table 1.8**

| $h$ (inches) | 68 | 69 | 70 | 71 | 72 | 73 | 74 | 75 |
|---|---|---|---|---|---|---|---|---|
| $w$ (pounds) | 166 | 171 | 176 | 181 | 186 | 191 | 196 | 201 |

Problems 27–32 concern the maximum heart rate (MHR), which is the maximum number of times a person's heart can safely beat in one minute. If MHR is in beats per minute and $a$ is age in years, the formulas used to estimate MHR, are

$$\text{For females: MHR} = 226 - a,$$

$$\text{For males: MHR} = 220 - a.$$

**27.** Which of the following is the correct statement?

    **(a)** As you age, your maximum heart rate decreases by one beat per year.

    **(b)** As you age, your maximum heart rate decreases by one beat per minute.

    **(c)** As you age, your maximum heart rate decreases by one beat per minute per year.

**28.** Which of the following is the correct statement for a male and female of the same age?

    **(a)** Their maximum heart rates are the same.

    **(b)** The male's maximum heart rate exceeds the female's.

    **(c)** The female's maximum heart rate exceeds the male's.

**29.** What can be said about the ages of a male and a female with the same maximum heart rate?

**30.** Recently[21] it has been suggested that a more accurate predictor of MHR for both males and females is given by

$$\text{MHR} = 208 - 0.7a.$$

    **(a)** At what age do the old and new formulas give the same MHR for females? For males?

    **(b)** Which of the following is true?

        **(i)** The new formula predicts a higher MHR for young people and a lower MHR for older people than the old formula.

        **(ii)** The new formula predicts a lower MHR for young people and a higher MHR for older people than the old formula.

    **(c)** When testing for heart disease, doctors ask patients to walk on a treadmill while the speed and incline are gradually increased until their heart rates reach 85 percent of the MHR. For a 65-year-old male, what is the difference in beats per minute between the heart rate reached if the old formula is used and the heart rate reached if the new formula is used?

**31.** Experiments[22] suggest that the female MHR decreases by 12 beats per minute by age 21, and by 19 beats per minute by age 33. Is this consistent with MHR being approximately linear with age?

**32.** Experiments[23] suggest that the male MHR decreases by 9 beats per minute by age 21, and by 26 beats per minute by age 33. Is this consistent with MHR being approximately linear with age?

**33.** Let $y$ be the percent increase in annual US national production during a year when the unemployment rate changes by $u$ percent. (For example, $u = 2$ if unemployment increases from 4% to 6%.) Okun's law states that

$$y = 3.5 - 2u.$$

    **(a)** What is the meaning of the number 3.5 in Okun's law?

    **(b)** What is the effect on national production of a year when unemployment rises from 5% to 8%?

    **(c)** What change in the unemployment rate corresponds to a year when production is the same as the year before?

    **(d)** What is the meaning of the coefficient $-2$ in Okun's law?

[19]Rosenzweig, M.L., *Species Diversity in Space and Time,* p. 292 (Cambridge: Cambridge University Press, 1995).

[20]Adapted from "Average Weight of Americans by Height and Age," *The World Almanac* (New Jersey: Funk and Wagnalls, 1992), p. 956.

[21]www.physsportsmed.com/issues/2001/07_01/jul01news.htm, accessed January 4, 2005.

[22]www.css.edu/users/tboone2/asep/May2002JEPonline.html, accessed January 4, 2005.

[23]www.css.edu/users/tboone2/asep/May2002JEPonline.html, accessed January 4, 2005.

**34.** An Australian[24] study found that, if other factors are constant (education, experience, etc.), taller people receive higher wages for the same work. The study reported a "height premium" for men of 3% of the hourly wage for a 10 cm increase in height; for women the height premium reported was 2%. We assume that hourly wages are a linear function of height, with slope given by the height premium at the average hourly wage for that gender.

(a) The average hourly wage[25] for a 178 cm Australian man is AU$29.40. Express the average hourly wage of an Australian man as a function of his height, $x$ cm.

(b) The average hourly wage for a 164 cm Australian woman is AU$24.78. Express the average hourly wage of an Australian woman as a function of her height, $y$ cm.

(c) What is the difference in average hourly wages between men and women of height 178 cm?

(d) Is there a height for which men and women are predicted to have the same wage? If so, what is it?

# 1.3  AVERAGE RATE OF CHANGE AND RELATIVE CHANGE

## Average Rate of Change

In the previous section, we saw that the height of the winning Olympic pole vault increased at an approximately constant rate of 2 inches/year between 1900 and 1912. Similarly, the world record for the mile decreased at an approximately constant rate of 0.4 seconds/year. We now see how to calculate rates of change when they are not constant.

**Example 1**    Table 1.9 shows the height of the winning pole vault at the Olympics[26] during the 1960s and 1990s. Find the rate of change of the winning height between 1960 and 1968, and between 1992 and 2000. In which of these two periods did the height increase faster than during the period 1900–1912?

**Table 1.9**    *Winning height in men's Olympic pole vault (approximate)*

| Year | 1960 | 1964 | 1968 | $\cdots$ | 1992 | 1996 | 2000 |
|---|---|---|---|---|---|---|---|
| Height (inches) | 185 | 201 | 213 | $\cdots$ | 228 | 233 | 232 |

**Solution**    From 1900 to 1912, the height increased by 2 inches/year. To compare the 1960s and 1990s, we calculate

$$\text{Average rate of change of height} \atop \text{1960 to 1968} = \frac{\text{Change in height}}{\text{Change in time}} = \frac{213 - 185}{1968 - 1960} = 3.5 \text{ inches/year}.$$

$$\text{Average rate of change of height} \atop \text{1992 to 2000} = \frac{\text{Change in height}}{\text{Change in time}} = \frac{232 - 228}{2000 - 1992} = 0.5 \text{ inches/year}.$$

Thus, on average, the height was increasing more quickly during the 1960s than from 1900 to 1912. During the 1990s, the height was increasing more slowly than from 1900 to 1912.

In Example 1, the function does not have a constant rate of change (it is not linear). However, we can compute an *average rate of change* over any interval. The word average is used because the rate of change may vary within the interval. We have the following general formula.

If $y$ is a function of $t$, so $y = f(t)$, then

$$\text{\textbf{Average rate of change} of } y \atop \text{between } t = a \text{ and } t = b = \frac{\Delta y}{\Delta t} = \frac{f(b) - f(a)}{b - a}.$$

The units of average rate of change of a function are units of $y$ per unit of $t$.

---

[24]"Study finds tall people at top of wages ladder", Yahoo News, May 17, 2009.
[25]Australian Fair Pay Commission, August 2007.
[26]*The World Almanac and Book of Facts, 2005*, p. 866 (New York).

The average rate of change of a linear function is the slope, and a function is linear if the average rate of change is the same on all intervals.

**Example 2**    Using Figure 1.25, estimate the average rate of change of the number of farms[27] in the US between 1950 and 1970.

**Figure 1.25**: Number of farms in the US (in millions)

Solution    Figure 1.25 shows that the number, $N$, of farms in the US was approximately 5.4 million in 1950 and approximately 2.8 million in 1970. If time, $t$, is in years, we have

$$\text{Average rate of change} = \frac{\Delta N}{\Delta t} = \frac{2.8 - 5.4}{1970 - 1950} = -0.13 \text{ million farms per year.}$$

The average rate of change is negative because the number of farms is decreasing. During this period, the number of farms decreased at an average rate of 0.13 million, or 130,000, per year.

We have looked at how an Olympic record and the number of farms change over time. In the next example, we look at average rate of change with respect to a quantity other than time.

**Example 3**    Polychlorinated biphenyl (PCB) is an industrial pollutant thought dangerous to wildlife. Table 1.10 shows data on PCB levels and the thickness of pelican egg shells.[28] (Thin shells break more easily.)
    Find the average rate of change in the thickness of the shell as the PCB concentration changes from 87 ppm to 452 ppm. Give units and explain what the sign of the answer tells us.

**Table 1.10**    *Thickness of pelican eggshells and PCB concentration in the eggshells*

| Concentration, $c$, in parts per million (ppm) | 87 | 147 | 204 | 289 | 356 | 452 |
|---|---|---|---|---|---|---|
| Thickness, $h$, in millimeters (mm) | 0.44 | 0.39 | 0.28 | 0.23 | 0.22 | 0.14 |

Solution    Since we are looking for the average rate of change of thickness with respect to change in PCB concentration, we have

$$\text{Average rate of change of thickness} = \frac{\text{Change in the thickness}}{\text{Change in the PCB level}} = \frac{\Delta h}{\Delta c} = \frac{0.14 - 0.44}{452 - 87}$$
$$= -0.00082 \frac{\text{mm}}{\text{ppm}}.$$

The units are thickness units (mm) over PCB concentration units (ppm), or millimeters over parts per million. The fact that the average rate of change is negative tells us that, for this data, the thickness of the eggshell decreases as the PCB concentration increases. The thickness of pelican eggs decreases by an average of 0.00082 mm for every additional part per million of PCB in the eggshell.

---

[27]*The World Almanac and Book of Facts, 2005*, p. 136 (New York).

[28]Risebrough, R. W., "Effects of environmental pollutants upon animals other than man." *Proceedings of the 6th Berkeley Symposium on Mathematics and Statistics, VI*, p. 443–463 (Berkeley: University of California Press, 1972). PCBs were banned in the US in 1979.

## Visualizing Rate of Change

For a function $y = f(x)$, the change in the value of the function between $x = a$ and $x = c$ is $\Delta y = f(c) - f(a)$. Since $\Delta y$ is a difference of two $y$-values, it is represented by the vertical distance in Figure 1.26. The average rate of change of $f$ between $x = a$ and $x = c$ is represented by the slope of the line joining the points $A$ and $C$ in Figure 1.27. This line is called the *secant line* between $x = a$ and $x = c$.

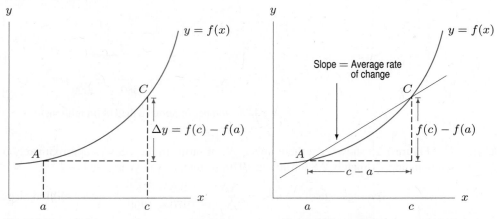

Figure 1.26: The change in a function is represented by a vertical distance

Figure 1.27: The average rate of change is represented by the slope of the line

**Example 4**   (a) Find the average rate of change of $y = f(x) = \sqrt{x}$ between $x = 1$ and $x = 4$.
(b) Graph $f(x)$ and represent this average rate of change as the slope of a line.
(c) Which is larger, the average rate of change of the function between $x = 1$ and $x = 4$ or the average rate of change between $x = 4$ and $x = 5$? What does this tell us about the graph of the function?

Solution   (a) Since $f(1) = \sqrt{1} = 1$ and $f(4) = \sqrt{4} = 2$, between $x = 1$ and $x = 4$, we have

$$\text{Average rate of change} = \frac{\Delta y}{\Delta x} = \frac{f(4) - f(1)}{4 - 1} = \frac{2 - 1}{3} = \frac{1}{3}.$$

(b) A graph of $f(x) = \sqrt{x}$ is given in Figure 1.28. The average rate of change of $f$ between 1 and 4 is the slope of the secant line between $x = 1$ and $x = 4$.
(c) Since the secant line between $x = 1$ and $x = 4$ is steeper than the secant line between $x = 4$ and $x = 5$, the average rate of change between $x = 1$ and $x = 4$ is larger than it is between $x = 4$ and $x = 5$. The rate of change is decreasing. This tells us that the graph of this function is bending downward.

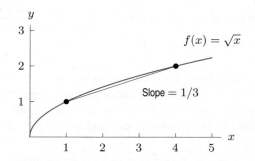

Figure 1.28: Average rate of change = Slope of secant line

## Concavity

We now look at the graphs of functions whose rates of change are increasing throughout an interval or decreasing throughout an interval.

Figure 1.28 shows a graph that is bending downward because the rate of change is decreasing. The graph in Figure 1.26 bends upward because the rate of change of the function is increasing. We make the following definitions.

> The graph of a function is **concave up** if it bends upward as we move left to right; the graph is **concave down** if it bends downward. (See Figure 1.29.) A line is neither concave up nor concave down.

**Figure 1.29**: Concavity of a graph

---

**Example 5**   Using Figure 1.30, estimate the intervals over which:
(a)   The function is increasing; decreasing.      (b)   The graph is concave up; concave down.

**Figure 1.30**

Solution
(a)   The graph suggests that the function is increasing for $x < 2$ and for $x > 6$. It appears to be decreasing for $2 < x < 6$.
(b)   The graph is concave down on the left and concave up on the right. It is difficult to tell exactly where the graph changes concavity, although it appears to be about $x = 4$. Approximately, the graph is concave down for $x < 4$ and concave up for $x > 4$.

---

**Example 6**   From the following values of $f(t)$, does $f$ appear to be increasing or decreasing? Do you think its graph is concave up or concave down?

| $t$ | 0 | 5 | 10 | 15 | 20 | 25 | 30 |
|------|------|------|------|------|------|------|------|
| $f(t)$ | 12.6 | 13.1 | 14.1 | 16.2 | 20.0 | 29.6 | 42.7 |

Solution   Since the given values of $f(t)$ increase as $t$ increases, $f$ appears to be increasing. As we read from left to right, the change in $f(t)$ starts small and gets larger (for constant change in $t$), so the graph is climbing faster. Thus, the graph appears to be concave up. Alternatively, plot the points and notice that a curve through these points bends up.

## Distance, Velocity, and Speed

A grapefruit is thrown up in the air. The height of the grapefruit above the ground first increases and then decreases. See Table 1.11.

**Table 1.11**  *Height, $y$, of the grapefruit above the ground $t$ seconds after it is thrown*

| $t$ (sec) | 0 | 1 | 2 | 3 | 4 | 5 | 6 |
|---|---|---|---|---|---|---|---|
| $y$ (feet) | 6 | 90 | 142 | 162 | 150 | 106 | 30 |

**Example 7**  Find the change and average rate of change of the height of the grapefruit during the first 3 seconds. Give units and interpret your answers.

**Solution**  The change in height during the first 3 seconds is $\Delta y = 162 - 6 = 156$ ft. This means that the grapefruit goes up a total of 156 feet during the first 3 seconds. The average rate of change during this 3 second interval is $156/3 = 52$ ft/sec. During the first 3 seconds, the grapefruit is rising at an average rate of 52 ft/sec.

The average rate of change of height with respect to time is *velocity*. You may recognize the units (feet per second) as units of velocity.

$$\text{Average velocity} = \frac{\text{Change in distance}}{\text{Change in time}} = \begin{array}{c} \text{Average rate of change of distance} \\ \text{with respect to time} \end{array}$$

There is a distinction between *velocity* and *speed*. Suppose an object moves along a line. If we pick one direction to be positive, the velocity is positive if the object is moving in that direction and negative if it is moving in the opposite direction. For the grapefruit, upward is positive and downward is negative. Speed is the magnitude of velocity, so it is always positive or zero.

**Example 8**  Find the average velocity of the grapefruit over the interval $t = 4$ to $t = 6$. Explain the sign of your answer.

**Solution**  Since the height is $y = 150$ feet at $t = 4$ and $y = 30$ feet at $t = 6$, we have

$$\text{Average velocity} = \frac{\text{Change in distance}}{\text{Change in time}} = \frac{\Delta y}{\Delta t} = \frac{30 - 150}{6 - 4} = -60 \text{ ft/sec.}$$

The negative sign means the height is decreasing and the grapefruit is moving downward.

**Example 9**  A car travels away from home on a straight road. Its distance from home at time $t$ is shown in Figure 1.31. Is the car's average velocity greater during the first hour or during the second hour?

**Figure 1.31:** Distance of car from home    **Figure 1.32:** Average velocities of the car

Solution    Average velocity is represented by the slope of a secant line. Figure 1.32 shows that the secant line between $t = 0$ and $t = 1$ is steeper than the secant line between $t = 1$ and $t = 2$. Thus, the average velocity is greater during the first hour.

## Relative Change

Is a population increase of 1000 a significant change? It depends on the original size of the community. If the town of Coyote, NM, population 1559, increases by 1000 people, the townspeople would definitely notice. On the other hand, if New York City, population 8.25 million, increases by 1000 people, almost no one will notice. To visualize the impact of the increase on the two different communities, we look at the change, 1000, as a fraction, or percentage, of the initial population. This percent change is called the *relative change*.

**Example 10**    If the population increases by 1000 people, find the relative change in the population for

(a)  Coyote, NM (population 1559)
(b)  New York City (population 8,250,000)

Solution    (a)  The population increases by 1000 from 1559 so

$$\text{Relative change} = \frac{\text{Change in population}}{\text{Initial population}} = \frac{1000}{1559} = 0.641.$$

The population has increased by 64.1%, a significant increase.
(b)  The population increases by 1000 from 8,250,000 so

$$\text{Relative change} = \frac{\text{Change in population}}{\text{Initial population}} = \frac{1000}{8,250,000} = 0.00012.$$

The population has increased by 0.012%, or less than one-tenth of one percent.

In general, when a quantity $P$ changes from $P_0$ to $P_1$, we define

$$\text{Relative change in } P = \frac{\text{Change in } P}{P_0} = \frac{P_1 - P_0}{P_0}.$$

The relative change is a number, without units. It is often expressed as a percentage.

**Example 11**    A price increase can be significant or inconsequential depending on the item. In each of the following cases, find the relative change in price of a $2 price increase; give your answer as a percent.

(a)   A gallon of gas costing $2.25          (b)   A cell phone costing $180

Solution    (a)  The change in the price is $2 so we have

$$\text{Relative change in price of gas} = \frac{\text{Change in price}}{\text{Initial price}} = \frac{2}{2.25} = 0.889.$$

The price of gas has gone up 88.9%.
(b)  We have

$$\text{Relative change in price of cell phone} = \frac{\text{Change in price}}{\text{Initial price}} = \frac{2}{180} = 0.011.$$

The price of the cell phone has gone up only 1.1%.

Relative change can be positive or negative, as we see in the following example.

**Example 12**    Find the relative change in the price of a $75.99 pair of jeans if the sale price is $52.99.

**Solution**    The price has dropped from $75.99 to $52.99. We have

$$\text{Relative change} = \frac{52.99 - 75.99}{75.99} = \frac{-23}{75.99} = -0.303.$$

The price has been reduced by 30.3% for the sale.

**Example 13**    The number of sales per week of a $75.99 pair of jeans is 25 pairs. The number of weekly sales goes up to 45 pairs when the price is reduced by 30.3%. Find the relative change in the weekly sales.

**Solution**    The quantity sold goes up from 25 pairs of jeans to 45 pairs. We have

$$\text{Relative change} = \frac{45 - 25}{25} = \frac{20}{25} = 0.8.$$

The number of sales per week grows by 80%.

### Ratio of Relative Changes: Elasticity

In Example 12 and 13 we see that a 30.3% reduction in the price of a $75.99 pair of jeans increased the weekly sales by 80%. If we are interested in the percent change in quantity as a result of a 1% change in price we look at the ratio:

$$\left| \frac{\text{Relative change in quantity}}{\text{Relative change in price}} \right| = \left| \frac{0.8}{-0.303} \right| = 2.64.$$

So the number of pair of jeans sold increases by 2.64% when the price drops by 1%. This ratio is called the elasticity. It gives information about how change in price of a product effects the change in quantity. Elasticity will be discussed in further detail in Section 4.6.

## Problems for Section 1.3

In Problems 1–4, decide whether the graph is concave up, concave down, or neither.

**1.**

**2.**

**5.** Table 1.12 gives values of a function $w = f(t)$. Is this function increasing or decreasing? Is the graph of this function concave up or concave down?

**Table 1.12**

| $t$ | 0 | 4 | 8 | 12 | 16 | 20 | 24 |
|-----|-----|-----|-----|-----|-----|-----|-----|
| $w$ | 100 | 58 | 32 | 24 | 20 | 18 | 17 |

**3.**

**4.**

**6.** Graph a function $f(x)$ which is increasing everywhere and concave up for negative $x$ and concave down for positive $x$.

**7.** For which pairs of consecutive points in Figure 1.33 is the function graphed:

   **(a)** Increasing and concave up?
   **(b)** Increasing and concave down?
   **(c)** Decreasing and concave up?
   **(d)** Decreasing and concave down?

**Figure 1.33**

**8.** Find the average rate of change of $f(x) = 2x^2$ between $x = 1$ and $x = 3$.

**9.** Find the average rate of change of $f(x) = 3x^2 + 4$ between $x = -2$ and $x = 1$. Illustrate your answer graphically.

**10.** When a deposit of $1000 is made into an account paying 8% interest, compounded annually, the balance, $B$, in the account after $t$ years is given by $B = 1000(1.08)^t$. Find the average rate of change in the balance over the interval $t = 0$ to $t = 5$. Give units and interpret your answer in terms of the balance in the account.

**11.** Table 1.13 gives the net sales of The Gap, Inc, which operates nearly 3000 clothing stores. [29]

   **(a)** Find the change in net sales between 2008 and 2010.
   **(b)** Find the average rate of change in net sales between 2005 and 2008. Give units and interpret your answer.
   **(c)** From 2005 to 2010, were there any one-year intervals during which the average rate of change was positive? If so, when?

**Table 1.13**  *Gap net sales, in millions of dollars*

| Year | 2005 | 2006 | 2007 | 2008 | 2009 | 2010 |
|------|------|------|------|------|------|------|
| Sales | 16,019 | 15,923 | 15,763 | 14,526 | 14,197 | 14,660 |

**12.** Table 1.14 shows world bicycle production. [30]

   **(a)** Find the change in bicycle production between 1950 and 2000. Give units.

   **(b)** Find the average rate of change in bicycle production between 1950 and 2000. Give units and interpret your answer in terms of bicycle production.

**Table 1.14**  *World bicycle production, in millions*

| Year | 1950 | 1960 | 1970 | 1980 | 1990 | 2000 |
|------|------|------|------|------|------|------|
| Bicycles | 11 | 20 | 36 | 62 | 92 | 101 |

**13.** Table 1.15 shows attendance at NFL football games. [31]

   **(a)** Find the average rate of change in the attendance from 2003 to 2007. Give units.
   **(b)** Find the annual increase in the attendance for each year from 2003 to 2007. (Your answer should be four numbers.)
   **(c)** Show that the average rate of change found in part (a) is the average of the four yearly changes found in part (b).

**Table 1.15**  *Attendance at NFL football games, in millions of fans*

| Year | 2003 | 2004 | 2005 | 2006 | 2007 |
|------|------|------|------|------|------|
| Attendance | 21.64 | 21.71 | 21.79 | 22.20 | 22.26 |

**14.** Figure 1.34 shows the total value of US imports, in billions of dollars. [32]

   **(a)** Was the value of the imports higher in 1985 or in 2003? Approximately how much higher?
   **(b)** Estimate the average rate of change of US imports between 1985 and 2003. Give units and interpret your answer in terms of imports.

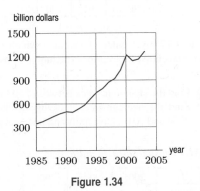

**Figure 1.34**

[29]http://www.sec.gov/Archives/edgar/data/39911/000119312510068386/d10k.html#tx95595_10, accessed May 2012.
[30]www.earth-policy.org/Indicators/indicator11_data1.htm, accessed April 19, 2005.
[31]*Statistical Abstracts of the United States 2009, Table 1204.*
[32]www.ita.doc.gov/td/industry/otea/usfth/aggregate/H03t26.pdf, accessed April 19, 2005.

**15.** Figure 1.35 shows a particle's distance from a point. What is the particle's average velocity from $t = 0$ to $t = 3$?

**Figure 1.35**

**16.** At time $t$ in seconds, a particle's distance $s(t)$, in cm, from a point is given in the table. What is the average velocity of the particle from $t = 3$ to $t = 10$?

| $t$ | 0 | 3 | 6 | 10 | 13 |
|---|---|---|---|---|---|
| $s(t)$ | 0 | 72 | 92 | 144 | 180 |

**17.** Table 1.16 shows world population, $P$, in billions of people, world passenger automobile production, $A$, in millions of cars, and world cell phone subscribers, $C$, in millions of subscribers.[33]

(a) Find the average rate of change, with units, for each of $P$, $A$, and $C$ between 1995 and 2005.

(b) Between 1995 and 2005, which increased faster:
  (i) Population or the number of automobiles?
  (ii) Population or the number of cell phone subscribers?

**Table 1.16**

| Year | 1995 | 2000 | 2005 |
|---|---|---|---|
| $P$ (billions) | 5.68 | 6.07 | 6.45 |
| $A$ (millions) | 36.1 | 41.3 | 45.9 |
| $C$ (millions) | 91 | 740 | 2168 |

**18.** Table 1.17 gives sales of Pepsico, which operates two major businesses: beverages (including Pepsi) and snack foods.[34]

(a) Find the change in sales between 2003 and 2010.

(b) Find the average rate of change in sales between 2003 and 2010. Give units and interpret your answer.

**Table 1.17**  *Pepsico sales, in millions of dollars*

| Year | 2003 | 2004 | 2005 | 2006 | 2007 | 2008 | 2009 | 2010 |
|---|---|---|---|---|---|---|---|---|
| Sales | 26,971 | 29,261 | 32,562 | 35,137 | 39,474 | 43,251 | 43,230 | 57,838 |

**19.** Figure 1.36 shows a particle's distance from a point. What is the particle's average velocity from $t = 1$ to $t = 3$?

**Figure 1.36**

**20.** Do you expect the average rate of change (in units per year) of each of the following to be positive or negative? Explain your reasoning.

(a) Number of acres of rain forest in the world.
(b) Population of the world.
(c) Number of polio cases each year in the US, since 1950.
(d) Height of a sand dune that is being eroded.
(e) Cost of living in the US.

**21.** Table 1.18 shows the production of tobacco in the US.[35]

(a) What is the average rate of change in tobacco production between 2003 and 2010? Give units and interpret your answer in terms of tobacco production.

(b) During this seven-year period, is there any interval during which the average rate of change was positive? If so, when?

**Table 1.18**  *Tobacco production, in millions of pounds*

| Year | 2003 | 2004 | 2005 | 2006 | 2007 | 2008 | 2009 | 2010 |
|---|---|---|---|---|---|---|---|---|
| Production | 802 | 882 | 645 | 728 | 788 | 801 | 823 | 719 |

**22.** Figure 1.37 shows the length, $L$, in cm, of a sturgeon (a type of fish) as a function of the time, $t$, in years.[36]

(a) Is the function increasing or decreasing? Is the graph concave up or concave down?

(b) Estimate the average rate of growth of the sturgeon between $t = 5$ and $t = 15$. Give units and interpret your answer in terms of the sturgeon.

**Figure 1.37**

[33] *Vital Signs 2007-2008*, The Worldwatch Institute, W.W. Norton & Company, 2007, p. 51 and 67.
[34] www.pepsico.com, accessed August, 2012.
[35] http://www.fda.gov/downloads/TobaccoProducts/NewsEvents/UCM242577.pdf, accessed August, 2012.
[36] Data from von Bertalanffy, L., *General System Theory*, p. 177 (New York: Braziller, 1968).

23. Table 1.19 shows the total US labor force, $L$. Find the average rate of change between 1940 and 2000; between 1940 and 1960; between 1980 and 2000. Give units and interpret your answers in terms of the labor force.[37]

**Table 1.19**   *US labor force, in thousands of workers*

| Year | 1940 | 1960 | 1980 | 2000 |
|------|------|------|------|------|
| $L$ | 47,520 | 65,778 | 99,303 | 136,891 |

24. The total world marine catch[38] of fish, in metric tons, was 17 million in 1950 and 99 million in 2001. What was the average rate of change in the marine catch during this period? Give units and interpret your answer.

25. Table 1.20 gives the revenues, $R$, of General Motors, formerly the world's largest auto manufacturer.[39]

    (a) Find the change in revenues between 2003 and 2008.
    (b) Find the average rate of change in revenues between 2003 and 2008. Give units and interpret your answer.
    (c) From 2003 to 2008, were there any one-year intervals during which the average rate of change was negative? If so, which?

**Table 1.20**   *GM revenues, billions of dollars*

| Year | 2003 | 2004 | 2005 | 2006 | 2007 | 2008 |
|------|------|------|------|------|------|------|
| $R$ | 184.0 | 192.9 | 193.1 | 205.6 | 181.1 | 149.0 |

26. The number of US households with cable television[40] was 12,168,450 in 1977 and 73,365,880 in 2003. Estimate the average rate of change in the number of US households with cable television during this 26-year period. Give units and interpret your answer.

27. Figure 1.38 shows the amount of nicotine $N = f(t)$, in mg, in a person's bloodstream as a function of the time, $t$, in hours, since the last cigarette.

    (a) Is the average rate of change in nicotine level positive or negative? Explain.
    (b) Find the average rate of change in the nicotine level between $t = 0$ and $t = 3$. Give units and interpret your answer in terms of nicotine.

**Figure 1.38**

28. Table 1.21 shows the concentration, $c$, of creatinine in the bloodstream of a dog.[41]

    (a) Including units, find the average rate at which the concentration is changing between the
        (i) $6^{\text{th}}$ and $8^{\text{th}}$ minutes. (ii) $8^{\text{th}}$ and $10^{\text{th}}$ minutes.
    (b) Explain the sign and relative magnitudes of your results in terms of creatinine.

**Table 1.21**

| $t$ (minutes) | 2 | 4 | 6 | 8 | 10 |
|------|------|------|------|------|------|
| $c$ ( mg/ml) | 0.439 | 0.383 | 0.336 | 0.298 | 0.266 |

29. The population of the world reached 1 billion in 1804, 2 billion in 1927, 3 billion in 1960, 4 billion in 1974, 5 billion in 1987 and 6 billion in 1999. Find the average rate of change of the population of the world, in people per minute, during each of these intervals (that is, from 1804 to 1927, 1927 to 1960, etc.).

Problems 30–31 refer to Figure 1.39, which shows the contraction velocity of a muscle as a function of the load it pulls against.

**Figure 1.39**

30. In terms of the muscle, interpret the
    (a) Vertical intercept    (b) Horizontal intercept

31. (a) Find the change in muscle contraction velocity when the load changes from 1 kg to 3 kg. Give units.
    (b) Find the average rate of change in the contraction velocity between 1 kg and 3 kg. Give units.

32. Table 1.22 gives the sales, $S$, of Intel Corporation, a leading manufacturer of integrated circuits.[42]

    (a) Find the change in sales between 2005 and 2010.
    (b) Find the average rate of change in sales between 2005 and 2010. Give units and interpret your answer.

**Table 1.22**   *Intel sales, in billions of dollars*

| Year | 2005 | 2006 | 2007 | 2008 | 2009 | 2010 |
|------|------|------|------|------|------|------|
| $S$ | 38.8 | 35.4 | 38.3 | 37.6 | 35.1 | 43.6 |

---

[37] *The World Almanac and Book of Facts 2005*, p. 144 (New York).
[38] *The World Almanac and Book of Facts 2005*, p. 143 (New York).
[39] www.gm.com/company/investor_information/earnings/hist_earnings/index.html, accessed May 23, 2009.
[40] *The World Almanac and Book of Facts 2005*, p. 310 (New York).
[41] From Cullen, M.R., *Linear Models in Biology* (Chichester: Ellis Horwood, 1985).
[42] Intel 2010 Annual Report, www.intel.com/intel/finance, accessed August, 2012.

**33.** Let $f(t)$ be the number of US billionaires in year $t$.

   **(a)** Express the following statements[43] in terms of $f$.
   - **(i)** In 1985 there were 13 US billionaires.
   - **(ii)** In 1990 there were 99 US billionaires.

   **(b)** Find the average yearly increase in the number of US billionaires between 1985 and 1990. Express this using $f$.

   **(c)** Assuming the yearly increase remains constant, find a formula predicting the number of US billionaires in year $t$.

**34.** Figure 1.40 shows the position of an object at time $t$.

   **(a)** Draw a line on the graph whose slope represents the average velocity between $t = 2$ and $t = 8$.

   **(b)** Is average velocity greater between $t = 0$ and $t = 3$ or between $t = 3$ and $t = 6$?

   **(c)** Is average velocity positive or negative between $t = 6$ and $t = 9$?

**Figure 1.40**

**35.** In an experiment, a lizard is encouraged to run as fast as possible. Figure 1.41 shows the distance run in meters as a function of the time in seconds.[44]

   **(a)** If the lizard were running faster and faster, what would be the concavity of the graph? Does this match what you see?

   **(b)** Estimate the average velocity of the lizard during this 0.8 second experiment.

**Figure 1.41**

**36.** Values of $F(t)$, $G(t)$, and $H(t)$ are in Table 1.23. Which graph is concave up and which is concave down? Which function is linear?

**Table 1.23**

| $t$ | $F(t)$ | $G(t)$ | $H(t)$ |
|---|---|---|---|
| 10 | 15 | 15 | 15 |
| 20 | 22 | 18 | 17 |
| 30 | 28 | 21 | 20 |
| 40 | 33 | 24 | 24 |
| 50 | 37 | 27 | 29 |
| 60 | 40 | 30 | 35 |

**37.** Experiments suggest that the male maximum heart rate (the most times a male's heart can safely beat in a minute) decreases by 9 beats per minute during the first 21 years of his life, and by 26 beats per minute during the first 33 years.[45] If you model the maximum heart rate as a function of age, should you use a function that is increasing or decreasing? Concave up or concave down?

**38.** A car starts slowly and then speeds up. Eventually the car slows down and stops. Graph the distance that the car has traveled against time.

In Problems 39–42, find the relative, or percent, change.

**39.** $B$ changes from 12,000 to 15,000

**40.** $S$ changes from 400 to 450

**41.** $W$ changes from 0.3 to 0.05

**42.** $R$ changes from 50 to 47

In Problems 43–46, which relative change is bigger in magnitude? Justify your answer.

**43.** The change in the Dow Jones average from 164.6 to 77.9 in 1931; the change in the Dow Jones average from 13261.8 to 8776.4 in 2008.

**44.** The change in the US population from 5.2 million to 7.2 million from 1800 to 1810; the change in the US population from 151.3 to 179.3 from 1950 to 1960.

**45.** An increase in class size from 5 to 10; an increase in class size from 30 to 50.

**46.** An increase in sales from \$100,000 to \$500,000; an increase in sales from \$20,000,000 to \$20,500,000.

**47.** Find the relative change of a population if it changes
   **(a)** From 1000 to 2000   **(b)** From 2000 to 1000
   **(c)** From 1,000,000 to 1,001,000

**48.** On Black Monday, October 28, 1929, the stock market on Wall Street crashed. The Dow Jones average dropped from 298.94 to 260.64 in one day. What was the relative change in the index?

**49.** On January 27, 2013, the cost to mail a letter in the US [46] was raised from 45 cents to 46 cents. Find the relative change in the cost.

[43]//hypertextbook.com/facts/2005/MichelleLee.shtml

[44]Data from Huey, R.B. and Hertz, P.E., "Effects of Body Size and Slope on the Acceleration of a Lizard," *J. Exp. Biol.*, Volume 110, 1984, p. 113-123.

[45]www.css.edu/users/tboone2/asep/May2002JEPonline.html, accessed January 4, 2005.

[46]http://en.wikipedia.org/wiki/History_of_United_States_postage_rates

**50.** The US Consumer Price Index (CPI) is a measure of the cost of living. The inflation rate is the annual relative rate of change of the CPI. Use the January data in Table 1.24[47] to estimate the inflation rate for each of years 2007–2012.

**Table 1.24**

| Year | 2007 | 2008 | 2009 | 2010 | 2011 | 2012 |
|------|------|------|------|------|------|------|
| CPI | 202.416 | 211.08 | 211.143 | 216.687 | 220.223 | 226.655 |

**51.** During 2008 the US economy stopped growing and began to shrink. Table 1.25[48] gives quarterly data on the US Gross Domestic Product (GDP), which measures the size of the economy.

(a) Estimate the relative growth rate (percent per year) at the first four times in the table.

(b) Economists often say an economy is in recession if the GDP decreases for two quarters in a row. Was the US in recession in 2008?

**Table 1.25**

| $t$ (years since 2008) | 0 | 0.25 | 0.5 | 0.75 | 1.0 |
|---|---|---|---|---|---|
| GDP (trillion dollars) | 14.15 | 14.29 | 14.41 | 14.2 | 14.09 |

**52.** An alternative to petroleum-based diesel fuel, biodiesel, is derived from renewable resources such as food crops, algae, and animal oils. The table shows the recent annual percent growth in US biodiesel consumption.[49]

| Year | 2005 | 2006 | 2007 | 2008 | 2009 |
|------|------|------|------|------|------|
| % growth over previous yr | 237 | 186.6 | 37.2 | −11.7 | 7.3 |

(a) Find the largest time interval over which the percentage growth in the US consumption of biodiesel was an increasing function of time. Interpret what increasing means, practically speaking, in this case.

(b) Find the largest time interval over which the actual US consumption of biodiesel was an increasing function of time. Interpret what increasing means, practically speaking, in this case.

**53.** Hydroelectric power is electric power generated by the force of moving water. Figure 1.42 shows[50] the annual percent growth in hydroelectric power consumption by the US industrial sector between 2004 and 2009.

(a) Find the largest time interval over which the percentage growth in the US consumption of hydroelectric power was a decreasing function of time. Interpret what decreasing means, practically speaking, in this case.

(b) Find the largest time interval over which the actual US consumption of hydroelectric power was a decreasing function of time. Interpret what decreasing means, practically speaking, in this case.

**Figure 1.42**

**54.** Solar panels are arrays of photovoltaic cells that convert solar radiation into electricity. The table shows the annual percent change in the US price per watt of a solar panel.[51]

| Year | 2004 | 2005 | 2006 | 2007 | 2008 |
|------|------|------|------|------|------|
| % growth over previous yr | −5.7 | 6.7 | 9.7 | −3.7 | 3.6 |

(a) Find the largest time interval over which the percentage growth in the US price per watt of a solar panel was an increasing function of time. Interpret what increasing means, practically speaking, in this case.

(b) Find the largest time interval over which the actual price per watt of a solar panel was an increasing function of time. Interpret what increasing means, practically speaking, in this case.

**55.** School organizations raise money by selling candy door to door. When the price is $1 a school organization sells 2765 candies and when the price goes up to $1.25 the quantity of sold candy drops down to 2440.

(a) Find the relative change in the price of candy.

(b) Find the relative change in the quantity of candy sold.

(c) Find and interpret the ratio

$$\left| \frac{\text{Relative change in quantity}}{\text{Relative change in price}} \right|$$

and interpret your answer.

---

[47] http://www.usinflationcalculator.com/, accessed August 2012.
[48] www.bea.gov/national/nipaweb, Table 1.1.5.
[49] http://www.eia.doe.gov/aer/renew.html. Accessed February 2011.
[50] Yearly values have been joined with segments to highlight trends in the data; however, values in between years should not be inferred from the segments. From http://www.eia.doe.gov/aer/renew.html. Accessed February 2011.
[51] We use the official price per peak watt, which uses the maximum number of watts a solar panel can produce under ideal conditions. From http://www.eia.doe.gov/aer/renew.html. Accessed February 2011.

# 1.4  APPLICATIONS OF FUNCTIONS TO ECONOMICS

In this section, we look at some of the functions of interest to decision-makers in a firm or industry.

## The Cost Function

> The **cost function**, $C(q)$, gives the total cost of producing a quantity $q$ of some good.

What sort of function do you expect $C$ to be? The more goods that are made, the higher the total cost, so $C$ is an increasing function. Costs of production can be separated into two parts: the *fixed costs,* which are incurred even if nothing is produced, and the *variable costs,* which depend on how many units are produced.

### An Example: Manufacturing Costs

Let's consider a company that makes radios. The factory and machinery needed to begin production are fixed costs, which are incurred even if no radios are made. The costs of labor and raw materials are variable costs since these quantities depend on how many radios are made. The fixed costs for this company are $24,000 and the variable costs are $7 per radio. Then,

$$\text{Total costs for the company} = \text{Fixed costs} + \text{Variable costs}$$
$$= 24{,}000 + 7 \cdot \text{Number of radios},$$

so, if $q$ is the number of radios produced,

$$C(q) = 24{,}000 + 7q.$$

This is the equation of a line with slope 7 and vertical intercept 24,000.

The variable cost for one additional unit is called the *marginal cost.* For a linear cost function, the marginal cost is the rate of change, or slope, of the cost function.

---

**Example 1**    Graph the cost function $C(q) = 24{,}000 + 7q$. Label the fixed costs and marginal cost.

Solution    The graph of $C(q)$ is the line in Figure 1.43. The fixed costs are represented by the vertical intercept of 24,000. The marginal cost is represented by the slope of 7, which is the change in cost corresponding to a unit change in production.

**Figure 1.43**: Cost function for the radio manufacturer

---

> If $C(q)$ is a linear cost function,
> - Fixed costs are represented by the vertical intercept.
> - Marginal cost is represented by the slope.

**Example 2**    In each case, draw a graph of a linear cost function satisfying the given conditions:

(a)  Fixed costs are large but marginal cost is small.
(b)  There are no fixed costs but marginal cost is high.

**Solution**    (a)  The graph is a line with a large vertical intercept and a small slope. See Figure 1.44.
(b)  The graph is a line with a vertical intercept of zero (so the line goes through the origin) and a large positive slope. See Figure 1.45. Figures 1.44 and 1.45 have the same scales.

Figure 1.44: Large fixed costs, small marginal cost    Figure 1.45: No fixed costs, high marginal cost

## The Revenue Function

> The **revenue function**, $R(q)$, gives the total revenue received by a firm from selling a quantity, $q$, of some good.

If the good sells for a price of $p$ per unit, and the quantity sold is $q$, then

$$\text{Revenue} = \text{Price} \cdot \text{Quantity}, \quad \text{so} \quad R = pq.$$

If the price does not depend on the quantity sold, so $p$ is a constant, the graph of revenue as a function of $q$ is a line through the origin, with slope equal to the price $p$.

**Example 3**    If radios sell for $15 each, sketch the manufacturer's revenue function. Show the price of a radio on the graph.

**Solution**    Since $R(q) = pq = 15q$, the revenue graph is a line through the origin with a slope of 15. See Figure 1.46. The price is the slope of the line.

Figure 1.46: Revenue function for the radio manufacturer

**Example 4**    Graph the cost function $C(q) = 24{,}000 + 7q$ and the revenue function $R(q) = 15q$ on the same axes. For what values of $q$ does the company make money?

Solution    The company makes money whenever revenues are greater than costs, so we find the values of $q$ for which the graph of $R(q)$ lies above the graph of $C(q)$. See Figure 1.47.

We find the point at which the graphs of $R(q)$ and $C(q)$ cross:

$$\text{Revenue} = \text{Cost}$$
$$15q = 24{,}000 + 7q$$
$$8q = 24{,}000$$
$$q = 3000.$$

The company makes a profit if it produces and sells more than 3000 radios. The company loses money if it produces and sells fewer than 3000 radios.

Figure 1.47: Cost and revenue functions for the radio manufacturer: What values of $q$ generate a profit?

## The Profit Function

Decisions are often made by considering the profit, usually written[52] as $\pi$ to distinguish it from the price, $p$. We have

$$\boxed{\text{Profit} = \text{Revenue} - \text{Cost} \quad \text{so} \quad \pi = R - C.}$$

The *break-even point* for a company is the point where the profit is zero and revenue equals cost. See Figure 1.47.

**Example 5**    Find a formula for the profit function of the radio manufacturer. Graph it, marking the break-even point.

Solution    Since $R(q) = 15q$ and $C(q) = 24{,}000 + 7q$, we have

$$\pi(q) = R(q) - C(q) = 15q - (24{,}000 + 7q) = -24{,}000 + 8q.$$

Notice that the negative of the fixed costs is the vertical intercept and the break-even point is the horizontal intercept. See Figure 1.48.

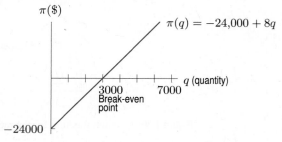

Figure 1.48: Profit for radio manufacturer

---

[52]This $\pi$ has nothing to do with the area of a circle, and merely stands for the Greek equivalent of the letter "p."

**Example 6**   (a) Using Table 1.26, estimate the break-even point for this company.
(b) Find the company's profit if 1000 units are produced.
(c) What price do you think the company is charging for its product?

Table 1.26   *Company's estimates of cost and revenue for a product*

| $q$ | 500 | 600 | 700 | 800 | 900 | 1000 | 1100 |
|---|---|---|---|---|---|---|---|
| $C(q)$, in $\$$ | 5000 | 5500 | 6000 | 6500 | 7000 | 7500 | 8000 |
| $R(q)$, in $\$$ | 4000 | 4800· | 5600 | 6400 | 7200 | 8000 | 8800 |

**Solution**   (a) The break-even point is the value of $q$ for which revenue equals cost. Since revenue is below cost at $q = 800$ and revenue is greater than cost at $q = 900$, the break-even point is between 800 and 900. The values in the table suggest that the break-even point is closer to 800, as the cost and revenue are closer there. A reasonable estimate for the break-even point is $q = 830$.
(b) If the company produces 1000 units, the cost is $\$7500$ and the revenue is $\$8000$, so the profit is $8000 - 7500 = 500$ dollars.
(c) From the table, it appears that $R(q) = 8q$. This indicates the company is selling the product for $\$8$ each.

## The Marginal Cost, Marginal Revenue, and Marginal Profit

Just as we used the term marginal cost to mean the rate of change, or slope, of a linear cost function, we use the terms *marginal revenue* and *marginal profit* to mean the rate of change, or slope, of linear revenue and profit functions, respectively. The term *marginal* is used because we are looking at how the cost, revenue, or profit change "at the margin," that is, by the addition of one more unit. For example, for the radio manufacturer, the marginal cost is 7 dollars/item (the additional cost of producing one more item is $\$7$), the marginal revenue is 15 dollars/item (the additional revenue from selling one more item is $\$15$), and the marginal profit is 8 dollars/item (the additional profit from selling one more item is $\$8$).

## The Depreciation Function

Suppose that the radio manufacturer has a machine that costs $\$20,000$ and is sold ten years later for $\$3000$. We say the value of the machine *depreciates* from $\$20,000$ today to a resale value of $\$3000$ in ten years. The depreciation formula gives the value, $V(t)$, in dollars, of the machine as a function of the number of years, $t$, since the machine was purchased. We assume that the value of the machine depreciates linearly.

The value of the machine when it is new ($t = 0$) is $\$20,000$, so $V(0) = 20,000$. The resale value at time $t = 10$ is $\$3000$, so $V(10) = 3000$. We have

$$\text{Slope} = m = \frac{3000 - 20,000}{10 - 0} = \frac{-17,000}{10} = -1700 \text{ dollars per year.}$$

This slope tells us that the value of the machine is decreasing at a rate of $\$1700$ per year. Since $V(0) = 20,000$, the vertical intercept is 20,000, so

$$V(t) = 20,000 - 1700t \text{ dollars.}$$

## Supply and Demand Curves

The quantity, $q$, of an item that is manufactured and sold depends on its price, $p$. As the price increases, manufacturers are usually willing to supply more of the product, whereas the quantity demanded by consumers falls.

> The **supply curve**, for a given item, relates the quantity, $q$, of the item that manufacturers are willing to make per unit time to the price, $p$, for which the item can be sold.
> The **demand curve** relates the quantity, $q$, of an item demanded by consumers per unit time to the price, $p$, of the item.

Economists often think of the quantities supplied and demanded as functions of price. However, for historical reasons, the economists put price (the independent variable) on the vertical axis and quantity (the dependent variable) on the horizontal axis. (The reason for this state of affairs is that economists originally took price to be the dependent variable and put it on the vertical axis. Later, when the point of view changed, the axes did not.) Thus, typical supply and demand curves look like those shown in Figure 1.49.

Figure 1.49: Supply and demand curves

**Example 7**    What is the economic meaning of the prices $p_0$ and $p_1$ and the quantity $q_1$ in Figure 1.49?

Solution    The vertical axis corresponds to a quantity of zero. Since the price $p_0$ is the vertical intercept on the supply curve, $p_0$ is the price at which the quantity supplied is zero. In other words, for prices below $p_0$, the suppliers will not produce anything. The price $p_1$ is the vertical intercept on the demand curve, so it corresponds to the price at which the quantity demanded is zero. In other words, for prices above $p_1$, consumers buy none of the product.

The horizontal axis corresponds to a price of zero, so the quantity $q_1$ on the demand curve is the quantity demanded if the price were zero—the quantity that could be given away free.

## Equilibrium Price and Quantity

If we plot the supply and demand curves on the same axes, as in Figure 1.50, the graphs cross at the *equilibrium point*. The values $p^*$ and $q^*$ at this point are called the *equilibrium price* and *equilibrium quantity*, respectively. It is assumed that the market naturally settles to this equilibrium point. (See Problem 28.)

Figure 1.50: The equilibrium price and quantity

**Example 8**    Find the equilibrium price and quantity if

$$\text{Quantity supplied} = 3p - 50 \quad \text{and} \quad \text{Quantity demanded} = 100 - 2p.$$

Solution    To find the equilibrium price and quantity, we find the point at which

$$\text{Supply} = \text{Demand}$$
$$3p - 50 = 100 - 2p$$
$$5p = 150$$
$$p = 30.$$

The equilibrium price is \$30. To find the equilibrium quantity, we use either the demand curve or the supply curve. At a price of \$30, the quantity produced is $100 - 2 \cdot 30 = 40$ items. The equilibrium quantity is 40 items. In Figure 1.51, the demand and supply curves intersect at $p^* = 30$ and $q^* = 40$.

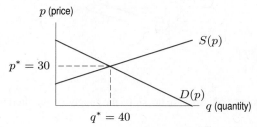

**Figure 1.51**: Equilibrium: $p^* = 30$, $q^* = 40$

## The Effect of Taxes on Equilibrium

What effect do taxes have on the equilibrium price and quantity for a product? We distinguish between two types of taxes.[53] A *specific tax* is a fixed amount per unit of a product sold regardless of the selling price. This is the case with such items as gasoline, alcohol, and cigarettes. A specific tax is usually imposed on the producer. A *sales tax* is a fixed percentage of the selling price. Many cities and states collect sales tax on a wide variety of items. A sales tax is usually imposed on the consumer. We consider a specific tax now; a sales tax is considered in Problems 43 and 44.

**Example 9**   A specific tax of \$5 per unit is now imposed upon suppliers in Example 8. What are the new equilibrium price and quantity?

**Solution**   The consumers pay $p$ dollars per unit, but the suppliers receive only $p - 5$ dollars per unit because \$5 goes to the government as taxes. Since

$$\text{Quantity supplied } = 3(\text{Amount per unit received by suppliers}) - 50,$$

the new supply equation is

$$\text{Quantity supplied } = 3(p - 5) - 50 = 3p - 65;$$

the demand equation is unchanged:

$$\text{Quantity demanded } = 100 - 2p.$$

At the equilibrium price, we have

$$\text{Demand} = \text{Supply}$$
$$100 - 2p = 3p - 65$$
$$165 = 5p$$
$$p = 33.$$

The equilibrium price is \$33. The equilibrium quantity is 34 units, since the quantity demanded is $q = 100 - 2 \cdot 33 = 34$.

In Example 8, the equilibrium price was \$30; with the imposition of a \$5 tax in Example 9, the equilibrium price is \$33. Thus the equilibrium price increases by \$3 as a result of the tax. Notice that this is less than the amount of the tax. The consumer ends up paying \$3 more than if the tax did not exist. However the government receives \$5 per item. The producer pays the other \$2 of the tax,

[53] Adapted from Barry Bressler, *A Unified Approach to Mathematical Economics*, p. 81–88 (New York: Harper & Row, 1975).

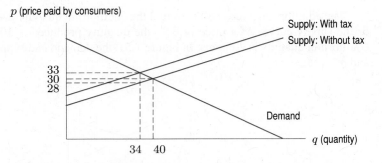

Figure 1.52: Specific tax shifts the supply curve, altering the equilibrium price and quantity

retaining \$28 of the price paid per item. Although the tax was imposed on the producer, some of the tax is passed on to the consumer in terms of higher prices. The tax has increased the price and reduced the number of items sold. See Figure 1.52. Notice that the taxes have the effect of moving the supply curve up by \$5 because suppliers have to be paid \$5 more to produce the same quantity.

## A Budget Constraint

An ongoing debate in the federal government concerns the allocation of money between defense and social programs. In general, the more that is spent on defense, the less that is available for social programs, and vice versa. Let's simplify the example to guns and butter. Assuming a constant budget, we show that the relationship between the number of guns and the quantity of butter is linear. Suppose that there is \$12,000 to be spent and that it is to be divided between guns, costing \$400 each, and butter, costing \$2000 a ton. Suppose the number of guns bought is $g$, and the number of tons of butter is $b$. Then the amount of money spent on guns is \$400$g$, and the amount spent on butter is \$2000$b$. Assuming all the money is spent,

$$\text{Amount spent on guns } + \text{ Amount spent on butter } = \$12,000$$

or

$$400g + 2000b = 12,000.$$

Thus, dividing both sides by 400,

$$g + 5b = 30.$$

This equation is the budget constraint. Since the budget constraint can be written as

$$g = 30 - 5b,$$

the graph of the budget constraint is a line. See Figure 1.53.

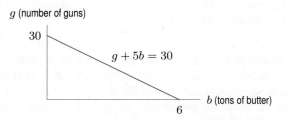

Figure 1.53: Budget constraint

# Problems for Section 1.4

**1.** In Figure 1.54, which shows the cost and revenue functions for a product, label each of the following:

    **(a)** Fixed costs         **(b)** Break-even quantity

    **(c)** Quantities at which the company:

        **(i)** Makes a profit       **(ii)** Loses money

**Figure 1.54**

**2.** Figure 1.55 shows cost and revenue for a company.

    **(a)** Approximately what quantity does this company have to produce to make a profit?

    **(b)** Estimate the profit generated by 600 units.

**Figure 1.55**

**3. (a)** Estimate the fixed costs and the marginal cost for the cost function in Figure 1.56.

    **(b)** Estimate $C(10)$ and interpret it in terms of cost.

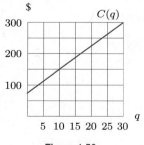

**Figure 1.56**

**4.** Values of a linear cost function are in Table 1.27. What are the fixed costs and the marginal cost? Find a formula for the cost function.

**Table 1.27**

| $q$ | 0 | 5 | 10 | 15 | 20 |
|------|------|------|------|------|------|
| $C(q)$ | 5000 | 5020 | 5040 | 5060 | 5080 |

**5.** The cost $C$, in millions of dollars, of producing $q$ items is given by $C = 5.7 + 0.002q$. Interpret the 5.7 and the 0.002 in terms of production. Give units.

**6. (a)** Give an example of a possible company where the fixed costs are zero (or very small).

    **(b)** Give an example of a possible company where the marginal cost is zero (or very small).

**7.** Suppose that $q = f(p)$ is the demand curve for a product, where $p$ is the selling price in dollars and $q$ is the quantity sold at that price.

    **(a)** What does the statement $f(12) = 60$ tell you about demand for this product?

    **(b)** Do you expect this function to be increasing or decreasing? Why?

**8.** A company has cost and revenue functions, in dollars, given by $C(q) = 6000 + 10q$ and $R(q) = 12q$.

    **(a)** Find the cost and revenue if the company produces 500 units. Does the company make a profit? What about 5000 units?

    **(b)** Find the break-even point and illustrate it graphically.

**9.** The demand curve for a quantity $q$ of a product is $q = 5500 - 100p$ where $p$ is price in dollars. Interpret the 5500 and the 100 in terms of demand. Give units.

**10.** A demand curve is given by $75p + 50q = 300$, where $p$ is the price of the product, in dollars, and $q$ is the quantity demanded at that price. Find $p$- and $q$-intercepts and interpret them in terms of consumer demand.

In Problems 11–14, give the cost, revenue, and profit functions.

**11.** An online seller of T-shirts pays $500 to start up the website and $6 per T-shirt, then sells the T-shirts for $12 each.

**12.** A car wash operator pays $35,000 for a franchise, then spends $10 per car wash, which costs the consumer $15.

**13.** A couple running a house-cleaning business invests $5000 in equipment, and they spend $15 in supplies to clean a house, for which they charge $60.

**14.** A lemonade stand operator sets up the stand for free in front of the neighbor's house, makes 5 quarts of lemonade for $4, then sells each 8-oz cup for 25 cents.

**15.** A company that makes Adirondack chairs has fixed costs of $5000 and variable costs of $30 per chair. The company sells the chairs for $50 each.

   **(a)** Find formulas for the cost and revenue functions.
   **(b)** Find the marginal cost and marginal revenue.
   **(c)** Graph the cost and the revenue functions on the same axes.
   **(d)** Find the break-even point.

**16.** An amusement park charges an admission fee of $21 per person as well as an additional $4.50 for each ride.

   **(a)** For one visitor, find the park's total revenue $R(n)$ as a function of the number of rides, $n$, taken.
   **(b)** Find $R(2)$ and $R(8)$ and interpret your answers in terms of amusement park fees.

**17.** A photocopying company has two different price lists. The first price list is $100 plus 3 cents per copy; the second price list is $200 plus 2 cents per copy.

   **(a)** For each price list, find the total cost as a function of the number of copies needed.
   **(b)** Determine which price list is cheaper for 5000 copies.
   **(c)** For what number of copies do both price lists charge the same amount?

**18.** A company has cost function $C(q) = 4000 + 2q$ dollars and revenue function $R(q) = 10q$ dollars.

   **(a)** What are the fixed costs for the company?
   **(b)** What is the marginal cost?
   **(c)** What price is the company charging for its product?
   **(d)** Graph $C(q)$ and $R(q)$ on the same axes and label the break-even point, $q_0$. Explain how you know the company makes a profit if the quantity produced is greater than $q_0$.
   **(e)** Find the break-even point $q_0$.

**19.** A movie theater has fixed costs of $5000 per day and variable costs averaging $6 per customer. The theater charges $11 per ticket.

   **(a)** How many customers per day does the theater need in order to make a profit?
   **(b)** Find the cost and revenue functions and graph them on the same axes. Mark the break-even point.

**20.** A company producing jigsaw puzzles has fixed costs of $6000 and variable costs of $2 per puzzle. The company sells the puzzles for $5 each.

   **(a)** Find formulas for the cost function, the revenue function, and the profit function.
   **(b)** Sketch a graph of $R(q)$ and $C(q)$ on the same axes. What is the break-even point, $q_0$, for the company?

**21.** Production costs for manufacturing running shoes consist of a fixed overhead of $650,000 plus variable costs of $20 per pair of shoes. Each pair of shoes sells for $70.

   **(a)** Find the total cost, $C(q)$, the total revenue, $R(q)$, and the total profit, $\pi(q)$, as a function of the number of pairs of shoes produced, $q$.
   **(b)** Find the marginal cost, marginal revenue, and marginal profit.
   **(c)** How many pairs of shoes must be produced and sold for the company to make a profit?

**22.** A $15,000 robot depreciates linearly to zero in 10 years.

   **(a)** Find a formula for its value as a function of time.
   **(b)** How much is the robot worth three years after it is purchased?

**23.** A $50,000 tractor has a resale value of $10,000 twenty years after it was purchased. Assume that the value of the tractor depreciates linearly from the time of purchase.

   **(a)** Find a formula for the value of the tractor as a function of the time since it was purchased.
   **(b)** Graph the value of the tractor against time.
   **(c)** Find the horizontal and vertical intercepts, give units, and interpret them.

**24.** A new bus worth $100,000 in 2010 depreciates linearly to $20,000 in 2030.

   **(a)** Find a formula for the value of the bus, $V$, as a function of time, $t$, in years since 2010.
   **(b)** What is the value of the bus in 2015?
   **(c)** Find and interpret the vertical and horizontal intercepts of the graph of the function.
   **(d)** What is the domain of the function?

**25.** A corporate office provides the demand curve in Figure 1.57 to its ice cream shop franchises. At a price of $1.00 per scoop, 240 scoops per day can be sold.

   **(a)** Estimate how many scoops could be sold per day at a price of 50¢ per scoop. Explain.
   **(b)** Estimate how many scoops per day could be sold at a price of $1.50 per scoop. Explain.

**Figure 1.57**

**26.** The table shows the cost of manufacturing various quantities of an item and the revenue obtained from their sale.

| Quantity | 0 | 10 | 20 | 30 | 40 | 50 | 60 | 70 | 80 |
|---|---|---|---|---|---|---|---|---|---|
| Cost ($) | 120 | 400 | 600 | 780 | 1000 | 1320 | 1800 | 2500 | 3400 |
| Revenue ($) | 0 | 300 | 600 | 900 | 1200 | 1500 | 1800 | 2100 | 2400 |

   **(a)** What range of production levels appears to be profitable?

**(b)** Calculate the profit or loss for each of the quantities shown. Estimate the most profitable production level.

**27.** One of Tables 1.28 and 1.29 represents a supply curve; the other represents a demand curve.

    **(a)** Which table represents which curve? Why?

    **(b)** At a price of $155, approximately how many items would consumers purchase?

    **(c)** At a price of $155, approximately how many items would manufacturers supply?

    **(d)** Will the market push prices higher or lower than $155?

    **(e)** What would the price have to be if you wanted consumers to buy at least 20 items?

    **(f)** What would the price have to be if you wanted manufacturers to supply at least 20 items?

**Table 1.28**

| $p$ ($/unit) | 182 | 167 | 153 | 143 | 133 | 125 | 118 |
|---|---|---|---|---|---|---|---|
| $q$ (quantity) | 5 | 10 | 15 | 20 | 25 | 30 | 35 |

**Table 1.29**

| $p$ ($/unit) | 6 | 35 | 66 | 110 | 166 | 235 | 316 |
|---|---|---|---|---|---|---|---|
| $q$ (quantity) | 5 | 10 | 15 | 20 | 25 | 30 | 35 |

**28.** Figure 1.58 shows supply and demand for a product.

    **(a)** What is the equilibrium price for this product? At this price, what quantity is produced?

    **(b)** Choose a price above the equilibrium price—for example, $p = 12$. At this price, how many items are suppliers willing to produce? How many items do consumers want to buy? Use your answers to these questions to explain why, if prices are above the equilibrium price, the market tends to push prices lower (toward the equilibrium).

    **(c)** Now choose a price below the equilibrium price—for example, $p = 8$. At this price, how many items are suppliers willing to produce? How many items do consumers want to buy? Use your answers to these questions to explain why, if prices are below the equilibrium price, the market tends to push prices higher (toward the equilibrium).

$p$ (price per unit)

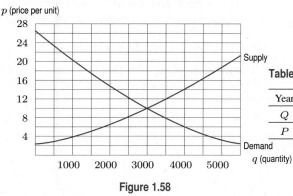

**Figure 1.58**

**29.** A company produces and sells shirts. The fixed costs are $7000 and the variable costs are $5 per shirt.

    **(a)** Shirts are sold for $12 each. Find cost and revenue as functions of the quantity of shirts, $q$.

    **(b)** The company is considering changing the selling price of the shirts. Demand is $q = 2000 - 40p$, where $p$ is price in dollars and $q$ is the number of shirts. What quantity is sold at the current price of $12? What profit is realized at this price?

    **(c)** Use the demand equation to write cost and revenue as functions of the price, $p$. Then write profit as a function of price.

    **(d)** Graph profit against price. Find the price that maximizes profits. What is this profit?

**30.** When the price, $p$, charged for a boat tour was $25, the average number of passengers per week, $N$, was 500. When the price was reduced to $20, the average number of passengers per week increased to 650. Find a formula for the demand curve, assuming that it is linear.

**31.** Table 1.30 gives data for the linear demand curve for a product, where $p$ is the price of the product and $q$ is the quantity sold every month at that price. Find formulas for the following functions. Interpret their slopes in terms of demand.

    **(a)** $q$ as a function of $p$.     **(b)** $p$ as a function of $q$.

**Table 1.30**

| $p$ (dollars) | 16 | 18 | 20 | 22 | 24 |
|---|---|---|---|---|---|
| $q$ (tons) | 500 | 460 | 420 | 380 | 340 |

**32.** The demand curve for a product is given by $q = 120{,}000 - 500p$ and the supply curve is given by $q = 1000p$ for $0 \le q \le 120{,}000$, where price is in dollars.

    **(a)** At a price of $100, what quantity are consumers willing to buy and what quantity are producers willing to supply? Will the market push prices up or down?

    **(b)** Find the equilibrium price and quantity. Does your answer to part (a) support the observation that market forces tend to push prices closer to the equilibrium price?

**33.** World production, $Q$, of zinc in thousands of metric tons and the value, $P$, in dollars per metric ton are given[54] in Table 1.31. Plot the value as a function of production. Sketch a possible supply curve.

**Table 1.31** *World zinc production*

| Year | 2003 | 2004 | 2005 | 2006 | 2007 | 2008 | 2009 | 2010 |
|---|---|---|---|---|---|---|---|---|
| $Q$ | 9520 | 9600 | 10,000 | 10,300 | 11,000 | 11,700 | 11,400 | 12,000 |
| $P$ | 896 | 1160 | 1480 | 3500 | 3400 | 1960 | 1720 | 2250 |

[54]http://minerals.usgs.gov/ds/2005/140/, accessed September, 2012.

**34.** A taxi company has an annual budget of $720,000 to spend on drivers and car replacement. Drivers cost the company $30,000 each and car replacements cost $20,000 each.

   **(a)** What is the company's budget constraint equation? Let $d$ be the number of drivers paid and $c$ be the number of cars replaced.

   **(b)** Find and interpret both intercepts of the graph of the equation.

**35.** A company has a total budget of $500,000 and spends this budget on raw materials and personnel. The company uses $m$ units of raw materials, at a cost of $100 per unit, and hires $r$ employees, at a cost of $25,000 each.

   **(a)** What is the equation of the company's budget constraint?

   **(b)** Solve for $m$ as a function of $r$.

   **(c)** Solve for $r$ as a function of $m$.

**36.** You have a budget of $2000 for the year to cover your books and social outings. Books cost (on average) $80 each and social outings cost (on average) $20 each. Let $b$ denote the number of books purchased per year and $s$ denote the number of social outings in a year.

   **(a)** What is the equation of your budget constraint?

   **(b)** Graph the budget constraint. (It does not matter which variable you put on which axis.)

   **(c)** Find the vertical and horizontal intercepts, and give a financial interpretation for each.

**37.** Linear supply and demand curves are shown in Figure 1.59, with price on the vertical axis.

   **(a)** Label the equilibrium price $p_0$ and the equilibrium quantity $q_0$ on the axes.

   **(b)** Explain the effect on equilibrium price and quantity if the slope, $\Delta p/\Delta q$, of the supply curve increases. Illustrate your answer graphically.

   **(c)** Explain the effect on equilibrium price and quantity if the slope, $\Delta p/\Delta q$, of the demand curve becomes more negative. Illustrate your answer graphically.

**Figure 1.59**

**38.** The demand for a product is given by $p = 90 - 10q$. Find the ratio

$$\left| \frac{\text{Relative change in demand}}{\text{Relative change in price}} \right|$$

if the price changes from $p = 50$ to $p = 51$. Interpret this ratio.

**39.** A demand curve has equation $q = 100 - 5p$, where $p$ is price in dollars. A $2 tax is imposed on consumers. Find the equation of the new demand curve. Sketch both curves.

**40.** A supply curve has equation $q = 4p - 20$, where $p$ is price in dollars. A $2 tax is imposed on suppliers. Find the equation of the new supply curve. Sketch both curves.

**41.** A tax of $8 per unit is imposed on the supplier of an item. The original supply curve is $q = 0.5p - 25$ and the demand curve is $q = 165 - 0.5p$, where $p$ is price in dollars. Find the equilibrium price and quantity before and after the tax is imposed.

**42.** The demand and supply curves for a product are given in terms of price, $p$, by

$$q = 2500 - 20p \quad \text{and} \quad q = 10p - 500.$$

   **(a)** Find the equilibrium price and quantity. Represent your answers on a graph.

   **(b)** A specific tax of $6 per unit is imposed on suppliers. Find the new equilibrium price and quantity. Represent your answers on the graph.

   **(c)** How much of the $6 tax is paid by consumers and how much by producers?

   **(d)** What is the total tax revenue received by the government?

**43.** In Example 8, the demand and supply curves are given by $q = 100 - 2p$ and $q = 3p - 50$, respectively; the equilibrium price is $30 and the equilibrium quantity is 40 units. A sales tax of 5% is imposed on the consumer.

   **(a)** Find the equation of the new demand and supply curves.

   **(b)** Find the new equilibrium price and quantity.

   **(c)** How much is paid in taxes on each unit? How much of this is paid by the consumer and how much by the producer?

   **(d)** How much tax does the government collect?

**44.** Answer the questions in Problem 43, assuming that the 5% sales tax is imposed on the supplier instead of the consumer.

# 1.5  EXPONENTIAL FUNCTIONS

The function $f(x) = 2^x$, where the power is variable, is an *exponential function*. The number 2 is called the base. Exponential functions of the form $f(x) = k \cdot a^x$, where $a$ is a positive constant, are used to represent many phenomena in the natural and social sciences.

## Population Growth

The population of Burkina Faso, a sub-Saharan African country,[55] from 2003 to 2009 is given in Table 1.32. To see how the population is growing, we look at the increase in population in the third column. If the population had been growing linearly, all the numbers in the third column would be the same.

**Table 1.32**  *Population of Burkina Faso (estimated), 2003–2009*

| Year | Population (millions) | Change in population (millions) |
|------|-----------------------|----------------------------------|
| 2003 | 12.853 | |
| | | 0.437 |
| 2004 | 13.290 | |
| | | 0.457 |
| 2005 | 13.747 | |
| | | 0.478 |
| 2006 | 14.225 | |
| | | 0.496 |
| 2007 | 14.721 | |
| | | 0.513 |
| 2008 | 15.234 | |
| | | 0.523 |
| 2009 | 15.757 | |

$P$ (population in millions)

$P = 12.853(1.034)^t$

$t$ (years since 2003)

**Figure 1.60**: Population of Burkina Faso (estimated): Exponential growth

Suppose we divide each year's population by the previous year's population. For example,

$$\frac{\text{Population in 2004}}{\text{Population in 2003}} = \frac{13.290 \text{ million}}{12.853 \text{ million}} = 1.034$$

$$\frac{\text{Population in 2005}}{\text{Population in 2004}} = \frac{13.747 \text{ million}}{13.290 \text{ million}} = 1.034.$$

The fact that both calculations give 1.034 shows the population grew by about 3.4% between 2003 and 2004 *and* between 2004 and 2005. Similar calculations for other years show that the population grew by a factor of about 1.034, or 3.4%, every year. Whenever we have a constant percent increase (here 3.4%), we have *exponential growth*. If $t$ is the number of years since 2003 and population is in millions,

When $t = 0$,  population $= 12.853 = 12.853(1.034)^0$.

When $t = 1$,  population $= 13.290 = 12.853(1.034)^1$.

When $t = 2$,  population $= 13.747 = 13.290(1.034) = 12.853(1.034)^2$.

When $t = 3$,  population $= 14.225 = 13.747(1.034) = 12.853(1.034)^3$.

So $P$, the population in millions $t$ years after 2003, is given by

$$P = 12.853(1.034)^t \text{ million}.$$

Since the variable $t$ is in the exponent, this is an exponential function. The base, 1.034, represents the factor by which the population grows each year and is called the *growth factor*. Assuming that the formula holds for 50 years, the population graph has the shape in Figure 1.60. The population is growing, so the function is increasing. Since the population grows faster as time passes, the graph is concave up. This behavior is typical of an exponential function. Even exponential functions that climb slowly at first, such as this one, eventually climb extremely quickly.

---

[55] dataworldbank.org, accessed January 12, 2011.

## Elimination of a Drug from the Body

Now we look at a quantity that is decreasing instead of increasing. When a patient is given medication, the drug enters the bloodstream. The rate at which the drug is metabolized and eliminated depends on the particular drug. For the antibiotic ampicillin, approximately 40% of the drug is eliminated every hour. A typical dose of ampicillin is 250 mg. Suppose $Q = f(t)$, where $Q$ is the quantity of ampicillin, in mg, in the bloodstream at time $t$ hours since the drug was given. At $t = 0$, we have $Q = 250$. Since the quantity remaining at the end of each hour is 60% of the quantity remaining the hour before, we have

$$f(0) = 250$$
$$f(1) = 250(0.6)$$
$$f(2) = 250(0.6)(0.6) = 250(0.6)^2$$
$$f(3) = 250(0.6)^2(0.6) = 250(0.6)^3.$$

So, after $t$ hours,

$$Q = f(t) = 250(0.6)^t.$$

This function is called an *exponential decay* function. As $t$ increases, the function values get arbitrarily close to zero. The $t$-axis is a *horizontal asymptote* for this function.

Notice the way the values in Table 1.33 are decreasing. Each additional hour a smaller quantity of drug is removed than the previous hour (100 mg the first hour, 60 mg the second, and so on). This is because as time passes, there is less of the drug in the body to be removed. Thus, the graph in Figure 1.61 bends upward. Compare this to the exponential growth in Figure 1.60, where each step upward is larger than the previous one. Notice that both graphs are concave up.

**Table 1.33** *Value of decay function*

| $t$ (hours) | $Q$ (mg) |
|---|---|
| 0 | 250 |
| 1 | 150 |
| 2 | 90 |
| 3 | 54 |
| 4 | 32.4 |
| 5 | 19.4 |

**Figure 1.61**: Drug elimination: Exponential decay

## The General Exponential Function

Exponential growth is often described in terms of percent growth rates. The population of Burkina Faso is growing at 3.4% per year, so it increases by a factor of $a = 1 + 0.034 = 1.034$ every year. Similarly, 40% of the ampicillin is removed every hour, so the quantity remaining decays by a factor of $a = 1 - 0.40 = 0.6$ each hour. We have the following general formulas.

We say that $P$ is an **exponential function** of $t$ with base $a$ if

$$P = P_0 a^t,$$

where $P_0$ is the initial quantity (when $t = 0$) and $a$ is the factor by which $P$ changes when $t$ increases by 1. If $a > 1$, we have **exponential growth**; if $0 < a < 1$, we have **exponential decay**. The factor $a$ is given by

$$a = 1 + r$$

where $r$ is the decimal representation of the percent rate of change; $r$ may be positive (for growth) or negative (for decay).

The largest possible domain for the exponential function is all real numbers,[56] provided $a > 0$.

## Comparison Between Linear and Exponential Functions

Every exponential function changes at a constant percent, or *relative*, rate. For example, the population of Burkina Faso increased approximately 3.4% per year. Every linear function changes at a constant absolute rate. For example, the Olympic pole vault record increased by 2 inches per year.

---

A **linear** function has a constant rate of change.
An **exponential** function has a constant percent, or relative, rate of change.

---

**Example 1**

The amount of adrenaline in the body can change rapidly. Suppose the initial amount is 15 mg. Find a formula for $A$, the amount in mg, at a time $t$ minutes later if $A$ is:

(a)  Increasing by 0.4 mg per minute.            (b)  Decreasing by 0.4 mg per minute.
(c)  Increasing by 3% per minute.               (d)  Decreasing by 3% per minute.

**Solution**

(a)  This is a linear function with initial quantity 15 and slope 0.4, so

$$A = 15 + 0.4t.$$

(b)  This is a linear function with initial quantity 15 and slope $-0.4$, so

$$A = 15 - 0.4t.$$

(c)  This is an exponential function with initial quantity 15 and base $1 + 0.03 = 1.03$, so

$$A = 15(1.03)^t.$$

(d)  This is an exponential function with initial quantity 15 and base $1 - 0.03 = 0.97$, so

$$A = 15(0.97)^t.$$

---

**Example 2**

Wolves were once common in the western US. By the 1990s, the wolf population in Wyoming had been wiped out by hunters and wolves put on the endangered species list. In 1995, wolves were reintroduced to Wyoming from Canada. Starting with 14 wolves, their number increased to 207 wolves in 2012.[57] Assuming the Wyoming wolf population was growing exponentially, find a function of the form $P = P_0 a^t$, where $P$ is the population $t$ years after 1995. What is the annual percent growth rate?

**Solution**

We know that $P_0 = 14$ when $t = 0$. In 2012, when $t = 17$, we have $P = 207$. Substituting in $P = P_0 a^t$ gives an equation we can solve for $a$:

$$207 = 14a^t.$$

Dividing both sides by 14 gives

$$\frac{207}{14} = a^{17}.$$

Taking the $17^{\text{th}}$ root of both sides, we get

$$a = (207/14)^{1/17} = 1.172.$$

Since $a = 1.172$, the Wyoming wolf population as a function of the number of years since 1995 is given by

$$P = 207(1.172)^t.$$

During this period, the population increased by about 17% per year.

---

[56]The reason we do not want $a \leq 0$ is that, for example, we cannot define $a^{1/2}$ if $a < 0$. Also, we do not usually have $a = 1$, since $P = P_0 a^t = P_0 1^t = P_0$ is then a constant function.

[57]Based on "Wyoming drops federal protection of gray wolves", BBC, August 31, 2012, and *Wyoming Wolf Program Status Report*, US Fish and Wildlife Services, September, 2012.

**Example 3**    Suppose that $Q = f(t)$ is an exponential function of $t$. If $f(20) = 88.2$ and $f(23) = 91.4$:

    (a)  Find the base.            (b)  Find the percent growth rate.

    (c)  Evaluate $f(25)$.

Solution    (a)  Let $Q = Q_0 a^t$. Substituting $t = 20, Q = 88.2$ and $t = 23, Q = 91.4$ gives two equations for $Q_0$ and $a$:

$$88.2 = Q_0 a^{20} \quad \text{and} \quad 91.4 = Q_0 a^{23}.$$

Dividing the two equations enables us to eliminate $Q_0$:

$$\frac{91.4}{88.2} = \frac{Q_0 a^{23}}{Q_0 a^{20}} = a^3.$$

Solving for the base, $a$, gives

$$a = \left(\frac{91.4}{88.2}\right)^{1/3} = 1.012.$$

    (b)  Since $a = 1.012$, the percent growth rate is 1.2%.

    (c)  We want to evaluate $f(25) = Q_0 a^{25} = Q_0 (1.012)^{25}$. First we find $Q_0$ from the equation

$$88.2 = Q_0 (1.012)^{20}.$$

Solving gives $Q_0 = 69.5$. Thus,

$$f(25) = 69.5(1.012)^{25} = 93.6.$$

## The Family of Exponential Functions and the Number $e$

The formula $P = P_0 a^t$ gives a family of exponential functions with parameters $P_0$ (the initial quantity) and $a$ (the base). The base tells us whether the function is increasing ($a > 1$) or decreasing ($0 < a < 1$). Since $a$ is the factor by which $P$ changes when $t$ is increased by 1, large values of $a$ mean fast growth; values of $a$ near 0 mean fast decay. (See Figures 1.62 and 1.63.) All members of the family $P = P_0 a^t$ are concave up if $P_0 > 0$.

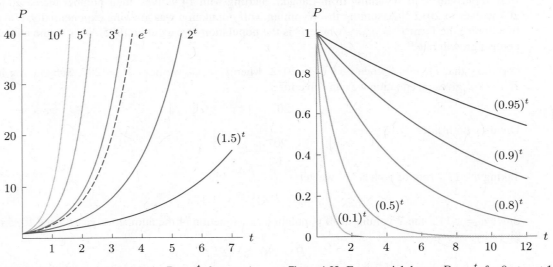

Figure 1.62: Exponential growth: $P = a^t$, for $a > 1$      Figure 1.63: Exponential decay: $P = a^t$, for $0 < a < 1$

In practice the most commonly used base is the number $e = 2.71828\ldots$. The fact that most calculators have an $e^x$ button is an indication of how important $e$ is. Since $e$ is between 2 and 3, the graph of $y = e^t$ in Figure 1.62 is between the graphs of $y = 2^t$ and $y = 3^t$.

The base $e$ is used so often that it is called the natural base. At first glance, this is somewhat mysterious: What could be natural about using 2.71828... as a base? The full answer to this question must wait until Chapter 3, where you will see that many calculus formulas come out more neatly when $e$ is used as the base. (See Appendix B for the relation to compound interest.)

## Problems for Section 1.5

1. The following functions give the populations of four towns with time $t$ in years.

   (i)  $P = 600(1.12)^t$     (ii)  $P = 1{,}000(1.03)^t$
   (iii)  $P = 200(1.08)^t$     (iv)  $P = 900(0.90)^t$

   (a) Which town has the largest percent growth rate? What is the percent growth rate?
   (b) Which town has the largest initial population? What is that initial population?
   (c) Are any of the towns decreasing in size? If so, which one(s)?

2. Each of the following functions gives the amount of a substance present at time $t$. In each case, give the amount present initially (at $t = 0$), state whether the function represents exponential growth or decay, and give the percent growth or decay rate.

   (a)  $A = 100(1.07)^t$     (b)  $A = 5.3(1.054)^t$
   (c)  $A = 3500(0.93)^t$    (d)  $A = 12(0.88)^t$

3. Figure 1.64 shows graphs of several cities' populations against time. Match each of the following descriptions to a graph and write a description to match each of the remaining graphs.

   (a) The population increased at 5% per year.
   (b) The population increased at 8% per year.
   (c) The population increased by 5000 people per year.
   (d) The population was stable.

Figure 1.64

Give a possible formula for the functions in Problems 4–5.

4.

5.

6. The gross domestic product, $G$, of Switzerland was 310 billion dollars in 2007. Give a formula for $G$ (in billions of dollars) $t$ years after 2007 if $G$ increases by
   (a) 3% per year        (b) 8 billion dollars per year

7. A town has a population of 1000 people at time $t = 0$. In each of the following cases, write a formula for the population, $P$, of the town as a function of year $t$.
   (a) The population increases by 50 people a year.
   (b) The population increases by 5% a year.

8. A product costs \$80 today. How much will the product cost in $t$ days if the price is reduced by
   (a) \$4 a day        (b) 5% a day

9. An air-freshener starts with 30 grams and evaporates. In each of the following cases, write a formula for the quantity, $Q$ grams, of air-freshener remaining $t$ days after the start and sketch a graph of the function. The decrease is:
   (a) 2 grams a day        (b) 12% a day

10. World population is approximately $P = 6.4(1.0126)^t$, with $P$ in billions and $t$ in years since 2004.
    (a) What is the yearly percent rate of growth of the world population?
    (b) What was the world population in 2004? What does this model predict for the world population in 2010?
    (c) Use part (b) to find the average rate of change of the world population between 2004 and 2010.

11. A 50 mg dose of quinine is given to a patient to prevent malaria. Quinine leaves the body at a rate of 6% per hour.
    (a) Find a formula for the amount, $A$ (in mg), of quinine in the body $t$ hours after the dose is given.
    (b) How much quinine is in the body after 24 hours?
    (c) Graph $A$ as a function of $t$.
    (d) Use the graph to estimate when 5 mg of quinine remains.

12. The consumer price index (CPI) for a given year is the amount of money in that year that has the same purchasing power as \$100 in 1983. At the start of 2009, the CPI was 211. Write a formula for the CPI as a function of $t$ years after 2009, assuming that the CPI increases by 2.8% every year.

13. During the 1980s, Costa Rica had the highest deforestation rate in the world, at 2.9% per year. (This is the rate at which land covered by forests is shrinking.) Assuming the rate continues, what percent of the land in Costa Rica covered by forests in 1980 will be forested in 2015?

**14.** Graph $y = 100e^{-0.4x}$. Describe what you see.

**15.** (a) Make a table of values for $y = e^x$ using $x = 0, 1, 2, 3$.

   (b) Plot the points found in part (a). Does the graph look like an exponential growth or decay function?

   (c) Make a table of values for $y = e^{-x}$ using $x = 0, 1, 2, 3$.

   (d) Plot the points found in part (c). Does the graph look like an exponential growth or decay function?

For Problems 16–17, find a possible formula for the function represented by the data.

**16.**

| $x$ | 0 | 1 | 2 | 3 |
|---|---|---|---|---|
| $f(x)$ | 4.30 | 6.02 | 8.43 | 11.80 |

**17.**

| $t$ | 0 | 1 | 2 | 3 |
|---|---|---|---|---|
| $g(t)$ | 5.50 | 4.40 | 3.52 | 2.82 |

In Problems 18–19, find all the tables that have the given characteristic.

(A)
| $x$ | 0 | 40 | 80 | 160 |
|---|---|---|---|---|
| $y$ | 2.2 | 2.2 | 2.2 | 2.2 |

(B)
| $x$ | −8 | −4 | 0 | 8 |
|---|---|---|---|---|
| $y$ | 51 | 62 | 73 | 95 |

(C)
| $x$ | −4 | −3 | 4 | 6 |
|---|---|---|---|---|
| $y$ | 18 | 0 | 4.5 | −2.25 |

(D)
| $x$ | 3 | 4 | 5 | 6 |
|---|---|---|---|---|
| $y$ | 18 | 9 | 4.5 | 2.25 |

**18.** $y$ could be a linear function of $x$.

**19.** $y$ could be an exponential function of $x$.

In Problems 20–23, a quantity $P$ is an exponential function of time $t$. Use the given information about the function $P = P_0 a^t$ to:

(a) Find values for the parameters $a$ and $P_0$.

(b) State the initial quantity and the percent rate of growth or decay.

**20.** $P_0 a^3 = 75$   and   $P_0 a^2 = 50$

**21.** $P_0 a^4 = 18$   and   $P_0 a^3 = 20$

**22.** $P = 320$ when $t = 5$ and $P = 500$ when $t = 3$

**23.** $P = 1600$ when $t = 3$ and $P = 1000$ when $t = 1$

**24.** If the world's population increased exponentially from 5.937 billion in 1998 to 6.771 billion in 2008 and continued to increase at the same percentage rate between 2008 and 2012, calculate what the world's population would have been in 2012. How does this compare to the Population Reference Bureau estimate of 7.07 billion in July 2012? [58]

**25.** The number of passengers using a railway fell from 190,205 to 174,989 during a 5-year period. Find the annual percentage decrease over this period.

**26.** The company that produces Cliffs Notes (abridged versions of classic literature) was started in 1958 with $4000 and sold in 1998 for $14,000,000. Find the annual percent increase in the value of this company over the 40 years.

**27.** Find a formula for the number of zebra mussels in a bay as a function of the number of years since 2010, given that there were 2700 at the start of 2010 and 3186 at the start of 2011.

   (a) Assume that the number of zebra mussels is growing linearly. Give units for the slope of the line and interpret it in terms of zebra mussels.

   (b) Assume that the number of zebra mussels is growing exponentially. What is the annual percent growth rate of the zebra mussel population?

**28.** Worldwide, wind energy[59] generating capacity, $W$, was 39,295 megawatts in 2003 and 120,903 megawatts in 2008.

   (a) Use the values given to write $W$, in megawatts, as a linear function of $t$, the number of years since 2003.

   (b) Use the values given to write $W$ as an exponential function of $t$.

   (c) Graph the functions found in parts (a) and (b) on the same axes. Label the given values.

   (d) Use the functions found in parts (a) and (b) to predict the wind energy generated in 2010. The actual wind energy generated in 2010 was 196,653 megawatts. Comment on the results: Which estimate is closer to the actual value?

**29.** (a) Which (if any) of the functions in the following table could be linear? Find formulas for those functions.

   (b) Which (if any) of these functions could be exponential? Find formulas for those functions.

| $x$ | $f(x)$ | $g(x)$ | $h(x)$ |
|---|---|---|---|
| −2 | 12 | 16 | 37 |
| −1 | 17 | 24 | 34 |
| 0 | 20 | 36 | 31 |
| 1 | 21 | 54 | 28 |
| 2 | 18 | 81 | 25 |

[58]ww.prb.org/Publications/Datasheets/2012/2012populationclock.aspx, accessed August 2012.
[59]http://www.wwindea.org/home/index.php, accessed September 2012.

**30.** Determine whether each of the following tables of values could correspond to a linear function, an exponential function, or neither. For each table of values that could correspond to a linear or an exponential function, find a formula for the function.

(a)

| $x$ | $f(x)$ |
|-----|--------|
| 0 | 10.5 |
| 1 | 12.7 |
| 2 | 18.9 |
| 3 | 36.7 |

(b)

| $t$ | $s(t)$ |
|-----|--------|
| −1 | 50.2 |
| 0 | 30.12 |
| 1 | 18.072 |
| 2 | 10.8432 |

(c)

| $u$ | $g(u)$ |
|-----|--------|
| 0 | 27 |
| 2 | 24 |
| 4 | 21 |
| 6 | 18 |

**31.** **(a)** Could the data on annual world soybean production[60] in Table 1.34 correspond to a linear function or an exponential function? If so, which?
**(b)** Find a formula for $P$, world soybean production in millions of tons, as a function of time, $t$, in years since 2000.
**(c)** What is the annual percent increase in soybean production?

**Table 1.34**  *Soybean production, in millions of tons*

| Year | 2000 | 2001 | 2002 | 2003 | 2004 | 2005 |
|------|------|------|------|------|------|------|
| Production | 161.0 | 170.3 | 180.2 | 190.7 | 201.8 | 213.5 |

**32.** The 2004 US presidential debates questioned whether the minimum wage has kept pace with inflation. Decide the question using the following information:[61] In 1938, the minimum wage was 25¢; in 2004, it was \$5.15. During the same period, inflation averaged 4.3%.

**33.** **(a)** Niki invested \$10,000 in the stock market. The investment was a loser, declining in value 10% per year each year for 10 years. How much was the investment worth after 10 years?
**(b)** After 10 years, the stock began to gain value at 10% per year. After how long will the investment regain its initial value (\$10,000)?

**34.** A photocopy machine can reduce copies to 80% of their original size. By copying an already reduced copy, further reductions can be made.

**(a)** If a page is reduced to 80%, what percent enlargement is needed to return it to its original size?
**(b)** Estimate the number of times in succession that a page must be copied to make the final copy less than 15% of the size of the original.

**35.** Whooping cough was thought to have been almost wiped out by vaccinations. It is now known that the vaccination wears off, leading to an increase in the number of cases, $w$, from 1248 in 1981 to 18,957 in 2004.

**(a)** With $t$ in years since 1980, find an exponential function that fits this data.
**(b)** What does your answer to part (a) give as the average annual percent growth rate of the number of cases?
**(c)** On May 4, 2005, the *Arizona Daily Star* reported (correctly) that the number of cases had more than doubled between 2000 and 2004. Does your model confirm this report? Explain.

**36.** Aircraft require longer takeoff distances, called takeoff rolls, at high altitude airports because of diminished air density. The table shows how the takeoff roll for a certain light airplane depends on the airport elevation. (Takeoff rolls are also strongly influenced by air temperature; the data shown assume a temperature of $0°$ C.) Determine a formula for this particular aircraft that gives the takeoff roll as an exponential function of airport elevation.

| Elevation (ft) | Sea level | 1000 | 2000 | 3000 | 4000 |
|----------------|-----------|------|------|------|------|
| Takeoff roll (ft) | 670 | 734 | 805 | 882 | 967 |

Problems 37–38 concern biodiesel, a fuel derived from renewable resources such as food crops, algae, and animal oils. The table shows the percent growth over the previous year in US biodiesel consumption.[62]

| Year | 2003 | 2004 | 2005 | 2006 | 2007 | 2008 | 2009 |
|------|------|------|------|------|------|------|------|
| % growth | −12.5 | 92.9 | 237 | 186.6 | 37.2 | −11.7 | 7.3 |

**37.** **(a)** According to the US Department of Energy, the US consumed 91 million gallons of biodiesel in 2005. Approximately how much biodiesel (in millions of gallons) did the US consume in 2006? In 2007?
**(b)** Graph the points showing the annual US consumption of biodiesel, in millions of gallons of biodiesel, for the years 2005 to 2009. Label the scales on the horizontal and vertical axes.

**38.** **(a)** True or false: The annual US consumption of biodiesel grew exponentially from 2003 to 2005. Justify your answer without doing any calculations.
**(b)** According to this data, during what single year(s), if any, did the US consumption of biodiesel at least double?
**(c)** According to this data, during what single year(s), if any, did the US consumption of biodiesel at least triple?

---

[60]*Vital Signs 2007-2008*, The Worldwatch Institute, W.W. Norton & Company, 2007, p. 23.
[61]http://www.dol.gov/esa/minwage/chart.htm#5.
[62]http://www.eia.doe.gov/aer/renew.html. Accessed February 2011.

**39.** Hydroelectric power is electric power generated by the force of moving water. The table shows the annual percent change in hydroelectric power consumption by the US industrial sector.[63]

percent growth over previous year

**Figure 1.65**

| Year | 2005 | 2006 | 2007 | 2008 | 2009 |
|------|------|------|------|------|------|
| % growth over previous yr | −1.9 | −10 | −45.4 | 5.1 | 11 |

**(a)** According to the US Department of Energy, the US industrial sector consumed about 29 trillion BTUs of hydroelectric power in 2006. Approximately how much hydroelectric power (in trillion BTUs) did the US consume in 2007? In 2005?

**(b)** Graph the points showing the annual US consumption of hydroelectric power, in trillion BTUs, for the years 2004 to 2009. Label the scales on the horizontal and vertical axes.

**(c)** According to this data, when did the largest yearly decrease, in trillion BTUs, in the US consumption of hydroelectric power occur? What was this decrease?

Problems 40–41 concern wind power, which has been used for centuries to propel ships and mill grain. Modern wind power is obtained from windmills that convert wind energy into electricity. Figure 1.65 shows the annual percent growth in US wind power consumption[64] between 2005 and 2009.

**40. (a)** According to the US Department of Energy, the US consumption of wind power was 341 trillion BTUs in 2007. How much wind power did the US consume in 2006? In 2008?

**(b)** Graph the points showing the annual US consumption of wind power, in trillion BTUs, for the years 2005 to 2009. Label the scales on the horizontal and vertical axes.

**(c)** Based on this data, in what year did the largest yearly increase, in trillion BTUs, in the US consumption of wind power occur? What was this increase?

**41. (a)** According to Figure 1.65, during what single year(s), if any, did the US consumption of wind power energy increase by at least 40%? Decrease by at least 40%?

**(b)** Did the US consumption of wind power energy double from 2006 to 2008?

# 1.6 THE NATURAL LOGARITHM

If $t$ is in years since 2000, the population of Nevada (in millions) can be modeled by the function

$$P = f(t) = 2.020(1.036)^t,$$

How do we find when the population is projected to reach 4 million? We want to find the value of $t$ for which

$$4 = f(t) = 2.020(1.036)^t.$$

We use logarithms to solve for a variable in an exponent.

## Definition and Properties of the Natural Logarithm

We define the natural logarithm of $x$, written $\ln x$, as follows:

---

The **natural logarithm** of $x$, written $\ln x$, is the power of $e$ needed to get $x$. In other words,

$$\ln x = c \quad \text{means} \quad e^c = x.$$

The natural logarithm is sometimes written $\log_e x$.

---

[63]From http://www.eia.doe.gov/aer/renew.html. Accessed February 2011.

[64]Yearly values have been joined with segments to highlight trends in the data. Actual values in between years should not be inferred from the segments. From http://www.eia.doe.gov/aer/renew.html. Accessed February 2011.

For example, $\ln e^3 = 3$ since 3 is the power of $e$ needed to give $e^3$. Similarly, $\ln(1/e) = \ln e^{-1} = -1$. A calculator gives $\ln 5 = 1.6094$, because $e^{1.6094} = 5$. However if we try to find $\ln(-7)$ on a calculator, we get an error message because $e$ to any power is never negative or 0. In general

$$\ln x \text{ is not defined if } x \text{ is negative or } 0.$$

To work with logarithms, we use the following properties:

**Properties of the Natural Logarithm**

1. $\ln(AB) = \ln A + \ln B$
2. $\ln\left(\dfrac{A}{B}\right) = \ln A - \ln B$
3. $\ln(A^p) = p \ln A$
4. $\ln e^x = x$
5. $e^{\ln x} = x$

In addition, $\ln 1 = 0$ because $e^0 = 1$, and $\ln e = 1$ because $e^1 = e$.

Using the $\boxed{\text{LN}}$ button on a calculator, we get the graph of $f(x) = \ln x$ in Figure 1.66. Observe that, for large $x$, the graph of $y = \ln x$ climbs very slowly as $x$ increases. The $x$-intercept is $x = 1$, since $\ln 1 = 0$. For $x > 1$, the value of $\ln x$ is positive; for $0 < x < 1$, the value of $\ln x$ is negative.

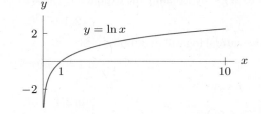

Figure 1.66: The natural logarithm function climbs very slowly

## Solving Equations Using Logarithms

Natural logs can be used to solve for unknown exponents.

**Example 1**    Find $t$ such that $3^t = 10$.

Solution    First, notice that we expect $t$ to be between 2 and 3, because $3^2 = 9$ and $3^3 = 27$. To find $t$ exactly, we take the natural logarithm of both sides and solve for $t$:

$$\ln(3^t) = \ln 10.$$

The third property of logarithms tells us that $\ln(3^t) = t \ln 3$, so we have

$$t \ln 3 = \ln 10$$
$$t = \frac{\ln 10}{\ln 3}.$$

Using a calculator to find the natural logs gives

$$t = 2.096.$$

**Example 2**  We return to the question of when the population of Nevada reaches 4 million. To get an answer, we solve $4 = 2.020(1.036)^t$ for $t$, using logs.

**Solution**  Dividing both sides of the equation by 2.020, we get

$$\frac{4}{2.020} = (1.036)^t.$$

Now take natural logs of both sides:

$$\ln\left(\frac{4}{2.020}\right) = \ln(1.036^t).$$

Using the fact that $\ln(1.036^t) = t\ln 1.036$, we get

$$\ln\left(\frac{4}{2.020}\right) = t\ln(1.036).$$

Solving this equation using a calculator to find the logs, we get

$$t = \frac{\ln(4/2.020)}{\ln(1.036)} = 19.317 \text{ years.}$$

Since $t = 0$ in 2000, this value of $t$ corresponds to the year 2019.

**Example 3**  Find $t$ such that $12 = 5e^{3t}$.

**Solution**  It is easiest to begin by isolating the exponential, so we divide both sides of the equation by 5:

$$2.4 = e^{3t}.$$

Now take the natural logarithm of both sides:

$$\ln 2.4 = \ln(e^{3t}).$$

Since $\ln(e^x) = x$, we have

$$\ln 2.4 = 3t,$$

so, using a calculator, we get

$$t = \frac{\ln 2.4}{3} = 0.2918.$$

## Exponential Functions with Base $e$

An exponential function with base $a$ has formula

$$P = P_0 a^t.$$

For any positive number $a$, we can write $a = e^k$ where $k = \ln a$. Thus, the exponential function can be rewritten as

$$P = P_0 a^t = P_0(e^k)^t = P_0 e^{kt}.$$

If $a > 1$, then $k$ is positive, and if $0 < a < 1$, then $k$ is negative. We conclude:

Writing $a = e^k$, so $k = \ln a$, any exponential function can be written in two forms

$$P = P_0 a^t \quad \text{or} \quad P = P_0 e^{kt}.$$

- If $a > 1$, we have exponential growth; if $0 < a < 1$, we have exponential decay.
- If $k > 0$, we have exponential growth; if $k < 0$, we have exponential decay.
- $k$ is called the *continuous* growth or decay rate.

The word continuous in continuous growth rate is used in the same way to describe continuous compounding of interest earned on money. (See Appendix A.)

**Example 4**    (a) Convert the function $P = 1000e^{0.05t}$ to the form $P = P_0 a^t$.
(b) Convert the function $P = 500(1.06)^t$ to the form $P = P_0 e^{kt}$.

**Solution**    (a) Since $P = 1000e^{0.05t}$, we have $P_0 = 1000$. We want to find $a$ so that

$$1000a^t = 1000e^{0.05t} = 1000(e^{0.05})^t.$$

We take $a = e^{0.05} = 1.0513$, so the following two functions give the same values:

$$P = 1000e^{0.05t} \qquad \text{and} \qquad P = 1000(1.0513)^t.$$

So a continuous growth rate of 5% is equivalent to a growth rate of 5.13% per unit time.
(b) We have $P_0 = 500$ and we want to find $k$ with

$$500(1.06)^t = 500(e^k)^t,$$

so we take

$$1.06 = e^k$$
$$k = \ln(1.06) = 0.0583.$$

The following two functions give the same values:

$$P = 500(1.06)^t \qquad \text{and} \qquad P = 500e^{0.0583t}.$$

So a growth rate of 6% per unit time is equivalent to a continuous growth rate of 5.83%.

**Example 5**    Sketch graphs of $P = e^{0.5t}$, a continuous growth rate of 50%, and $Q = 5e^{-0.2t}$, a continuous decay rate of 20%.

**Solution**    The graph of $P = e^{0.5t}$ is in Figure 1.67. Notice that the graph is the same shape as the previous exponential growth curves: increasing and concave up. The graph of $Q = 5e^{-0.2t}$ is in Figure 1.68; it has the same shape as other exponential decay functions.

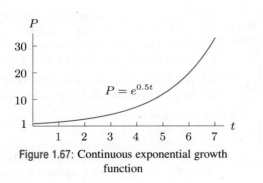

Figure 1.67: Continuous exponential growth function

Figure 1.68: Continuous exponential decay function

# Problems for Section 1.6

For Problems 1–16, solve for $t$ using natural logarithms.

**1.** $10 = 2^t$

**2.** $5^t = 7$

**3.** $2 = (1.02)^t$

**4.** $130 = 10^t$

**5.** $10 = e^t$

**6.** $100 = 25(1.5)^t$

**7.** $50 = 10 \cdot 3^t$

**8.** $5 = 2e^t$

**9.** $e^{3t} = 100$

**10.** $10 = 6e^{0.5t}$

**11.** $40 = 100e^{-0.03t}$

**12.** $a = b^t$

**13.** $B = Pe^{rt}$

**14.** $2P = Pe^{0.3t}$

**15.** $7 \cdot 3^t = 5 \cdot 2^t$

**16.** $5e^{3t} = 8e^{2t}$

The functions in Problems 17–20 represent exponential growth or decay. What is the initial quantity? What is the growth rate? State if the growth rate is continuous.

**17.** $P = 5(1.07)^t$

**18.** $P = 7.7(0.92)^t$

**19.** $P = 15e^{-0.06t}$

**20.** $P = 3.2e^{0.03t}$

Write the functions in Problems 21–24 in the form $P = P_0a^t$. Which represent exponential growth and which represent exponential decay?

**21.** $P = 15e^{0.25t}$

**22.** $P = 2e^{-0.5t}$

**23.** $P = P_0e^{0.2t}$

**24.** $P = 7e^{-\pi t}$

In Problems 25–28, put the functions in the form $P = P_0e^{kt}$.

**25.** $P = 15(1.5)^t$

**26.** $P = 10(1.7)^t$

**27.** $P = 174(0.9)^t$

**28.** $P = 4(0.55)^t$

In Problems 29–30, a quantity $P$ is an exponential function of time $t$. Use the given information about the function $P = P_0e^{kt}$ to:

**(a)** Find values for the parameters $k$ and $P_0$.

**(b)** State the initial quantity and the continuous percent rate of growth or decay.

**29.** $P = 140$ when $t = 3$ and $P = 100$ when $t = 1$

**30.** $P = 40$ when $t = 4$ and $P = 50$ when $t = 3$

**31.** **(a)** What is the continuous percent growth rate for $P = 100e^{0.06t}$, with time, $t$, in years?

**(b)** Write this function in the form $P = P_0a^t$. What is the annual percent growth rate?

**32.** **(a)** What is the annual percent decay rate for $P = 25(0.88)^t$, with time, $t$, in years?

**(b)** Write this function in the form $P = P_0e^{kt}$. What is the continuous percent decay rate?

**33.** What annual percent growth rate is equivalent to a continuous percent growth rate of 8%?

**34.** What continuous percent growth rate is equivalent to an annual percent growth rate of 10%?

**35.** The following formulas give the populations of four different towns, $A$, $B$, $C$, and $D$, with $t$ in years from now.

$$P_A = 600e^{0.08t} \qquad P_B = 1000e^{-0.02t}$$
$$P_C = 1200e^{0.03t} \qquad P_D = 900e^{0.12t}$$

**(a)** Which town is growing fastest (that is, has the largest percentage growth rate)?

**(b)** Which town is the largest now?

**(c)** Are any of the towns decreasing in size? If so, which one(s)?

**36.** A city's population is 1000 and growing at 5% a year.

**(a)** Find a formula for the population at time $t$ years from now assuming that the 5% per year is an:

  (i)  Annual rate        (ii)  Continuous annual rate

**(b)** In each case in part (a), estimate the population of the city in 10 years.

**37.** The population, $P$, in millions, of Nicaragua was 5.4 million in 2004 and growing at an annual rate of 3.4%. Let $t$ be time in years since 2004.

**(a)** Express $P$ as a function in the form $P = P_0a^t$.

**(b)** Express $P$ as an exponential function using base $e$.

**(c)** Compare the annual and continuous growth rates.

**38.** The gross world product is $W = 32.4(1.036)^t$, where $W$ is in trillions of dollars and $t$ is years since 2001. Find a formula for gross world product using a continuous growth rate.

**39.** The population of the world can be represented by $P = 7(1.0115)^t$, where $P$ is in billions of people and $t$ is years since 2012. Find a formula for the population of the world using a continuous growth rate.

**40.** A fishery stocks a pond with 1000 young trout. The number of trout $t$ years later is given by $P(t) = 1000e^{-0.5t}$.

**(a)** How many trout are left after six months? After 1 year?

**(b)** Find $P(3)$ and interpret it in terms of trout.

**(c)** At what time are there 100 trout left?

**(d)** Graph the number of trout against time, and describe how the population is changing. What might be causing this?

**41.** The Hershey Company is the largest US producer of chocolate. In 2011, annual net sales were 6.1 billion dollars and were increasing at a continuous rate of 4.2% per year.[65]

   **(a)** Write a formula for annual net sales, $S$, as a function of time, $t$, in years since 2011.

   **(b)** Estimate annual net sales in 2015.

   **(c)** Use a graph to estimate the year in which annual net sales are expected to pass 8 billion dollars and check your estimate using logarithms.

**42.** During a recession a firm's revenue declines continuously so that the revenue, $R$ (measured in millions of dollars), in $t$ years' time is given by $R = 5e^{-0.15t}$.

   **(a)** Calculate the current revenue and the revenue in two years' time.

   **(b)** After how many years will the revenue decline to $2.7 million?

**43.** The population of a city is 50,000 in 2008 and is growing at a continuous yearly rate of 4.5%.

   **(a)** Give the population of the city as a function of the number of years since 2008. Sketch a graph of the population against time.

   **(b)** What will be the city's population in the year 2018?

   **(c)** Calculate the time for the population of the city to reach 100,000. This is called the doubling time of the population.

**44.** For children and adults with diseases such as asthma, the number of respiratory deaths per year increases by 0.33% when pollution particles increase by a microgram per cubic meter of air.[66]

   **(a)** Write a formula for the number of respiratory deaths per year as a function of quantity of pollution in the air. (Let $Q_0$ be the number of deaths per year with no pollution.)

   **(b)** What quantity of air pollution results in twice as many respiratory deaths per year as there would be without pollution?

**45.** The concentration of the car exhaust fume nitrous oxide, $NO_2$, in the air near a busy road is a function of distance from the road. The concentration decays exponentially at a continuous rate of 2.54% per meter.[67] At what distance from the road is the concentration of $NO_2$ half what it is on the road?

**46.** With time, $t$, in years since the start of 1980, textbook prices have increased at 6.7% per year while inflation has been 3.3% per year.[68] Assume both rates are continuous growth rates.

   **(a)** Find a formula for $B(t)$, the price of a textbook in year $t$ if it cost $B_0$ in 1980.

   **(b)** Find a formula for $P(t)$, the price of an item in year $t$ if it cost $P_0$ in 1980 and its price rose according to inflation.

   **(c)** A textbook cost $50 in 1980. When is its price predicted to be double the price that would have resulted from inflation alone?

**47.** In 2011, the populations of China and India were approximately 1.34 and 1.19 billion people[69], respectively. However, due to central control the annual population growth rate of China was 0.4% while the population of India was growing by 1.37% each year. If these growth rates remain constant, when will the population of India exceed that of China?

**48.** In 2010, there were about 246 million vehicles (cars and trucks) and about 308.7 million people in the US.[70] The number of vehicles grew 15.5% over the previous decade, while the population has been growing at 9.7% per decade. If the growth rates remain constant, when will there be, on average, one vehicle per person?

# 1.7 EXPONENTIAL GROWTH AND DECAY

Many quantities in nature change according to an exponential growth or decay function of the form $P = P_0e^{kt}$, where $P_0$ is the initial quantity and $k$ is the continuous growth or decay rate.

**Example 1**   The Environmental Protection Agency (EPA) investigated a spill of radioactive iodine. The radiation level at the site was about 2.4 millirems/hour (four times the maximum acceptable limit of 0.6 millirems/hour), so the EPA ordered an evacuation of the surrounding area. The level of radiation from an iodine source decays at a continuous hourly rate of $k = -0.004$.

[65] 2011 Annual Report to Stockholders, accessed at www.thehersheycompany.com, August 2012.

[66] Brook, R. D., Franklin, B., Cascio, W., Hong, Y., Howard, G., Lipsett, M., Luepker, R., Mittleman, M., Samet, J., and Smith, S. C. (2004). "Air pollution and cardiovascular disease." *Circulation,* 109(21):2655267.

[67] Rickwood, P. and Knight, D. (2009). "The health impacts of local traffic pollution on primary school age children." *State of Australian Cities 2009 Conference Proceedings.*

[68] Data from "Textbooks headed for ash heap of history", http://educationtechnews.com, Vol 5, 2010.

[69] http://www.indexmundi.com/. Accessed April 17, 2011.

[70] http://www.autoblog.com/2010/01/04/report-number-of-cars-in-the-u-s-dropped-by-four-million-in-20/ and http://2010.census.gov/news/releases/operations/cb10-cn93.html. Accessed February 2012.

(a) What was the level of radiation 24 hours later?

(b) Find the number of hours until the level of radiation reached the maximum acceptable limit, and the inhabitants could return.

Solution

(a) The level of radiation, $R$, in millirems/hour, at time $t$, in hours since the initial measurement, is given by

$$R = 2.4e^{-0.004t},$$

so the level of radiation 24 hours later was

$$R = 2.4e^{(-0.004)(24)} = 2.18 \text{ millirems per hour.}$$

(b) A graph of $R = 2.4e^{-0.004t}$ is in Figure 1.69. The maximum acceptable value of $R$ is 0.6 millirems per hour, which occurs at approximately $t = 350$. Using logarithms, we have

$$0.6 = 2.4e^{-0.004t}$$
$$0.25 = e^{-0.004t}$$
$$\ln 0.25 = -0.004t$$
$$t = \frac{\ln 0.25}{-0.004} = 346.57.$$

The inhabitants will not be able to return for 346.57 hours, or about 15 days.

Figure 1.69: The level of radiation from radioactive iodine

**Example 2**

The population of Kenya[71] was 19.5 million in 1984 and 39.0 million in 2009. Assuming the population increases exponentially, find a formula for the population of Kenya as a function of time.

Solution

We measure the population, $P$, in millions and time, $t$, in years since 1984. We can express $P$ in terms of $t$ using the continuous growth rate $k$ by

$$P = P_0 e^{kt} = 19.5 e^{kt},$$

where $P_0 = 19.5$ is the initial value of $P$. We find $k$ using the fact that $P = 39.0$ when $t = 25$:

$$39.0 = 19.5 e^{k \cdot 25}.$$

Divide both sides by 19.5, giving

$$\frac{39.0}{19.5} = e^{25k}.$$

Take natural logs of both sides:

$$\ln\left(\frac{39.0}{19.5}\right) = \ln(e^{25k}).$$

Since $\ln(e^{25k}) = 25k$, this becomes

$$\ln\left(\frac{39.0}{19.5}\right) = 25k.$$

---

[71] www.cia.gov/library/publications/the-world-factbook.

We get

$$k = \frac{1}{25} \ln \left( \frac{39.0}{19.5} \right) = 0.028,$$

and therefore

$$P = 19.5 e^{0.028t}.$$

Since $k = 0.028 = 2.8\%$, the population of Kenya was growing at a continuous rate of 2.8% per year.

## Doubling Time and Half-Life

Every exponential growth function has a constant doubling time and every exponential decay function has a constant half-life.

> The **doubling time** of an exponentially increasing quantity is the time required for the quantity to double.
> The **half-life** of an exponentially decaying quantity is the time required for the quantity to be reduced by a factor of one half.

**Example 3**    Show algebraically that every exponentially growing function has a fixed doubling time.

**Solution**    Consider the exponential function $P = P_0 a^t$. For any base $a$ with $a > 1$, there is a positive number $d$ such that $a^d = 2$. We show that $d$ is the doubling time. If the population is $P$ at time $t$, then at time $t + d$, the population is

$$P_0 a^{t+d} = P_0 a^t a^d = (P_0 a^t)(2) = 2P.$$

So, no matter what the initial quantity and no matter what the initial time, the size of the population is doubled $d$ time units later.

**Example 4**    The release of chlorofluorocarbons used in air conditioners and household sprays (hair spray, shaving cream, etc.) destroys the ozone in the upper atmosphere. The quantity of ozone, $Q$, is decaying exponentially at a continuous rate of 0.25% per year. What is the half-life of ozone? In other words, at this rate, how long will it take for half the ozone to disappear?

**Solution**    If $Q_0$ is the initial quantity of ozone and $t$ is in years, then

$$Q = Q_0 e^{-0.0025t}.$$

We want to find the value of $t$ making $Q = Q_0/2$, so

$$\frac{Q_0}{2} = Q_0 e^{-0.0025t}.$$

Dividing both sides by $Q_0$ and taking natural logs gives

$$\ln \left( \frac{1}{2} \right) = -0.0025t,$$

so

$$t = \frac{\ln(1/2)}{-0.0025} = 277 \text{ years.}$$

Half the present atmospheric ozone will be gone in 277 years.

## Financial Applications: Compound Interest

We deposit $100 in a bank paying interest at a rate of 8% per year. How much is in the account at the end of the year? This depends on how often the interest is compounded. If the interest is paid into the account *annually*, that is, only at the end of the year, then the balance in the account after one year is $108. However, if the interest is paid twice a year, then 4% is paid at the end of the first six months and 4% at the end of the year. Slightly more money is earned this way, since the interest paid early in the year will earn interest during the rest of the year. This effect is called *compounding*.

In general, the more often interest is compounded, the more money is earned (although the increase may not be large). What happens if interest is compounded more frequently, such as every minute or every second? The benefit of increasing the frequency of compounding becomes negligible beyond a certain point. When that point is reached, we find the balance using the number $e$ and we say that the interest per year is *compounded continuously*. If we have deposited $100 in an account paying 8% interest per year compounded continuously, the balance after one year is $100e^{0.08} = \$108.33$. Compounding is discussed further in Appendix B. In general:

---

An amount $P_0$ is deposited in an account paying interest at a rate of $r$ per year. Let $P$ be the balance in the account after $t$ years.
- If interest is compounded annually, then $P = P_0(1 + r)^t$.
- If interest is compounded continuously, then $P = P_0 e^{rt}$, where $e = 2.71828....$

---

We write $P_0$ for the initial deposit because it is the value of $P$ when $t = 0$. Note that for a 7% interest rate, $r = 0.07$. If a rate is continuous, we will say so explicitly.

---

**Example 5**   A bank advertises an interest rate of 8% per year. If you deposit $5000, how much is in the account 3 years later if the interest is compounded  (a)   Annually?        (b)   Continuously?

**Solution**   (a)  For annual compounding, $P = P_0(1 + r)^t = 5000(1.08)^3 = \$6298.56$.
(b)  For continuous compounding, $P = P_0 e^{rt} = 5000e^{0.08 \cdot 3} = \$6356.25$. As expected, the amount in the account 3 years later is larger if the interest is compounded continuously ($6356.25) than if the interest is compounded annually ($6298.56).

---

**Example 6**   If $10,000 is deposited in an account paying interest at a rate of 5% per year, compounded continuously, how long does it take for the balance in the account to reach $15,000?

**Solution**   Since interest is compounded continuously, we use $P = P_0 e^{rt}$ with $r = 0.05$ and $P_0 = 10,000$. We want to find the value of $t$ for which $P = 15,000$. The equation is

$$15,000 = 10,000e^{0.05t}.$$

Now divide both sides by 10,000, then take logarithms and solve for $t$:

$$1.5 = e^{0.05t}$$
$$\ln(1.5) = \ln(e^{0.05t})$$
$$\ln(1.5) = 0.05t$$
$$t = \frac{\ln(1.5)}{0.05} = 8.1093.$$

It takes about 8.1 years for the balance in the account to reach $15,000.

---

**Example 7**   (a)  Calculate the doubling time, $D$, for interest rates of 2%, 3%, 4%, and 5% per year, compounded annually.
(b)  Use your answers to part (a) to check that an interest rate of $i$% gives a doubling time approximated for small values of $i$ by

$$D \approx \frac{70}{i} \text{ years}.$$

This is the "Rule of 70" used by bankers: To compute the approximate doubling time of an investment, divide 70 by the percent annual interest rate.

**Solution**    (a) We find the doubling time for an interest rate of 2% per year using the formula $P = P_0(1.02)^t$ with $t$ in years. To find the value of $t$ for which $P = 2P_0$, we solve

$$2P_0 = P_0(1.02)^t$$
$$2 = (1.02)^t$$
$$\ln 2 = \ln(1.02)^t$$
$$\ln 2 = t\ln(1.02) \qquad \text{(using the third property of logarithms)}$$
$$t = \frac{\ln 2}{\ln 1.02} = 35.003 \text{ years.}$$

With an annual interest rate of 2%, it takes about 35 years for an investment to double in value. Similarly, we find the doubling times for 3%, 4%, and 5% in Table 1.35.

**Table 1.35**    *Doubling time as a function of interest rate*

| $i$ (% annual growth rate) | 2 | 3 | 4 | 5 |
|---|---|---|---|---|
| $D$ (doubling time in years) | 35.003 | 23.450 | 17.673 | 14.207 |

(b) We compute $(70/i)$ for $i = 2, 3, 4, 5$. The results are shown in Table 1.36.

**Table 1.36**    *Approximate doubling time as a function of interest rate: Rule of 70*

| $i$ (% annual growth rate) | 2 | 3 | 4 | 5 |
|---|---|---|---|---|
| $(70/i)$ (Approximate doubling time in years) | 35.000 | 23.333 | 17.500 | 14.000 |

Comparing Tables 1.35 and 1.36, we see that the quantity $(70/i)$ gives a reasonably accurate approximation to the doubling time, $D$, for the small interest rates we considered.

## Present and Future Value

Many business deals involve payments in the future. For example, when a car is bought on credit, payments are made over a period of time. Being paid $100 in the future is clearly worse than being paid $100 today for many reasons. If we are given the money today, we can do something else with it—for example, put it in the bank, invest it somewhere, or spend it. Thus, even without considering inflation, if we are to accept payment in the future, we would expect to be paid more to compensate for this loss of potential earnings.[72] The question we consider now is, how much more?

To simplify matters, we consider only what we would lose by not earning interest; we do not consider the effect of inflation. Let's look at some specific numbers. Suppose we deposit $100 in an account that earns 7% interest per year compounded annually, so that in a year's time we have $107. Thus, $100 today is worth $107 a year from now. We say that the $107 is the *future value* of the $100, and that the $100 is the *present value* of the $107. In general, we say the following:

- The **future value**, $B$, of a payment, $P$, is the amount to which the $P$ would have grown if deposited today in an interest-bearing bank account.
- The **present value**, $P$, of a future payment, $B$, is the amount that would have to be deposited in a bank account today to produce exactly $B$ in the account at the relevant time in the future.

Due to the interest earned, the future value is larger than the present value. The relation between the present and future values depends on the interest rate, as follows.

---

[72]This is referred to as the time value of money.

Suppose $B$ is the *future value* of $P$ and $P$ is the *present value* of $B$. If interest is compounded annually at a rate $r$ for $t$ years, then

$$B = P(1 + r)^t, \quad \text{or equivalently,} \quad P = \frac{B}{(1 + r)^t}.$$

If interest is compounded continuously at a rate $r$ for $t$ years, then

$$B = Pe^{rt}, \quad \text{or equivalently,} \quad P = \frac{B}{e^{rt}} = Be^{-rt}.$$

The rate, $r$, is sometimes called the *discount rate*. The present value is often denoted by $PV$ and the future value by $FV$.

**Example 8**

You win the lottery and are offered the choice between \$1 million in four yearly installments of \$250,000 each, starting now, and a lump-sum payment of \$920,000 now. Assuming a 6% interest rate per year, compounded continuously, and ignoring taxes, which should you choose?

**Solution**

We assume that you pick the option with the largest present value. The first of the four \$250,000 payments is made now, so

$$\text{Present value of first payment} = \$250,000.$$

The second payment is made one year from now and so

$$\text{Present value of second payment} = \$250,000e^{-0.06(1)}.$$

Calculating the present value of the third and fourth payments similarly, we find:

$$\begin{aligned}
\text{Total present value} &= \$250,000 + \$250,000e^{-0.06(1)} + \$250,000e^{-0.06(2)} + \$250,000e^{-0.06(3)} \\
&= \$250,000 + \$235,441 + \$221,730 + \$208,818 \\
&= \$915,989.
\end{aligned}$$

Since the present value of the four payments is less than \$920,000, you are better off taking the \$920,000 now.

Alternatively, we can compare the future values of the two pay schemes. We calculate the future value of both schemes three years from now, on the date of the last \$250,000 payment. At that time,

$$\text{Future value of the lump-sum payment} = \$920,000e^{0.06(3)} = \$1,101,440.$$

The future value of the first \$250,000 payment is $\$250,000e^{0.06(3)}$. Calculating the future value of the other payments similarly, we find:

$$\begin{aligned}
\text{Total future value} &= \$250,000e^{0.06(3)} + \$250,000e^{0.06(2)} + \$250,000e^{0.06(1)} + \$250,000 \\
&= \$299,304 + \$281,874 + \$265,459 + \$250,000 \\
&= \$1,096,637.
\end{aligned}$$

As we expect, the future value of the \$920,000 payment is greater, so you are better off taking the \$920,000 now.[73]

---

[73] If you read the fine print, you will find that many lotteries do not make their payments right away, but often spread them out, sometimes far into the future. This is to reduce the present value of the payments made, so that the value of the prizes is less than it might first appear!

## Problems for Section 1.7

1. Figure 1.70 shows the balances in two bank accounts. Both accounts pay the same interest rate, but one compounds continuously and the other compounds annually. Which curve corresponds to which compounding method? What is the initial deposit in each case?

**Figure 1.70**

2. The exponential function $y(x) = Ce^{\alpha x}$ satisfies the conditions $y(0) = 2$ and $y(1) = 1$. Find the constants $C$ and $\alpha$. What is $y(2)$?

3. Suppose $1000 is invested in an account paying interest at a rate of 5.5% per year. How much is in the account after 8 years if the interest is compounded

   (a) Annually?          (b) Continuously?

4. If you deposit $10,000 in an account earning interest at an 8% annual rate compounded continuously, how much money is in the account after five years?

5. If you need $20,000 in your bank account in 6 years, how much must be deposited now? The interest rate is 10%, compounded continuously.

6. If $12,000 is deposited in an account paying 8% interest per year, compounded continuously, how long will it take for the balance to reach $20,000?

7. If a bank pays 6% per year interest compounded continuously, how long does it take for the balance in an account to double?

8. Find the doubling time of a quantity that is increasing by 7% per year.

9. The half-life of nicotine in the blood is 2 hours. A person absorbs 0.4 mg of nicotine by smoking a cigarette. Fill in the following table with the amount of nicotine remaining in the blood after $t$ hours. Estimate the length of time until the amount of nicotine is reduced to 0.04 mg.

| $t$ (hours) | 0 | 2 | 4 | 6 | 8 | 10 |
|---|---|---|---|---|---|---|
| Nicotine (mg) | 0.4 | | | | | |

10. World wind energy generating[74] capacity, $W$, was 18,000 megawatts in 2000 and has been increasing at a continuous rate of approximately 27% per year. Assume this rate continues.

   (a) Give a formula for $W$, in megawatts, as a function of time, $t$, in years since 2000.

   (b) When is wind capacity predicted to pass 250,000 megawatts?

11. From October 2002 to October 2006 the number $N(t)$ of Wikipedia articles was approximated by $N(t) = N_0 e^{t/500}$, where $t$ is the number of days after October 1, 2002. Find the doubling time for the number of Wikipedia articles during this period.

12. You want to invest money for your child's education in a certificate of deposit (CD). You want it to be worth $12,000 in 10 years. How much should you invest if the CD pays interest at a 9% annual rate compounded
   (a) Annually?          (b) Continuously?

13. A cup of coffee contains 100 mg of caffeine, which leaves the body at a continuous rate of 17% per hour.

   (a) Write a formula for the amount, $A$ mg, of caffeine in the body $t$ hours after drinking a cup of coffee.
   (b) Graph the function from part (a). Use the graph to estimate the half-life of caffeine.
   (c) Use logarithms to find the half-life of caffeine.

14. A population, currently 200, is growing at 5% per year.

   (a) Write a formula for the population, $P$, as a function of time, $t$, years in the future.
   (b) Graph $P$ against $t$.
   (c) Estimate the population 10 years from now.
   (d) Use the graph to estimate the doubling time of the population.

15. Air pressure, $P$, decreases exponentially with height, $h$, above sea level. If $P_0$ is the air pressure at sea level and $h$ is in meters, then

$$P = P_0 e^{-0.00012h}.$$

   (a) At the top of Mount McKinley, height 6194 meters (about 20,320 feet), what is the air pressure, as a percent of the pressure at sea level?
   (b) The maximum cruising altitude of an ordinary commercial jet is around 12,000 meters (about 39,000 feet). At that height, what is the air pressure, as a percent of the sea level value?

16. The antidepressant fluoxetine (or Prozac) has a half-life of about 3 days. What percentage of a dose remains in the body after one day? After one week?

17. A firm decides to increase output at a constant relative rate from its current level of 20,000 to 30,000 units during the next five years. Calculate the annual percent rate of increase required to achieve this growth.

---

[74]World Wind Energy Association, www.wwindea.org, accessed September 6, 2009.

**18.** The half-life of a radioactive substance is 12 days. There are 10.32 grams initially.

    **(a)** Write an equation for the amount, $A$, of the substance as a function of time.

    **(b)** When is the substance reduced to 1 gram?

**19.** One of the main contaminants of a nuclear accident, such as that at Chernobyl, is strontium-90, which decays exponentially at a rate of approximately 2.5% per year.

    **(a)** Write the percent of strontium-90 remaining, $P$, as a function of years, $t$, since the nuclear accident. [Hint: 100% of the contaminant remains at $t = 0$.]

    **(b)** Graph $P$ against $t$.

    **(c)** Estimate the half-life of strontium-90.

    **(d)** After the Chernobyl disaster, it was predicted that the region would not be safe for human habitation for 100 years. Estimate the percent of original strontium-90 remaining at this time.

**20.** The number of people living with HIV infections increased worldwide approximately exponentially from 2.5 million in 1985 to 34 million in 2010.[75] (HIV is the virus that causes AIDS.)

    **(a)** Give a formula for the number of HIV infections, $H$, (in millions) as a function of years, $t$, since 1985. Use the form $H = H_0 e^{kt}$. Graph this function.

    **(b)** What was the yearly continuous percent change in the number of HIV infections between 1985 and 2010?

**21.** **(a)** Figure 1.71 shows exponential growth. Starting at $t = 0$, estimate the time for the population to double.

    **(b)** Repeat part (a), but this time start at $t = 3$.

    **(c)** Pick any other value of $t$ for the starting point, and notice that the doubling time is the same no matter where you start.

**Figure 1.71**

**22.** An exponentially growing animal population numbers 500 at time $t = 0$; two years later, it is 1500. Find a formula for the size of the population in $t$ years and find the size of the population at $t = 5$.

**23.** If the quantity of a substance decreases by 4% in 10 hours, find its half-life.

**24.** Pregnant women metabolize some drugs at a slower rate than the rest of the population. The half-life of caffeine is about 4 hours for most people. In pregnant women, it is 10 hours.[76] (This is important because caffeine, like all psychoactive drugs, crosses the placenta to the fetus.) If a pregnant woman and her husband each have a cup of coffee containing 100 mg of caffeine at 8 am, how much caffeine does each have left in the body at 10 pm?

**25.** The half-life of radioactive strontium-90 is 29 years. In 1960, radioactive strontium-90 was released into the atmosphere during testing of nuclear weapons, and was absorbed into people's bones. How many years does it take until only 10% of the original amount absorbed remains?

**26.** In 1923, koalas were introduced on Kangaroo Island off the coast of Australia. In 1996, the population was 5000. By 2005, the population had grown to 27,000, prompting a debate on how to control their growth and avoid koalas dying of starvation.[77] Assuming exponential growth, find the (continuous) rate of growth of the koala population between 1996 and 2005. Find a formula for the population as a function of the number of years since 1996, and estimate the population in the year 2020.

**27.** The population of the US was 281.4 million in 2000 and 308.7 million in 2010.[78] Assuming exponential growth,

    **(a)** In what year is the population expected to go over 350 million?

    **(b)** What population is predicted for the 2020 census?

**28.** In 2012, the world's population was 7 billion, and the population is projected[79] to reach 8 billion by the year 2025. What annual growth rate is projected?

**29.** A picture supposedly painted by Vermeer (1632–1675) contains 99.5% of its carbon-14 (half-life 5730 years). From this information decide whether the picture is a fake. Explain your reasoning.

**30.** In November 2010, a "tiger summit" was held in St. Petersburg, Russia.[80] In 1900, there were 100,000 wild tigers worldwide; in 2010 the number was 3200.

    **(a)** Assuming the tiger population has decreased exponentially, find a formula for $f(t)$, the number of wild tigers $t$ years since 1900.

[75] http://www.unaids.org/en/media/unaids/contentassets/restore/AIDS30_KEY_FINDINGS_en.pdf, accessed September 2012.

[76] From Robert M. Julien, *A Primer of Drug Action*, 7th ed., p. 159 (New York: W. H. Freeman, 1995).

[77] news.yahoo.com/s/afp/australiaanimalskoalas, accessed June 1, 2005.

[78] http://2010.census.gov/2010census/. Accessed April 17, 2011.

[79] http://geography.about.com/od/obtainpopulationdata/a/worldpopulation.htm, accessed September 2012.

[80] "Tigers would be extinct in Russia if unprotected," Yahoo! News, Nov. 21, 2010.

**(b)** Between 2000 and 2010, the number of wild tigers decreased by 40%. Is this percentage larger or smaller than the decrease in the tiger population predicted by your answer to part (a)?

**31.** The world population was 6.9 billion at the end of 2010 and is predicted to reach 9 billion by the end of 2050.[81]

**(a)** Assuming the population is growing exponentially, what is the continuous growth rate per year?

**(b)** The United Nations celebrated the "Day of 5 Billion" on July 11, 1987, and the "Day of 6 Billion" on October 12, 1999. Using the growth rate in part (a), when is the "Day of 7 Billion" predicted to be?

**32.** The number of alternative fuel vehicles[82] running on E85, fuel that is up to 85% plant-derived ethanol, increased exponentially in the US between 2003 and 2008.

**(a)** Use this information to complete the missing table values.

**(b)** How many E85-powered vehicles were there in the US in 2003?

**(c)** By what percent did the number of E85-powered vehicles grow from 2004 to 2008?

| Year | 2004 | 2005 | 2006 | 2007 | 2008 |
|---|---|---|---|---|---|
| Number of E85 vehicles | 211,800 | ? | ? | ? | 450,327 |

**33.** Find the future value in 8 years of a $10,000 payment today, if the interest rate is 3% per year compounded continuously.

**34.** Find the future value in 15 years of a $20,000 payment today, if the interest rate is 3.8% per year compounded continuously.

**35.** Find the present value of an $8000 payment to be made in 5 years. The interest rate is 4% per year compounded continuously.

**36.** Find the present value of a $20,000 payment to be made in 10 years. Assume an interest rate of 3.2% per year compounded continuously.

**37.** Interest is compounded annually. Consider the following choices of payments to you:

Choice 1: $1500 now and $3000 one year from now

Choice 2: $1900 now and $2500 one year from now

**(a)** If the interest rate on savings were 5% per year, which would you prefer?

**(b)** Is there an interest rate that would lead you to make a different choice? Explain.

**38.** The island of Manhattan was sold for $24 in 1626. Suppose the money had been invested in an account which compounded interest continuously.

**(a)** How much money would be in the account in the year 2012 if the yearly interest rate was

(i)  5%?          (ii)  7%?

**(b)** If the yearly interest rate was 6%, in what year would the account be worth one billion dollars?

**39.** **(a)** Use the Rule of 70 to predict the doubling time of an investment which is earning 8% interest per year.

**(b)** Find the doubling time exactly, and compare your answer to part (a).

**40.** A business associate who owes you $3000 offers to pay you $2800 now, or else pay you three yearly installments of $1000 each, with the first installment paid now. If you use only financial reasons to make your decision, which option should you choose? Justify your answer, assuming a 6% interest rate per year, compounded continuously.

**41.** A person is to be paid $2000 for work done over a year. Three payment options are being considered. Option 1 is to pay the $2000 in full now. Option 2 is to pay $1000 now and $1000 in a year. Option 3 is to pay the full $2000 in a year. Assume an annual interest rate of 5% a year, compounded continuously.

**(a)** Without doing any calculations, which option is the best option financially for the worker? Explain.

**(b)** Find the future value, in one year's time, of all three options.

**(c)** Find the present value of all three options.

**42.** A company is considering whether to buy a new machine, which costs $97,000. The cash flows (adjusted for taxes and depreciation) that would be generated by the new machine are given in the following table:

| Year | 1 | 2 | 3 | 4 |
|---|---|---|---|---|
| Cash flow | $50,000 | $40,000 | $25,000 | $20,000 |

**(a)** Find the total present value of the cash flows. Treat each year's cash flow as a lump sum at the end of the year and use an interest rate of 7.5% per year, compounded annually.

**(b)** Based on a comparison of the cost of the machine and the present value of the cash flows, would you recommend purchasing the machine?

**43.** Big Tree McGee is negotiating his rookie contract with a professional basketball team. They have agreed to a three-year deal which will pay Big Tree a fixed amount at the end of each of the three years, plus a signing bonus at the beginning of his first year. They are still haggling about the amounts and Big Tree must decide between a big signing bonus and fixed payments per year, or a smaller bonus with payments increasing each year. The

---

[81]"Reviewing the Bidding on the Climate Files", in About Dot Earth, *New York Times*, Nov. 19, 2010.
[82]http://www.eia.doe.gov/aer/renew.html

two options are summarized in the table. All values are payments in millions of dollars.

|  | Signing bonus | Year 1 | Year 2 | Year 3 |
|---|---|---|---|---|
| Option #1 | 6.0 | 2.0 | 2.0 | 2.0 |
| Option #2 | 1.0 | 2.0 | 4.0 | 6.0 |

(a) Big Tree decides to invest all income in stock funds which he expects to grow at a rate of 10% per year, compounded continuously. He would like to choose the contract option which gives him the greater future value at the end of the three years when the last payment is made. Which option should he choose?

(b) Calculate the present value of each contract offer.

**44.** You win $38,000 in the state lottery to be paid in two installments—$19,000 now and $19,000 one year from now. A friend offers you $36,000 in return for your two lottery payments. Instead of accepting your friend's offer, you take out a one-year loan at an interest rate of 8.25% per year, compounded annually. The loan will be paid back by a single payment of $19,000 (your second lottery check) at the end of the year. Which is better, your friend's offer or the loan?

**45.** You are considering whether to buy or lease a machine whose purchase price is $12,000. Taxes on the machine will be $580 due in one year, $464 due in two years, and $290 due in three years. If you buy the machine, you expect to be able to sell it after three years for $5,000. If you lease the machine for three years, you make an initial payment of $2650 and then three payments of $2650 at the end of each of the next three years. The leasing company will pay the taxes. The interest rate is 7.75% per year, compounded annually. Should you buy or lease the machine? Explain.

**46.** You are buying a car that comes with a one-year warranty and are considering whether to purchase an extended warranty for $375. The extended warranty covers the two years immediately after the one-year warranty expires. You estimate that the yearly expenses that would have been covered by the extended warranty are $150 at the end of the first year of the extension and $250 at the end of the second year of the extension. The interest rate is 5% per year, compounded annually. Should you buy the extended warranty? Explain.

# 1.8  NEW FUNCTIONS FROM OLD

We have studied linear and exponential functions and the logarithm function. In this section, we learn how to create new functions by composing, stretching, and shifting functions we already know.

## Composite Functions

A drop of water falls onto a paper towel. The area, $A$ of the circular damp spot is a function of $r$, its radius, which is a function of time, $t$. We know $A = f(r) = \pi r^2$; suppose $r = g(t) = t + 1$. By substitution, we express $A$ as a function of $t$:

$$A = f(g(t)) = \pi(t + 1)^2.$$

The function $f(g(t))$ is a "function of a function," or a *composite function*, in which there is an *inside function* and an *outside function*. To find $f(g(2))$, we first add one ($g(2) = 2 + 1 = 3$) and then square and multiply by $\pi$. We have

$$f(g(2)) = \pi(2 + 1)^2 \quad = \quad \pi 3^2 \quad = \quad 9\pi.$$

First calculation      Second calculation

The inside function is $t + 1$ and the outside function is squaring and multiplying by $\pi$. In general, the inside function represents the calculation that is done first and the outside function represents the calculation done second.

**Example 1**  If $f(t) = t^2$ and $g(t) = t + 2$, find

(a)  $f(t + 1)$     (b)  $f(t) + 3$     (c)  $f(t + h)$     (d)  $f(g(t))$     (e)  $g(f(t))$

**Solution**
(a) Since $t + 1$ is the inside function, $f(t + 1) = (t + 1)^2$.
(b) Here 3 is added to $f(t)$, so $f(t) + 3 = t^2 + 3$.
(c) Since $t + h$ is the inside function, $f(t + h) = (t + h)^2$.
(d) Since $g(t) = t + 2$, substituting $t + 2$ into $f$ gives $f(g(t)) = f(t + 2) = (t + 2)^2$.
(e) Since $f(t) = t^2$, substituting $t^2$ into $g$ gives $g(f(t)) = g(t^2) = t^2 + 2$.

**Example 2**    If $f(x) = e^x$ and $g(x) = 5x + 1$, find  (a)  $f(g(x))$     (b)  $g(f(x))$

Solution    (a) Substituting $g(x) = 5x + 1$ into $f$ gives $f(g(x)) = f(5x + 1) = e^{5x+1}$.
(b) Substituting $f(x) = e^x$ into $g$ gives $g(f(x)) = g(e^x) = 5e^x + 1$.

**Example 3**    Using the following table, find $g(f(0))$, $f(g(0))$, $f(g(1))$, and $g(f(1))$.

| $x$ | 0 | 1 | 2 | 3 |
|---|---|---|---|---|
| $f(x)$ | 3 | 1 | $-1$ | $-3$ |
| $g(x)$ | 0 | 2 | 4 | 6 |

Solution    To find $g(f(0))$, we first find $f(0) = 3$ from the table. Then we have $g(f(0)) = g(3) = 6$.
For $f(g(0))$, we must find $g(0)$ first. Since $g(0) = 0$, we have $f(g(0)) = f(0) = 3$.
Similar reasoning leads to $f(g(1)) = f(2) = -1$ and $g(f(1)) = g(1) = 2$.

We can write a composite function using a new variable $u$ to represent the value of the inside function. For example

$$y = (t + 1)^4 \quad \text{is the same as} \quad y = u^4 \quad \text{with} \quad u = t + 1.$$

Other expressions for $u$, such as $u = (t + 1)^2$, with $y = u^2$, are also possible.

**Example 4**    Use a new variable $u$ for the inside function to express each of the following as a composite function:
(a)  $y = \ln(3t)$      (b)  $w = 5(2r + 3)^2$      (c)  $P = e^{-0.03t}$

Solution    (a) We take the inside function to be $3t$, so $y = \ln u$ with $u = 3t$.
(b) We take the inside function to be $2r + 3$, so $w = 5u^2$ with $u = 2r + 3$.
(c) We take the inside function to be $-0.03t$, so $P = e^u$ with $u = -0.03t$.

## Stretches of Graphs

If the demand function is linear, the graph of a possible revenue function $R = f(p)$ is in Figure 1.72. What does the graph of $R = 3f(p)$ look like? The factor 3 in the function $R = 3f(p)$ stretches each $f(p)$ revenue value by multiplying it by 3. See Figure 1.73. If $c$ is positive, the graph of $R = cf(p)$ is the graph of $R = f(p)$ stretched or shrunk vertically by $c$ units. If $c$ is negative, the function no longer makes sense as a revenue function, but we can still draw the graph. What does the graph of $R = -2f(p)$ look like? The factor $-2$ in the function $R = -2f(p)$ stretches $f(p)$ by multiplying by 2 and reflecting it about the $x$-axis. See Figure 1.73.

> Multiplying a function by a constant, $c$, stretches the graph vertically (if $c > 1$) or shrinks the graph vertically (if $0 < c < 1$). A negative sign (if $c < 0$) reflects the graph about the $x$-axis, in addition to shrinking or stretching.

Figure 1.72: Graph of $f(p)$          Figure 1.73: Multiples of the function $f(p)$

## Shifted Graphs

Consider the function $y = x^2 + 4$. The $y$-coordinates for this function are exactly 4 units larger than the corresponding $y$-coordinates of the function $y = x^2$. So the graph of $y = x^2 + 4$ is obtained from the graph of $y = x^2$ by adding 4 to the $y$-coordinate of each point, that is, by moving the graph of $y = x^2$ up 4 units. (See Figure 1.74.)

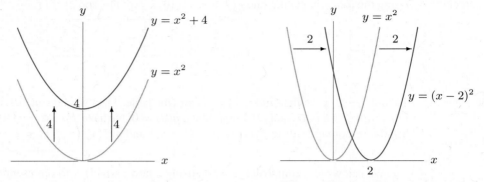

Figure 1.74: Vertical shift: Graphs of $y = x^2$ and $y = x^2 + 4$

Figure 1.75: Horizontal shift: Graphs of $y = x^2$ and $y = (x - 2)^2$

A graph can also be shifted to the left or to the right. In Figure 1.75, we see that the graph of $y = (x - 2)^2$ is the graph of $y = x^2$ shifted to the right 2 units. In general,

- The graph of $y = f(x) + k$ is the graph of $y = f(x)$ moved up $k$ units (down if $k$ is negative).
- The graph of $y = f(x - k)$ is the graph of $y = f(x)$ moved to the right $k$ units (to the left if $k$ is negative).

**Example 5**   (a) A cost function, $C(q)$, for a company is shown in Figure 1.76. The fixed cost increases by $1000. Sketch a graph of the new cost function.
(b) A supply curve, $S$, for a product is given in Figure 1.77. A new factory opens and produces 100 units of the product no matter what the price. Sketch a graph of the new supply curve.

Figure 1.76: A cost function

Figure 1.77: A supply function

**Solution**   (a) For each quantity, the new cost is $1000 more than the old cost. The new cost function is $C(q) + 1000$, whose graph is the graph of $C(q)$ shifted vertically up 1000 units. (See Figure 1.78.)
(b) To see the effect of the new factory, look at an example. At a price of 10 dollars, approximately 800 units are currently produced. With the new factory, this amount increases by 100 units, so the new amount produced is 900 units. At each price, the quantity produced increases by 100, so the new supply curve is $S$ shifted horizontally to the right by 100 units. (See Figure 1.79.)

Figure 1.78: New cost function (original curve dashed)

Figure 1.79: New supply curve (original curve dashed)

## Problems for Section 1.8

In Problems 1–3, find the following:

(a) $f(g(x))$     (b) $g(f(x))$     (c) $f(f(x))$

1. $f(x) = 5x - 1$ and $g(x) = 3x + 2$
2. $f(x) = x - 2$ and $g(x) = x^2 + 8$
3. $f(x) = 3x$ and $g(x) = e^{2x}$
4. Let $f(x) = x^2$ and $g(x) = 3x - 1$. Find the following:

   (a) $f(2) + g(2)$         (b) $f(2) \cdot g(2)$
   (c) $f(g(2))$             (d) $g(f(2))$

5. For $g(x) = x^2 + 2x + 3$, find and simplify:

   (a) $g(2 + h)$            (b) $g(2)$
   (c) $g(2 + h) - g(2)$

6. If $f(x) = x^2 + 1$, find and simplify:

   (a) $f(t + 1)$   (b) $f(t^2 + 1)$   (c) $f(2)$
   (d) $2f(t)$      (e) $(f(t))^2 + 1$

For the functions $f$ and $g$ in Problems 7–10, find

(a) $f(g(1))$      (b) $g(f(1))$      (c) $f(g(x))$
(d) $g(f(x))$      (e) $f(t)g(t)$

7. $f(x) = x^2$, $g(x) = x + 1$
8. $f(x) = \sqrt{x + 4}$, $g(x) = x^2$
9. $f(x) = e^x$, $g(x) = x^2$
10. $f(x) = 1/x$, $g(x) = 3x + 4$
11. Use Table 1.37 to find:

    (a) $f(g(1))$   (b) $g(f(1))$   (c) $f(g(4))$
    (d) $g(f(4))$   (e) $f(g(6))$   (f) $g(f(6))$

### Table 1.37

| $x$    | 1 | 2 | 3 | 4 | 5 | 6 |
|--------|---|---|---|---|---|---|
| $f(x)$ | 5 | 4 | 3 | 3 | 4 | 5 |
| $g(x)$ | 6 | 5 | 4 | 3 | 2 | 1 |

12. Use Table 1.38 to find:

    (a) $f(g(0))$   (b) $f(g(1))$   (c) $f(g(2))$
    (d) $g(f(2))$   (e) $g(f(3))$

### Table 1.38

| $x$    | 0  | 1 | 2 | 3 | 4  | 5  |
|--------|----|---|---|---|----|----|
| $f(x)$ | 10 | 6 | 3 | 4 | 7  | 11 |
| $g(x)$ | 2  | 3 | 5 | 8 | 12 | 15 |

13. Make a table of values for each of the following functions using Table 1.38:

    (a) $f(x) + 3$    (b) $f(x - 2)$    (c) $5g(x)$
    (d) $-f(x) + 2$   (e) $g(x - 3)$    (f) $f(x) + g(x)$

14. Use the variable $u$ for the inside function to express each of the following as a composite function:

    (a) $y = (5t^2 - 2)^6$       (b) $P = 12e^{-0.6t}$
    (c) $C = 12\ln(q^3 + 1)$

15. Use the variable $u$ for the inside function to express each of the following as a composite function:

    (a) $y = 2^{3x-1}$           (b) $P = \sqrt{5t^2 + 10}$
    (c) $w = 2\ln(3r + 4)$

Simplify the quantities in Problems 16–19 using $m(z) = z^2$.

16. $m(z + 1) - m(z)$          17. $m(z + h) - m(z)$

18. $m(z) - m(z - h)$          19. $m(z+h) - m(z-h)$

For Problems 20–25, use the graphs in Figure 1.80.

**Figure 1.80**

**20.** Estimate $f(g(1))$.　　**21.** Estimate $g(f(1))$.

**22.** Estimate $f(g(4))$.　　**23.** Estimate $g(f(4))$.

**24.** Estimate $f(f(2))$.　　**25.** Estimate $g(g(2))$.

For Problems 26–29, use the graphs in Figure 1.81.

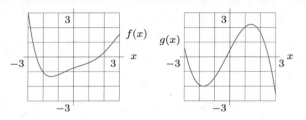

**Figure 1.81**

**26.** Estimate $f(g(1))$.　　**27.** Estimate $g(f(2))$.

**28.** Estimate $f(f(1))$.　　**29.** Estimate $f(g(3))$.

**30.** Using Table 1.39, create a table of values for $f(g(x))$ and for $g(f(x))$.

Table 1.39

| $x$ | −3 | −2 | −1 | 0 | 1 | 2 | 3 |
|-----|----|----|----|---|---|---|---|
| $f(x)$ | 0 | 1 | 2 | 3 | 2 | 1 | 0 |
| $g(x)$ | 3 | 2 | 2 | 0 | −2 | −2 | −3 |

**31.** A tree of height $y$ meters has, on average, $B$ branches, where $B = y - 1$. Each branch has, on average, $n$ leaves, where $n = 2B^2 - B$. Find the average number of leaves on a tree as a function of height.

In Problems 32–35, use Figure 1.82 to estimate the function value or explain why it cannot be done.

**Figure 1.82**

**32.** $u(v(10))$　　**33.** $u(v(40))$

**34.** $v(u(10))$　　**35.** $v(u(40))$

**36.** The Heaviside step function, $H$, is graphed in Figure 1.83. Graph the following functions.

**(a)** $2H(x)$　　**(b)** $H(x) + 1$　　**(c)** $H(x + 1)$

**(d)** $-H(x)$　　**(e)** $H(-x)$

**Figure 1.83**

In Problems 37–42, use Figure 1.84 to graph the function.

**Figure 1.84**

**37.** $y = f(x) + 1$

**38.** $y = f(x - 2)$

**39.** $y = 3f(x)$

**40.** $y = f(x + 1) - 2$

**41.** $y = -f(x) + 3$

**42.** $y = -2f(x - 1)$

For the functions $f$ in Problems 43–45, graph:

**(a)** $f(x + 2)$　　**(b)** $f(x - 1)$　　**(c)** $f(x) - 4$

**(d)** $f(x + 1) + 3$　　**(e)** $3f(x)$　　**(f)** $-f(x) + 1$

**43.**　　　　　　　　　　**44.**

**45.**

In Problems 46–51, use Figure 1.85 to graph the function.

Figure 1.85

Figure 1.86

**46.** $y = f(x) + 2$

**47.** $y = 2f(x)$

**48.** $y = f(x - 1)$

**49.** $y = -3f(x)$

**50.** $y = 2f(x) - 1$

**51.** $y = 2 - f(x)$

**52.** Morphine, a pain-relieving drug, is administered to a patient intravenously starting at 8 am. The drug saturation curve $Q = f(t)$ in Figure 1.86 gives the quantity, $Q$, of morphine in the blood $t$ hours after 8 am.

(a) Draw the drug saturation curve $Q = g(t)$ if the IV line is started at noon instead of 8 am.

(b) Is $g$ one of the following transformations of $f$: vertical shift, vertical stretch, horizontal shift, horizontal stretch? If so, which?

(c) Write $g(t)$ in terms of the function $f$.

**53.** (a) Write an equation for a graph obtained by vertically stretching the graph of $y = x^2$ by a factor of 2, followed by a vertical upward shift of 1 unit. Sketch it.

(b) What is the equation if the order of the transformations (stretching and shifting) in part (a) is interchanged?

(c) Are the two graphs the same? Explain the effect of reversing the order of transformations.

In Problems 54–57 the functions $r = f(t)$ and $V = g(r)$ give the radius and the volume of a commercial hot air balloon being inflated for testing. The variable $t$ is in minutes, $r$ is in feet, and $V$ is in cubic feet. The inflation begins at $t = 0$. In each case, give a mathematical expression that represents the given statement.

**54.** The volume of the balloon $t$ minutes after inflation began.

**55.** The volume of the balloon if its radius were twice as big.

**56.** The time that has elapsed when the radius of the balloon is 30 feet.

**57.** The time that has elapsed when the volume of the balloon is 10,000 cubic feet.

# 1.9    PROPORTIONALITY AND POWER FUNCTIONS

## Proportionality

A common functional relationship occurs when one quantity is *proportional* to another. For example, if apples are \$1.40 a pound, we say the price you pay, $p$ dollars, is proportional to the weight you buy, $w$ pounds, because

$$p = f(w) = 1.40w.$$

As another example, the area, $A$, of a circle is proportional to the square of the radius, $r$:

$$A = f(r) = \pi r^2.$$

> We say $y$ is (directly) **proportional** to $x$ if there is a nonzero constant $k$ such that
>
> $$y = kx.$$
>
> This $k$ is called the constant of proportionality.

We also say that one quantity is *inversely proportional* to another if one is proportional to the reciprocal of the other. For example, the speed, $v$, at which you make a 50-mile trip is inversely proportional to the time, $t$, taken, because $v$ is proportional to $1/t$:

$$v = 50 \left( \frac{1}{t} \right) = \frac{50}{t}.$$

Notice that if $y$ is directly proportional to $x$, then the magnitude of one variable increases (decreases) when the magnitude of the other increases (decreases). If, however, $y$ is inversely proportional to $x$, then the magnitude of one variable increases when the magnitude of the other decreases.

**Example 1**    The heart mass of a mammal is proportional to its body mass.[83]

    (a) Write a formula for heart mass, $H$, as a function of body mass, $B$.

    (b) A human with a body mass of 70 kilograms has a heart mass of 0.42 kilograms. Use this information to find the constant of proportionality.

    (c) Estimate the heart mass of a horse with a body mass of 650 kg.

Solution    (a) Since $H$ is proportional to $B$, for some constant $k$, we have

$$H = kB.$$

    (b) We use the fact that $H = 0.42$ when $B = 70$ to solve for $k$:

$$H = kB$$
$$0.42 = k(70)$$
$$k = \frac{0.42}{70} = 0.006.$$

    (c) Since $k = 0.006$, we have $H = 0.006B$, so the heart mass of the horse is given by

$$H = 0.006(650) = 3.9 \text{ kilograms}.$$

**Example 2**    The period of a pendulum, $T$, is the amount of time required for the pendulum to make one complete swing. For small swings, the period, $T$, is approximately proportional to the square root of $l$, the pendulum's length. So

$$T = k\sqrt{l} \quad \text{where } k \text{ is a constant}.$$

Notice that $T$ is not directly proportional to $l$, but $T$ is proportional to $\sqrt{l}$.

**Example 3**    An object's weight, $w$, is inversely proportional to the square of its distance, $r$, from the earth's center. So, for some constant $k$,

$$w = \frac{k}{r^2}.$$

Here $w$ is not inversely proportional to $r$, but to $r^2$.

## Power Functions

In each of the previous examples, one quantity is proportional to the power of another quantity. We make the following definition:

> We say that $Q(x)$ is a **power function** of $x$ if $Q(x)$ is proportional to a constant power of $x$. If $k$ is the constant of proportionality, and if $p$ is the power, then
>
> $$Q(x) = k \cdot x^p.$$

[83]K. Schmidt-Nielson: *Scaling—Why is Animal Size So Important?* (Cambridge: CUP, 1984).

For example, the function $H = 0.006B$ is a power function with $p = 1$. The function $T = k\sqrt{l} = kl^{1/2}$ is a power function with $p = 1/2$, and the function $w = k/r^2 = kr^{-2}$ is a power function with $p = -2$.

**Example 4**    Which of the following are power functions? For those which are, write the function in the form $y = kx^p$, and give the coefficient $k$ and the exponent $p$.

(a)  $y = \dfrac{5}{x^3}$  (b)  $y = \dfrac{2}{3x}$  (c)  $y = \dfrac{5x^2}{2}$

(d)  $y = 5 \cdot 2^x$  (e)  $y = 3\sqrt{x}$  (f)  $y = (3x^2)^3$

**Solution**    (a)  Since $y = 5x^{-3}$, this is a power function with $k = 5$ and $p = -3$.
(b)  Since $y = (2/3)x^{-1}$, this is a power function with $k = 2/3$ and $p = -1$.
(c)  Since $y = (5/2)x^2$, this is a power function with $k = 5/2 = 2.5$ and $p = 2$.
(d)  This is not a power function. It is an exponential function.
(e)  Since $y = 3x^{1/2}$, this is a power function with $k = 3$ and $p = 1/2$.
(f)  Since $y = 3^3 \cdot (x^2)^3 = 27x^6$, this is a power function with $k = 27$ and $p = 6$.

## Graphs of Power Functions

The graph of $y = x^2$ is shown in Figure 1.87. It is decreasing for negative $x$ and increasing for positive $x$. Notice that it is bending upward, or concave up, for all $x$. The graph of $y = x^3$ is shown in Figure 1.88. Notice that it is bending downward, or concave down for negative $x$ and bending upward, or concave up for positive $x$. The graph of $y = \sqrt{x} = x^{1/2}$ is shown in Figure 1.89. Notice that the graph is increasing and concave down.

Since $x^2$ increases without bound as $x$ increases, we often say that it tends to infinity as $x$ approaches infinity, which we write in symbols as

$$x^2 \to \infty \quad \text{as} \quad x \to \infty.$$

Since $x^3$ decreases without bound as $x$ decreases, we write

$$x^3 \to -\infty \quad \text{as} \quad x \to -\infty.$$

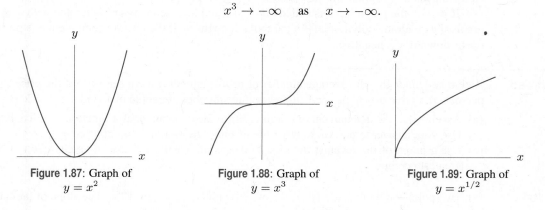

Figure 1.87: Graph of $y = x^2$

Figure 1.88: Graph of $y = x^3$

Figure 1.89: Graph of $y = x^{1/2}$

**Example 5**    If $N$ is the average number of species found on an island and $A$ is the area of the island, observations have shown[84] that $N$ is approximately proportional to the cube root of $A$. Write a formula for $N$ as a function of $A$ and describe the shape of the graph of this function.

**Solution**    For some positive constant $k$, we have

$$N = k\sqrt[3]{A} = kA^{1/3}.$$

[84]*Scientific American*, p. 112 (September, 1989).

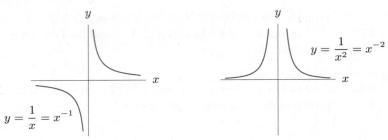

Figure 1.90: Graphs of negative powers of $x$

It turns out that the value of $k$ depends on the region of the world in which the island is found. The graph of $N$ against $A$ (for $A > 0$) has a shape similar to the graph in Figure 1.89. It is increasing and concave down. Thus, larger islands have more species on them (as we would expect), but the increase slows as the island gets larger.

The function $y = x^0 = 1$ has a graph that is a horizontal line. For negative powers, rewriting

$$y = x^{-1} = \frac{1}{x} \quad \text{and} \quad y = x^{-2} = \frac{1}{x^2}$$

makes it clear that as $x > 0$ increases, the denominators increase and the functions decrease. The graphs of $y = x^{-1}$ and $y = x^{-2}$ have both the $x$- and $y$-axes as asymptotes. (See Figure 1.90.)

## Quadratic Functions and Polynomials

Sums of power functions with nonnegative integer exponents are called *polynomials*, which are functions of the form

$$y = p(x) = a_n x^n + a_{n-1} x^{n-1} + \cdots + a_1 x + a_0.$$

Here, $n$ is a nonnegative integer, called the *degree* of the polynomial, and $a_n$ is a nonzero number called the *leading coefficient*. We call $a_n x^n$ the *leading term*.

If $n = 2$, the polynomial is called *quadratic* and has the form $ax^2 + bx + c$ with $a \neq 0$. The graph of a quadratic polynomial is a parabola. It opens up if the leading coefficient $a$ is positive and opens down if $a$ is negative.

**Example 6**    A company finds that the average number of people attending a concert is 75 if the price is $50 per person. At a price of $35 per person, the average number of people in attendance is 120.

(a) Assume that the demand curve is a line. Write the demand, $q$, as a function of price, $p$.
(b) Use your answer to part (a) to write the revenue, $R$, as a function of price, $p$.
(c) Use a graph of the revenue function to determine what price should be charged to obtain the greatest revenue.

Solution    (a) Two points on the line are $(p, q) = (50, 75)$ and $(p, q) = (35, 120)$. The slope of the line is

$$m = \frac{120 - 75}{35 - 50} = \frac{45}{-15} = -3 \text{ people/dollar.}$$

To find the vertical intercept of the line, we use the slope and one of the points:

$$75 = b + (-3)(50)$$
$$225 = b$$

The demand function is $q = 225 - 3p$.
(b) Since $R = pq$ and $q = 225 - 3p$, we see that $R = p(225 - 3p) = 225p - 3p^2$.

(c) The revenue function is the quadratic polynomial graphed in Figure 1.91. The maximum revenue occurs at $p = 37.5$. Thus, the company maximizes revenue by charging $37.50 per person.

Figure 1.91: Revenue function for concert ticket sales

## Problems for Section 1.9

In Problems 1–12, determine whether or not the function is a power function. If it is a power function, write it in the form $y = kx^p$ and give the values of $k$ and $p$.

1. $y = \dfrac{x}{5}$

2. $y = 5\sqrt{x}$

3. $y = \dfrac{8}{x}$

4. $y = \dfrac{3}{x^2}$

5. $y = 2^x$

6. $y = \dfrac{3}{8x}$

7. $y = (3x^5)^2$

8. $y = \dfrac{5}{2\sqrt{x}}$

9. $y = 3 \cdot 5^x$

10. $y = \dfrac{2x^2}{10}$

11. $y = (5x)^3$

12. $y = 3x^2 + 4$

In Problems 13–16, write a formula representing the function.

13. The strength, $S$, of a beam is proportional to the square of its thickness, $h$.

14. The energy, $E$, expended by a swimming dolphin is proportional to the cube of the speed, $v$, of the dolphin.

15. The average velocity, $v$, for a trip over a fixed distance, $d$, is inversely proportional to the time of travel, $t$.

16. The gravitational force, $F$, between two bodies is inversely proportional to the square of the distance $d$ between them.

17. Use shifts of power functions to find a possible formula for each of the graphs:

(a)

(b)

18. The surface area of a mammal, $S$, satisfies the equation $S = kM^{2/3}$, where $M$ is the body mass, and the constant of proportionality $k$ depends on the body shape of the mammal. A human of body mass 70 kilograms has surface area 18,600 cm². Find the constant of proportionality for humans. Find the surface area of a human with body mass 60 kilograms.

19. The number of species of lizards, $N$, found on an island off Baja California is proportional to the fourth root of the area, $A$, of the island.[85] Write a formula for $N$ as a function of $A$. Graph this function. Is it increasing or decreasing? Is the graph concave up or concave down? What does this tell you about lizards and island area?

20. The blood mass of a mammal is proportional to its body mass. A rhinoceros with body mass 3000 kilograms has blood mass of 150 kilograms. Find a formula for the blood mass of a mammal as a function of the body mass and estimate the blood mass of a human with body mass 70 kilograms.

21. Kleiber's Law states that the metabolic needs (such as calorie requirements) of a mammal are proportional to its body weight raised to the 0.75 power.[86] Surprisingly, the daily diets of mammals conform to this relation well. Assuming Kleiber's Law holds:

(a) Write a formula for $C$, daily calorie consumption, as a function of body weight, $W$.

(b) Sketch a graph of this function. (You do not need scales on the axes.)

(c) If a human weighing 150 pounds needs to consume 1800 calories a day, estimate the daily calorie requirement of a horse weighing 700 lbs and of a rabbit weighing 9 lbs.

(d) On a per-pound basis, which animal requires more calories: a mouse or an elephant?

[85]Rosenzweig, M.L., *Species Diversity in Space and Time*, p. 143 (Cambridge: Cambridge University Press, 1995).

[86]Strogatz, S., "Math and the City", The New York Times, May 20, 2009. Kleiber originally estimated the exponent as 0.74; it is now believed to be 0.75.

22. Allometry is the study of the relative size of different parts of a body as a consequence of growth. In this problem, you will check the accuracy of an allometric equation: the weight of a fish is proportional to the cube of its length.[87] Table 1.40 relates the weight, $y$, in gm, of plaice (a type of fish) to its length, $x$, in cm. Does this data support the hypothesis that (approximately) $y = kx^3$? If so, estimate the constant of proportionality, $k$.

Table 1.40

| $x$ | $y$ | $x$ | $y$ | $x$ | $y$ |
|------|------|------|------|------|------|
| 33.5 | 332 | 37.5 | 455 | 41.5 | 623 |
| 34.5 | 363 | 38.5 | 500 | 42.5 | 674 |
| 35.5 | 391 | 39.5 | 538 | 43.5 | 724 |
| 36.5 | 419 | 40.5 | 574 | | |

23. Biologists estimate that the number of animal species of a certain body length is inversely proportional to the square of the body length.[88] Write a formula for the number of animal species, $N$, of a certain body length as a function of the length, $L$. Are there more species at large lengths or at small lengths? Explain.

24. The specific heat, $s$, of an element is the number of calories of heat required to raise the temperature of one gram of the element by one degree Celsius. Use the following table to decide if $s$ is proportional or inversely proportional to the atomic weight, $w$, of the element. If so, find the constant of proportionality.

| Element | Li | Mg | Al | Fe | Ag | Pb | Hg |
|---------|------|------|------|------|-------|-------|-------|
| $w$ | 6.9 | 24.3 | 27.0 | 55.8 | 107.9 | 207.2 | 200.6 |
| $s$ | 0.92 | 0.25 | 0.21 | 0.11 | 0.056 | 0.031 | .033 |

25. The circulation time of a mammal (that is, the average time it takes for all the blood in the body to circulate once and return to the heart) is proportional to the fourth root of the body mass of the mammal.

   (a) Write a formula for the circulation time, $T$, in terms of the body mass, $B$.
   (b) If an elephant of body mass 5230 kilograms has a circulation time of 148 seconds, find the constant of proportionality.
   (c) What is the circulation time of a human with body mass 70 kilograms?

26. Zipf's Law, developed by George Zipf in 1949, states that in a given country, the population of a city is inversely proportional to the city's rank by size in the country.[89] Assuming Zipf's Law:

   (a) Write a formula for the population, $P$, of a city as a function of its rank, $R$.

   (b) If the constant of proportionality $k$ is 300,000, what is the approximate population of the largest city (rank 1)? The second largest city (rank 2)? The third largest city?
   (c) Answer the questions of part (b) if $k = 6$ million.
   (d) Interpret the meaning of the constant of proportionality $k$ in this context.

27. The infrastructure needs of a region (for example, the number of miles of electrical cable, the number of miles of roads, the number of gas stations) depend on its population. Cities enjoy economies of scale.[90] For example, the number of gas stations is proportional to the population raised to the power of 0.77.

   (a) Write a formula for the number, $N$, of gas stations in a city as a function of the population, $P$, of the city.
   (b) If city A is 10 times bigger than city B, how do their number of gas stations compare?
   (c) Which is expected to have more gas stations per person, a town of 10,000 people or a city of 500,000 people?

28. According to the National Association of Realtors,[91] the minimum annual gross income, $m$, in thousands of dollars, needed to obtain a 30-year home loan of $A$ thousand dollars at 9% is given in Table 1.41. Note that the larger the loan, the greater the income needed. Of course, not every mortgage is financed at 9%. In fact, excepting for slight variations, mortgage interest rates are generally determined not by individual banks but by the economy as a whole. The minimum annual gross income, $m$, in thousands of dollars, needed for a home loan of $100,000 at various interest rates, $r$, is given in Table 1.42. Note that obtaining a loan at a time when interest rates are high requires a larger income.

   (a) Is the size of the loan, $A$, proportional to the minimum annual gross income, $m$?
   (b) Is the percentage rate, $r$, proportional to the minimum annual gross income, $m$?

Table 1.41

| $A$ | 50 | 75 | 100 | 150 | 200 |
|-----|------|------|------|------|------|
| $m$ | 17.242 | 25.863 | 34.484 | 51.726 | 68.968 |

Table 1.42

| $r$ | 8 | 9 | 10 | 11 | 12 |
|-----|------|------|------|------|------|
| $m$ | 31.447 | 34.484 | 37.611 | 40.814 | 44.084 |

---

[87] Adapted from "On the Dynamics of Exploited Fish Populations" by R. J. H. Beverton and S. J. Holt, *Fishery Investigations*, Series II, 19, 1957.

[88] *US News & World Report*, August 18, 1997, p. 79.

[89] Strogatz, S., "Math and the City", The New York Times, May 20, 2009.

[90] Strogatz, S., "Math and the City", *The New York Times*, May 20, 2009.

[91] "Income Needed to Get a Mortgage," *The World Almanac 1992*, p. 720.

**29.** A sporting goods wholesaler finds that when the price of a product is $25, the company sells 500 units per week. When the price is $30, the number sold per week decreases to 460 units.

   **(a)** Find the demand, $q$, as a function of price, $p$, assuming that the demand curve is linear.

   **(b)** Use your answer to part (a) to write revenue as a function of price.

   **(c)** Graph the revenue function in part (b). Find the price that maximizes revenue. What is the revenue at this price?

**30.** A health club has cost and revenue functions given by $C = 10,000 + 35q$ and $R = pq$, where $q$ is the number of annual club members and $p$ is the price of a one-year membership. The demand function for the club is $q = 3000 - 20p$.

   **(a)** Use the demand function to write cost and revenue as functions of $p$.

   **(b)** Graph cost and revenue as a function of $p$, on the same axes. (Note that price does not go above $170 and that the annual costs of running the club reach $120,000.)

   **(c)** Explain why the graph of the revenue function has the shape it does.

   **(d)** For what prices does the club make a profit?

   **(e)** Estimate the annual membership fee that maximizes profit. Mark this point on your graph.

# 1.10 PERIODIC FUNCTIONS

## What Are Periodic Functions?

Many functions have graphs that oscillate, resembling a wave. Figure 1.92 shows the number of new housing construction starts (one-family units) in the US, 2002–2005, where $t$ is time in quarter-years.[92] Notice that few new homes begin construction during the first quarter of a year (January, February, and March), whereas many new homes are begun in the second quarter (April, May, and June). Since 2008, as the economy has slowed, the pattern of oscillations has been replaced by a sharp drop in housing construction.

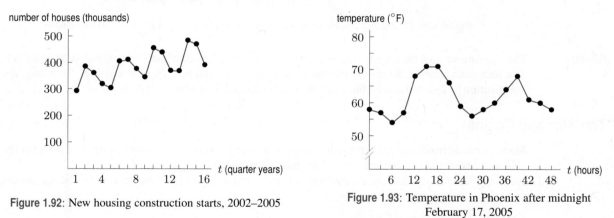

Figure 1.92: New housing construction starts, 2002–2005

Figure 1.93: Temperature in Phoenix after midnight February 17, 2005

Let's look at another example. Figure 1.93 is a graph of the temperature (in °C) in Phoenix, AZ, in hours after midnight, February 17, 2005. Notice that the maximum is in the afternoon and the minimum is in the early morning.[93] Again, the graph looks like a wave.

Functions whose values repeat at regular intervals are called *periodic*. Many processes, such as the number of housing starts or the temperature, are approximately periodic. The water level in a tidal basin, the blood pressure in a heart, retail sales in the US, and the position of air molecules transmitting a musical note are also all periodic functions of time.

## Amplitude and Period

Periodic functions repeat exactly the same cycle forever. If we know one cycle of the graph, we know the entire graph.

---

[92] http://www.census.gov/const/www/quarterly_starts_completions.pdf, accessed May 25, 2009.
[93] http://www.weather.com, accessed February 20, 2005.

> For any periodic function of time:
> - The **amplitude** is half the difference between its maximum and minimum values.
> - The **period** is the time for the function to execute one complete cycle.

**Example 1**   Estimate the amplitude and period of the new housing starts function shown in Figure 1.92.

**Solution**    Figure 1.92 is not exactly periodic, since the maximum and minimum are not the same for each cycle. Nonetheless, the minimum is about 300, and the maximum is about 450. The difference between them is 150, so the amplitude is about $\frac{1}{2}(150) = 75$ thousand houses.

     The wave completes a cycle between $t = 1$ and $t = 5$, so the period is $t = 4$ quarter-years, or one year. The business cycle for new housing construction is one year.

**Example 2**   Figure 1.94 shows the temperature in an unopened freezer. Estimate the temperature in the freezer at 12:30 and at 2:45.

Figure 1.94: Oscillating freezer temperature. Estimate the temperature at 12:30 and 2:45

**Solution**    The maximum and minimum values each occur every 25 minutes, so the period is 25 minutes. The temperature at 12:30 should be the same as at 12:55 and at 1:20, namely, 2°F. Similarly, the temperature at 2:45 should be the same as at 2:20 and 1:55, or about $-1.5$°F.

## The Sine and Cosine

Many periodic functions are represented using the functions called *sine* and *cosine*. The keys for the sine and cosine on a calculator are usually labeled as sin and cos.

*Warning*: Your calculator can be in either "degree" mode or "radian" mode. For this book, always use "radian" mode.

### Graphs of the Sine and Cosine

The graphs of the sine and the cosine functions are periodic; see Figures 1.95 and 1.96. Notice that the graph of the cosine function is the graph of the sine function, shifted $\pi/2$ to the left.

Figure 1.95: Graph of $\sin t$                            Figure 1.96: Graph of $\cos t$

     The maximum and minimum values of $\sin t$ are $+1$ and $-1$, so the amplitude of the sine function is 1. The graph of $y = \sin t$ completes a cycle between $t = 0$ and $t = 2\pi$; the rest of the graph repeats this portion. The period of the sine function is $2\pi$.

**Example 3**    Use a graph of $y = 3 \sin 2t$ to estimate the amplitude and period of this function.

**Solution**    In Figure 1.97, the waves have a maximum of $+3$ and a minimum of $-3$, so the amplitude is 3. The graph completes one complete cycle between $t = 0$ and $t = \pi$, so the period is $\pi$.

Figure 1.97: The amplitude is 3 and the period is $\pi$

**Example 4**    Explain how the graphs of each of the following functions differ from the graph of $y = \sin t$.

(a)   $y = 6 \sin t$          (b)   $y = 5 + \sin t$          (c)   $y = \sin(t + \frac{\pi}{2})$

**Solution**    (a) The graph of $y = 6 \sin t$ is in Figure 1.98. The maximum and minimum values are $+6$ and $-6$, so the amplitude is 6. This is the graph of $y = \sin t$ stretched vertically by a factor of 6.

(b) The graph of $y = 5 + \sin t$ is in Figure 1.99. The maximum and minimum values of this function are 6 and 4, so the amplitude is $(6 - 4)/2 = 1$. The amplitude (or size of the wave) is the same as for $y = \sin t$, since this is a graph of $y = \sin t$ shifted up 5 units.

(c) The graph of $y = \sin(t + \pi/2)$ is in Figure 1.100. This has the same amplitude, namely 1, and period, namely $2\pi$, as the graph of $y = \sin t$. It is the graph of $y = \sin t$ shifted $\pi/2$ units to the left. (In fact, this is the graph of $y = \cos t$.)

Figure 1.98: Graph of
$y = 6 \sin t$

Figure 1.99: Graph of
$y = 5 + \sin t$

Figure 1.100: Graph of
$y = \sin(t + \frac{\pi}{2})$

## Families of Curves: The Graph of $y = A \sin(Bt)$

The constants $A$ and $B$ in the expression $y = A \sin(Bt)$ are called *parameters*. We can study families of curves by varying one parameter at a time and studying the result.

**Example 5**    (a) Graph $y = A \sin t$ for several positive values of $A$. Describe the effect of $A$ on the graph.
(b) Graph $y = \sin(Bt)$ for several positive values of $B$. Describe the effect of $B$ on the graph.

**Solution**    (a) From the graphs of $y = A \sin t$ for $A = 1, 2, 3$ in Figure 1.101, we see that $A$ is the amplitude.

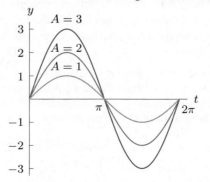

Figure 1.101: Graphs of $y = A \sin t$ with $A = 1, 2, 3$

(b) The graphs of $y = \sin(Bt)$ for $B = \frac{1}{2}, B = 1$, and $B = 2$ are shown in Figure 1.102. When $B = 1$, the period is $2\pi$; when $B = 2$, the period is $\pi$; and when $B = \frac{1}{2}$, the period is $4\pi$. The parameter $B$ affects the period of the function. The graphs suggest that the larger $B$ is, the shorter the period. In fact, the period is $2\pi/B$.

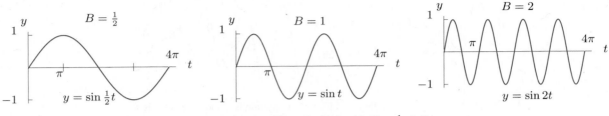

Figure 1.102: Graphs of $y = \sin(Bt)$ with $B = \frac{1}{2}, 1, 2$

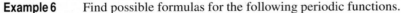

In Example 5, the amplitude of $y = A\sin(Bt)$ was determined by the parameter $A$, and the period was determined by the parameter $B$. In general, we have

---

The functions $y = A\sin(Bt) + C$ and $y = A\cos(Bt) + C$ are periodic with

$$\text{Amplitude} = |A|, \qquad \text{Period} = \frac{2\pi}{|B|}, \qquad \text{Vertical shift} = C$$

---

**Example 6**   Find possible formulas for the following periodic functions.

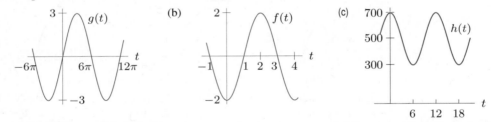

**Solution**

(a) This function looks like a sine function of amplitude 3, so $g(t) = 3\sin(Bt)$. Since the function executes one full oscillation between $t = 0$ and $t = 12\pi$, when $t$ changes by $12\pi$, the quantity $Bt$ changes by $2\pi$. This means $B \cdot 12\pi = 2\pi$, so $B = 1/6$. Therefore, $g(t) = 3\sin(t/6)$ has the graph shown.

(b) This function looks like an upside-down cosine function with amplitude 2, so $f(t) = -2\cos(Bt)$. The function completes one oscillation between $t = 0$ and $t = 4$. Thus, when $t$ changes by 4, the quantity $Bt$ changes by $2\pi$, so $B \cdot 4 = 2\pi$, or $B = \pi/2$. Therefore, $f(t) = -2\cos(\pi t/2)$ has the graph shown.

(c) This function looks like a cosine function. The maximum is 700 and the minimum is 300, so the amplitude is $\frac{1}{2}(700 - 300) = 200$. The height halfway between the maximum and minimum is 500, so the cosine curve has been shifted up 500 units, so $h(t) = 500 + 200\cos(Bt)$. The period is 12, so $B \cdot 12 = 2\pi$. Thus, $B = \pi/6$. The function $h(t) = 500 + 200\cos(\pi t/6)$ has the graph shown.

---

**Example 7**   On June 23, 2009, high tide in Portland, Maine was at midnight.[94] The height of the water in the harbor is a periodic function, since it oscillates between high and low tide. If $t$ is in hours since midnight, the height (in feet) is approximated by the formula

$$y = 4.9 + 4.4\cos\left(\frac{\pi}{6}t\right).$$

(a) Graph this function from $t = 0$ to $t = 24$.

---

[94]www.maineboats.com/tidecharts/tides?T=junpt09.

(b) What was the water level at high tide?

(c) When was low tide, and what was the water level at that time?

(d) What is the period of this function, and what does it represent in terms of tides?

(e) What is the amplitude of this function, and what does it represent in terms of tides?

Solution

(a) See Figure 1.103.

(b) The water level at high tide was 9.3 feet (given by the $y$-intercept on the graph).

(c) Low tide occurs at $t = 6$ (6 am) and at $t = 18$ (6 pm). The water level at this time is 0.5 feet.

(d) The period is 12 hours and represents the interval between successive high tides or successive low tides. Of course, there is something wrong with the assumption in the model that the period is 12 hours. If so, the high tide would always be at noon or midnight, instead of progressing slowly through the day, as it in fact does. The interval between successive high tides actually averages about 12 hours 39 minutes, which could be taken into account in a more precise mathematical model.

(e) The maximum is 9.3, and the minimum is 0.5, so the amplitude is $(9.3 - 0.5)/2$, which is 4.4 feet. This represents half the difference between the depths at high and low tide.

Figure 1.103: Graph of the function approximating the depth of the water in Portland, Maine on June 23, 2009

## Problems for Section 1.10

In Problems 1–6, graph the function. What is the amplitude and period?

**1.** $y = 3 \sin x$

**2.** $y = 4 \cos 2x$

**3.** $y = -3 \sin 2\theta$

**4.** $y = 3 \sin 2x$

**5.** $y = 5 - \sin 2t$

**6.** $y = 4 \cos(\frac{1}{2}t)$

**7.** Figure 1.104 shows quarterly beer production during the period 1997 to 1999. Quarter 1 reflects production during the first three months of the year, etc.[95]

(a) Explain why a periodic function should be used to model these data.

(b) Approximately when does the maximum occur? The minimum? Why does this make sense?

(c) What are the period and amplitude for these data?

Figure 1.104

[95] www.beerinstitute.org/pdfs/PRODUCTION_AND_WITHDRAWALS_OF_MALT_BEVERAGES_1997_1999.pdf, accessed May 7, 2005.

8. Sketch a possible graph of sales of sunscreen in the northeastern US over a 3-year period, as a function of months since January 1 of the first year. Explain why your graph should be periodic. What is the period?

9. The following table shows values of a periodic function $f(x)$. The maximum value attained by the function is 5.

(a) What is the amplitude of this function?
(b) What is the period of this function?
(c) Find a formula for this periodic function.

| $x$ | 0 | 2 | 4 | 6 | 8 | 10 | 12 |
|-----|---|---|---|---|---|----|----|
| $f(x)$ | 5 | 0 | −5 | 0 | 5 | 0 | −5 |

10. A person breathes in and out every three seconds. The volume of air in the person's lungs varies between a minimum of 2 liters and a maximum of 4 liters. Which of the following is the best formula for the volume of air in the person's lungs as a function of time?

(a) $y = 2 + 2\sin\left(\frac{\pi}{3}t\right)$   (b) $y = 3 + \sin\left(\frac{2\pi}{3}t\right)$

(c) $y = 2 + 2\sin\left(\frac{2\pi}{3}t\right)$   (d) $y = 3 + \sin\left(\frac{\pi}{3}t\right)$

11. Values of a function are given in the following table. Explain why this function appears to be periodic. Approximately what are the period and amplitude of the function? Assuming that the function is periodic, estimate its value at $t = 15$, at $t = 75$, and at $t = 135$.

| $t$ | 20 | 25 | 30 | 35 | 40 | 45 | 50 | 55 | 60 |
|-----|----|----|----|----|----|----|----|----|----|
| $f(t)$ | 1.8 | 1.4 | 1.7 | 2.3 | 2.0 | 1.8 | 1.4 | 1.7 | 2.3 |

12. Average daily high temperatures in Ottawa, the capital of Canada, range from a low of $-6°$ Celsius on January 1 to a high of $26°$ Celsius on July 1 six months later. See Figure 1.105. Find a formula for $H$, the average daily high temperature in Ottawa in, $°C$, as a function of $t$, the number of months since January 1.

Figure 1.105

13. Figure 1.106 shows the levels of the hormones estrogen and progesterone during the monthly ovarian cycles in females.[96] Is the level of both hormones periodic? What is the period in each case? Approximately when in the monthly cycle is estrogen at a peak? Approximately when in the monthly cycle is progesterone at a peak?

Figure 1.106

14. Delta Cephei is one of the most visible stars in the night sky. Its brightness has periods of 5.4 days, the average brightness is 4.0 and its brightness varies by $\pm0.35$. Find a formula that models the brightness of Delta Cephei as a function of time, $t$, with $t = 0$ at peak brightness.

15. Most breeding birds in the northeast US migrate elsewhere during the winter. The number of bird species in an Ohio forest preserve oscillates between a high of 28 in June and a low of 10 in December.[97]

(a) Graph the number of bird species in this preserve as a function of $t$, the number of months since June. Include at least three years on your graph.
(b) What are the amplitude and period of this function?
(c) Find a formula for the number of bird species, $B$, as a function of the number of months, $t$ since June.

In Problems 16–27, find a possible formula for the graph.

[96]Robert M. Julien, *A Primer of Drug Action*, Seventh Edition, p. 360 (W. H. Freeman and Co., New York: 1995).
[97]M. L. Rosenzweig, *Species Diversity in Space and Time*, p. 71 (Cambridge University Press, 1995).

**20.**

**21.**

**22.**

**23.**

**24.**

**25.**

**26.**

**27.**

**30.** The desert temperature, $H$, oscillates daily between $40°F$ at 5 am and $80°F$ at 5 pm. Write a possible formula for $H$ in terms of $t$, measured in hours from 5 am.

**31.** Table 1.43 gives values for $g(t)$, a periodic function.

   **(a)** Estimate the period and amplitude for this function.

   **(b)** Estimate $g(34)$ and $g(60)$.

**Table 1.43**

| $t$ | 0 | 2 | 4 | 6 | 8 | 10 | 12 | 14 |
|---|---|---|---|---|---|---|---|---|
| $g(t)$ | 14 | 19 | 17 | 15 | 13 | 11 | 14 | 19 |

| $t$ | 16 | 18 | 20 | 22 | 24 | 26 | 28 |
|---|---|---|---|---|---|---|---|
| $g(t)$ | 17 | 15 | 13 | 11 | 14 | 19 | 17 |

**32.** In Figure 1.107, the blue curve shows monthly mean carbon dioxide ($CO_2$) concentration, in parts per million (ppm) at Mauna Loa Observatory, Hawaii, as a function of $t$, in months, since December 2005. The black curve shows the monthly mean concentration adjusted for seasonal $CO_2$ variation.[98]

   **(a)** Approximately how much did the monthly mean $CO_2$ increase between December 2005 and December 2010?

   **(b)** Find the average monthly rate of increase of the monthly mean $CO_2$ between December 2005 and December 2010. Use this information to find a linear function that approximates the black curve.

   **(c)** The seasonal $CO_2$ variation between December 2005 and December 2010 can be approximated by a sinusoidal function of the form $A \sin Bt$. What is the approximate period of the function? What is its amplitude? Give a formula for the function.

   **(d)** The blue curve may be approximated by a function of the form $h(t) = f(t) + g(t)$, where $f(t)$ is sinusoidal and $g(t)$ is linear. Using your work in parts (b) and (c), find a possible formula for $h(t)$. Graph $h(t)$ using the scale in Figure 1.107.

**Figure 1.107**

**28.** The Bay of Fundy in Canada has the largest tides in the world. The difference between low and high water levels is 15 meters (nearly 50 feet). At a particular point the depth of the water, $y$ meters, is given as a function of time, $t$, in hours since midnight by

$$y = D + A \cos\left(B(t - C)\right).$$

   **(a)** What is the physical meaning of $D$?

   **(b)** What is the value of $A$?

   **(c)** What is the value of $B$? Assume the time between successive high tides is 12.4 hours.

   **(d)** What is the physical meaning of $C$?

**29.** The depth of water in a tank oscillates once every 6 hours. If the smallest depth is 5.5 feet and the largest depth is 8.5 feet, find a possible formula for the depth in terms of time in hours.

[98]http://www.esrl.noaa.gov/gmd/ccgg/trends/. Accessed March 2011. Monthly means joined by segments to highlight trends.

## CHAPTER SUMMARY

- **Function terminology**
  Domain/range, increasing/decreasing, concavity, intercepts.
- **Linear functions**
  Slope, $y$-intercept. Grow by equal amounts in equal times.
- **Economic applications**
  Cost, revenue, and profit functions, break-even point. Supply and demand curves, equilibrium point. Depreciation function. Budget constraint. Present and future value.
- **Change, average rate of change, relative change**

- **Exponential functions**
  Exponential growth and decay, growth rate, the number $e$, continuous growth rate, doubling time, half-life, compound interest. Grow by equal percentages in equal times.
- **The natural logarithm function**
- **New functions from old**
  Composition, shifting, stretching.
- **Power functions and proportionality**
- **Polynomials**
- **Periodic functions**
  Sine, cosine, amplitude, period.

## REVIEW PROBLEMS FOR CHAPTER ONE

1. The population of a city, $P$, in millions, is a function of $t$, the number of years since 1970, so $P = f(t)$. Explain the meaning of the statement $f(35) = 12$ in terms of the population of this city.

2. The time $T$, in minutes, that it takes Dan to run $x$ kilometers is a function $T = f(x)$. Explain the meaning of the statement $f(5) = 23$ in terms of running.

3. Describe what Figure 1.108 tells you about an assembly line whose productivity is represented as a function of the number of workers on the line.

**Figure 1.108**

4. It warmed up throughout the morning, and then suddenly got much cooler around noon, when a storm came through. After the storm, it warmed up before cooling off at sunset. Sketch temperature as a function of time.

5. A gas tank 6 meters underground springs a leak. Gas seeps out and contaminates the soil around it. Graph the amount of contamination as a function of the depth (in meters) below ground.

6. You drive at a constant speed from Chicago to Detroit, a distance of 275 miles. About 120 miles from Chicago you pass through Kalamazoo, Michigan. Sketch a graph of your distance from Kalamazoo as a function of time.

7. The graphs in Figure 1.109 represent the temperature, $H$, of four loaves of bread each put into an oven at time $t = 0$.

   (a) Which curve corresponds to the bread that was put into the hottest oven?

(b) Which curve corresponds to the bread that had the lowest temperature at the time that it was put into the oven?

(c) Which two curves correspond to loaves of bread that were at the same temperature when they were put into the oven?

(d) Write a sentence describing any differences between the curves shown in (II) and (III). In terms of bread, what might cause this difference?

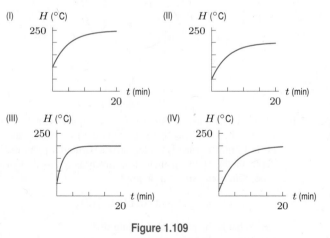

**Figure 1.109**

Find the equation of the line passing through the points in Problems 8–11.

8. $(0, -1)$ and $(2, 3)$

9. $(-1, 3)$ and $(2, 2)$

10. $(0, 2)$ and $(2, 2)$

11. $(-1, 3)$ and $(-1, 4)$

**12.** Match the graphs in Figure 1.110 with the following equations. (Note that the $x$ and $y$ scales may be unequal.)

   (a)   $y = x - 5$           (b)   $-3x + 4 = y$

   (c)   $5 = y$                (d)   $y = -4x - 5$

   (e)   $y = x + 6$         (f)   $y = x/2$

**Figure 1.110**

**13.** Find a linear function that generates the values in Table 1.44.

**Table 1.44**

| $x$ | 5.2 | 5.3 | 5.4 | 5.5 | 5.6 |
|-----|-----|-----|-----|-----|-----|
| $y$ | 27.8 | 29.2 | 30.6 | 32.0 | 33.4 |

**14.** Residents of the town of Maple Grove who are connected to the municipal water supply are billed a fixed amount monthly plus a charge for each cubic foot of water used. A household using 1000 cubic feet was billed \$40, while one using 1600 cubic feet was billed \$55.

   (a) What is the charge per cubic foot?

   (b) Write an equation for the total cost of a resident's water as a function of cubic feet of water used.

   (c) How many cubic feet of water used would lead to a bill of \$100?

**15.** A controversial 1992 Danish study[99] reported that men's average sperm count decreased from 113 million per milliliter in 1940 to 66 million per milliliter in 1990.

   (a) Express the average sperm count, $S$, as a linear function of the number of years, $t$, since 1940.

   (b) A man's fertility is affected if his sperm count drops below about 20 million per milliliter. If the linear model found in part (a) is accurate, in what year will the average male sperm count fall below this level?

**16.** Let $y = f(x) = 3x - 5$.

   (a) What is $f(1)$?

   (b) Find the value of $y$ when $x$ is 5.

   (c) Find the value of $x$ when $y$ is 4.

   (d) Find the average rate of change of $f$ between $x = 2$ and $x = 4$.

In Problems 17–22, find the average velocity for the position function $s(t)$, in mm, over the interval $1 \le t \le 3$, where $t$ is in seconds.

**17.** $s(t) = 12t - t^2$         **18.** $s(t) = \ln(t)$

**19.**

| $t$ | 0 | 1 | 2 | 3 |
|-----|---|---|---|---|
| $s(t)$ | 7 | 3 | 7 | 11 |

**20.**

| $t$ | 0 | 1 | 2 | 3 |
|-----|---|---|---|---|
| $s(t)$ | .8 | 4 | 2 | 4 |

**21.**     **22.**

**23.** The yield, $Y$, of an apple orchard (in bushels) as a function of the amount, $a$, of fertilizer (in pounds) used on the orchard is shown in Figure 1.111.

   (a) Describe the effect of the amount of fertilizer on the yield of the orchard.

   (b) What is the vertical intercept? Explain what it means in terms of apples and fertilizer.

   (c) What is the horizontal intercept? Explain what it means in terms of apples and fertilizer.

   (d) What is the range of this function for $0 \le a \le 80$?

   (e) Is the function increasing or decreasing at $a = 60$?

   (f) Is the graph concave up or down near $a = 40$?

**Figure 1.111**

**24.** Sketch reasonable graphs for the following. Pay particular attention to the concavity of the graphs.

   (a) The total revenue generated by a car rental business, plotted against the amount spent on advertising.

   (b) The temperature of a cup of hot coffee standing in a room, plotted as a function of time.

---

[99]"Investigating the Next Silent Spring," *US News and World Report*, pp. 50–52 (March 11, 1996).

**25.** Each of the functions $g$, $h$, $k$ in Table 1.45 is increasing, but each increases in a different way. Which of the graphs in Figure 1.112 best fits each function?

**Table 1.45**

| $t$ | $g(t)$ | $h(t)$ | $k(t)$ |
|-----|--------|--------|--------|
| 1 | 23 | 10 | 2.2 |
| 2 | 24 | 20 | 2.5 |
| 3 | 26 | 29 | 2.8 |
| 4 | 29 | 37 | 3.1 |
| 5 | 33 | 44 | 3.4 |
| 6 | 38 | 50 | 3.7 |

**Figure 1.112**

**26.** When a new product is advertised, more and more people try it. However, the rate at which new people try it slows as time goes on.

  **(a)** Graph the total number of people who have tried such a product against time.
  **(b)** What do you know about the concavity of the graph?

**27.** Figure 1.113 shows the age-adjusted death rates from different types of cancer among US males.[100]

  **(a)** Discuss how the death rate has changed for the different types of cancers.
  **(b)** For which type of cancer has the average rate of change between 1930 and 1967 been the largest? Estimate the average rate of change for this cancer type. Interpret your answer.
  **(c)** For which type of cancer has the average rate of change between 1930 and 1967 been the most negative? Estimate the average rate of change for this cancer type. Interpret your answer.

**28.** Find the average rate of change between $x = 0$ and $x = 10$ of each of the following functions: $y = x$, $y = x^2$, $y = x^3$, and $y = x^4$. Which has the largest average rate of change? Graph the four functions, and draw lines whose slopes represent these average rates of change.

**29.** The volume of water in a pond over a period of 20 weeks is shown in Figure 1.114.

  **(a)** Is the average rate of change of volume positive or negative over the following intervals?
    (i)   $t = 0$ and $t = 5$    (ii)   $t = 0$ and $t = 10$
    (iii)  $t = 0$ and $t = 15$   (iv)  $t = 0$ and $t = 20$
  **(b)** During which of the following time intervals was the average rate of change larger?
    (i)  $0 \le t \le 5$ or $0 \le t \le 10$
    (ii)  $0 \le t \le 10$ or $0 \le t \le 20$
  **(c)** Estimate the average rate of change between $t = 0$ and $t = 10$. Interpret your answer in terms of water.

**Figure 1.114**

**30. (a)** What are the fixed costs and the marginal cost for the cost function in Figure 1.115?
  **(b)** Explain what $C(100) = 2500$ tells you about costs.

**Figure 1.115**

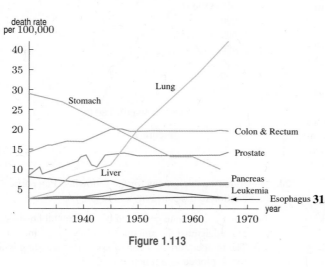

**Figure 1.113**

**31.** The Quick-Food company provides a college meal-service plan. Quick-Food has fixed costs of $350,000 per term and variable costs of $400 per student. Quick-Food charges $800 per student per term. How many students must sign up with the Quick-Food plan in order for the company to make a profit?

---

[100] Abraham M. Lilienfeld, *Foundations of Epidemiology*, p. 67 (New York; Oxford University Press, 1976).

**32.** For tax purposes, you may have to report the value of your assets, such as cars or refrigerators. The value you report drops with time. "Straight-line depreciation" assumes that the value is a linear function of time. If a $950 refrigerator depreciates completely in seven years, find a formula for its value as a function of time.

**33.** One of the graphs in Figure 1.116 is a supply curve, and the other is a demand curve. Which is which? Explain how you made your decision using what you know about the effect of price on supply and demand.

**Figure 1.116**

**34.** Figure 1.117 shows supply and demand curves.

(a) What is the equilibrium price for this product? At this price, what quantity is produced?

(b) Choose a price above the equilibrium price—for example, $p = 300$. At this price, how many items are suppliers willing to produce? How many items do consumers want to buy? Use your answers to these questions to explain why, if prices are above the equilibrium price, the market tends to push prices lower (toward the equilibrium).

(c) Now choose a price below the equilibrium price—for example, $p = 200$. At this price, how many items are suppliers willing to produce? How many items do consumers want to buy? Use your answers to these questions to explain why, if prices are below the equilibrium price, the market tends to push prices higher (toward the equilibrium).

**Figure 1.117**

Find possible formulas for the graphs in Problems 35–40.

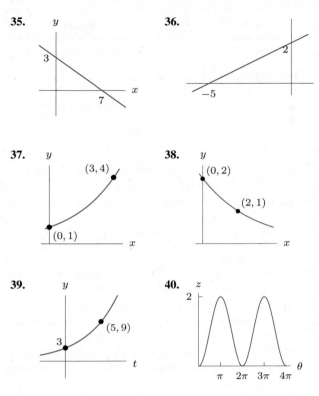

**41.** Table 1.46 gives values for three functions. Which functions could be linear? Which could be exponential? Which are neither? For those which could be linear or exponential, give a possible formula for the function.

**Table 1.46**

| $x$ | $f(x)$ | $g(x)$ | $h(x)$ |
|---|---|---|---|
| 0 | 25 | 30.8 | 15,000 |
| 1 | 20 | 27.6 | 9,000 |
| 2 | 14 | 24.4 | 5,400 |
| 3 | 7 | 21.2 | 3,240 |

**42.** The worldwide carbon dioxide emission[101], $C$, from consumption of fossil fuels was 22.0 billion tons in 1995 and 28.2 billion tons in 2005. Find a formula for the emission $C$ in $t$ years after 1995 if:

(a) $C$ is a linear function of $t$. What is the annual rate of increase in carbon dioxide emission?

(b) $C$ is an exponential function of $t$. What is the annual percent rate of increase in carbon dioxide emission?

---

[101] *Statistical Abstracts of the United States 2009*, Table 1304.

**43.** The population of a region is growing exponentially. There were 40,000,000 people in 2000 ($t = 0$) and 48,000,000 in 2010. Find an expression for the population at any time $t$, in years. What population would you predict for the year 2020? What is the doubling time?

For Problems 44–47, solve for $x$ using logs.

**44.** $3^x = 11$

**45.** $20 = 50(1.04)^x$

**46.** $e^{5x} = 100$

**47.** $25e^{3x} = 10$

**48.** Write the exponential functions $P = e^{0.08t}$ and $Q = e^{-0.3t}$ in the form $P = a^t$ and $Q = b^t$.

**49.** **(a)** What is the continuous percent growth rate for the function $P = 10e^{0.15t}$?
**(b)** Write this function in the form $P = P_0 a^t$.
**(c)** What is the annual (not continuous) percent growth rate for this function?
**(d)** Graph $P = 10e^{0.15t}$ and your answer to part (b) on the same axes. Explain what you see.

**50.** You need $10,000 in your account 3 years from now and the interest rate is 8% per year, compounded continuously. How much should you deposit now?

**51.** If $Q_0$ is the quantity of radioactive carbon-14 in an organism at the time of death, the quantity, $Q$, remaining $t$ years later is given by

$$Q = Q_0 e^{-0.000121t}.$$

**(a)** A skull uncovered at an archeological dig has 15% of the original amount of carbon-14 present. Estimate its age.
**(b)** Calculate the half-life of carbon-14.

**52.** A radioactive substance has a half-life of 8 years. If 200 grams are present initially, how much remains at the end of 12 years? How long until only 10% of the original amount remains?

**53.** The size of an exponentially growing bacteria colony doubles in 5 hours. How long will it take for the number of bacteria to triple?

**54.** When the Olympic Games were held outside Mexico City in 1968, there was much discussion about the effect the high altitude (7340 feet) would have on the athletes. Assuming air pressure decays exponentially by 0.4% every 100 feet, by what percentage is air pressure reduced by moving from sea level to Mexico City?

**55.** The third-quarter revenue of Apple® went from $3.68 billion[102] in 2005 to $15.68 billion[103] in 2010. Find an exponential function to model the revenue as a function of years since 2005. What is the continuous percent growth rate, per year, of revenue?

**56.** The total world marine catch in 1950 was 17 million tons and in 2001 was 99 million tons.[104] If the marine catch is increasing exponentially, find the (continuous) rate of increase. Use it to predict the total world marine catch in the year 2020.

**57.** You have the option of renewing the service contract on your three-year old dishwasher. The new service contract is for three years at a price of $200. The interest rate is 7.25% per year, compounded annually, and you estimate that the costs of repairs if you do not buy the service contract will be $50 at the end of the first year, $100 at the end of the second year, and $150 at the end of the third year. Should you buy the service contract? Explain.

**58.** If $h(x) = x^3 + 1$ and $g(x) = \sqrt{x}$, find

**(a)** $g(h(x))$      **(b)** $h(g(x))$
**(c)** $h(h(x))$      **(d)** $g(x) + 1$
**(e)** $g(x + 1)$

**59.** Let $f(x) = 2x + 3$ and $g(x) = \ln x$. Find formulas for each of the following functions.

**(a)** $g(f(x))$   **(b)** $f(g(x))$   **(c)** $f(f(x))$

In Problems 60–62, find the following:

**(a)** $f(g(x))$   **(b)** $g(f(x))$   **(c)** $f(f(x))$

**60.** $f(x) = 2x^2$ and $g(x) = x + 3$

**61.** $f(x) = 2x + 3$ and $g(x) = 5x^2$

**62.** $f(x) = x^2 + 1$ and $g(x) = \ln x$

In Problems 63–65, use Figure 1.118 to graph the function.

**Figure 1.118**

**63.** $5f(x)$        **64.** $f(x + 5)$        **65.** $f(x) + 5$

For the functions $f(x)$ in Problems 66–69, graph:

**(a)** $y = f(x) + 2$        **(b)** $y = f(x - 1)$
**(c)** $y = 3f(x)$           **(d)** $y = -f(x)$

[102]http://www.apple.com/pr/library/2005/oct/11results.html. Accessed April 27, 2011.
[103]http://www.apple.com/pr/library/2010/01/25results.html. Accessed April 27, 2011.
[104]*The World Almanac and Book of Facts 2005*, p. 143 (New York).

**66.**

**67.**

**68.**

**69.**

In Problems 70–73, use Figure 1.119 to graph the functions.

**Figure 1.119**

**70.** $n(t) = m(t) + 2$

**71.** $p(t) = m(t - 1)$

**72.** $k(t) = m(t + 1.5)$

**73.** $w(t) = m(t - 0.5) - 2.5$

**74.** A plan is adopted to reduce the pollution in a lake to the legal limit. The quantity $Q$ of pollutants in the lake after $t$ weeks of clean-up is modeled by the function $Q = f(t)$ where $f(t) = A + Be^{Ct}$.

  **(a)** What are the signs of $A$, $B$ and $C$?
  **(b)** What is the initial quantity of pollution in the lake?
  **(c)** What is the legal limit of pollution in the lake?

In Problems 75–76, use shifts of a power function to find a possible formula for the graph.

**75.** $(-3, 2)$

**76.**

**77.** The following table gives values for a function $p = f(t)$. Could $p$ be proportional to $t$?

| $t$ | 0 | 10 | 20 | 30 | 40 | 50 |
|---|---|---|---|---|---|---|
| $p$ | 0 | 25 | 60 | 100 | 140 | 200 |

**78.** The DuBois formula relates a person's surface area $s$, in m², to weight $w$, in kg, and height $h$, in cm, by

$$s = 0.01w^{0.25}h^{0.75}.$$

  **(a)** What is the surface area of a person who weighs 65 kg and is 160 cm tall?
  **(b)** What is the weight of a person whose height is 180 cm and who has a surface area of 1.5 m²?
  **(c)** For people of fixed weight 70 kg, solve for $h$ as a function of $s$. Simplify your answer.

Find the period and amplitude in Problems 79–81.

**79.** $y = 7\sin(3t)$
**80.** $z = 3\cos(u/4) + 5$
**81.** $r = 0.1\sin(\pi t) + 2$

**82.** A graduate student in environmental science studied the temperature fluctuations of a river. Figure 1.120 shows the temperature of the river (in °C) every hour, with hour 0 being midnight of the first day.

  **(a)** Explain why a periodic function could be used to model these data.
  **(b)** Approximately when does the maximum occur? The minimum? Why does this make sense?
  **(c)** What is the period for these data? What is the amplitude?

**Figure 1.120**

**83.** Figure 1.121 shows the number of reported[105] cases of mumps by month, in the US, for 1972–73.

  **(a)** Find the period and amplitude of this function, and interpret each in terms of mumps.

[105]Center for Disease Control, 1974, *Reported Morbidity and Mortality in the United States 1973*, Vol. 22, No. 53. Prior to the licensing of the vaccine in 1967, 100,000–200,000 cases of mumps were reported annually. Since 1995, fewer than 1000 cases are reported annually. Source: CDC.

**(b)** Predict the number of cases of mumps 30 months and 45 months after January 1, 1972.

**Figure 1.121**

**84.** A population of animals varies periodically between a low of 700 on January 1 and a high of 900 on July 1. Graph the population against time.

For Problems 85–86, find a possible formula for each graph.

**85.**

**86.**

# STRENGTHEN YOUR UNDERSTANDING

In Problems 1–105, indicate whether the statement is true or false.

**1.** The domain is the set of outputs of a function.

**2.** If $V = f(a)$, where $V$ is the value of a car (in thousands of dollars) and $a$ is the car's age (in years), then $f(10)$ is the age of a car valued at $10,000.

**3.** If $f(x) = x^2$, then the point $(2, 4)$ is on the graph of $f(x)$.

**4.** The set of numbers between 3 and 4, including 3 and 4, is written $(3, 4)$.

**5.** The function $D = f(r)$ given by $D = -3r + 10$ has vertical intercept 10.

**6.** A function is always given by a formula.

**7.** If $f(x) = x^2 + 2x + 1$ then $f(3) = 16$.

**8.** The graph of a function can have more than one horizontal intercept.

**9.** The graph of a function can have more than one vertical intercept.

**10.** The vertical intercept on the graph of $C = f(q)$, where $C$ is the cost to produce $q$ items, represents the cost to produce no items.

**11.** The slope of the graph of a linear function $f(p)$ is $(f(p_2) - f(p_1))/(p_2 - p_1)$.

**12.** The graph of the linear function with formula $m(x) = 3x + 2$ has slope 2.

**13.** The slope of the graph of a linear function can be zero.

**14.** An equation of a line with slope $-1$ that passes through the point $(2, 5)$ is $y = -x + 7$.

**15.** The function whose values are shown in the following table could be linear:

| $s$ | 2 | 4 | 6 | 8 |
|---|---|---|---|---|
| $h(s)$ | $-1$ | $-5$ | $-9$ | $-13$ |

**16.** The graphs of two different linear functions must intersect in a point.

**17.** A line with positive slope must also have a positive $y$-intercept.

**18.** The linear function $f(x)$ with $f(4) = 2$ and $f(9) = 3$ has slope 5.

**19.** If number of acres of harvested land is a linear function of elevation in meters, the units of the slope are meters per acre.

**20.** If $(2, 5)$ is a point on the graph of a line with slope 3, then $(3, 8)$ is also a point on the line.

**21.** The function $D = f(r)$ given by $D = -3r + 10$ is an increasing function of $r$.

**22.** The average rate of change of a linear function $f(t)$ between $t = a$ and $t = b$ is $(f(b) - f(a))/(b - a)$.

**23.** If $C(n)$ is the total cost, in dollars, to feed $n$ students in the campus cafeteria, then the average rate of change of $C(n)$ has units of students per dollar.

**24.** If $s(z) = z^2$, then the average rate of change between $z = -1$ and $z = 2$ is positive.

**25.** A function $f(x)$ can be both increasing and concave down over the interval $0 \le x \le 1$.

**26.** The function $Q(r)$ given in the following table appears to be concave up:

| $r$ | 1 | 2 | 3 | 4 |
|---|---|---|---|---|
| $Q(r)$ | 10 | 15 | 17 | 18 |

27. The speed and velocity of a moving object are the same.

28. The average rate of change of a function is the slope of the line between two points on the graph of the function.

29. A particle whose position $s$, in feet, at time $t$, in seconds, is given by $s(t) = 3t + 2$ has average velocity 3 feet per second.

30. If the graph of a function is concave up, the function must be increasing.

31. The relative change in a quantity is the change divided by the size of the quantity before the change.

32. If production is measured in tons, the units of the percent change of production is also measured in tons.

33. If cost is $1000 for a quantity of 500 and percent change is 15% when the quantity increases by 100 units, then the cost to produce 600 units is $1150.

34. Relative change is always positive.

35. If $P$ in grams is a function of $t$ in hours, then the relative rate of change is measured in grams per hour.

36. Profit is the sum of cost and revenue.

37. Revenue from selling a product is the selling price times the quantity sold.

38. The graph of the cost function $C(q)$ always passes through the origin.

39. The cost function $C(q)$ is a decreasing function of quantity $q$.

40. If the selling price is constant, the revenue function $R(q)$ is an increasing function of quantity $q$.

41. Demand is always greater than supply.

42. At equilibrium price $p^*$ and quantity $q^*$, the supply and demand curves intersect.

43. The units of marginal cost are the same as the units of marginal revenue.

44. The marginal profit is the marginal revenue minus marginal cost.

45. The imposition of a sales tax won't change the equilibrium price and quantity.

46. The function $Q(t) = 5 \cdot 3^t$ is exponential.

47. An exponential function has a constant percent growth or decay rate.

48. Exponential functions are always increasing.

49. The function $P(t) = 10 \cdot (1.03)^t$ has a 30% growth rate.

50. The function $Q(x) = 35(1/3)^x$ has $Q(2)/Q(1) = 1/3$.

51. The function $R(s) = 16 \cdot 5^s$ has a vertical intercept of 16.

52. The number $e$ satisfies $2 < e < 3$.

53. The function $f(t) = 5^t$ grows more quickly than the function $g(t) = e^t$.

54. If $P = 25(1.15)^t$ gives the size of a population in year $t$, then the population is growing by 15% per year.

55. The function $Q(r)$ given in the following table could be exponential:

| $r$ | 0 | 0.1 | 0.2 | 0.3 |
|-----|---|-----|-----|-----|
| $Q(r)$ | 5 | 6.2 | 7.4 | 8.6 |

56. The value of $\ln(0)$ is 1.

57. The value of $\ln(1)$ is 0.

58. For all $a > 0$ and $b > 0$, we have $\ln(a + b) = \ln(a) \cdot \ln(b)$.

59. The value of $\ln(e^2)$ is 2.

60. The function $f(x) = \ln(x)$ is an increasing function of $x$.

61. If $5^t = 36$, then $t \ln 5 = \ln 36$.

62. The function $P = 10e^{5t}$ is an exponential growth function.

63. When $b > 0$, we have $e^{\ln b} = \ln(e^b)$.

64. When $B > 0$, we have $\ln(2B) = 2\ln(B)$.

65. When $A > 0$ and $B > 0$, we have $\ln(A^B) = B \ln(A)$.

66. The doubling time of $P(t) = 3e^{5t}$ and $Q(t) = 6e^{5t}$ is the same.

67. If the half-life of a quantity is 6 years, then 100 mg of the substance will decay to 25 mg in 9 years.

68. The half-life of $P(t) = 2e^{-0.6t}$ is twice the half-life of $Q(t) = e^{-0.6t}$.

69. An amount of $1000 invested in a bank account at an interest rate of 3% compounded annually has a balance after $t$ years of $1000e^{0.03t}$.

70. The doubling time of a continuous rate of 6% is more than the doubling time of a continuous rate of 3%.

71. To find the doubling time of $P(t) = 5e^{2t}$, we can solve $10 = 5e^{2t}$ for $t$.

72. Present value is always less than future value if interest rates are greater than zero.

73. Assuming continuous growth rate of 3%, the future value five years from now of a $1000 payment today is $1000e^{0.15}$.

74. The future value in five years of a $1000 payment made today is less than its future value in ten years (assuming an annual interest rate of 2%).

**75.** The present value of a payment of $1000 five years from now is less than the present value of a $1000 payment made ten years from now (assuming an annual interest rate of 2%).

**76.** The graph of $f(x + 5)$ is the same as the graph of $f(x) + 5$.

**77.** If the graph of $f(x)$ is always increasing, then so is the graph of $f(x + k)$.

**78.** If the graph of $g(t)$ is concave up, then the graph of $-2g(t)$ is concave down.

**79.** If the graph of $f(x)$ crosses the $x$-axis at $x = 1$, then so does the graph of $5f(x)$.

**80.** If the graph of $f(x)$ crosses the $x$-axis at $x = 1$, then the graph of $f(x + 1)$ crosses the $x$-axis at $x = 0$.

**81.** If $g(s) = s^2$ then $g(3 + h) = 9 + h^2$.

**82.** If $f(t) = t^2$ and $g(t) = t + 1$ then $f(g(t)) = g(f(t))$.

**83.** If $f(x) = x^3 - 5$ and $g(x) = \ln x$ then $f(g(x)) = (\ln x)^3 - 5$.

**84.** The function $h(x) = (3x^2 + 2)^3$ can be written $g(u(x))$ where $g(t) = t^3$ and $u(x) = 3x^2 + 2$.

**85.** If $f(x) = x^2 - 1$ then $f(x + h) - f(x) = h^2$.

**86.** If $A$ is proportional to $B$, then $A = kB$ for some nonzero constant $k$.

**87.** If $A$ is inversely proportional to $B$, then $A = -kB$ for some nonzero constant $k$.

**88.** The function $f(x) = 3x^{10}$ is a power function.

**89.** The function $h(s) = 3 \cdot 10^s$ is a power function.

**90.** The function $h(x) = 3/\sqrt{x}$ can be written as a power function in the form $h(x) = 3x^{-2}$.

**91.** The function $g(x) = 3/(2x^2)$ can be written as a power function in the form $g(x) = 6x^{-2}$.

**92.** The function $f(x) = (3\sqrt{x})/2$ can be written as the power function $f(x) = 1.5x^{1/2}$.

**93.** If $w = 10.25r^3$, then $w$ is proportional to the cube of $r$.

**94.** If $S = 25/\sqrt[3]{t}$, then $S$ is inversely proportional to the cube root of $t$.

**95.** If $p$ is proportional to $q$, then the ratio $p/q$ is constant.

**96.** The amplitude of $f(x) = 3 \sin x$ is $3/2$.

**97.** The period of $g(x) = \cos x + 2$ is $2\pi$.

**98.** The value of $\sin(3t)/\sin(5t)$ is $3/5$.

**99.** The graph of $y = \cos x$ is a horizontal shift of the graph of $y = \sin x$.

**100.** The period of $y = 3\cos(5t) + 7$ is 5.

**101.** The period of $y = \sin(2t)$ is twice the period of $y = \sin(t)$.

**102.** The functions $f(t) = 5 \sin t$ and $g(t) = 8 + 5 \sin t$ have the same amplitude.

**103.** The graphs of $y = (\sin x)^2$ and $y = \sin(x^2)$ are the same.

**104.** For all $x$, we have $0 \le \sin(x) \le 1$.

**105.** For all $x$, we have $\sin^2 x + \cos^2 x = 1$.

## PROJECTS FOR CHAPTER ONE

**1. Compound Interest**

The newspaper article below is from *The New York Times*, May 27, 1990. Fill in the three blanks. (For the first blank, assume that daily compounding is essentially the same as continuous compounding. For the last blank, assume the interest has been compounded yearly, and give your answer in dollars. Ignore the occurrence of leap years.)

### *213 Years After Loan, Uncle Sam Is Dunned*

#### By LISA BELKIN

Special to The New York Times

SAN ANTONIO, May 26 — More than 200 years ago, a wealthy Pennsylvania merchant named Jacob DeHaven lent $450,000 to the Continental Congress to rescue the troops at Valley Forge. That loan was apparently never repaid.

So Mr. DeHaven's descendants are taking the United States Government to court to collect what they believe they are owed.

The total: ____ in today's dollars if the interest is compounded daily at 6 percent, the going rate at the time. If compounded yearly, the bill is only ____.

#### Family Is Flexible

The descendants say that they are willing to be flexible about the amount of a settlement and that they might even accept a heartfelt thank you or perhaps a DeHaven statue. But they also note that interest is accumulating at ____ a second.

PROJECTS FOR CHAPTER ONE

## 2. Population Center of the US

Since the opening up of the West, the US population has moved westward. To observe this, we look at the "population center" of the US, which is the point at which the country would balance if it were a flat plate with no weight, and every person had equal weight. In 1790 the population center was east of Baltimore, Maryland. It has been moving westward ever since, and in 2000 it was in Edgar Springs, Missouri. During the second half of the $20^{\text{th}}$ century, the population center has moved about 50 miles west every 10 years.

**(a)** Let us measure position westward from Edgar Springs along the line running through Baltimore. For the years since 2000, express the approximate position of the population center as a function of time in years from 2000.

**(b)** The distance from Baltimore to Edgar Springs is a bit over 1000 miles. Could the population center have been moving at roughly the same rate for the last two centuries?

**(c)** Could the function in part (a) continue to apply for the next four centuries? Why or why not? [Hint: You may want to look at a map. Note that distances are in air miles and are not driving distances.]

## 3. Medical Case Study: Anaphylaxis[106]

During surgery, a patient's blood pressure was observed to be dangerously low. One possible cause is a severe allergic reaction called *anaphylaxis*. A diagnosis of anaphylaxis is based in part on a blood test showing the elevation of the serum *tryptase*, a molecule released by allergic cells. In anaphylaxis, the concentration of tryptase in the blood rises rapidly and then decays back to baseline in a few hours.

However, low blood pressure from an entirely different cause (say from a heart problem) can also lead to an elevation in tryptase. Before diagnosing anaphylaxis, the medical team needs to make sure that the observed tryptase elevation is the result of an allergy problem, not a heart problem. To do this, they need to know the peak level reached by the serum tryptase. The normal range for the serum tryptase is 0–15 ng/ml (nanograms per milliliter). Mild to moderate elevations from low blood pressure are common, but if the peak were three times the normal maximum (that is, above 45 ng/ml), then a diagnosis of anaphylaxis would be made.

The surgeons who resuscitated this patient ran two blood tests to measure $T_r$, the serum tryptase concentration; the results are in Table 1.47. Use the test results to estimate the peak serum tryptase level at the time of surgery assuming that tryptase decays exponentially. Did this patient experience anaphylaxis?

Table 1.47    *Serum tryptase levels*

| $t$, hours since surgery | 4 | 19.5 |
|---|---|---|
| $T_r$, concentration in ng/ml | 37 | 13 |

---

[106]From David E. Sloane, M.D., drawing from an actual episode in his clinic.

# Chapter Two

# RATE OF CHANGE: THE DERIVATIVE

## Contents

# 2.1  INSTANTANEOUS RATE OF CHANGE

Chapter 1 introduced the average rate of change of a function over an interval. In this section, we consider the rate of change of a function at a point. We saw in Chapter 1 that when an object is moving along a straight line, the average rate of change of position with respect to time is the average velocity. If position is expressed as $y = f(t)$, where $t$ is time, then

$$\text{Average rate of change in position between } t = a \text{ and } t = b = \frac{\Delta y}{\Delta t} = \frac{f(b) - f(a)}{b - a}.$$

If you drive 200 miles in 4 hours, your average velocity is $200/4 = 50$ miles per hour. Of course, this does not mean that you travel at exactly 50 mph the entire trip. Your velocity at a given instant during the trip is shown on your speedometer, and this is the quantity that we investigate now.

## Instantaneous Velocity

We throw a grapefruit straight upward into the air. Table 2.1 gives its height, $y$, at time $t$. What is the velocity of the grapefruit at exactly $t = 1$? We use average velocities to estimate this quantity.

Table 2.1   *Height of the grapefruit above the ground*

| $t$ (sec) | 0 | 1 | 2 | 3 | 4 | 5 | 6 |
|---|---|---|---|---|---|---|---|
| $y = s(t)$ (feet) | 6 | 90 | 142 | 162 | 150 | 106 | 30 |

The average velocity on the interval $0 \leq t \leq 1$ is 84 ft/sec and the average velocity on the interval $1 \leq t \leq 2$ is 52 ft/sec. Notice that the average velocity before $t = 1$ is larger than the average velocity after $t = 1$ since the grapefruit is slowing down. We expect the velocity *at $t = 1$* to be between these two average velocities. How can we find the velocity at *exactly $t = 1$*? We look at what happens near $t = 1$ in more detail. Suppose that we find the average velocities on either side of $t = 1$ over smaller and smaller intervals, as in Figure 2.1. Then, for example,

$$\text{Average velocity between } t = 1 \text{ and } t = 1.01 = \frac{\Delta y}{\Delta t} = \frac{s(1.01) - s(1)}{1.01 - 1} = \frac{90.678 - 90}{0.01} = 67.8 \text{ ft/sec.}$$

We expect the instantaneous velocity at $t = 1$ to be between the average velocities on either side of $t = 1$. In Figure 2.1, the values of the average velocity before $t = 1$ and the average velocity after $t = 1$ get closer together as the size of the interval shrinks. For the smallest intervals in Figure 2.1, both velocities are 68.0 ft/sec (to one decimal place), so we say the velocity at $t = 1$ is 68.0 ft/sec (to one decimal place).

| $t$ | 0 | 0.9 | 0.99 | 0.999 | 1 | 1.001 | 1.01 | 1.1 | 2 |
|---|---|---|---|---|---|---|---|---|---|
| $y = s(t)$ | 6.000 | 83.040 | 89.318 | 89.932 | 90.000 | 90.068 | 90.678 | 96.640 | 142.000 |

Figure 2.1: Average velocities over intervals on either side of $t = 1$ showing successively smaller intervals

Of course, if we showed more decimal places, the average velocities before and after $t = 1$ would no longer agree. To calculate the velocity at $t = 1$ to more decimal places of accuracy, we take smaller and smaller intervals on either side of $t = 1$ until the average velocities agree to the number of decimal places we want. In this way, we can estimate the velocity at $t = 1$ to any accuracy.

## Defining Instantaneous Velocity Using the Idea of a Limit

When we take smaller intervals near $t = 1$, it turns out that the average velocities for the grapefruit are always just above or just below 68 ft/sec. It seems natural, then, to define velocity at the instant $t = 1$ to be 68 ft/sec. This is called the *instantaneous velocity* at this point. Its definition depends on our being convinced that smaller and smaller intervals provide average velocities that come arbitrarily close to 68. This process is referred to as *taking the limit*.

> The **instantaneous velocity** of an object at time $t$ is defined to be the limit of the average velocity of the object over shorter and shorter time intervals containing $t$.

Notice that the instantaneous velocity seems to be exactly 68, but what if it were 68.000001? How can we be sure that we have taken small enough intervals? Showing that the limit is exactly 68 requires more precise knowledge of how the velocities were calculated and of the limiting process; see the Focus on Theory section.

## Instantaneous Rate of Change

We can define the *instantaneous rate of change* of any function $y = f(t)$ at a point $t = a$. We mimic what we did for velocity and look at the average rate of change over smaller and smaller intervals.

> The **instantaneous rate of change** of $f$ at $a$, also called the **rate of change** of $f$ at $a$, is defined to be the limit of the average rates of change of $f$ over shorter and shorter intervals around $a$.

Since the average rate of change is a difference quotient of the form $\Delta y / \Delta t$, the instantaneous rate of change is a limit of difference quotients. In practice, we often approximate a rate of change by one of these difference quotients.

**Example 1**    The quantity (in mg) of a drug in the blood at time $t$ (in minutes) is given by $Q = 25(0.8)^t$. Estimate the rate of change of the quantity at $t = 3$ and interpret your answer.

Solution    We estimate the rate of change at $t = 3$ by computing the average rate of change over intervals near $t = 3$. We can make our estimate as accurate as we like by choosing our intervals small enough. Let's look at the average rate of change over the interval $3 \leq t \leq 3.01$:

$$\text{Average rate of change} = \frac{\Delta Q}{\Delta t} = \frac{25(0.8)^{3.01} - 25(0.8)^3}{3.01 - 3.00} = \frac{12.7715 - 12.80}{3.01 - 3.00} = -2.85.$$

A reasonable estimate for the rate of change of the quantity at $t = 3$ is $-2.85$. Since $Q$ is in mg and $t$ in minutes, the units of $\Delta Q / \Delta t$ are mg/minute. Since the rate of change is negative, the quantity of the drug is decreasing. After 3 minutes, the quantity of the drug in the body is decreasing at 2.85 mg/minute.

In Example 1, we estimated the rate of change using an interval to the right of the point ($t = 3$ to $t = 3.01$). In the next section we briefly consider other ways of making estimates.

## The Derivative at a Point

The instantaneous rate of change of a function $f$ at a point $a$ is so important that it is given its own name, the *derivative of $f$ at $a$*, denoted $f'(a)$ (read "$f$-prime of a"). If we want to emphasize that $f'(a)$ is the rate of change of $f(x)$ as the variable $x$ increases, we call $f'(a)$ the derivative of $f$ *with respect to $x$* at $x = a$. Notice that the derivative is just a new name for the rate of change of a function.

> The **derivative of $f$ at $a$**, written $f'(a)$, is defined to be the instantaneous rate of change of $f$ at the point $a$.

A definition of the derivative using a formula is given in the Focus on Theory section.

**Example 2**    Estimate $f'(2)$ if $f(x) = x^3$.

Solution    Since $f'(2)$ is the derivative, or rate of change, of $f(x) = x^3$ at 2, we look at the average rate of change over intervals near 2. Using the interval $2 \le x \le 2.001$, we see that

$$\text{Average rate of change on } 2 \le x \le 2.001 = \frac{(2.001)^3 - 2^3}{2.001 - 2} = \frac{8.0120 - 8}{0.001} = 12.0.$$

The rate of change of $f(x)$ at $x = 2$ appears to be approximately 12, so we estimate $f'(2) = 12$.

## Visualizing the Derivative: Slope of the Graph and Slope of the Tangent Line

Figure 2.2 shows the average rate of change of a function represented by the slope of the secant line joining points $A$ and $B$. The derivative is found by taking the average rate of change over smaller and smaller intervals. In Figure 2.3, as point $B$ moves toward point $A$, the secant line approaches the tangent line at point $A$. Thus, the derivative is represented by the slope of the tangent line to the graph at the point.

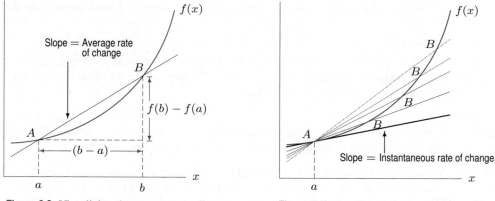

Figure 2.2: Visualizing the average rate of change of $f$ between $a$ and $b$

Figure 2.3: Visualizing the instantaneous rate of change of $f$ at $a$

Alternatively, take the graph of a function around a point and "zoom in" to get a close-up view. (See Figure 2.4.) The more we zoom in, the more the graph appears to be straight. We call the slope of this line the *slope of the graph* at the point; it also represents the derivative.

> The derivative of a function at the point $A$ is equal to
>
> - The slope of the graph of the function at $A$.
> - The slope of the line tangent to the curve at $A$.

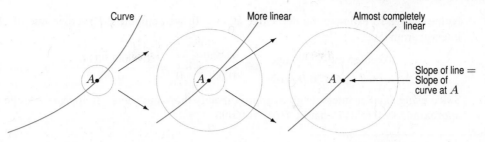

Figure 2.4: Finding the slope of a curve at a point by "zooming in"

The slope interpretation is often useful in gaining rough information about the derivative, as the following examples show.

---

**Example 3**     Use a graph of $f(x) = x^2$ to determine whether each of the following quantities is positive, negative, or zero:  (a)  $f'(1)$    (b)  $f'(-1)$    (c)  $f'(2)$    (d)  $f'(0)$

**Solution**     Figure 2.5 shows tangent line segments to the graph of $f(x) = x^2$ at the points $x = 1$, $x = -1$, $x = 2$, and $x = 0$. Since the derivative is the slope of the tangent line at the point, we have:

(a)  $f'(1)$ is positive.
(b)  $f'(-1)$ is negative.
(c)  $f'(2)$ is positive (and larger than $f'(1)$).
(d)  $f'(0) = 0$ since the graph has a horizontal tangent at $x = 0$.

Figure 2.5: Tangent lines showing sign of derivative of $f(x) = x^2$

---

**Example 4**     Estimate the derivative of $f(x) = 2^x$ at $x = 0$ graphically and numerically.

**Solution**     Graphically: If we draw a tangent line at $x = 0$ to the exponential curve in Figure 2.6, we see that it has a positive slope between 0.5 and 1.

Figure 2.6: Graph of $f(x) = 2^x$ showing the derivative at $x = 0$

Numerically: To estimate the derivative at $x = 0$, we compute the average rate of change on an interval around 0.

$$\text{Average rate of change on } 0 \le x \le 0.0001 = \frac{2^{0.0001} - 2^0}{0.0001 - 0} = \frac{1.000069317 - 1}{0.0001} = 0.69317.$$

Since using smaller intervals gives approximately the same values, it appears that the derivative is approximately 0.69317; that is, $f'(0) \approx 0.693$.

**Example 5**    The graph of a function $y = f(x)$ is shown in Figure 2.7. Indicate whether each of the following quantities is positive or negative, and illustrate your answers graphically.

(a)   $f'(1)$                  (b)   $\dfrac{f(3) - f(1)}{3 - 1}$                  (c)   $f(4) - f(2)$

Figure 2.7

**Solution**    (a)  Since $f'(1)$ is the slope of the graph at $x = 1$, we see in Figure 2.8 that $f'(1)$ is positive.

Figure 2.8                          Figure 2.9                          Figure 2.10

(b)  The difference quotient $(f(3) - f(1))/(3 - 1)$ is the slope of the secant line between $x = 1$ and $x = 3$. We see from Figure 2.9 that this slope is positive.

(c)  Since $f(4)$ is the value of the function at $x = 4$ and $f(2)$ is the value of the function at $x = 2$, the expression $f(4) - f(2)$ is the change in the function between $x = 2$ and $x = 4$. Since $f(4)$ lies below $f(2)$, this change is negative. See Figure 2.10.

## Estimating the Derivative of a Function Given Numerically

If we are given a table of values for a function, we can estimate values of its derivative. To do this, we have to assume that the points in the table are close enough together that the function does not change wildly between them.

**Example 6**    The total acreage of farms in the US[1] has decreased since 1980. See Table 2.2.

Table 2.2    *Total farm land in million acres*

| Year | 1980 | 1985 | 1990 | 1995 | 2000 |
|---|---|---|---|---|---|
| Farm land (million acres) | 1039 | 1012 | 987 | 963 | 945 |

(a)  What was the average rate of change in farm land between 1980 and 2000?

(b)  Estimate $f'(1995)$ and interpret your answer in terms of farm land.

---

[1] *Statistical Abstracts of the United States 2004–2005*, Table 796.

Solution        (a) Between 1980 and 2000,

$$\text{Average rate of change} = \frac{945 - 1039}{2000 - 1980} = \frac{-94}{20} = -4.7 \text{ million acres per year.}$$

Between 1980 and 2000, the amount of farm land was decreasing at an average rate of 4.7 million acres per year.

(b) We use the interval from 1995 to 2000 to estimate the instantaneous rate of change at 1995:

$$f'(1995) = \begin{array}{c} \text{Rate of change} \\ \text{in 1995} \end{array} \approx \frac{945 - 963}{2000 - 1995} = \frac{-18}{5} = -3.6 \text{ million acres per year.}$$

In 1995, the amount of farm land was decreasing at a rate of approximately 3.6 million acres per year.

## Problems for Section 2.1

1. Figure 2.11 shows $N = f(t)$, the number of farms in the US[2] between 1930 and 2000 as a function of year, $t$.

   (a) Is $f'(1950)$ positive or negative? What does this tell you about the number of farms?
   (b) Which is more negative: $f'(1960)$ or $f'(1980)$? Explain.

millions of farms

Figure 2.11

2. Use the graph in Figure 2.7 to decide if each of the following quantities is positive, negative or approximately zero. Illustrate your answers graphically.

   (a) The average rate of change of $f(x)$ between $x = 3$ and $x = 7$.
   (b) The instantaneous rate of change of $f(x)$ at $x = 3$.

3. The position $s$ of a car at time $t$ is given in the following table.

| $t$ (sec) | 0 | 0.2 | 0.4 | 0.6 | 0.8 | 1.0 |
|---|---|---|---|---|---|---|
| $s$ (ft) | 0 | 0.5 | 1.8 | 3.8 | 6.5 | 9.6 |

   (a) Find the average velocity over the interval $0 \leq t \leq 0.2$.

   (b) Find the average velocity over the interval $0.2 \leq t \leq 0.4$.
   (c) Use the previous answers to estimate the instantaneous velocity of the car at $t = 0.2$.

4. In a time of $t$ seconds, a particle moves a distance of $s$ meters from its starting point, where $s = 4t^2 + 3$.

   (a) Find the average velocity between $t = 1$ and $t = 1 + h$ if:
   
       (i) $h = 0.1$,   (ii) $h = 0.01$,   (iii) $h = 0.001$.

   (b) Use your answers to part (a) to estimate the instantaneous velocity of the particle at time $t = 1$.

5. Figure 2.12 shows the cost, $y = f(x)$, of manufacturing $x$ kilograms of a chemical.

   (a) Is the average rate of change of the cost greater between $x = 0$ and $x = 3$, or between $x = 3$ and $x = 5$? Explain your answer graphically.
   (b) Is the instantaneous rate of change of the cost of producing $x$ kilograms greater at $x = 1$ or at $x = 4$? Explain your answer graphically.
   (c) What are the units of these rates of change?

$y$ (thousand $)

$x$ (kg)

Figure 2.12

---

[2] www.nass.usda.gov:81/ipedb/farmnum.htm, accessed April 11, 2005.

**6.** The distance (in feet) of an object from a point is given by $s(t) = t^2$, where time $t$ is in seconds.

  **(a)** What is the average velocity of the object between $t = 2$ and $t = 5$?

  **(b)** By using smaller and smaller intervals around 2, estimate the instantaneous velocity at time $t = 2$.

**7. (a)** Using Table 2.3, find the average rate of change in the world's population, $P$, between 1975 and 2010.[3] Give units.

  **(b)** If $P = f(t)$ with $t$ in years, estimate $f'(2010)$ and give units.

**Table 2.3**   *World population, in billions of people*

| Year | 1975 | 1980 | 1985 | 1990 | 1995 | 2000 | 2005 | 2010 |
|---|---|---|---|---|---|---|---|---|
| Population | 4.08 | 4.45 | 4.84 | 5.27 | 5.68 | 6.07 | 6.45 | 6.89 |

**8.** The size, $S$, of a tumor (in cubic millimeters) is given by $S = 2^t$, where $t$ is the number of months since the tumor was discovered. Give units with your answers.

  **(a)** What is the total change in the size of the tumor during the first six months?

  **(b)** What is the average rate of change in the size of the tumor during the first six months?

  **(c)** Estimate the rate at which the tumor is growing at $t = 6$. (Use smaller and smaller intervals.)

**9.** Let $g(x) = 4^x$. Use small intervals to estimate $g'(1)$.

**10. (a)** Let $g(t) = (0.8)^t$. Use a graph to determine whether $g'(2)$ is positive, negative, or zero.

  **(b)** Use a small interval to estimate $g'(2)$.

**11.** For the function shown in Figure 2.13, at what labeled points is the slope of the graph positive? Negative? At which labeled point does the graph have the greatest (i.e., most positive) slope? The least slope (i.e., negative and with the largest magnitude)?

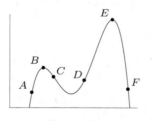

**Figure 2.13**

**12.** Match the points labeled on the curve in Figure 2.14 with the given slopes.

| Slope | Point |
|---|---|
| $-3$ | |
| $-1$ | |
| $0$ | |
| $1/2$ | |
| $1$ | |
| $2$ | |

**Figure 2.14**

**13.** For the function $f(x) = 3^x$, estimate $f'(1)$. From the graph of $f(x)$, would you expect your estimate to be greater than or less than the true value of $f'(1)$?

**14.** Table 2.4 gives $P = f(t)$, the number of households, in millions, in the US with cable television $t$ years since 1998.[4]

  **(a)** Does $f'(4)$ appear to be positive or negative? What does this tell you about the percent of households with cable television?

  **(b)** Estimate $f'(2)$. Estimate $f'(10)$. Explain what each is telling you, in terms of cable television.

**Table 2.4**

| $t$ | 0 | 2 | 4 | 6 | 8 | 10 | 12 |
|---|---|---|---|---|---|---|---|
| $P$ | 64.65 | 66.25 | 66.732 | 65.727 | 65.141 | 64.874 | 60.958 |

**15.** The following table gives the percent of the US population living in urban areas as a function of year.[5]

| Year | 1800 | 1830 | 1860 | 1890 | 1920 |
|---|---|---|---|---|---|
| Percent | 6.0 | 9.0 | 19.8 | 35.1 | 51.2 |

| Year | 1950 | 1980 | 1990 | 2000 | 2005 |
|---|---|---|---|---|---|
| Percent | 64.0 | 73.7 | 75.2 | 79.0 | 79.0 |

  **(a)** Find the average rate of change of the percent of the population living in urban areas between 1890 and 1990.

  **(b)** Estimate the rate at which this percent is increasing at the year 1990.

  **(c)** Estimate the rate of change of this function for the year 1830 and explain what it is telling you.

**16. (a)** Graph $f(x) = x^2$ and $g(x) = x^2 + 3$ on the same axes. What can you say about the slopes of the tangent lines to the two graphs at the point $x = 0$? $x = 1$? $x = 2$? $x = a$, where $a$ is any value?

  **(b)** Explain why adding a constant to any function will not change the value of the derivative at any point.

---

[3]http://www.prb.org/Publications/Datasheets/2010/2010wpds, accessed September 2012.

[4]http://2010.census.gov/2010census/, accessed September 2012.

[5]*Statistical Abstracts of the US*, 1985, US Department of Commerce, Bureau of the Census, p. 22, and http://www.census.gov/compendia/statab/cats/population/estimates_and_projections–states_metropolitan_areas_cities.html, accessed September 2012.

**17.** The function in Figure 2.15 has $f(4) = 25$ and $f'(4) = 1.5$. Find the coordinates of the points $A, B, C$.

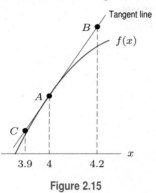

**Figure 2.15**

**18.** Use Figure 2.16 to fill in the blanks in the following statements about the function $f$ at point $A$.
(a) $f(\_\_) = \_\_$      (b) $f'(\_\_) = \_\_$

**Figure 2.16**

**19.** Show how to represent the following on Figure 2.17.
(a) $f(4)$                      (b) $f(4) - f(2)$
(c) $\dfrac{f(5) - f(2)}{5 - 2}$      (d) $f'(3)$

**Figure 2.17**

**20.** For each of the following pairs of numbers, use Figure 2.17 to decide which is larger. Explain your answer.

(a) $f(3)$ or $f(4)$?
(b) $f(3) - f(2)$ or $f(2) - f(1)$?

(c) $\dfrac{f(2) - f(1)}{2 - 1}$ or $\dfrac{f(3) - f(1)}{3 - 1}$?
(d) $f'(1)$ or $f'(4)$?

**21.** Estimate the instantaneous rate of change of the function $f(x) = x \ln x$ at $x = 1$ and at $x = 2$. What do these values suggest about the concavity of the graph between 1 and 2?

**22.** On October 17, 2006, in an article called "US Population Reaches 300 Million," the BBC reported that the US gains 1 person every 11 seconds. If $f(t)$ is the US population in millions $t$ years after October 17, 2006, find $f(0)$ and $f'(0)$.

**23.** The following table shows the number of hours worked in a week, $f(t)$, hourly earnings, $g(t)$, in dollars, and weekly earnings, $h(t)$, in dollars, of production workers as functions of $t$, the year.[6]

(a) Indicate whether each of the following derivatives is positive, negative, or zero: $f'(t)$, $g'(t)$, $h'(t)$. Interpret each answer in terms of hours or earnings.
(b) Estimate each of the following derivatives, and interpret your answers:

(i) $f'(1970)$ and $f'(1995)$

(ii) $g'(1970)$ and $g'(1995)$

(iii) $h'(1970)$ and $h'(1995)$

| $t$ | 1970 | 1975 | 1980 | 1985 | 1990 | 1995 | 2000 |
|---|---|---|---|---|---|---|---|
| $f(t)$ | 37.0 | 36.0 | 35.2 | 34.9 | 34.3 | 34.3 | 34.3 |
| $g(t)$ | 3.40 | 4.73 | 6.84 | 8.73 | 10.09 | 11.64 | 14.00 |
| $h(t)$ | 125.80 | 170.28 | 240.77 | 304.68 | 349.29 | 399.53 | 480.41 |

## 2.2  THE DERIVATIVE FUNCTION

In Section 2.1 we looked at the derivative of a function at a point. In general, the derivative takes on different values at different points and is itself a function. Recall that the derivative is the slope of the tangent line to the graph at the point.

---

[6]*The World Almanac and Book of Facts 2005*, p. 151 (New York). Production workers include nonsupervisory workers in mining, manufacturing, construction, transportation, public utilities, wholesale and retail trade, finance, insurance, real estate, and services.

## Finding the Derivative of a Function Given Graphically

**Example 1**    Estimate the derivative of the function $f(x)$ graphed in Figure 2.18 at $x = -2, -1, 0, 1, 2, 3, 4, 5$.

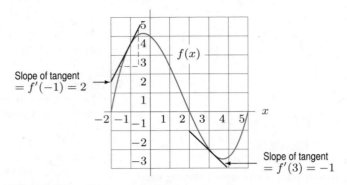

Figure 2.18: Estimating the derivative graphically as the slope of a tangent line

**Solution**    From the graph, we estimate the derivative at any point by placing a straightedge so that it forms the tangent line at that point, and then using the grid to estimate the slope of the tangent line. For example, the tangent at $x = -1$ is drawn in Figure 2.18, and has a slope of about 2, so $f'(-1) \approx 2$. Notice that the slope at $x = -2$ is positive and fairly large; the slope at $x = -1$ is positive but smaller. At $x = 0$, the slope is negative, by $x = 1$ it has become more negative, and so on. Some estimates of the derivative, to the nearest integer, are listed in Table 2.5. You should check these values yourself. Is the derivative positive where you expect? Negative?

Table 2.5    *Estimated values of derivative of function in Figure 2.18*

| $x$ | $-2$ | $-1$ | 0 | 1 | 2 | 3 | 4 | 5 |
|---|---|---|---|---|---|---|---|---|
| Derivative at $x$ | 6 | 2 | $-1$ | $-2$ | $-2$ | $-1$ | 1 | 4 |

The important point to notice is that for every $x$-value, there is a corresponding value of the derivative. The derivative, therefore, is a function of $x$.

---

For a function $f$, we define the **derivative function**, $f'$, by

$$f'(x) = \text{Instantaneous rate of change of } f \text{ at } x.$$

---

**Example 2**    Plot the values of the derivative function calculated in Example 1. Compare the graphs of $f'$ and $f$.

**Solution**    Graphs of $f$ and $f'$ are in Figures 2.19 and 2.20, respectively. Notice that $f'$ is positive (its graph is above the $x$-axis) where $f$ is increasing, and $f'$ is negative (its graph is below the $x$-axis) where $f$ is decreasing. The value of $f'(x)$ is 0 where $f$ has a maximum or minimum value (at approximately $x = -0.4$ and $x = 3.7$).

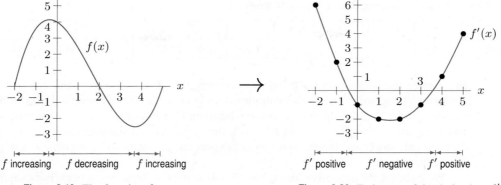

Figure 2.19: The function $f$                    Figure 2.20: Estimates of the derivative, $f'$

**Example 3**    The graph of $f$ is in Figure 2.21. Which of the graphs (a)–(c) is a graph of the derivative, $f'$?

Figure 2.21

(a)                                  (b)                                  (c)

**Solution**    Since the tangent of $f(x)$ is horizontal at $x = -1$ and $x = 2$, the derivative is zero there. Therefore, the graph of $f'(x)$ has $x$-intercepts at $x = -1$ and $x = 2$.

The function $f$ is decreasing for $x < -1$, increasing for $-1 < x < 2$, and decreasing for $x > 2$. The derivative is positive (its graph is above the $x$-axis) where $f$ is increasing, and the derivative is negative (its graph is below the $x$-axis) where $f$ is decreasing. The correct graph is (c).

## What Does the Derivative Tell Us Graphically?

Where the derivative, $f'$, of a function is positive, the tangent to the graph of $f$ is sloping up; where $f'$ is negative, the tangent is sloping down. If $f' = 0$ everywhere, then the tangent is horizontal everywhere and so $f$ is constant. The sign of the derivative $f'$ tells us whether the function $f$ is increasing or decreasing.

> If $f' > 0$ on an interval, then $f$ is *increasing* on that interval.
> If $f' < 0$ on an interval, then $f$ is *decreasing* on that interval.
> If $f' = 0$ on an interval, then $f$ is *constant* on that interval.

The magnitude of the derivative gives us the magnitude of the rate of change of $f$. If $f'$ is large in magnitude, then the graph of $f$ is steep (up if $f'$ is positive or down if $f'$ is negative); if $f'$ is small in magnitude, the graph of $f$ is gently sloping.

## Estimating the Derivative of a Function Given Numerically

If we are given a table of function values instead of a graph of the function, we can estimate values of the derivative.

**Example 4**    Table 2.6 gives values of $c(t)$, the concentration (mg/cc) of a drug in the bloodstream at time $t$ (min). Construct a table of estimated values for $c'(t)$, the rate of change of $c(t)$ with respect to $t$.

**Table 2.6**   *Concentration of a drug as a function of time*

| $t$ (min) | 0 | 0.1 | 0.2 | 0.3 | 0.4 | 0.5 | 0.6 | 0.7 | 0.8 | 0.9 | 1.0 |
|---|---|---|---|---|---|---|---|---|---|---|---|
| $c(t)$ (mg/cc) | 0.84 | 0.89 | 0.94 | 0.98 | 1.00 | 1.00 | 0.97 | 0.90 | 0.79 | 0.63 | 0.41 |

Solution

To estimate the derivative of $c$ using the values in the table, we assume that the data points are close enough together that the concentration does not change wildly between them. From the table, we see that the concentration is increasing between $t = 0$ and $t = 0.4$, so we expect a positive derivative there. From $t = 0.5$ to $t = 1.0$, the concentration starts to decrease, and the rate of decrease gets larger and larger, so we would expect the derivative to be negative and of greater and greater magnitude.

We estimate the derivative for each value of $t$ using a difference quotient. For example,

$$c'(0) \approx \frac{c(0.1) - c(0)}{0.1 - 0} = \frac{0.89 - 0.84}{0.1} = 0.5 \text{ (mg/cc) per minute.}$$

Similarly, we get the estimates

$$c'(0.1) \approx \frac{c(0.2) - c(0.1)}{0.2 - 0.1} = \frac{0.94 - 0.89}{0.1} = 0.5$$

$$c'(0.2) \approx \frac{c(0.3) - c(0.2)}{0.3 - 0.2} = \frac{0.98 - 0.94}{0.1} = 0.4$$

and so on. These values are tabulated in Table 2.7. Notice that the derivative has small positive values up until $t = 0.4$, and then it gets more and more negative, as we expected.

**Table 2.7**   *Derivative of concentration*

| $t$ | 0 | 0.1 | 0.2 | 0.3 | 0.4 | 0.5 | 0.6 | 0.7 | 0.8 | 0.9 |
|---|---|---|---|---|---|---|---|---|---|---|
| $c'(t)$ | 0.5 | 0.5 | 0.4 | 0.2 | 0.0 | $-0.3$ | $-0.7$ | $-1.1$ | $-1.6$ | $-2.2$ |

## Improving Numerical Estimates for the Derivative

In the previous example, our estimate for the derivative of $c(t)$ at $t = 0.2$ used the point to the right. We found the average rate of change between $t = 0.2$ and $t = 0.3$. However, we could equally well have gone to the left and used the rate of change between $t = 0.1$ and $t = 0.2$ to approximate the derivative at 0.2. For a more accurate result, we could average these slopes, getting the approximation

$$c'(0.2) \approx \frac{1}{2} \left( \begin{array}{c} \text{Slope to left} \\ \text{of 0.2} \end{array} + \begin{array}{c} \text{Slope to right} \\ \text{of 0.2} \end{array} \right) = \frac{0.5 + 0.4}{2} = 0.45.$$

Each of these methods of approximating the derivative gives a reasonable answer. We will usually estimate the derivative by going to the right.

## Finding the Derivative of a Function Given by a Formula

If we are given a formula for a function $f$, can we come up with a formula for $f'$? Using the definition of the derivative, we often can. Indeed, much of the power of calculus depends on our ability to find formulas for the derivatives of all the familiar functions. This is explained in detail in Chapter 3. In the next example, we see how to guess a formula for the derivative.

**Example 5**   Guess a formula for the derivative of $f(x) = x^2$.

Solution

We use difference quotients to estimate the values of $f'(1)$, $f'(2)$, and $f'(3)$. Then we look for a pattern in these values which we use to guess a formula for $f'(x)$.

Near $x = 1$, we have

$$f'(1) \approx \frac{1.001^2 - 1^2}{0.001} = \frac{1.002 - 1}{0.001} = \frac{0.002}{0.001} = 2.$$

Similarly,

$$f'(2) \approx \frac{2.001^2 - 2^2}{0.001} = \frac{4.004 - 4}{0.001} = \frac{0.004}{0.001} = 4$$

$$f'(3) \approx \frac{3.001^2 - 3^2}{0.001} = \frac{9.006 - 9}{0.001} = \frac{0.006}{0.001} = 6.$$

Knowing the value of $f'$ at specific points cannot tell us the formula for $f'$, but it can be suggestive: knowing $f'(1) \approx 2$, $f'(2) \approx 4$, $f'(3) \approx 6$ suggests that $f'(x) = 2x$. In Chapter 3, we show that this is indeed the case.

## Problems for Section 2.2

For Problems 1–6, graph the derivative of the given functions.

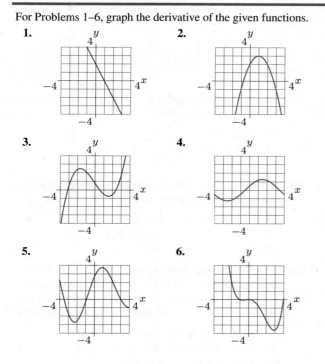

1.

2.

3.

4.

5.

6.

**Figure 2.23**

**9.** In the graph of $f$ in Figure 2.24, at which of the labeled $x$-values is

   **(a)** $f(x)$ greatest?    **(b)** $f(x)$ least?

   **(c)** $f'(x)$ greatest?    **(d)** $f'(x)$ least?

**Figure 2.24**

**7.** The graph of $f(x)$ is given in Figure 2.22. Draw tangent lines to the graph at $x = -2$, $x = -1$, $x = 0$, and $x = 2$. Estimate $f'(-2)$, $f'(-1)$, $f'(0)$, and $f'(2)$.

**Figure 2.22**

**10.** Find approximate values for $f'(x)$ at each of the $x$-values given in the following table.

| $x$ | 0 | 5 | 10 | 15 | 20 |
|---|---|---|---|---|---|
| $f(x)$ | 100 | 70 | 55 | 46 | 40 |

**8.** The graph of $f(x)$ is given in Figure 2.23. Estimate $f'(1)$, $f'(2)$, $f'(3)$, $f'(4)$, and $f'(5)$.

**11.** Using slopes to left and right of 0, estimate $R'(0)$ if $R(x) = 100(1.1)^x$.

For Problems 12–17, sketch the graph of $f'(x)$.

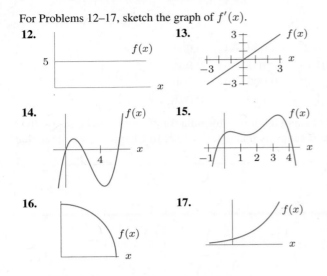

**12.**

**13.**

**14.**

**15.**

**16.**

**17.**

Match the functions in Problems 18–21 with one of the derivatives in Figure 2.25.

(I)   (II)   (III)   (IV)   (V)   (VI)   (VII)   (VIII)

**Figure 2.25**

**18.**

**19.**

**20.**

**21.**

**22.** A city grew in population throughout the 1980s and into the early 1990s. The population was at its largest in 1995, and then shrank until 2010. Let $P = f(t)$ represent the population of the city $t$ years since 1980. Sketch graphs of $f(t)$ and $f'(t)$, labeling the units on the axes.

**23.** Values of $x$ and $g(x)$ are given in the table. For what value of $x$ does $g'(x)$ appear to be closest to 3?

| $x$ | 2.7 | 3.2 | 3.7 | 4.2 | 4.7 | 5.2 | 5.7 | 6.2 |
|---|---|---|---|---|---|---|---|---|
| $g(x)$ | 3.4 | 4.4 | 5.0 | 5.4 | 6.0 | 7.4 | 9.0 | 11.0 |

**24.** Draw a possible graph of $y = f(x)$ given the following information about its derivative.

- $f'(x) > 0$ for $x < -1$
- $f'(x) < 0$ for $x > -1$
- $f'(x) = 0$ at $x = -1$

**25.** Draw a possible graph of a continuous function $y = f(x)$ that satisfies the following three conditions:

- $f'(x) > 0$ for $1 < x < 3$
- $f'(x) < 0$ for $x < 1$ and $x > 3$
- $f'(x) = 0$ at $x = 1$ and $x = 3$

**26.** A vehicle moving along a straight road has distance $f(t)$ from its starting point at time $t$. Which of the graphs in Figure 2.26 could be $f'(t)$ for the following scenarios? (Assume the scales on the vertical axes are all the same.)

**(a)** A bus on a popular route, with no traffic
**(b)** A car with no traffic and all green lights
**(c)** A car in heavy traffic conditions

(I)   (II)   (III)

**Figure 2.26**

**27. (a)** Let $f(x) = \ln x$. Use small intervals to estimate $f'(1)$, $f'(2)$, $f'(3)$, $f'(4)$, and $f'(5)$.
**(b)** Use your answers to part (a) to guess a formula for the derivative of $f(x) = \ln x$.

**28.** Suppose $f(x) = \frac{1}{3}x^3$. Estimate $f'(2)$, $f'(3)$, and $f'(4)$. What do you notice? Can you guess a formula for $f'(x)$?

**29.** Match each property (a)–(d) with one or more of graphs (I)–(IV) of functions.

(a) $f'(x) = 1$ for all $0 \le x \le 4$.
(b) $f'(x) > 0$ for all $0 \le x \le 4$
(c) $f'(2) = 1$
(d) $f'(1) = 2$

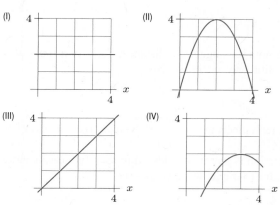

**30.** A child inflates a balloon, admires it for a while and then lets the air out at a constant rate. If $V(t)$ gives the volume of the balloon at time $t$, then Figure 2.27 shows $V'(t)$ as a function of $t$. At what time does the child:

(a) Begin to inflate the balloon?
(b) Finish inflating the balloon?
(c) Begin to let the air out?
(d) What would the graph of $V'(t)$ look like if the child had alternated between pinching and releasing the open end of the balloon, instead of letting the air out at a constant rate?

Figure 2.27

# 2.3  INTERPRETATIONS OF THE DERIVATIVE

We have seen the derivative interpreted as a slope and as a rate of change. In this section, we see other interpretations. The purpose of these examples is not to make a catalog of interpretations but to illustrate the process of obtaining them. There is another notation for the derivative that is often helpful.

## An Alternative Notation for the Derivative

So far we have used the notation $f'$ to stand for the derivative of the function $f$. An alternative notation for derivatives was introduced by the German mathematician Gottfried Wilhelm Leibniz (1646–1716) when calculus was first being developed. We know that $f'(x)$ is approximated by the average rate of change over a small interval. If $y = f(x)$, then the average rate of change is given by $\Delta y / \Delta x$. For small $\Delta x$, we have

$$f'(x) \approx \frac{\Delta y}{\Delta x}.$$

Leibniz's notation for the derivative, $dy/dx$, is meant to remind us of this. If $y = f(x)$, then we write

$$f'(x) = \frac{dy}{dx}.$$

Leibniz's notation is quite suggestive, especially if we think of the letter $d$ in $dy/dx$ as standing for "small difference in . . . ." The notation $dy/dx$ reminds us that the derivative is a limit of ratios of the form

$$\frac{\text{Difference in } y\text{-values}}{\text{Difference in } x\text{-values}}.$$

The notation $dy/dx$ is useful for determining the units for the derivative: the units for $dy/dx$ are the units for $y$ divided by (or "per") the units for $x$.

The separate entities $dy$ and $dx$ officially have no independent meaning: they are part of one notation. In fact, a good formal way to view the notation $dy/dx$ is to think of $d/dx$ as a single symbol meaning "the derivative with respect to $x$ of . . .". Thus, $dy/dx$ could be viewed as

$$\frac{d}{dx}(y), \quad \text{meaning "the derivative with respect to } x \text{ of } y."$$

On the other hand, many scientists and mathematicians really do think of $dy$ and $dx$ as separate entities representing "infinitesimally" small differences in $y$ and $x$, even though it is difficult to say exactly how small "infinitesimal" is. It may not be formally correct, but it is very helpful intuitively to think of $dy/dx$ as a very small change in $y$ divided by a very small change in $x$.

For example, recall that if $s = f(t)$ is the position of a moving object at time $t$, then $v = f'(t)$ is the velocity of the object at time $t$. Writing

$$v = \frac{ds}{dt}$$

reminds us that $v$ is a velocity since the notation suggests a distance, $ds$, over a time, $dt$, and we know that distance over time is velocity. Similarly, we recognize

$$\frac{dy}{dx} = f'(x)$$

as the slope of the graph of $y = f(x)$ by remembering that slope is vertical rise, $dy$, over horizontal run, $dx$.

The disadvantage of the Leibniz notation is that it is awkward to specify the value at which a derivative is evaluated. To specify $f'(2)$, for example, we have to write

$$\left. \frac{dy}{dx} \right|_{x=2}.$$

## Using Units to Interpret the Derivative

Suppose a body moves along a straight line. If $s = f(t)$ gives the position in meters of the body from a fixed point on the line as a function of time, $t$, in seconds, then knowing that

$$\frac{ds}{dt} = f'(2) = 10 \text{ meters/sec}$$

tells us that when $t = 2$ sec, the body is moving at a velocity of 10 meters/sec. If the body continues to move at this velocity for a whole second (from $t = 2$ to $t = 3$), it would move an additional 10 meters.

In other words, if $\Delta s$ represents the change in position during a time interval $\Delta t$, and if the body continues to move at this velocity, we have $\Delta s = 10\Delta t$, so

$$\Delta s = f'(2)\,\Delta t = 10\,\Delta t.$$

If the velocity is varying, this relationship is no longer exact. For small values of $\Delta t$, we have the *Tangent Line Approximation*

$$\Delta s \approx f'(t)\Delta t.$$

(See also page 107.) Notice that, for a given positive $\Delta t$, a large derivative gives large change in $s$; a small derivative gives small change in $s$. In general:

---

- The units of the derivative of a function are the units of the dependent variable divided by the units of the independent variable. In other words, the units of $dA/dB$ are the units of $A$ divided by the units of $B$.
- If the derivative of a function is not changing rapidly near a point, then the derivative is approximately equal to the change in the function when the independent variable increases by 1 unit.

---

The following examples illustrate how useful units can be in suggesting interpretations of the derivative.

**Example 1**   The cost $C$ (in dollars) of building a house $A$ square feet in area is given by the function $C = f(A)$. What are the units and the practical interpretation of the function $f'(A)$?

**Solution**   In the Leibniz notation,

$$f'(A) = \frac{dC}{dA}.$$

This is a cost divided by an area, so it is measured in dollars per square foot. You can think of $dC$ as the extra cost of building an extra $dA$ square feet of house. So if you are planning to build a house with area $A$ square feet, $f'(A)$ is approximately the cost per square foot of the *extra* area involved in building a house 1 square foot larger, and is called the *marginal cost*.

**Example 2**   The cost of extracting $T$ tons of ore from a copper mine is $C = f(T)$ dollars. What does it mean to say that $f'(2000) = 100$?

**Solution**   In the Leibniz notation,

$$f'(2000) = \left.\frac{dC}{dT}\right|_{T=2000}.$$

Since $C$ is measured in dollars and $T$ is measured in tons, $dC/dT$ is measured in dollars per ton. You can think of $dC$ as the extra cost of extracting an extra $dT$ tons of ore. So the statement

$$\left.\frac{dC}{dT}\right|_{T=2000} = 100$$

says that when 2000 tons of ore have already been extracted from the mine, the cost of extracting the next ton is approximately \$100. Another way of saying this is that it costs about \$100 to extract the $2001^{\text{st}}$ ton.

**Example 3**   If $q = f(p)$ gives the number of thousands of tons of zinc produced when the price is $p$ dollars per ton, then what are the units and the meaning of

$$\left.\frac{dq}{dp}\right|_{p=900} = 0.2?$$

**Solution**   The units of $dq/dp$ are the units of $q$ over the units of $p$, or thousands of tons per dollar. You can think of $dq$ as the extra zinc produced when the price increases by $dp$. The statement

$$\left.\frac{dq}{dp}\right|_{p=900} = f'(900) = 0.2 \text{ thousand tons per dollar}$$

tells us that the instantaneous rate of change of $q$ with respect to $p$ is 0.2 when $p = 900$. This means that when the price is \$900, the quantity produced increases by about 0.2 thousand tons, or 200 tons more for a one-dollar increase in price.

**Example 4**   The time, $L$ (in hours), that a drug stays in a person's system is a function of the quantity administered, $q$, in mg, so $L = f(q)$.

(a) Interpret the statement $f(10) = 6$. Give units for the numbers 10 and 6.
(b) Write the derivative of the function $L = f(q)$ in Leibniz notation. If $f'(10) = 0.5$, what are the units of the 0.5?
(c) Interpret the statement $f'(10) = 0.5$ in terms of dose and duration.

**Solution**   (a) We know that $f(q) = L$. In the statement $f(10) = 6$, we have $q = 10$ and $L = 6$, so the units are 10 mg and 6 hours. The statement $f(10) = 6$ tells us that a dose of 10 mg lasts 6 hours.
(b) Since $L = f(q)$, we see that $L$ depends on $q$. The derivative of this function is $dL/dq$. Since $L$ is in hours and $q$ is in mg, the units of the derivative are hours per mg. In the statement $f'(10) = 0.5$, the 0.5 is the derivative and the units are hours per mg.

(c) The statement $f'(10) = 0.5$ tells us that, at a dose of 10 mg, the instantaneous rate of change of duration is 0.5 hour per mg. In other words, if we increase the dose by 1 mg, the drug stays in the body approximately 30 minutes longer.

---

In the previous example, notice that $f'(10) = 0.5$ tells us that a 1 mg increase in dose leads to about a 0.5-hour increase in duration. If, on the other hand, we had had $f'(10) = 20$, we would have known that a 1-mg increase in dose leads to about a 20-hour increase in duration. Thus the derivative is the multiplier relating changes in dose to changes in duration. The magnitude of the derivative tells us how sensitive the time is to changes in dose.

We define the derivative of velocity, $dv/dt$, as *acceleration*.

**Example 5**    If the velocity of a body at time $t$ seconds is measured in meters/sec, what are the units of the acceleration?

Solution    Since acceleration, $dv/dt$, is the derivative of velocity, the units of acceleration are units of velocity divided by units of time, or (meters/sec)/sec, written meters/sec$^2$.

---

## Using the Derivative to Estimate Values of a Function

Since the derivative tells us how fast the value of a function is changing, we can use the derivative at a point to estimate values of the function at nearby points.

**Example 6**    Fertilizers can improve agricultural production. A Cornell University study[7] on maize (corn) production in Kenya found that the average value, $y = f(x)$, in Kenyan shillings of the yearly maize production from an average plot of land is a function of the quantity, $x$, of fertilizer used in kilograms. (The shilling is the Kenyan unit of currency.)

(a) Interpret the statements $f(5) = 11,500$ and $f'(5) = 350$.
(b) Use the statements in part (a) to estimate $f(6)$ and $f(10)$.
(c) The value of the derivative, $f'$, is increasing for $x$ near 5. Which estimate in part (b) is more reliable?

Solution    (a) The statement $f(5) = 11,500$ tells us that $y = 11,500$ when $x = 5$. This means that if 5 kg of fertilizer are applied, maize worth 11,500 Kenyan shillings is produced. Since the derivative is $dy/dx$, the statement $f'(5) = 350$ tells us that

$$\frac{dy}{dx} = 350 \quad \text{when } x = 5.$$

This means that if the amount of fertilizer used is 5 kg and increases by 1 kg, then maize production increases by about 350 Kenyan shillings.

(b) We want to estimate $f(6)$, that is the production when 6 kg of fertilizer are used. If instead of 5 kg of fertilizer, one more kilogram is used, giving 6 kg altogether, we expect production, in Kenyan shillings, to increase from 11,500 by about 350. Thus,

$$f(6) \approx 11,500 + 350 = 11,850.$$

Similarly, if 5 kg more fertilizer is used, so 10 kg are used altogether, we expect production to increase by about $5 \cdot 350 = 1750$ Kenyan shillings, so production is approximately

$$f(10) \approx 11,500 + 1750 = 13,250.$$

(c) To estimate $f(6)$, we assume that production increases at rate of 350 Kenyan shillings per kilogram between $x = 5$ and $x = 6$ kg. To estimate $f(10)$, we assume that production continues to increase at the same rate all the way from $x = 5$ to $x = 10$ kg. Since the derivative is increasing for $x$ near 5, the estimate of $f(6)$ is more reliable.

---

[7]"State-conditional fertilizer yield response on western Kenyan farms", by P. Marenya, C. Barrett, Social Science Research Network, abstract = 1141937, 2009.

In Example 6, representing the change in $y$ by $\Delta y$ and the change in $x$ by $\Delta x$, we used the result introduced earlier in this section:

---

### Tangent Line Approximation: Local Linearity

If $y = f(x)$ and $\Delta x$ is near 0, then $\Delta y \approx f'(x)\Delta x$. For $x$ near $a$, we have $\Delta y = f(x) - f(a)$ and $\Delta x = x - a$, so

$$f(x) \approx f(a) + f'(a)\Delta x.$$

---

## Relative Rate of Change

In Section 1.5, we saw that an exponential function has a constant percent rate of change. Now we link this idea to derivatives. Analogous to the relative change, we look at the rate of change as a fraction of the original quantity.

---

The **relative rate of change** of $y = f(t)$ at $t = a$ is defined to be

$$\begin{array}{c} \text{Relative rate of change} \\ \text{of } y \text{ at } a \end{array} = \frac{dy/dt}{y} = \frac{f'(a)}{f(a)}.$$

---

We see in Section 3.3 that an exponential function has a constant relative rate of change. If the independent variable is time, the relative rate is often given as a percent change per unit time.

---

**Example 7**   Annual world soybean production, $W = f(t)$, in million tons, is a function of $t$ years since the start of 2000.

(a) Interpret the statements $f(8) = 253$ and $f'(8) = 17$ in terms of soybean production.
(b) Calculate the relative rate of change of $W$ at $t = 8$; interpret it in terms of soybean production.

**Solution**   (a) The statement $f(8) = 253$ tells us that 253 million tons of soybeans were produced in the year 2008. The statement $f'(8) = 17$ tells us that in 2008 annual soybean production was increasing at a rate of 17 million tons per year.

(b) We have

$$\text{Relative rate of change of soybean production} = \frac{f'(8)}{f(8)} = \frac{17}{253} = 0.067.$$

In 2008, annual soybean production was increasing at a continuous rate of 6.7% per year.

---

**Example 8**   Solar photovoltaic (PV) cells are the world's fastest growing energy source. At time $t$ in years since 2005, peak PV energy-generating capacity worldwide was approximately $E = 4.6e^{0.43t}$ gigawatts.[8] Estimate the relative rate of change of PV energy-generating capacity in 2015 using this model and

(a)   $\Delta t = 1$                    (b)   $\Delta t = 0.1$                    (c)   $\Delta t = 0.01$

**Solution**   Let $E = f(t)$. In 2015 we have $t = 10$. The relative rate of change of $f$ in 2015 is $f'(10)/f(10)$. We estimate $f'(10)$ using a difference quotient.

(a) Estimating the relative rate of change using $\Delta t = 1$ at $t = 10$, we have

$$\frac{dE/dt}{E} = \frac{f'(10)}{f(10)} \approx \frac{1}{f(10)}\frac{f(11) - f(10)}{1} = 0.537 = 53.7\% \text{ per year.}$$

---

[8] en.wikipedia.org/wiki/Photovoltaics. Accessed February 2013. A gigawatt measures power and can be used to measure energy-generating capacity.

(b) With $\Delta t = 0.1$ and $t = 10$, we have

$$\frac{dE/dt}{E} = \frac{f'(10)}{f(10)} \approx \frac{1}{f(10)} \frac{f(10.1) - f(10)}{0.1} = 0.439 = 43.9\% \text{ per year.}$$

(c) With $\Delta t = 0.01$ and $t = 10$, we have

$$\frac{dE/dt}{E} = \frac{f'(10)}{f(10)} \approx \frac{1}{f(10)} \frac{f(10.01) - f(10)}{0.01} = 0.431 = 43.1\% \text{ per year.}$$

The relative rate of change is approximately 43.1% per year. From Section 1.6, we know that the exponential function $E = 4.6e^{0.43t}$ has a continuous rate of change of 43% per year for all $t$, so the exact relative rate of change is 43%.

---

**Example 9**     In April 2009, the US Bureau of Economic Analysis announced that the US gross domestic product (GDP) was decreasing at an annual rate of 6.1%. The GDP of the US at that time was 13.84 trillion dollars. Calculate the annual rate of change of the US GDP in April 2009.

**Solution**     The Bureau of Economic Analysis is reporting the relative rate of change. In April 2009, the relative rate of change of GDP was $-0.061$ per year. To find the rate of change, we use:

$$\text{Relative rate of change in April 2009} = \frac{\text{Rate of change in April 2009}}{\text{GDP in April 2009}}$$

$$-0.061 = \frac{\text{Rate of change}}{13.84}$$

$$\text{Rate of change in April 2009} = -0.061 \cdot 13.84 = -0.84424 \text{ trillion dollars per year.}$$

The GDP of the US was decreasing at a continuous rate of 844.24 billion dollars per year in April 2009.

---

## Problems for Section 2.3

In Problems 1–4, write the Leibniz notation for the derivative of the given function and include units.

**1.** The distance to the ground, $D$, in feet, of a skydiver is a function of the time $t$ in minutes since the skydiver jumped out of the airplane.

**2.** The cost, $C$, of a steak, in dollars, is a function of the weight, $W$, of the steak, in pounds.

**3.** The number, $N$, of gallons of gas left in a gas tank is a function of the distance, $D$, in miles, the car has been driven.

**4.** An employee's pay, $P$, in dollars, for a week is a function of the number of hours worked, $H$.

**5.** The time for a chemical reaction, $T$ (in minutes), is a function of the amount of catalyst present, $a$ (in milliliters), so $T = f(a)$.

    (a) If $f(5) = 18$, what are the units of 5? What are the units of 18? What does this statement tell us about the reaction?

    (b) If $f'(5) = -3$, what are the units of 5? What are the units of $-3$? What does this statement tell us?

**6.** An economist is interested in how the price of a certain item affects its sales. At a price of $\$p$, a quantity, $q$, of the item is sold. If $q = f(p)$, explain the meaning of each of the following statements:

    (a) $f(150) = 2000$       (b) $f'(150) = -25$

**7.** The cost, $C = f(w)$, in dollars of buying a chemical is a function of the weight bought, $w$, in pounds.

    (a) In the statement $f(12) = 5$, what are the units of the 12? What are the units of the 5? Explain what this is saying about the cost of buying the chemical.

    (b) Do you expect the derivative $f'$ to be positive or negative? Why?

    (c) In the statement $f'(12) = 0.4$, what are the units of the 12? What are the units of the 0.4? Explain what this is saying about the cost of buying the chemical.

8. Figure 2.28 shows world solar energy output, in megawatts, as a function of years since 1990.[9] Estimate $f'(6)$. Give units and interpret your answer.

solar power (megawatts)

**Figure 2.28**

9. When you breathe, a muscle (called the diaphragm) reduces the pressure around your lungs and they expand to fill with air. The table shows the volume of a lung as a function of the reduction in pressure from the diaphragm. Pulmonologists (lung doctors) define the *compliance* of the lung as the derivative of this function.[10]

   (a) What are the units of compliance?
   (b) Estimate the maximum compliance of the lung.
   (c) Explain why the compliance gets small when the lung is nearly full (around 1 liter).

| Pressure reduction (cm of water) | Volume (liters) |
|---|---|
| 0 | 0.20 |
| 5 | 0.29 |
| 10 | 0.49 |
| 15 | 0.70 |
| 20 | 0.86 |
| 25 | 0.95 |
| 30 | 1.00 |

10. On May 9, 2007, CBS Evening News had a 4.3 point rating. (Ratings measure the number of viewers.) News executives estimated that a 0.1 drop in the ratings for the CBS Evening News corresponds to a \$5.5 million drop in revenue.[11] Express this information as a derivative. Specify the function, the variables, the units, and the point at which the derivative is evaluated.

11. A yam has just been taken out of the oven and is cooling off before being eaten. The temperature, $T$, of the yam (measured in degrees Fahrenheit) is a function of how long it has been out of the oven, $t$ (measured in minutes). Thus, we have $T = f(t)$.

    (a) Is $f'(t)$ positive or negative? Why?
    (b) What are the units for $f'(t)$?

12. Let $f(x)$ be the elevation in feet of the Mississippi River $x$ miles from its source. What are the units of $f'(x)$? What can you say about the sign of $f'(x)$?

13. Meteorologists define the temperature lapse rate to be $-dT/dz$ where $T$ is the air temperature in Celsius at altitude $z$ kilometers above the ground.

    (a) What are the units of the lapse rate?
    (b) What is the practical meaning of a lapse rate of 6.5?

14. Investing \$1000 at an annual interest rate of $r\%$, compounded continuously, for 10 years gives you a balance of \$$B$, where $B = g(r)$. Give a financial interpretation of the statements:

    (a) $g(5) \approx 1649$.
    (b) $g'(5) \approx 165$. What are the units of $g'(5)$?

15. Table 2.8 shows world gold production,[12] $G = f(t)$, as a function of year, $t$.

    (a) Does $f'(t)$ appear to be positive or negative? What does this mean in terms of gold production?
    (b) In which time interval does $f'(t)$ appear to be least?
    (c) Estimate $f'(2002)$. Give units and interpret your answer in terms of gold production.
    (d) Use the estimated value of $f'(2009)$ to estimate $f(2010)$ and $f(2015)$, and interpret your answers.

**Table 2.8** *World gold production*

| $t$ (year) | 2005 | 2006 | 2007 | 2008 | 2009 |
|---|---|---|---|---|---|
| $G$ (metric tons) | 2470 | 2370 | 2360 | 2290 | 2450 |

16. The average weight, $W$, in pounds, of an adult is a function, $W = f(c)$, of the average number of Calories per day, $c$, consumed.

    (a) Interpret the statements $f(1800) = 155$ and $f'(2000) = 0$ in terms of diet and weight.
    (b) What are the units of $f'(c) = dW/dc$?

17. The cost, $C$ (in dollars), to produce $g$ gallons of a chemical can be expressed as $C = f(g)$. Using units, explain the meaning of the following statements in terms of the chemical:

    (a) $f(200) = 1300$    (b) $f'(200) = 6$

18. Let $G$ be annual US government purchases, $T$ be annual US tax revenues, and $Y$ be annual US output of all goods and services. All three quantities are given in dollars. Interpret the statements about the two derivatives, called fiscal policy multipliers.

    (a) $dY/dG = 0.60$    (b) $dY/dT = -0.26$

---

[9]The Worldwatch Institute, *Vital Signs* 2001, p. 47 (New York: W.W. Norton, 2001).
[10]Adapted from John B. West, *Respiratory Physiology*, 4th Ed. (New York: Williams and Wilkins, 1990).
[11]*OC Register*, May 9, 2007; *The New York Times*, May 14, 2007.
[12]http://minerals.usgs.gov/ds/2005/140/gold.pdf, accessed September 2012.

19. The weight, $W$, in lbs, of a child is a function of its age, $a$, in years, so $W = f(a)$.

   (a) Do you expect $f'(a)$ to be positive or negative? Why?

   (b) What does $f(8) = 45$ tell you? Give units for the numbers 8 and 45.

   (c) What are the units of $f'(a)$? Explain what $f'(a)$ tells you in terms of age and weight.

   (d) What does $f'(8) = 4$ tell you about age and weight?

   (e) As $a$ increases, do you expect $f'(a)$ to increase or decrease? Explain.

20. A recent study reports that men who retired late developed Alzheimer's at a later stage than those who stopped work earlier. Each additional year of employment was associated with about a six-week later age of onset. Express these results as a statement about the derivative of a function. State clearly what function you use, including the units of the dependent and independent variables.

21. The thickness, $P$, in mm, of pelican eggshells depends on the concentration, $c$, of PCBs in the eggshell, measured in ppm (parts per million); that is, $P = f(c)$.

   (a) The derivative $f'(c)$ is negative. What does this tell you?

   (b) Give units and interpret $f(200) = 0.28$ and $f'(200) = -0.0005$ in terms of PCBs and eggshells.

22. Suppose that $f(t)$ is a function with $f(25) = 3.6$ and $f'(25) = -0.2$. Estimate $f(26)$ and $f(30)$.

23. For a function $f(x)$, we know that $f(20) = 68$ and $f'(20) = -3$. Estimate $f(21)$, $f(19)$ and $f(25)$.

Problems 24–27 concern $g(t)$ in Figure 2.29, which gives the weight of a human fetus as a function of its age.

weight (kg)

Figure 2.29

24. (a) What are the units of $g'(24)$?

   (b) What is the biological meaning of $g'(24) = 0.096$?

25. (a) Which is greater, $g'(20)$ or $g'(36)$?

   (b) What does your answer say about fetal growth?

26. Is the instantaneous weight growth rate greater or less than the average rate of change of weight over the 40-week period

   (a)  At week 20?     (b)  At week 36?

27. Estimate (a)  $g'(20)$    (b)  $g'(36)$

   (c) The average rate of change of weight for the entire 40-week gestation.

28. Annual net sales, in billion of dollars, for the Hershey Company, the largest US producer of chocolate, is a function $S = f(t)$ of time, $t$, in years since 2000.

   (a) Interpret the statements $f(8) = 5.1$ and $f'(8) = 0.22$ in terms of Hershey sales.[13]

   (b) Estimate $f(12)$ and interpret it in terms of Hershey sales.

29. For some painkillers, the size of the dose, $D$, given depends on the weight of the patient, $W$. Thus, $D = f(W)$, where $D$ is in milligrams and $W$ is in pounds.

   (a) Interpret the statements $f(140) = 120$ and $f'(140) = 3$ in terms of this painkiller.

   (b) Use the information in the statements in part (a) to estimate $f(145)$.

30. US meat[14] production, $M = f(t)$, in millions of metric tons, is a function of $t$, years since 2000.

   (a) Interpret $f(10) = 92.63$ and $f'(10) = 0.64$ in terms of meat production.

   (b) Estimate $f(15)$ and interpret it in terms of meat production.

31. The quantity, $Q$ mg, of nicotine in the body $t$ minutes after a cigarette is smoked is given by $Q = f(t)$.

   (a) Interpret the statements $f(20) = 0.36$ and $f'(20) = -0.002$ in terms of nicotine. What are the units of the numbers 20, 0.36, and $-0.002$?

   (b) Use the information given in part (a) to estimate $f(21)$ and $f(30)$. Justify your answers.

32. A mutual fund is currently valued at $80 per share and its value per share is increasing at a rate of $0.50 a day. Let $V = f(t)$ be the value of the share $t$ days from now.

   (a) Express the information given about the mutual fund in term of $f$ and $f'$.

   (b) Assuming that the rate of growth stays constant, estimate and interpret $f(10)$.

33. Figure 2.30 shows how the contraction velocity, $v(x)$, of a muscle changes as the load on it changes.

   (a) Find the slope of the line tangent to the graph of contraction velocity at a load of 2 kg. Give units.

   (b) Using your answer to part (a), estimate the change in the contraction velocity if the load is increased from 2 kg by adding 50 grams.

[13] 2008 Annual Report to Stockholders, accessed at www.thehersheycompany.com.
[14] http://www.fao.org/economic/ess/ess-publications/ess-yearbook/ess-yearbook2010/en/, accessed September 2012.

**(c)** Express your answer to part (a) as a derivative of $v(x)$.

**Figure 2.30**

**34.** Figure 2.31 shows how the pumping rate of a person's heart changes after bleeding.

**(a)** Find the slope of the line tangent to the graph at time 2 hours. Give units.
**(b)** Using your answer to part (a), estimate how much the pumping rate increases during the minute beginning at time 2 hours.
**(c)** Express your answer to part (a) as a derivative of $g(t)$.

**Figure 2.31**

**35.** Suppose $C(r)$ is the total cost of paying off a car loan borrowed at an annual interest rate of $r\%$. What are the units of $C'(r)$? What is the practical meaning of $C'(r)$? What is its sign?

Problems 36–40 refer to Figure 2.32, which shows the depletion of food stores in the human body during starvation.

**Figure 2.32**

**36.** Which is being consumed at a greater rate, fat or protein, during the

**(a)** Third week?      **(b)** Seventh week?

**37.** The fat storage graph is linear for the first four weeks. What does this tell you about the use of stored fat?

**38.** Estimate the rate of fat consumption after

**(a)** 3 weeks     **(b)** 6 weeks     **(c)** 8 weeks

**39.** What seems to happen during the sixth week? Why do you think this happens?

**40.** Figure 2.33 shows the derivatives of the protein and fat storage functions. Which graph is which?

**Figure 2.33**

**41.** A person with a certain liver disease first exhibits larger and larger concentrations of certain enzymes (called SGOT and SGPT) in the blood. As the disease progresses, the concentration of these enzymes drops, first to the predisease level and eventually to zero (when almost all of the liver cells have died). Monitoring the levels of these enzymes allows doctors to track the progress of a patient with this disease. If $C = f(t)$ is the concentration of the enzymes in the blood as a function of time,

**(a)** Sketch a possible graph of $C = f(t)$.
**(b)** Mark on the graph the intervals where $f' > 0$ and where $f' < 0$.
**(c)** What does $f'(t)$ represent, in practical terms?

**42.** A company's revenue from car sales, $C$ (in thousands of dollars), is a function of advertising expenditure, $a$, in thousands of dollars, so $C = f(a)$.

**(a)** What does the company hope is true about the sign of $f'$?
**(b)** What does the statement $f'(100) = 2$ mean in practical terms? How about $f'(100) = 0.5$?
**(c)** Suppose the company plans to spend about $100,000 on advertising. If $f'(100) = 2$, should the company spend more or less than $100,000 on advertising? What if $f'(100) = 0.5$?

**43.** A company making solar panels spends $x$ dollars on materials, and the revenue from the sale of the solar panels is $f(x)$ dollars.

(a) What does the statement $f'(80,000) = 2$ mean in practical terms? How about $f'(80,000) = 0.5$?

(b) Suppose the company plans to spend about $80,000 on materials. If $f'(80,000) = 2$, should the company spend more than $80,000 on materials? What if $f'(100) = 0.5$?

**44.** For a new type of biofuel, scientists estimate that it takes $A = f(g)$ gallons of gasoline to produce the raw materials to generate $g$ gallons of biofuel. Assume the biofuel is equal in efficiency to the gasoline.

(a) At a certain level of production, we have $dA/dg = 1.3$. Interpret this in practical terms. Is this level of production sustainable? Explain.

(b) Repeat part (a) if $dA/dg = 0.2$.

**45.** In 2011, the Greenland Ice Sheet was melting at a rate between 82 and 224 cubic km per year.[15]

(a) What derivative does this tell us about? Define the function and give units for each variable.

(b) What numerical statement can you make about the derivative? Give units.

**46.** The area of Brazil's rain forest, $R = f(t)$, in million acres, is a function of the number of years, $t$, since 2000.

(a) Interpret $f(9) = 740$ and $f'(9) = -2.7$ in terms of Brazil's rain forests.[16]

(b) Find and interpret the relative rate of change of $f(t)$ when $t = 9$.

**47.** The number of active Facebook users hit 175 million at the end of February 2009 and 200 million[17] at the end of April 2009. With $t$ in months since the start of 2009, let $f(t)$ be the number of active users in millions. Estimate $f(4)$ and $f'(4)$ and the relative rate of change of $f$ at $t = 4$. Interpret your answers in terms of Facebook users.

**48.** Estimate the relative rate of change of $f(t) = t^2$ at $t = 4$. Use $\Delta t = 0.01$.

**49.** Estimate the relative rate of change of $f(t) = t^2$ at $t = 10$. Use $\Delta t = 0.01$.

**50.** The world population in billions is predicted to be approximately $P = 7.1e^{0.011t}$ where $t$ is in years since 2013.[18] Estimate the relative rate of change of population in 2020 using this model and

(a) $\Delta t = 1$     (b) $\Delta t = 0.1$     (c) $\Delta t = 0.01$

**51.** The weight, $w$, in kilograms, of a baby is a function $f(t)$ of her age, $t$, in months.

(a) What does $f(2.5) = 5.67$ tell you?

(b) What does $f'(2.5)/f(2.5) = 0.13$ tell you?

**52.** Downloads of Apple Apps, $D = g(t)$, in billions of downloads from iTunes, is a function of $t$ months since its inception in June, 2008.[19]

(a) Interpret the statements $g(36) = 15$ and $g'(36) = 0.93$ in terms of App downloads.

(b) Calculate the relative rate of change of $P$ at $t = 36$; interpret it in terms of App downloads.

**53.** The number of barrels of oil produced from North Dakota oil wells is estimated to be $B = 21.88e^{0.059t}$ million barrels, where $t$ is in months since Sept 2012.[20] Estimate the relative rate of change of oil production in December 2012 using

(a) $\Delta t = 1$     (b) $\Delta t = 0.1$     (c) $\Delta t = 0.01$

**54.** During the 1970s and 1980s, the buildup of chlorofluorocarbons (CFCs) created a hole in the ozone layer over Antarctica. After the 1987 Montreal Protocol, an agreement to phase out CFC production, the ozone hole has shrunk. The ODGI (ozone depleting gas index) shows the level of CFCs present.[21] Let $O(t)$ be the ODGI for Antarctica in year $t$; then $O(2000) = 95$ and $O'(2000) = -1.25$. Assuming that the ODGI decreases at a constant rate, estimate when the ozone hole will have recovered, which occurs when ODGI = 0.

# 2.4   THE SECOND DERIVATIVE

Since the derivative is itself a function, we can calculate its derivative. For a function $f$, the derivative of its derivative is called the *second derivative*, and written $f''$. If $y = f(x)$, the second derivative can also be written as $\dfrac{d^2y}{dx^2}$, which means $\dfrac{d}{dx}\left(\dfrac{dy}{dx}\right)$, the derivative of $\dfrac{dy}{dx}$.

---

[15] www.climate.org/topics/sea-level, accessed June 5, 2011.
[16] www.rain-tree.com/facts.htm, accessed June 2009.
[17] www.facebook.com/press, accessed June 2009.
[18] www.census.gov/population/international/data/worldpop. Accessed February 2013.
[19] www.asymco.com/2011/07/13/itunes-app-total-downloads-finally-overtook-song-downloads/, accessed January 21, 2013.
[20] www.mjperry.blogspot.com/2011/11/ndakota-oil-continues-exponential.html, accessed January 21, 2013.
[21] www.esrl.noaa.gov/gmd/odgi

## What Does the Second Derivative Tell Us?

Recall that the derivative of a function tells us whether the function is increasing or decreasing:

If $f' > 0$ on an interval, then $f$ is increasing on that interval.

If $f' < 0$ on an interval, then $f$ is decreasing on that interval.

Since $f''$ is the derivative of $f'$, we have

If $f'' > 0$ on an interval, then $f'$ is increasing on that interval.

If $f'' < 0$ on an interval, then $f'$ is decreasing on that interval.

So the question becomes: What does it mean for $f'$ to be increasing or decreasing? The case in which $f'$ is increasing is shown in Figure 2.34, where the graph of $f$ is bending upward, or is *concave up*. In the case when $f'$ is decreasing, shown in Figure 2.35, the graph is bending downward, or is *concave down*. We have the following result:

> If $f'' > 0$ on an interval, then $f'$ is increasing and the graph of $f$ is concave up on that interval.
> If $f'' < 0$ on an interval, then $f'$ is decreasing and the graph of $f$ is concave down on that interval.

Figure 2.34: Meaning of $f''$: The slope increases from negative to positive as you move from left to right, so $f''$ is positive and $f$ is concave up

Figure 2.35: Meaning of $f''$: The slope decreases from positive to negative as you move from left to right, so $f''$ is negative and $f$ is concave down

**Example 1**    For the functions whose graphs are given in Figure 2.36, decide where their second derivatives are positive and where they are negative.

Figure 2.36: What signs do the second derivatives have?

**Solution**    From the graphs it appears that

(a) $f'' > 0$ everywhere, because the graph of $f$ is concave up everywhere.

(b) $g'' < 0$ everywhere, because the graph is concave down everywhere.

(c) $h'' > 0$ for $x > 0$, because the graph of $h$ is concave up there; $h'' < 0$ for $x < 0$, because the graph of $h$ is concave down there.

## Interpretation of the Second Derivative as a Rate of Change

If we think of the derivative as a rate of change, then the second derivative is a rate of change of a rate of change. If the second derivative is positive, the rate of change is increasing; if the second derivative is negative, the rate of change is decreasing.

The second derivative is often a matter of practical concern. In 1985 a newspaper headline reported the Secretary of Defense as saying that Congress and the Senate had cut the defense budget. As his opponents pointed out, however, Congress had merely cut the rate at which the defense budget was increasing.[22] In other words, the derivative of the defense budget was still positive (the budget was increasing), but the second derivative was negative (the budget's rate of increase had slowed).

**Example 2**    A population, $P$, growing in a confined environment often follows a *logistic* growth curve, like the graph shown in Figure 2.37. Describe how the rate at which the population is increasing changes over time. What is the sign of the second derivative $d^2P/dt^2$? What is the practical interpretation of $t^*$ and $L$?

Figure 2.37: Logistic growth curve

**Solution**    Initially, the population is increasing, and at an increasing rate. So, initially $dP/dt$ is increasing and $d^2P/dt^2 > 0$. At $t^*$, the rate at which the population is increasing is a maximum; the population is growing fastest then. Beyond $t^*$, the rate at which the population is growing is decreasing, so $d^2P/dt^2 < 0$. At $t^*$, the graph changes from concave up to concave down and $d^2P/dt^2 = 0$.

The quantity $L$ represents the limiting value of the population that is approached as $t$ tends to infinity; $L$ is called the *carrying capacity* of the environment and represents the maximum population that the environment can support.

**Example 3**    Table 2.9 shows the number of abortions per year, $A$, reported in the US in the year $t$.[23]

Table 2.9    *Abortions reported in the US (1972–2000)*

| Year, $t$ | 1972 | 1975 | 1980 | 1985 | 1990 | 1995 | 2000 | 2005 |
|---|---|---|---|---|---|---|---|---|
| 1000s of abortions reported, $A$ | 587 | 1034 | 1554 | 1589 | 1609 | 1359 | 1313 | 1206 |

(a) Calculate the average rate of change for the time intervals shown between 1972 and 2005.
(b) What can you say about the sign of $d^2A/dt^2$ during the period 1972–1995?

**Solution**    (a) For each time interval we can calculate the average rate of change of the number of abortions per year over this interval. For example, between 1972 and 1975

$$\frac{\text{Average rate}}{\text{of change}} = \frac{\Delta A}{\Delta t} = \frac{1034 - 587}{1975 - 1972} = \frac{447}{3} = 149.$$

Thus, between 1972 and 1975, there were approximately 149,000 more abortions reported each year. Values of $\Delta A/\Delta t$ are listed in Table 2.10.

---

[22] In the *Boston Globe*, March 13, 1985, Representative William Gray (D–Pa.) was reported as saying: "It's confusing to the American people to imply that Congress threatens national security with reductions when you're really talking about a reduction in the increase."

[23] *Statistical Abstracts of the United States 2004–2009*, Table 99.

**Table 2.10**  *Rate of change of number of abortions reported*

| Time | 1972–75 | 1975–80 | 1980–85 | 1985–90 | 1990–95 | 1995–2000 | 2000–05 |
|------|---------|---------|---------|---------|---------|-----------|---------|
| Average rate of change, $\Delta A/\Delta t$ (1000s/year) | 149 | 104 | 7 | 4 | −50 | −9.2 | −21.4 |

(b) We assume the data lies on a smooth curve. Since the values of $\Delta A/\Delta t$ are decreasing dramatically for 1975–1995, we can be pretty certain that $dA/dt$ also decreases, so $d^2A/dt^2$ is negative for this period. For 1972–1975, the sign of $d^2A/dt^2$ is less clear; abortion data from 1968 would help. Figure 2.38 confirms this; the graph appears to be concave down for 1975–1995. The fact that $dA/dt$ is positive during the period 1972–1980 corresponds to the fact that the number of abortions reported increased from 1972 to 1980. The fact that $dA/dt$ is negative during the period 1990–2005 corresponds to the fact that the number of abortions reported decreased from 1990 to 2005. The fact that $d^2A/dt^2$ is negative for 1975–1995 reflects the fact that the rate of increase slowed over this period.

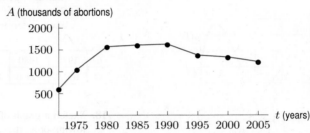

**Figure 2.38:** How the number of reported abortions in the US is changing with time

## Problems for Section 2.4

**1.** For the function $g(x)$ graphed in Figure 2.39, are the following nonzero quantities positive or negative?

   **(a)**  $g'(0)$          **(b)**  $g''(0)$

**Figure 2.39**

**2.** At one of the labeled points on the graph in Figure 2.40 both $dy/dx$ and $d^2y/dx^2$ are negative. Which is it?

**Figure 2.40**

**3.** Graph the functions described in parts (a)–(d).

   **(a)** First and second derivatives everywhere positive.
   **(b)** Second derivative everywhere negative; first derivative everywhere positive.
   **(c)** Second derivative everywhere positive; first derivative everywhere negative.
   **(d)** First and second derivatives everywhere negative.

For Problems 4–9, give the signs of the first and second derivatives for the following functions. Each derivative is either positive everywhere, zero everywhere, or negative everywhere.

**8.**

**9.**

In Problems 10–11, use the graph given for each function.
  **(a)** Estimate the intervals on which the derivative is positive and the intervals on which the derivative is negative.
  **(b)** Estimate the intervals on which the second derivative is positive and the intervals on which the second derivative is negative.

**10.**

**11.**

In Problems 12–13, use the values given for each function.
  **(a)** Does the derivative of the function appear to be positive or negative over the given interval? Explain.
  **(b)** Does the second derivative of the function appear to be positive or negative over the given interval? Explain.

**12.**

| $t$ | 100 | 110 | 120 | 130 | 140 |
|---|---|---|---|---|---|
| $w(t)$ | 10.7 | 6.3 | 4.2 | 3.5 | 3.3 |

**13.**

| $t$ | 0 | 1 | 2 | 3 | 4 | 5 |
|---|---|---|---|---|---|---|
| $s(t)$ | 12 | 14 | 17 | 20 | 31 | 55 |

**14.** Sketch the graph of a function whose first derivative is everywhere negative and whose second derivative is positive for some $x$-values and negative for other $x$-values.

**15.** IBM-Peru uses second derivatives to assess the relative success of various advertising campaigns. They assume that all campaigns produce some increase in sales. If a graph of sales against time shows a positive second derivative during a new advertising campaign, what does this suggest to IBM management? Why? What does a negative second derivative suggest?

**16.** Values of $f(t)$ are given in the following table.
  **(a)** Does this function appear to have a positive or negative first derivative? Second derivative? Explain.
  **(b)** Estimate $f'(2)$ and $f'(8)$.

| $t$ | 0 | 2 | 4 | 6 | 8 | 10 |
|---|---|---|---|---|---|---|
| $f(t)$ | 150 | 145 | 137 | 122 | 98 | 56 |

**17.** The table gives the number of passenger cars, $C = f(t)$, in millions,[24] in the US in the year $t$.
  **(a)** Do $f'(t)$ and $f''(t)$ appear to be positive or negative during the period 1975–1990?
  **(b)** Do $f'(t)$ and $f''(t)$ appear to be positive or negative during the period 1990-2000?
  **(c)** Estimate $f'(2005)$. Using units, interpret your answer in terms of passenger cars.

| $t$ | 1975 | 1980 | 1985 | 1990 | 1995 | 2000 | 2005 |
|---|---|---|---|---|---|---|---|
| $C$ | 106.7 | 121.6 | 127.9 | 133.7 | 128.4 | 133.6 | 136.6 |

**18.** Sketch a graph of a continuous function $f$ with the following properties:
  - $f'(x) > 0$ for all $x$
  - $f''(x) < 0$ for $x < 2$ and $f''(x) > 0$ for $x > 2$.

**19.** Sketch the graph of a function $f$ such that $f(2) = 5$, $f'(2) = 1/2$, and $f''(2) > 0$.

**20.** At exactly two of the labeled points in Figure 2.41, the derivative $f'$ is 0; the second derivative $f''$ is not zero at any of the labeled points. On a copy of the table, give the signs of $f$, $f'$, $f''$ at each marked point.

| Point | $f$ | $f'$ | $f''$ |
|---|---|---|---|
| A | | | |
| B | | | |
| C | | | |
| D | | | |

**Figure 2.41**

**21.** For three minutes the temperature of a feverish person has had positive first derivative and negative second derivative. Which of the following is correct?
  **(a)** The temperature rose in the last minute more than it rose in the minute before.
  **(b)** The temperature rose in the last minute, but less than it rose in the minute before.
  **(c)** The temperature fell in the last minute but less than it fell in the minute before.
  **(d)** The temperature rose for two minutes but fell in the last minute.

[24] www.bts.gov/publications/national_transportation_statistics/html/table_01_11.html. Accessed April 27, 2011.

**22.** Yesterday's temperature at $t$ hours past midnight was $f(t)$ °C. At noon the temperature was 20°C. The first derivative, $f'(t)$, decreased all morning, reaching a low of 2°C/hour at noon, then increased for the rest of the day. Which one of the following must be correct?

  **(a)** The temperature fell in the morning and rose in the afternoon.
  **(b)** At 1 pm the temperature was 18°C.
  **(c)** At 1 pm the temperature was 22°C.
  **(d)** The temperature was lower at noon than at any other time.
  **(e)** The temperature rose all day.

**23.** A function $f$ has $f(5) = 20$, $f'(5) = 2$, and $f''(x) < 0$, for $x \geq 5$. Which of the following are possible values for $f(7)$ and which are impossible?

  **(a)**  26     **(b)**  24     **(c)**  22

**24.** An industry is being charged by the Environmental Protection Agency (EPA) with dumping unacceptable levels of toxic pollutants in a lake. Over a period of several months, an engineering firm makes daily measurements of the rate at which pollutants are being discharged into the lake. The engineers produce a graph similar to either Figure 2.42(a) or Figure 2.42(b). For each case, give an idea of what argument the EPA might make in court against the industry and of the industry's defense.

**Figure 2.42**

**25.** "Winning the war on poverty" has been described cynically as slowing the rate at which people are slipping below the poverty line. Assuming that this is happening:

  **(a)** Graph the total number of people in poverty against time.
  **(b)** If $N$ is the number of people below the poverty line at time $t$, what are the signs of $dN/dt$ and $d^2N/dt^2$? Explain.

**26.** In economics, *total utility* refers to the total satisfaction from consuming some commodity. According to the economist Samuelson:[25]

  As you consume more of the same good, the total (psychological) utility increases. However, …with successive new units of the good, your total utility will grow at a slower and slower rate because of a fundamental tendency for your psychological ability to appreciate more of the good to become less keen.

  **(a)** Sketch the total utility as a function of the number of units consumed.
  **(b)** In terms of derivatives, what is Samuelson saying?

**27.** Let $P(t)$ represent the price of a share of stock of a corporation at time $t$. What does each of the following statements tell us about the signs of the first and second derivatives of $P(t)$?

  **(a)** "The price of the stock is rising faster and faster."
  **(b)** "The price of the stock is close to bottoming out."

**28.** Each of the graphs in Figure 2.43 shows the position of a particle moving along the $x$-axis as a function of time, $0 \leq t \leq 5$. The vertical scales of the graphs are the same. During this time interval, which particle has

  **(a)** Constant velocity?
  **(b)** The greatest initial velocity?
  **(c)** The greatest average velocity?
  **(d)** Zero average velocity?
  **(e)** Zero acceleration?
  **(f)** Positive acceleration throughout?

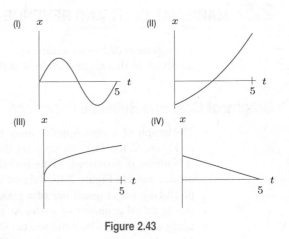

**Figure 2.43**

**29.** In 2009, a study was done on the impact of sea-level rise in the mid-Atlantic states.[26] Let $a(t)$ be the depth of the sea in millimeters (mm) at a typical point on the Atlantic Coast, and let $m(t)$ be the depth of the sea in mm at a typical point on the Gulf of Mexico, with time $t$ in years since data collection started.

  **(a)** The study reports "Sea level is rising and there is evidence that the rate is accelerating." What does this statement tell us about $a(t)$ and $m(t)$?

---

[25]From Paul A. Samuelson, *Economics*, 11th edition (New York: McGraw-Hill, 1981).

[26]www.epa.gov/climatechange/effects/coastal/sap4-1.html, *Coastal Sensitivity to Sea-Level Rise: A Focus on the Mid-Atlantic Region*, US Climate Change Science Program, January 2009.

**(b)** The study also reports "The Atlantic Coast and the Gulf of Mexico experience higher rates of sea-level rise (2 to 4 mm per year and 2 to 10 mm per year, respectively) than the current global average (1.7 mm per year)." What does this tell us about $a(t)$ and $m(t)$?

**(c)** Assume the rates at which the sea level rises on the Atlantic Coast and the Gulf of Mexico are constant for a century and within the ranges given in the report.

   (i) What is the largest amount the sea could rise on the Atlantic Coast during a century? Your answer should be a range of values.

   (ii) What is the shortest amount of time in which the sea level in the Gulf of Mexico could rise 1 meter?

**30.** Table 2.11 shows the number of Facebook subscribers, $N$ in millions, worldwide at 3-month intervals.[27]

   **(a)** Calculate the average rate of change of $N$ per month for the time intervals shown between March 2011 and March 2012.

   **(b)** What can you say about the sign of $d^2N/dt^2$ during the period March 2011–March 2012?

**Table 2.11**

| Month, $t$ | Mar 2011 | Jun 2011 | Sep 2011 | Dec 2011 | Mar 2012 |
|------------|----------|----------|----------|----------|----------|
| $N$ | 664.0 | 710.7 | 756.9 | 799.1 | 835.5 |

**31.** In 1913, Carlson[28] conducted the classic experiment in which he grew yeast, *Saccharomyces cerevisiae*, in laboratory cultures and collected data every hour for 18 hours. Table 2.12 shows the yeast population, $P$, at representative times $t$ in hours.

   **(a)** Calculate the average rate of change of $P$ per hour for the time intervals shown between 0 and 18 hours.

   **(b)** What can you say about the sign of $d^2P/dt^2$ during the period 0–18 hours?

**Table 2.12**

| $t$ | 0 | 2 | 4 | 6 | 8 | 10 | 12 | 14 | 16 | 18 |
|-----|-----|------|------|-------|-------|-------|-------|-------|-------|-------|
| $P$ | 9.6 | 29.0 | 71.1 | 174.6 | 350.7 | 513.3 | 594.8 | 640.8 | 655.9 | 661.8 |

# 2.5   MARGINAL COST AND REVENUE

Management decisions within a particular firm or industry usually depend on the costs and revenues involved. In this section we look at the cost and revenue functions.

## Graphs of Cost and Revenue Functions

The graph of a cost function may be linear, as in Figure 2.44, or it may have the shape shown in Figure 2.45. The intercept on the $C$-axis represents the fixed costs, which are incurred even if nothing is produced. (This includes, for instance, the cost of the machinery needed to begin production.) In Figure 2.45, the cost function increases quickly at first and then more slowly because producing larger quantities of a good is usually more efficient than producing smaller quantities— this is called *economy of scale*. At still higher production levels, the cost function increases faster again as resources become scarce; sharp increases may occur when new factories have to be built. Thus, the graph of a cost function, $C$, may start out concave down and become concave up later on.

**Figure 2.44:** A linear cost function        **Figure 2.45:** A nonlinear cost function

[27]www.internetworldstats.com/facebook.htm, accessed January 21, 2013.

[28]T. Carlson, "Über Geschwindigkeit und Grösse der Hefevermehrung in Würze", *Biochem. Z.*, 1913.

The revenue function is $R = pq$, where $p$ is price and $q$ is quantity. If the price, $p$, is a constant, the graph of $R$ against $q$ is a straight line through the origin with slope equal to the price. (See Figure 2.46.) In practice, for large values of $q$, the market may become glutted, causing the price to drop and giving $R$ the shape in Figure 2.47.

Figure 2.46: Revenue: Constant price          Figure 2.47: Revenue: Decreasing price

**Example 1**   If cost, $C$, and revenue, $R$, are given by the graph in Figure 2.48, for what production quantities does the firm make a profit?

Figure 2.48: Costs and revenues for Example 1

Solution   The firm makes a profit whenever revenues are greater than costs, that is, when $R > C$. The graph of $R$ is above the graph of $C$ approximately when $130 < q < 215$. Production between 130 units and 215 units will generate a profit.

## Marginal Analysis

Many economic decisions are based on an analysis of the costs and revenues "at the margin." Let's look at this idea through an example.

Suppose you are running an airline and you are trying to decide whether to offer an additional flight. How should you decide? We'll assume that the decision is to be made purely on financial grounds: if the flight will make money for the company, it should be added. Obviously you need to consider the costs and revenues involved. Since the choice is between adding this flight and leaving things the way they are, the crucial question is whether the *additional costs* incurred are greater or smaller than the *additional revenues* generated by the flight. These additional costs and revenues are called *marginal costs* and *marginal revenues*.

Suppose $C(q)$ is the function giving the cost of running $q$ flights. If the airline had originally planned to run 100 flights, its costs would be $C(100)$. With the additional flight, its costs would be $C(101)$. Therefore,

$$\text{Additional cost "at the margin"} = C(101) - C(100).$$

Now

$$C(101) - C(100) = \frac{C(101) - C(100)}{101 - 100},$$

and this quantity is the average rate of change of cost between 100 and 101 flights. In Figure 2.49 the average rate of change is the slope of the secant line. If the graph of the cost function is not curving too fast near the point, the slope of the secant line is close to the slope of the tangent line

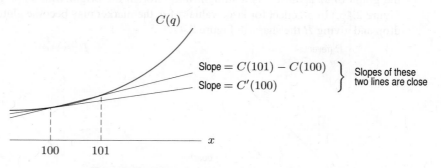

Figure 2.49: Marginal cost: Slope of one of these lines

there. Therefore, the average rate of change is close to the instantaneous rate of change. Since these rates of change are not very different, many economists choose to define marginal cost, $MC$, as the instantaneous rate of change of cost with respect to quantity:

Marginal cost $= MC = C'(q)$    so    Marginal cost $\approx C(q+1) - C(q)$.

Marginal cost is represented by the slope of the cost curve.

Similarly if the revenue generated by $q$ flights is $R(q)$ and the number of flights increases from 100 to 101, then

Additional revenue "at the margin" $= R(101) - R(100)$.

Now $R(101) - R(100)$ is the average rate of change of revenue between 100 and 101 flights. As before, the average rate of change is approximately equal to the instantaneous rate of change, so economists often define

Marginal revenue $= MR = R'(q)$    so    Marginal revenue $\approx R(q+1) - R(q)$.

**Example 2**    If $C(q)$ and $R(q)$ for the airline are given in Figure 2.50, should the company add the 101$^{\text{st}}$ flight?

Solution    The marginal revenue is the slope of the revenue curve at $q = 100$. The marginal cost is the slope of the graph of $C$ at $q = 100$. Figure 2.50 suggests that the slope at point $A$ is smaller than the slope at $B$, so $MC < MR$ for $q = 100$. This means that the airline will make more in extra revenue than it will spend in extra costs if it runs another flight, so it should go ahead and run the 101$^{\text{st}}$ flight.

Figure 2.50: Cost and revenue for Example 2

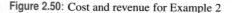

**Example 3**     The graph of a cost function is given in Figure 2.51. Does it cost more to produce the $500^{\text{th}}$ item or the $2000^{\text{th}}$? Does it cost more to produce the $3000^{\text{th}}$ item or the $4000^{\text{th}}$? At approximately what production level is marginal cost smallest? What is the total cost at this production level?

Figure 2.51: Estimating marginal cost: Where is marginal cost smallest?

**Solution**     The cost to produce an additional item is the marginal cost, which is represented by the slope of the cost curve. Since the slope of the cost function in Figure 2.51 is greater at $q = 0.5$ (when the quantity produced is 0.5 thousand, or 500) than at $q = 2$, it costs more to produce the $500^{\text{th}}$ item than the $2000^{\text{th}}$ item. Since the slope is greater at $q = 4$ than $q = 3$, it costs more to produce the $4000^{\text{th}}$ item than the $3000^{\text{th}}$ item.

The slope of the cost function is close to zero at $q = 2$, and is positive everywhere else, so the slope is smallest at $q = 2$. The marginal cost is smallest at a production level of 2000 units. Since $C(2) \approx 10,000$, the total cost to produce 2000 units is about $10,000.

**Example 4**     If the revenue and cost functions, $R$ and $C$, are given by the graphs in Figure 2.52, sketch graphs of the marginal revenue and marginal cost functions, $MR$ and $MC$.

Figure 2.52: Total revenue and total cost for Example 4

**Solution**     The revenue graph is a line through the origin, with equation

$$R = pq$$

where $p$ represents the constant price, so the slope is $p$ and

$$MR = R'(q) = p.$$

The total cost is increasing, so the marginal cost is always positive. For small $q$ values, the graph of the cost function is concave down, so the marginal cost is decreasing. For larger $q$, say $q > 100$, the graph of the cost function is concave up and the marginal cost is increasing. Thus, the marginal cost has a minimum at about $q = 100$. (See Figure 2.53.)

Figure 2.53: Marginal revenue and costs for Example 4

# Problems for Section 2.5

**1.** It costs \$4800 to produce 1295 items and it costs \$4830 to produce 1305 items. What is the approximate marginal cost at a production level of 1300 items?

**2.** The function $C(q)$ gives the cost in dollars to produce $q$ barrels of olive oil.

  **(a)** What are the units of marginal cost?
  **(b)** What is the practical meaning of the statement $MC = 3$ for $q = 100$?

**3.** In Figure 2.54, estimate the marginal revenue when the level of production is 600 units and interpret it.

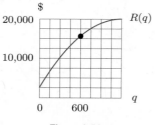

**Figure 2.54**

**4.** In Figure 2.55, is marginal cost greater at $q = 5$ or at $q = 30$? At $q = 20$ or at $q = 40$? Explain.

**Figure 2.55**

**5.** In Figure 2.56, estimate the marginal cost when the level of production is 10,000 units and interpret it.

**Figure 2.56**

**6.** For $q$ units of a product, a manufacturer's cost is $C(q)$ dollars and revenue is $R(q)$ dollars, with $C(500) = 7200$, $R(500) = 9400$, $MC(500) = 15$, and $MR(500) = 20$.

  **(a)** What is the profit or loss at $q = 500$?
  **(b)** If production is increased from 500 to 501 units, by approximately how much does profit change?

**7.** The cost of recycling $q$ tons of paper is given in the following table. Estimate the marginal cost at $q = 2000$. Give units and interpret your answer in terms of cost. At approximately what production level does marginal cost appear smallest?

| $q$ (tons)      | 1000 | 1500 | 2000 | 2500 | 3000 | 3500 |
|-----------------|------|------|------|------|------|------|
| $C(q)$ (dollars) | 2500 | 3200 | 3640 | 3825 | 3900 | 4400 |

8. Figure 2.57 shows part of the graph of cost and revenue for a car manufacturer. Which is greater, marginal cost or marginal revenue, at

(a)  $q_1$?                          (b)  $q_2$?

**Figure 2.57**

9. Let $C(q)$ represent the total cost of producing $q$ items. Suppose $C(15) = 2300$ and $C'(15) = 108$. Estimate the total cost of producing: (a) 16 items (b) 14 items.

10. To produce 1000 items, the total cost is $5000 and the marginal cost is $25 per item. Estimate the costs of producing 1001 items, 999 items, and 1100 items.

11. Let $C(q)$ represent the cost and $R(q)$ represent the revenue, in dollars, of producing $q$ items.

(a) If $C(50) = 4300$ and $C'(50) = 24$, estimate $C(52)$.

(b) If $C'(50) = 24$ and $R'(50) = 35$, approximately how much profit is earned by the 51st item?

(c) If $C'(100) = 38$ and $R'(100) = 35$, should the company produce the 101st item? Why or why not?

12. Cost and revenue functions for a charter bus company are shown in Figure 2.58. Should the company add a 50th bus? How about a 90th? Explain your answers using marginal revenue and marginal cost.

**Figure 2.58**

13. An industrial production process costs $C(q)$ million dollars to produce $q$ million units; these units then sell for $R(q)$ million dollars. If $C(2.1) = 5.1$, $R(2.1) = 6.9$, $MC(2.1) = 0.6$, and $MR(2.1) = 0.7$, calculate

(a) The profit earned by producing 2.1 million units
(b) The approximate change in revenue if production increases from 2.1 to 2.14 million units.
(c) The approximate change in revenue if production decreases from 2.1 to 2.05 million units.
(d) The approximate change in profit in parts (b) and (c).

14. A company's cost of producing $q$ liters of a chemical is $C(q)$ dollars; this quantity can be sold for $R(q)$ dollars. Suppose $C(2000) = 5930$ and $R(2000) = 7780$.

(a) What is the profit at a production level of 2000?
(b) If $MC(2000) = 2.1$ and $MR(2000) = 2.5$, what is the approximate change in profit if $q$ is increased from 2000 to 2001? Should the company increase or decrease production from $q = 2000$?
(c) If $MC(2000) = 4.77$ and $MR(2000) = 4.32$, should the company increase or decrease production from $q = 2000$?

15. Table 2.13 shows the cost, $C(q)$, and revenue, $R(q)$, in terms of quantity $q$. Estimate the marginal cost, $C'(q)$, and marginal revenue, $R'(q)$, for $q$ between 0 and 7.

**Table 2.13**

| $q$ | 0 | 1 | 2 | 3 | 4 | 5 | 6 | 7 |
|---|---|---|---|---|---|---|---|---|
| $C(q)$ | 9 | 10 | 12 | 15 | 19 | 24 | 30 | 37 |
| $R(q)$ | 0 | 5 | 10 | 15 | 20 | 25 | 30 | 35 |

16. Table 2.14 shows the cost, $C(q)$, and revenue, $R(q)$, in terms of quantity $q$. Estimate the marginal cost, $MC(q)$, and marginal revenue, $MR(q)$, for $q$ between 0 and 6.

**Table 2.14**

| $q$ | 1 | 2 | 3 | 4 | 5 | 6 |
|---|---|---|---|---|---|---|
| $C(q)$ | 20 | 60 | 120 | 200 | 300 | 420 |
| $R(q)$ | 100 | 220 | 330 | 410 | 450 | 480 |

# CHAPTER SUMMARY

- **Rate of change**
  Average, instantaneous

- **Estimating derivatives**
  Estimate derivatives from a graph, table of values, or formula

- **Interpretation of derivatives**
  Rate of change, slope, using units, instantaneous velocity

- **Relative rate of change**
  Calculation and interpretation

- **Marginality**
  Marginal cost and marginal revenue

- **Second derivative**
  Concavity

- **Derivatives and graphs**
  Understand relation between sign of $f'$ and whether $f$ is increasing or decreasing. Sketch graph of $f'$ from graph of $f$. Marginal analysis

# REVIEW PROBLEMS FOR CHAPTER TWO

1. In a time of $t$ seconds, a particle moves a distance of $s$ meters from its starting point, where $s = 3t^2$.

   **(a)** Find the average velocity between $t = 1$ and $t = 1 + h$ if:

   (i)  $h = 0.1$,  (ii)  $h = 0.01$,  (iii)  $h = 0.001$.

   **(b)** Use your answers to part (a) to estimate the instantaneous velocity of the particle at time $t = 1$.

2. Figure 2.59 shows the graph of $f$. Match the derivatives in the table with the points $a, b, c, d, e$.

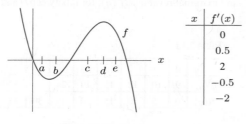

| $x$ | $f'(x)$ |
|---|---|
|  | 0 |
|  | 0.5 |
|  | 2 |
|  | $-0.5$ |
|  | $-2$ |

**Figure 2.59**

3. **(a)** Use a graph of $f(x) = 2 - x^3$ to decide whether $f'(1)$ is positive or negative. Give reasons.
   **(b)** Use a small interval to estimate $f'(1)$.

4. Estimate $f'(2)$ for $f(x) = 3^x$. Explain your reasoning.

5. **(a)** The function $f$ is given in Figure 2.60. At which of the labeled points is $f'(x)$ positive? Negative? Zero?
   **(b)** At which labeled point is $f'$ largest? At which labeled point is $f'$ most negative?

**Figure 2.60**

6. Use Figure 2.61 to fill in the blanks in the following statements about the function $g$ at point $B$.

   **(a)**  $g(\underline{\quad}) = \underline{\quad}$    **(b)**  $g'(\underline{\quad}) = \underline{\quad}$

**Figure 2.61**

7. In a time of $t$ seconds, a particle moves a distance of $s$ meters from its starting point, where $s = \sin(2t)$.

   **(a)** Find the average velocity between $t = 1$ and $t = 1 + h$ if:

   (i)  $h = 0.1$,  (ii)  $h = 0.01$,  (iii)  $h = 0.001$.

   **(b)** Use your answers to part (a) to estimate the instantaneous velocity of the particle at time $t = 1$.

8. The distance (in feet) of an object from a point is given by $s(t) = t^2$, where time $t$ is in seconds.

   **(a)** What is the average velocity of the object between $t = 3$ and $t = 5$?
   **(b)** By using smaller and smaller intervals around 3, estimate the instantaneous velocity at time $t = 3$.

9. Let $f(x) = 5^x$. Use small intervals to estimate $f'(2)$.

10. Using slopes to left and right of 0, estimate $P'(0)$ if $P(t) = 200(1.05)^t$.

Sketch the graphs of the derivatives of the functions shown in Problems 11–20. Be sure your sketches are consistent with the important features of the graphs of the original functions.

**11.**

**12.**

**13.**

**14.**

**15.**

**16.**

**17.**

**18.**

**19.**

**20.**

**21. (a)** Estimate $f'(2)$ using the values of $f$ in the table.
**(b)** For what values of $x$ does $f'(x)$ appear to be positive? Negative?

| $x$ | 0 | 2 | 4 | 6 | 8 | 10 | 12 |
|---|---|---|---|---|---|---|---|
| $f(x)$ | 10 | 18 | 24 | 21 | 20 | 18 | 15 |

**22.** Figure 2.62 is the graph of $f'$, the derivative of a function $f$. On what interval(s) is the function $f$

**(a)** Increasing?      **(b)** Decreasing?

**Figure 2.62**: Graph of $f'$, not $f$

**23.** The average weight $W$ of an oak tree in kilograms that is $x$ meters tall is given by the function $W = f(x)$. What are the units of measurement of $f'(x)$?

**24.** The percent, $P$, of US households with a personal computer is a function of the number of years, $t$, since 1982 (when the percent was essentially zero), so $P = f(t)$. Interpret the statements $f(20) = 57$ and $f'(20) = 3$.

**25.** The temperature, $T$, in degrees Fahrenheit, of a cold yam placed in a hot oven is given by $T = f(t)$, where $t$ is the time in minutes since the yam was put in the oven.

**(a)** What is the sign of $f'(t)$? Why?
**(b)** What are the units of $f'(20)$? What is the practical meaning of the statement $f'(20) = 2$?

**26.** The quantity sold, $q$, of a certain product is a function of the price, $p$, so $q = f(p)$. Interpret each of the following statements in terms of demand for the product:

**(a)** $f(15) = 200$      **(b)** $f'(15) = -25$.

**27.** Figure 2.63 shows the length, $L$, in cm, of a sturgeon (a type of fish) as a function of the time, $t$, in years.[29] Estimate $f'(10)$. Give units and interpret your answer.

**Figure 2.63**

**28.** Suppose that $f(x)$ is a function with $f(20) = 345$ and $f'(20) = 6$. Estimate $f(22)$.

**29.** The wind speed $W$ in meters per second at a distance $x$ kilometers from the center of a hurricane is given by the function $W = h(x)$. What does the fact that $h'(15) > 0$ tell you about the hurricane?

**30.** You drop a rock from a high tower. After it falls $x$ meters its speed $S$ in meters per second is $S = h(x)$. What is the meaning of $h'(20) = 0.5$ ?

[29] Data from L. von Bertalanffy, *General System Theory*, p. 177 (New York: Braziller, 1968).

**31.** If $t$ is the number of years since 2011, the population, $P$, of China, in billions, can be approximated by the function

$$P = f(t) = 1.34(1.004)^t.$$

Estimate $f(9)$ and $f'(9)$, giving units. What do these two numbers tell you about the population of China?

**32.** After investing \$1000 at an annual interest rate of 7% compounded continuously for $t$ years, your balance is \$$B$, where $B = f(t)$. What are the units of $dB/dt$? What is the financial interpretation of $dB/dt$?

**33.** Let $f(t)$ be the depth, in centimeters, of water in a tank at time $t$, in minutes.

  (a) What does the sign of $f'(t)$ tell us?
  (b) Explain the meaning of $f'(30) = 20$. Include units.
  (c) Using the information in part (b), at time $t = 30$ minutes, find the rate of change of depth, in meters, with respect to time in hours. Give units.

**34.** For the function graphed in Figure 2.64, are the following nonzero quantities positive or negative?

  (a)  $f(2)$       (b)  $f'(2)$       (c)  $f''(2)$

Figure 2.64

**35.** At one of the labeled points on the graph in Figure 2.65 both $dy/dx$ and $d^2y/dx^2$ are positive. Which is it?

Figure 2.65

**36.** A climber on Mount Everest is 6000 meters from the start of a trail and at elevation 8000 meters above sea level. At $x$ meters from the start, the elevation of the trail is $h(x)$ meters above sea level. If $h'(x) = 0.5$ for $x$ near 6000, what is the approximate elevation another 3 meters along the trail?

**37.** Let $f(v)$ be the gas consumption (in liters/km) of a car going at velocity $v$ (in km/hr). In other words, $f(v)$ tells you how many liters of gas the car uses to go one kilometer at velocity $v$. Explain what the following statements tell you about gas consumption:

$$f(80) = 0.05 \quad \text{and} \quad f'(80) = 0.0005.$$

**38.** To study traffic flow, a city installs a device which records $C(t)$, the total number of cars that have passed by $t$ hours after 4:00 am. The graph of $C(t)$ is in Figure 2.66.

  (a) When is the traffic flow the greatest?
  (b) Estimate $C'(2)$.
  (c) What does $C'(2)$ mean in practical terms?

Figure 2.66

**39.** The temperature, $H$, in degrees Celsius, of a cup of coffee placed on the kitchen counter is given by $H = f(t)$, where $t$ is in minutes since the coffee was put on the counter.

  (a) Is $f'(t)$ positive or negative? Give a reason for your answer.
  (b) What are the units of $f'(20)$? What is its practical meaning in terms of the temperature of the coffee?

**40.** Suppose that $f(x)$ is a function with $f(100) = 35$ and $f'(100) = 3$. Estimate $f(102)$.

**41.** Suppose $P(t)$ is the monthly payment, in dollars, on a mortgage which will take $t$ years to pay off. What are the units of $P'(t)$? What is the practical meaning of $P'(t)$? What is its sign?

**42.** The population, $P$, of a city (in thousands) at time $t$ (in years) is $P = 700e^{0.035t}$. Estimate the relative rate of change of the population at $t = 3$ using

  (a)  $\Delta t = 1$    (b)  $\Delta t = 0.1$    (c)  $\Delta t = 0.01$

**43.** For each part below, sketch a graph of a function that satisfies the given conditions. There are many possible correct answers.

  (a) $f' > 0$ and $f'' > 0$.
  (b) $f' > 0$ and $f'' < 0$.
  (c) $f' < 0$ and $f'' > 0$.
  (d) $f' < 0$ and $f'' < 0$.

**44.** For each function, do the signs of the first and second derivatives of the function appear to be positive or negative over the given interval?

**(a)**

| $x$ | 1.0 | 1.1 | 1.2 | 1.3 | 1.4 | 1.5 |
|---|---|---|---|---|---|---|
| $f(x)$ | 10.1 | 11.2 | 13.7 | 16.0 | 21.2 | 27.7 |

**(b)**

| $x$ | 1.0 | 1.1 | 1.2 | 1.3 | 1.4 | 1.5 |
|---|---|---|---|---|---|---|
| $f(x)$ | 10.1 | 9.9 | 8.1 | 6.0 | 3.9 | 0.1 |

**(c)**

| $x$ | 1.0 | 1.1 | 1.2 | 1.3 | 1.4 | 1.5 |
|---|---|---|---|---|---|---|
| $f(x)$ | 1000 | 1010 | 1015 | 1018 | 1020 | 1021 |

**45.** The length $L$ of the day in minutes (sunrise to sunset) $x$ kilometers north of the equator on June 21 is given by $L = f(x)$. What are the units of

**(a)** $f'(3000)$?  **(b)** $f''(3000)$?

**46.** Sketch the graph of a function whose first and second derivatives are everywhere positive.

**47.** At which of the marked $x$-values in Figure 2.67 can the following statements be true?

**(a)** $f(x) < 0$
**(b)** $f'(x) < 0$
**(c)** $f(x)$ is decreasing
**(d)** $f'(x)$ is decreasing
**(e)** Slope of $f(x)$ is positive
**(f)** Slope of $f(x)$ is increasing

**Figure 2.67**

**48.** Sketch the graph of the height of a particle against time if velocity is positive and acceleration is negative.

**49.** Figure 2.68 gives the position, $f(t)$, of a particle at time $t$. At which of the marked values of $t$ can the following statements be true?

**(a)** The position is positive
**(b)** The velocity is positive
**(c)** The acceleration is positive
**(d)** The position is decreasing
**(e)** The velocity is decreasing

**Figure 2.68**

**50.** A high school principal is concerned about the drop in the percentage of students who graduate from her school, shown in the following table, compared with the fall in national average from 69.2% in 2006 to 68.8% in 2007.[30]

| Year entered school, $t$ | 1995 | 1998 | 2001 | 2004 | 2007 |
|---|---|---|---|---|---|
| Percent graduating, $P$ | 62.4 | 54.1 | 48.0 | 43.5 | 41.8 |

**(a)** Calculate the average rate of change of $P$ for each of the three-year intervals between 1995 and 2007.
**(b)** Does $d^2P/dt^2$ appear to be positive or negative between 1995 and 2007?
**(c)** Explain why the values of $P$ and $dP/dt$ are troublesome to the principal.
**(d)** Explain why the sign of $d^2P/dt^2$ and the magnitude of $dP/dt$ in the year 2004 may give the principal some cause for optimism.

**51.** Students were asked to evaluate $f'(4)$ from the following table which shows values of the function $f$:

| $x$ | 1 | 2 | 3 | 4 | 5 | 6 |
|---|---|---|---|---|---|---|
| $f(x)$ | 4.2 | 4.1 | 4.2 | 4.5 | 5.0 | 5.7 |

- Student A estimated the derivative as $f'(4) \approx \dfrac{f(5) - f(4)}{5 - 4} = 0.5$.
- Student B estimated the derivative as $f'(4) \approx \dfrac{f(4) - f(3)}{4 - 3} = 0.3$.
- Student C suggested that they should split the difference and estimate the average of these two results, that is, $f'(4) \approx \frac{1}{2}(0.5 + 0.3) = 0.4$.

**(a)** Sketch the graph of $f$, and indicate how the three estimates are represented on the graph.
**(b)** Explain which answer is likely to be best.

[30] http://www.csmonitor.com/USA/Education/2010/0610/Graduation-rate-for-US-high-schoolers-falls-for-second-straight-year, accessed September 2012.

**52.** Figure 2.69 shows the rate at which energy, $f(v)$, is consumed by a bird flying at speed $v$ meters/sec.

   **(a)** What rate of energy consumption is needed by the bird to keep aloft, without moving forward?

   **(b)** What does the shape of the graph tell you about how birds fly?

   **(c)** Sketch $f'(v)$.

**Figure 2.69**

## STRENGTHEN YOUR UNDERSTANDING

In Problems 1–55, indicate whether the statement is true or false.

**1.** The derivative of $f$ at $a$ is the instantaneous rate of change of $f$ at the point $a$.

**2.** If $f(x) = x^2$ then $f'(1)$ is positive.

**3.** If $g(t) = 2^t$ then $g'(1) \approx (2^{1.001} - 2^1)/(1.001 - 1)$.

**4.** The slope of the graph of $H(x) = \sqrt{x}$ is negative at $x = 2$.

**5.** A function $f$ cannot have both $f(a) = 0$ and $f'(a) = 0$.

**6.** The average rate of change of $f$ between 0 and 1 is always less than the slope of the graph of $f$ at 0.

**7.** The function $r$ in the following table appears to have a negative derivative at $t = 0.5$:

| $t$ | 0.3 | 0.5 | 0.7 | 0.9 |
|---|---|---|---|---|
| $r(t)$ | 1.2 | 6.5 | 9.7 | 13.4 |

**8.** The derivative of $f$ at 3 is given by the difference quotient $(f(3) - f(0))/(3 - 0)$.

**9.** If $R(w) = w^3$ then $R'(-2)$ is negative.

**10.** A function can have more than one point where the derivative is 0.

**11.** If $f' > 0$ on an interval, then $f$ is increasing on that interval.

**12.** The $f$ is negative on an interval, then the derivative of $f$ is decreasing on that interval.

**13.** If $f$ is always increasing, then $f'$ is always increasing.

**14.** If $f(2) > g(2)$ then $f'(2) > g'(2)$.

**15.** The derivative of the constant function $q(x) = 5$ is $q'(x) = 0$.

**16.** The derivative of a function that is always decreasing is also always decreasing.

**17.** The function $g(t) = \ln(t)$ has $g'(1) < 0$.

**18.** If $f$ is a function with $f(3) = 0$ then $f'(3) = 0$.

**19.** If $f'$ is zero at all points in an interval, then the graph of $f$ is a horizontal line on that interval.

**20.** If $f'$ is negative at all points in an interval, then $f$ is decreasing on that interval.

**21.** If the cost $C$ (in dollars) of feeding $x$ students in the dining center is given by $C = f(x)$, then the units of $dC/dx$ are dollars per student.

**22.** If $y = f(x)$ then $dy/dx$ and $f'(x)$ mean the same thing.

**23.** If the cost $C$ (in dollars) of extracting $T$ tons of ore is given by $C = f(T)$ then $f'(2000)$ is the approximate cost to extract the 2001$^{\text{st}}$ ton.

**24.** If $f(10) = 20$ and $f'(10) = 3$, then 23 is a reasonable approximation of $f(11)$.

**25.** The units of $dA/dB$ are the units of $A$ divided by the units of $B$.

**26.** If $A = f(B)$ then the units of $f'(B)$ are the units of $B$ divided by the units of $A$.

**27.** If $f'(100) = 2$ and the derivative of $f$ is not changing rapidly, then $f(101) - f(100) \approx 2$.

**28.** If $t$ (in minutes) is the time that a dose of $D$ milligrams of morphine is effective as a painkiller, so that $t = f(D)$, then the units of $f'(D)$ are minutes per milligram.

**29.** If $h = f(a)$ gives height $h$ (in inches) of a child aged $a$ years, then $dh/da$ is positive when $0 < a < 10$.

**30.** If $W = f(R)$ and $f'(R)$ is negative, then we expect $W$ to decrease as $R$ increases.

**31.** If $f'' > 0$ on an interval, then $f$ is increasing on that interval.

**32.** If $f'' < 0$ on an interval, then $f$ is concave down on that interval.

**33.** If $f'' > 0$ on an interval, then $f' > 0$ on that interval.

**34.** If $f'$ is decreasing on an interval, then $f$ is concave down on that interval.

**35.** If a car is slowing down, then the second derivative of its distance as a function of time is negative.

**36.** There is a function with $f > 0$ and $f' > 0$ and $f'' > 0$ everywhere.

**37.** There is a function with $f > 0$ and $f' < 0$ and $f'' > 0$ everywhere.

**38.** There is a function with $f'' = 0$ everywhere.

**39.** The function $f(x) = e^x$ has $f'' > 0$ everywhere.

**40.** The function $f(x) = \ln(x)$ has $f'' > 0$ for $x > 0$.

**41.** Marginal cost is the instantaneous rate of change of cost with respect to quantity.

**42.** Marginal revenue is the derivative of the revenue function with respect to quantity.

**43.** If marginal revenue is greater than marginal cost when quantity is 1000, then increasing the quantity to 1001 will increase the profit.

**44.** Marginal cost is always greater than or equal to zero.

**45.** If the revenue function is linear with slope 5, then marginal revenue is always zero.

**46.** The units of marginal cost are quantity per dollar.

**47.** The units of marginal revenue are the same as the units of marginal cost.

**48.** Marginal cost is never equal to marginal revenue.

**49.** If the graphs of the cost and revenue functions $C(q)$ and $R(q)$ cross at $q^*$, then marginal revenue is equal to marginal cost at $q^*$.

**50.** If the graphs of the marginal cost and marginal revenue functions $C'(q)$ and $R'(q)$ cross at $q^*$, then marginal revenue is equal to marginal cost at $q^*$.

**51.** If $P$ is a function of $t$, then the relative rate of change of $P$ is $(1/P)(dP/dt)$.

**52.** If $f(25) = 10$ gallons and $f'(25) = 2$ gallons per minute, then at $t = 25$, the function $f$ is changing at a rate of 20% per minute.

**53.** If a quantity is 100 and has relative rate of change $-3\%$ per minute, we expect the quantity to be about 97 one minute later.

**54.** If a population of animals changes from 500 to 400 in one month, then the relative rate of change is about $-100$ animals per month.

**55.** Linear functions have constant rate of change and exponential functions have constant relative rate of change.

# PROJECTS FOR CHAPTER TWO

### 1. Estimating the Temperature of a Yam

You put a yam in a hot oven, maintained at a constant temperature of 200°C. As the yam picks up heat from the oven, its temperature rises.[31]

**(a)** Draw a possible graph of the temperature $T$ of the yam against time $t$ (minutes) since it is put into the oven. Explain any interesting features of the graph, and in particular explain its concavity.

**(b)** At $t = 30$, the temperature $T$ of the yam is 120° and increasing at the (instantaneous) rate of 2°/min. Using this information and the shape of the graph, estimate the temperature at time $t = 40$.

**(c)** In addition, you are told that at $t = 60$, the temperature of the yam is 165°. Can you improve your estimate of the temperature at $t = 40$?

**(d)** Assuming all the data given so far, estimate the time at which the temperature of the yam is 150°.

### 2. Temperature and Illumination

Alone in your dim, unheated room, you light a single candle rather than curse the darkness. Depressed with the situation, you walk directly away from the candle, sighing. The temperature (in degrees Fahrenheit) and illumination (in % of one candle power) decrease as your distance (in feet) from the candle increases. In fact, you have tables showing this information.

---

[31]From Peter D. Taylor, *Calculus: The Analysis of Functions* (Toronto: Wall & Emerson, Inc., 1992).

| Distance (feet) | Temperature (°F) | Distance (feet) | Illumination (%) |
|---|---|---|---|
| 0 | 55 | 0 | 100 |
| 1 | 54.5 | 1 | 85 |
| 2 | 53.5 | 2 | 75 |
| 3 | 52 | 3 | 67 |
| 4 | 50 | 4 | 60 |
| 5 | 47 | 5 | 56 |
| 6 | 43.5 | 6 | 53 |

You are cold when the temperature is below 40°. You are in the dark when the illumination is at most 50% of one candle power.

**(a)** Two graphs are shown in Figures 2.70 and 2.71. One is temperature as a function of distance and one is illumination as a function of distance. Which is which? Explain.

Figure 2.70                              Figure 2.71

**(b)** What is the average rate at which the temperature is changing when the illumination drops from 75% to 56%?

**(c)** You can still read your watch when the illumination is about 65%. Can you still read your watch at 3.5 feet? Explain.

**(d)** Suppose you know that at 6 feet the instantaneous rate of change of the temperature is −4.5°F/ft and the instantaneous rate of change of illumination is −3% candle power/ft. Estimate the temperature and the illumination at 7 feet.

**(e)** Are you in the dark before you are cold, or vice versa?

**3. Chlorofluorocarbons (CFCs) in the Atmosphere**

Chlorofluorocarbons (CFCs) were used as propellants in spray cans until their buildup in the atmosphere started destroying the ozone, which protects us from ultraviolet rays. Since the 1987 Montreal Protocol (an agreement to curb CFCs), the CFCs in the atmosphere above the US have been reduced from a high of 3200 parts per trillion (ppt) in 1994 to 2750 ppt in 2010.[32] The reduction has been approximately linear. Let $C(t)$ be the concentration of CFCs in ppt in year $t$.

**(a)** Find $C(1994)$ and $C(2010)$.

**(b)** Estimate $C'(1994)$ and $C'(2010)$.

**(c)** Assuming $C(t)$ is linear, find a formula for $C(t)$.

**(d)** When is $C(t)$ expected to reach 1850 ppt, the level before CFCs were introduced?

**(e)** If you were told that in the future, $C(t)$ would not be exactly linear, and that $C''(t) > 0$, would your answer to part (d) be too early or too late?

---

[32]www.esrl.noaa.gov/gmd/odgi

# FOCUS ON THEORY

## LIMITS, CONTINUITY, AND THE DEFINITION OF THE DERIVATIVE

The velocity at a single instant in time is surprisingly difficult to define precisely. Consider the statement "At the instant it crossed the finish line, the horse was traveling at 42 mph." How can such a claim be substantiated? A photograph taken at that instant will show the horse motionless—it is no help at all. There is some paradox in trying to quantify the property of motion at a particular instant in time, since by focusing on a single instant we stop the motion!

A similar difficulty arises whenever we attempt to measure the rate of change of anything—for example, oil leaking out of a damaged tanker. The statement "One hour after the ship's hull ruptured, oil was leaking at a rate of 200 barrels per second" seems not to make sense. We could argue that at any given instant *no* oil is leaking.

Problems of motion were of central concern to Zeno and other philosophers as early as the fifth century BC. The approach that we took, made famous by Newton's calculus, is to stop looking for a simple notion of speed at an instant, and instead to look at speed over small intervals containing the instant. This method sidesteps the philosophical problems mentioned earlier but brings new ones of its own.

### Definition of the Derivative Using Average Rates

In Section 2.1, we defined the derivative as the instantaneous rate of change of a function. We can estimate a derivative by computing average rates of change over smaller and smaller intervals. We use this idea to give a symbolic definition of the derivative. Letting $h$ represent the size of the interval, we have

$$\text{Average rate of change between } x \text{ and } x+h = \frac{f(x+h) - f(x)}{(x+h) - x} = \frac{f(x+h) - f(x)}{h}.$$

To find the derivative, or instantaneous rate of change at the point $x$, we use smaller and smaller intervals. To find the derivative exactly, we take the limit as $h$, the size of the interval, shrinks to zero, so we say

$$\text{Derivative} = \text{Limit, as } h \text{ approaches zero, of } \frac{f(x+h) - f(x)}{h}.$$

Finally, instead of writing the phrase "limit, as $h$ approaches 0," we use the notation $\lim_{h \to 0}$. This leads to the following symbolic definition:

For any function $f$, we define the **derivative function**, $f'$, by

$$f'(x) = \lim_{h \to 0} \frac{f(x+h) - f(x)}{h},$$

provided the limit exists. The function $f$ is said to be **differentiable** at any point $x$ at which the derivative function is defined.

Notice that we have replaced the original difficulty of computing velocity at a point by an argument that the average rates of change approach a number as the time intervals shrink in size. In a sense, we have traded one hard question for another, since we don't yet have any idea how to be certain what number the average velocities are approaching.

## The Idea of a Limit

We used a limit to define the derivative. Now we look a bit more at the idea of the limit of a function at the point $c$. Provided the limit exists:

> We write $\lim_{x \to c} f(x)$ to represent the number approached by $f(x)$ as $x$ approaches $c$.

**Example 1**    Investigate $\lim_{x \to 2} x^2$.

**Solution**    Notice that we can make $x^2$ as close to 4 as we like by taking $x$ sufficiently close to 2. (Look at the values of $1.9^2$, $1.99^2$, $1.999^2$, and $2.1^2$, $2.01^2$, $2.001^2$ in Table 2.15; they seem to be approaching 4.) We write

$$\lim_{x \to 2} x^2 = 4,$$

which is read "the limit, as $x$ approaches 2, of $x^2$ is 4." Notice that the limit does not ask what happens *at* $x = 2$, so it is not sufficient to substitute 2 to find the answer. The limit describes behavior of a function *near* a point, not *at* the point.

Table 2.15    *Values of $x^2$ near $x = 2$*

| $x$ | 1.9 | 1.99 | 1.999 | 2.001 | 2.01 | 2.1 |
|-----|-----|------|-------|-------|------|-----|
| $x^2$ | 3.61 | 3.96 | 3.996 | 4.004 | 4.04 | 4.41 |

**Example 2**    Use a graph to estimate $\lim_{x \to 0} \dfrac{2^x - 1}{x}$.

Figure 2.72: Find the limit as $x \to 0$ of $\dfrac{2^x - 1}{x}$

**Solution**    Notice that the expression $\dfrac{2^x - 1}{x}$ is undefined at $x = 0$. To find out what happens to this expression as $x$ approaches 0, look at a graph of $f(x) = \dfrac{2^x - 1}{x}$. Figure 2.72 shows that as $x$ approaches 0 from either side, the value of $\dfrac{2^x - 1}{x}$ appears to approach 0.7. If we zoom in on the graph near $x = 0$, we can estimate the limit with greater accuracy, giving

$$\lim_{x \to 0} \frac{2^x - 1}{x} \approx 0.693.$$

**Example 3**    Estimate $\lim_{h \to 0} \dfrac{(3 + h)^2 - 9}{h}$ numerically.

**Solution**    The limit is the value approached by this expression as $h$ approaches 0. The values in Table 2.16 seem to be approaching 6 as $h \to 0$. So it is a reasonable guess that

$$\lim_{h \to 0} \frac{(3 + h)^2 - 9}{h} = 6.$$

However, we cannot be sure that the limit is *exactly* 6 by looking at the table. To calculate the limit exactly requires algebra.

Table 2.16    *Values of* $\left((3+h)^2 - 9\right)/h$

| $h$ | $-0.1$ | $-0.01$ | $-0.001$ | $0.001$ | $0.01$ | $0.1$ |
|---|---|---|---|---|---|---|
| $\left((3+h)^2 - 9\right)/h$ | 5.9 | 5.99 | 5.999 | 6.001 | 6.01 | 6.1 |

**Example 4**   Use algebra to find $\lim\limits_{h \to 0} \dfrac{(3+h)^2 - 9}{h}$.

**Solution**   Expanding the numerator gives

$$\frac{(3+h)^2 - 9}{h} = \frac{9 + 6h + h^2 - 9}{h} = \frac{6h + h^2}{h}.$$

Since taking the limit as $h \to 0$ means looking at values of $h$ near, but not equal, to 0, we can cancel a common factor of $h$, giving

$$\lim_{h \to 0} \frac{(3+h)^2 - 9}{h} = \lim_{h \to 0} \frac{6h + h^2}{h} = \lim_{h \to 0} (6+h).$$

As $h$ approaches 0, the values of $(6+h)$ approach 6, so

$$\lim_{h \to 0} \frac{(3+h)^2 - 9}{h} = \lim_{h \to 0} (6+h) = 6.$$

## Continuity

Roughly speaking, a function is said to be *continuous* on an interval if its graph has no breaks, jumps, or holes in that interval. A continuous function has a graph that can be drawn without lifting the pencil from the paper.

*Example:* The function $f(x) = 3x^2 - x^2 + 2x + 1$ is continuous on any interval. (See Figure 2.73.)

*Example:* The function $f(x) = 1/x$ is not defined at $x = 0$. It is continuous on any interval not containing the origin. (See Figure 2.74.)

*Example:* Suppose $p(x)$ is the price of mailing a first-class letter weighing $x$ ounces. It costs 46¢ for one ounce or less, 66¢ between the first and second ounces, and so on. So the graph (in Figure 2.75) is a series of steps. This function is not continuous on intervals such as $(0, 2)$ because the graph jumps at $x = 1$.

Figure 2.73: The graph of $f(x) = 3x^3 - x^2 + 2x - 1$

Figure 2.74: Graph of $f(x) = 1/x$: Not defined at 0

Figure 2.75: Cost of mailing a letter

### What Does Continuity Mean Numerically?

Continuity is important in practical work because it means that small errors in the independent variable lead to small errors in the value of the function.

*Example:* Suppose that $f(x) = x^2$ and that we want to compute $f(\pi)$. Knowing $f$ is continuous tells us that taking $x = 3.14$ should give a good approximation to $f(\pi)$, and that we can get a better approximation to $f(\pi)$ by using more decimals of $\pi$.

*Example:* If $p(x)$ is the cost of mailing a letter weighing $x$ ounces, then $p(0.99) = p(1) = 46¢$, whereas $p(1.01) = 66¢$, because as soon as we get over 1 ounce, the price jumps up to $66¢$. So a small difference in the weight of a letter can lead to a significant difference in its mailing cost. Hence $p$ is not continuous at $x = 1$.

## Definition of Continuity

We now define continuity using limits. The idea of continuity rules out breaks, jumps, or holes by demanding that the behavior of a function *near* a point be consistent with its behavior *at* the point:

> The function $f$ is **continuous** at $x = c$ if $f$ is defined at $x = c$ and
>
> $$\lim_{x \to c} f(x) = f(c).$$
>
> The function is **continuous on an interval** $(a, b)$ if it is continuous at every point in the interval.

## Which Functions Are Continuous?

Requiring a function to be continuous on an interval is not asking very much, as any function whose graph is an unbroken curve over the interval is continuous. For example, exponential functions, polynomials, and sine and cosine are continuous on every interval. Functions created by adding, multiplying, or composing continuous functions are also continuous.

# Using the Definition to Calculate Derivatives

By estimating the derivative of the function $f(x) = x^2$ at several points, we guessed in Example 5 of Section 2.2 that the derivative of $x^2$ is $f'(x) = 2x$. In order to show that this formula is correct, we have to use the symbolic definition of the derivative given earlier in this section.

In evaluating the expression

$$\lim_{h \to 0} \frac{f(x + h) - f(x)}{h},$$

we simplify the difference quotient first, and then take the limit as $h$ approaches zero.

**Example 5**    Show that the derivative of $f(x) = x^2$ is $f'(x) = 2x$.

Solution    Using the definition of the derivative with $f(x) = x^2$, we have

$$f'(x) = \lim_{h \to 0} \frac{f(x + h) - f(x)}{h} = \lim_{h \to 0} \frac{(x + h)^2 - x^2}{h}$$

$$= \lim_{h \to 0} \frac{x^2 + 2xh + h^2 - x^2}{h} = \lim_{h \to 0} \frac{2xh + h^2}{h}$$

$$= \lim_{h \to 0} \frac{h(2x + h)}{h}.$$

To take the limit, look at what happens when $h$ is close to 0, but do not let $h = 0$. Since $h \neq 0$, we cancel the common factor of $h$, giving

$$f'(x) = \lim_{h \to 0} \frac{h(2x + h)}{h} = \lim_{h \to 0} (2x + h) = 2x,$$

because as $h$ gets close to zero, $2x + h$ gets close to $2x$. So

$$f'(x) = \frac{d}{dx}(x^2) = 2x.$$

**Example 6**     Show that if $f(x) = 3x - 2$, then $f'(x) = 3$.

Solution     Since the slope of the linear function $f(x) = 3x - 2$ is 3 and the derivative is the slope, we see that $f'(x) = 3$. We can also use the definition to get this result:

$$f'(x) = \lim_{h \to 0} \frac{f(x+h) - f(x)}{h} = \lim_{h \to 0} \frac{(3(x+h) - 2) - (3x - 2)}{h}$$
$$= \lim_{h \to 0} \frac{3x + 3h - 2 - 3x + 2}{h} = \lim_{h \to 0} \frac{3h}{h}.$$

To find the limit, look at what happens when $h$ is close to, but not equal to, 0. Simplifying, we get

$$f'(x) = \lim_{h \to 0} \frac{3h}{h} = \lim_{h \to 0} 3 = 3.$$

# Problems on Limits and the Definition of the Derivative

**1.** On Figure 2.76, mark lengths that represent the quantities in parts (a) – (e). (Pick any $h$, with $h > 0$.)

(a)  $a + h$        (b)  $h$        (c)  $f(a)$

(d)  $f(a + h)$     (e)  $f(a+h) - f(a)$

(f)  Using your answers to parts (a)–(e), show how the quantity $\dfrac{f(a+h) - f(a)}{h}$ can be represented as the slope of a line on the graph.

**Figure 2.77**

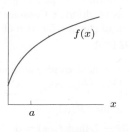

**Figure 2.76**

For the expressions in Problems 3–6,
(a)  What is the result when we substitute $h = 0$?
(b)  Find the values when we substitute $h = 0.1$, $h = 0.01$, $h = 0.001$, and $h = 0.0001$.
(c)  Use the results of part (b) to estimate the limit as $h$ goes to zero.

**3.** $\dfrac{e^{5h} - 1}{h}$          **4.** $\dfrac{2e^{3h} - 2}{h}$

**5.** $\dfrac{\ln(h + 1)}{h}$          **6.** $\dfrac{\sin(3h)}{h}$ (in radians)

**2.** On Figure 2.77, mark lengths that represent the quantities in parts (a)–(e). (Pick any $h$, with $h > 0$.)

(a)  $a + h$        (b)  $h$        (c)  $f(a)$

(d)  $f(a + h)$     (e)  $f(a+h) - f(a)$

(f)  Using your answers to parts (a)–(e), represent the quantity $\dfrac{f(a+h) - f(a)}{h}$ as the slope of a line on the graph.

Use a graph to estimate the limits in Problems 7–8.

**7.** $\lim_{x \to 0} \dfrac{5^x - 1}{x}$

**8.** $\lim_{x \to 0} \dfrac{\sin x}{x}$ (with $x$ in radians)

Estimate the limits in Problems 9–12 by substituting smaller and smaller values of $h$. For trigonometric functions, use radians. Give answers to one decimal place.

**9.** $\lim\limits_{h\to 0} \dfrac{7^h - 1}{h}$

**10.** $\lim\limits_{h\to 0} \dfrac{(3+h)^3 - 27}{h}$

**11.** $\lim\limits_{h\to 0} \dfrac{\cos h - 1}{h}$

**12.** $\lim\limits_{h\to 0} \dfrac{e^{1+h} - e}{h}$

**20.** $\lim\limits_{h\to 0} \dfrac{(3h - 7) + 7}{h}$

**21.** $\lim\limits_{h\to 0} \dfrac{(h+1)^2 - 1}{h}$

**22.** $\lim\limits_{h\to 0} \dfrac{(h-2)^2 - 4}{h}$

In Problems 13–16, does the function $f(x)$ appear to be continuous on the interval $0 \le x \le 2$? If not, what about on the interval $0 \le x \le 0.5$?

**13.**    **14.**

**15.**    **16.**

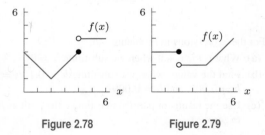

**17.** The graph of $y = f(x)$ is in Figure 2.78. Does the function $f(x)$ appear to be continuous on the given interval?

(a) $1 \le x \le 3$
(b) $0.5 \le x \le 1.5$
(c) $3 \le x \le 5$
(d) $2 \le x \le 6$

Figure 2.78          Figure 2.79

**18.** The graph of $y = f(x)$ is in Figure 2.79. Does the function $f(x)$ appear to be continuous on the given interval?

(a) $1 \le x \le 3$
(b) $0.5 \le x \le 1.5$
(c) $3 \le x \le 5$
(d) $4 \le x \le 5$

In Problems 19–22, find the limit by simplifying the expression.

**19.** $\lim\limits_{h\to 0} \dfrac{(5 + 2h) - 5}{h}$

Are the functions in Problems 23–28 continuous on the given intervals?

**23.** $f(x) = x + 2$      on   $-3 \le x \le 3$

**24.** $f(x) = 2^x$      on   $0 \le x \le 10$

**25.** $f(x) = x^2 + 2$      on   $0 \le x \le 5$

**26.** $f(x) = \dfrac{1}{x - 1}$      on   $2 \le x \le 3$

**27.** $f(x) = \dfrac{1}{x - 1}$      on   $0 \le x \le 2$

**28.** $f(x) = \dfrac{1}{x^2 + 1}$      on   $0 \le x \le 2$

Which of the functions described in Problems 29–33 are continuous?

**29.** The number of people in a village as a function of time.

**30.** The distance traveled by a car in stop-and-go traffic as a function of time.

**31.** The weight of a baby as a function of time during the second month of the baby's life.

**32.** The number of pairs of pants as a function of the number of yards of cloth from which they are made. Each pair requires 3 yards.

**33.** You start in North Carolina and go westward on Interstate 40 toward California. Consider the function giving the local time of day as a function of your distance from your starting point.

Use the definition of the derivative to show how the formulas in Problems 34–43 are obtained.

**34.** If $f(x) = 5x$, then $f'(x) = 5$.

**35.** If $f(x) = 3x - 2$, then $f'(x) = 3$.

**36.** If $f(x) = x^2 + 4$, then $f'(x) = 2x$.

**37.** If $f(x) = 3x^2$, then $f'(x) = 6x$.

**38.** If $f(x) = x - x^2$, then $f'(x) = 1 - 2x$.

**39.** If $f(x) = 5x^2 + 1$, then $f'(x) = 10x$.

**40.** If $f(x) = 2x^2 + x$, then $f'(x) = 4x + 1$.

**41.** If $f(x) = -2x^3$, then $f'(x) = -6x^2$.

**42.** If $f(x) = 1 - x^3$, then $f'(x) = -3x^2$.

**43.** If $f(x) = 1/x$, then $f'(x) = -1/x^2$.

# Chapter Three

# SHORTCUTS TO DIFFERENTATION

## Contents

# 3.1  DERIVATIVE FORMULAS FOR POWERS AND POLYNOMIALS

The derivative of a function at a point represents a slope and a rate of change. In Chapter 2, we learned how to estimate values of the derivative of a function given by a graph or by a table. Now, we learn how to find a formula for the derivative of a function given by a formula.

## Derivative of a Constant Function

The graph of a constant function $f(x) = k$ is a horizontal line, with a slope of 0 everywhere. Therefore, its derivative is 0 everywhere. (See Figure 3.1.)

$$\text{If } f(x) = k, \text{ then } f'(x) = 0.$$

For example, $\dfrac{d}{dx}(5) = 0$.

**Figure 3.1**: A constant function

## Derivative of a Linear Function

We already know that the slope of a line is constant. This tells us that the derivative of a linear function is constant.

$$\text{If } f(x) = b + mx, \text{ then } f'(x) = \text{Slope} = m.$$

For example, $\dfrac{d}{dx}\left(5 - \dfrac{3}{2}x\right) = -\dfrac{3}{2}$.

## Derivative of a Constant Times a Function

Figure 3.2 shows the graph of $y = f(x)$ and of three multiples: $y = 3f(x)$, $y = \frac{1}{2}f(x)$, and $y = -2f(x)$. How are the derivatives of these functions related? In other words, for a particular $x$-value, how are the slopes of these graphs related?

**Figure 3.2**: A function and its multiples: Derivative of multiple is multiple of derivative

Multiplying by a constant stretches or shrinks the graph (and reflects it about the $x$-axis if the constant is negative). This changes the slope of the curve at each point. If the graph has been stretched, the "rises" have all been increased by the same factor, whereas the "runs" remain the same. Thus, the slopes are all steeper by the same factor. If the graph has been shrunk, the slopes are all smaller by the same factor. If the graph has been reflected about the $x$-axis, the slopes will all have their signs reversed. Thus, if a function is multiplied by a constant, $c$, so is its derivative:

---

### Derivative of a Constant Multiple

If $c$ is a constant,

$$\frac{d}{dx}\left[cf(x)\right] = cf'(x).$$

---

## Derivatives of Sums and Differences

Values of two functions, $f(x)$ and $g(x)$, and their sum $f(x) + g(x)$ are listed in Table 3.1.

**Table 3.1**  *Sum of functions*

| $x$ | $f(x)$ | $g(x)$ | $f(x) + g(x)$ |
|---|---|---|---|
| 0 | 100 | 0 | 100 |
| 1 | 110 | 0.2 | 110.2 |
| 2 | 130 | 0.4 | 130.4 |
| 3 | 160 | 0.6 | 160.6 |
| 4 | 200 | 0.8 | 200.8 |

We see that adding the increments of $f(x)$ and the increments of $g(x)$ gives the increments of $f(x) + g(x)$. For example, as $x$ increases from 0 to 1, $f(x)$ increases by 10 and $g(x)$ increases by 0.2, while $f(x) + g(x)$ increases by $110.2 - 100 = 10.2$. Similarly, as $x$ increases from 3 to 4, $f(x)$ increases by 40 and $g(x)$ by 0.2, while $f(x) + g(x)$ increases by $200.8 - 160.6 = 40.2$.

This example suggests that the rate at which $f(x) + g(x)$ is increasing is the sum of the rates at which $f(x)$ and $g(x)$ are increasing. Similar reasoning applies to the difference, $f(x) - g(x)$. In terms of derivatives:

---

### Derivative of Sum and Difference

$$\frac{d}{dx}\left[f(x) + g(x)\right] = f'(x) + g'(x) \qquad \text{and} \qquad \frac{d}{dx}\left[f(x) - g(x)\right] = f'(x) - g'(x).$$

---

## Powers of $x$

We start by looking at $f(x) = x^2$ and $g(x) = x^3$. We show in the Focus on Theory section at the end of this chapter that

$$f'(x) = \frac{d}{dx}\left(x^2\right) = 2x \quad \text{and} \quad g'(x) = \frac{d}{dx}\left(x^3\right) = 3x^2.$$

The graphs of $f(x) = x^2$ and $g(x) = x^3$ and their derivatives are shown in Figures 3.3 and 3.4. Notice $f'(x) = 2x$ has the behavior we expect. It is negative for $x < 0$ (when $f$ is decreasing), zero for $x = 0$, and positive for $x > 0$ (when $f$ is increasing). Similarly, $g'(x) = 3x^2$ is zero when $x = 0$, but positive everywhere else, as $g$ is increasing everywhere else. These examples are special cases of the power rule.

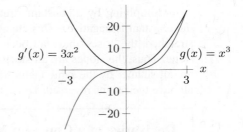

Figure 3.3: Graphs of $f(x) = x^2$ and its derivative $f'(x) = 2x$

Figure 3.4: Graphs of $g(x) = x^3$ and its derivative $g'(x) = 3x^2$

---

## The Power Rule

For any constant real number $n$,

$$\frac{d}{dx}(x^n) = nx^{n-1}.$$

---

**Example 1**    Find the derivative of (a)   $h(x) = x^8$        (b)   $P(t) = t^7$.

**Solution**    (a)   $h'(x) = 8x^7$.        (b)   $P'(t) = 7t^6$.

---

We can use the power rule to differentiate negative and fractional powers.

---

**Example 2**    Use the power rule to differentiate (a)   $\dfrac{1}{x^3}$      (b)   $\sqrt{x}$      (c)   $2t^{4.5}$.

**Solution**    (a) For $n = -3$:     $\dfrac{d}{dx}\left(\dfrac{1}{x^3}\right) = \dfrac{d}{dx}(x^{-3}) = -3x^{-3-1} = -3x^{-4} = -\dfrac{3}{x^4}$.

(b) For $n = 1/2$:     $\dfrac{d}{dx}(\sqrt{x}) = \dfrac{d}{dx}\left(x^{1/2}\right) = \dfrac{1}{2}x^{(1/2)-1} = \dfrac{1}{2}x^{-1/2} = \dfrac{1}{2\sqrt{x}}$.

(c) For $n = 4.5$:     $\dfrac{d}{dt}\left(2t^{4.5}\right) = 2\left(4.5t^{4.5-1}\right) = 9t^{3.5}$.

---

## Derivatives of Polynomials

Using the derivatives of powers, constant multiples, and sums, we can differentiate any polynomial.

---

**Example 3**    Differentiate:

(a)   $A(t) = 3t^5$                               (b)   $r(p) = p^5 + p^3$

(c)   $f(x) = 5x^2 - 7x^3$                      (d)   $g(t) = \dfrac{t^2}{4} + 3$

**Solution**    (a) Using the constant multiple rule: $A'(t) = \dfrac{d}{dt}(3t^5) = 3\dfrac{d}{dt}(t^5) = 3 \cdot 5t^4 = 15t^4$.

(b) Using the sum rule: $r'(p) = \dfrac{d}{dp}(p^5 + p^3) = \dfrac{d}{dp}(p^5) + \dfrac{d}{dp}(p^3) = 5p^4 + 3p^2$.

(c) Using all three rules together:

$$f'(x) = \frac{d}{dx}(5x^2 - 7x^3) = \frac{d}{dx}(5x^2) - \frac{d}{dx}(7x^3) \quad \text{Derivative of difference}$$

$$= 5\frac{d}{dx}(x^2) - 7\frac{d}{dx}(x^3) \quad \text{Derivative of multiple}$$

$$= 5(2x) - 7(3x^2) = 10x - 21x^2 \quad \text{Power rule.}$$

(d) Using both rules:

$$g'(t) = \frac{d}{dt}\left(\frac{t^2}{4} + 3\right) = \frac{1}{4}\frac{d}{dt}(t^2) + \frac{d}{dt}(3)$$

$$= \frac{1}{4}(2t) + 0 = \frac{t}{2}. \quad \text{Since the derivative of a constant, } \frac{d}{dt}(3)\text{, is zero.}$$

## Using the Derivative Formulas

Since the slope of the tangent line to a curve is given by the derivative, we use differentiation to find the equation of the tangent line.

**Example 4**  Find an equation for the tangent line at $x = 1$ to the graph of

$$y = x^3 + 2x^2 - 5x + 7.$$

Sketch the graph of the curve and its tangent line on the same axes.

**Solution**  Differentiating gives

$$\frac{dy}{dx} = 3x^2 + 2(2x) - 5(1) + 0 = 3x^2 + 4x - 5,$$

so the slope of the tangent line at $x = 1$ is

$$m = \left.\frac{dy}{dx}\right|_{x=1} = 3(1)^2 + 4(1) - 5 = 2.$$

When $x = 1$, we have $y = 1^3 + 2(1^2) - 5(1) + 7 = 5$, so the point $(1, 5)$ lies on the tangent line. Using the formula $y - y_0 = m(x - x_0)$ gives

$$y - 5 = 2(x - 1)$$
$$y = 3 + 2x.$$

The equation of the tangent line is $y = 3 + 2x$. See Figure 3.5.

Figure 3.5: Find the equation for this tangent line

**Example 5**  Find and interpret the second derivatives of (a)  $f(x) = x^2$  (b)  $g(x) = x^3$.

**Solution**  (a) Differentiating $f(x) = x^2$ gives $f'(x) = 2x$, so $f''(x) = \frac{d}{dx}(2x) = 2$. Since $f''$ is always positive, the graph of $f$ is concave up, as expected for a parabola opening upward. (See Figure 3.6.)

(b) Differentiating $g(x) = x^3$ gives $g'(x) = 3x^2$, so $g''(x) = \dfrac{d}{dx}(3x^2) = 3\dfrac{d}{dx}(x^2) = 3 \cdot 2x = 6x$.

Since $6x$ is positive for $x > 0$ and negative for $x < 0$, the graph of $g(x) = x^3$ is concave up for $x > 0$ and concave down for $x < 0$. (See Figure 3.7.)

Figure 3.6: Graph of $f(x) = x^2$ with $f''(x) = 2$     Figure 3.7: Graph of $g(x) = x^3$ with $g''(x) = 6x$

---

**Example 6**     The revenue (in dollars) from producing $q$ units of a product is given by

$$R(q) = 1000q - 3q^2.$$

Find $R(125)$ and $R'(125)$. Give units and interpret your answers.

**Solution**     We have

$$R(125) = 1000 \cdot 125 - 3 \cdot 125^2 = 78{,}125 \text{ dollars}.$$

Since $R'(q) = 1000 - 6q$, we have

$$R'(125) = 1000 - 6 \cdot 125 = 250 \text{ dollars per unit}.$$

If 125 units are sold, the revenue is 78,125 dollars. If an additional unit is then sold, the revenue increases by about \$250.

---

**Example 7**     Figure 3.8 shows the graph of a cubic polynomial. Both graphically and algebraically, describe the behavior of the derivative of this cubic.

Figure 3.8: The cubic of Example 7          Figure 3.9: Derivative of the cubic of Example 7

**Solution**     Graphical approach: Suppose we move along the curve from left to right. To the left of $A$, the slope is positive; it starts very positive and decreases until the curve reaches $A$, where the slope is 0. Between $A$ and $C$ the slope is negative. Between $A$ and $B$ the slope is decreasing (getting more negative); it is most negative at $B$. Between $B$ and $C$ the slope is negative but increasing; at $C$ the slope is zero. From $C$ to the right, the slope is positive and increasing. The graph of the derivative function is shown in Figure 3.9.

Algebraic approach: $f$ is a cubic that goes to $+\infty$ as $x \to +\infty$, so

$$f(x) = ax^3 + bx^2 + cx + d$$

with $a > 0$. Hence,

$$f'(x) = 3ax^2 + 2bx + c,$$

whose graph is a parabola opening upward because the coefficient of $x^2$ is positive, as in Figure 3.9.

## Problems for Section 3.1

For Problems 1–38, find the derivative. Assume $a$, $b$, $c$, $k$ are constants.

**1.** $y = 3x$

**2.** $y = 5$

**3.** $y = x^{-12}$

**4.** $y = x^{12}$

**5.** $y = 8t^3$

**6.** $y = x^{4/3}$

**7.** $y = 5x + 13$

**8.** $y = 3t^4 - 2t^2$

**9.** $f(q) = q^3 + 10$

**10.** $f(x) = \dfrac{1}{x^4}$

**11.** $y = 6x^3 + 4x^2 - 2x$

**12.** $y = x^2 + 5x + 9$

**13.** $y = 8t^3 - 4t^2 + 12t - 3$

**14.** $y = 3x^2 + 7x - 9$

**15.** $y = -3x^4 - 4x^3 - 6x$

**16.** $y = 4.2q^2 - 0.5q + 11.27$

**17.** $f(z) = -\dfrac{1}{z^{6.1}}$

**18.** $g(t) = \dfrac{1}{t^5}$

**19.** $y = \sqrt{x}$

**20.** $y = \dfrac{1}{r^{7/2}}$

**21.** $f(x) = \sqrt{\dfrac{1}{x^3}}$

**22.** $h(\theta) = \dfrac{1}{\sqrt[3]{\theta}}$

**23.** $z = (t-1)(t+1)$

**24.** $R = (s^2 + 1)^2$

**25.** $y = z^2 + \dfrac{1}{2z}$

**26.** $y = 3t^5 - 5\sqrt{t} + \dfrac{7}{t}$

**27.** $h(t) = \dfrac{3}{t} + \dfrac{4}{t^2}$

**28.** $y = 3t^2 + \dfrac{12}{\sqrt{t}} - \dfrac{1}{t^2}$

**29.** $h(\theta) = \theta(\theta^{-1/2} - \theta^{-2})$

**30.** $y = \sqrt{x}(x+1)$

**31.** $y = ax^2 + bx + c$

**32.** $f(x) = kx^2$

**33.** $v = at^2 + \dfrac{b}{t^2}$

**34.** $Q = aP^2 + bP^3$

**35.** $V = \frac{4}{3}\pi r^2 b$

**36.** $P = a + b\sqrt{t}$

**37.** $h(x) = \dfrac{ax+b}{c}$

**38.** $w = 3ab^2 q$

**39. (a)** Use a graph of $P(q) = 6q - q^2$ to determine whether each of the following derivatives is positive, negative, or zero: $P'(1)$, $P'(3)$, $P'(4)$. Explain.
**(b)** Find $P'(q)$ and the three derivatives in part (a).

**40.** Let $f(x) = x^3 - 4x^2 + 7x - 11$. Find $f'(0)$, $f'(2)$, $f'(-1)$.

**41.** Let $f(t) = t^2 - 4t + 5$.
**(a)** Find $f'(t)$.
**(b)** Find $f'(1)$ and $f'(2)$.
**(c)** Use a graph of $f(t)$ to check that your answers to part (b) are reasonable. Explain.

**42.** Find the rate of change of a population of size $P(t) = t^3 + 4t + 1$ at time $t = 2$.

**43.** The height of a sand dune (in centimeters) is represented by $f(t) = 700 - 3t^2$, where $t$ is measured in years since 2005. Find $f(5)$ and $f'(5)$. Using units, explain what each means in terms of the sand dune.

In Problems 44–45, find the relative rate of change $f'(t)/f(t)$ at the given value of $t$. Assume $t$ is in years and give your answer as a percent.

**44.** $f(t) = 3t + 2$;   $t = 5$

**45.** $f(t) = 2t^3 + 10$;   $t = 4$

**46.** The number, $N$, of acres of harvested land in a region is given by
$$N = f(t) = 120\sqrt{t},$$
where $t$ is the number of years since farming began in the region. Find $f(9)$, $f'(9)$, and the relative rate of change $f'/f$ at $t = 9$. Interpret your answers in terms of harvested land.

**47.** Zebra mussels are freshwater shellfish that first appeared in the St. Lawrence River in the early 1980s and have spread throughout the Great Lakes. Suppose that $t$ months after they appeared in a small bay, the number of zebra mussels is given by $Z(t) = 300t^2$. How many zebra mussels are in the bay after four months? At what rate is the population growing at that time? Give units.

**48.** The quantity, $Q$, in tons, of material at a municipal waste site is a function of the number of years since 2000, with
$$Q = f(t) = 3t^2 + 100.$$
Find $f(10)$, $f'(10)$, and the relative rate of change $f'/f$ at $t = 10$. Interpret your answers in terms of waste.

**49.** If $f(t) = 2t^3 - 4t^2 + 3t - 1$, find $f'(t)$ and $f''(t)$.

**50.** If $f(t) = t^4 - 3t^2 + 5t$, find $f'(t)$ and $f''(t)$.

**51.** Find the equation of the line tangent to the graph of $f(x) = 2x^3 - 5x^2 + 3x - 5$ at $x = 1$.

**52. (a)** Find the equation of the tangent line to $f(x) = x^3$ at the point where $x = 2$.
**(b)** Graph the tangent line and the function on the same axes. If the tangent line is used to estimate values of the function near $x = 2$, will the estimates be overestimates or underestimates?

**53.** Find the equation of the line tangent to the graph of $f(t) = 6t - t^2$ at $t = 4$. Sketch the graph of $f(t)$ and the tangent line on the same axes.

**54.** The time, $T$, in seconds for one complete oscillation of a pendulum is given by $T = f(L) = 1.111\sqrt{L}$, where $L$ is the length of the pendulum in feet. Find the following quantities, with units, and interpret in terms of the pendulum.

(a) $f(100)$          (b) $f'(100)$.

**55.** Kleiber's Law states that the daily calorie requirement, $C(w)$, of a mammal is proportional to the mammal's body weight $w$ raised to the 0.75 power.[1] If body weight is measured in pounds, the constant of proportionality is approximately 42.

(a) Give formulas for $C(w)$ and $C'(w)$.
(b) Find and interpret
    (i) $C(10)$ and $C'(10)$
    (ii) $C(100)$ and $C'(100)$
    (iii) $C(1000)$ and $C'(1000)$

**56.** If you are outdoors, the wind may make it feel a lot colder than the thermometer reads. You feel the windchill temperature, which, if the air temperature is $20°F$, is given in $°F$ by $W(v) = 48.17 - 27.2v^{0.16}$, where $v$ is the wind velocity in mph for $5 \leq v \leq 60$.[2]

(a) If the air temperature is $20°F$, and the wind is blowing at 40 mph, what is the windchill temperature, to the nearest degree?
(b) Find $W'(40)$, and explain what this means in terms of windchill.

**57.** (a) Use the formula for the area of a circle of radius $r$, $A = \pi r^2$, to find $dA/dr$.
(b) The result from part (a) should look familiar. What does $dA/dr$ represent geometrically?
(c) Use the difference quotient to explain the observation you made in part (b).

**58.** Suppose $W$ is proportional to $r^3$. The derivative $dW/dr$ is proportional to what power of $r$?

**59.** Show that for any power function $f(x) = x^n$, we have $f'(1) = n$.

**60.** The cost to produce $q$ items is $C(q) = 1000 + 2q^2$ dollars. Find the marginal cost of producing the 25$^{\text{th}}$ item. Interpret your answer in terms of costs.

**61.** The demand curve for a product is given by $q = 300 - 3p$, where $p$ is the price of the product and $q$ is the quantity that consumers buy at this price.

(a) Write the revenue as a function, $R(p)$, of price.
(b) Find $R'(10)$ and interpret your answer in terms of revenue.
(c) For what prices is $R'(p)$ positive? For what prices is it negative?

**62.** A ball is dropped from the top of the Empire State Building. The height, $y$, of the ball above the ground (in feet) is given as a function of time, $t$, (in seconds) by

$$y = 1250 - 16t^2.$$

(a) Find the velocity of the ball at time $t$. What is the sign of the velocity? Why is this to be expected?
(b) When does the ball hit the ground, and how fast is it going at that time? Give your answer in feet per second and in miles per hour (1 ft/sec = 15/22 mph).

**63.** The yield, $Y$, of an apple orchard (measured in bushels of apples per acre) is a function of the amount $x$ of fertilizer in pounds used per acre. Suppose

$$Y = f(x) = 320 + 140x - 10x^2.$$

(a) What is the yield if 5 pounds of fertilizer is used per acre?
(b) Find $f'(5)$. Give units with your answer and interpret it in terms of apples and fertilizer.
(c) Given your answer to part (b), should more or less fertilizer be used? Explain.

**64.** The demand for a product is given, for $p, q \geq 0$, by

$$p = f(q) = 50 - 0.03q^2.$$

(a) Find the $p$- and $q$-intercepts for this function and interpret them in terms of demand for this product.
(b) Find $f(20)$ and give units with your answer. Explain what it tells you in terms of demand.
(c) Find $f'(20)$ and give units with your answer. Explain what it tells you in terms of demand.

**65.** The cost (in dollars) of producing $q$ items is given by $C(q) = 0.08q^3 + 75q + 1000$.

(a) Find the marginal cost function.
(b) Find $C(50)$ and $C'(50)$. Give units with your answers and explain what each is telling you about costs of production.

**66.** Let $f(x) = x^3 - 6x^2 - 15x + 20$. Find $f'(x)$ and all values of $x$ for which $f'(x) = 0$. Explain the relationship between these values of $x$ and the graph of $f(x)$.

**67.** If the demand curve is a line, we can write $p = b + mq$, where $p$ is the price of the product, $q$ is the quantity sold at that price, and $b$ and $m$ are constants.

(a) Write the revenue as a function of quantity sold.
(b) Find the marginal revenue function.

---

[1] Strogatz, S., "Math and the City", *The New York Times*, May 20, 2009.
[2] www.weather.gov/om/windchill/index.shtml Accessed April 21, 2009.

## 3.2  EXPONENTIAL AND LOGARITHMIC FUNCTIONS

### The Exponential Function

What do we expect the graph of the derivative of the exponential function $f(x) = a^x$ to look like? The graph of an exponential function with $a > 1$ is shown in Figure 3.10. The function increases slowly for $x < 0$ and more rapidly for $x > 0$, so the values of $f'$ are small for $x < 0$ and larger for $x > 0$. Since the function is increasing for all values of $x$, the graph of the derivative must lie above the $x$-axis. In fact, the graph of $f'$ resembles the graph of $f$ itself. We will see how this observation holds for $f(x) = 2^x$ and $g(x) = 3^x$.

**Figure 3.10:** $f(x) = a^x$, with $a > 1$

### The Derivatives of $2^x$ and $3^x$

In Section 2.1, we estimated the derivative of $f(x) = 2^x$ at $x = 0$:

$$f'(0) \approx 0.693.$$

By estimating the derivative at other values of $x$, we obtain the graph in Figure 3.11. Since the graph of $f'$ looks like the graph of $f$ shrunk vertically, we assume that $f'$ is a multiple of $f$. Since $f'(0) \approx 0.693 = 0.693 \cdot 1 = 0.693f(0)$, the multiplier is approximately 0.693, which suggests that

$$\frac{d}{dx}(2^x) = f'(x) \approx (0.693)2^x.$$

Similarly, in Figure 3.12, the derivative of $g(x) = 3^x$ is a multiple of $g$, with multiplier $g'(0) \approx 1.0986$. So

$$\frac{d}{dx}(3^x) = g'(x) \approx (1.0986)3^x.$$

**Figure 3.11:** Graph of $f(x) = 2^x$ and its derivative

**Figure 3.12:** Graph of $g(x) = 3^x$ and its derivative

### The Derivative of $a^x$ and the Number $e$

The calculation of the derivative of $f(x) = a^x$, for $a > 0$, is similar to that of $2^x$ and $3^x$. The derivative is again proportional to the original function. When $a = 2$, the constant of proportionality (0.6931) is less than 1, and the derivative is smaller than the original function. When $a = 3$, the constant of proportionality (1.0986) is more than 1, and the derivative is greater than the original function. Is there an in-between case, when derivative and function are exactly equal? In other words:

$$\text{Is there a value of } a \text{ that makes } \frac{d}{dx}(a^x) = a^x?$$

The answer is yes: the value is $a \approx 2.718\ldots$, the number $e$ introduced in Chapter 1. This means that the function $e^x$ is its own derivative:

$$\frac{d}{dx}(e^x) = e^x.$$

It turns out that the constants involved in the derivatives of $2^x$ and $3^x$ are natural logarithms. In fact, since $0.6931 \approx \ln 2$ and $1.0986 \approx \ln 3$, we (correctly) guess that

$$\frac{d}{dx}(2^x) = (\ln 2)2^x \quad \text{and} \quad \frac{d}{dx}(3^x) = (\ln 3)3^x.$$

In the Focus on Theory section at the end of this chapter, we show that, in general:

## The Exponential Rule

For any positive constant $a$,

$$\frac{d}{dx}(a^x) = (\ln a)a^x.$$

Since $\ln a$ is a constant, the derivative of $a^x$ is proportional to $a^x$. Many quantities have rates of change that are proportional to themselves; for example, the simplest model of population growth has this property. The fact that the constant of proportionality is 1 when $a = e$ makes $e$ a particularly useful base for exponential functions.

**Example 1**    Differentiate $2 \cdot 3^x + 5e^x$.

**Solution**    We have $\dfrac{d}{dx}(2 \cdot 3^x + 5e^x) = 2\dfrac{d}{dx}(3^x) + 5\dfrac{d}{dx}(e^x) = 2\ln 3 \cdot 3^x + 5e^x.$

### The Derivative of $e^{kt}$

Since functions of the form $e^{kt}$ where $k$ is a constant are often useful, we calculate the derivative of $e^{kt}$. Since $e^{kt} = (e^k)^t$, the derivative is $(\ln(e^k))(e^k)^t = (k\ln e)(e^{kt}) = ke^{kt}$. Thus, if $k$ is a constant,

$$\frac{d}{dt}(e^{kt}) = ke^{kt}.$$

**Example 2**    Find the derivative of $P = 5 + 3x^2 - 7e^{-0.2x}$.

**Solution**    The derivative is

$$\frac{dP}{dx} = 0 + 3(2x) - 7(-0.2e^{-0.2x}) = 6x + 1.4e^{-0.2x}.$$

## The Derivative of $\ln x$

What does the graph of the derivative of the logarithmic function $f(x) = \ln x$ look like? Figure 3.13 shows that $\ln x$ is increasing, so its derivative is positive. The graph of $f(x) = \ln x$ is concave down, so the derivative is decreasing. Furthermore, the slope of $f(x) = \ln x$ is very large near $x = 0$ and very small for large $x$, so the derivative tends to $+\infty$ for $x$ near 0 and tends to 0 for very large $x$. See Figure 3.14. It turns out that

$$\frac{d}{dx}(\ln x) = \frac{1}{x}.$$

We give an algebraic justification for this rule in the Focus on Theory section.

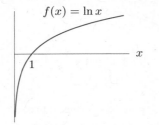

Figure 3.13: Graph of $f(x) = \ln x$

Figure 3.14: Graph of the derivative of $f(x) = \ln x$

---

**Example 3**    Differentiate $y = 5 \ln t + 7e^t - 4t^2 + 12$.

Solution        We have

$$\frac{d}{dt}(5 \ln t + 7e^t - 4t^2 + 12) = 5\frac{d}{dt}(\ln t) + 7\frac{d}{dt}(e^t) - 4\frac{d}{dt}(t^2) + \frac{d}{dt}(12)$$

$$= 5\left(\frac{1}{t}\right) + 7(e^t) - 4(2t) + 0$$

$$= \frac{5}{t} + 7e^t - 8t.$$

---

## Using the Derivative Formulas

**Example 4**    In Chapter 1, we saw that if $t$ is in years since the start of 2000, the population of Nevada, $P$, in millions, can be approximated by

$$P = 2.020(1.036)^t.$$

At what rate was the population growing at the beginning of 2009? Give units with your answer.

Solution        The instantaneous rate of growth is the derivative, so we want $dP/dt$ when $t = 9$. We have:

$$\frac{dP}{dt} = \frac{d}{dt}(2.020(1.036)^t) = 2.020(\ln 1.036)(1.036)^t = 0.0714(1.036)^t.$$

Substituting $t = 9$ gives

$$\frac{dP}{dt} = 0.0714(1.036)^9 = 0.0982.$$

The population of Nevada was growing at a rate of about 0.0982 million, or 98,200, people per year at the start of 2009.

---

**Example 5**    Find the equation of the tangent line to the graph of $f(x) = \ln x$ at the point where $x = 2$. Draw a graph with $f(x)$ and the tangent line on the same axes.

Solution    Since $f'(x) = 1/x$, the slope of the tangent line at $x = 2$ is $f'(2) = 1/2 = 0.5$. When $x = 2$, $y = \ln 2 = 0.693$, so a point on the tangent line is $(2, 0.693)$. Substituting into the equation for a line, we have:

$$y - 0.693 = 0.5(x - 2)$$
$$y = -0.307 + 0.5x.$$

The equation of the tangent line is $y = -0.307 + 0.5x$. See Figure 3.15.

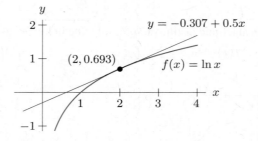

Figure 3.15: Graph of $f(x) = \ln x$ and a tangent line

---

**Example 6**    Suppose $1000 is deposited into a bank account that pays 8% annual interest, compounded continuously.

(a) Find a formula $f(t)$ for the balance $t$ years after the initial deposit.
(b) Find $f(10)$ and $f'(10)$ and explain what your answers mean in terms of money.

Solution    (a) The balance is $f(t) = 1000e^{0.08t}$.
(b) Substituting $t = 10$ gives

$$f(10) = 1000e^{(0.08)(10)} = 2225.54.$$

This means that the balance is $2225.54 after 10 years.
To find $f'(10)$, we compute $f'(t) = 1000(0.08e^{0.08t}) = 80e^{0.08t}$. Therefore,

$$f'(10) = 80e^{(0.08)(10)} = 178.04.$$

This means that after 10 years, the balance is growing at the rate of about $178 per year.

---

## Problems for Section 3.2

Differentiate the functions in Problems 1–28. Assume that $A$, $B$, and $C$ are constants.

**1.** $P = 3t^3 + 2e^t$

**2.** $f(x) = 2e^x + x^2$

**3.** $f(x) = x^3 + 3^x$

**4.** $y = 5t^2 + 4e^t$

**5.** $y = 5 \cdot 5^t + 6 \cdot 6^t$

**6.** $y = 2^x + \dfrac{2}{x^3}$

**7.** $y = 4 \cdot 10^x - x^3$

**8.** $f(x) = 2^x + 2 \cdot 3^x$

**9.** $y = 5 \cdot 2^x - 5x + 4$

**10.** $y = 3x - 2 \cdot 4^x$

**11.** $y = e^{0.7t}$

**12.** $f(t) = e^{3t}$

**13.** $P = e^{-0.2t}$

**14.** $y = e^{-4t}$

**15.** $P = 200e^{0.12t}$

**16.** $P = 50e^{-0.6t}$

**17.** $P(t) = 12.41(0.94)^t$

**18.** $P(t) = 3000(1.02)^t$

**19.** $y = B + Ae^t$

**20.** $P(t) = Ce^t.$

**21.** $y = 10^x + \dfrac{10}{x}$

**22.** $f(x) = Ae^x - Bx^2 + C$

**23.** $D = 10 - \ln p$

**24.** $R = 3 \ln q$

**25.** $R(q) = q^2 - 2 \ln q$

**26.** $y = t^2 + 5 \ln t$

**27.** $f(t) = Ae^t + B \ln t$

**28.** $y = x^2 + 4x - 3 \ln x$

In Problems 29–34, find the relative rate of change, $f'(t)/f(t)$, of the function $f(t)$.

**29.** $f(t) = 15t + 12$

**30.** $f(t) = 10t + 5$

**31.** $f(t) = 30e^{-7t}$

**32.** $f(t) = 8e^{5t}$

**33.** $f(t) = 35t^{-4}$

**34.** $f(t) = 6t^2$

**35.** For $f(t) = 4 - 2e^t$, find $f'(-1)$, $f'(0)$, and $f'(1)$. Graph $f(t)$, and draw tangent lines at $t = -1$, $t = 0$, and $t = 1$. Do the slopes of the lines match the derivatives you found?

**36.** Find the equation of the tangent line to the graph of $y = 3^x$ at $x = 1$. Check your work by sketching a graph of the function and the tangent line on the same axes.

**37.** Find the equation of the tangent line to $y = e^{-2t}$ at $t = 0$. Check by sketching the graphs of $y = e^{-2t}$ and the tangent line on the same axes.

**38.** Find the equation of the tangent line to $f(x) = 10e^{-0.2x}$ at $x = 4$.

**39.** A fish population is approximated by $P(t) = 10e^{0.6t}$, where $t$ is in months. Calculate and use units to explain what each of the following tells us about the population:

    **(a)** $P(12)$         **(b)** $P'(12)$

**40.** The world's population[3] is about $f(t) = 6.91e^{0.011t}$ billion, where $t$ is time in years since 2010. Find $f(0)$, $f'(0)$, $f(10)$, and $f'(10)$. Using units, interpret your answers in terms of population.

**41.** The demand curve for a product is given by

$$q = f(p) = 10{,}000e^{-0.25p},$$

where $q$ is the quantity sold and $p$ is the price of the product, in dollars. Find $f(2)$ and $f'(2)$. Explain in economic terms what information each of these answers gives you.

**42.** The value of an automobile purchased in 2009 can be approximated by the function $V(t) = 25(0.85)^t$, where $t$ is the time, in years, from the date of purchase, and $V(t)$ is the value, in thousands of dollars.

    **(a)** Evaluate and interpret $V(4)$, including units.

    **(b)** Find an expression for $V'(t)$, including units.

    **(c)** Evaluate and interpret $V'(4)$, including units.

    **(d)** Use $V(t)$, $V'(t)$, and any other considerations you think are relevant to write a paragraph in support of or in opposition to the following statement: "From a monetary point of view, it is best to keep this vehicle as long as possible."

**43.** A new DVD is available for sale in a store one week after its release. The cumulative revenue, $\$R$, from sales of the DVD in this store in week $t$ after its release is

$$R = f(t) = 350 \ln t \quad \text{with} \quad t > 1.$$

Find $f(5)$, $f'(5)$, and the relative rate of change $f'/f$ at $t = 5$. Interpret your answers in terms of revenue.

**44.** In 2009, the population of Hungary[4] was approximated by

$$P = 9.906(0.997)^t,$$

where $P$ is in millions and $t$ is in years since 2009. Assume the trend continues.

    **(a)** What does this model predict for the population of Hungary in the year 2020?

    **(b)** How fast (in people/year) does this model predict Hungary's population will be decreasing in 2020?

**45.** With $t$ in years since January 1, 2010, the population $P$ of Slim Chance is predicted by

$$P = 35{,}000(0.98)^t.$$

At what rate will the population be changing on January 1, 2023?

**46.** With a yearly inflation rate of 5%, prices are given by

$$P = P_0(1.05)^t,$$

where $P_0$ is the price in dollars when $t = 0$ and $t$ is time in years. Suppose $P_0 = 1$. How fast (in cents/year) are prices rising when $t = 10$?

**47.** Find the value of $c$ in Figure 3.16, where the line $l$ tangent to the graph of $y = 2^x$ at $(0, 1)$ intersects the $x$-axis.

**Figure 3.16**

**48.** At a time $t$ hours after it was administered, the concentration of a drug in the body is $f(t) = 27e^{-0.14t}$ ng/ml. What is the concentration 4 hours after it was administered? At what rate is the concentration changing at that time?

**49.** The cost of producing a quantity, $q$, of a product is given by

$$C(q) = 1000 + 30e^{0.05q} \quad \text{dollars.}$$

Find the cost and the marginal cost when $q = 50$. Interpret these answers in economic terms.

---

[3]http://www.indexmundi.com/world/. Accessed April 27, 2011.
[4]https://www.cia.gov/library/publications/the-world-factbook/print/hu.html, accessed April 14, 2009.

**50.** Carbon-14 is a radioactive isotope used to date objects. If $A_0$ represents the initial amount of carbon-14 in the object, then the quantity remaining at time $t$, in years, is

$$A(t) = A_0 e^{-0.000121t}.$$

(a) A tree, originally containing 185 micrograms of carbon-14, is now 500 years old. At what rate is the carbon-14 decaying now?

(b) In 1988, scientists found that the Shroud of Turin, which was reputed to be the burial cloth of Jesus, contained 91% of the amount of carbon-14 in freshly made cloth of the same material.[5] According to this data, how old was the Shroud of Turin in 1988?

**51.** For the cost function $C = 1000 + 300 \ln q$ (in dollars), find the cost and the marginal cost at a production level of 500. Interpret your answers in economic terms.

**52.** In 2009, the population of Mexico was 111 million and growing 1.13% annually, while the population of the US was 307 million and growing 0.975% annually.[6] If we measure growth rates in people/year, which population was growing faster in 2009?

**53.** In 2009, the population, $P$, of India was 1.166 billion and growing at 1.5% annually.[7]

(a) Give a formula for $P$ in terms of time, $t$, measured in years since 2009.

(b) Find $\dfrac{dP}{dt}$, $\dfrac{dP}{dt}\bigg|_{t=0}$, and $\dfrac{dP}{dt}\bigg|_{t=25}$. What do each of these represent in practical terms?

**54.** (a) Find the equation of the tangent line to $y = \ln x$ at $x = 1$.

(b) Use it to calculate approximate values for $\ln(1.1)$ and $\ln(2)$.

(c) Using a graph, explain whether the approximate values are smaller or larger than the true values. Would the same result have held if you had used the tangent line to estimate $\ln(0.9)$ and $\ln(0.5)$? Why?

**55.** Find the quadratic polynomial $g(x) = ax^2 + bx + c$ which best fits the function $f(x) = e^x$ at $x = 0$, in the sense that

$$g(0) = f(0), \text{ and } g'(0) = f'(0), \text{ and } g''(0) = f''(0).$$

Using a computer or calculator, sketch graphs of $f$ and $g$ on the same axes. What do you notice?

# 3.3  THE CHAIN RULE

We now see how to differentiate composite functions such as $f(t) = \ln(3t)$ and $g(x) = e^{-x^2}$.

## The Derivative of a Composition of Functions

Suppose $y = f(z)$ with $z = g(t)$ for some inside function $g$ and outside function $f$, where $f$ and $g$ are differentiable. A small change in $t$, called $\Delta t$, generates a small change in $z$, called $\Delta z$. In turn, $\Delta z$ generates a small change in $y$, called $\Delta y$. Provided $\Delta t$ and $\Delta z$ are not zero, we can say

$$\frac{\Delta y}{\Delta t} = \frac{\Delta y}{\Delta z} \cdot \frac{\Delta z}{\Delta t}.$$

Since the derivative $\dfrac{dy}{dt}$ is the limit of the quotient $\dfrac{\Delta y}{\Delta t}$ as $\Delta t$ gets smaller and smaller, this suggests

---

**The Chain Rule**

If $y = f(z)$ and $z = g(t)$ are differentiable, then the derivative of $y = f(g(t))$ is given by

$$\frac{dy}{dt} = \frac{dy}{dz} \cdot \frac{dz}{dt}.$$

In words, the derivative of a composite function is the derivative of the outside function times the derivative of the inside function:

$$\frac{d}{dt}(f(g(t))) = f'(g(t)) \cdot g'(t).$$

---

[5] The New York Times, October 18, 1988.

[6] https://www.cia.gov/library/publications/the-world-factbook/print/ms.html and https://www.cia.gov/library/publications/the-world-factbook/print/us.html, accessed April 14, 2009.

[7] https://www.cia.gov/library/publications/the-world-factbook/print/in.html, accessed April 14, 2009.

The following example shows us how to interpret the chain rule in practical terms.

**Example 1**    The amount of gas, $G$, in gallons, consumed by a car depends on the distance traveled, $s$, in miles, and $s$ depends on the time, $t$, in hours. If 0.05 gallons of gas are consumed for each mile traveled, and the car is traveling at 30 miles/hr, how fast is gas being consumed? Give units.

Solution    We expect the rate of gas consumption to be in gallons/hr. We are told that

$$\text{Rate gas is consumed with respect to distance} = \frac{dG}{ds} = 0.05 \text{ gallons/mile}$$

$$\text{Rate distance is increasing with respect to time} = \frac{ds}{dt} = 30 \text{ miles/hr.}$$

We want to calculate the rate at which gas is being consumed with respect to time, or $dG/dt$. We think of $G$ as a function of $s$, and $s$ as a function of $t$. By the chain rule we know that

$$\frac{dG}{dt} = \frac{dG}{ds} \cdot \frac{ds}{dt} = \left(0.05 \frac{\text{gallons}}{\text{mile}}\right) \cdot \left(30 \frac{\text{miles}}{\text{hour}}\right) = 1.5 \text{ gallons/hour.}$$

Thus, gas is being consumed at a rate of 1.5 gallons/hour.

## The Chain Rule for Functions Given by Formulas

In order to use the chain rule to differentiate a composite function, we first rewrite the function using a new variable $z$ to represent the inside function:

$$y = (t+1)^4 \quad \text{is the same as} \quad y = z^4 \quad \text{where} \quad z = t+1.$$

**Example 2**    Use a new variable $z$ for the inside function to express each of the following as a composite function:
(a)  $y = \ln(3t)$      (b)  $P = e^{-0.03t}$      (c)  $w = 5(2r+3)^2.$

Solution    (a) The inside function is $3t$, so we have $y = \ln z$ with $z = 3t$.
(b) The inside function is $-0.03t$, so we have $P = e^z$ with $z = -0.03t$.
(c) The inside function is $2r+3$, so we have $w = 5z^2$ with $z = 2r+3$.

**Example 3**    Find the derivative of the following functions:  (a)  $y = (4t^2+1)^7$      (b)  $P = e^{3t}.$

Solution    (a) Here $z = 4t^2+1$ is the inside function; $y = z^7$ is the outside function. Since $dy/dz = 7z^6$ and $dz/dt = 8t$, we have

$$\frac{dy}{dt} = \frac{dy}{dz} \cdot \frac{dz}{dt} = (7z^6)(8t) = 7(4t^2+1)^6(8t) = 56t(4t^2+1)^6.$$

(b) Let $z = 3t$ and $P = e^z$. Then $dP/dz = e^z$ and $dz/dt = 3$, so

$$\frac{dP}{dt} = \frac{dP}{dz} \cdot \frac{dz}{dt} = e^z \cdot 3 = e^{3t} \cdot 3 = 3e^{3t}.$$

Notice that the derivative formula for $e^{kt}$ introduced in Section 3.2 is just a special case of the chain rule.

The derivative rules give us

$$\frac{d}{dt}(t^n) = nt^{n-1} \qquad \frac{d}{dt}(e^t) = e^t \qquad \frac{d}{dt}(\ln t) = \frac{1}{t}.$$

Using the chain rule in addition, we have the following results.

If $z$ is a differentiable function of $t$, then

$$\frac{d}{dt}(z^n) = nz^{n-1}\frac{dz}{dt}, \qquad \frac{d}{dt}(e^z) = e^z\frac{dz}{dt}, \qquad \frac{d}{dt}(\ln z) = \frac{1}{z}\frac{dz}{dt}.$$

**Example 4**  Differentiate (a)  $(3t^3 - t)^5$  (b)  $\ln(q^2 + 1)$  (c)  $e^{-x^2}$.

**Solution**  (a) Let $z = 3t^3 - t$, giving

$$\frac{d}{dt}(3t^3 - t)^5 = \frac{d}{dt}(z^5) = 5z^4\frac{dz}{dt} = 5(3t^3 - t)^4(9t^2 - 1).$$

(b) We have $z = q^2 + 1$, so

$$\frac{d}{dq}(\ln(q^2 + 1)) = \frac{d}{dq}(\ln z) = \frac{1}{z}\frac{dz}{dq} = \frac{1}{q^2 + 1}(2q).$$

(c) Taking $z = -x^2$, the derivative is

$$\frac{d}{dx}(e^{-x^2}) = \frac{d}{dx}(e^z) = e^z\frac{dz}{dx} = e^{-x^2}(-2x) = -2xe^{-x^2}.$$

As we see in the following example, it is often faster to use the chain rule without introducing the new variable, $z$.

**Example 5**  Differentiate
(a)  $(x^2 + 4)^3$  (b)  $5\ln(2t^2 + 3)$  (c)  $\sqrt{1 + 2e^{5t}}$

**Solution**  (a) We have

$$\begin{aligned}
\frac{d}{dx}\left((x^2 + 4)^3\right) &= 3(x^2 + 4)^2 \cdot \frac{d}{dx}(x^2 + 4) \\
&= 3(x^2 + 4)^2 \cdot 2x \\
&= 6x(x^2 + 4)^2.
\end{aligned}$$

(b) We have

$$\begin{aligned}
\frac{d}{dt}\left(5\ln(2t^2 + 3)\right) &= 5 \cdot \frac{1}{2t^2 + 3} \cdot \frac{d}{dt}(2t^2 + 3) \\
&= 5 \cdot \frac{1}{2t^2 + 3} \cdot 4t \\
&= \frac{20t}{2t^2 + 3}.
\end{aligned}$$

(c) Here we use the chain rule twice, giving

$$\begin{aligned}
\frac{d}{dt}\left((1 + 2e^{5t})^{1/2}\right) &= \frac{1}{2}(1 + 2e^{5t})^{-1/2} \cdot \frac{d}{dt}(1 + 2e^{5t}) \\
&= \frac{1}{2}(1 + 2e^{5t})^{-1/2} \cdot 2e^{5t} \cdot \frac{d}{dt}(5t) \\
&= \frac{1}{2}(1 + 2e^{5t})^{-1/2} \cdot 2e^{5t} \cdot 5 \\
&= \frac{5e^{5t}}{\sqrt{1 + 2e^{5t}}}.
\end{aligned}$$

**Example 6**    Let $h(x) = f(g(x))$ and $k(x) = g(f(x))$. Evaluate    (a) $h'(1)$  (b) $k'(1)$    given that

$$f(1) = 1, \quad f'(0) = 0, \quad f'(1) = 3, \quad g(1) = 0, \quad g'(1) = 1.$$

Solution    (a) The chain rule tells us that $h'(x) = f'(g(x)) \cdot g'(x)$, so

$$h'(1) = f'(g(1)) \cdot g'(1)$$
$$= f'(0) \cdot g'(1)$$
$$= 0 \cdot 1$$
$$= 0.$$

(b) The chain rule tells us that $k'(x) = g'(f(x)) \cdot f'(x)$, so

$$k'(1) = g'(f(1)) \cdot f'(1)$$
$$= g'(1) \cdot f'(1)$$
$$= 1 \cdot 3$$
$$= 3.$$

**Example 7**    Let $h(x) = f(g(x))$ and $k(x) = g(f(x))$. Use Figure 3.17 to estimate:    (a) $h'(1)$    (b) $k'(2)$

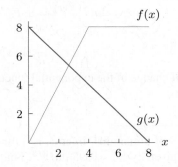

**Figure 3.17**: Graphs of $f$ and $g$ for Example 7

Solution    (a) The chain rule tells us that $h'(x) = f'(g(x)) \cdot g'(x)$, so

$$h'(1) = f'(g(1)) \cdot g'(1)$$
$$= f'(7) \cdot g'(1)$$
$$= 0 \cdot (-1)$$
$$= 0.$$

We use the slopes of the lines in Figure 3.17 to find the derivatives $f'(7) = 0$ and $g'(1) = -1$.

(b) The chain rule tells us that $k'(x) = g'(f(x)) \cdot f'(x)$, so

$$k'(2) = g'(f(2)) \cdot f'(2)$$
$$= g'(4) \cdot f'(2)$$
$$= (-1) \cdot 2$$
$$= -2.$$

We use slopes to compute the derivatives $g'(4) = -1$ and $f'(2) = 2$.

## Relative Rates and Logarithms

In Section 2.3 we defined the relative rate of change of a function $z = f(t)$ to be

$$\text{Relative rate of change} = \frac{f'(t)}{f(t)} = \frac{1}{z}\frac{dz}{dt}.$$

Since

$$\frac{d}{dt}(\ln z) = \frac{1}{z}\frac{dz}{dt},$$

we have the following result:

For any positive function $f(t)$,

$$\begin{array}{l}\text{Relative rate of change}\\ \text{of } f(t)\end{array} = \frac{d}{dt}(\ln f(t)).$$

Just as linear functions have constant rates of change, in the following example we see that exponential functions have constant relative rates of change.

**Example 8**    Find the relative rate of change of the exponential function $z = P_0 e^{kt}$.

Solution    Since

$$\ln z = \ln(P_0 e^{kt}) = \ln P_0 + \ln(e^{kt}) = \ln P_0 + kt,$$

we have

$$\frac{d}{dt}(\ln z) = k.$$

The relative rate of change of the exponential function $P_0 e^{kt}$ is the constant $k$.

**Example 9**    The surface area $S$ of a mammal, in $\text{cm}^2$, is a function of the body mass, $M$, of the mammal, in kilograms, and is given by $S = 1095 \cdot M^{2/3}$. Find the relative rate of change of $S$ with respect to $M$ and evaluate for a human with body mass 70 kilograms. Interpret your answer.

Solution    We have

$$\ln S = \ln(1095 \cdot M^{2/3}) = \ln(1095) + \ln(M^{2/3}) = \ln(1095) + \frac{2}{3}\ln M.$$

Thus,

$$\begin{aligned}\text{Relative rate of change} &= \frac{d}{dM}(\ln S)\\ &= \frac{d}{dM}\left(\ln(1095) + \frac{2}{3}\ln M\right)\\ &= \frac{2}{3}\cdot\frac{1}{M}.\end{aligned}$$

For a human with body mass $M = 70$ kilograms, we have

$$\text{Relative rate} = \frac{2}{3}\frac{1}{70} = 0.0095 = 0.95\% \text{ per kg}.$$

The surface area of a human with body mass 70 kilograms increases by about 0.95% if body mass increases by 1 kilogram.

## Problems for Section 3.3

Find the derivative of the functions in Problems 1–27.

**1.** $f(x) = (x+1)^{99}$     **2.** $g(x) = (4x^2+1)^7$

**3.** $w = (t^2+1)^{100}$     **4.** $R = (q^2+1)^4$

**5.** $w = (5r-6)^3$     **6.** $f(x) = (x^3+x^2)^{-90}$

**7.** $y = 12 - 3x^2 + 2e^{3x}$     **8.** $y = \sqrt{s^3+1}$

**9.** $f(x) = 6e^{5x} + e^{-x^2}$     **10.** $C = 12(3q^2-5)^3$

**11.** $w = e^{-3t^2}$     **12.** $y = 5e^{5t+1}$

**13.** $y = \ln(5t+1)$     **14.** $w = e^{\sqrt{s}}$

**15.** $f(t) = \ln(t^2+1)$     **16.** $f(x) = \ln(1-x)$

**17.** $f(x) = \ln(e^x+1)$     **18.** $f(x) = \ln(1-e^{-x})$

**19.** $f(x) = \ln(\ln x)$     **20.** $f(x) = (\ln x)^3$

**21.** $y = 5 + \ln(3t+2)$     **22.** $y = (5+e^x)^2$

**23.** $y = 5x + \ln(x+2)$     **24.** $y = \sqrt{e^x+1}$

**25.** $P = (1+\ln x)^{0.5}$     **26.** $f(\theta) = (e^\theta + e^{-\theta})^{-1}$

**27.** $f(x) = \sqrt{2+\sqrt{x}}$

In Problems 28–29, find the relative rate of change $f'(t)/f(t)$ at the given value of $t$. Assume $t$ is in years and give your answer as a percent.

**28.** $f(t) = 2e^{0.3t}; \quad t = 7$

**29.** $f(t) = \ln(t^2+1); \quad t = 2$

In Problems 30–33, find the relative rate of change of $f(t)$ using the formula $\frac{d}{dt} \ln f(t)$.

**30.** $f(t) = 6.8e^{-0.5t}$     **31.** $f(t) = 5e^{1.5t}$

**32.** $f(t) = 4.5t^{-4}$     **33.** $f(t) = 3t^2$

**34.** Find the equation of the tangent line to $f(x) = (x-1)^3$ at the point where $x = 2$.

**35.** If you invest $P$ dollars in a bank account at an annual interest rate of $r\%$, then after $t$ years you will have $B$ dollars, where

$$B = P\left(1 + \frac{r}{100}\right)^t.$$

**(a)** Find $dB/dt$, assuming $P$ and $r$ are constant. In terms of money, what does $dB/dt$ represent?

**(b)** Find $dB/dr$, assuming $P$ and $t$ are constant. In terms of money, what does $dB/dr$ represent?

**36.** A firm estimates that the total revenue, $R$, received from the sale of $q$ goods is given by

$$R = \ln(1 + 1000q^2).$$

Calculate the marginal revenue when $q = 10$.

**37.** The distance, $s$, of a moving body from a fixed point is given as a function of time by $s = 20e^{t/2}$. Find the velocity, $v$, of the body as a function of $t$.

**38.** The distance traveled, $D$ in feet, is a function of time, $t$, in seconds, with $D = f(t) = \sqrt{t^3+1}$. Find $f(10)$, $f'(10)$, and the relative rate of change $f'/f$ at $t = 10$. Interpret your answers in terms of distance traveled.

For Problems 39–42, let $h(x) = f(g(x))$ and $k(x) = g(f(x))$. Use Figure 3.18 to estimate the derivatives.

**Figure 3.18**

**39.** $h'(1)$     **40.** $k'(1)$

**41.** $h'(2)$     **42.** $k'(2)$

In Problems 43–48, use Figure 3.19 to evaluate the derivative.

**Figure 3.19**

**43.** $\frac{d}{dx} f(g(x))|_{x=30}$     **44.** $\frac{d}{dx} f(g(x))|_{x=70}$

**45.** $\frac{d}{dx} g(f(x))|_{x=30}$     **46.** $\frac{d}{dx} g(f(x))|_{x=70}$

**47.** $\frac{d}{dx} f(g(x))|_{x=20}$     **48.** $\frac{d}{dx} g(f(x))|_{x=60}$

**49.** Given $y = f(x)$ with $f(1) = 4$ and $f'(1) = 3$, find

    **(a)** $g'(1)$ if $g(x) = \sqrt{f(x)}$.
    **(b)** $h'(1)$ if $h(x) = f(\sqrt{x})$.

**50.** Some economists suggest that an extra year of education increases a person's wages, on average, by about 14%. Assume you could make $10 per hour with your current level of education and that inflation increases wages at a continuous rate of 3.5% per year.

    **(a)** How much would you make per hour with four ad-

ditional years of education?

    **(b)** What is the difference between your wages in 20 years' time with and without the additional four years of education?

    **(c)** Is the difference you found in part (b) increasing with time? If so, at what rate? (Assume the number of additional years of education stays fixed at four.)

**51.** Show that if the graphs of $f(t)$ and $h(t) = Ae^{kt}$ are tangent at $t = a$, then $k$ is the relative rate of change of $f$ at $t = a$.

## 3.4  THE PRODUCT AND QUOTIENT RULES

This section shows how to find the derivatives of products and quotients of functions.

### The Product Rule

Suppose we know the derivatives of $f(x)$ and $g(x)$ and want to calculate the derivative of the product, $f(x)g(x)$. We start by looking at an example. Let $f(x) = x$ and $g(x) = x^2$. Then

$$f(x)g(x) = x \cdot x^2 = x^3,$$

so the derivative of the product is $3x^2$. Notice that the derivative of the product is *not* equal to the product of the derivatives, since $f'(x) = 1$ and $g'(x) = 2x$, so $f'(x)g'(x) = (1)(2x) = 2x$. In general, we have the following rule, which is justified in the Focus on Theory section at the end of this chapter.

---

**The Product Rule**

If $u = f(x)$ and $v = g(x)$ are differentiable functions, then

$$(fg)' = f'g + fg'.$$

The product rule can also be written

$$\frac{d(uv)}{dx} = \frac{du}{dx} \cdot v + u \cdot \frac{dv}{dx}.$$

In words:
    The derivative of a product is the derivative of the first times the second, plus the first times the derivative of the second.

---

We check that this rule gives the correct answers for $f(x) = x$ and $g(x) = x^2$. The derivative of $f(x)g(x)$ is

$$f'(x)g(x) + f(x)g'(x) = 1(x^2) + x(2x) = x^2 + 2x^2 = 3x^2.$$

This is the answer we expect for the derivative of $f(x)g(x) = x \cdot x^2 = x^3$.

---

**Example 1**    Differentiate (a) $x^2 e^{2x}$    (b) $t^3 \ln(t+1)$    (c) $(3x^2 + 5x)e^x$.

Solution        (a)  Using the product rule, we have

$$\frac{d}{dx}(x^2 e^{2x}) = \frac{d}{dx}(x^2) \cdot e^{2x} + x^2 \frac{d}{dx}(e^{2x})$$
$$= (2x)e^{2x} + x^2(2e^{2x})$$
$$= 2xe^{2x} + 2x^2 e^{2x}.$$

(b)  Differentiating using the product rule gives

$$\frac{d}{dt}(t^3 \ln(t+1)) = \frac{d}{dt}(t^3) \cdot \ln(t+1) + t^3 \frac{d}{dt}(\ln(t+1))$$
$$= (3t^2)\ln(t+1) + t^3 \left(\frac{1}{t+1}\right)$$
$$= 3t^2 \ln(t+1) + \frac{t^3}{t+1}.$$

(c)  The product rule gives

$$\frac{d}{dx}((3x^2 + 5x)e^x) = \left(\frac{d}{dx}(3x^2 + 5x)\right)e^x + (3x^2 + 5x)\frac{d}{dx}(e^x)$$
$$= (6x + 5)e^x + (3x^2 + 5x)e^x$$
$$= (3x^2 + 11x + 5)e^x.$$

**Example 2**   Find the derivative of $C = \dfrac{e^{2t}}{t}$.

Solution       We write $C = e^{2t}t^{-1}$ and use the product rule:

$$\frac{d}{dt}(e^{2t}t^{-1}) = \frac{d}{dt}(e^{2t}) \cdot t^{-1} + e^{2t}\frac{d}{dt}(t^{-1})$$
$$= (2e^{2t}) \cdot t^{-1} + e^{2t}(-1)t^{-2}$$
$$= \frac{2e^{2t}}{t} - \frac{e^{2t}}{t^2}.$$

**Example 3**   A demand curve for a product has the equation $p = 80e^{-0.003q}$, where $p$ is price and $q$ is quantity sold.

(a)  Find the revenue as a function of quantity sold.
(b)  Find the marginal revenue function.

Solution       (a)  Since Revenue = Price × Quantity, we have $R = pq = (80e^{-0.003q})q = 80qe^{-0.003q}$.
(b)  The marginal revenue function is the derivative of revenue with respect to quantity. The product rule gives

$$\text{Marginal Revenue} = \frac{d}{dq}(80qe^{-0.003q})$$
$$= \left(\frac{d}{dq}(80q)\right)e^{-0.003q} + 80q\left(\frac{d}{dq}(e^{-0.003q})\right)$$
$$= (80)e^{-0.003q} + 80q(-0.003e^{-0.003q})$$
$$= (80 - 0.24q)e^{-0.003q}.$$

## The Quotient Rule

Suppose we want to differentiate a function of the form $Q(x) = f(x)/g(x)$. (Of course, we have to avoid points where $g(x) = 0$.) We want a formula for $Q'$ in terms of $f'$ and $g'$. We have the following rule, which is justified in the Focus on Theory section at the end of this chapter.

---

### The Quotient Rule

If $u = f(x)$ and $v = g(x)$ are differentiable functions, then

$$\left(\frac{f}{g}\right)' = \frac{f'g - fg'}{g^2},$$

or equivalently,

$$\frac{d}{dx}\left(\frac{u}{v}\right) = \frac{\frac{du}{dx}\cdot v - u\cdot\frac{dv}{dx}}{v^2}.$$

In words:

The derivative of a quotient is the derivative of the numerator times the denominator minus the numerator times the derivative of the denominator, all over the denominator squared.

---

**Example 4**    Differentiate  (a) $\dfrac{5x^2}{x^3 + 1}$    (b) $\dfrac{1}{1 + e^x}$    (c) $\dfrac{e^x}{x^2}$.

**Solution**    (a) Using the quotient rule

$$\frac{d}{dx}\left(\frac{5x^2}{x^3 + 1}\right) = \frac{\left(\frac{d}{dx}(5x^2)\right)(x^3 + 1) - 5x^2\frac{d}{dx}(x^3 + 1)}{(x^3 + 1)^2} = \frac{10x(x^3 + 1) - 5x^2(3x^2)}{(x^3 + 1)^2}$$

$$= \frac{-5x^4 + 10x}{(x^3 + 1)^2}.$$

(b) Differentiating using the quotient rule yields

$$\frac{d}{dx}\left(\frac{1}{1 + e^x}\right) = \frac{\left(\frac{d}{dx}(1)\right)(1 + e^x) - 1\frac{d}{dx}(1 + e^x)}{(1 + e^x)^2} = \frac{0(1 + e^x) - 1(0 + e^x)}{(1 + e^x)^2}$$

$$= \frac{-e^x}{(1 + e^x)^2}.$$

(c) The quotient rule gives

$$\frac{d}{dx}\left(\frac{e^x}{x^2}\right) = \frac{\left(\frac{d}{dx}(e^x)\right)x^2 - e^x\left(\frac{d}{dx}(x^2)\right)}{(x^2)^2} = \frac{e^x x^2 - e^x(2x)}{x^4}$$

$$= e^x\left(\frac{x^2 - 2x}{x^4}\right) = e^x\left(\frac{x - 2}{x^3}\right).$$

**Example 5**    If $f(2) = 1$, $f'(2) = 5$, $g(2) = 3$ and $g'(2) = 6$, find

(a)  $h'(2)$ if $h(x) = f(x)g(x)$

(b)  $k'(2)$ if $k(x) = f(x)/g(x)$.

Solution    (a)  Differentiating using the product rule yields

$$h'(x) = f'(x)g(x) + f(x)g'(x),$$

so

$$h'(2) = f'(2)g(2) + f(2)g'(2) = 5 \cdot 3 + 1 \cdot 6 = 21.$$

(b)  Differentiating using the quotient rule yields

$$k'(x) = \frac{f'(x)g(x) - f(x)g'(x)}{[g(x)]^2},$$

so

$$k'(2) = \frac{f'(2)g(2) - f(2)g'(2)}{[g(2)]^2} = \frac{5 \cdot 3 - 1 \cdot 6}{3^2} = 1.$$

**Example 6**    Let $h(x) = f(x)g(x)$ and $k(x) = f(x)/g(x)$. Use Figure 3.20 to estimate:    (a) $h'(2)$    (b) $k'(6)$

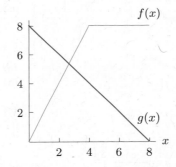

Figure 3.20: Graphs of $f$ and $g$ for Example 6

Solution    (a)  The product rule tells us that $h'(x) = f'(x)g(x) + f(x)g'(x)$, so

$$h'(2) = f'(2)g(2) + f(2)g'(2)$$
$$= 2 \cdot 6 + 4 \cdot (-1)$$
$$= 8.$$

We use the slopes of the lines in Figure 3.20 to find the derivatives $f'(2) = 2$ and $g'(2) = -1$.

(b)  The quotient rule tells us that $k'(x) = (f'(x)g(x) - f(x)g'(x))/[g(x)]^2$, so

$$k'(6) = \frac{f'(6)g(6) - f(6)g'(6)}{[g(6)]^2}$$
$$= \frac{0 \cdot 2 - 8 \cdot (-1)}{2^2}$$
$$= 2.$$

We use slopes to compute the derivatives $f'(6) = 0$ and $g'(6) = -1$.

## Problems for Section 3.4

1. If $f(x) = x^2(x^3 + 5)$, find $f'(x)$ two ways: by using the product rule and by multiplying out before taking the derivative. Do you get the same result? Should you?

2. If $f(x) = (2x + 1)(3x - 2)$, find $f'(x)$ two ways: by using the product rule and by multiplying out. Do you get the same result?

For Problems 3–32, find the derivative. Assume that $a$, $b$, $c$, and $k$ are constants.

3. $f(t) = te^{-2t}$

4. $f(x) = xe^x$

5. $y = t^2(3t + 1)^3$

6. $y = 5xe^{x^2}$

7. $y = x \ln x$

8. $y = (t^2 + 3)e^t$

9. $y = (t^3 - 7t^2 + 1)e^t$

10. $z = (3t + 1)(5t + 2)$

11. $R = 3qe^{-q}$

12. $P = t^2 \ln t$

13. $f(x) = \dfrac{x^2 + 3}{x}$

14. $f(z) = \sqrt{z}e^{-z}$

15. $y = te^{-t^2}$

16. $f(t) = te^{5-2t}$

17. $g(p) = p \ln(2p + 1)$

18. $y = x \cdot 2^x$

19. $f(w) = (5w^2 + 3)e^{w^2}$

20. $w = (t^3 + 5t)(t^2 - 7t + 2)$

21. $z = (te^{3t} + e^{5t})^9$

22. $f(x) = \dfrac{x}{e^x}$

23. $z = \dfrac{1 - t}{1 + t}$

24. $w = \dfrac{3z}{1 + 2z}$

25. $w = \dfrac{3y + y^2}{5 + y}$

26. $y = \dfrac{e^x}{1 + e^x}$

27. $f(x) = \dfrac{ax + b}{cx + k}$

28. $y = \dfrac{1 + z}{\ln z}$

29. $f(x) = axe^{-bx}$

30. $f(x) = (ax^2 + b)^3$

31. $g(\alpha) = e^{\alpha e^{-2\alpha}}$

32. $f(t) = ae^{bt}$

33. If $f(x) = (3x + 8)(2x - 5)$, find $f'(x)$ and $f''(x)$.

34. Find the equation of the tangent line to the graph of $f(x) = \dfrac{2x - 5}{x + 1}$ at the point at which $x = 0$.

35. Find the equation of the tangent line to the graph of $f(x) = x^2 e^{-x}$ at $x = 0$. Check by graphing this function and the tangent line on the same axes.

36. The quantity of a drug, $Q$ mg, present in the body $t$ hours after an injection of the drug is given is
$$Q = f(t) = 100te^{-0.5t}.$$
Find $f(1)$, $f'(1)$, $f(5)$, and $f'(5)$. Give units and interpret the answers.

37. A drug concentration curve is given by $C = f(t) = 20te^{-0.04t}$, with $C$ in mg/ml and $t$ in minutes.

   (a) Graph $C$ against $t$. Is $f'(15)$ positive or negative? Is $f'(45)$ positive or negative? Explain.
   (b) Find $f(30)$ and $f'(30)$ analytically. Interpret them in terms of the concentration of the drug in the body.

38. If $p$ is price in dollars and $q$ is quantity, demand for a product is given by
$$q = 5000e^{-0.08p}.$$

   (a) What quantity is sold at a price of $10?
   (b) Find the derivative of demand with respect to price when the price is $10 and interpret your answer in terms of demand.

39. The demand for a product is given in Problem 38. Find the revenue and the derivative of revenue with respect to price at a price of $10. Interpret your answers in economic terms.

40. The quantity demanded of a certain product, $q$, is given in terms of $p$, the price, by
$$q = 1000e^{-0.02p}$$

   (a) Write revenue, $R$, as a function of price.
   (b) Find the rate of change of revenue with respect to price.
   (c) Find the revenue and rate of change of revenue with respect to price when the price is $10. Interpret your answers in economic terms.

41. If $\dfrac{d}{dt}(tf(t)) = 1 + f(t)$, what is $f'(t)$?

42. The quantity, $q$, of a certain skateboard sold depends on the selling price, $p$, in dollars, so we write $q = f(p)$. You are given that $f(140) = 15{,}000$ and $f'(140) = -100$.

   (a) What do $f(140) = 15{,}000$ and $f'(140) = -100$ tell you about the sales of skateboards?
   (b) The total revenue, $R$, earned by the sale of skateboards is given by $R = pq$. Find $\left.\dfrac{dR}{dp}\right|_{p=140}$.
   (c) What is the sign of $\left.\dfrac{dR}{dp}\right|_{p=140}$? If the skateboards are currently selling for $140, what happens to revenue if the price is increased to $141?

43. Show that the relative rate of change of a product $fg$ is the sum of the relative rates of change of $f$ and $g$.

44. Show that the relative rate of change of a quotient $f/g$ is the difference between the relative rates of change of $f$ and $g$.

**45.** If $h = f^n$, show that

$$\frac{(f^n)'}{f^n} = n\frac{f'}{f}.$$

**46.** For positive constants $c$ and $k$, the *Monod growth curve* describes the growth of a population, $P$, as a function of the available quantity of a resource, $r$:

$$P = \frac{cr}{k+r}.$$

Find $dP/dr$ and interpret it in terms of the growth of the population.

**47.** If a someone is lost in the wilderness, the search and rescue team identifies the boundaries of the search area and then uses probabilities to help optimize the chances of finding the person, assuming the subject is immobile. The probability, $O$, of the person being outside the search area after the search has begun and the person has not been found, is given by

$$O(E) = \frac{I}{1 - (1-I)E},$$

where $I$ is the probability of the person being outside the search area at the start of the search and $E$ is the search effort, a measure of how well the search area has been covered by the resources in the field.

**(a)** If there was a 20% chance that the subject was not in the search area at the start of the search, and the search effort was 80%, what is the current probability of the person being outside the search area? (Probabilities are between 0 and 1, so 20% = 0.2 and 80% = 0.8.)

**(b)** In practical terms, what does $I = 1$ mean? Is this realistic?

**(c)** Evaluate $O'(E)$. Is it positive or negative? What does that tell you about $O$ as $E$ increases?

# 3.5 DERIVATIVES OF PERIODIC FUNCTIONS

Since the sine and cosine functions are periodic, their derivatives must be periodic also. (Why?) Let's look at the graph of $f(x) = \sin x$ in Figure 3.21 and estimate the derivative function graphically.

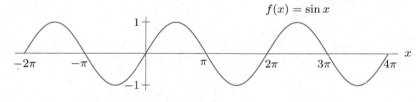

Figure 3.21: The sine function

First we might ask ourselves where the derivative is zero. (At $x = \pm\pi/2, \pm 3\pi/2, \pm 5\pi/2$, etc.) Then ask where the derivative is positive and where it is negative. (Positive for $-\pi/2 < x < \pi/2$; negative for $\pi/2 < x < 3\pi/2$, etc.) Since the largest positive slopes are at $x = 0, 2\pi$, and so on, and the largest negative slopes are at $x = \pi, 3\pi$, and so on, we get something like the graph in Figure 3.22.

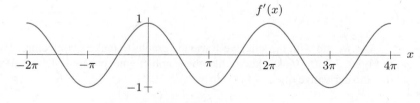

Figure 3.22: Derivative of $f(x) = \sin x$

The graph of the derivative in Figure 3.22 looks suspiciously like the graph of the cosine function. This might lead us to conjecture, quite correctly, that the derivative of the sine is the cosine. However, we cannot be sure just from the graphs.

One thing we can do is to check that the derivative function in Figure 3.22 has amplitude 1 (as it must if it is the cosine). That means we have to convince ourselves that the derivative of $f(x) = \sin x$ is 1 when $x = 0$. The next example suggests that this is true when $x$ is in radians.

**Example 1**    Using a calculator, estimate the derivative of $f(x) = \sin x$ at $x = 0$. Make sure your calculator is set in radians.

Solution    We use the average rate of change of $\sin x$ on the small interval $0 \le x \le 0.01$ to compute

$$f'(0) \approx \frac{\sin(0.01) - \sin(0)}{0.01 - 0} = \frac{0.0099998 - 0}{0.01} = 0.99998 \approx 1.0.$$

The derivative of $f(x) = \sin x$ at $x = 0$ is approximately 1.0.

**Warning:**  It is important to notice that in the previous example $x$ was in *radians*; any conclusions we have drawn about the derivative of $\sin x$ are valid *only* when $x$ is in radians.

**Example 2**    Starting with the graph of the cosine function, sketch a graph of its derivative.

Solution    The graph of $g(x) = \cos x$ is in Figure 3.23(a). Its derivative is 0 at $x = 0, \pm\pi, \pm 2\pi$, and so on; it is positive for $-\pi < x < 0$, $\pi < x < 2\pi$, and so on, and it is negative for $0 < x < \pi$, $2\pi < x < 3\pi$, and so on. The derivative is in Figure 3.23(b).

Figure 3.23: $g(x) = \cos x$ and its derivative, $g'(x)$

As we did with the sine, we'll use the graphs to make a conjecture. The derivative of the cosine in Figure 3.23(b) looks exactly like the graph of sine, except reflected about the $x$-axis. It turns out that the derivative of $\cos x$ is $-\sin x$.

For $x$ in radians,

$$\frac{d}{dx}(\sin x) = \cos x \quad \text{and} \quad \frac{d}{dx}(\cos x) = -\sin x.$$

**Example 3**    Differentiate (a)   $5 \sin t - 8 \cos t$        (b)   $5 - 3 \sin x + x^3$

Solution      (a) Differentiating gives

$$\frac{d}{dt}(5 \sin t - 8 \cos t) = 5 \frac{d}{dt}(\sin t) - 8 \frac{d}{dt}(\cos t) = 5(\cos t) - 8(-\sin t) = 5 \cos t + 8 \sin t.$$

(b) We have

$$\frac{d}{dx}(5 - 3 \sin x + x^3) = \frac{d}{dx}(5) - 3 \frac{d}{dx}(\sin x) + \frac{d}{dx}(x^3) = 0 - 3(\cos x) + 3x^2 = -3 \cos x + 3x^2.$$

The chain rule tells us how to differentiate composite functions involving the sine and cosine. Suppose $y = \sin(3t)$, so $y = \sin z$ and $z = 3t$, so

$$\frac{dy}{dt} = \frac{dy}{dz} \cdot \frac{dz}{dt} = \cos z \frac{dz}{dt} = \cos(3t) \cdot 3 = 3 \cos(3t).$$

In general,

> If $z$ is a differentiable function of $t$, then
>
> $$\frac{d}{dt}(\sin z) = \cos z \frac{dz}{dt} \quad \text{and} \quad \frac{d}{dt}(\cos z) = -\sin z \frac{dz}{dt}$$

In many applications, $z = kt$ for some constant $k$. Then we have:

> If $k$ is a constant, then
>
> $$\frac{d}{dt}(\sin kt) = k \cos kt \quad \text{and} \quad \frac{d}{dt}(\cos kt) = -k \sin kt$$

**Example 4**    Differentiate:
(a)   $\sin(t^2)$                (b)   $5 \cos(2t)$                (c)   $t \sin t.$

Solution      (a) We have $y = \sin z$ with $z = t^2$, so

$$\frac{d}{dt}(\sin(t^2)) = \frac{d}{dt}(\sin z) = \cos z \frac{dz}{dt} = \cos(t^2) \cdot 2t = 2t \cos(t^2).$$

(b) We have $y = 5 \cos z$ with $z = 2t$, so

$$\frac{d}{dt}(5 \cos(2t)) = 5 \frac{d}{dt}(\cos(2t)) = 5(-2 \sin(2t)) = -10 \sin(2t).$$

(c) We use the product rule:

$$\frac{d}{dt}(t \sin t) = \frac{d}{dt}(t) \cdot \sin t + t \frac{d}{dt}(\sin t) = 1 \cdot \sin t + t(\cos t) = \sin t + t \cos t.$$

## Problems for Section 3.5

Differentiate the functions in Problems 1–20. Assume that $A$ and $B$ are constants.

**1.** $P = 3 + \cos t$

**2.** $y = 5 \sin x$

**3.** $y = B + A \sin t$

**4.** $y = t^2 + 5 \cos t$

**5.** $y = 5 \sin x - 5x + 4$

**6.** $R(q) = q^2 - 2 \cos q$

**7.** $R = \sin(5t)$

**8.** $f(x) = \sin(3x)$

**9.** $y = 2 \cos(5t)$

**10.** $W = 4 \cos(t^2)$

**11.** $y = A \sin(Bt)$

**12.** $y = \sin(x^2)$

**13.** $y = 6 \sin(2t) + \cos(4t)$

**14.** $z = \cos(4\theta)$

**15.** $f(x) = 2x \sin(3x)$

**16.** $f(x) = x^2 \cos x$

**17.** $z = \dfrac{e^{t^2} + t}{\sin(2t)}$

**18.** $f(\theta) = \theta^3 \cos \theta$

**19.** $f(\theta) = \dfrac{\sin \theta}{\theta}$

**20.** $f(t) = \dfrac{t^2}{\cos t}$

**21.** Find the equation of the tangent line to the graph of $y = \sin x$ at $x = \pi$. Graph the function and the tangent line on the same axes.

**22.** Is the graph of $y = \sin(x^4)$ increasing or decreasing when $x = 10$? Is it concave up or concave down?

**23.** Find the equations of the tangent lines to the graph of $f(x) = \sin x$ at $x = 0$ and at $x = \pi/3$. Use each tangent line to approximate $\sin(\pi/6)$. Would you expect these results to be equally accurate, since they are taken equally far away from $x = \pi/6$ but on opposite sides? If the accuracy is different, can you account for the difference?

**24.** If $t$ is the number of months since June, the number of bird species, $N$, found in an Ohio forest oscillates approximately according to the formula

$$N = f(t) = 19 + 9 \cos\left(\frac{\pi}{6}t\right).$$

**(a)** Graph $f(t)$ for $0 \le t \le 24$ and describe what it shows. Use the graph to decide whether $f'(1)$ and $f'(10)$ are positive or negative.

**(b)** Find $f'(t)$.

**(c)** Find and interpret $f(1)$, $f'(1)$, $f(10)$, and $f'(10)$.

**25.** The average adult takes about 12 breaths per minute. As a patient inhales, the volume of air in the lung increases. As the patient exhales, the volume of air in the lung decreases. For $t$ in seconds since start of the breathing cycle, the volume of air inhaled or exhaled since $t = 0$ is given,[8] in hundreds of cubic centimeters, by

$$A(t) = -2 \cos\left(\frac{2\pi}{5}t\right) + 2.$$

**(a)** How long is one breathing cycle?

**(b)** Find $A'(1)$ and explain what it means.

**26.** A company's monthly sales, $S(t)$, are seasonal and given as a function of time, $t$, in months, by

$$S(t) = 2000 + 600 \sin\left(\frac{\pi}{6}t\right).$$

**(a)** Graph $S(t)$ for $t = 0$ to $t = 12$. What is the maximum monthly sales? What is the minimum monthly sales? If $t = 0$ is January 1, when during the year are sales highest?

**(b)** Find $S(2)$ and $S'(2)$. Interpret in terms of sales.

**27.** A boat at anchor is bobbing up and down in the sea. The vertical distance, $y$, in feet, between the sea floor and the boat is given as a function of time, $t$, in minutes, by

$$y = 15 + \sin(2\pi t).$$

**(a)** Find the vertical velocity, $v$, of the boat at time $t$.

**(b)** Make rough sketches of $y$ and $v$ against $t$.

**28.** The depth of the water, $y$, in meters, in the Bay of Fundy, Canada, is given as a function of time, $t$, in hours after midnight, by the function

$$y = 10 + 7.5 \cos(0.507t).$$

How quickly is the tide rising or falling (in meters/hour) at each of the following times?

**(a)**  6:00 am

**(b)**  9:00 am

**(c)**  Noon

**(d)**  6:00 pm

**29.** Paris, France, has a latitude of approximately $49°$ N. If $t$ is the number of days since the start of 2009, the number of hours of daylight in Paris can be approximated by

$$D(t) = 4 \cos\left(\frac{2\pi}{365}(t - 172)\right) + 12.$$

**(a)** Find $D(40)$ and $D'(40)$. Explain what this tells about daylight in Paris.

**(b)** Find $D(172)$ and $D'(172)$. Explain what this tells about daylight in Paris.

**30.** On July 7, 2009, there was a full moon in the Eastern time zone.[9] If $t$ is the number of days since July 7th, the percent of moon illuminated can be represented by

$$H(t) = 50 + 50 \cos\left(\frac{\pi}{15}t\right).$$

**(a)** Find $H'(t)$. Explain what this tells about the moon.

**(b)** For $0 \le t \le 30$, when is $H'(t) = 0$? What does this tell us about the moon?

**(c)** For $0 \le t \le 30$, when is $H'(t)$ negative? When is it positive? Explain what positive and negative values of $H'(t)$ tell us about the moon.

---

[8]Based upon information obtained from Dr. Gadi Avshalomov on August 14, 2008.

[9]www.aa.usno.navy.mil/feq/docs/moon_phases.php, accessed on April 14, 2009.

## CHAPTER SUMMARY

- **Derivatives of elementary functions**
  Powers, polynomials, exponential functions, logarithms, periodic functions
- **Derivatives of sums, differences, constant multiples**
- **Chain rule**

- **Product and quotient rules**
- **Relative rates of change**
  Using logarithms
- **Tangent line approximation**
- **Interpreting derivatives found using formulas**

## REVIEW PROBLEMS FOR CHAPTER THREE

Find the derivatives for the functions in Problems 1–40. Assume $k$ is a constant.

**1.** $f(t) = 6t^4$

**2.** $f(x) = x^3 - 3x^2 + 5x$

**3.** $P(t) = e^{2t}$

**4.** $W = r^3 + 5r - 12$

**5.** $C = e^{0.08q}$

**6.** $y = 5e^{-0.2t}$

**7.** $y = xe^{3x}$

**8.** $s(t) = (t^2 + 4)(5t - 1)$

**9.** $g(t) = e^{(1+3t)^2}$

**10.** $f(x) = x^2 + 3\ln x$

**11.** $Q(t) = 5t + 3e^{1.2t}$

**12.** $g(z) = (z^2 + 5)^3$

**13.** $f(x) = 6(5x - 1)^3$

**14.** $f(z) = \ln(z^2 + 1)$

**15.** $h(x) = (1 + e^x)^{10}$

**16.** $q = 100e^{-0.05p}$

**17.** $y = x^2 \ln x$

**18.** $s(t) = t^2 + 2\ln t$

**19.** $P = 4t^2 + 7\sin t$

**20.** $R(t) = (\sin t)^5$

**21.** $h(t) = \ln\left(e^{-t} - t\right)$

**22.** $f(x) = \sin(2x)$

**23.** $g(x) = \dfrac{25x^2}{e^x}$

**24.** $h(t) = \dfrac{t + 4}{t - 4}$

**25.** $y = x^2 \cos x$

**26.** $h(x) = \ln(1 + e^x)$

**27.** $h(w) = e^{\ln w + 1}$

**28.** $h(x) = \ln(x^3 + x)$

**29.** $q(x) = \dfrac{1 + e^x}{1 - e^{-x}}$

**30.** $q(x) = \dfrac{x}{1 + x}$

**31.** $f(x) = xe^x$

**32.** $h(x) = \sin(e^x)$

**33.** $h(x) = \cos(x^3)$

**34.** $z = \dfrac{3t + 1}{5t + 2}$

**35.** $z = \dfrac{t^2 + 5t + 2}{t + 3}$

**36.** $h(p) = \dfrac{1 + p^2}{3 + 2p^2}$

**37.** $y = \dfrac{3^x}{3} + \dfrac{33}{\sqrt{x}}$

**38.** $f(t) = \sin\sqrt{e^t + 1}$

**39.** $f(t) = \dfrac{7}{e^{kt}}$

**40.** $g(t) = \dfrac{\ln(kt) + t}{\ln(kt) - t}$

**41.** Let $f(x) = x^2 + 1$. Compute the derivatives $f'(0)$, $f'(1)$, $f'(2)$, and $f'(-1)$. Check your answers graphically.

**42.** Let $f(x) = x^2 + 3x - 5$. Find $f'(0)$, $f'(3)$, $f'(-2)$.

**43.** Find the equation of the line tangent to the graph of $f$ at $(1, 1)$, where $f$ is given by $f(x) = 2x^3 - 2x^2 + 1$.

**44.** Some antique furniture increased very rapidly in price over the past decade. For example, the price of a particular rocking chair is well approximated by

$$V = 75(1.35)^t,$$

where $V$ is in dollars and $t$ is in years since 2000. Find the rate, in dollars per year, at which the price is increasing at time $t$.

**45.** According to the US Census, the world population $P$, in billions, was approximately[10]

$$P = 6.8e^{0.012t}$$

where $t$ is in years since January 1, 2009. At what rate was the world's population increasing on that date? Give your answer in millions of people per year.

**46.** A football player kicks a ball at an angle of $30°$ from the ground with an initial velocity of 64 feet per second. Its height $t$ seconds later is $h(t) = 32t - 16t^2$.

   **(a)** Graph the height of the ball as a function of the time.
   **(b)** Find $v(t)$, the velocity of the ball at time $t$.
   **(c)** Find $v(1)$, and explain what is happening to the ball at this time. What is the height of the ball at this time?

**47.** The graph of $y = x^3 - 9x^2 - 16x + 1$ has a slope of 5 at two points. Find the coordinates of the points.

**48.** **(a)** Find the slope of the graph of $f(x) = 1 - e^x$ at the point where it crosses the $x$-axis.
   **(b)** Find the equation of the tangent line to the curve at this point.

---

[10]Based on *2009 World Population Data Sheet* from http://www.prb.org/pdf09/09wpds_eng.pdf. Accessed March 10, 2013.

**49.** Find the equation of the tangent line to the graph of $P(t) = t \ln t$ at $t = 2$. Graph the function $P(t)$ and the tangent line $Q(t)$ on the same axes.

**50.** The balance, $B$, in a bank account $t$ years after a deposit of \$5000 is given by $B = 5000e^{0.08t}$. At what rate is the balance in the account changing at $t = 5$ years? Use units to interpret your answer in financial terms.

**51.** If a cup of coffee is left on a counter top, it cools off slowly. The temperature in degrees Fahrenheit $t$ minutes after it was left on the counter is given by

$$C(t) = 74 + 103e^{-0.033t}.$$

(a) What was the temperature of the coffee when it was left on the counter?
(b) If the coffee was left on the counter for a long time, what is the lowest temperature the coffee would reach? What does that temperature represent?
(c) Find $C(5)$ and $C'(5)$. Explain what this tells about the temperature of the coffee.
(d) Without calculation, decide if the magnitude of $C'(50)$ is greater or less than the magnitude of $C'(5)$? Why?

**52.** With length, $l$, in meters, the period $T$, in seconds, of a pendulum is given by

$$T = 2\pi \sqrt{\frac{l}{9.8}}.$$

(a) How fast does the period increase as $l$ increases?
(b) Does this rate of change increase or decrease as $l$ increases?

**53.** One gram of radioactive carbon-14 decays according to the formula
$$Q = e^{-0.000121t},$$
where $Q$ is the number of grams of carbon-14 remaining after $t$ years.

(a) Find the rate at which carbon-14 is decaying (in grams/year).
(b) Sketch the rate you found in part (a) against time.

**54.** The temperature, $H$, in degrees Fahrenheit (°F), of a can of soda that is put into a refrigerator to cool is given as a function of time, $t$, in hours, by

$$H = 40 + 30e^{-2t}.$$

(a) Find the rate at which the temperature of the soda is changing (in °F/hour).
(b) What is the sign of $dH/dt$? Explain.
(c) When, for $t \geq 0$, is the magnitude of $dH/dt$ largest? In terms of the can of soda, why is this?

**55.** Explain for which values of $a$ the function $a^x$ is increasing and for which values it is decreasing. Use the fact that, for $a > 0$,

$$\frac{d}{dx}(a^x) = (\ln a)a^x.$$

**56.** Worldwide production of solar power, in megawatts, can be modeled by $f(t) = 1040(1.3)^t$, where $t$ is years[11] since 2000. Find $f(0)$, $f'(0)$, $f(15)$, and $f'(15)$. Give units and interpret your answers in terms of solar power.

**57.** The temperature $Y$ in degrees Fahrenheit of a yam in a hot oven $t$ minutes after it is placed there is given by

$$Y(t) = 350(1 - 0.7e^{-0.008t}).$$

(a) What was the temperature of the yam when it was placed in the oven?
(b) What is the temperature of the oven?
(c) When does the yam reach 175° F?
(d) Estimate the rate at which the temperature of the yam is increasing when $t = 20$.

**58.** Kepler's third law of planetary motion states that $P^2 = kd^3$, where $P$ represents the time, in earth days, it takes a planet to orbit the sun once, $d$ is the planet's average distance, in miles, from the sun, and $k$ is a constant.[12]

(a) If $k = 1.65864 \cdot 10^{-19}$, write $P$ as a function of $d$.
(b) Mercury is approximately 36 million miles from the sun. How long does it take Mercury to orbit the sun?
(c) Find $P'(d)$. What does the sign of the derivative tell us about the time it takes a planet to orbit the sun? Why does this make sense from a practical viewpoint?

**59.** Imagine you are zooming in on the graph of each of the following functions near the origin:

$$y = x \qquad\qquad y = \sqrt{x} \qquad\quad y = x^2$$
$$y = x^3 + \tfrac{1}{2}x^2 \quad y = x^3 \qquad\quad y = \ln(x+1)$$
$$y = \tfrac{1}{2}\ln(x^2 + 1) \; y = \sqrt{2x - x^2}$$

Which of them look the same? Group together those functions which become indistinguishable near the origin, and give the equations of the lines they look like.

**60.** Given a power function of the form $f(x) = ax^n$, with $f'(2) = 3$ and $f'(4) = 24$, find $n$ and $a$.

**61.** Given $r(2) = 4$, $s(2) = 1$, $s(4) = 2$, $r'(2) = -1$, $s'(2) = 3$, and $s'(4) = 3$, compute the following derivatives, or state what additional information you would need to be able to compute the derivative.

(a) $H'(2)$ if $H(x) = r(x) + s(x)$
(b) $H'(2)$ if $H(x) = 5s(x)$
(c) $H'(2)$ if $H(x) = r(x) \cdot s(x)$
(d) $H'(2)$ if $H(x) = \sqrt{r(x)}$

---

[11]https://www.solarbuzz.com/FastFactsIndustry.htm, accessed April 14, 2009.
[12]www.exploratorium.edu/ronh/age/index.html, accessed May 3, 2009.

**62.** Given $F(2) = 1, F'(2) = 5, F(4) = 3, F'(4) = 7$ and $G(4) = 2, G'(4) = 6, G(3) = 4, G'(3) = 8$, find:

(a) $H(4)$ if $H(x) = F(G(x))$
(b) $H'(4)$ if $H(x) = F(G(x))$
(c) $H(4)$ if $H(x) = G(F(x))$
(d) $H'(4)$ if $H(x) = G(F(x))$

**63.** A dose, $D$, of a drug causes a temperature change, $T$, in a patient. For $C$ a positive constant, $T$ is given by

$$T = \left(\frac{C}{2} - \frac{D}{3}\right) D^2.$$

(a) What is the rate of change of temperature change with respect to dose?
(b) For what doses does the temperature change increase as the dose increases?

**64.** A yam is put in a hot oven, maintained at a constant temperature 200°C. At time $t = 30$ minutes, the temperature $T$ of the yam is 120° and is increasing at an (instantaneous) rate of 2°/min. Newton's law of cooling (or, in our case, warming) implies that the temperature at time $t$ is given by
$$T(t) = 200 - ae^{-bt}.$$
Find $a$ and $b$.

For Problems 65–70, let $h(x) = f(x) \cdot g(x)$, and $k(x) = f(x)/g(x)$, and $l(x) = g(x)/f(x)$. Use Figure 3.24 to estimate the derivatives.

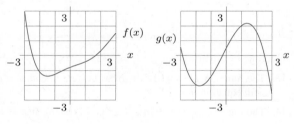

**Figure 3.24**

**65.** $h'(1)$          **66.** $k'(1)$

**67.** $h'(2)$          **68.** $k'(2)$

**69.** $l'(1)$          **70.** $l'(2)$

**71.** On what intervals is the graph of $f(x) = x^4 - 4x^3$ both decreasing and concave up?

**72.** Given $p(x) = x^n - x$, find the intervals over which $p$ is a decreasing function when:

(a) $n = 2$     (b) $n = \frac{1}{2}$     (c) $n = -1$

**73.** Using the equation of the tangent line to the graph of $e^x$ at $x = 0$, show that

$$e^x \geq 1 + x$$

for all values of $x$. A sketch may be helpful.

**74.** In Section 1.10 the depth, $y$, in feet, of water in Portland, Maine is given in terms of $t$, the number of hours since midnight, by

$$y = 4.9 + 4.4\cos\left(\frac{\pi}{6}t\right).$$

(a) Find $dy/dt$. What does $dy/dt$ represent, in terms of water level?
(b) For $0 \leq t \leq 24$, when is $dy/dt$ zero? (Figure 1.103 may be helpful.) Explain what it means (in terms of water level) for $dy/dt$ to be zero.

**75.** Using a graph to help you, find the equations of all lines through the origin tangent to the parabola

$$y = x^2 - 2x + 4.$$

Sketch the lines on the graph.

**76.** A museum has decided to sell one of its paintings and to invest the proceeds. If the picture is sold between the years 2000 and 2020 and the money from the sale is invested in a bank account earning 5% interest per year compounded annually, then $B(t)$, the balance in the year 2020, depends on the year, $t$, in which the painting is sold and the sale price $P(t)$. If $t$ is measured from the year 2000 so that $0 < t < 20$ then

$$B(t) = P(t)(1.05)^{20-t}.$$

(a) Explain why $B(t)$ is given by this formula.
(b) Show that the formula for $B(t)$ is equivalent to

$$B(t) = (1.05)^{20}\frac{P(t)}{(1.05)^t}.$$

(c) Find $B'(10)$, given that $P(10) = 150{,}000$ and $P'(10) = 5000$.

**77.** Figure 3.25 shows the number of gallons, $G$, of gasoline used on a trip of $M$ miles.

(a) The function $f$ is linear on each of the intervals $0 < M < 70$ and $70 < M < 100$. What is the slope of these lines? What are the units of these slopes?
(b) What is gas consumption (in miles per gallon) during the first 70 miles of this trip? During the next 30 miles?
(c) Figure 3.26 shows distance traveled, $M$ (in miles), as a function of time $t$, in hours since the start of the trip. Describe this trip in words. Give a possible explanation for what happens one hour into the trip. What do your answers to part (b) tell you about the trip?
(d) If we let $G = k(t) = f(h(t))$, estimate $k(0.5)$ and interpret your answer in terms of the trip.
(e) Find $k'(0.5)$ and $k'(1.5)$. Give units and interpret your answers.

**Figure 3.25**

**Figure 3.26**

**78.** The 2010 Census[13] determined the population of the US was 308.75 million on April 1, 2010. If the population was increasing exponentially at a rate of 2.85 million per year on that date, find a formula for the population as a function of time, $t$, in years since that date.

**79.** The speed of sound in dry air is

$$f(T) = 331.3\sqrt{1 + \frac{T}{273.15}} \text{ meters/second}$$

where $T$ is the temperature in degrees Celsius. Find a linear function that approximates the speed of sound for temperatures near $0°C$.

**80.** Global temperatures have been rising, on average, for more than a century, sparking concern that the polar ice will melt and sea levels will rise. With $t$ in years since 1880, fitting functions to the data[14] gives three models for the average global temperature in Celsius:

$$f(t) = 13.625 + 0.006t$$
$$g(t) = 0.00006t^2 - 0.0017t + 13.788$$
$$h(t) = 13.63e^{0.0004t}.$$

(a) What family of functions is used in each model?
(b) Find the rate of change of temperature in 2010 in each of the three models. Give units.
(c) For each model, find the change in temperature over a 130-year period if the temperature had been changing at the rate you found in part (b) for that model.
(d) For each model, find the predicted change in temperature for the 130 years from 1880 to 2010.
(e) For which model, if any, are the answers equal in parts (c) and (d)?
(f) For which model is the discrepancy largest between the answers in parts (c) and (d)?

## STRENGTHEN YOUR UNDERSTANDING

In Problems 1–50, indicate whether the statement is true or false.

**1.** If $f(x) = 5x^2 + 1$ then $f'(-1) = -10$.

**2.** The two functions $f(x) = 3x^5$ and $g(x) = 3x^5 + 7$ have the same derivative.

**3.** The derivative of $h(t) = (3t^2 + 1)(2t)$ is $h'(t) = (6t)(2) = 12t$.

**4.** If $k(s) = \sqrt{s^3}$ then $k'(s) = \sqrt{3s^2}$.

**5.** The equation of the line tangent to $f(x) = x^5 + 5$ at $x = 1$ is $y = 9x - 3$.

**6.** The derivative of $f(r) = 1/r^5$ is $f'(r) = 1/5r^4$.

**7.** The function $g(w) = w^3 - 3w$ has exactly two places where $g'(w) = 0$.

**8.** If $f(x) = 3x^3 - x^2 + 2x$ then $f$ is decreasing at $x = 1$.

**9.** If $f(x) = 3x^3 - x^2 + 2x$ then the graph of $f$ is concave up at $x = 1$.

**10.** If $g(t) = t^\pi$ then $g'(1) = \pi$.

**11.** If $f(x) = e^x$ then $f'(x) = xe^{x-1}$.

**12.** If $g(s) = 5\ln(s)$ then $g'(2) = 5/2$.

**13.** The function $f(x) = 3e^x + x$ has tangent line at $x = 0$ with equation $y = 4x + 3$.

**14.** The function $h(x) = 2\ln x - x^2$ is decreasing at $x = 1$.

**15.** The graph of $h(x) = 2\ln x - x^2$ is concave down at $x = 1$.

**16.** If $f(x) = \ln 2$ then $f'(x) = 1/2$.

**17.** If $f(x) = e^{2x}$ then $f'(x) = e^{2x}$.

**18.** If $w(q) = 10^q$ then $w'(q) = \log(10) \cdot 10^q$.

**19.** If $k(p) = 5 \cdot e^p$ then $k'(p) = \ln 5 \cdot e^p$.

**20.** If $f(x) = 3e^{5x}$ then $f'(x) = 15e^{5x}$.

**21.** The derivative of $f(t) = e^{t^2}$ is $f'(t) = 2e^{2t}$.

**22.** If $y = (x + x^2)^5$ then $dy/dx = 5(1 + 2x)^4$.

**23.** If $y = \ln(x^2 + 4)$ then $dy/dx = (2x)/(x^2 + 4)$.

**24.** If $y = \sqrt{1 - 2t}$ then $y' = 1/(2\sqrt{1 - 2t})$.

**25.** If $y = e^{-x}$ then $dy/dx = -e^{-x}$.

**26.** The chain rule says $d/dt(f(g(t))) = f(g'(t)) \cdot g(t)$.

[13]http://2010.census.gov/2010census/, accessed March 10, 2013.
[14]From data.giss.nasa.gov/gistemp/tabledate/GLB.Ts.txt, accessed April 2012.

27. If $g(x) = \ln(x^2 + 3x)$ then $g'(x) = (1/x)(2x + 3)$.

28. The function $f(x) = e^{1-x}$ is decreasing at $x = 1$.

29. The graph of $f(x) = e^{1-x}$ is concave up at $x = 1$.

30. If $B = 30(1 + 2r)^5$ then $dB/dr = 150(1 + 2r)^4$.

31. If $y = e^x \ln(x)$ then $y' = e^x/x$.

32. If $y = (x^2 + 1)2^x$ then $y' = 2x(\ln 2)2^x$.

33. If $y = x/e^x$ then $y' = (e^x - xe^x)/e^{2x} = (1 - x)/e^x$.

34. If $z = 2/(1 + t^2)$ then $z' = -4t/(1 + t^2)^2$.

35. If $s = w^2 e^w$ then $s' = 2we^w$.

36. If $P = q\ln(q^2 + 1)$ then $P' = q/(q^2 + 1) + \ln(q^2 + 1)$.

37. If $y = e^{x \ln x}$ then $y' = e^{x \ln x}(1 + \ln x)$.

38. Using the product rule to differentiate $x^2 \cdot x^2$ gives the same result as differentiating $x^4$ directly.

39. The derivative of the product of two functions is the product of their derivatives.

40. The derivative of the quotient of two functions is the quotient of their derivatives.

41. The derivative of $\sin t + \cos t$ is $\cos t - \sin t$.

42. The second derivative of $f(t) = \sin t$ is $f''(t) = \sin t$.

43. The second derivative of $g(t) = \cos t$ is $g''(t) = -\cos t$.

44. If $y = \sin 2t$ then $y' = \cos 2t$.

45. If $y = \cos t^2$ then $y' = -\sin 2t$.

46. If $z = (\sin 2t)\cos 3t$ then $z' = -6(\cos 2t)\sin 3t$.

47. If $y = \sin(\cos t)$ then $y' = \cos(\cos t) + \sin(-\sin t)$.

48. If $P = 1/\sin q$ then $dP/dq = 1/\cos q$.

49. If $Q = \cos(\pi - t)$ then $dQ/dt = \sin(\pi - t)$.

50. If $Q = \sin(\pi t + 1)$ then $dQ/dt = \pi\cos(\pi t + 1)$.

## PROJECTS FOR CHAPTER THREE

1. **Coroner's Rule of Thumb**

   Coroners estimate time of death using the rule of thumb that a body cools about 2°F during the first hour after death and about 1°F for each additional hour. Assuming an air temperature of 68°F and a living body temperature of 98.6°F, the temperature $T(t)$ in °F of a body at a time $t$ hours since death is given by

   $$T(t) = 68 + 30.6e^{-kt}.$$

   (a) For what value of $k$ will the body cool by 2°F in the first hour?

   (b) Using the value of $k$ found in part (a), after how many hours will the temperature of the body be decreasing at a rate of 1°F per hour?

   (c) Using the value of $k$ found in part (a), show that, 24 hours after death, the coroner's rule of thumb gives approximately the same temperature as the formula.

2. **Air Pressure and Altitude**

   Air pressure at sea level is 30 inches of mercury. At an altitude of $h$ feet above sea level, the air pressure, $P$, in inches of mercury, is given by

   $$P = 30e^{-3.23 \times 10^{-5}h}$$

   (a) Sketch a graph of $P$ against $h$.

   (b) Find the equation of the tangent line at $h = 0$.

   (c) A rule of thumb used by travelers is that air pressure drops about 1 inch for every 1000-foot increase in height above sea level. Write a formula for the air pressure given by this rule of thumb.

   (d) What is the relation between your answers to parts (b) and (c)? Explain why the rule of thumb works.

   (e) Are the predictions made by the rule of thumb too large or too small? Why?

3. **Relative Growth Rates: Population, GDP, and GDP per Capita**

   (a) Let $Y$ be the world's annual production (GDP). The world GDP per capita is given by $Y/P$ where $P$ is world population. Figure 3.27 shows relative growth rate of GDP and GDP per capita for 1952–2000.[15]

---

[15] Angus Maddison, *The World Economy: Historical Statistics*, OECD, 2003.

(i) Explain why the vertical distance between the two curves gives the relative rate of growth of the world population.

(ii) Estimate the relative rate of population growth in 1970 and 2000.

(b) In 2006 the relative rate of change of the GDP in developing countries was 4.5% per year, and the relative rate of change of the population was 1.2%. What was the relative rate of change of the per capita GDP in developing countries?

(c) In 2006 the relative rate of change of the world's total production (GDP) was 3.8% per year, and the relative rate of change of the world's per capita production was 2.6% per year. What was the relative rate of change of the world population?

Figure 3.27

## 4. Keeling Curve: Atmospheric Carbon Dioxide

Since the 1950s, the carbon dioxide concentration in the air has been recorded at the Mauna Loa Observatory in Hawaii.[16] A graph of this data is called the Keeling Curve, after Charles Keeling, who started recording the data. With $t$ in years since 1950, fitting functions to the data gives three models for the carbon dioxide concentration in parts per million (ppm):

$$f(t) = 303 + 1.3t$$
$$g(t) = 304e^{0.0038t}$$
$$h(t) = 0.0135t^2 + 0.5133t + 310.5.$$

(a) What family of function is used in each model?

(b) Find the rate of change of carbon dioxide in 2010 in each of the three models. Give units.

(c) Arrange the three models in increasing order of the rates of change they give for 2010. (Which model predicts the largest rate of change in 2010? Which predicts the smallest?)

(d) Consider the same three models for all positive time $t$. Will the ordering in part (c) remain the same for all $t$? If not, how will it change?

---

[16]www.esrl.noaa.gov/gmd/ccgg/, accessed March 10, 2013.

# FOCUS ON THEORY

## ESTABLISHING THE DERIVATIVE FORMULAS

The graph of $f(x) = x^2$ suggests that the derivative of $x^2$ is $f'(x) = 2x$. However, as we saw in the Focus on Theory section in Chapter 2, to be sure that this formula is correct, we have to use the definition:

$$f'(x) = \lim_{h \to 0} \frac{f(x+h) - f(x)}{h}.$$

As in Chapter 2, we simplify the difference quotient and then take the limit as $h$ approaches zero.

**Example 1**  Confirm that the derivative of $g(x) = x^3$ is $g'(x) = 3x^2$.

Solution  Using the definition, we calculate $g'(x)$:

$$g'(x) = \lim_{h \to 0} \frac{g(x+h) - g(x)}{h} = \lim_{h \to 0} \frac{(x+h)^3 - x^3}{h}$$

$$\text{Multiplying out} \longrightarrow = \lim_{h \to 0} \frac{x^3 + 3x^2h + 3xh^2 + h^3 - x^3}{h}$$

$$= \lim_{h \to 0} \frac{3x^2h + 3xh^2 + h^3}{h}$$

$$\text{Simplifying} \longrightarrow = \lim_{h \to 0} (3x^2 + 3xh + h^2) = 3x^2.$$

$$\nwarrow \text{Looking at what happens as } h \to 0$$

So $g'(x) = \dfrac{d}{dx}(x^3) = 3x^2$.

**Example 2**  Give an informal justification that the derivative of $f(x) = e^x$ is $f'(x) = e^x$.

Solution  Using $f(x) = e^x$, we have

$$f'(x) = \lim_{h \to 0} \frac{f(x+h) - f(x)}{h} = \lim_{h \to 0} \frac{e^{x+h} - e^x}{h}$$

$$= \lim_{h \to 0} \frac{e^x e^h - e^x}{h} = \lim_{h \to 0} e^x \left( \frac{e^h - 1}{h} \right).$$

What is the limit of $\dfrac{e^h - 1}{h}$ as $h \to 0$? The graph of $\dfrac{e^h - 1}{h}$ in Figure 3.28 suggests that $\dfrac{e^h - 1}{h}$ approaches 1 as $h \to 0$. In fact, it can be proved that the limit equals 1, so

$$f'(x) = \lim_{h \to 0} e^x \left( \frac{e^h - 1}{h} \right) = e^x \cdot 1 = e^x.$$

Figure 3.28: What is $\lim\limits_{h \to 0} \frac{e^h - 1}{h}$?

**Example 3**  Show that if $f(x) = 2x^2 + 1$, then $f'(x) = 4x$.

Solution  We use the definition of the derivative with $f(x) = 2x^2 + 1$:

$$f'(x) = \lim_{h \to 0} \frac{f(x+h) - f(x)}{h} = \lim_{h \to 0} \frac{(2(x+h)^2 + 1) - (2x^2 + 1)}{h}$$

$$= \lim_{h \to 0} \frac{2(x^2 + 2xh + h^2) + 1 - 2x^2 - 1}{h} = \lim_{h \to 0} \frac{2x^2 + 4xh + 2h^2 + 1 - 2x^2 - 1}{h}$$

$$= \lim_{h \to 0} \frac{4xh + 2h^2}{h} = \lim_{h \to 0} \frac{h(4x + 2h)}{h}.$$

To find the limit, look at what happens when $h$ is close to 0, but $h \neq 0$. Simplifying, we have

$$f'(x) = \lim_{h \to 0} \frac{h(4x + 2h)}{h} = \lim_{h \to 0} (4x + 2h) = 4x$$

because as $h$ gets close to 0, we know that $4x + 2h$ gets close to $4x$.

## Using the Chain Rule to Establish Derivative Formulas

We use the chain rule to justify the formulas for derivatives of $\ln x$ and of $a^x$.

### Derivative of $\ln x$

We'll differentiate an identity that involves $\ln x$. In Section 1.6, we have $e^{\ln x} = x$. Differentiating gives

$$\frac{d}{dx}(e^{\ln x}) = \frac{d}{dx}(x) = 1.$$

On the left side, since $e^x$ is the outside function and $\ln x$ is the inside function, the chain rule gives

$$\frac{d}{dx}(e^{\ln x}) = e^{\ln x} \cdot \frac{d}{dx}(\ln x).$$

Thus, solving for $\frac{d}{dx}(\ln x)$, we have the result in Section 3.2,

$$\frac{d}{dx}(\ln x) = \frac{1}{e^{\ln x}} = \frac{1}{x}.$$

### Derivative of $a^x$

Graphical arguments suggest that the derivative of $a^x$ is proportional to $a^x$. Now we show that the constant of proportionality is $\ln a$. For $a > 0$, we use the identity from Section 1.6:

$$\ln(a^x) = x \ln a.$$

On the left side, using $\frac{d}{dx}(\ln x) = \frac{1}{x}$ and the chain rule gives

$$\frac{d}{dx}(\ln a^x) = \frac{1}{a^x} \cdot \frac{d}{dx}(a^x).$$

Since $\ln a$ is a constant, differentiating the right side gives

$$\frac{d}{dx}(x \ln a) = \ln a.$$

Since the two sides are equal, we have

$$\frac{1}{a^x} \frac{d}{dx}(a^x) = \ln a.$$

Solving for $\frac{d}{dx}(a^x)$ gives the result of Section 3.2. For $a > 0$,

$$\frac{d}{dx}(a^x) = (\ln a)a^x.$$

## The Product Rule

Suppose we want to calculate the derivative of the product of differentiable functions, $f(x)g(x)$, using the definition of the derivative. Notice that in the second step below, we are adding and subtracting the same quantity: $f(x)g(x + h)$.

$$\frac{d[f(x)g(x)]}{dx} = \lim_{h \to 0} \frac{f(x + h)g(x + h) - f(x)g(x)}{h}$$

$$= \lim_{h \to 0} \frac{f(x + h)g(x + h) - f(x)g(x + h) + f(x)g(x + h) - f(x)g(x)}{h}$$

$$= \lim_{h \to 0} \left[ \frac{f(x + h) - f(x)}{h} \cdot g(x + h) + f(x) \cdot \frac{g(x + h) - g(x)}{h} \right].$$

Taking the limit as $h \to 0$ gives the product rule:

$$(f(x)g(x))' = f'(x) \cdot g(x) + f(x) \cdot g'(x).$$

## The Quotient Rule

Let $Q(x) = f(x)/g(x)$ be the quotient of differentiable functions. Assuming that $Q(x)$ is differentiable, we can use the product rule on $f(x) = Q(x)g(x)$:

$$f'(x) = Q'(x)g(x) + Q(x)g'(x).$$

Substituting for $Q(x)$ gives

$$f'(x) = Q'(x)g(x) + \frac{f(x)}{g(x)}g'(x).$$

Solving for $Q'(x)$ gives

$$Q'(x) = \frac{f'(x) - \dfrac{f(x)}{g(x)}g'(x)}{g(x)}.$$

Multiplying the top and bottom by $g(x)$ to simplify gives the quotient rule:

$$\left( \frac{f(x)}{g(x)} \right)' = \frac{f'(x)g(x) - f(x)g'(x)}{(g(x))^2}.$$

## Problems on Establishing the Derivative Formulas

For Problems 1–7, use the definition of the derivative to obtain the following results.

1. If $f(x) = 2x + 1$, then $f'(x) = 2$.
2. If $f(x) = 5x^2$, then $f'(x) = 10x$.
3. If $f(x) = 2x^2 + 3$, then $f'(x) = 4x$.
4. If $f(x) = x^2 + x$, then $f'(x) = 2x + 1$.
5. If $f(x) = 4x^2 + 1$, then $f'(x) = 8x$.
6. If $f(x) = x^4$, then $f'(x) = 4x^3$. [Hint: $(x + h)^4 = x^4 + 4x^3h + 6x^2h^2 + 4xh^3 + h^4$.]
7. If $f(x) = x^5$, then $f'(x) = 5x^4$. [Hint: $(x + h)^5 = x^5 + 5x^4h + 10x^3h^2 + 10x^2h^3 + 5xh^4 + h^5$.]
8. (a) Use a graph of $g(h) = \dfrac{2^h - 1}{h}$ to explain why we believe that $\lim_{h \to 0} \dfrac{2^h - 1}{h} \approx 0.6931$.

(b) Use the definition of the derivative and the result from part (a) to explain why, if $f(x) = 2^x$, we believe that $f'(x) \approx (0.6931)2^x$.

9. Use the definition of the derivative to show that if $f(x) = C$, where $C$ is a constant, then $f'(x) = 0$.

10. Use the definition of the derivative to show that if $f(x) = b + mx$, for constants $m$ and $b$, then $f'(x) = m$.

11. Use the definition of the derivative to show that if $f(x) = k \cdot u(x)$, where $k$ is a constant and $u(x)$ is a function, then $f'(x) = k \cdot u'(x)$.

12. Use the definition of the derivative to show that if $f(x) = u(x) + v(x)$, for functions $u(x)$ and $v(x)$, then $f'(x) = u'(x) + v'(x)$.

# FOCUS ON PRACTICE

Find derivatives for the functions in Problems 1–63. Assume $a, b, c$, and $k$ are constants.

1. $f(t) = t^2 + t^4$

2. $g(x) = 5x^4$

3. $y = 5x^3 + 7x^2 - 3x + 1$

4. $s(t) = 6t^{-2} + 3t^3 - 4t^{1/2}$

5. $f(x) = \dfrac{1}{x^2} + 5\sqrt{x} - 7$

6. $P(t) = 100e^{0.05t}$

7. $f(x) = 5e^{2x} - 2 \cdot 3^x$

8. $P(t) = 1{,}000(1.07)^t$

9. $D(p) = e^{p^2} + 5p^2$

10. $y = t^2 e^{5t}$

11. $y = x^2\sqrt{x^2 + 1}$

12. $f(x) = \ln\left(x^2 + 1\right)$

13. $s(t) = 8\ln(2t + 1)$

14. $g(w) = w^2\ln(w)$

15. $f(x) = 2^x + x^2 + 1$

16. $P(t) = \sqrt{t^2 + 4}$

17. $C(q) = (2q + 1)^3$

18. $g(x) = 5x(x + 3)^2$

19. $P(t) = be^{kt}$

20. $f(x) = ax^2 + bx + c$

21. $y = x^2\ln(2x + 1)$

22. $f(t) = \left(e^t + 4\right)^3$

23. $f(x) = 5\sin(2x)$

24. $W(r) = r^2\cos r$

25. $g(t) = 3\sin(5t) + 4$

26. $y = e^{3t}\sin(2t)$

27. $y = 2e^x + 3\sin x + 5$

28. $f(t) = 3t^2 - 4t + 1$

29. $y = 17x + 24x^{1/2}$

30. $g(x) = -\frac{1}{2}(x^5 + 2x - 9)$

31. $f(x) = 5x^4 + \dfrac{1}{x^2}$

32. $y = \dfrac{e^{2x}}{x^2 + 1}$

33. $f(x) = \dfrac{x^2 + 3x + 2}{x + 1}$

34. $y = \left(\dfrac{x^2 + 2}{3}\right)^2$

35. $g(x) = \sin(2 - 3x)$

36. $f(z) = \dfrac{z^2 + 1}{3z}$

37. $q(r) = \dfrac{3r}{5r + 2}$

38. $y = x\ln x - x + 2$

39. $j(x) = \ln(e^{ax} + b)$

40. $g(t) = \dfrac{t - 4}{t + 4}$

41. $h(w) = (w^4 - 2w)^5$

42. $h(w) = w^3\ln(10w)$

43. $f(x) = \ln(\sin x + \cos x)$

44. $w(r) = \sqrt{r^4 + 1}$

45. $h(w) = -2w^{-3} + 3\sqrt{w}$

46. $h(x) = \sqrt{\dfrac{x^2 + 9}{x + 3}}$

47. $v(t) = t^2 e^{-ct}$

48. $f(x) = \dfrac{x}{1 + \ln x}$

49. $g(\theta) = e^{\sin\theta}$

50. $p(t) = e^{4t+2}$

51. $j(x) = \dfrac{x^3}{a} + \dfrac{a}{b}x^2 - cx$

52. $f(z) = \dfrac{z^2 + 1}{\sqrt{z}}$

53. $h(r) = \dfrac{r^2}{2r + 1}$

54. $g(x) = 2x - \dfrac{1}{\sqrt[3]{x}} + 3^x - e$

55. $f(t) = 2te^t - \dfrac{1}{\sqrt{t}}$

56. $w = \dfrac{5 - 3z}{5 + 3z}$

57. $f(x) = \dfrac{x^3}{9}(3\ln x - 1)$

58. $g(x) = \dfrac{x^2 + \sqrt{x} + 1}{x^{3/2}}$

59. $y = \left(x^2 + 5\right)^3 \left(3x^3 - 2\right)^2$

60. $f(x) = \dfrac{a^2 - x^2}{a^2 + x^2}$

61. $w(r) = \dfrac{ar^2}{b + r^3}$

62. $H(t) = (at^2 + b)e^{-ct}$

63. $g(w) = \dfrac{5}{(a^2 - w^2)^2}$

## Chapter Four

# USING THE DERIVATIVE

## Contents

# 4.1 LOCAL MAXIMA AND MINIMA

## What Derivatives Tell Us About a Function and Its Graph

As we saw in Chapter 2, values of a function and its derivatives are related as follows:
- If $f' > 0$ on an interval, then $f$ is increasing on that interval.
- If $f' < 0$ on an interval, then $f$ is decreasing on that interval.
- If $f'' > 0$ on an interval, then the graph of $f$ is concave up on that interval.
- If $f'' < 0$ on an interval, then the graph of $f$ is concave down on that interval.

We now use these principles in conjunction with the derivative formulas from Chapter 3. For example, when we graph a function on a computer or calculator, we often see only part of the picture. The first and second derivatives can help identify regions with interesting behavior.

**Example 1**    Use a computer or calculator to sketch a useful graph of the function
$$f(x) = x^3 - 9x^2 - 48x + 52.$$

Solution    Since $f$ is a cubic polynomial, we expect a graph that is roughly S-shaped. Graphing this function with $-10 \leq x \leq 10$, $-10 \leq y \leq 10$ gives the two nearly vertical lines in Figure 4.1. We know that there is more going on than this, but how do we know where to look?

**Figure 4.1**: Unhelpful graph of $f(x) = x^3 - 9x^2 - 48x + 52$

We use the derivative to determine where the function is increasing and where it is decreasing. The derivative of $f$ is
$$f'(x) = 3x^2 - 18x - 48.$$
To find where $f' > 0$ or $f' < 0$, we first find where $f' = 0$; that is, where $3x^2 - 18x - 48 = 0$. Factoring gives
$$3(x - 8)(x + 2) = 0,$$
so $x = -2$ or $x = 8$. Since $f' = 0$ *only* at $x = -2$ and $x = 8$, and since $f'$ is continuous, $f'$ cannot change sign on any of the three intervals $x < -2$, or $-2 < x < 8$, or $8 < x$.

How can we tell the sign of $f'$ on each of these intervals? The easiest way is to pick a point and substitute into $f'$. For example, since $f'(-3) = 33 > 0$, we know $f'$ is positive for $x < -2$, so $f$ is increasing for $x < -2$. Similarly, since $f'(0) = -48$ and $f'(10) = 72$, we know that $f$ decreases between $x = -2$ and $x = 8$ and increases for $x > 8$. Summarizing:

| | $x = -2$ | | $x = 8$ | |
|---|---|---|---|---|
| $f$ increasing ↗ | | $f$ decreasing ↘ | | $f$ increasing ↗ |
| $f' > 0$ | $f' = 0$ | $f' < 0$ | $f' = 0$ | $f' > 0$ |

We find that $f(-2) = 104$ and $f(8) = -396$. Hence, on the interval $-2 < x < 8$ the function decreases from a high of 104 to a low of $-396$. (Now we see why not much showed up in our first calculator graph.)

One more point on the graph is easy to get: the $y$-intercept, $f(0) = 52$. With just these three points we can get a much more helpful graph. By setting the plotting window to $-10 \leq x \leq 20$ and $-400 \leq y \leq 400$, we get Figure 4.2, which gives much more insight into the behavior of $f(x)$ than the graph in Figure 4.1.

In Figure 4.2, we see that part of the graph is concave up and part is concave down. We can use the second derivative to analyze concavity. We have

$$f''(x) = 6x - 18.$$

Thus, $f''(x) < 0$ when $x < 3$ and $f''(x) > 0$ when $x > 3$, so the graph of $f$ is concave down for $x < 3$ and concave up for $x > 3$. At $x = 3$, we have $f''(x) = 0$. See Figure 4.2. Summarizing:

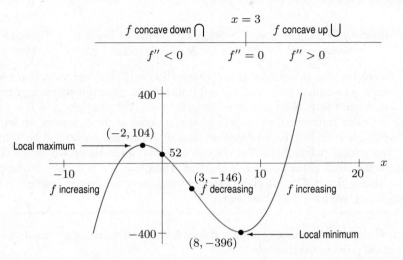

Figure 4.2: Useful graph of $f(x) = x^3 - 9x^2 - 48x + 52$. Notice that the scales on the $x$-and $y$-axes are different.

## Local Maxima and Minima

We are often interested in points such as those marked local maximum and local minimum in Figure 4.2. We have the following definition:

> Suppose $p$ is a point in the domain of $f$:
> - $f$ has a **local minimum** at $p$ if $f(p)$ is less than or equal to the values of $f$ for points near $p$.
> - $f$ has a **local maximum** at $p$ if $f(p)$ is greater than or equal to the values of $f$ for points near $p$.

We use the adjective "local" because we are describing only what happens near $p$. Local maxima and minima are sometimes called local extrema.

## How Do We Detect a Local Maximum or Minimum?

In the preceding example, the points $x = -2$ and $x = 8$, where $f'(x) = 0$, played a key role in leading us to local maxima and minima. We give a name to such points:

> For any function $f$, a point $p$ in the domain of $f$ where $f'(p) = 0$ or $f'(p)$ is undefined is called a **critical point** of the function. In addition, the point $(p, f(p))$ on the graph of $f$ is also called a **critical point**. A **critical value** of $f$ is the value, $f(p)$, at a critical point, $p$.

Notice that "critical point of $f$" can refer either to points in the domain of $f$ or to points on the graph of $f$. You will know which meaning is intended from the context. A function may have any number of critical points or none at all. (See Figures 4.3–4.5.)

**Figure 4.3:** A quadratic: One critical point

**Figure 4.4:** $f(x) = x^3 + x + 1$: No critical points

**Figure 4.5:** $g(x) = \sin x$: Many critical points

Geometrically, at a critical point where $f'(p) = 0$, the line tangent to the graph of $f$ at $p$ is horizontal. At a critical point where $f'(p)$ is undefined, there is no horizontal tangent to the graph—there is either a vertical tangent or no tangent at all. (For example, $x = 0$ is a critical point for the absolute value function $f(x) = |x|$.) However, most of the functions we will work with will be differentiable everywhere, and therefore most of our critical points will be of the $f'(p) = 0$ variety.

The critical points divide the domain of $f$ into intervals on which the sign of the derivative remains the same, either positive or negative. Therefore, if $f$ is defined on the interval between two successive critical points, its graph cannot change direction on that interval; it is either going up or going down. We have the following result:

---

If a function, continuous on the real line, has a local maximum or minimum at $p$, then $p$ is a critical point of the function.

---

If a continuous function $f$ has domain the interval $a \leq x \leq b$, then $f$ may have local maxima or minima at the endpoints $x = a$ and $x = b$, even if these points are not critical points of $f$.

## Testing For Local Maxima and Minima

If $f'$ has different signs on either side of a critical point $p$ with $f'(p) = 0$, then the graph changes direction at $p$ and looks like one of those in Figure 4.6. We have the following criteria:

---

### The First-Derivative Test for Local Maxima and Minima

Suppose $p$ is a critical point of a continuous function $f$. Moving from left to right:
- If $f'$ changes from negative to positive at $p$, then $f$ has a local minimum at $p$.
- If $f'$ changes from positive to negative at $p$, then $f$ has a local maximum at $p$.

---

**Figure 4.6:** Changes in direction at a critical point, $p$: Local maxima and minima

Knowing the concavity of a function can also be useful in testing if a critical point is a local maximum or a local minimum. Suppose $p$ is a critical point of $f$, with $f'(p) = 0$, so that the graph of $f$ has a horizontal tangent line at $p$. If the graph is concave up at $p$, then $f$ has a local minimum at $p$. Likewise, if the graph is concave down, $f$ has a local maximum. (See Figure 4.7.) This suggests:

Figure 4.7: Local maxima and minima and concavity

---

### The Second-Derivative Test for Local Maxima and Minima

Suppose $p$ is a critical point of a continuous function $f$, and $f'(p) = 0$.

- If $f''(p) > 0$, then $f$ has a local minimum at $p$.
- If $f''(p) < 0$, then $f$ has a local maximum at $p$.
- If $f''(p) = 0$, then the test tells us nothing.

---

**Example 2**

Use the second-derivative test to confirm that $f(x) = x^3 - 9x^2 - 48x + 52$ has a local maximum at $x = -2$ and a local minimum at $x = 8$.

**Solution**

In Example 1, we calculated $f'(x) = 3x^2 - 18x - 48 = 3(x-8)(x+2)$, so $f'(8) = f'(-2) = 0$. Differentiating again gives $f''(x) = 6x - 18$. Since

$$f''(8) = 6 \cdot 8 - 18 = 30 \qquad \text{and} \qquad f''(-2) = 6(-2) - 18 = -30,$$

the second-derivative test confirms that $x = 8$ is a local minimum and $x = -2$ is a local maximum.

---

**Example 3**

(a) Graph a function $f$ with the following properties:
- $f(x)$ has critical points at $x = 2$ and $x = 5$;
- $f'(x)$ is positive to the left of 2 and positive to the right of 5;
- $f'(x)$ is negative between 2 and 5.

(b) Identify the critical points as local maxima, local minima, or neither.

**Solution**

(a) We know that $f(x)$ is increasing when $f'(x)$ is positive, and $f(x)$ is decreasing when $f'(x)$ is negative. The function is increasing to the left of 2 and increasing to the right of 5, and it is decreasing between 2 and 5. A possible sketch is given in Figure 4.8.

(b) We see that the function has a local maximum at $x = 2$ and a local minimum at $x = 5$.

Figure 4.8: A function with critical points at $x = 2$ and $x = 5$

---

### Warning!

*Not every critical point of a function is a local maximum or minimum.* For instance, consider $f(x) = x^3$, graphed in Figure 4.9. The derivative is $f'(x) = 3x^2$ so $x = 0$ is a critical point. But $f'(x) = 3x^2$ is positive on both sides of $x = 0$, so $f$ increases on both sides of $x = 0$. There is neither a local maximum nor a local minimum for $f(x)$ at $x = 0$.

$$f(x) = x^3$$

Critical point

Figure 4.9: A critical point that is neither a local maximum nor minimum.

**Example 4**    The value of an investment at time $t$ is given by $S(t)$. The rate of change, $S'(t)$, of the value of the investment is shown in Figure 4.10.

(a) What are the critical points of the function $S(t)$?
(b) Identify each critical point as a local maximum, a local minimum, or neither.
(c) Explain the financial significance of each of the critical points.

rate of change
of value

$S'(t)$

$t$ (time)

1   2   3   4   5   6   7

Figure 4.10: Graph of $S'(t)$, the rate of change of the value of the investment

**Solution**    (a) The critical points of $S$ occur at times $t$ when $S'(t) = 0$. We see in Figure 4.10 that $S'(t) = 0$ at $t = 1$, 4, and 6, so the critical points occur at $t = 1$, 4, and 6.

(b) In Figure 4.10, we see that $S'(t)$ is positive to the left of 1 and between 1 and 4, that $S'(t)$ is negative between 4 and 6, and that $S'(t)$ is positive to the right of 6. Therefore $S(t)$ is increasing to the left of 1 and between 1 and 4 (with a slope of zero at 1), decreasing between 4 and 6, and increasing again to the right of 6. A possible sketch of $S(t)$ is given in Figure 4.11. We see that $S$ has neither a local maximum nor a local minimum at the critical point $t = 1$, but that it has a local maximum at $t = 4$ and a local minimum at $t = 6$.

value

$S(t)$

$t$ (time)

1  2  3  4  5  6  7

Figure 4.11: Possible graph of the function representing the value of the investment at time $t$

(c) At time $t = 1$ the investment momentarily stopped increasing in value, though it started increasing again immediately afterward. At $t = 4$, the value peaked and began to decline. At $t = 6$, it started increasing again.

**Example 5**    Find the critical point of the function $f(x) = x^2 + bx + c$. What is its graphical significance?

**Solution**    Since $f'(x) = 2x + b$, the critical point $x$ satisfies the equation $2x + b = 0$. Thus, the critical point is at $x = -b/2$. The graph of $f$ is a parabola and the critical point is its vertex. See Figure 4.12.

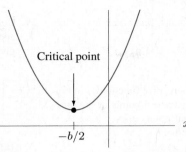

Figure 4.12: Critical point of the parabola $f(x) = x^2 + bx + c$. (Sketched with $b, c > 0$)

## Problems for Section 4.1

In Problems 1–4, indicate all critical points of the function $f$. How many critical points are there? Identify each critical point as a local maximum, a local minimum, or neither.

5. **(a)** Graph a function with two local minima and one local maximum.
   **(b)** Graph a function with two critical points. One of these critical points should be a local minimum, and the other should be neither a local maximum nor a local minimum.

6. Graph two continuous functions $f$ and $g$, each of which has exactly five critical points, the points $A$–$E$ in Figure 4.13, and that satisfy the following conditions:
   **(a)** $f(x) \to \infty$ as $x \to -\infty$   and
        $f(x) \to \infty$ as $x \to \infty$
   **(b)** $g(x) \to -\infty$ as $x \to -\infty$   and
        $g(x) \to 0$ as $x \to \infty$

Figure 4.13

7. During an illness a person ran a fever. His temperature rose steadily for eighteen hours, then went steadily down for twenty hours. When was there a critical point for his temperature as a function of time?

Using a calculator or computer, graph the functions in Problems 8–13. Describe in words the interesting features of the graph, including the location of the critical points and where the function is monotonic (that is, increasing or decreasing). Then use the derivative and algebra to explain the shape of the graph.

8. $f(x) = x^3 + 6x + 1$   9. $f(x) = x^3 - 6x + 1$

10. $f(x) = 3x^5 - 5x^3$   11. $f(x) = e^x - 10x$

12. $f(x) = x \ln x, \quad x > 0$   13. $f(x) = x + 2\sin x$

In Problems 14–15, find the critical points of the function and classify them as local maxima or local minima or neither.

14. $g(x) = xe^{-3x}$   15. $h(x) = x + 1/x$

In Problems 16–19, find all critical points and then use the first-derivative test to determine local maxima and minima. Check your answer by graphing.

16. $f(x) = 3x^4 - 4x^3 + 6$   17. $f(x) = (x^2 - 4)^7$

18. $f(x) = (x^3 - 8)^4$   19. $f(x) = \dfrac{x}{x^2 + 1}$

20. The function $f(x) = x^4 - 4x^3 + 8x$ has a critical point at $x = 1$. Use the second-derivative test to identify it as a local maximum or local minimum.

21. Find and classify the critical points of $f(x) = x^3(1-x)^4$ as local maxima and minima.

**22.** If $U$ and $V$ are positive constants, find all critical points of
$$F(t) = Ue^t + Ve^{-t}.$$

**23.** Indicate on the graph of the derivative function $f'$ in Figure 4.14 the $x$-values that are critical points of the function $f$ itself. At which critical points does $f$ have local maxima, local minima, or neither?

**Figure 4.14**

In Problems 24–27, the function $f$ is defined for all $x$. Use the graph of $f'$ to decide:
(a) Over what intervals is $f$ increasing? Decreasing?
(b) Does $f$ have local maxima or minima? If so, which, and where?

**24.**                                   **25.**

**26.**                                   **27.**

**28.** Figure 4.15 is a graph of $f'$. For what values of $x$ does $f$ have a local maximum? A local minimum?

**Figure 4.15**: Graph of $f'$ (not $f$)

**29.** Consumer demand for a product is changing over time, and the rate of change of demand, $f'(t)$, in units/week, is given, in week $t$, for $0 \le t \le 10$, in the following table.

| $t$ | 0 | 1 | 2 | 3 | 4 | 5 | 6 | 7 | 8 | 9 | 10 |
|---|---|---|---|---|---|---|---|---|---|---|---|
| $f'(t)$ | 12 | 10 | 4 | $-2$ | $-3$ | $-1$ | 3 | 7 | 11 | 15 | 10 |

(a) When is the demand for this product increasing? When is it decreasing?
(b) Approximately when is demand at a local maximum? A local minimum?

**30.** Suppose $f$ has a continuous derivative whose values are given in the following table.

(a) Estimate the $x$-coordinates of critical points of $f$ for $0 \le x \le 10$.
(b) For each critical point, indicate if it is a local maximum of $f$, local minimum, or neither.

| $x$ | 0 | 1 | 2 | 3 | 4 | 5 | 6 | 7 | 8 | 9 | 10 |
|---|---|---|---|---|---|---|---|---|---|---|---|
| $f'(x)$ | 5 | 2 | 1 | $-2$ | $-5$ | $-3$ | $-1$ | 2 | 3 | 1 | $-1$ |

**31.** The derivative of $f(t)$ is given by $f'(t) = t^3 - 6t^2 + 8t$ for $0 \le t \le 5$. Graph $f'(t)$, and describe how the function $f(t)$ changes over the interval $t = 0$ to $t = 5$. When is $f(t)$ increasing and when is it decreasing? Where does $f(t)$ have a local maximum and where does it have a local minimum?

In Problems 32–33, find constants $a$ and $b$ so that the minimum for the parabola $f(x) = x^2 + ax + b$ is at the given point. [Hint: Begin by finding the critical point in terms of $a$.]

**32.** $(3, 5)$                         **33.** $(-2, -3)$

**34.** Find the value of $a$ so that the function $f(x) = xe^{ax}$ has a critical point at $x = 3$.

**35.** For what values of $a$ and $b$ does $f(x) = a(x - b\ln x)$ have a local minimum at the point $(2, 5)$? Figure 4.16 shows a graph of $f(x)$ with $a = 1$ and $b = 1$.

**Figure 4.16**

**36.** Sketch several members of the family $y = x^3 - ax^2$ on the same axes. Discuss the effect of the parameter $a$ on the graph. Find all critical points for this function.

**37.** **(a)** For $a$ a positive constant, find all critical points of $f(x) = x - a\sqrt{x}$.
**(b)** What value of $a$ gives a critical point at $x = 5$? Does $f(x)$ have a local maximum or a local minimum at this critical point?

**38.** Find constants $a$ and $b$ in the function $f(x) = axe^{bx}$ such that $f(\frac{1}{3}) = 1$ and the function has a local maximum at $x = \frac{1}{3}$.

In Problems 39–41, investigate the one-parameter family of

functions. Assume that $a$ is positive.
**(a)** Graph $f(x)$ using three different values for $a$.
**(b)** Using your graph in part (a), describe the critical points of $f$ and how they appear to move as $a$ increases.
**(c)** Find a formula for the $x$-coordinates of the critical point(s) of $f$ in terms of $a$.

**39.** $f(x) = (x - a)^2$

**40.** $f(x) = x^3 - ax$

**41.** $f(x) = x^2 e^{-ax}$

**42.** If $m, n \geq 2$ are integers, find and classify the critical points of $f(x) = x^m(1 - x)^n$.

# 4.2 INFLECTION POINTS

## Concavity and Inflection Points

A study of the points on the graph of a function where the slope changes sign led us to critical points. Now we will study the points on the graph where the concavity changes, either from concave up to concave down, or from concave down to concave up.

> A point at which the graph of a function $f$ changes concavity is called an **inflection point** of $f$.

The words "inflection point of $f$" can refer either to a point in the domain of $f$ or to a point on the graph of $f$. The context of the problem will tell you which is meant.

### How Do You Locate an Inflection Point?

Since the concavity of the graph of $f$ changes at an inflection point, the sign of $f''$ changes there: it is positive on one side of the inflection point and negative on the other. Thus, at the inflection point, $f''$ is zero or undefined. (See Figure 4.17.)

> Suppose $f''$ is defined on both sides of a point $p$:
> • If $f''$ is zero or undefined at $p$, then $p$ is a possible inflection point.
> • To test whether $p$ is an inflection point, check whether $f''$ changes sign at $p$.

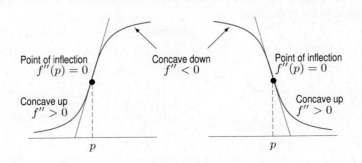

Figure 4.17: Change in concavity (from positive to negative or vice versa) at point $p$

**Example 1**    Find the inflection points of $f(x) = x^3 - 9x^2 - 48x + 52$.

Solution    In Figure 4.18, part of the graph of $f$ is concave up and part is concave down, so the function must have an inflection point. However, it is difficult to locate the inflection point accurately by examining the graph. To find the inflection point exactly, we calculate where the second derivative is zero. Since $f'(x) = 3x^2 - 18x - 48$,

$$f''(x) = 6x - 18 \qquad \text{so} \qquad f''(x) = 0 \quad \text{when} \quad x = 3.$$

We can see that the graph of $f(x)$ changes concavity at $x = 3$, so $x = 3$ is an inflection point.

**Figure 4.18**: Graph of $f(x) = x^3 - 9x^2 - 48x + 52$ showing the inflection point at $x = 3$

**Example 2**    Graph a function $f$ with the following properties: $f$ has a critical point at $x = 4$ and an inflection point at $x = 8$; the value of $f'$ is negative to the left of 4 and positive to the right of 4; the value of $f''$ is positive to the left of 8 and negative to the right of 8.

Solution    Since $f'$ is negative to the left of 4 and positive to the right of 4, the value of $f(x)$ is decreasing to the left of 4 and increasing to the right of 4. The values of $f''$ tell us that the graph of $f(x)$ is concave up to the left of 8 and concave down to the right of 8. A possible sketch is given in Figure 4.19.

**Figure 4.19**: A function with a critical point at $x = 4$ and an inflection point at $x = 8$

**Example 3**    Figure 4.20 shows a population growing toward a limiting population, $L$. There is an inflection point on the graph at the point where the population reaches $L/2$. What is the significance of the inflection point to the population?

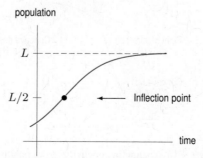

**Figure 4.20**: Inflection point on graph of a population growing toward a limiting population, $L$

Solution    At times before the inflection point, the population is increasing faster every year. At times after the
            inflection point, the population is increasing slower every year. At the inflection point, the population
            is growing fastest.

Example 4   (a)  How many critical points and how many inflection points does the function $f(x) = xe^{-x}$ have?
            (b)  Use derivatives to find the critical points and inflection points exactly.

Figure 4.21: Graph of $f(x) = xe^{-x}$

Solution    (a)  Figure 4.21 shows the graph of $f(x) = xe^{-x}$. It appears to have one critical point, which is a
                 local maximum. Are there any inflection points? Since the graph of the function is concave down
                 at the critical point and concave up for large $x$, the graph of the function changes concavity, so
                 there must be an inflection point to the right of the critical point.
            (b)  To find the critical point, find the point where the first derivative of $f$ is zero or undefined. The
                 product rule gives
                 $$f'(x) = x(-e^{-x}) + (1)(e^{-x}) = (1 - x)e^{-x}.$$
                 We have $f'(x) = 0$ when $x = 1$, so the critical point is at $x = 1$. To find the inflection point, we
                 find where the second derivative of $f$ changes sign. Using the product rule on the first derivative,
                 we have
                 $$f''(x) = (1 - x)(-e^{-x}) + (-1)(e^{-x}) = (x - 2)e^{-x}.$$
                 We have $f''(x) = 0$ when $x = 2$. Since $f''(x) > 0$ for $x > 2$ and $f''(x) < 0$ for $x < 2$, the
                 concavity changes sign at $x = 2$. So the inflection point is at $x = 2$.

### Warning!

*Not every point $x$ where $f''(x) = 0$ (or $f''$ is undefined) is an inflection point* (just as not every
point where $f' = 0$ is a local maximum or minimum). For instance, $f(x) = x^4$ has $f''(x) = 12x^2$
so $f''(0) = 0$, but $f'' > 0$ when $x > 0$ and when $x < 0$, so the graph of $f$ is concave up on both
sides of $x = 0$. There is *no* change in concavity at $x = 0$. (See Figure 4.22.)

Figure 4.22: Graph of $f(x) = x^4$

**Example 5**    Suppose that water is being poured into the vase in Figure 4.23 at a constant rate measured in liters per minute. Graph $y = f(t)$, the depth of the water against time, $t$. Explain the concavity, and indicate the inflection points.

Solution    Notice that the volume of water in the vase increases at a constant rate.

At first the water level, $y$, rises quite slowly because the base of the vase is wide, and so it takes a lot of water to make the depth increase. However, as the vase narrows, the rate at which the water level rises increases. This means that initially $y$ is increasing at an increasing rate, and the graph is concave up. The water level is rising fastest, so the rate of change of the depth $y$ is at a maximum, when the water reaches the middle of the vase, where the diameter is smallest; this is an inflection point. (See Figure 4.24.) After that, the rate at which the water level changes starts to decrease, and so the graph is concave down.

Figure 4.23: A vase

Figure 4.24: Graph of depth of water in the vase, $y$, against time, $t$

**Example 6**    What is the concavity of the graph of $f(x) = ax^2 + bx + c$?

Solution    We have $f'(x) = 2ax + b$ and $f''(x) = 2a$. The second derivative of $f$ has the same sign as $a$. If $a > 0$, the graph is concave up everywhere, an upward-opening parabola. If $a < 0$, the graph is concave down everywhere, a downward-opening parabola. (See Figure 4.25.) If $a = 0$, the function is linear and the graph is a straight line.

Figure 4.25: Concavity of $f(x) = ax^2 + bx + c$

## Problems for Section 4.2

In Problems 1–4, indicate the approximate locations of all inflection points. How many inflection points are there?

**5.** Graph a function with only one critical point (at $x = 5$) and one inflection point (at $x = 10$). Label the critical point and the inflection point on your graph.

**6. (a)** Graph a polynomial with two local maxima and two local minima.
   **(b)** What is the least number of inflection points this function must have? Label the inflection points.

**7.** Graph a function which has a critical point and an inflection point at the same place.

**8.** During a flood, the water level in a river first rose faster and faster, then rose more and more slowly until it reached its highest point, then went back down to its pre-flood level. Consider water depth as a function of time.

   **(a)** Is the time of highest water level a critical point or an inflection point of this function?
   **(b)** Is the time when the water first began to rise more slowly a critical point or an inflection point?

**9.** When I got up in the morning I put on only a light jacket because, although the temperature was dropping, it seemed that the temperature would not go much lower. But I was wrong. Around noon a northerly wind blew up and the temperature began to drop faster and faster. The worst was around 6 pm when, fortunately, the temperature started going back up.

   **(a)** When was there a critical point in the graph of temperature as a function of time?
   **(b)** When was there an inflection point in the graph of temperature as a function of time?

**10.** For $f(x) = x^3 - 18x^2 - 10x + 6$, find the inflection point algebraically. Graph the function with a calculator or computer and confirm your answer.

**11.** Find the inflection points of $f(x) = x^4 + x^3 - 3x^2 + 2$.

In each of Problems 12–21, use the first derivative to find all critical points and use the second derivative to find all inflection points. Use a graph to identify each critical point as a local maximum, a local minimum, or neither.

**12.** $f(x) = x^2 - 5x + 3$

**13.** $f(x) = x^3 - 3x + 10$

**14.** $f(x) = 2x^3 + 3x^2 - 36x + 5$

**15.** $f(x) = \dfrac{x^3}{6} + \dfrac{x^2}{4} - x + 2$

**16.** $f(x) = x^4 - 2x^2$

**17.** $f(x) = 3x^4 - 4x^3 + 6$

**18.** $f(x) = x^4 - 8x^2 + 5$

**19.** $f(x) = x^4 - 4x^3 + 10$

**20.** $f(x) = x^5 - 5x^4 + 35$

**21.** $f(x) = 3x^5 - 5x^3$

**22. (a)** Use a graph to estimate the $x$-values of any critical points and inflection points of $f(x) = e^{-x^2}$.
   **(b)** Use derivatives to find the $x$-values of any critical points and inflection points exactly.

**23. (a)** Find all critical points and all inflection points of the function $f(x) = x^4 - 2ax^2 + b$. Assume $a$ and $b$ are positive constants.
   **(b)** Find values of the parameters $a$ and $b$ if $f$ has a critical point at the point $(2, 5)$.
   **(c)** If there is a critical point at $(2, 5)$, where are the inflection points?

**24.** Indicate on the graph of the derivative $f'$ in Figure 4.26 the $x$-values that are inflection points of the function $f$.

**Figure 4.26**

**25.** Indicate on the graph of the second derivative $f''$ in Figure 4.27 the $x$-values that are inflection points of the function $f$.

**Figure 4.27**

For Problems 26–29, sketch a possible graph of $y = f(x)$, using the given information about the derivatives $y' = f'(x)$ and $y'' = f''(x)$. Assume that the function is defined and continuous for all real $x$.

**26.**

$$y' = 0 \qquad\qquad y' = 0$$
$$y' > 0 \mid \qquad y' > 0 \qquad \mid y' < 0$$
$$\xrightarrow{\qquad\qquad\qquad\qquad\qquad\qquad} x$$
$$\quad x_1 \qquad\qquad x_2 \qquad\qquad x_3$$

$$y'' = 0 \quad y'' = 0$$
$$y'' < 0 \mid y'' > 0 \mid \qquad y'' < 0$$
$$\xrightarrow{\qquad\qquad\qquad\qquad\qquad\qquad} x$$

**27.**

$$y' < 0$$
$$\xrightarrow{\qquad\qquad\qquad\qquad\qquad\qquad} x$$
$$\quad x_1 \qquad\qquad x_2 \qquad\qquad x_3$$

$$y'' = 0 \quad y'' = 0 \quad y'' = 0$$
$$y'' > 0 \mid y'' < 0 \mid y'' > 0 \mid y'' < 0$$
$$\xrightarrow{\qquad\qquad\qquad\qquad\qquad\qquad} x$$

**28.**

**29.**

**30.** Indicate on Figure 4.28 approximately where the inflection points of $f(x)$ are if the graph shows

**(a)** The function $f(x)$　　**(b)** The derivative $f'(x)$
**(c)** The second derivative $f''(x)$

Figure 4.28

Problems 31–34 concern $f(t)$ in Figure 4.29, which gives the length of a human fetus as a function of its age.

length (cm)

Figure 4.29

**31. (a)** What are the units of $f'(24)$?
　　**(b)** What is the biological meaning of $f'(24) = 1.6$?
**32. (a)** Which is greater, $f'(20)$ or $f'(36)$?
　　**(b)** What does your answer say about fetal growth?
**33. (a)** At what time does the inflection point occur?
　　**(b)** What is the biological significance of this point?
**34.** Estimate

　　**(a)** $f'(20)$　　　　　**(b)** $f'(36)$

　　**(c)** The average rate of change of length over the 40 weeks shown.

**35. (a)** Water is flowing at a constant rate (i.e., constant volume per unit time) into a cylindrical container standing vertically. Sketch a graph showing the depth of water against time.
　　**(b)** Water is flowing at a constant rate into a cone-shaped container standing on its point. Sketch a graph showing the depth of the water against time.

**36.** If water is flowing at a constant rate (i.e., constant volume per unit time) into the Grecian urn in Figure 4.30, sketch a graph of the depth of the water against time. Mark on the graph the time at which the water reaches the widest point of the urn.

Figure 4.30

**37.** The vase in Figure 4.31 is filled with water at a constant rate (i.e., constant volume per unit time).

　　**(a)** Graph $y = f(t)$, the depth of the water, against time, $t$. Show on your graph the points at which the concavity changes.
　　**(b)** At what depth is $y = f(t)$ growing most quickly? Most slowly? Estimate the ratio between the growth rates at these two depths.

Figure 4.31

Find formulas for the functions described in Problems 38–40.

**38.** A cubic polynomial, $ax^3 + bx^2 + cx + d$, with a critical point at $x = 2$, an inflection point at $(1, 4)$, and a leading coefficient of 1.

**39.** A function of the form $y = \dfrac{a}{1 + be^{-t}}$ with $y$-intercept 2 and an inflection point at $t = 1$.

**40.** A curve of the form $y = e^{-(x-a)^2/b}$ for $b > 0$ with a local maximum at $x = 2$ and points of inflection at $x = 1$ and $x = 3$.

# 4.3 GLOBAL MAXIMA AND MINIMA

## Global Maxima and Minima

The techniques for finding maximum and minimum values make up the field called *optimization*. Local maxima and minima occur where a function takes larger or smaller values than at nearby points. However, we are often interested in where a function is larger or smaller than at all other points. For example, a firm trying to maximize its profit may do so by minimizing its costs. We make the following definition:

> For any function $f$:
> - $f$ has a **global minimum** at $p$ if $f(p)$ is less than or equal to all values of $f$.
> - $f$ has a **global maximum** at $p$ if $f(p)$ is greater than or equal to all values of $f$.

### How Do We Find Global Maxima and Minima?

If $f$ is a continuous function defined on an interval $a \leq x \leq b$ (including its endpoints), Figure 4.32 illustrates that the global maximum or minimum of $f$ occurs at a local maximum or a local minimum, respectively, which could be at one of the endpoints, $x = a$ or $x = b$.

> **To find the global maximum and minimum of a continuous function on an interval including endpoints:** Compare values of the function at all the critical points in the interval and at the endpoints.

What if the continuous function is defined on an interval $a < x < b$ (excluding its endpoints), or on the entire real line which has no endpoints? The function graphed in Figure 4.33 has no global maximum because the function has no largest value. The global minimum of this function coincides with one of the local minima and is marked. A function defined on the entire real line or on an interval excluding endpoints may or may not have a global maximum or a global minimum.

> **To find the global maximum and minimum of a continuous function on an interval excluding endpoints or on the entire real line:** Find the values of the function at all the critical points and sketch a graph.

Figure 4.32: Global maximum and minimum on an interval domain, $a \leq x \leq b$

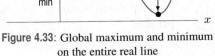

Figure 4.33: Global maximum and minimum on the entire real line

**Example 1**    Find the global maximum and minimum of $f(x) = x^3 - 9x^2 - 48x + 52$ on the interval $-5 \leq x \leq 14$.

Solution    We have calculated the critical points of this function previously using

$$f'(x) = 3x^2 - 18x - 48 = 3(x + 2)(x - 8),$$

so $x = -2$ and $x = 8$ are critical points. Since the global maxima and minima occur at a critical point or at an endpoint of the interval, we evaluate $f$ at these four points:

$$f(-5) = -58, \qquad f(-2) = 104, \qquad f(8) = -396, \qquad f(14) = 360.$$

Comparing these four values, we see that the global maximum is 360 and occurs at $x = 14$, and that the global minimum is $-396$ and occurs at $x = 8$. See Figure 4.34.

Figure 4.34: Global maximum and minimum on the interval $-5 \leq x \leq 14$

Figure 4.35: Maximum rate of photosynthesis

**Example 2**    For time, $t \geq 0$, in days, the rate at which photosynthesis takes place in the leaf of a plant, represented by the rate at which oxygen is produced, is approximated by[1]

$$p(t) = 100(e^{-0.02t} - e^{-0.1t}).$$

When is photosynthesis occurring fastest? What is that rate?

**Solution**    To find the global maximum value of $p(t)$, we first find critical points. We differentiate, set equal to zero, and solve for $t$:

$$p'(t) = 100(-0.02e^{-0.02t} + 0.1e^{-0.1t}) = 0$$
$$-0.02e^{-0.02t} = -0.1e^{-0.1t}$$
$$\frac{e^{-0.02t}}{e^{-0.1t}} = \frac{0.1}{0.02}$$
$$e^{-0.02t+0.1t} = 5$$
$$e^{0.08t} = 5$$
$$0.08t = \ln 5$$
$$t = \frac{\ln 5}{0.08} = 20.12 \text{ days.}$$

Differentiating again gives

$$p''(t) = 100(0.0004e^{-0.02t} - 0.01e^{-0.1t})$$

and substituting $t = 20.12$ gives $p''(20.12) = -0.107$, so $t = 20.12$ is a local maximum.

Since $t = 20.12$ is the only critical point and it is a local maximum, $t = 20.12$ must give the global maximum. See Figure 4.35. The maximum rate is

$$p(20.12) = 100 \left( e^{-0.02(20.12)} - e^{-0.1(20.12)} \right) = 53.50.$$

Photosynthesis occurs fastest after about 20 days. The maximum rate is about 53.5 units of oxygen per day.

## A Graphical Example: Minimizing Gas Consumption

Next we look at an example in which a function is given graphically and the maximum and minimum values are read from a graph. We already know how to estimate the maximum and minimum values

[1]Examples adapted from Rodney Gentry, *Introduction to Calculus for the Biological and Health Sciences* (Reading: Addison-Wesley, 1978).

of $f(x)$ from a graph of $f(x)$—read off the highest and lowest values. In this example, we see how to estimate the minimum value of the quantity $f(x)/x$ from a graph of $f(x)$ against $x$.

The question we investigate is how to set driving speeds to maximize fuel efficiency.[2] We assume that gas consumption, $g$ (in gallons/hour), as a function of velocity, $v$ (in mph) is as shown in Figure 4.36. We want to minimize the gas consumption per *mile*, not the gas consumption per hour. Notice that

$$\text{Units of } \frac{g}{v} = \frac{\text{gallons/hour}}{\text{miles/hour}} = \frac{\text{gallons}}{\text{miles}},$$

suggesting we minimize $G = g/v$.

Figure 4.36: Gas consumption versus velocity

**Example 3**    Using Figure 4.36, estimate the velocity which minimizes $G = g/v$.

Solution    We want to find the minimum value of $G = g/v$ when $g$ and $v$ are related by the graph in Figure 4.36. We could use Figure 4.36 to sketch a graph of $G$ against $v$ and estimate a critical point. But there is an easier way. Figure 4.37 shows that $g/v$ is the slope of the line from the origin to the point $P$. Where on the curve should $P$ be to make the slope a minimum? From the possible positions of the line shown in Figure 4.37, we see that the slope of the line is both a local and global minimum when the line is tangent to the curve. From Figure 4.38, we can see that the velocity at this point is about 50 mph. Thus to minimize gas consumption per mile, we should drive about 50 mph.

Figure 4.37: Graphical representation of gas consumption per mile, $G = g/v$

Figure 4.38: Velocity for maximum gas efficiency

# Problems for Section 4.3

For Problems 1–2, indicate all critical points on the given graphs. Determine which correspond to local minima, local maxima, global minima, global maxima, or none of these. (Note that the graphs are on closed intervals.)

[2] Adapted from Peter D. Taylor, *Calculus: The Analysis of Functions* (Toronto: Wall & Emerson, 1992).

3. For each interval, use Figure 4.39 to choose the statement that gives the location of the global maximum and global minimum of $f$ on the interval.

(a)  $4 \leq x \leq 12$        (b)  $11 \leq x \leq 16$

(c)  $4 \leq x \leq 9$         (d)  $8 \leq x \leq 18$

(I) Maximum at right endpoint, minimum at left endpoint.

(II) Maximum at right endpoint, minimum at critical point.

(III) Maximum at left endpoint, minimum at right endpoint.

(IV) Maximum at left endpoint, minimum at critical point.

**Figure 4.39**

In Problems 4–7, graph a function with the given properties.

4. Has local minimum and global minimum at $x = 3$ but no local or global maximum.

5. Has local minimum at $x = 3$, local maximum at $x = 8$, but no global maximum or minimum.

6. Has no local or global maxima or minima.

7. Has local and global minimum at $x = 3$, local and global maximum at $x = 8$.

8. True or false? Give an explanation for your answer. The global maximum of $f(x) = x^2$ on every closed interval is at one of the endpoints of the interval.

9. Plot the graph of $f(x) = x^3 - e^x$ using a graphing calculator or computer to find all local and global maxima and minima for: (a)  $-1 \leq x \leq 4$   (b)  $-3 \leq x \leq 2$

In Problems 10–13, sketch the graph of a function on the interval $0 \leq x \leq 10$ with the given properties.

10. Has local minimum at $x = 3$, local maximum at $x = 8$, but global maximum and global minimum at the endpoints of the interval.

11. Has local and global maximum at $x = 3$, local and global minimum at $x = 10$.

12. Has global maximum at $x = 0$, global minimum at $x = 10$, and no other local maxima or minima.

13. Has local and global minimum at $x = 3$, local and global maximum at $x = 8$.

14. The function $y = t(x)$ is positive and continuous with a global maximum at the point $(3, 3)$. Graph $t(x)$ if $t'(x)$ and $t''(x)$ have the same sign for $x < 3$, but opposite signs for $x > 3$.

15. Figure 4.40 shows the rate at which photosynthesis is taking place in a leaf.

(a) At what time, approximately, is photosynthesis proceeding fastest for $t \geq 0$?

(b) If the leaf grows at a rate proportional to the rate of photosynthesis, for what part of the interval $0 \leq t \leq 200$ is the leaf growing? When is it growing fastest?

**Figure 4.40**

For the functions in Problems 16–19, do the following:

(a) Find $f'$ and $f''$.

(b) Find the critical points of $f$.

(c) Find any inflection points of $f$.

(d) Evaluate $f$ at its critical points and at the endpoints of the given interval. Identify local and global maxima and minima of $f$ in the interval.

(e) Graph $f$.

16. $f(x) = x^3 - 3x^2$   $(-1 \leq x \leq 3)$

17. $f(x) = 2x^3 - 9x^2 + 12x + 1$ $(-0.5 \leq x \leq 3)$

18. $f(x) = x^3 - 3x^2 - 9x + 15$   $(-5 \leq x \leq 4)$

19. $f(x) = x + \sin x$   $(0 \leq x \leq 2\pi)$

20. Find the value of $x$ that maximizes $y = 12 + 18x - 5x^2$ and the corresponding value of $y$, by

(a) Estimating the values from a graph of $y$.

(b) Finding the values using calculus.

21. Find the value(s) of $x$ that give critical points of $y = ax^2 + bx + c$, where $a$, $b$, $c$ are constants. Under what conditions on $a$, $b$, $c$ is the critical value a maximum? A minimum?

22. A grapefruit is tossed straight up with an initial velocity of 50 ft/sec. The grapefruit is 5 feet above the ground when it is released. Its height, in feet, at time $t$ seconds is given by

$$y = -16t^2 + 50t + 5.$$

How high does it go before returning to the ground?

**23.** The sum of two nonnegative numbers is 100. What is the maximum value of the product of these two numbers?

**24.** The product of two positive numbers is 784. What is the minimum value of their sum?

**25.** The sum of three nonnegative numbers is 36, and one of the numbers is twice one of the other numbers. What is the maximum value of the product of these three numbers?

**26.** The perimeter of a rectangle is 64 cm. Find the lengths of the sides of the rectangle giving the maximum area.

In Problems 27–32, find the exact global maximum and minimum values of the function. The domain is all real numbers unless otherwise specified.

**27.** $g(x) = 4x - x^2 - 5$

**28.** $f(x) = x + 1/x$ for $x > 0$

**29.** $g(t) = te^{-t}$ for $t > 0$

**30.** $f(x) = x - \ln x$ for $x > 0$

**31.** $f(t) = \dfrac{t}{1 + t^2}$

**32.** $f(t) = (\sin^2 t + 2)\cos t$

**33.** What value of $w$ minimizes $S$ if $S - 5pw = 3qw^2 - 6pq$ and $p$ and $q$ are positive constants?

**34.** The energy expended by a bird per day, $E$, depends on the time spent foraging for food per day, $F$ hours. Foraging for a shorter time requires better territory, which then requires more energy for its defense.[3] Find the foraging time that minimizes energy expenditure if

$$E = 0.25F + \frac{1.7}{F^2}.$$

**35.** A rectangular swimming pool is to be built with an area of 1800 square feet. The owner wants 5-foot-wide decks along either side and 10-foot-wide decks at the two ends. Find the dimensions of the smallest piece of property on which the pool can be built satisfying these conditions.

**36.** If you have 100 feet of fencing and want to enclose a rectangular area up against a long, straight wall, what is the largest area you can enclose?

**37.** An apple tree produces, on average, 400 kg of fruit each season. However, if more than 200 trees are planted per km$^2$, crowding reduces the yield by 1 kg for each tree over 200.

(a) Express the total yield, $y$, from one square kilometer as a function of the number of trees on it. Graph this function.

(b) How many trees should a farmer plant on each square kilometer to maximize yield?

**38.** On the west coast of Canada, crows eat whelks (a shellfish). To open the whelks, the crows drop them from the air onto a rock. If the shell does not smash the first time, the whelk is dropped again.[4] The average number of drops, $n$, needed when the whelk is dropped from a height of $x$ meters is approximated by

$$n(x) = 1 + \frac{27}{x^2}.$$

(a) Give the total vertical distance the crow travels upward to open a whelk as a function of drop height, $x$.

(b) Crows are observed to drop whelks from the height that minimizes the total vertical upward distance traveled per whelk. What is this height?

**39.** During a flu outbreak in a school of 763 children, the number of infected children, $I$, was expressed in terms of the number of susceptible (but still healthy) children, $S$, by the function[5]

$$I = 192\ln\left(\frac{S}{762}\right) - S + 763.$$

What is the maximum possible number of infected children?

**40.** The number of offspring in a population may not be a linear function of the number of adults. The Ricker curve, used to model fish populations, claims that $y = axe^{-bx}$, where $x$ is the number of adults, $y$ is the number of offspring, and $a$ and $b$ are positive constants.

(a) Find and classify all critical points of the Ricker curve.

(b) Is there a global maximum? What does this imply about populations?

**41.** The oxygen supply, $S$, in the blood depends on the hematocrit, $H$, the percentage of red blood cells in the blood:

$$S = aHe^{-bH} \quad \text{for positive constants } a, b.$$

(a) What value of $H$ maximizes the oxygen supply? What is the maximum oxygen supply?

(b) How does increasing the value of the constants $a$ and $b$ change the maximum value of $S$?

**42.** The quantity of a drug in the bloodstream $t$ hours after a tablet is swallowed is given, in mg, by

$$q(t) = 20(e^{-t} - e^{-2t}).$$

(a) How much of the drug is in the bloodstream at time $t = 0$?

(b) When is the maximum quantity of drug in the bloodstream? What is that maximum?

(c) In the long run, what happens to the quantity?

---

[3] Adapted from Graham Pyke, reported by J. R. Krebs and N. B. Davis in *An Introduction to Behavioural Ecology* (Oxford: Blackwell, 1987).

[4] Adapted from Reto Zach, reported by J. R. Krebs and N. B. Davis in *An Introduction to Behavioural Ecology* (Oxford: Blackwell, 1987).

[5] Data from Communicable Disease Surveillance Centre (UK), reported in "Influenza in a Boarding School", *British Medical Journal*, March 4, 1978.

**43.** When birds lay eggs, they do so in clutches of several at a time. When the eggs hatch, each clutch gives rise to a brood of baby birds. We want to determine the clutch size which maximizes the number of birds surviving to adulthood per brood. If the clutch is small, there are few baby birds in the brood; if the clutch is large, there are so many baby birds to feed that most die of starvation. The number of surviving birds per brood as a function of clutch size is shown by the benefit curve in Figure 4.41.[6]

(a) Estimate the clutch size which maximizes the number of survivors per brood.

(b) Suppose also that there is a biological cost to having a larger clutch: the female survival rate is reduced by large clutches. This cost is represented by the dotted line in Figure 4.41. If we take cost into account by assuming that the optimal clutch size in fact maximizes the vertical distance between the curves, what is the new optimal clutch size?

**Figure 4.41**

**44.** Let $f(v)$ be the amount of energy consumed by a flying bird, measured in joules per second (a joule is a unit of energy), as a function of its speed $v$ (in meters/sec). Let $a(v)$ be the amount of energy consumed by the same bird, measured in joules per meter.

(a) Suggest a reason in terms of the way birds fly for the shape of the graph of $f(v)$ in Figure 4.42.

(b) What is the relationship between $f(v)$ and $a(v)$?

(c) Where on the graph is $a(v)$ a minimum?

(d) Should the bird try to minimize $f(v)$ or $a(v)$ when it is flying? Why?

**Figure 4.42**

**45.** A person's blood pressure, $p$, in millimeters of mercury (mm Hg) is given, for $t$ in seconds, by

$$p = 100 + 20\sin(2.5\pi t).$$

(a) What are the maximum and minimum values of blood pressure?

(b) What is the time between successive maxima?

(c) Show your answers on a graph of blood pressure against time.

**46.** A chemical reaction converts substance $A$ to substance $Y$. At the start of the reaction, the quantity of $A$ present is $a$ grams. At time $t$ seconds later, the quantity of $Y$ present is $y$ grams. The rate of the reaction, in grams/sec, is given by

$$\text{Rate } = ky(a - y), \quad k \text{ is a positive constant.}$$

(a) For what values of $y$ is the rate nonnegative? Graph the rate against $y$.

(b) For what values of $y$ is the rate a maximum?

**47.** In a chemical reaction, substance $A$ combines with substance $B$ to form substance $Y$. At the start of the reaction, the quantity of $A$ present is $a$ grams, and the quantity of $B$ present is $b$ grams. At time $t$ seconds after the start of the reaction, the quantity of $Y$ present is $y$ grams. Assume $a < b$ and $y \leq a$. For certain types of reactions, the rate of the reaction, in grams/sec, is given by

$$\text{Rate } = k(a - y)(b - y), \quad k \text{ is a positive constant.}$$

(a) For what values of $y$ is the rate nonnegative? Graph the rate against $y$.

(b) Use your graph to find the value of $y$ at which the rate of the reaction is fastest.

# 4.4  PROFIT, COST, AND REVENUE

## Maximizing Profit

A fundamental issue for a producer of goods is how to maximize profit. For a quantity, $q$, the profit $\pi(q)$ is the difference between the revenue, $R(q)$, and the cost, $C(q)$, of supplying that quantity. Thus, $\pi(q) = R(q) - C(q)$. The marginal cost, $MC = C'$, is the derivative of $C$; marginal revenue is $MR = R'$.

---

[6]Data from C. M. Perrins and D. Lack, reported by J. R. Krebs and N. B. Davies in *An Introduction to Behavioural Ecology* (Oxford: Blackwell, 1987).

Now we look at how to maximize total profit, given functions for revenue and cost. The next example suggests a criterion for identifying the optimal production level.

**Example 1**   Estimate the maximum profit if the revenue and cost are given by the curves $R$ and $C$, respectively, in Figure 4.43.

Figure 4.43: Maximum profit at $q = 140$

**Solution**   Since profit is revenue minus cost, the profit is represented by the vertical distance between the cost and revenue curves, marked by the vertical arrows in Figure 4.43. When revenue is below cost, the company is taking a loss; when revenue is above cost, the company is making a profit. The maximum profit must occur between about $q = 70$ and $q = 200$, which is the interval in which the company is making a profit. Profit is maximized when the vertical distance between the curves is largest (and revenue is above cost). This occurs at approximately $q = 140$.

The profit accrued at $q = 140$ is the vertical distance between the curves, so the maximum profit = $\$80,000 - \$60,000 = \$20,000$.

## Maximum Profit Can Occur Where $MR = MC$

We now analyze the marginal costs and marginal revenues near the optimal point. Zooming in on Figure 4.43 around $q = 140$ gives Figure 4.44.

At a production level $q_1$ to the left of 140 in Figure 4.44, marginal cost is less than marginal revenue. The company would make more money by producing more units, so production should be increased (toward a production level of 140). At any production level $q_2$ to the right of 140, marginal cost is greater than marginal revenue. The company would lose money by producing more units and would make more money by producing fewer units. Production should be adjusted down toward 140.

What about the marginal revenue and marginal cost at $q = 140$? Since $MC < MR$ to the left of 140, and $MC > MR$ to the right of 140, we expect $MC = MR$ at 140. In this example, profit is maximized at the point where the slopes of the cost and revenue graphs are equal.

Figure 4.44: Example 1: Maximum profit occurs where $MC = MR$

We can get the same result analytically. Global maxima and minima of a function can only occur at critical points of the function or at the endpoints of the interval. To find critical points of $\pi$, look for zeros of the derivative:

$$\pi'(q) = R'(q) - C'(q) = 0.$$

So

$$R'(q) = C'(q),$$

that is, the slopes of the graphs of $R(q)$ and $C(q)$ are equal at $q$. In economic language,

---

The maximum (or minimum) profit can occur where

Marginal profit = 0,

that is, where

Marginal revenue = Marginal cost.

---

Of course, maximum or minimum profit does not *have* to occur where $MR = MC$; either one could occur at an endpoint. Example 2 shows how to visualize maxima and minima of the profit on a graph of marginal revenue and marginal cost.

---

**Example 2**    The total revenue and total cost curves for a product are given in Figure 4.45.

(a) Sketch the marginal revenue and marginal cost, $MR$ and $MC$, on the same axes. Mark the two quantities where marginal revenue equals marginal cost. What is the significance of these two quantities? At which quantity is profit maximized?

(b) Graph the profit function $\pi(q)$.

Figure 4.45: Total revenue and total cost

**Solution**    (a) Since $R(q)$ is a straight line with positive slope, the graph of its derivative, $MR$, is a horizontal line. (See Figure 4.46.) Since $C(q)$ is always increasing, its derivative, $MC$, is always positive. As $q$ increases, the cost curve changes from concave down to concave up, so the derivative of the cost function, $MC$, changes from decreasing to increasing. (See Figure 4.46.) The local minimum on the marginal cost curve corresponds to the inflection point of $C(q)$.

Where is profit maximized? We know that the maximum profit can occur when Marginal revenue = Marginal cost, that is where the curves in Figure 4.46 cross at $q_1$ and $q_2$. Do these points give the maximum profit?

We first consider $q_1$. To the left of $q_1$, we have $MR < MC$, so $\pi' = MR - MC$ is negative and the profit function is decreasing there. To the right of $q_1$, we have $MR > MC$, so $\pi'$ is positive and the profit function is increasing. This behavior, decreasing and then increasing, means that the profit function has a local minimum at $q_1$. This is certainly not the production level we want.

What happens at $q_2$? To the left of $q_2$, we have $MR > MC$, so $\pi'$ is positive and the profit function is increasing. To the right of $q_2$, we have $MR < MC$, so $\pi'$ is negative and the profit function is decreasing. This behavior, increasing and then decreasing, means that the profit function has a local maximum at $q_2$. The global maximum profit occurs either at the production level $q_2$ or at an endpoint (the largest and smallest possible production levels). Since the profit is negative at the endpoints (see Figure 4.45), the global maximum occurs at $q_2$.

Figure 4.46: Marginal revenue and marginal cost

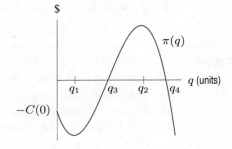

Figure 4.47: Profit function

(b) The graph of the profit function is in Figure 4.47. At the maximum and minimum, the slope of the profit curve is zero:

$$\pi'(q_1) = \pi'(q_2) = 0.$$

Note that since $R(0) = 0$ and $C(0)$ represents the fixed costs of production, we have

$$\pi(0) = R(0) - C(0) = -C(0).$$

Therefore the vertical intercept of the profit function is a negative number, equal in magnitude to the size of the fixed cost.

---

**Example 3**    Find the quantity which maximizes profit if the total revenue and total cost (in dollars) are given by

$$R(q) = 5q - 0.003q^2$$
$$C(q) = 300 + 1.1q$$

where $q$ is quantity and $0 \le q \le 1000$ units. What production level gives the minimum profit?

**Solution**    We begin by looking for production levels that give Marginal revenue = Marginal cost. Since

$$MR = R'(q) = 5 - 0.006q$$
$$MC = C'(q) = 1.1,$$

$MR = MC$ leads to

$$5 - 0.006q = 1.1$$
$$q = \frac{3.9}{0.006} = 650 \text{ units.}$$

Does this represent a local maximum or minimum of the profit $\pi$? To decide, look to the left and right of 650 units.

When $q = 649$, we have $MR = \$1.106$ per unit, which is greater than $MC = \$1.10$ per unit.

Thus, producing one more unit (the $650^{\text{th}}$) brings in more revenue than it costs, so profit increases.

When $q = 651$, we have $MR = \$1.094$ per unit, which is less than $MC = \$1.10$ per unit.

It is not profitable to produce the $651^{\text{st}}$ unit. We conclude that $q = 650$ gives a local maximum for the profit function $\pi$.

To check whether $q = 650$ gives a global maximum, we compare the profit at the endpoints, $q = 0$ and $q = 1000$, with the profit at $q = 650$.

At $q = 0$, the only cost is $300 (the fixed costs) and there is no revenue, so $\pi(0) = -\$300$.

At $q = 1000$, we have $R(1000) = \$2000$ and $C(1000) = \$1400$, so $\pi(1000) = \$600$.

At $q = 650$, we have $R(650) = \$1982.50$ and $C(650) = \$1015$, so $\pi(650) = \$967.50$.

Therefore, the maximum profit is obtained at a production level of $q = 650$ units. The minimum profit (a loss) occurs when $q = 0$ and there is no production at all.

## Maximizing Revenue

For some companies, costs do not depend on the number of items sold. For example, a city bus company with a fixed schedule has the same costs no matter how many people ride the buses. In such a situation, profit is maximized by maximizing revenue.

**Example 4**    At a price of $80 for a half-day trip, a white-water rafting company attracts 300 customers. Every $5 decrease in price attracts an additional 30 customers.

(a) Find the demand equation.
(b) Express revenue as a function of price.
(c) What price should the company charge per trip to maximize revenue?

**Solution**    (a) We first find the equation relating price to demand. If price, $p$, is 80, the number of trips sold, $q$, is 300. If $p$ is 75, then $q$ is 330, and so on. See Table 4.1. Because demand changes by a constant (30 people) for every $5 drop in price, $q$ is a linear function of $p$. Then

$$\text{Slope} = \frac{300 - 330}{80 - 75} = -\frac{30}{5} = -6 \text{ people/dollar,}$$

so the demand equation is $q = -6p + b$. Since $p = 80$ when $q = 300$, we have

$$300 = -6 \cdot 80 + b$$
$$b = 300 + 6 \cdot 80 = 780.$$

The demand equation is $q = -6p + 780$.

(b) Since revenue $R = p \cdot q$, revenue as a function of price is

$$R(p) = p(-6p + 780) = -6p^2 + 780p.$$

(c) Figure 4.48 shows this revenue function has a maximum. To find it, we differentiate:

$$R'(q) = -12p + 780 = 0$$
$$p = \frac{780}{12} = 65.$$

The maximum revenue is achieved when the price is $65.

Table 4.1  *Demand for rafting trips*

| Price, $p$ | Number of trips sold, $q$ |
|---|---|
| 80 | 300 |
| 75 | 330 |
| 70 | 360 |
| 65 | 390 |
| . . . | . . . |

Figure 4.48: Revenue for a rafting company as a function of price

## Problems for Section 4.4

1. Figure 4.49 shows cost and revenue. For what production levels is the profit function positive? Negative? Estimate the production at which profit is maximized.

**Figure 4.49**

2. The revenue from selling $q$ items is $R(q) = 500q - q^2$, and the total cost is $C(q) = 150 + 10q$. Write a function that gives the total profit earned, and find the quantity which maximizes the profit.

3. Revenue is given by $R(q) = 450q$ and cost is given by $C(q) = 10,000 + 3q^2$. At what quantity is profit maximized? What is the total profit at this production level?

4. Using the cost and revenue graphs in Figure 4.50, sketch the following functions. Label the points $q_1$ and $q_2$.

   (a)   Total profit       (b)   Marginal cost
   (c)   Marginal revenue

**Figure 4.50**

5. Figure 4.46 in Section 4.4 shows the points, $q_1$ and $q_2$, where marginal revenue equals marginal cost.

   (a) On the graph of the corresponding total cost and total revenue functions in Figure 4.51, label the points $q_1$ and $q_2$. Using slopes, explain the significance of these points.
   (b) Explain in terms of profit why one is a local minimum and one is a local maximum.

**Figure 4.51**

6. Let $C(q)$ be the total cost of producing a quantity $q$ of a certain product. See Figure 4.52.

   (a) What is the meaning of $C(0)$?
   (b) Describe in words how the marginal cost changes as the quantity produced increases.
   (c) Explain the concavity of the graph (in terms of economics).
   (d) Explain the economic significance (in terms of marginal cost) of the point at which the concavity changes.
   (e) Do you expect the graph of $C(q)$ to look like this for all types of products?

**Figure 4.52**

7. Let $C(q)$ represent the cost, $R(q)$ the revenue, and $\pi(q)$ the total profit, in dollars, of producing $q$ items.

   (a) If $C'(50) = 75$ and $R'(50) = 84$, approximately how much profit is earned by the $51^{st}$ item?
   (b) If $C'(90) = 71$ and $R'(90) = 68$, approximately how much profit is earned by the $91^{st}$ item?
   (c) If $\pi(q)$ is a maximum when $q = 78$, how do you think $C'(78)$ and $R'(78)$ compare? Explain.

8. Table 4.2 shows cost, $C(q)$, and revenue, $R(q)$.

   (a) At approximately what production level, $q$, is profit maximized? Explain your reasoning.
   (b) What is the price of the product?
   (c) What are the fixed costs?

**Table 4.2**

| $q$ | 0 | 500 | 1000 | 1500 | 2000 | 2500 | 3000 |
|------|------|------|------|------|------|------|------|
| $R(q)$ | 0 | 1500 | 3000 | 4500 | 6000 | 7500 | 9000 |
| $C(q)$ | 3000 | 3800 | 4200 | 4500 | 4800 | 5500 | 7400 |

9. Table 4.3 shows marginal cost, $MC$, and marginal revenue, $MR$.

   (a) Use the marginal cost and marginal revenue at a production of $q = 5000$ to determine whether production should be increased or decreased from 5000.
   (b) Estimate the production level that maximizes profit.

**Table 4.3**

| $q$ | 5000 | 6000 | 7000 | 8000 | 9000 | 10000 |
|------|------|------|------|------|------|------|
| $MR$ | 60 | 58 | 56 | 55 | 54 | 53 |
| $MC$ | 48 | 52 | 54 | 55 | 58 | 63 |

**10.** Figure 4.53 shows graphs of marginal cost and marginal revenue. Estimate the production levels that could maximize profit. Explain your reasoning.

**Figure 4.53**

**11.** The marginal cost and marginal revenue of a company are $MC(q) = 0.03q^2 - 1.4q + 34$ and $MR(q) = 30$, where $q$ is the number of items manufactured. To increase profits, should the company increase or decrease production from each of the following levels?

(a) 25 items     (b) 50 items     (c) 80 items

**12.** A manufacturing process has marginal costs given in the table; the item sells for $30 per unit. At how many quantities, $q$, does the profit appear to be a maximum? In what intervals do these quantities appear to lie?

| $q$ | 0 | 10 | 20 | 30 | 40 | 50 | 60 |
|---|---|---|---|---|---|---|---|
| MC ($/unit) | 34 | 23 | 18 | 19 | 26 | 39 | 58 |

**13.** Cost and revenue functions are given in Figure 4.54. Approximately what quantity maximizes profits?

**Figure 4.54**

**14.** Cost and revenue functions are given in Figure 4.54.

(a) At a production level of $q = 3000$, is marginal cost or marginal revenue greater? Explain what this tells you about whether production should be increased or decreased.

(b) Answer the same questions for $q = 5000$.

**15.** When production is 2000, marginal revenue is $4 per unit and marginal cost is $3.25 per unit. Do you expect maximum profit to occur at a production level above or below 2000? Explain.

**16.** Revenue and cost functions for a company are given in Figure 4.55.

(a) Estimate the marginal cost at $q = 400$.
(b) Should the company produce the 500$^{\text{th}}$ item? Why?
(c) Estimate the quantity which maximizes profit.

**Figure 4.55**

**17.** A company estimates that the total revenue, $R$, in dollars, received from the sale of $q$ items is $R = \ln(1 + 1000q^2)$. Calculate and interpret the marginal revenue if $q = 10$.

**18.** The demand equation for a product is $p = 45 - 0.01q$. Write the revenue as a function of $q$ and find the quantity that maximizes revenue. What price corresponds to this quantity? What is the total revenue at this price?

**19.** The demand for tickets to an amusement park is given by $p = 70 - 0.02q$, where $p$ is the price of a ticket in dollars and $q$ is the number of people attending at that price.

(a) What price generates an attendance of 3000 people? What is the total revenue at that price? What is the total revenue if the price is $20?
(b) Write the revenue function as a function of attendance, $q$, at the amusement park.
(c) What attendance maximizes revenue?
(d) What price should be charged to maximize revenue?
(e) What is the maximum revenue? Can we determine the corresponding profit?

**20.** An ice cream company finds that at a price of $4.00, demand is 4000 units. For every $0.25 decrease in price, demand increases by 200 units. Find the price and quantity sold that maximize revenue.

**21.** At a price of $8 per ticket, a musical theater group can fill every seat in the theater, which has a capacity of 1500. For every additional dollar charged, the number of people buying tickets decreases by 75. What ticket price maximizes revenue?

**22.** The demand equation for a quantity $q$ of a product at price $p$, in dollars, is $p = -5q + 4000$. Companies producing the product report the cost, $C$, in dollars, to produce a quantity $q$ is $C = 6q + 5$ dollars.

(a) Express a company's profit, in dollars, as a function of $q$.
(b) What production level earns the company the largest profit?
(c) What is the largest profit possible?

**23. (a)** Production of an item has fixed costs of $10,000 and variable costs of $2 per item. Express the cost, $C$, of producing $q$ items.

**(b)** The relationship between price, $p$, and quantity, $q$, demanded is linear. Market research shows that 10,100 items are sold when the price is $5 and 12,872 items are sold when the price is $4.50. Express $q$ as a function of price $p$.

**(c)** Express the profit earned as a function of $q$.

**(d)** How many items should the company produce to maximize profit? (Give your answer to the nearest integer.) What is the profit at that production level?

**24.** An online seller of knitted sweaters finds that it costs $35 to make her first sweater. Her cost for each additional sweater goes down until it reaches $25 for her $100^{th}$ sweater, and after that it starts to rise again. If she can sell each sweater for $35, is the quantity sold that maximizes her profit less than 100? Greater than 100?

**25.** A landscape architect plans to enclose a 3000 square-foot rectangular region in a botanical garden. She will use shrubs costing $45 per foot along three sides and fencing costing $20 per foot along the fourth side. Find the minimum total cost.

**26.** You run a small furniture business. You sign a deal with a customer to deliver up to 400 chairs, the exact number to be determined by the customer later. The price will be $90 per chair up to 300 chairs, and above 300, the price will be reduced by $0.25 per chair (on the whole order) for every additional chair over 300 ordered. What are the largest and smallest revenues your company can make under this deal?

**27.** A warehouse selling cement has to decide how often and in what quantities to reorder. It is cheaper, on average, to place large orders, because this reduces the ordering cost per unit. On the other hand, larger orders mean higher storage costs. The warehouse always reorders cement in the same quantity, $q$. The total weekly cost, $C$, of ordering and storage is given by

$$C = \frac{a}{q} + bq, \quad \text{where } a, b \text{ are positive constants.}$$

**(a)** Which of the terms, $a/q$ and $bq$, represents the ordering cost and which represents the storage cost?

**(b)** What value of $q$ gives the minimum total cost?

**28.** A demand function is $p = 400 - 2q$, where $q$ is the quantity of the good sold for price $p$.

**(a)** Find an expression for the total revenue, $R$, in terms of $q$.

**(b)** Differentiate $R$ with respect to $q$ to find the marginal revenue, $MR$, in terms of $q$. Calculate the marginal revenue when $q = 10$.

**(c)** Calculate the change in total revenue when production increases from $q = 10$ to $q = 11$ units. Confirm that a one-unit increase in $q$ gives a reasonable approximation to the exact value of $MR$ obtained in part (b).

**29.** A business sells an item at a constant rate of $r$ units per month. It reorders in batches of $q$ units, at a cost of $a + bq$ dollars per order. Storage costs are $k$ dollars per item per month, and, on average, $q/2$ items are in storage, waiting to be sold. [Assume $r, a, b, k$ are positive constants.]

**(a)** How often does the business reorder?

**(b)** What is the average monthly cost of reordering?

**(c)** What is the total monthly cost, $C$ of ordering and storage?

**(d)** Obtain Wilson's lot size formula, the optimal batch size which minimizes cost.

**30. (a)** A cruise line offers a trip for $2000 per passenger. If at least 100 passengers sign up, the price is reduced for *all* the passengers by $10 for every additional passenger (beyond 100) who goes on the trip. The boat can accommodate 250 passengers. What number of passengers maximizes the cruise line's total revenue? What price does each passenger pay then?

**(b)** The cost to the cruise line for $n$ passengers is $80,000 + 400n$. What is the maximum profit that the cruise line can make on one trip? How many passengers must sign up for the maximum to be reached and what price will each pay?

**31.** A company manufactures only one product. The quantity, $q$, of this product produced per month depends on the amount of capital, $K$, invested (i.e., the number of machines the company owns, the size of its building, and so on) and the amount of labor, $L$, available each month. We assume that $q$ can be expressed as a *Cobb-Douglas production function*:

$$q = cK^{\alpha}L^{\beta},$$

where $c$, $\alpha$, $\beta$ are positive constants, with $0 < \alpha < 1$ and $0 < \beta < 1$. In this problem we will see how the Russian government could use a Cobb-Douglas function to estimate how many people a newly privatized industry might employ. A company in such an industry has only a small amount of capital available to it and needs to use all of it, so $K$ is fixed. Suppose $L$ is measured in man-hours per month, and that each man-hour costs the company $w$ rubles (a ruble is the unit of Russian currency). Suppose the company has no other costs besides labor, and that each unit of the good can be sold for a fixed price of $p$ rubles. How many man-hours of labor per month should the company use in order to maximize its profit?

**32.** A company can produce and sell $f(L)$ tons of a product per month using $L$ hours of labor per month. The wage of the workers is $w$ dollars per hour, and the finished product sells for $p$ dollars per ton.

**(a)** The function $f(L)$ is the company's production function. Give the units of $f(L)$. What is the practical significance of $f(1000) = 400$?

**(b)** The derivative $f'(L)$ is the company's marginal product of labor. Give the units of $f'(L)$. What is the practical significance of $f'(1000) = 2$?

(c) The real wage of the workers is the quantity of product that can be bought with one hour's wages. Show that the real wage is $w/p$ tons per hour.

(d) Show that the monthly profit of the company is

$$\pi(L) = pf(L) - wL.$$

(e) Show that when operating at maximum profit, the company's marginal product of labor equals the real wage:

$$f'(L) = \frac{w}{p}.$$

# 4.5  AVERAGE COST

To stay in business, a company needs to know whether it can turn a profit—which is possible if the price of its product can be set above the average cost of production.

In this section, we see how average cost can be calculated and visualized, and the relationship between average cost and marginal cost.

## What Is Average Cost?

The average cost is the cost per unit of producing a certain quantity; it is the total cost divided by the number of units produced.

If the cost of producing a quantity $q$ is $C(q)$, then the **average cost**, $a(q)$, of producing a quantity $q$ is given by

$$a(q) = \frac{C(q)}{q}.$$

Although both are measured in the same units, for example, dollars per item, be careful not to confuse the average cost with the marginal cost (the cost of producing the next item).

**Example 1**  A salsa company has cost function $C(q) = 0.01q^3 - 0.6q^2 + 13q + 1000$ (in dollars), where $q$ is the number of cases of salsa produced. If 100 cases are produced, find the average cost per case.

**Solution**  The total cost of producing the 100 cases is given by

$$C(100) = 0.01(100^3) - 0.6(100^2) + 13(100) + 1000 = \$6300.$$

We find the average cost per case by dividing by 100, the number of cases produced.

$$\text{Average cost} = \frac{6300}{100} = 63 \text{ dollars/case.}$$

If 100 cases of salsa are produced, the average cost is $63 per case.

### Visualizing Average Cost on the Total Cost Curve

We know that average cost is $a(q) = C(q)/q$. Since we can subtract zero from any number without changing it, we can write

$$a(q) = \frac{C(q)}{q} = \frac{C(q) - 0}{q - 0}.$$

This expression gives the slope of the line joining the points $(0,0)$ and $(q, C(q))$ on the cost curve. See Figure 4.56.

$$\begin{array}{c} \text{Average cost} \\ \text{to produce } q \text{ items} \end{array} = \frac{C(q)}{q} = \begin{array}{c} \text{Slope of the line from the origin} \\ \text{to point } (q, C(q)) \text{ on cost curve.} \end{array}$$

Figure 4.56: Average cost is the slope of the line from the origin to a point on the cost curve

## Minimizing Average Cost

We use the graphical representation of average cost to investigate the relationship between average and marginal cost, and to identify the production level which minimizes average cost.

**Example 2**   A cost function, in dollars, is $C(q) = 1000 + 20q$, where $q$ is the number of units produced. Find and compare the marginal cost to produce the $100^{\text{th}}$ unit and the average cost of producing 100 units. Illustrate your answer on a graph.

Solution   The cost function is linear with fixed costs of $1000 and variable costs of $20 per unit. Thus,

$$\text{Marginal cost} = C'(q) = 20 \text{ dollars per unit.}$$

This means that after 99 units have been produced, it costs an additional $20 to produce the next unit. In contrast,

$$\text{Average cost of producing 100 units} = a(100) = \frac{C(100)}{100} = \frac{3000}{100} = 30 \text{ dollars/unit.}$$

Notice that the average cost includes the fixed costs of $1000 spread over the entire production, whereas marginal cost does not. Thus, the average cost is greater than the marginal cost in this example. See Figure 4.57.

Figure 4.57: Average cost > Marginal cost

**Example 3**   Mark on the cost graph in Figure 4.58 the quantity at which the average cost is minimized.

Solution   In Figure 4.59, the average costs at $q_1$, $q_2$, $q_3$, and $q_4$ are given by the slopes of the lines from the origin to the curve. These slopes are steep for small $q$, become less steep as $q$ increases, and then get steeper again. Thus, as $q$ increases, the average cost decreases and then increases, so there is a minimum value. In Figure 4.59 the minimum occurs at the point $q_0$ where the line from the origin is tangent to the cost curve.

**Figure 4.58**: A cost function

**Figure 4.59**: Minimum average cost occurs at $q_0$ where line is tangent to cost curve

In Figure 4.59, notice that average cost is a minimum (at $q_0$) when average cost equals marginal cost. The next example shows what happens when marginal cost and average cost are not equal.

**Example 4**   Suppose 100 items are produced at an average cost of \$2 per item. Find the average cost of producing 101 items if the marginal cost to produce the $101^{st}$ item is:   (a) \$1    (b) \$3.

Solution   If 100 items are produced at an average cost of \$2 per item, the total cost of producing the items is $100 \cdot \$2 = \$200$.

(a)  Since the marginal, or additional, cost to produce the $101^{st}$ item is \$1, the total cost of producing 101 items is $\$200 + \$1 = \$201$. The average cost to produce these items is $201/101$, or \$1.99 per item. The average cost has gone down.

(b)  In this case, the marginal cost to produce the $101^{st}$ item is \$3. The total cost to produce 101 items is \$203 and the average cost is $203/101$, or \$2.01 per item. The average cost has gone up.

Notice that in Example 4(a), where it costs less than the average to produce an additional item, average cost decreases as production increases. In Example 4(b), where it costs more than the average to produce an additional item, average cost increases with production. We summarize:

---

### Relationship Between Average Cost and Marginal Cost

- If marginal cost is less than average cost, then increasing production decreases average cost.

- If marginal cost is greater than average cost, then increasing production increases average cost.

- Marginal cost equals average cost at critical points of average cost.

---

**Example 5**    Show analytically that critical points of average cost occur when marginal cost equals average cost.

**Solution**    Since $a(q) = C(q)/q = C(q)q^{-1}$, we use the product rule to find $a'(q)$:

$$a'(q) = C'(q)(q^{-1}) + C(q)(-q^{-2}) = \frac{C'(q)}{q} + \frac{-C(q)}{q^2} = \frac{qC'(q) - C(q)}{q^2}.$$

At critical points we have $a'(q) = 0$, so

$$\frac{qC'(q) - C(q)}{q^2} = 0$$

Therefore, we have

$$qC'(q) - C(q) = 0$$
$$qC'(q) = C(q)$$
$$C'(q) = \frac{C(q)}{q}.$$

In other words, at a critical point:

$$\text{Marginal cost } = \text{ Average cost.}$$

**Example 6**    A total cost function, in thousands of dollars, is given by $C(q) = q^3 - 6q^2 + 15q$, where $q$ is in thousands and $0 \le q \le 5$.

(a) Graph $C(q)$. Estimate visually the quantity at which average cost is minimized.
(b) Graph the average cost function. Use it to estimate the minimum average cost.
(c) Determine analytically the exact value of $q$ at which average cost is minimized.
(d) Graph the marginal cost function on the same axes as the average cost.
(e) Show that at the minimum average cost, Marginal cost $=$ Average cost. Explain how you can see this result on your graph of average and marginal costs.

**Solution**    (a) A graph of $C(q)$ is in Figure 4.60. Average cost is minimized at the point where a line from the origin to the point on the curve has minimum slope. This occurs where the line is tangent to the curve, which is at approximately $q = 3$, corresponding to a production of 3000 units.
(b) Since average cost is total cost divided by quantity, we have

$$a(q) = \frac{C(q)}{q} = \frac{q^3 - 6q^2 + 15q}{q} = q^2 - 6q + 15.$$

Figure 4.61 suggests that the minimum average cost occurs at $q = 3$.
(c) Average cost is minimized at a critical point of $a(q) = q^2 - 6q + 15$. Differentiating gives

$$a'(q) = 2q - 6 = 0$$
$$q = 3.$$

The minimum occurs at $q = 3$.
(d) See Figure 4.61. Marginal cost is the derivative of $C(q) = q^3 - 6q^2 + 15q$,

$$MC(q) = 3q^2 - 12q + 15.$$

(e) At $q = 3$, we have

$$\text{Marginal cost } = 3 \cdot 3^2 - 12 \cdot 3 + 15 = 6.$$
$$\text{Average cost } = 3^2 - 6 \cdot 3 + 15 = 6.$$

Thus, marginal and average cost are equal at $q = 3$. This result can be seen in Figure 4.61 since the marginal cost curve cuts the average cost curve at the minimum average cost.

$ (thousands)

Figure 4.60: Cost function, showing the minimum average cost

$ (thousands) per unit

Figure 4.61: Average and marginal cost functions, showing minimum average cost

## Problems for Section 4.5

**1.** For each cost function in Figure 4.62, is there a value of $q$ at which average cost is minimized? If so, approximately where? Explain your answer.

Figure 4.62

**2.** Figure 4.63 shows cost with $q = 10,000$ marked.

  **(a)** Find the average cost when the production level is 10,000 units and interpret it.
  **(b)** Represent your answer to part (a) graphically.
  **(c)** At approximately what production level is average cost minimized?

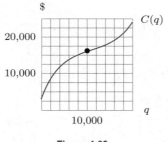

Figure 4.63

**3.** The graph of a cost function is given in Figure 4.64.

  **(a)** At $q = 25$, estimate the following quantities and represent your answers graphically.

  (i)  Average cost        (ii)  Marginal cost

  **(b)** At approximately what value of $q$ is average cost minimized?

Figure 4.64

**4.** The cost of producing $q$ items is $C(q) = 2500 + 12q$ dollars.

  **(a)** What is the marginal cost of producing the $100^{\text{th}}$ item? the $1000^{\text{th}}$ item?
  **(b)** What is the average cost of producing 100 items? 1000 items?

**5.** The cost function is $C(q) = 1000 + 20q$. Find the marginal cost to produce the $200^{\text{th}}$ unit and the average cost of producing 200 units.

6. Graph the average cost function corresponding to the total cost function shown in Figure 4.65.

**Figure 4.65**

7. The total cost of production, in thousands of dollars, is $C(q) = q^3 - 12q^2 + 60q$, where $q$ is in thousands and $0 \leq q \leq 8$.

   (a) Graph $C(q)$. Estimate visually the quantity at which average cost is minimized.
   (b) Determine analytically the exact value of $q$ at which average cost is minimized.

8. You are the manager of a firm that produces slippers that sell for $20 a pair. You are producing 1200 pairs of slippers each month, at an average cost of $2 each. The marginal cost at a production level of 1200 is $3 per pair.

   (a) Are you making or losing money?
   (b) Will increasing production increase or decrease your average cost? Your profit?
   (c) Would you recommend that production be increased or decreased?

9. The average cost per item to produce $q$ items is given by

   $$a(q) = 0.01q^2 - 0.6q + 13, \quad \text{for} \quad q > 0.$$

   (a) What is the total cost, $C(q)$, of producing $q$ goods?
   (b) What is the minimum marginal cost? What is the practical interpretation of this result?
   (c) At what production level is the average cost a minimum? What is the lowest average cost?
   (d) Compute the marginal cost at $q = 30$. How does this relate to your answer to part (c)? Explain this relationship both analytically and in words.

10. The marginal cost at a production level of 2000 units of an item is $10 per unit and the average cost of producing 2000 units is $15 per unit. If the production level were increased slightly above 2000, would the following quantities increase or decrease, or is it impossible to tell?

    (a)  Average cost          (b)  Profit

11. An agricultural worker in Uganda is planting clover to increase the number of bees making their home in the region. There are 100 bees in the region naturally, and for every acre put under clover, 20 more bees are found in the region.

    (a) Draw a graph of the total number, $N(x)$, of bees as a function of $x$, the number of acres devoted to clover.

    (b) Explain, both geometrically and algebraically, the shape of the graph of:
       (i) The marginal rate of increase of the number of bees with acres of clover, $N'(x)$.
       (ii) The average number of bees per acre of clover, $N(x)/x$.

12. A developer has recently purchased a laundromat and an adjacent factory. For years, the laundromat has taken pains to keep the smoke from the factory from soiling the air used by its clothes dryers. Now that the developer owns both the laundromat and the factory, she could install filters in the factory's smokestacks to reduce the emission of smoke, instead of merely protecting the laundromat from it. The cost of filters for the factory and the cost of protecting the laundromat against smoke depend on the number of filters used, as shown in the table.

| Number of filters | Total cost of filters | Total cost of protecting laundromat from smoke |
|---|---|---|
| 0 | $0 | $127 |
| 1 | $5 | $63 |
| 2 | $11 | $31 |
| 3 | $18 | $15 |
| 4 | $26 | $6 |
| 5 | $35 | $3 |
| 6 | $45 | $0 |
| 7 | $56 | $0 |

    (a) Make a table which shows, for each possible number of filters (0 through 7), the marginal cost of the filter, the average cost of the filters, and the marginal savings in protecting the laundromat from smoke.
    (b) Since the developer wishes to minimize the total costs to both her businesses, what should she do? Use the table from part (a) to explain your answer.
    (c) What should the developer do if, in addition to the cost of the filters, the filters must be mounted on a rack which costs $100?
    (d) What should the developer do if the rack costs $50?

13. Show analytically that if marginal cost is less than average cost, then the derivative of average cost with respect to quantity satisfies $a'(q) < 0$.

14. Show analytically that if marginal cost is greater than average cost, then the derivative of average cost with respect to quantity satisfies $a'(q) > 0$.

15. A reasonably realistic model of a firm's costs is given by the *short-run Cobb-Douglas cost curve*

    $$C(q) = Kq^{1/a} + F,$$

    where $a$ is a positive constant, $F$ is the fixed cost, and $K$ measures the technology available to the firm.

    (a) Show that $C$ is concave down if $a > 1$.
    (b) Assuming that $a < 1$, find what value of $q$ minimizes the average cost.

# 4.6  ELASTICITY OF DEMAND

The sensitivity of demand to changes in price varies with the product. For example, a change in the price of light bulbs may not affect the demand for light bulbs much, because people need light bulbs no matter what their price. However, a change in the price of a particular make of car may have a significant effect on the demand for that car, because people can switch to another make.

## Elasticity of Demand

We want to find a way to measure this sensitivity of demand to price changes. Our measure should work for products as diverse as light bulbs and cars. The prices of these two items are so different that it makes little sense to talk about absolute changes in price: Changing the price of light bulbs by $1 is a substantial change, whereas changing the price of a car by $1 is not. Instead, we use the percent change in price. How, for example, does a 1% increase in price affect the demand for the product?

Let $\Delta p$ denote the change in the price $p$ of a product and $\Delta q$ denote the corresponding change in quantity $q$ demanded. The percent change in price is $\Delta p/p$ and the percent change in quantity demanded is $\Delta q/q$. We assume in this book that $\Delta p$ and $\Delta q$ have opposite signs (because increasing the price usually decreases the quantity demanded). Then the effect of a price change on demand is measured by the absolute value of the ratio

$$\left| \frac{\text{Percent change in demand}}{\text{Percent change in price}} \right| = \left| \frac{\Delta q/q}{\Delta p/p} \right| = \left| \frac{\Delta q}{q} \cdot \frac{p}{\Delta p} \right| = \left| \frac{p}{q} \cdot \frac{\Delta q}{\Delta p} \right|$$

For small changes in $p$, we approximate $\Delta q/\Delta p$ by the derivative $dq/dp$. We define:

---

The **elasticity of demand**[7] for a product, $E$, is given approximately by

$$E \approx \left| \frac{\Delta q/q}{\Delta p/p} \right|, \quad \text{or exactly by} \quad E = \left| \frac{p}{q} \cdot \frac{dq}{dp} \right|.$$

---

Increasing the price of an item by 1% causes a drop of approximately $E\%$ in the quantity of goods demanded. For small changes, $\Delta p$, in price,

$$\frac{\Delta q}{q} \approx -E \frac{\Delta p}{p}.$$

If $E > 1$, a 1% increase in price causes demand to drop by more than 1%, and we say that demand is *elastic*. If $0 \leq E < 1$, a 1% increase in price causes demand to drop by less than 1%, and we say that demand is *inelastic*. In general, a larger elasticity causes a larger percent change in demand for a given percent change in price.

---

**Example 1**    Raising the price of hotel rooms from $75 to $80 per night reduces weekly sales from 100 rooms to 90 rooms.

(a) Approximate the elasticity of demand for rooms at a price of $75.
(b) Should the owner raise the price?

**Solution**     (a) The percent change in the price is

$$\frac{\Delta p}{p} = \frac{5}{75} = 0.067 = 6.7\%,$$

---

[7]When it is necessary to distinguish it from other elasticities, this quantity is called the elasticity of demand with respect to price, or the price elasticity of demand.

and the percent change in demand is

$$\frac{\Delta q}{q} = \frac{-10}{100} = -0.1 = -10\%.$$

The elasticity of demand is approximated by the ratio

$$E \approx \left|\frac{\Delta q/q}{\Delta p/p}\right| = \frac{0.10}{0.067} = 1.5.$$

The elasticity is greater than 1 because the percent change in the demand is greater than the percent change in the price.

(b) At a price of $75 per room,

$$\text{Revenue} = (100 \text{ rooms})(\$75 \text{ per room}) = \$7500 \text{ per week.}$$

At a price of $80 per room,

$$\text{Revenue} = (90 \text{ rooms})(\$80 \text{ per room}) = \$7200 \text{ per week.}$$

A price increase results in loss of revenue, so the price should not be raised.

---

**Example 2**    The demand curve for a product is given by $q = 1000 - 2p^2$, where $p$ is the price. Find the elasticity at $p = 10$ and at $p = 15$. Interpret your answers.

**Solution**    We first find the derivative $dq/dp = -4p$. At a price of $p = 10$, we have $dq/dp = -4 \cdot 10 = -40$, and the quantity demanded is $q = 1000 - 2 \cdot 10^2 = 800$. At this price, the elasticity is

$$E = \left|\frac{p}{q} \cdot \frac{dq}{dp}\right| = \left|\frac{10}{800}(-40)\right| = 0.5.$$

The demand is inelastic at a price of $p = 10$: a 1% increase in price results in approximately a 0.5% decrease in demand.

At a price of $15, we have $q = 550$ and $dq/dp = -60$. The elasticity is

$$E = \left|\frac{p}{q} \cdot \frac{dq}{dp}\right| = \left|\frac{15}{550}(-60)\right| = 1.64.$$

The demand is elastic: a 1% increase in price results in approximately a 1.64% decrease in demand.

---

## Revenue and Elasticity of Demand

Elasticity enables us to analyze the effect of a price change on revenue. An increase in price usually leads to a fall in demand. However, the revenue may increase or decrease. The revenue $R = pq$ is the product of two quantities, and as one increases, the other decreases. Elasticity measures the relative significance of these two competing changes.

---

**Example 3**    Three hundred units of an item are sold when the price of the item is $10. When the price of the item is raised by $1, what is the effect on revenue if the quantity sold drops by

(a)   10 units?                                    (b)   100 units?

**Solution**    Since Revenue = Price · Quantity, when the price is $10, we have

$$\text{Revenue} = 10 \cdot 300 = \$3000.$$

(a) At a price of $11, the quantity sold is $300 - 10 = 290$, so

$$\text{Revenue} = 11 \cdot 290 = \$3190.$$

Thus, raising the price has increased revenue.

(b) At a price of $11, the quantity sold is $300 - 100 = 200$, so

$$\text{Revenue} = 11 \cdot 200 = \$2200.$$

Thus, raising the price has decreased revenue.

---

Elasticity allows us to predict whether revenue increases or decreases with a price increase.

---

**Example 4**    The item in Example 3(a) is wool whose demand equation is $q = 400 - 10p$. The item in Example 3(b) is houseplants, whose demand equation is $q = 1300 - 100p$. Find the elasticity of wool and houseplants.

Solution    For wool, $q = 400 - 10p$, so $dq/dp = -10$. Thus,

$$E_{\text{Wool}} = \left| \frac{p}{q} \frac{dq}{dp} \right| = \left| \frac{10}{300}(-10) \right| = \frac{1}{3}.$$

For houseplants, $q = 1300 - 100p$, so $dq/dp = -100$. Thus,

$$E_{\text{Houseplants}} = \left| \frac{p}{q} \frac{dq}{dp} \right| = \left| \frac{10}{300}(-100) \right| = \frac{10}{3}.$$

Notice that $E_{\text{Wool}} < 1$ and revenue increases with an increase in price; $E_{\text{Houseplants}} > 1$ and revenue decreases with an increase in price. In the next example we see the relationship between elasticity and maximum revenue.

---

**Example 5**    Table 4.4 shows the demand, $q$, revenue, $R$, and elasticity, $E$, for the product in Example 2 at several prices. What price brings in the greatest revenue? What is the elasticity at that price?

Solution    Table 4.4 suggests that maximum revenue is achieved at a price of about $13, and at that price, $E$ is about 1. At prices below $13, we have $E < 1$, so the reduction in demand caused by a price increase is small; thus, raising the price increases revenue. At prices above $13, we have $E > 1$, so the increase in demand caused by a price decrease is relatively large; thus lowering the price increases revenue.

**Table 4.4**    *Revenue and elasticity at different points*

| Price $p$ | 10 | 11 | 12 | 13 | 14 | 15 |
|---|---|---|---|---|---|---|
| Demand $q$ | 800 | 758 | 712 | 662 | 608 | 550 |
| Revenue $R$ | 8000 | 8338 | 8544 | 8606 | 8512 | 8250 |
| Elasticity $E$ | 0.5 | 0.64 | 0.81 | 1.02 | 1.29 | 1.64 |
|  | Inelastic | Inelastic | Inelastic | Elastic | Elastic | Elastic |

---

Example 6 shows that revenue does have a local maximum when $E = 1$. We summarize as follows:

**Relationship Between Elasticity and Revenue**

- If $E < 1$, demand is inelastic and revenue is increased by raising the price.
- If $E > 1$, demand is elastic and revenue is increased by lowering the price.
- $E = 1$ occurs at critical points of the revenue function.

**Example 6** Show analytically that critical points of the revenue function occur when $E = 1$.

**Solution** We think of revenue as a function of price. Using the product rule to differentiate $R = pq$, we have

$$\frac{dR}{dp} = \frac{d}{dp}(pq) = p\frac{dq}{dp} + \frac{dp}{dp}q = p\frac{dq}{dp} + q.$$

At a critical point the derivative $dR/dp$ equals zero, so we have

$$p\frac{dq}{dp} + q = 0$$

$$p\frac{dq}{dp} = -q$$

$$\frac{p}{q}\frac{dq}{dp} = -1$$

$$E = 1.$$

## Elasticity of Demand for Different Products

Different products generally have different elasticities. See Table 4.5. If there are close substitutes for a product, or if the product is a luxury rather than a necessity, a change in price generally has a large effect on demand, and the demand for the product is elastic. On the other hand, if there are no close substitutes or if the product is a necessity, changes in price have a relatively small effect on demand, and the demand is inelastic. For example, demand for salt, penicillin, eyeglasses, and lightbulbs is inelastic over the usual range of prices for these products.

**Table 4.5** *Elasticity of demand (with respect to price) for selected farm products*[8]

| | | | | |
|---|---|---|---|---|
| Cabbage | 0.25 | | Oranges | 0.62 |
| Potatoes | 0.27 | | Cream | 0.69 |
| Wool | 0.33 | | Apples | 1.27 |
| Peanuts | 0.38 | | Peaches | 1.49 |
| Eggs | 0.43 | | Fresh tomatoes | 2.22 |
| Milk | 0.49 | | Lettuce | 2.58 |
| Butter | 0.62 | | Fresh peas | 2.83 |

## Problems for Section 4.6

1. The elasticity of a good is $E = 0.5$. What is the effect on the quantity demanded of:

   (a) A 3% price increase? (b) A 3% price decrease?

2. The elasticity of a good is $E = 2$. What is the effect on the quantity demanded of:

   (a) A 3% price increase? (b) A 3% price decrease?

3. What are the units of elasticity if:

   (a) Price $p$ is in dollars and quantity $q$ is in tons?
   (b) Price $p$ is in yen and quantity $q$ is in liters?
   (c) What can you conclude in general?

4. There are many brands of laundry detergent. Would you expect the elasticity of demand for any particular brand to be high or low? Explain.

5. Would you expect the demand for high-definition television sets to be elastic or inelastic? Explain.

6. There is only one company offering local telephone service in a town. Would you expect the elasticity of demand for telephone service to be high or low? Explain.

---

[8]Estimated by the US Department of Agriculture and reported in W. Adams & J. Brock, *The Structure of American Industry*, 10th ed (Englewood Cliffs: Prentice Hall, 2000).

**7.** What is the elasticity for peaches in Table 4.5? Explain what this number tells you about the effect of price increases on the demand for peaches. Is the demand for peaches elastic or inelastic? Is this what you expect? Explain.

**8.** What is the elasticity for potatoes in Table 4.5? Explain what this number tells you about the effect of price increases on the demand for potatoes. Is the demand for potatoes elastic or inelastic? Is this what you expect? Explain.

**9.** The demand for a product is given by $q = 200 - 2p^2$. Find the elasticity of demand when the price is \$5. Is the demand inelastic or elastic, or neither?

**10.** The demand for a product is given by $p = 90 - 10q$. Find the elasticity of demand when $p = 50$. If this price rises by 2%, calculate the corresponding percentage change in demand.

**11.** School organizations raise money by selling candy door to door. The table shows $p$, the price of the candy, and $q$, the quantity sold at that price.

| $p$ | \$1.00 | \$1.25 | \$1.50 | \$1.75 | \$2.00 | \$2.25 | \$2.50 |
|-----|--------|--------|--------|--------|--------|--------|--------|
| $q$ | 2765 | 2440 | 1980 | 1660 | 1175 | 800 | 430 |

 

(a) Estimate the elasticity of demand at a price of \$1.00. At this price, is the demand elastic or inelastic?
(b) Estimate the elasticity at each of the prices shown. What do you notice? Give an explanation for why this might be so.
(c) At approximately what price is elasticity equal to 1?
(d) Find the total revenue at each of the prices shown. Confirm that the total revenue appears to be maximized at approximately the price where $E = 1$.

**12.** The demand for yams is given by $q = 5000 - 10p^2$, where $q$ is in pounds of yams and $p$ is the price of a pound of yams.

(a) If the current price of yams is \$2 per pound, how many pounds will be sold?
(b) Is the demand at \$2 elastic or inelastic? Is it more accurate to say "People want yams and will buy them no matter what the price" or "Yams are a luxury item and people will stop buying them if the price gets too high"?

**13.** The demand for yams is given in Problem 12.

(a) At a price of \$2 per pound, what is the total revenue for the yam farmer?
(b) Write revenue as a function of price, and then find the price that maximizes revenue.
(c) What quantity is sold at the price you found in part (b), and what is the total revenue?
(d) Show that $E = 1$ at the price you found in part (b).

**14.** It has been estimated that the elasticity of demand for slaves in the American South before the Civil War was equal to 0.86 (fairly high) in the cities and equal to 0.05 (very low) in the countryside.[9]

(a) Why might this be?
(b) Where do you think the staunchest defenders of slavery were from, the cities or the countryside?

**15.** Find the exact price that maximizes revenue for sales of the product in Example 2.

**16.** If $E = 2$ for all prices $p$, how can you maximize revenue?

**17.** If $E = 0.5$ for all prices $p$, how can you maximize revenue?

**18.** (a) Let $p$ be the price and $q$ be the quantity sold of a good with a high elasticity of demand, $E$. Explain intuitively (without formulas) the effect of raising the price on the revenue, $R$.
(b) Derive an expression for $dR/dp$ in terms of $q$ and $E$. Show all the steps and reasoning.
(c) Explain how your answer to part (b) confirms your answer to part (a).

**19.** (a) If the demand equation is $pq = k$ for a positive constant $k$, compute the elasticity of demand.
(b) Explain the answer to part (a) in terms of the revenue function.

**20.** Show that a demand equation $q = k/p^r$, where $r$ is a positive constant, gives constant elasticity $E = r$.

**21.** If $p$ is price and $E$ is the elasticity of demand for a good, show analytically that

$$\text{Marginal revenue} = p(1 - 1/E).$$

**22.** Suppose cost is proportional to quantity, $C(q) = kq$. Show that a firm earns maximum profit when

$$\frac{\text{Profit}}{\text{Revenue}} = \frac{1}{E}$$

[Hint: Combine the result of Problem 21 with the fact that profit is maximized when $MR = MC$.]

**23.** A linear demand function is given in Figure 4.66. Economists compute elasticity of demand $E$ for any quantity $q_0$ using the formula

$$E = d_1/d_2,$$

where $d_1$ and $d_2$ are the vertical distances shown in Figure 4.66.

(a) Explain why this formula works.
(b) Determine the prices, $p$, at which   (i) $E > 1$   (ii) $E < 1$   (iii) $E = 1$

---

[9]Donald McCloskey, *The Applied Theory of Price*, p. 134 (New York: Macmillan, 1982).

**Figure 4.66**

for chicken with respect to the price of beef is defined as $E_{\text{cross}} = |p/q \cdot dq/dp|$. What does $E_{\text{cross}}$ tell you about the sensitivity of the quantity of chicken bought to changes in the price of beef?

24. Show analytically that if elasticity of demand satisfies $E > 1$, then the derivative of revenue with respect to price satisfies $dR/dp < 0$.

25. Show analytically that if elasticity of demand satisfies $E < 1$, then the derivative of revenue with respect to price satisfies $dR/dp > 0$.

26. If $q$ is the quantity of chicken demanded as a function of the price $p$ of beef, the *cross-price* elasticity of demand

27. Dwell time, $t$, is the time in minutes that shoppers spend in a store. Sales, $s$, is the number of dollars they spend in the store. The elasticity of sales with respect to dwell time is 1.3. Explain what this means in simple language.

28. Elasticity of cost with respect to quantity is defined as $E_{C,q} = q/C \cdot dC/dq$.

    (a) What does this elasticity tell you about sensitivity of cost to quantity produced?
    (b) Show that $E_{C,q} =$ Marginal cost/Average cost.

29. The *income* elasticity of demand for a product is defined as $E_{\text{income}} = |I/q \cdot dq/dI|$ where $q$ is the quantity demanded as a function of the income $I$ of the consumer. What does $E_{\text{income}}$ tell you about the sensitivity of the quantity of the product purchased to changes in the income of the consumer?

# 4.7 LOGISTIC GROWTH

In 1923, eighteen koalas were introduced to Kangaroo Island, off the coast of Australia.[10] The koalas thrived on the island and their population grew to about 5000 in 1997. Is it reasonable to expect the population to continue growing exponentially? Since there is only a finite amount of space on the island, the population cannot grow without bound forever. Instead we expect that there is a maximum population that the island can sustain. Population growth with an upper bound can be modeled with a *logistic* or *inhibited growth model*.

## Modeling the US Population

Population projections first became important to political philosophers in the late eighteenth century. As concern for scarce resources has grown, so has the interest in accurate population projections. In the US, the population is recorded every ten years by a census. The first such census was in 1790. Table 4.6 contains the census data from 1790 to 2010.

**Table 4.6**    *US population,[11] in millions, 1790-2010*

| Year | Population | Year | Population | Year | Population | Year | Population |
|------|-----------|------|-----------|------|-----------|------|-----------|
| 1790 | 3.9 | 1850 | 23.2 | 1910 | 92.2 | 1970 | 203.2 |
| 1800 | 5.3 | 1860 | 31.4 | 1920 | 106.0 | 1980 | 226.5 |
| 1810 | 7.2 | 1870 | 38.6 | 1930 | 123.2 | 1990 | 248.7 |
| 1820 | 9.6 | 1880 | 50.2 | 1940 | 132.2 | 2000 | 281.4 |
| 1830 | 12.9 | 1890 | 63.0 | 1950 | 151.3 | 2010 | 308.7 |
| 1840 | 17.1 | 1900 | 76.2 | 1960 | 179.3 | | |

---

[10]*Watertown Daily Times*, April 18, 1997.
[11]www.census.gov. Accessed February 12, 2012.

Figure 4.67: US population, 1790-1860                    Figure 4.68: US population, 1790-1940

Figure 4.67 suggests that the population grew exponentially during the years 1790-1860. However, after 1860 the rate of growth began to decrease. See Figure 4.68.

### The Years 1790-1860: An Exponential Model

We begin by modeling the US population for the years 1790-1860 using an exponential function. If $t$ is the number of years since 1790 and $P$ is the population in millions, regression gives the exponential function that fits the data as approximately[12]

$$P = 3.9(1.03)^t.$$

Thus, between 1790 and 1860, the US population was growing at an annual rate of about 3%.

The function $P = 3.9(1.03)^t$ is plotted in Figure 4.69 with the data; it fits the data remarkably well. Of course, since we used the data from throughout the 70-year period, we should expect good agreement throughout that period. What is surprising is that if we had used only the populations in 1790 and 1800 to create our exponential function, the predictions would still be very accurate. It is amazing that a person in 1800 could predict the population 60 years later so accurately, especially when one considers all the wars, recessions, epidemics, additions of new territory, and immigration that took place from 1800 to 1860.

Figure 4.69: An exponential model for          Figure 4.70: The exponential model and the US population,
the US population, 1790-1860                    1790-1940. Not a good fit beyond 1860

### The Years 1790-1940: A Logistic Model

How well does the exponential function fit the US population beyond 1860? Figure 4.70 shows a graph of the US population from 1790 until 1940 with the exponential function $P = 3.9(1.03)^t$. The exponential function which fit the data so well for the years 1790-1860 does not fit very well beyond 1860. We must look for another way to model this data.

The graph of the function given by the data in Figure 4.68 is concave up for small values of $t$, but then appears to become concave down and to be leveling off. This kind of growth is modeled with a *logistic function*. If $t$ is in years since 1790, the function

$$P = \frac{192}{1 + 48e^{-0.0317t}},$$

[12]See Appendix A: Fitting Formulas to Data. Different algorithms may give different formulas.

which is graphed in Figure 4.71, fits the data well up to 1940. Such a formula is found by logistic regression on a calculator or computer.[13]

Figure 4.71: A logistic model for US population, 1790-1940

## The Logistic Function

A logistic function, such as that used to model the US population, is everywhere increasing. Its graph is concave up at first, then becomes concave down, and levels off at a horizontal asymptote. As we saw in the US population model, a logistic function is approximately exponential for small[14] values of $t$. A logistic function can be used to model the sales of a new product and the spread of a virus.

> For positive constants $L$, $C$, and $k$, a **logistic function** has the form
>
> $$P = f(t) = \frac{L}{1 + Ce^{-kt}}.$$

The general logistic function has three parameters: $L$, $C$, and $k$. In Example 1, we investigate the effect of two of these parameters on the graph; Problem 2 at the end of the section considers the third.

**Example 1**    Consider the logistic function $P = \dfrac{L}{1 + 100e^{-kt}}$.

(a) Let $k = 1$. Graph $P$ for several values for $L$. Explain the effect of the parameter $L$.
(b) Now let $L = 1$. Graph $P$ for several values for $k$. Explain the effect of the parameter $k$.

Solution    (a) See Figure 4.72. Notice that the graph levels off at the value $L$. The parameter $L$ determines the horizontal asymptote and the upper bound for $P$.

Figure 4.72: Graph of $P = \dfrac{L}{1 + 100e^{-t}}$ for various values of $L$

Figure 4.73: Graph of $P = \dfrac{1}{1 + 100e^{-kt}}$ with various values of $k$

(b) See Figure 4.73. Notice that as $k$ increases, the curve approaches the asymptote more rapidly. The parameter $k$ affects the steepness of the curve.

---

[13] See Appendix A: Fitting Formulas to Data.
[14] Just how small is small enough depends on the values of the parameters $C$ and $k$.

## The Carrying Capacity and the Point of Diminishing Returns

Example 1 suggests that the parameter $L$ of the logistic function is the value at which $P$ levels off, where

$$P = \frac{L}{1 + Ce^{-kt}}.$$

This value $L$ is called the *carrying capacity* and represents the largest population an environment can support.

One way to estimate the carrying capacity is to find the inflection point. The graph of a logistic curve is concave up at first and then concave down. At the inflection point, where the concavity changes, the slope is largest. To the left of this point, the graph is concave up and the rate of growth is increasing. To the right of this point, the graph is concave down and the rate of growth is diminishing. The inflection point is called the *point of diminishing returns*. Problem 70 in the Review Problems shows that this point is at $P = L/2$. See Figure 4.74. Companies sometimes watch for this concavity change in the sales of a new product and use it to estimate the maximum potential sales.

---

Properties of the logistic function $P = \dfrac{L}{1 + Ce^{-kt}}$:

- The limiting value $L$ represents the carrying capacity for $P$.

- The point of diminishing returns is the inflection point where $P$ is growing the fastest. It occurs where $P = L/2$.

- The logistic function is approximately exponential for small values of $t$, with growth rate $k$.

---

**Figure 4.74:** Logistic growth

## The Years 1790-2010: Another Look at the US Population

We used a logistic function to model the US population between 1790 and 1940. How well does this model fit the US population since 1940? We now look at all the population data from 1790 to 2010.

**Example 2**    If $t$ is in years since 1790 and $P$ is in millions, we used the following logistic function to model the US population between 1790 and 1940:

$$P = \frac{192}{1 + 48e^{-0.0317t}}.$$

According to this function, what is the maximum US population? Is this prediction accurate? How well does this logistic model fit the growth of the US population since 1940?

**Table 4.7**  *Predicted versus actual US population, in millions, 1940-2010 (logistic model)*

| Year | 1940 | 1950 | 1960 | 1970 | 1980 | 1990 | 2000 | 2010 |
|------|------|------|------|------|------|------|------|------|
| Actual | 132.2 | 151.3 | 179.3 | 203.2 | 226.5 | 248.7 | 281.4 | 308.7 |
| Predicted | 136.0 | 147.7 | 157.6 | 165.7 | 172.2 | 177.2 | 181.0 | 183.9 |

Solution          Table 4.7 shows the actual US population between 1940 and 2010 and the predicted values using
                  this logistic model. According to the formula for the logistic function, the upper bound for the
                  population is $L = 192$ million. However, Table 4.7 shows that the actual US population was above
                  this figure by 1970. The fit between the logistic function and the actual population is not a good one
                  beyond 1940. See Figure 4.75.

Figure 4.75: The logistic model and the US population, 1790-2010

Despite World War II, which depressed population growth between 1942 and 1945, in the last
half of the 1940s the US population surged. The 1950s saw a population growth of 28 million,
leaving our logistic model in the dust. This surge in population is referred to as the baby boom.

Once again we have reached a point where our model is no longer useful. This should not lead
you to believe that a reasonable mathematical model cannot be found; rather, it points out that no
model is perfect and that when one model fails, we seek a better one. Just as we abandoned the
exponential model in favor of the logistic model for the US population, we could look further.

## Sales Predictions

Total sales of a new product often follow a logistic model. For example, when a new application
(app) for a mobile device comes on the market, sales first increase rapidly as word of the app spreads.
Eventually, most of the people who want the app have already bought it and sales slow down. The
graph of total sales against time is concave up at first and then concave down, with the upper bound
$L$ equal to the maximum potential sales.

Example 3          Table 4.8 shows the total sales (in thousands) of new app since it was introduced.

                   (a) Find the point where concavity changes in this function. Use it to estimate the maximum poten-
                       tial sales, $L$.
                   (b) Using logistic regression, fit a logistic function to this data. What maximum potential sales does
                       this function predict?

Table 4.8    *Total sales of a new app since its introduction*

| $t$ (months)              | 0   | 1 | 2 | 3  | 4  | 5   | 6   | 7   |
|---------------------------|-----|---|---|----|----|-----|-----|-----|
| $P$ (total sales in 1000s) | 0.5 | 2 | 8 | 33 | 95 | 258 | 403 | 496 |

Solution           (a) The rate of change of total sales increases until $t = 5$ and decreases after $t = 5$, so the inflection
                       point is at approximately $t = 5$, when $P = 258$. So $L/2 = 258$ and $L = 516$. The maximum
                       potential sales for this app are estimated to be 516,000.
                   (b) Logistic regression gives the following function:

$$P = \frac{532}{1 + 869e^{-1.33t}}.$$

Maximum potential sales predicted by this function are $L = 532$, or about 532,000. See Figure 4.76.

Figure 4.76: Logistic growth: Total sales of an app

## Dose-Response Curves

A *dose-response curve* plots the intensity of physiological response to a drug as a function of the dose administered. As the dose increases, the intensity of the response increases, so a dose-response function is increasing. The intensity of the response is generally scaled as a percentage of the maximum response. The curve cannot go above the maximum response (or 100%), so the curve levels off at a horizontal asymptote. Dose-response curves are generally concave up for low doses and concave down for high doses. A dose-response curve can be modeled by a logistic function with the independent variable being the dose of the drug, not time.

A dose-response curve shows the amount of drug needed to produce the desired effect, as well as the maximum effect attainable and the dose required to obtain it. The slope of the dose-response curve gives information about the therapeutic safety margin of the drug.

Drugs need to be administered in a dose which is large enough to be effective but not so large as to be dangerous. Figure 4.77 shows two different dose-response curves: one with a small slope and one with a large slope. In Figure 4.77(a), there is a broad range of dosages at which the drug is both safe and effective. In Figure 4.77(b), where the slope of the curve is steep, the range of dosages at which the drug is both safe and effective is small. If the slope of the dose-response curve is steep, a small mistake in the dosage can have dangerous results. Administration of such a drug is difficult.

Figure 4.77: What does the slope of the dose-response curve tell us?

**Example 4**    Figure 4.78 shows dose-response curves for three different drugs used for the same purpose. Discuss the advantages and disadvantages of the three drugs.

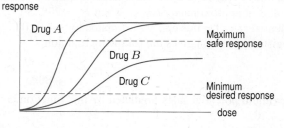

Figure 4.78: What are the advantages and disadvantages of each of these drugs?

Solution    Drugs $A$ and $B$ show the same maximum response, both above the maximum safe level. Drug $A$ reaches this level more quickly. The maximum response of Drug $C$ is significantly lower, while still reaching the minimum desired level. Thus, Drug $C$ may be the preferred drug despite its lower maximum effect because it is the safest to administer.

## Problems for Section 4.7

1. If $t$ is in years since 1990, one model for the population of the world, $P$, in billions, is

$$P = \frac{40}{1 + 11e^{-0.08t}}.$$

   (a) What does this model predict for the maximum sustainable population of the world?
   (b) Graph $P$ against $t$.
   (c) According to this model, when will the earth's population reach 20 billion? 39.9 billion?

2. Investigate the effect of the parameter $C$ on the logistic curve

$$P = \frac{10}{1 + Ce^{-t}}.$$

   Substitute several values for $C$ and explain, with a graph and with words, the effect of $C$ on the graph.

3. The following table shows the total sales, in thousands, since a new game was brought to market.

   (a) Plot this data and mark on your plot the point of diminishing returns.
   (b) Predict total possible sales of this game, using the point of diminishing returns.

| Month | 0 | 2 | 4 | 6 | 8 | 10 | 12 | 14 |
|---|---|---|---|---|---|---|---|---|
| Sales | 0 | 2.3 | 5.5 | 9.6 | 18.2 | 31.8 | 42.0 | 50.8 |

4. Write a paragraph explaining why sales of a new product often follow a logistic curve. Explain the benefit to the company of watching for the point of diminishing returns.

5. (a) Draw a logistic curve. Label the carrying capacity $L$ and the point of diminishing returns $t_0$.
   (b) Draw the derivative of the logistic curve. Mark the point $t_0$ on the horizontal axis.
   (c) A company keeps track of the rate of sales (for example, sales per week) rather than total sales. Explain how the company can tell on a graph of rate of sales when the point of diminishing returns is reached.

6. The following table gives the percentage, $P$, of households with cable television between 1977 and 2003.[15]

| Year | 1977 | 1978 | 1979 | 1980 | 1981 | 1982 | 1983 |
|---|---|---|---|---|---|---|---|
| $P$ | 16.6 | 17.9 | 19.4 | 22.6 | 28.3 | 35.0 | 40.5 |
| Year | 1984 | 1985 | 1986 | 1987 | 1988 | 1989 | 1990 |
| $P$ | 43.7 | 46.2 | 48.1 | 50.5 | 53.8 | 57.1 | 59.0 |
| Year | 1991 | 1992 | 1993 | 1994 | 1995 | 1996 | 1997 |
| $P$ | 60.6 | 61.5 | 62.5 | 63.4 | 65.7 | 66.7 | 67.3 |
| Year | 1998 | 1999 | 2000 | 2001 | 2002 | 2003 | |
| $P$ | 67.4 | 68.0 | 67.8 | 69.2 | 68.9 | 68.0 | |

   (a) Explain why a logistic model is reasonable for this data.
   (b) Estimate the point of diminishing returns. What limiting value $L$ does this point predict? Does this limiting value appear to be accurate, given the percentages for 2002 and 2003?
   (c) If $t$ is in years since 1977, the best fitting logistic function for this data turns out to be

$$P = \frac{68.8}{1 + 3.486e^{-0.237t}},$$

   What limiting value does this function predict?
   (d) Explain in terms of percentages of households what the limiting value is telling you. Do you think your answer to part (c) is an accurate prediction?

7. The Tojolobal Mayan Indian community in Southern Mexico has available a fixed amount of land.[16] The proportion, $P$, of land in use for farming $t$ years after 1935 is modeled with the logistic function

$$P = \frac{1}{1 + 3e^{-0.0275t}}.$$

   (a) What proportion of the land was in use for farming in 1935?
   (b) What is the long-run prediction of this model?
   (c) When was half the land in use for farming?
   (d) When is the proportion of land used for farming increasing most rapidly?

[15] *The World Almanac and Book of Facts 2005*, p. 310 (New York).
[16] Adapted from J. S. Thomas and M. C. Robbins, "The Limits to Growth in a Tojolobal Maya Ejido," *Geoscience and Man* 26, pp. 9–16 (Baton Rouge: Geoscience Publications, 1988).

8. In the spring of 2003, SARS (Severe Acute Respiratory Syndrome) spread rapidly in several Asian countries and Canada. Table 4.9 gives the total number, $P$, of SARS cases reported in Hong Kong[17] by day $t$, where $t = 0$ is March 17, 2003.

(a) Find the average rate of change of $P$ for each interval in Table 4.9.

(b) In early April 2003, there was fear that the disease would spread at an ever-increasing rate for a long time. What is the earliest date by which epidemiologists had evidence to indicate that the rate of new cases had begun to slow?

(c) Explain why an exponential model for $P$ is not appropriate.

(d) It turns out that a logistic model fits the data well. Estimate the value of $t$ at the inflection point. What limiting value of $P$ does this point predict?

(e) The best-fitting logistic function for this data turns out to be

$$P = \frac{1760}{1 + 17.53e^{-0.1408t}}.$$

What limiting value of $P$ does this function predict?

**Table 4.9** *Total number of SARS cases in Hong Kong by day t (where t = 0 is March 17, 2003)*

| $t$ | $P$ | $t$ | $P$ | $t$ | $P$ | $t$ | $P$ |
|-----|-----|-----|-----|-----|-----|-----|-----|
| 0 | 95 | 26 | 1108 | 54 | 1674 | 75 | 1739 |
| 5 | 222 | 33 | 1358 | 61 | 1710 | 81 | 1750 |
| 12 | 470 | 40 | 1527 | 68 | 1724 | 87 | 1755 |
| 19 | 800 | 47 | 1621 | | | | |

9. Substitute $t = 0, 10, 20, \ldots, 70$ into the exponential function used in this section to model the US population 1790–1860. Compare the predicted values of the population with the actual values.

10. On page 214, a logistic function was used to model the US population. Use this function to predict the US population in each of the census years from 1790–1940. Compare the predicted and actual values.

11. A curve representing the total number of people, $P$, infected with a virus often has the shape of a logistic curve of the form

$$P = \frac{L}{1 + Ce^{-kt}},$$

with time $t$ in weeks. Suppose that 10 people originally have the virus and that in the early stages the number of people infected is increasing approximately exponentially, with a continuous growth rate of 1.78. It is estimated that, in the long run, approximately 5000 people will become infected.

(a) What should we use for the parameters $k$ and $L$?

(b) Use the fact that when $t = 0$, we have $P = 10$, to find $C$.

(c) Now that you have estimated $L$, $k$, and $C$, what is the logistic function you are using to model the data? Graph this function.

(d) Estimate the length of time until the rate at which people are becoming infected starts to decrease. What is the value of $P$ at this point?

12. Find the point where the following curve is steepest:

$$y = \frac{50}{1 + 6e^{-2t}} \qquad \text{for } t \geq 0.$$

13. A dose-response curve is given by $R = f(x)$, where $R$ is percent of maximum response and $x$ is the dose of the drug in mg. The curve has the shape shown in Figure 4.77. The inflection point is at $(15, 50)$ and $f'(15) = 11$.

(a) Explain what $f'(15)$ tells you in terms of dose and response for this drug.

(b) Is $f'(10)$ greater than or less than 11? Is $f'(20)$ greater than or less than 11? Explain.

14. If $R$ is percent of maximum response and $x$ is dose in mg, the dose-response curve for a drug is given by

$$R = \frac{100}{1 + 100e^{-0.1x}}.$$

(a) Graph this function.

(b) What dose corresponds to a response of 50% of the maximum? This is the inflection point, at which the response is increasing the fastest.

(c) For this drug, the minimum desired response is 20% and the maximum safe response is 70%. What range of doses is both safe and effective for this drug?

15. Dose-response curves for three different products are given in Figure 4.79.

(a) For the desired response, which drug requires the largest dose? The smallest dose?

(b) Which drug has the largest maximum response? The smallest?

(c) Which drug is the safest to administer? Explain.

Figure 4.79

intensity of response

Product $A$    Product $C$

Product $B$    Maximum safe response

Minimum desired response

dose (mg)

---

[17]www.who.int/csr/country/en, accessed July 13, 2003.

**16.** Explain why it is safer to use a drug for which the derivative of the dose-response curve is smaller.

There are two kinds of dose-response curves. One type, discussed in this section, plots the intensity of response against the dose of the drug. We now consider a dose-response curve in which the percentage of subjects showing a specific response is plotted against the dose of the drug. In Problems 17–18, the curve on the left shows the percentage of subjects exhibiting the desired response at the given dose, and the curve on the right shows the percentage of subjects for which the given dose is lethal.

**17.** In Figure 4.80, what range of doses appears to be both safe and effective for 99% of all patients?

**Figure 4.80**

**18.** In Figure 4.81, discuss the possible outcomes and what percent of patients fall in each outcome when 50 mg of the drug is administered.

**Figure 4.81**

**19.** A population, $P$, growing logistically is given by

$$P = \frac{L}{1 + Ce^{-kt}}.$$

**(a)** Show that

$$\frac{L - P}{P} = Ce^{-kt}.$$

**(b)** Explain why part (a) shows that the ratio of the additional population the environment can support to the existing population decays exponentially.

**20.** Cell membranes contain ion channels. The fraction, $f$, of channels that are open is a function of the membrane potential $V$ (the voltage inside the cell minus voltage outside), in millivolts (mV), given by

$$f(V) = \frac{1}{1 + e^{-(V+25)/2}}.$$

**(a)** Find the values of $L$, $k$, and $C$ in the logistic formula for $f$:

$$f(V) = \frac{L}{1 + Ce^{-kV}}.$$

**(b)** At what voltages $V$ are 10%, 50% and 90% of the channels open?

# 4.8  THE SURGE FUNCTION AND DRUG CONCENTRATION

## Nicotine in the Blood

When a person smokes a cigarette, the nicotine from the cigarette enters the body through the lungs, is absorbed into the blood, and spreads throughout the body. Most cigarettes contain between 0.5 and 2.0 mg of nicotine; approximately 20% (between 0.1 and 0.4 mg) is actually inhaled and absorbed into the person's bloodstream. As the nicotine leaves the blood, the smoker feels the need for another cigarette. The half-life of nicotine in the bloodstream is about two hours. The lethal dose is considered to be about 60 mg.

The nicotine level in the blood rises as a person smokes, and tapers off when smoking ceases. Table 4.10 shows blood nicotine concentration (in ng/ml) during and after the use of cigarettes. (Smoking occurred during the first ten minutes and the experimental data shown represent average values for ten people.)[18]

The points in Table 4.10 are plotted in Figure 4.82. Functions with this behavior are called *surge functions*. They have equations of the form $y = ate^{-bt}$, where $a$ and $b$ are positive constants.

[18]Benowitz, Porched, Skeiner, Jacog, "Nicotine Absorption and Cardiovascular Effects with Smokeless Tobacco Use: Comparison with Cigarettes and Nicotine Gum," *Clinical Pharmacology and Therapeutics* 44 (1988): 24.

**Table 4.10**    *Blood nicotine concentrations during and after the use of cigarettes*

| $t$ (minutes) | 0 | 5 | 10 | 15 | 20 | 25 | 30 | 45 | 60 | 75 | 90 | 105 | 120 |
|---|---|---|---|---|---|---|---|---|---|---|---|---|---|
| $C$ (ng/ml) | 4 | 12 | 17 | 14 | 13 | 12 | 11 | 9 | 8 | 7.5 | 7 | 6.5 | 6 |

**Figure 4.82**: Blood nicotine concentrations during and after the use of cigarettes

**Figure 4.83**: One member of the family $y = ate^{-bt}$, with $a = 1$ and $b = 1$

## The Family of Functions $y = ate^{-bt}$

What effect do the positive parameters $a$ and $b$ have on the shape of the graph of $y = ate^{-bt}$? Start by looking at the graph with $a = 1$ and $b = 1$. See Figure 4.83. We consider the effect of the parameter $b$ on the graph of $y = ate^{-bt}$ now; the parameter $a$ is considered in Problem 2 of this section.

### The Effect of the Parameter $b$ on $y = te^{-bt}$

Graphs of $y = te^{-bt}$ for different positive values of $b$ are shown in Figure 4.84. The general shape of the curve does not change as $b$ changes, but as $b$ decreases, the curve rises for a longer period of time and to a higher value.

**Figure 4.84**: Graph of $y = te^{-bt}$, with $b$ varying

**Figure 4.85**: How does the maximum depend on $b$?

We see in Figure 4.85 that, when $b = 1$, the maximum occurs at about $t = 1$. When $b = 2$, it occurs at about $t = \frac{1}{2}$, and when $b = 3$, it occurs at about $t = \frac{1}{3}$. The next example shows that the maximum of the function $y = te^{-bt}$ occurs at $t = 1/b$.

---

**Example 1**    For $b > 0$, show that the maximum value of $y = te^{-bt}$ occurs at $t = 1/b$ and increases as $b$ decreases.

**Solution**    The maximum occurs at a critical point where $dy/dt = 0$. Differentiating gives

$$\frac{dy}{dt} = 1 \cdot e^{-bt} + t\left(-be^{-bt}\right) = e^{-bt} - bte^{-bt} = e^{-bt}(1 - bt).$$

So $dy/dt = 0$ where

$$1 - bt = 0$$
$$t = \frac{1}{b}.$$

Substituting $t = 1/b$ shows that at the maximum,

$$y = \frac{1}{b}e^{-b(1/b)} = \frac{e^{-1}}{b}.$$

So, for $b > 0$, as $b$ increases, the maximum value of $y$ decreases and vice versa.

---

The **surge function** $y = ate^{-bt}$, for positive constants $a$ and $b$, increases rapidly and then decreases toward zero with a maximum at $t = 1/b$. See Figure 4.86.

---

Figure 4.86: Curve showing drug concentration as a function of time

## Drug Concentration Curves

As with nicotine, the graph of concentration against time is called the *drug concentration curve*. If $t$ is the time since the drug was administered, the concentration, $C$, can be modeled by the surge function $C = ate^{-bt}$, where $a$ and $b$ are positive constants. (See Figure 4.86.)

### Factors Affecting Drug Absorption

Drug interactions and the age of the patient can affect the drug concentration curve. In Problems 11 and 13, we see that food intake can also affect the rate of absorption of a drug, and (perhaps most surprising) that drug concentration curves can vary markedly between different commercial versions of the same drug.

---

**Example 2**    Figure 4.87 shows the drug concentration curves for paracetamol (acetaminophen) alone and for paracetamol taken in conjunction with propantheline. Figure 4.88 shows drug concentration curves for patients known to be slow absorbers of the drug, for paracetamol alone and for paracetamol in conjunction with metoclopramide. Discuss the effects of the additional drugs on peak concentration and the time to reach peak concentration.[19]

Figure 4.87: Drug concentration curves for paracetamol, normal patients

Figure 4.88: Drug concentration curves for paracetamol, patients with slow absorption

[19]Graeme S. Avery, ed. *Drug Treatment: Principle and Practice of Clinical Pharmacology and Therapeutics* (Sydney: Adis Press, 1976).

Solution    Figure 4.87 shows it takes about 1.5 hours for the paracetamol to reach its peak concentration, and that the maximum concentration reached is about 23 μg of paracetamol per ml of blood. However, if propantheline is administered with the paracetamol, it takes much longer to reach the peak concentration (about three hours, or approximately double the time), and the peak concentration is much lower, at about 16 μg/ml.

Comparing the curves for paracetamol alone in Figures 4.87 and 4.88 shows that the time to reach peak concentration is the same (about 1.5 hours), but the maximum concentration is lower for patients with slow absorption. When metoclopramide is given with paracetamol in Figure 4.88, the peak concentration is reached faster and is higher.

## Minimum Effective Concentration

The minimum effective concentration of a drug is the blood concentration necessary to achieve a pharmacological response. The time at which this concentration is reached is referred to as onset; termination occurs when the drug concentration falls below this level. See Figure 4.89.

Figure 4.89: When is the drug effective?

**Example 3**    Depo-Provera was approved for use in the US in 1992 as a contraceptive. Figure 4.90 shows the drug concentration curve for a dose of 150 mg given intramuscularly.[20] The minimum effective concentration is about 4 ng/ml. How often should the drug be administered?

Figure 4.90: Drug concentration curve for Depo-Provera    Figure 4.91: When should the next dose be administered?

Solution    The minimum effective concentration on the drug concentration curve is plotted as a dotted horizontal line at 4 ng/ml. See Figure 4.91. We see that the drug becomes effective almost immediately and ceases to be effective after about four months. Doses should be given about every four months.

Although the dosage interval is four months, notice that it takes ten months after injections are discontinued for Depo-Provera to be entirely eliminated from the body. Fertility during that period is unpredictable.

[20]Robert M. Julien, *A Primer of Drug Action* (W. H. Freeman and Co, 1995).

# Problems for Section 4.8

1. If time, $t$, is in hours and concentration, $C$, is in ng/ml, the drug concentration curve for a drug is given by

$$C = 12.4te^{-0.2t}.$$

   (a) Graph this curve.
   (b) How many hours does it take for the drug to reach its peak concentration? What is the concentration at that time?
   (c) If the minimum effective concentration is 10 ng/ml, during what time period is the drug effective?
   (d) Complications can arise whenever the level of the drug is above 4 ng/ml. How long must a patient wait before being safe from complications?

2. Let $b = 1$, and graph $C = ate^{-bt}$ using different values for $a$. Explain the effect of the parameter $a$.

3. If $t$ is in hours, the drug concentration curve for a drug is given by $C = 17.2te^{-0.4t}$ ng/ml. The minimum effective concentration is 10 ng/ml.

   (a) If the second dose of the drug is to be administered when the first dose becomes ineffective, when should the second dose be given?
   (b) If you want the onset of effectiveness of the second dose to coincide with termination of effectiveness of the first dose, when should the second dose be given?

4. Figure 4.92 shows drug concentration curves for anhydrous ampicillin for newborn babies and adults.[21] Discuss the differences between newborns and adults in the absorption of this drug.

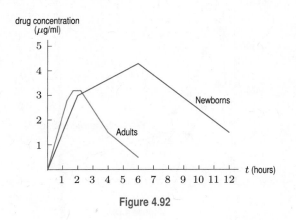

**Figure 4.92**

5. Absorption of different forms of the antibiotic erythromycin may be increased, decreased, delayed or not affected by food. Figure 4.93 shows the drug concentration levels of erythromycin in healthy, fasting human volunteers who received single oral doses of 500 mg erythromycin tablets, together with either large (250 ml) or small (20 ml) accompanying volumes of water.[22] Discuss the effect of the water on the concentration of erythromycin in the blood. How are the peak concentration and the time to reach peak concentration affected? When does the effect of the volume of water wear off?

**Figure 4.93**

6. Hydrocodone bitartrate is a cough suppressant usually administered in a 10 mg oral dose. The peak concentration of the drug in the blood occurs 1.3 hours after consumption and the peak concentration is 23.6 ng/ml. Draw the drug concentration curve for hydrocodone bitartrate.

7. Figure 4.82 shows the concentration of nicotine in the blood during and after smoking a cigarette. Figure 4.94 shows the concentration of nicotine in the blood during and after using chewing tobacco or nicotine gum. (The chewing occurred during the first 30 minutes and the experimental data shown represent the average values for ten patients.)[23] Compare the three nicotine concentration curves (for cigarettes, chewing tobacco and nicotine gum) in terms of peak concentration, the time until peak concentration, and the rate at which the nicotine is eliminated from the bloodstream.

---

[21]*Pediatrics*, 1973, 51, 578.

[22]J. W. Bridges and L.F. Chasseaud, *Progress in Drug Metabolism* (New York: John Wiley and Sons, 1980).

[23]Benowitz, Porchet, Skeiner, Jacob, "Nicotine Absorption and Cardiovascular Effects with Smokeless Tobacco Use: Comparison with Cigarettes and Nicotine Gum," *Clinical Pharmacology and Therapeutics* 44 (1988): 24.

Figure 4.94

Figure 4.95

**10.** This problem shows how a surge can be modeled with a difference of exponential decay functions.

   **(a)** Using graphs of $e^{-t}$ and $e^{-2t}$, explain why the graph of $f(t) = e^{-t} - e^{-2t}$ has the shape of a surge.

   **(b)** Find the critical point and inflection point of $f$.

**11.** Figure 4.96 shows the plasma levels of canrenone in a healthy volunteer after a single oral dose of spironolactone given on a fasting stomach and together with a standardized breakfast. (Spironolactone is a diuretic agent that is partially converted into canrenone in the body.)[24] Discuss the effect of food on peak concentration and time to reach peak concentration. Is the effect of the food strongest during the first 8 hours, or after 8 hours?

**8.** If $t$ is in minutes since the drug was administered, the concentration, $C(t)$ in ng/ml, of a drug in a patient's bloodstream is given by

$$C(t) = 20te^{-0.03t}.$$

   **(a)** How long does it take for the drug to reach peak concentration? What is the peak concentration?

   **(b)** What is the concentration of the drug in the body after 15 minutes? After an hour?

   **(c)** If the minimum effective concentration is 10 ng/ml, when should the next dose be administered?

Figure 4.96

**9.** For time $t \geq 0$, the function $C = ate^{-bt}$ with positive constants $a$ and $b$ gives the concentration, $C$, of a drug in the body. Figure 4.95 shows the maximum concentration reached (in nanograms per milliliter, ng/ml) after a 10 mg dose of the cough medicine hydrocodone bitartrate. Find the values of $a$ and $b$.

**12.** The method of administering a drug can have a strong influence on the drug concentration curve. Figure 4.97 shows drug concentration curves for penicillin following various routes of administration. Three milligrams per

[24]Welling & Tse, *Pharmacokinetics of Cardiovascular, Central Nervous System, and Antimicrobial Drugs* (The Royal Society of Chemistry, 1985).

[25]J. W. Bridges and L. F. Chasseaud, *Progress in Drug Metabolism* (New York: John Wiley and Sons, 1980).

kilogram of body weight were dissolved in water and administered intravenously (IV), intramuscularly (IM), subcutaneously (SC), and orally (PO). The same quantity of penicillin dissolved in oil was administered intramuscularly (P-IM). The minimum effective concentration (MEC) is labeled on the graph.[25]

(a) Which method reaches peak concentration the fastest? The slowest?

(b) Which method has the largest peak concentration? The smallest?

(c) Which method wears off the fastest? The slowest?

(d) Which method has the longest effective duration? The shortest?

(e) When penicillin is administered orally, for approximately what time interval is it effective?

**Figure 4.98**

**Figure 4.97**

**14.** Figure 4.99 shows a graph of the percentage of drug dissolved against time for four tetracycline products $A$, $B$, $C$, and $D$. Figure 4.100 shows the drug concentration curves for the same four tetracycline products.[27] Discuss the effect of dissolution rate on peak concentration and time to reach peak concentration.

**Figure 4.99**

**13.** Figure 4.98 shows drug concentration curves after oral administration of 0.5 mg of four digoxin products. All the tablets met current USP standards of potency, disintegration time, and dissolution rate.[26]

(a) Discuss differences and similarities in the peak concentration and the time to reach peak concentration.

(b) Give possible values for minimum effective concentration and maximum safe concentration that would make Product $C$ or Product $D$ the preferred drug.

(c) Give possible values for minimum effective concentration and maximum safe concentration that would make Product $A$ the preferred drug.

**Figure 4.100**

[26]Graeme S. Avery, ed. *Drug Treatment: Principles and Practice of Clinical Pharmacology and Therapeutics* (Sydney: Adis Press, 1976).

[27]J. W. Bridges and L.F. Chasseaud, *Progress in Drug Metabolism* (New York: John Wiley and Sons, 1980).

## CHAPTER SUMMARY

- **Using the first derivative**
  Critical points, local maxima and minima
- **Using the second derivative**
  Inflection points, concavity
- **Optimization**
  Global maxima and minima
- **Maximizing profit and revenue**

- **Average cost**
  Minimizing average cost
- **Elasticity**
- **Families of functions**
  Parameters. The surge function, drug concentration curves. The logistic function, carrying capacity, point of diminishing returns.

## REVIEW PROBLEMS FOR CHAPTER FOUR

For Problems 1–2, indicate all critical points on the given graphs. Which correspond to local minima, local maxima, global maxima, global minima, or none of these? (Note that the graphs are on closed intervals.)

**1.**

**2.**

**13.** On the graph of $f'$ in Figure 4.101, indicate the $x$-values that are critical points of the function $f$ itself. Are they local maxima, local minima, or neither?

Figure 4.101: Graph of $f'$ (not $f$)

In Problems 3–7, use derivatives to find the critical points and inflection points.

**3.** $f(x) = x^3 - 9x^2 + 24x + 5$

**4.** $f(x) = x^5 - 10x^3 - 8$

**5.** $f(x) = x^5 + 15x^4 + 25$

**6.** $f(x) = 5x - 3\ln x$

**7.** $f(x) = 4xe^{3x}$

In Problems 8–9, find the value(s) of $x$ for which:
(a) $f(x)$ has a local maximum or local minimum. Indicate which ones are maxima and which are minima.
(b) $f(x)$ has a global maximum or global minimum.

**8.** $f(x) = x^{10} - 10x$, and $0 \le x \le 2$

**9.** $f(x) = x - \ln x$, and $0.1 \le x \le 2$

**10.** (a) Find the critical points of $p(1-p)^4$.
(b) Classify the critical points as local maxima, local minima, or neither.
(c) What are the maximum and minimum values of $p(1-p)^4$ on $0 \le x \le 1$?

**11.** On July 1, the price of a stock had a critical point. How could the price have been changing during the time around July 1?

**12.** (a) Show that if $a$ is a positive constant, then $x = 0$ is the only critical point of $f(x) = x + a\sqrt{x}$.
(b) Use derivatives to show that $f$ is increasing and its graph is concave down for all $x > 0$.

Problems 14–15 show the graph of a derivative function $f'$. Indicate on a sketch the $x$-values that are critical points of the function $f$ itself. Identify each critical point as a local maximum, a local minimum, or neither.

**14.**                                   **15.**

**16.** Suppose $f$ has a continuous derivative. From the values of $f'(\theta)$ in the following table, estimate the $\theta$ values with $1 < \theta < 2.1$ at which $f(\theta)$ has a local maximum or minimum. Identify which is which.

| $\theta$ | 1.0 | 1.1 | 1.2 | 1.3 | 1.4 | 1.5 |
|---|---|---|---|---|---|---|
| $f'(\theta)$ | 2.4 | 0.3 | −2.0 | −3.5 | −3.3 | −1.7 |
| $\theta$ | 1.6 | 1.7 | 1.8 | 1.9 | 2.0 | 2.1 |
| $f'(\theta)$ | 0.8 | 2.8 | 3.6 | 2.8 | 0.7 | −1.6 |

**17. (a)** Find the derivative of $f(x) = x^5 + x + 7$. What is its sign?

**(b)** How many real roots does the equation $x^5 + x + 7 = 0$ have? How do you know?

[Hint: How many critical points does this function have?]

**18. (a)** If $b$ is a positive constant and $x > 0$, find all critical points of $f(x) = x - b \ln x$.

**(b)** Use the second-derivative test to determine whether the function has a local maximum or local minimum at each critical point.

**19.** If $a$ and $b$ are nonzero constants, find the domain and all critical points of

$$f(x) = \frac{ax^2}{x - b}.$$

**20. (a)** On a computer or calculator, graph $f(\theta) = \theta - \sin \theta$. Can you tell whether the function has any zeros in the interval $0 \leq \theta \leq 1$?

**(b)** Find $f'$. What does the sign of $f'$ tell you about the zeros of $f$ in the interval $0 \leq \theta \leq 1$?

**21.** For the function, $f$, graphed in Figure 4.102:

**(a)** Sketch $f'(x)$.

**(b)** Where does $f'(x)$ change its sign?

**(c)** Where does $f'(x)$ have local maxima or minima?

**Figure 4.102**

**22.** Using your answer to Problem 21 as a guide, write a short paragraph (using complete sentences) which describes the relationships between the following features of a function $f$:

- The local maxima and minima of $f$.
- The points at which the graph of $f$ changes concavity.
- The sign changes of $f'$.
- The local maxima and minima of $f'$.

**23.** The graphs of $f(x) = 1 + e^{-ax}$ for $a = 1, 2$, and 5, are in Figure 4.103. Without a calculator, identify the graphs by looking at $f'(0)$.

**Figure 4.103**

**24.** The graphs of $f(x) = xe^{-ax}$ for $a = 1, 2$, and 3, are in Figure 4.104. Without a calculator, identify the graphs by locating the critical points of $f(x)$.

**Figure 4.104**

**25.** If water is flowing at a constant rate (i.e., constant volume per unit time) into the vase in Figure 4.105, sketch a graph of the depth of the water against time. Mark on the graph the time at which the water reaches the corner of the vase.

**Figure 4.105**

**26.** Water flows at a constant rate into the left side of the W-shaped container in Figure 4.106. Sketch a graph of the height, $H$, of the water in the left side of the container as a function of time, $t$. The container starts empty.

**Figure 4.106**

**27.** In 1774, Captain James Cook left 10 rabbits on a small Pacific island. The rabbit population is approximated by

$$P(t) = \frac{2000}{1 + e^{5.3-0.4t}}$$

with $t$ measured in years since 1774. Using a calculator or computer:

**(a)** Graph $P$. Does the population level off?
**(b)** Estimate when the rabbit population grew most rapidly. How large was the population at that time?
**(c)** Find the inflection point on the graph and explain its significance for the rabbit population.
**(d)** What natural causes could lead to the shape of the graph of $P$?

**28.** The polynomial $f$ has exactly two local maxima and one local minimum; these are the only critical points of $f$.

**(a)** Sketch a possible graph of $f$.
**(b)** What is the largest number of zeros $f$ could have?
**(c)** What is the smallest number of zeros $f$ could have?
**(d)** What is the smallest number of inflection points $f$ could have?
**(e)** What is the smallest degree $f$ could have?
**(f)** Find a possible formula for $f(x)$.

**29.** For $f(x) = \sin(x^2)$ between $x = 0$ and $x = 3$, find the coordinates of all intercepts, critical points, and inflection points to two decimal points.

**30.** **(a)** Graph $f(x) = x + a\sin x$ for $a = 0.5$ and $a = 3$.
**(b)** For what values of $a$ is $f(x)$ increasing for all $x$?

**31.** **(a)** Graph $f(x) = x^2 + a\sin x$ for $a = 1$ and $a = 20$.
**(b)** For what values of $a$ is $f(x)$ concave up for all $x$?

**32.** Figure 4.107 gives the derivative of $g(x)$ on $-2 \le x \le 2$.

**(a)** Write a few sentences describing the behavior of $g(x)$ on this interval.
**(b)** Does the graph of $g(x)$ have any inflection points? If so, give the approximate $x$-coordinates of their locations. Explain your reasoning.
**(c)** What are the global maxima and minima of $g$ on $[-2, 2]$?
**(d)** If $g(-2) = 5$, what do you know about $g(0)$ and $g(2)$? Explain.

**Figure 4.107**

**33.** For some positive constant $C$, a patient's temperature change, $T$, due to a dose, $D$, of a drug is given by

$$T = \left(\frac{C}{2} - \frac{D}{3}\right) D^2.$$

**(a)** What dosage maximizes the temperature change?
**(b)** The sensitivity of the body to the drug is defined as $dT/dD$. What dosage maximizes sensitivity?

**34.** A rectangle has one side on the $x$-axis and two corners on the top half of the circle of radius 1 centered at the origin. Find the maximum area of such a rectangle. What are the coordinates of its vertices?

**35.** A closed box has a fixed surface area $A$ and a square base with side $x$.

**(a)** Find a formula for its volume, $V$, as a function of $x$.
**(b)** Sketch a graph of $V$ against $x$.
**(c)** Find the maximum value of $V$.

**36.** As an epidemic spreads through a population, the number of infected people, $I$, is expressed as a function of the number of susceptible people, $S$, by

$$I = k\ln\left(\frac{S}{S_0}\right) - S + S_0 + I_0, \quad \text{for } k, S_0, I_0 > 0.$$

**(a)** Find the maximum number of infected people.
**(b)** The constant $k$ is a characteristic of the particular disease; the constants $S_0$ and $I_0$ are the values of $S$ and $I$ when the disease starts. Which of the following affects the maximum possible value of $I$? Explain.

- The particular disease, but not how it starts.
- How the disease starts, but not the particular disease.
- Both the particular disease and how it starts.

**37.** The hypotenuse of a right triangle has one end at the origin and one end on the curve $y = x^2e^{-3x}$, with $x \ge 0$. One of the other two sides is on the $x$-axis, the other side is parallel to the $y$-axis. Find the maximum area of such a triangle. At what $x$-value does it occur?

In Problems 38–39 a vertical line divides a region into two pieces. Find the value of the coordinate $x$ that maximizes the product of the two areas.

**38.**                                        **39.**

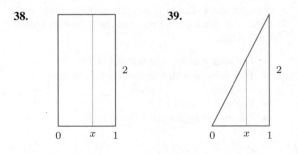

**40.** Which point on the curve $y = \sqrt{1-x}$ is closest to the origin?

**41.** Find the point(s) on the ellipse

$$\frac{x^2}{9} + y^2 = 1$$

   (a) Closest to the point $(2, 0)$.
   (b) Closest to the focus $(\sqrt{8}, 0)$.

[Hint: Minimize the square of the distance—this avoids square roots.]

**42.** What are the dimensions of the closed cylindrical can that has surface area 280 square centimeters and contains the maximum volume?

**43.** The following table gives the cost and revenue, in dollars, for different production levels, $q$.

   (a) At approximately what production level is profit maximized?
   (b) What price is charged per unit for this product?
   (c) What are the fixed costs of production?

| $q$ | 0 | 100 | 200 | 300 | 400 | 500 |
|---|---|---|---|---|---|---|
| $R(q)$ | 0 | 500 | 1000 | 1500 | 2000 | 2500 |
| $C(q)$ | 700 | 900 | 1000 | 1100 | 1300 | 1900 |

**44.** Figure 4.108 gives cost and revenue. What are fixed costs? What quantity maximizes profit, and what is the maximum profit earned?

**Figure 4.108**

**45.** Marginal revenue and marginal cost are given in the following table. Estimate the production levels that could maximize profit. Explain.

| $q$ | 1000 | 2000 | 3000 | 4000 | 5000 | 6000 |
|---|---|---|---|---|---|---|
| $MR$ | 78 | 76 | 74 | 72 | 70 | 68 |
| $MC$ | 100 | 80 | 70 | 65 | 75 | 90 |

**46.** Figure 4.109 shows cost and revenue for a product.

   (a) Estimate the production level that maximizes profit.
   (b) Graph marginal revenue and marginal cost for this product on the same axes. Label on this graph the production level that maximizes profit.

**Figure 4.109**

**47.** The marginal revenue and marginal cost for a certain item are graphed in Figure 4.110. Do the following quantities maximize profit for the company? Explain your answer.

   (a) $q = a$           (b) $q = b$

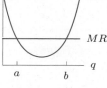

**Figure 4.110**

**48.** The total cost of producing $q$ units of a product is given by $C(q) = q^3 - 60q^2 + 1400q + 1000$ for $0 \leq q \leq 50$; the product sells for $788 per unit. What production level maximizes profit? Find the total cost, total revenue, and total profit at this production level. Graph the cost and revenue functions on the same axes, and label the production level at which profit is maximized and the corresponding cost, revenue, and profit. [Hint: Costs can go as high as $46,000.]

**49.** The total cost $C(q)$ of producing $q$ goods is given by:

$$C(q) = 0.01q^3 - 0.6q^2 + 13q.$$

   (a) What is the fixed cost?
   (b) What is the maximum profit if each item is sold for $7? (Assume you sell everything you produce.)
   (c) Suppose exactly 34 goods are produced. They all sell when the price is $7 each, but for each $1 increase in price, 2 fewer goods are sold. Should the price be raised, and if so by how much?

**50.** The demand equation for a product is $p = b_1 - a_1 q$ and the cost function is $C(q) = b_2 + a_2 q$, where $p$ is the price of the product and $q$ is the quantity sold. Find the value of $q$, in terms of the positive constants $b_1$, $a_1$, $b_2$, $a_2$, that maximizes profit.

**51.** A manufacturer's cost of producing a product is given in Figure 4.111. The manufacturer can sell the product for a price $p$ each (regardless of the quantity sold), so that the total revenue from selling a quantity $q$ is $R(q) = pq$.

   **(a)** The difference $\pi(q) = R(q) - C(q)$ is the total profit. For which quantity $q_0$ is the profit a maximum? Mark your answer on a sketch of the graph.
   **(b)** What is the relationship between $p$ and $C'(q_0)$? Explain your result both graphically and analytically. What does this mean in terms of economics? (Note that $p$ is the slope of the line $R(q) = pq$. Note also that $\pi(q)$ has a maximum at $q = q_0$, so $\pi'(q_0) = 0$.)
   **(c)** Graph $C'(q)$ and $p$ (as a horizontal line) on the same axes. Mark $q_0$ on the $q$-axis.

Figure 4.111

**52.** Let $C(q) = 0.04q^3 - 3q^2 + 75q + 96$ be the total cost of producing $q$ items.

   **(a)** Find the average cost per item as a function of $q$.
   **(b)** Use a graphing calculator or computer to graph average cost against $q$.
   **(c)** For what values of $q$ is the average cost per item decreasing? Increasing?
   **(d)** For what value of $q$ is the average cost per item smallest? What is the smallest average cost per item at that point?

**53.** Graph a cost function where the minimum average cost of $25 per unit is achieved by producing 15,000 units.

**54.** Figure 4.112 shows the cost, $C(q)$, and the revenue, $R(q)$, for a quantity $q$. Label the following points on the graph:

   **(a)** The point $F$ representing the fixed costs.
   **(b)** The point $B$ representing the break-even level of production.
   **(c)** The point $M$ representing the level of production at which marginal cost is a minimum.
   **(d)** The point $A$ representing the level of production at which average cost $a(q) = C(q)/q$ is a minimum.

   **(e)** The point $P$ representing the level of production at which profit is a maximum.

Figure 4.112

In Problems 55–60, cost, $C(q)$, is a positive, increasing, concave-down function of quantity produced, $q$. Which one of the two numbers is the larger?

**55.** $C'(2)$ and $C'(3)$

**56.** $C'(5)$ and $\dfrac{C(5) - C(3)}{5 - 3}$

**57.** $\dfrac{C(100) - C(50)}{50}$ and $\dfrac{C(75) - C(50)}{25}$

**58.** $\dfrac{C(100) - C(50)}{50}$ and $\dfrac{C(75) - C(25)}{50}$

**59.** $C'(3)$ and $C(3)/3$

**60.** $C(10)/10$ and $C(25)/25$

**61.** The demand for a product is $q = 2000 - 5p$ where $q$ is units sold at a price of $p$ dollars. Find the elasticity if the price is $20, and interpret your answer in terms of demand.

**62.** Each of the graphs in Figure 4.113 belongs to one of the following families of functions. In each case, identify which family is most likely:

   an exponential function,

   a logarithmic function,

   a polynomial (What is the degree? Is the leading coefficient positive or negative?),

   a logistic function,

   a surge function.

(a)      (b)

(c)      (d)

(e)      (f)

(g)

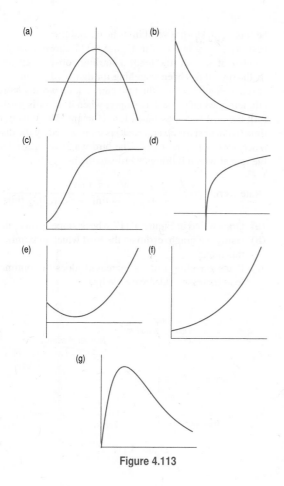

**Figure 4.113**

**63.** Find the dimensions of the rectangle with perimeter 200 meters that has the largest area.

**64.** A square-bottomed box with a top has a fixed volume, $V$. What dimensions minimize the surface area?

**65.** A right triangle has one vertex at the origin and one vertex on the curve $y = e^{-x/3}$ for $1 \leq x \leq 5$. One of the two perpendicular sides is along the $x$-axis; the other is parallel to the $y$-axis. Find the maximum and minimum areas for such a triangle.

**66.** A line goes through the origin and a point on the curve $y = x^2 e^{-3x}$, for $x \geq 0$. Find the maximum slope of such a line. At what $x$-value does it occur?

**67.** A rectangle has one side on the $x$-axis, one side on the $y$-axis, one vertex at the origin and one on the curve $y = e^{-2x}$ for $x \geq 0$. Find the

(a)  Maximum area      (b)  Minimum perimeter

**68.** A pigeon is released from a boat (point $B$ in Figure 4.114) floating on a lake. Because of falling air over the cool water, the energy required to fly one meter over the lake is twice the corresponding energy $e$ required for flying over the bank ($e = 3$ joule/meter). To minimize

the energy required to fly from $B$ to the loft, $L$, the pigeon heads to a point $P$ on the bank and then flies along the bank to $L$. The distance $\overline{AL}$ is 2000 m, and $\overline{AB}$ is 500 m. The angle at $A$ is a right angle.

**(a)** Express the energy required to fly from $B$ to $L$ via $P$ as a function of the angle $\theta$ (the angle $BPA$).
**(b)** What is the optimal angle $\theta$?
**(c)** Does your answer change if $\overline{AL}$, $\overline{AB}$, and $e$ have different numerical values?

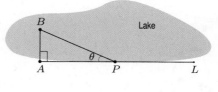

**Figure 4.114**

**69.** The bell-shaped curve of statistics has formula

$$p(x) = \frac{1}{\sigma\sqrt{2\pi}} e^{-(x-\mu)^2/(2\sigma^2)}$$

where $\mu$ is the mean and $\sigma$ is the standard deviation.

**(a)** Where does $p(x)$ have a maximum?
**(b)** Does $p(x)$ have a point of inflection? If so, where?

**70.** Consider a population $P$ satisfying the *logistic equation*

$$\frac{dP}{dt} = kP\left(1 - \frac{P}{L}\right).$$

**(a)** Use the chain rule to find $d^2P/dt^2$.
**(b)** Show that the point of diminishing returns, where $d^2P/dt^2 = 0$, occurs where $P = L/2$.

**71.** Let $C = ate^{-bt}$ represent a drug concentration curve.

**(a)** Discuss the effect on peak concentration and time to reach peak concentration of varying the parameter $a$ while keeping $b$ fixed.
**(b)** Discuss the effect on peak concentration and time to reach peak concentration of varying the parameter $b$ while keeping $a$ fixed.
**(c)** Suppose $a = b$, so $C = ate^{-at}$. Discuss the effect on peak concentration and time to reach peak concentration of varying the parameter $a$.

**72.** The rate of sales of an automobile anti-theft device are given in the following table.

**(a)** When is the point of diminishing returns reached?
**(b)** What are the total sales at this point?
**(c)** Assuming logistic sales growth, use your answer to part (b) to estimate total potential sales of the device.

| Months | 1 | 2 | 3 | 4 | 5 | 6 |
|---|---|---|---|---|---|---|
| Sales per month | 140 | 520 | 680 | 750 | 700 | 550 |

**73.** Figure 4.115 shows the concentration of bemetizide (a diuretic) in the blood after single oral doses of 25 mg alone, or 25 mg bemetizide and 50 mg triamterene in combination.[28] If the minimum effective concentration in a patient is 40 ng/ml, compare the effect of combining bemetizide with triamterene on peak concentration, time to reach peak concentration, time until onset of effectiveness, and duration of effectiveness. Under what circumstances might it be wise to use the triamterene with the bemetizide?

concentration of
bemetizide (ng/ml)

Bemetezide alone

Bemetezide + triamterene

*t* (hours)

**Figure 4.115**

**74.** The distance, *s*, traveled by a cyclist, who starts at 1 pm, is given in Figure 4.116. Time, *t*, is in hours since noon.

(a) Explain why the quantity $s/t$ is represented by the slope of a line from the origin to the point $(t, s)$ on the graph.

(b) Estimate the time at which the quantity $s/t$ is a maximum.

(c) What is the relationship between the quantity $s/t$ and the instantaneous speed of the cyclist at the time you found in part (b)?

*s* (km)

*t* (hours)

**Figure 4.116**

**75.** A bird such as a starling feeds worms to its young. To collect worms, the bird flies to a site where worms are to be found, picks up several in its beak, and flies back to its nest. The *loading curve* in Figure 4.117 shows how the number of worms (the load) a starling collects depends on the time it has been searching for them.[29] The curve is concave down because the bird can pick up worms more efficiently when its beak is empty; when its beak is partly full, the bird becomes much less efficient. The traveling time (from nest to site and back) is represented by the distance $PO$ in Figure 4.117. The bird wants to maximize the rate at which it brings worms to the nest, where

$$\text{Rate worms arrive} = \frac{\text{Load}}{\text{Traveling time} + \text{Searching time}}$$

(a) Draw a line in Figure 4.117 whose slope is this rate.

(b) Using the graph, estimate the load which maximizes this rate.

(c) If the traveling time is increased, does the optimal load increase or decrease? Why?

load
(number of worms)

Number of worms

*P*

Traveling time   *O*   Searching time

time

**Figure 4.117**

**76.** Table 4.11 shows the total number of cars in a University of Arizona parking lot at 30-minute intervals.[30]

(a) Graph the total number of cars in the parking lot as a function of time. Estimate the capacity of the parking lot, and when it was full.

(b) Construct a table, and then plot a graph, of the rate of arrival of cars as a function of time.

(c) From your graph in part (b), estimate when rush hour occurred.

(d) Explain the relationship between the points on the graphs in parts (a) and (b) where rush hour occurred.

**Table 4.11**    *Total number of cars, C, at time t*

| *t* | 5:00 | 5:30 | 6:00 | 6:30 | 7:00 | 7:30 | 8:00 | 8:30 | 9:00 |
|-----|------|------|------|------|------|------|------|------|------|
| *C* | 4 | 5 | 8 | 18 | 50 | 110 | 170 | 200 | 200 |

---

[28] Welling & Tse, *Pharmacokinetics of Cardiovascular, Central Nervous System, and Antimicrobial Drugs* (The Royal Society of Chemistry, 1985).

[29] Alex Kacelnick (1984). Reported by J. R. Krebs and N. B. Davis, *An Introduction to Behavioural Ecology* (Oxford: Blackwell, 1987).

[30] Adapted from Nancy Roberts et al., *Introduction to Computer Simulation*, p. 93 (Reading: Addison-Wesley, 1983).

**77.** A single cell of a bee's honey comb has the shape shown in Figure 4.118. The surface area of this cell is given by

$$A = 6hs + \frac{3}{2}s^2 \left( \frac{-\cos\theta}{\sin\theta} + \frac{\sqrt{3}}{\sin\theta} \right)$$

where $h$, $s$, $\theta$ are as shown in the picture.

**(a)** Keeping $h$ and $s$ fixed, for what angle, $\theta$, is the surface area a minimum?

**(b)** Measurements on bee's cells have shown that the angle actually used by bees is about $\theta = 55°$. Comment.

Figure 4.118

**78.** An organism has size $W$ at time $t$. For positive constants $A$, $b$, and $c$, the Gompertz growth function gives

$$W = Ae^{-e^{b-ct}}, \quad t \geq 0.$$

**(a)** Find the intercepts and asymptotes.

**(b)** Find the critical points and inflection points.

**(c)** Graph $W$ for various values of $A$, $b$, and $c$.

**(d)** A certain organism grows fastest when it is about 1/3 of its final size. Would the Gompertz growth function be useful in modeling its growth? Explain.

# STRENGTHEN YOUR UNDERSTANDING

In Problems 1–80, indicate whether the statement is true or false.

**1.** The function $f$ has a local maximum at $p$ if $f(p) \leq f(x)$ for points $x$ near $p$.

**2.** If $f'(p) = 0$ then $p$ is a critical point of $f$.

**3.** If $p$ is a critical point of $f$ then $f'(p) = 0$.

**4.** If $f$ is increasing at all points to the left of $p$ and decreasing at all points to the right of $p$ then $f$ has a local maximum at $p$.

**5.** If $f'(p) = 0$ and $f''(p) > 0$ then $f$ has a local maximum at $p$.

**6.** If $f'(p) = 0$ and $f''(p) > 0$ then $f$ has a local minimum at $p$.

**7.** If $f''(p) > 0$ then $f$ has a local minimum at $p$.

**8.** Every critical point of $f$ is either a local maximum or local minimum of $f$.

**9.** A function $f$ must have at least one critical point.

**10.** If $f$ has a local minimum at $x = p$ then $f'(p) = 0$.

**11.** A point at which a graph changes concavity is called an inflection point.

**12.** If $f''(p) = 0$ then $p$ is an inflection point of $f$.

**13.** A point $p$ can be both a critical point and an inflection point of a function $f$.

**14.** The function $f(x) = x^3$ has an inflection point at $x = 0$.

**15.** The function $H(x) = x^4$ has an inflection point at $x = 0$.

**16.** A function $f$ can have one inflection point and no critical points.

**17.** A function $f$ can have 2 critical points and 3 inflection points.

**18.** If $f''(x) = x(x + 1)$ then $f$ has an inflection point at $x = -1$.

**19.** If $f''(x) = x(x + 1)^2$ then $f$ has an inflection point at $x = -1$.

**20.** If $f''(x) = e^x(x + 1)$ then $f$ has an inflection point at $x = -1$. is an inflection point.

**21.** A local maximum of $f$ can also be a global maximum of $f$.

22. A global maximum of $f$ on the interval $1 \leq x \leq 2$ always occurs at a critical point.

23. Every function has a global minimum.

24. If function $y = f(x)$ is increasing on the interval $a \leq x \leq b$, then the global maximum of $f$ on this interval occurs at $x = b$.

25. If a function $y = f(x)$ has $f'(x) < 0$ for all $x$ in the interval $a \leq x \leq b$, then the global maximum of $f$ on this interval occurs at $x = b$.

26. A function $S(x)$ could have a different global maximum on each of the intervals $1 \leq x \leq 2$ and $2 \leq x \leq 3$.

27. The function $k(x) = 1/x$ has a global maximum when $x > 0$.

28. The function $f$ has a global maximum on the interval $-5 \leq x \leq 5$ at $p$ if $f(p) \leq f(x)$ for all $-5 \leq x \leq 5$.

29. The function $f$ has a global minimum on the interval $-5 \leq x \leq 5$ at $p$ if $f(p) \leq f(x)$ for all $-5 \leq x \leq 5$.

30. If $f'(p) = 0$ and $f''(p) > 0$ then $p$ is a global minimum of $f$.

31. If marginal cost is less than marginal revenue, then increasing quantity sold will increase profit.

32. If marginal cost is greater than marginal revenue, then decreasing quantity sold will increase profit.

33. When marginal revenue equals marginal cost there is maximum profit.

34. If revenue is greater than cost, profit is the vertical distance between the cost and revenue curves.

35. Maximum profit occurs at a critical point of the cost function.

36. Maximum profit can occur when marginal profit is zero.

37. Profit is maximized where the cost and revenue curves cross.

38. Profit is zero where the graphs of the cost and revenue curves cross.

39. If prices are constant, the graph of marginal revenue is a horizontal line.

40. If prices are constant, the graph of revenue is a horizontal line.

41. Average cost is total cost for $q$ items divided by $q$.

42. Marginal cost and average cost have the same units.

43. Marginal cost is the same thing as average cost.

44. The average cost of $q$ items is the slope of the tangent line to the cost curve at $q$.

45. If marginal cost is less than average cost, increasing production increases average cost.

46. Marginal cost equals average cost at critical points of marginal cost.

47. If marginal cost is greater than average cost, then increasing production increases average cost.

48. Average cost has a critical point at a quantity where the line from the origin to the cost curve is also tangent to the cost curve.

49. Average cost is a decreasing function of quantity.

50. Marginal and average cost functions are both minimized at the same quantity.

51. The elasticity of demand is given by $E = |q/p \cdot dq/dp|$.

52. If elasticity, $E$, is greater than one, then demand is inelastic.

53. If elasticity, $E$, is such that $0 \leq E < 1$ then demand is elastic.

54. Elasticity is a measure of the effect on demand of a change in price.

55. If a product is considered a necessity, the demand is generally elastic.

56. An increase in price always causes an increase in revenue.

57. If elasticity $E > 1$ then revenue increases when price increases.

58. At a critical point of the revenue function, demand is neither elastic nor inelastic.

59. If elasticity $E < 1$ then profit increases with an increase in price.

60. An increase in price always causes an increase in profit.

61. If $P = 1000/(1 + 2e^{-3t})$ then $P$ is a logistic function.

62. If $P = 1000/(1 + 2e^{3t})$ then $P$ is a logistic function.

63. The function $P = 1000/(1 + 2e^{-3t})$ has an inflection point when $t = 500$.

64. The function $P = 1000/(1 + 2e^{-3t})$ has an inflection point when $P = 500$.

65. The logistic function $P = L/(1 + Ce^{-kt})$ approaches $L$ as $t$ increases.

66. If the slope of the dose/response curve is large, a small change in the dose will have a large effect on the response.

67. The carrying capacity of a population growing logistically is the largest population the environment can support.

68. The parameter $k$ in the logistic function $P = L/(1 + Ce^{-kt})$ affects the rate at which the curve approaches its asymptote $L$.

69. The logistic function $P = L/(1 + Ce^{-kt})$ is concave up for $P < L/2$.

70. The logistic function $P = L/(1 + Ce^{-kt})$ is always increasing.

71. The surge function is an exponential decay function.

**72.** The surge function has one critical point, which is a global maximum.

**73.** The surge function is always concave down.

**74.** If minimum effective concentration is positive and less than peak concentration, then the surge function will intersect the minimum effective concentration line at two points.

**75.** If minimum effective concentration is greater than peak concentration, then the drug will be effective only for the first half of the time interval.

**76.** The surge function has exactly one inflection point, and it is always at a $t$-value greater than the $t$-value of the critical point.

**77.** The minimum effective concentration of a drug is the blood concentration necessary to achieve a specific pharmacologic response.

**78.** The function $y = t/(12e^{3t})$ is a surge function.

**79.** The function $y = t/(12e^{-3t})$ is a surge function.

**80.** The surge function $y = 5te^{-3t}$ has maximum at $t = 1/3$.

## PROJECTS FOR CHAPTER FOUR

### 1. Average and Marginal Costs

The total cost of producing a quantity $q$ is $C(q)$. The average cost $a(q)$ is given in Figure 4.119. The following rule is used by economists to determine the marginal cost $C'(q_0)$, for any $q_0$:

- Construct the tangent line $t_1$ to $a(q)$ at $q_0$.
- Let $t_2$ be the line with the same vertical intercept as $t_1$ but with twice the slope of $t_1$.

Then $C'(q_0)$ is the vertical distance shown in Figure 4.119. Explain why this rule works.

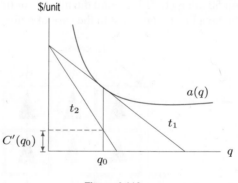

**Figure 4.119**

### 2. Firebreaks

The summer of 2000 was devastating for forests in the western US: over 3.5 million acres of trees were lost to fires, making this the worst fire season in 30 years. This project studies a fire management technique called *firebreaks*, which reduce the damage done by forest fires. A firebreak is a strip where trees have been removed in a forest so that a fire started on one side of the strip will not spread to the other side. Having many firebreaks helps confine a fire to a small area. On the other hand, having too many firebreaks involves removing large swaths of trees.[31]

**(a)** A forest in the shape of a 50 km by 50 km square has firebreaks in rectangular strips 50 km by 0.01 km. The trees between two firebreaks are called a stand of trees. All firebreaks in this forest are parallel to each other and to one edge of the forest, with the first firebreak at the edge of the forest. The firebreaks are evenly spaced throughout the forest. (For example, Figure 4.120 shows four firebreaks.) The total area lost in the case of a fire is the area of the stand of trees in which the fire started plus the area of all the firebreaks.

---

[31] Adapted from D. Quinney and R. Harding, *Calculus Connections* (New York: John Wiley & Sons, 1996).

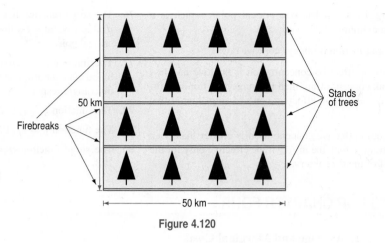

**Figure 4.120**

(i) Find the number of firebreaks that minimizes the total area lost to the forest in the case of a fire.

(ii) If a firebreak is 50 km by $b$ km, find the optimal number of firebreaks as a function of $b$. If the width, $b$, of a firebreak is quadrupled, how does the optimal number of firebreaks change?

**(b)** Now suppose firebreaks are arranged in two equally spaced sets of parallel lines, as shown in Figure 4.121. The forest is a 50 km by 50 km square, and each firebreak is a rectangular strip 50 km by 0.01 km. Find the number of firebreaks in each direction that minimizes the total area lost to the forest in the case of a fire.

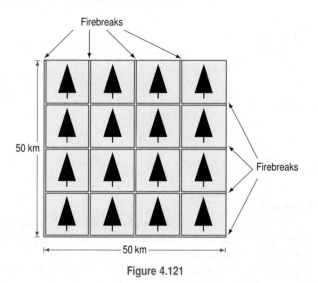

**Figure 4.121**

**3. Production and the Price of Raw Materials**

The production function $f(x)$ gives the number of units of an item that a manufacturing company can produce from $x$ units of raw material. The company buys the raw material at price $w$ dollars per unit and sells all it produces at a price of $p$ dollars per unit. The quantity of raw material that maximizes profit is denoted by $x^*$.

**(a)** Do you expect the derivative $f'(x)$ to be positive or negative? Justify your answer.

**(b)** Explain why the formula $\pi(x) = pf(x) - wx$ gives the profit $\pi(x)$ that the company earns as a function of the quantity $x$ of raw materials that it uses.

(c) Evaluate $f'(x^*)$.

(d) Assuming it is nonzero, is $f''(x^*)$ positive or negative?

(e) If the supplier of the raw materials is likely to change the price $w$, then it is appropriate to treat $x^*$ as a function of $w$. Find a formula for the derivative $dx^*/dw$ and decide whether it is positive or negative.

(f) If the price $w$ goes up, should the manufacturing company buy more or less of the raw material?

4. **Medical Case Study: Impact of Asthma on Breathing**[32]

Asthma is a common breathing disease in which inflammation in the airways of the lungs causes episodes of shortness of breath, coughing, and chest tightness. Patients with asthma often have wheezing, an abnormal sound heard on exhalation due to turbulent airflow. Turbulent airflow is caused by swelling, mucus secretion, and constriction of muscle in the walls of the airways, shrinking the radius of the air passages leading to increased resistance to airflow and making it harder for patients to exhale.

An important breathing test for asthma is called *spirometry*. In this test, a patient takes in as deep a breath as he or she can, and then exhales as rapidly, forcefully, and for as long as possible through a tube connected to an analyzer. The analyzer measures a number of parameters and generates two graphs.

(a) Figure 4.122 is a volume-time curve for an asthma-free patient, showing the volume of air exhaled, $V$, as a function of time, $t$, since the test began.[33]

  (i) What is the physical interpretation of the slope of the volume-time curve?

  (ii) The volume VC shown on the volume-time graph is called the (forced) vital capacity (FVC or simply VC). Describe the physical meaning of VC.

(b) Figure 4.123 is the flow-volume curve for the same patient.[34] The flow-volume curve shows the flow rate, $dV/dt$, of air as a function of $V$, the volume of air exhaled.

  (i) What is the physical interpretation of the slope of the flow-volume curve?

  (ii) Describe how the slope of the flow-volume curve changes as $V$ increases from 0 to 5.5 liters. Explain what this means for the patient's breath.

  (iii) Sketch the slope of the flow-volume curve.

  (iv) What is the volume of air that has been exhaled when the flow rate is a maximum, and what is that maximal rate, the *peak expiratory flow*? Explain how this maximal rate is identified on the flow-volume curve and how the volume at which the maximal rate occurs is identified on the slope curve in part (b)(iii).

(c) How do you imagine the volume-time curve and the flow-volume curve would be different for a patient with acute asthma? Draw curves to illustrate your thinking.

Figure 4.122: Volume-time curve

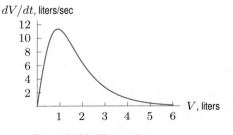

Figure 4.123: Flow-volume curve

---

[32]From David E. Sloane, M.D.

[33]Image based on www.aafp.org/afp/2004/0301/p1107.html, accessed July 9, 2011.

[34]Image from http://www.aafp.org/afp/2004/0301/p1107.html, accessed July 9, 2011.

# Chapter Five

# ACCUMULATED CHANGE: THE DEFINITE INTEGRAL

## Contents

# 5.1 DISTANCE AND ACCUMULATED CHANGE

In Chapter 2, we used the derivative to find the rate of change of a function. Here we see how to go in the other direction. If we know the rate of change, can we find the original function? We start by finding the distance traveled from its rate of change, the velocity. For positive constant velocities, we can find the distance traveled using the formula

$$\text{Distance} = \text{Velocity} \times \text{Time}.$$

In this section we see how to estimate the distance when the velocity is not a constant.

## A Thought Experiment: How Far Did the Car Go?

Suppose a car is moving with increasing velocity and that we measure the car's velocity every two seconds, obtaining the data in Table 5.1:

**Table 5.1**  *Velocity of car every two seconds*

| Time (sec)       | 0  | 2  | 4  | 6  | 8  | 10 |
|------------------|----|----|----|----|----|----|
| Velocity (ft/sec)| 20 | 30 | 38 | 44 | 48 | 50 |

How far has the car traveled? Since we don't know how fast the car is moving at every moment, we can't calculate the distance exactly, but we can make an estimate. The velocity is increasing, so the car is going at least 20 ft/sec for the first two seconds. Since Distance = Velocity × Time, the car goes at least $20 \cdot 2 = 40$ feet during the first two seconds. Likewise, it goes at least $30 \cdot 2 = 60$ feet during the next two seconds, and so on. During the ten-second period it goes at least

$$20 \cdot 2 + 30 \cdot 2 + 38 \cdot 2 + 44 \cdot 2 + 48 \cdot 2 = 360 \text{ feet.}$$

Thus, 360 feet is an underestimate of the total distance traveled during the ten seconds.

To get an overestimate, we can reason in a similar way: During the first two seconds, the car's velocity is at most 30 ft/sec, so it moves at most $30 \cdot 2 = 60$ feet. In the next two seconds it moves at most $38 \cdot 2 = 76$ feet, and so on. Therefore, over the ten-second period it moves at most

$$30 \cdot 2 + 38 \cdot 2 + 44 \cdot 2 + 48 \cdot 2 + 50 \cdot 2 = 420 \text{ feet.}$$

Therefore,

$$360 \text{ feet} \leq \text{Total distance traveled} \leq 420 \text{ feet.}$$

There is a difference of 60 feet between the upper and lower estimates. A better estimate would be the average of the upper and lower estimates,

$$\frac{360 + 420}{2} = 390 \text{ feet.}$$

## Visualizing Distance on the Velocity Graph

We can represent both upper and lower estimates on a graph of the velocity against time. The velocity can be graphed by plotting the data in Table 5.1 and drawing a curve through the data points. (See Figure 5.1.)

The area of the first dark rectangle is $20 \cdot 2 = 40$, the lower estimate of the distance moved during the first two seconds. The area of the second dark rectangle is $30 \cdot 2 = 60$, the lower estimate for the distance moved in the next two seconds. The total area of the dark rectangles represents the lower estimate for the total distance moved during the ten seconds.

If the dark and light rectangles are considered together, the first area is $30 \cdot 2 = 60$, the upper estimate for the distance moved in the first two seconds. The second area is $38 \cdot 2 = 76$, the upper estimate for the next two seconds. Continuing this calculation suggests that the upper estimate for the total distance is represented by the sum of the areas of the dark and light rectangles.

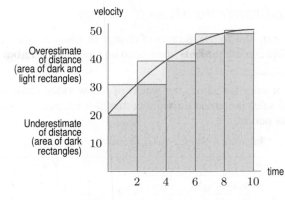

Figure 5.1: Shaded area estimates distance traveled. Velocity measured every 2 seconds

## Visualizing Distance on the Velocity Graph: Area Under Curve

As we make more frequent velocity measurements, the rectangles used to estimate the distance traveled fit the curve more closely. See Figures 5.2 and 5.3. In the limit, as the number of subdivisions increases, we see that the distance traveled is given by the area between the velocity curve and the horizontal axis. See Figure 5.4. In general:

> If the velocity is positive, the total distance traveled is the area under the velocity curve.

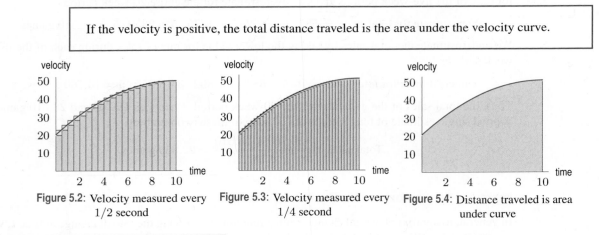

Figure 5.2: Velocity measured every 1/2 second

Figure 5.3: Velocity measured every 1/4 second

Figure 5.4: Distance traveled is area under curve

**Example 1**    With time $t$ in seconds, the velocity of a bicycle, in feet per second, is given by $v(t) = 5t$. How far does the bicycle travel in 3 seconds?

Solution    The velocity is linear. See Figure 5.5. The distance traveled is the area between the line $v(t) = 5t$ and the $t$-axis. Since this region is a triangle of height 15 and base 3

$$\text{Distance traveled } = \text{ Area of triangle } = \frac{1}{2} \cdot 15 \cdot 3 = 22.5 \text{ feet.}$$

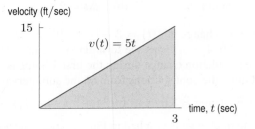

Figure 5.5: Shaded area represents distance traveled

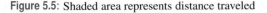

## Approximating Total Change from Rate of Change

We have seen how to use the rate of change of distance (the velocity) to calculate the total distance traveled. We can use the same method to find total change from the rate of change of other quantities.

**Example 2**    The rate of sales (in games per week) of a new video game is shown in Table 5.2. Assuming that the rate of sales increased throughout the 20-week period, estimate the total number of games sold during this period.

Table 5.2    *Weekly sales of a video game*

| Time (weeks) | 0 | 5 | 10 | 15 | 20 |
|---|---|---|---|---|---|
| Rate of sales (games per week) | 0 | 585 | 892 | 1875 | 2350 |

**Solution**    If the rate of sales is constant, we have

$$\text{Total sales} = \text{Rate of sales per week} \times \text{Number of weeks.}$$

How many games were sold during the first five weeks? During this time, sales went from 0 to 585 games per week. If we assume that 585 games were sold every week, we get an overestimate for the sales in the first five weeks of $(585 \text{ games/week})(5 \text{ weeks}) = 2925$ games. Similar overestimates for each of the five-week periods gives an overestimate for the entire 20-week period:

$$\text{Overestimate for total sales} = 585 \cdot 5 + 892 \cdot 5 + 1875 \cdot 5 + 2350 \cdot 5 = 28{,}510 \text{ games.}$$

We underestimate the total sales by taking the lower value for rate of sales during each of the five-week periods:

$$\text{Underestimate for total sales} = 0 \cdot 5 + 585 \cdot 5 + 892 \cdot 5 + 1875 \cdot 5 = 16{,}760 \text{ games.}$$

Thus, the total sales of the game during the 20-week period is between 16,760 and 28,510 games. A good single estimate of total sales is the average of these two numbers:

$$\text{Total sales} \approx \frac{16{,}760 + 28{,}510}{2} = 22{,}635 \text{ games.}$$

### Improving the Approximation: The Role of $n$ and $\Delta t$

In general, to approximate total change from a function $f(t)$ giving the rate of change at time $t$, we construct a sum. We use the notation $\Delta t$ for the size of the $t$-intervals used. We use $n$ to represent the number of subintervals of length $\Delta t$. In the following example, we see how decreasing $\Delta t$ (and increasing $n$) improves the accuracy of the approximation.

**Example 3**    If $t$ is in hours since the start of a 20-hour period, a bacteria population increases at a rate given by

$$f(t) = 3 + 0.1t^2 \text{ millions of bacteria per hour.}$$

Make an underestimate of the total change in the number of bacteria over this period using

(a)   $\Delta t = 4$ hours          (b)   $\Delta t = 2$ hours          (c)   $\Delta t = 1$ hour

**Solution**    (a) The rate of change is $f(t) = 3 + 0.1t^2$. If we use $\Delta t = 4$, we measure the rate every 4 hours and $n = 20/4 = 5$. Using the formula to calculate $f(t)$, we obtain Table 5.3. An underestimate for the population change during the first 4 hours is $(3.0 \text{ million/hour})(4 \text{ hours}) = 12$ million. Combining the contributions from all the subintervals gives the underestimate:

$$\text{Total change} \approx 3.0 \cdot 4 + 4.6 \cdot 4 + 9.4 \cdot 4 + 17.4 \cdot 4 + 28.6 \cdot 4 = 252.0 \text{ million bacteria.}$$

The rate of change is graphed in Figure 5.6(a); the area of the shaded rectangles represents this underestimate. Notice that $n = 5$ is the number of rectangles in the graph.

**Table 5.3** *Rate of change with $\Delta t = 4$ using $f(t) = 3 + 0.1t^2$ million bacteria/hour*

| $t$ (hours) | 0 | 4 | 8 | 12 | 16 | 20 |
|---|---|---|---|---|---|---|
| $f(t)$ | 3.0 | 4.6 | 9.4 | 17.4 | 28.6 | 43.0 |

(b) If we use $\Delta t = 2$, we measure $f(t)$ every 2 hours and $n = 20/2 = 10$. See Table 5.4. The underestimate is

$$\text{Total change} \approx 3.0 \cdot 2 + 3.4 \cdot 2 + 4.6 \cdot 2 + \cdots + 35.4 \cdot 2 = 288.0 \text{ million bacteria.}$$

Figure 5.6(b) suggests that this estimate is more accurate than the estimate made in part (a).

**Table 5.4** *Rate of change with $\Delta t = 2$ using $f(t) = 3 + 0.1t^2$ million bacteria/hour*

| $t$ (hours) | 0 | 2 | 4 | 6 | 8 | 10 | 12 | 14 | 16 | 18 | 20 |
|---|---|---|---|---|---|---|---|---|---|---|---|
| $f(t)$ | 3.0 | 3.4 | 4.6 | 6.6 | 9.4 | 13.0 | 17.4 | 22.6 | 28.6 | 35.4 | 43.0 |

(c) If we use $\Delta t = 1$, then $n = 20$ and a similar calculation shows that we have

$$\text{Total change} \approx 307.0 \text{ million bacteria.}$$

The shaded area in Figure 5.6(c) represents this estimate; it is the most accurate of the three.

**Figure 5.6:** More and more accurate estimates of total change from rate of change. In each case, $f(t)$ is the rate of change, and the shaded area approximates total change. Largest $n$ and smallest $\Delta t$ give the best estimate.

Notice that as $n$ gets larger, the estimate improves and the area of the shaded rectangles approaches the area under the curve.

## Left- and Right-Hand Sums

Now we see how to express these sums for any function $f(t)$ that is continuous for $a \le t \le b$. We divide the interval from $a$ to $b$ into $n$ equal subdivisions, each of width $\Delta t$, so

$$\Delta t = \frac{b - a}{n}.$$

We let $t_0, t_1, t_2, \ldots, t_n$ be endpoints of the subdivisions, as in Figures 5.7 and 5.8. We construct two sums, similar to the overestimates and underestimates earlier in this section. For a *left-hand sum*, we use the values of the function from the left end of the interval. For a *right-hand sum*, we use the values of the function from the right end of the interval. We have:

$$\text{Left-hand sum} = f(t_0)\Delta t + f(t_1)\Delta t + \cdots + f(t_{n-1})\Delta t$$

$$\text{Right-hand sum} = f(t_1)\Delta t + f(t_2)\Delta t + \cdots + f(t_n)\Delta t.$$

These sums represent the shaded areas in Figures 5.7 and 5.8, provided $f(t) \geq 0$. In Figure 5.7, the first rectangle has width $\Delta t$ and height $f(t_0)$, since the top of its left edge just touches the curve, and hence it has area $f(t_0)\Delta t$. The second rectangle has width $\Delta t$ and height $f(t_1)$, and hence has area $f(t_1)\Delta t$, and so on. The sum of all these areas is the left-hand sum. The right-hand sum, shown in Figure 5.8, is constructed in the same way, except that each rectangle touches the curve on its right edge instead of its left.

Figure 5.7: Left-hand sum: Area of rectangles

Figure 5.8: Right-hand sum: Area of rectangles

## Writing Left- and Right-Hand Sums Using Sigma Notation

Both the left-hand and right-hand sums can be written more compactly using *sigma*, or summation, notation. The symbol $\sum$ is a capital sigma, or Greek letter "S." We write

$$\text{Right-hand sum} = \sum_{i=1}^{n} f(t_i)\Delta t = f(t_1)\Delta t + f(t_2)\Delta t + \cdots + f(t_n)\Delta t.$$

The $\sum$ tells us to add terms of the form $f(t_i)\Delta t$. The "$i = 1$" at the base of the sigma sign tells us to start at $i = 1$, and the "$n$" at the top tells us to stop at $i = n$.

In the left-hand sum we start at $i = 0$ and stop at $i = n - 1$, so we write

$$\text{Left-hand sum} = \sum_{i=0}^{n-1} f(t_i)\Delta t = f(t_0)\Delta t + f(t_1)\Delta t + \cdots + f(t_{n-1})\Delta t.$$

## Problems for Section 5.1

1. Suppose that you travel 30 miles/hour for 2 hours, then 40 miles/hour for 1/2 hour, then 20 miles/hour for 4 hours.

   (a) What is the total distance you traveled?
   (b) Sketch a graph of the velocity function for this trip.
   (c) Represent the total distance traveled on your graph in part (b).

2. Figure 5.9 shows the velocity of a car for $0 \leq t \leq 12$ and the rectangles used to estimate the distance traveled.

   (a) Do the rectangles represent a left or a right sum?
   (b) Do the rectangles lead to an upper or a lower estimate?
   (c) What is the value of $n$?
   (d) What is the value of $\Delta t$?

   (e) Give an approximate value for the estimate.

Figure 5.9

3. Figure 5.10 shows the velocity of a runner for $0 \leq t \leq 15$ and the rectangles used to estimate the distance traveled.

   (a) Do the rectangles represent a left or a right sum?

**(b)** Do the rectangles lead to an upper or a lower estimate?

**(c)** What is the value of $n$?

**(d)** What is the value of $\Delta t$?

**(e)** Give an approximate value for the estimate.

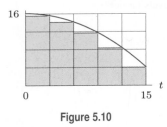

**Figure 5.10**

**4.** A car comes to a stop six seconds after the driver applies the brakes. While the brakes are on, the velocities recorded are in Table 5.5.

**Table 5.5**

| Time since brakes applied (sec) | 0 | 2 | 4 | 6 |
|---|---|---|---|---|
| Velocity (ft/sec) | 88 | 45 | 16 | 0 |

**(a)** Give lower and upper estimates for the distance the car traveled after the brakes were applied.

**(b)** On a sketch of velocity against time, show the lower and upper estimates of part (a).

**5.** A car starts moving at time $t = 0$ and goes faster and faster. Its velocity is shown in the following table. Estimate how far the car travels during the 12 seconds.

| $t$ (seconds) | 0 | 3 | 6 | 9 | 12 |
|---|---|---|---|---|---|
| Velocity (ft/sec) | 0 | 10 | 25 | 45 | 75 |

**6.** Graph the rate of sales against time for the video game data in Example 2. Represent graphically the overestimate and the underestimate calculated in that example.

**7.** Figure 5.11 shows the velocity, $v$, of an object (in meters/sec). Estimate the total distance the object traveled between $t = 0$ and $t = 6$.

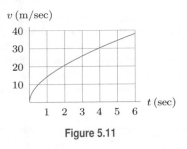

**Figure 5.11**

**8.** Roger runs a marathon. His friend Jeff rides behind him on a bicycle and clocks his speed every 15 minutes. Roger starts out strong, but after an hour and a half he is so exhausted that he has to stop. Jeff's data follow:

| Time since start (min) | 0 | 15 | 30 | 45 | 60 | 75 | 90 |
|---|---|---|---|---|---|---|---|
| Speed (mph) | 12 | 11 | 10 | 10 | 8 | 7 | 0 |

**(a)** Assuming that Roger's speed is never increasing, give upper and lower estimates for the distance Roger ran during the first half hour.

**(b)** Give upper and lower estimates for the distance Roger ran in total during the entire hour and a half.

**9.** The following table gives world oil consumption, in billions of barrels per year.[1] Estimate total oil consumption during this 25-year period.

| Year | 1985 | 1990 | 1995 | 2000 | 2005 | 2010 |
|---|---|---|---|---|---|---|
| Oil (bn barrels/yr) | 20.9 | 23.3 | 25.6 | 28.0 | 30.7 | 31.7 |

**10.** A car accelerates smoothly from 0 to 60 mph in 10 seconds with the velocity given in Figure 5.12. Estimate how far the car travels during the 10-second period.

**Figure 5.12**

**11.** The velocity of a car is $f(t) = 5t$ meters/sec. Use a graph of $f(t)$ to find the exact distance traveled by the car, in meters, from $t = 0$ to $t = 10$ seconds.

**12.** A village wishes to measure the quantity of water that is piped to a factory during a typical morning. A gauge on the water line gives the flow rate (in cubic meters per hour) at any instant. The flow rate is about 100 m$^3$/hr at 6 am and increases steadily to about 280 m$^3$/hr at 9 am.

Using only this information, give your best estimate of the total volume of water used by the factory between 6 am and 9 am.

[1]http://www.indexmundi.com/energy.aspx, accessed May 2012.

**13.** Filters at a water treatment plant become less effective over time. The rate at which pollution passes through the filters into a nearby lake is given in the following table.

    **(a)** Estimate the total quantity of pollution entering the lake during the 30-day period.

    **(b)** Your answer to part (a) is only an estimate. Give bounds (lower and upper estimates) between which the true quantity of pollution must lie. (Assume the rate of pollution is continually increasing.)

| Day | 0 | 6 | 12 | 18 | 24 | 30 |
|-----|---|---|----|----|----|----|
| Rate (kg/day) | 7 | 8 | 10 | 13 | 18 | 35 |

**14.** A car initially going 50 ft/sec brakes at a constant rate (constant negative acceleration), coming to a stop in 5 seconds.

    **(a)** Graph the velocity from $t = 0$ to $t = 5$.

    **(b)** How far does the car travel?

    **(c)** How far does the car travel if its initial velocity is doubled, but it brakes at the same constant rate?

**15.** Figure 5.13 shows the rate of change of a fish population. Estimate the total change in the population during this 12-month period.

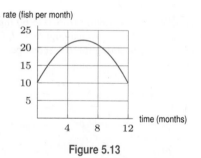

**Figure 5.13**

**16.** Two cars travel in the same direction along a straight road. Figure 5.14 shows the velocity, $v$, of each car at time $t$. Car $B$ starts 2 hours after car $A$ and car $B$ reaches a maximum velocity of 50 km/hr.

    **(a)** For approximately how long does each car travel?

    **(b)** Estimate car $A$'s maximum velocity.

    **(c)** Approximately how far does each car travel?

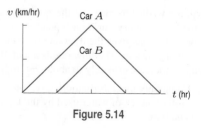

**Figure 5.14**

**17.** Two cars start at the same time and travel in the same direction along a straight road. Figure 5.15 gives the velocity, $v$, of each car as a function of time, $t$. Which car:

    **(a)** Attains the larger maximum velocity?

    **(b)** Stops first?

    **(c)** Travels farther?

**Figure 5.15**

**18.** Your velocity is given by $v(t) = t^2 + 1$ in m/sec, with $t$ in seconds. Estimate the distance, $s$, traveled between $t = 0$ and $t = 5$. Explain how you arrived at your estimate.

**19.** The value of a mutual fund increases at a rate of $R = 500e^{0.04t}$ dollars per year, with $t$ in years since 2010.

    **(a)** Using $t = 0, 2, 4, 6, 8, 10$, make a table of values for $R$.

    **(b)** Use the table to estimate the total change in the value of the mutual fund between 2010 and 2020.

**20.** An old rowboat has sprung a leak. Water is flowing into the boat at a rate, $r(t)$, given in the table.

    **(a)** Compute upper and lower estimates for the volume of water that has flowed into the boat during the 15 minutes.

    **(b)** Draw a graph to illustrate the lower estimate.

| $t$ minutes | 0 | 5 | 10 | 15 |
|-------------|---|---|----|----|
| $r(t)$ liters/min | 12 | 20 | 24 | 16 |

**21.** The rate of change of the world's population, in millions of people per year, is given in the following table.

    **(a)** Use this data to estimate the total change in the world's population between 1950 and 2000.

    **(b)** The world population was 2555 million people in 1950 and 6085 million people in 2000. Calculate the true value of the total change in the population. How does this compare with your estimate in part (a)?

| Year | 1950 | 1960 | 1970 | 1980 | 1990 | 2000 |
|------|------|------|------|------|------|------|
| Rate of change | 37 | 41 | 78 | 77 | 86 | 79 |

**22.** A car speeds up at a constant rate from 10 to 70 mph over a period of half an hour. Its fuel efficiency (in miles per gallon) increases with speed; values are in the table. Make lower and upper estimates of the quantity of fuel used during the half hour.

| Speed (mph) | 10 | 20 | 30 | 40 | 50 | 60 | 70 |
|---|---|---|---|---|---|---|---|
| Fuel efficiency (mpg) | 15 | 18 | 21 | 23 | 24 | 25 | 26 |

Problems 23–26 concern hybrid cars such as the Toyota Prius that are powered by a gas-engine, electric-motor combination, but can also function in Electric-Vehicle (EV) only mode. Figure 5.16 shows the velocity, $v$, of a 2010 Prius Plug-in Hybrid Prototype operating in normal hybrid mode and EV-only mode, respectively, while accelerating from a stoplight.[2]

**Figure 5.16**

**23.** Could the car travel half a mile in EV-only mode during the first 25 seconds of movement?

**24.** About how far, in feet, does the 2010 Prius Prototype travel in EV-only mode during the first 15 seconds of movement?

**25.** Assume two identical cars, one running in normal hybrid mode and one running in EV-only mode, accelerate together in a straight path from a stoplight. Approximately how far apart are the cars after 5 seconds?

**26.** Assume two identical cars, one running in normal hybrid mode and one running in EV-only mode, accelerate together in a straight path from a stoplight. Approximately how far apart are the cars after 15 seconds?

**27.** A car is traveling at 80 feet per second (approximately 55 miles per hour) and slows down as it passes through a busy intersection. The car's velocity is shown in the following table.

| Time since brakes applied (seconds) | 0 | 3 | 6 | 9 | 12 |
|---|---|---|---|---|---|
| velocity (ft/sec) | 80 | 62 | 47 | 32 | 22 |

(a) Use a left sum to approximate the total distance the car has traveled over the 12 second interval.

(b) Is your answer in part (a) a lower or upper estimate? How can you tell?

(c) Use a right sum to approximate the total distance the car has traveled over the 12 second interval.

(d) Is your answer in part (c) a lower or upper estimate? How can you tell?

(e) Using your answers in parts (a) and (c), find a better estimate for the total distance the car has traveled.

**28.** The following table gives the total world emissions of $CO_2$ from fossil fuels, in billions of tons per year.[3]

| Year | 1981 | 1986 | 1991 | 1996 | 2001 | 2006 | 2011 |
|---|---|---|---|---|---|---|---|
| $CO_2$ (bn tons per year) | 20.1 | 21.3 | 21.9 | 23.4 | 24.2 | 29.1 | 34.7 |

(a) Use this data to estimate the total world $CO_2$ emissions between 1981 and 2011 using a left sum with $n = 6$.

(b) Is your answer in part (a) an upper or lower estimate? How can you tell?

(c) Use this data to estimate the total world $CO_2$ emissions between 1981 and 2011 using a right sum with $n = 3$.

(d) Is your answer in part (c) an upper or lower estimate? How can you tell?

**29.** The rate of change of a quantity is given by $f(t) = t^2 + 1$. Make an underestimate and an overestimate of the total change in the quantity between $t = 0$ and $t = 8$ using

  **(a)** $\Delta t = 4$    **(b)** $\Delta t = 2$    **(c)** $\Delta t = 1$

What is $n$ in each case? Graph $f(t)$ and shade rectangles to represent each of your six answers.

**30.** Use the expressions for left and right sums on page 245 and Table 5.6.

(a) If $n = 4$, what is $\Delta t$? What are $t_0, t_1, t_2, t_3, t_4$? What are $f(t_0), f(t_1), f(t_2), f(t_3), f(t_4)$?

(b) Find the left and right sums using $n = 4$.

(c) If $n = 2$, what is $\Delta t$? What are $t_0, t_1, t_2$? What are $f(t_0), f(t_1), f(t_2)$?

(d) Find the left and right sums using $n = 2$.

**Table 5.6**

| $t$ | 15 | 17 | 19 | 21 | 23 |
|---|---|---|---|---|---|
| $f(t)$ | 10 | 13 | 18 | 20 | 30 |

**31.** Use the expressions for left and right sums on page 245 and Table 5.7.

(a) If $n = 4$, what is $\Delta t$? What are $t_0, t_1, t_2, t_3, t_4$? What are $f(t_0), f(t_1), f(t_2), f(t_3), f(t_4)$?

(b) Find the left and right sums using $n = 4$.

(c) If $n = 2$, what is $\Delta t$? What are $t_0, t_1, t_2$? What are $f(t_0), f(t_1), f(t_2)$?

(d) Find the left and right sums using $n = 2$.

**Table 5.7**

| $t$ | 0 | 4 | 8 | 12 | 16 |
|---|---|---|---|---|---|
| $f(t)$ | 25 | 23 | 22 | 20 | 17 |

[2] www.motortrend.com/, accessed May 2011.

[3] http://cdiac.ornl.gov/trends/emis/meth_reg.html, Accessed January 2013.

# 5.2  THE DEFINITE INTEGRAL

In Section 5.1 we saw how to approximate total change given the rate of change. In this section we define a new quantity, the definite integral, which gives the total change exactly.

## Taking the Limit to Obtain the Definite Integral

If $f$ is a rate of change of some quantity, then the left-hand sum and the right-hand sum approximate the total change in the quantity. For most functions $f$, the approximation is improved by increasing the value of $n$. To find the total change exactly, we take larger and larger values of $n$ and look at the values approached by the left and right sums. This is called taking the *limit* of these sums as $n$ goes to infinity and is written $\lim_{n \to \infty}$. If $f$ is continuous for $a \leq t \leq b$, the limits of the left- and right-hand sums exist and are equal. The *definite integral* is the common limit of these sums.

---

Suppose $f$ is continuous for $a \leq t \leq b$. The **definite integral** of $f$ from $a$ to $b$, written

$$\int_a^b f(t)\, dt,$$

is the limit of the left-hand or right-hand sums with $n$ subdivisions of $[a, b]$ as $n$ gets arbitrarily large. In other words, if $t_0, t_1, \ldots t_n$ are the endpoints of the subdivisions,

$$\int_a^b f(t)\, dt = \lim_{n \to \infty} (\text{Left-hand sum}) = \lim_{n \to \infty} \left( \sum_{i=0}^{n-1} f(t_i) \Delta t \right)$$

and

$$\int_a^b f(t)\, dt = \lim_{n \to \infty} (\text{Right-hand sum}) = \lim_{n \to \infty} \left( \sum_{i=1}^{n} f(t_i) \Delta t \right).$$

Each of these sums is called a *Riemann sum*, $f$ is called the *integrand*, and $a$ and $b$ are called the *limits of integration*.

---

The "$\int$" notation comes from an old-fashioned "S," which stands for "sum" in the same way that $\sum$ does. The "$dt$" in the integral comes from the factor $\Delta t$. Notice that the limits on the $\sum$ symbol are 0 and $n - 1$ for the left-hand sum, and 1 and $n$ for the right-hand sum, whereas the limits on the $\int$ sign are $a$ and $b$.

When $f(t)$ is positive, the left- and right-hand sums are represented by the sums of areas of rectangles, so the definite integral is represented graphically by an area.

---

**Example 1**    Write the result of Example 3 in the previous section using integral notation.

Solution    Part (c) gave 307.0 million as the best estimate of the total change in the bacteria population. In integral notation

$$\int_0^{20} f(t)\, dt = \int_0^{20} (3 + 0.1t^2)\, dt \approx 307.0 \text{ million.}$$

---

## Computing a Definite Integral

In practice, many calculators and computers calculate definite integrals by automatically computing sums for larger and larger values of $n$.

**Example 2**   Compute $\int_0^1 e^{-t^2}\,dt$ and represent this integral as an area.

**Solution**   Using a calculator or computer, we find

$$\int_0^1 e^{-t^2}\,dt = 0.747.$$

The integral represents the area between $t = 0$ and $t = 1$ under the curve $f(t) = e^{-t^2}$. See Figure 5.17.

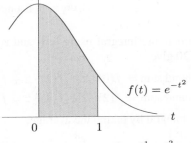

Figure 5.17: Shaded area $= \int_0^1 e^{-t^2}\,dt$

## Estimating a Definite Integral from a Table or Graph

If we have a formula for the integrand, $f(x)$, we can calculate the integral $\int_a^b f(x)\,dx$ using a calculator or computer. If, however, we have only a table of values or a graph of $f(x)$, we can still estimate the integral. Note that we can use any letter ($x$, $t$, $y$, $q$, etc.) for the independent variable.

**Example 3**   Values for a function $f(t)$ are in the following table. Estimate $\int_{20}^{30} f(t)dt$.

| $t$ | 20 | 22 | 24 | 26 | 28 | 30 |
|------|----|----|----|----|----|----|
| $f(t)$ | 5 | 7 | 11 | 18 | 29 | 45 |

**Solution**   Since we have only a table of values, we use left- and right-hand sums to approximate the integral. The values of $f(t)$ are spaced 2 units apart, so $\Delta t = 2$ and $n = (30 - 20)/2 = 5$. Calculating the left-hand and right-hand sums gives

$$\text{Left-hand sum} = f(20) \cdot 2 + f(22) \cdot 2 + f(24) \cdot 2 + f(26) \cdot 2 + f(28) \cdot 2$$
$$= 5 \cdot 2 + 7 \cdot 2 + 11 \cdot 2 + 18 \cdot 2 + 29 \cdot 2$$
$$= 140.$$

$$\text{Right-hand sum} = f(22) \cdot 2 + f(24) \cdot 2 + f(26) \cdot 2 + f(28) \cdot 2 + f(30) \cdot 2$$
$$= 7 \cdot 2 + 11 \cdot 2 + 18 \cdot 2 + 29 \cdot 2 + 45 \cdot 2$$
$$= 220.$$

Both left- and right-hand sums approximate the integral. We generally get a better estimate by averaging the two:

$$\int_{20}^{30} f(t)dt \approx \frac{140 + 220}{2} = 180.$$

**Example 4**   The function $f(x)$ is graphed in Figure 5.18. Estimate $\int_0^6 f(x)\,dx$.

Figure 5.18: Estimate $\int_0^6 f(x)\,dx$

Solution    We can approximate the integral using left- and right-hand sums with $n = 3$, so $\Delta x = 2$. Figures 5.19 and 5.20 give

$$\text{Left-hand sum} = f(0) \cdot 2 + f(2) \cdot 2 + f(4) \cdot 2 = 21 \cdot 2 + 11 \cdot 2 + 5 \cdot 2 = 74,$$
$$\text{Right-hand sum} = f(2) \cdot 2 + f(4) \cdot 2 + f(6) \cdot 2 = 11 \cdot 2 + 5 \cdot 2 + 3 \cdot 2 = 38.$$

We estimate the integral by taking the average:

$$\int_0^6 f(x)\,dx \approx \frac{74 + 38}{2} = 56.$$

Alternatively, since the integral equals the area under the curve between $x = 0$ and $x = 6$, we can estimate it by counting grid boxes. Each grid box has area $5 \cdot 1 = 5$, and the region under $f(x)$ includes about 10.5 grid boxes, so the area is about $10.5 \cdot 5 = 52.5$.

Figure 5.19: Area of shaded region is left-hand sum with $n = 3$

Figure 5.20: Area of shaded region is right-hand sum with $n = 3$

## Rough Estimates of a Definite Integral

When calculating an integral using a calculator or computer, it is useful to have a rough idea of the value you expect. This helps detect errors in entering the integral.

**Example 5**    Figure 5.21 shows the graph of a function $f(t)$. Which of the numbers 0.023, 1.099, 1.526, and 11.984 could be the value of $\int_1^3 f(t)\,dt$? Explain your reasoning.

Solution    Figure 5.21 shows left- and right-hand approximations to $\int_1^3 f(t)\,dt$ with $n = 1$. We see that the right-hand sum $2(1/3)$ is an underestimate of $\int_1^3 f(t)\,dt$. Since 0.023 is less than $2/3$, this value must be wrong. Similarly, we see that the left-hand sum $2(1)$ is an overestimate of the integral. Since 11.984 is larger than 2, this value is wrong. Since the graph is concave up, the value of the integral is closer to the smaller value of the two sums, $2/3$, than to the larger value, 2. Thus, the integral is less than the average of the two sums, $4/3$. Since $1.526 > 4/3$, this value is wrong too. Since $2/3 < 1.099 < 4/3$, the value 1.099 could be correct.

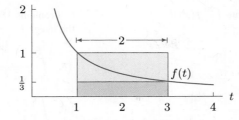

Figure 5.21: Left- and right-hand sums with $n = 1$

# Problems for Section 5.2

In Problems 1–2, rectangles have been drawn to approximate $\int_0^6 g(x)\,dx$.

(a) Do the rectangles represent a left or a right sum?

(b) Do the rectangles lead to an upper or a lower estimate?

(c) What is the value of $n$?

(d) What is the value of $\Delta x$?

1.

2.

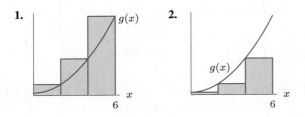

3. Estimate $\displaystyle\int_0^6 2^x\,dx$ using a left-hand sum with $n = 2$.

4. Estimate $\displaystyle\int_0^{12} \frac{1}{x+1}\,dx$ using a left-hand sum with $n = 3$.

5. Estimate $\int_0^1 e^{-x^2}\,dx$ using $n = 5$ rectangles to form a

(a) Left-hand sum    (b) Right-hand sum

6. Use the following table to estimate $\int_{10}^{26} f(x)\,dx$.

| $x$ | 10 | 14 | 18 | 22 | 26 |
|---|---|---|---|---|---|
| $f(x)$ | 100 | 88 | 72 | 50 | 28 |

7. Use the table to estimate $\int_0^{40} f(x)dx$. What values of $n$ and $\Delta x$ did you use?

| $x$ | 0 | 10 | 20 | 30 | 40 |
|---|---|---|---|---|---|
| $f(x)$ | 350 | 410 | 435 | 450 | 460 |

8. Use the following table to estimate $\int_0^{15} f(x)\,dx$.

| $x$ | 0 | 3 | 6 | 9 | 12 | 15 |
|---|---|---|---|---|---|---|
| $f(x)$ | 50 | 48 | 44 | 36 | 24 | 8 |

9. Use the following table to estimate $\int_3^4 W(t)\,dt$. What are $n$ and $\Delta t$?

| $t$ | 3.0 | 3.2 | 3.4 | 3.6 | 3.8 | 4.0 |
|---|---|---|---|---|---|---|
| $W(t)$ | 25 | 23 | 20 | 15 | 9 | 2 |

10. Using Figure 5.22, draw rectangles representing each of the following Riemann sums for the function $f$ on the interval $0 \le t \le 8$. Calculate the value of each sum.

(a) Left-hand sum with $\Delta t = 4$

(b) Right-hand sum with $\Delta t = 4$

(c) Left-hand sum with $\Delta t = 2$

(d) Right-hand sum with $\Delta t = 2$

Figure 5.22

**11.** Use Figure 5.23 to estimate $\int_0^{20} f(x)\, dx$.

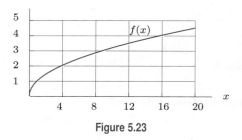

**Figure 5.23**

**12.** Use Figure 5.24 to estimate $\int_{-10}^{15} f(x)dx$.

**Figure 5.24**

Use the graphs in Problems 13–14 to estimate $\int_0^3 f(x)\, dx$.

**13.**    **14.**

**15.** Using Figure 5.25, find the value of $\int_1^6 f(x)\, dx$.

**Figure 5.25**

**16.** Without calculation, what can you say about the relationship between the values of the two integrals:

$$\int_0^2 e^{x^2}\, dx \quad \text{and} \quad \int_0^2 e^{t^2}\, dt?$$

**17.** If we know $\int_2^5 f(x)\, dx = 4$, what is the value of

$$3\left(\int_2^5 f(x)\, dx\right) + 1?$$

In Problems 18–25, use a calculator or computer to evaluate the integral.

**18.** $\displaystyle\int_1^4 \frac{1}{\sqrt{1+x^2}}\, dx$

**19.** $\displaystyle\int_{-1}^1 \frac{1}{e^t}\, dt$

**20.** $\displaystyle\int_{-1}^1 \frac{x^2+1}{x^2-4}\, dx$

**21.** $\displaystyle\int_{1.1}^{1.7} e^t \ln t\, dt$

**22.** $\displaystyle\int_0^3 \ln(y^2+1)\, dy$

**23.** $\displaystyle\int_3^4 \sqrt{e^z + z}\, dz$

**24.** $\displaystyle\int_0^2 \frac{1}{1+x^2}\, dx + \int_0^2 \frac{1}{1+y^2}\, dy$

**25.** $\displaystyle\int_0^2 \sqrt{4+t^2}\, dt - \int_0^2 \sqrt{4+x^2}\, dx$

For Problems 26–29:

  **(a)** Use a graph of the integrand to make a rough estimate of the integral. Explain your reasoning.
  **(b)** Use a computer or calculator to find the value of the definite integral.

**26.** $\displaystyle\int_0^1 x^3\, dx$

**27.** $\displaystyle\int_0^3 \sqrt{x}\, dx$

**28.** $\displaystyle\int_0^1 3^t\, dt$

**29.** $\displaystyle\int_1^2 x^x\, dx$

**30.** The graph of $f(t)$ is in Figure 5.26. Which of the following four numbers could be an estimate of $\int_0^1 f(t)dt$ accurate to two decimal places? Explain your choice.

  I.  $-98.35$   II.  $71.84$   III.  $100.12$   IV.  $93.47$

**Figure 5.26**

**31. (a)** Use a calculator or computer to find $\int_0^6 (x^2+1)\, dx$. Represent this value as the area under a curve.
  **(b)** Estimate $\int_0^6 (x^2+1)\, dx$ using a left-hand sum with $n=3$. Represent this sum graphically on a sketch of $f(x) = x^2+1$. Is this sum an overestimate or underestimate of the true value found in part (a)?
  **(c)** Estimate $\int_0^6 (x^2+1)\, dx$ using a right-hand sum with $n=3$. Represent this sum on your sketch. Is this sum an overestimate or underestimate?

# 5.3   THE DEFINITE INTEGRAL AS AREA

## Relationship Between Definite Integral and Area

If $f(x)$ is continuous and positive, each term $f(x_0)\Delta x$, $f(x_1)\Delta x, \ldots$ in a left- or right-hand Riemann sum represents the area of a rectangle. See Figure 5.27. As the width $\Delta x$ of the rectangles approaches zero, the rectangles fit the curve of the graph more exactly, and the sum of their areas gets closer to the area under the curve shaded in Figure 5.28. In other words:

---

When $f(x)$ is positive and $a < b$:

$$\text{Area under graph of } f \atop \text{between } a \text{ and } b = \int_a^b f(x)\,dx.$$

---

We assumed in drawing Figure 5.28 that the graph of $f(x)$ lies above the $x$-axis. If the graph lies below the $x$-axis, then each value of $f(x)$ is negative, so each $f(x)\,\Delta x$ is negative, and the area is counted negatively. In that case, the definite integral is the negative of the area between the graph of $f$ and the horizontal axis.

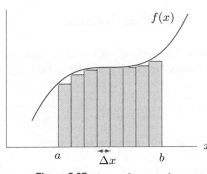

Figure 5.27: Area of rectangles approximating the area under the curve

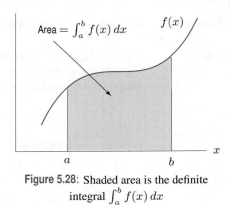

Figure 5.28: Shaded area is the definite integral $\int_a^b f(x)\,dx$

---

**Example 1**   What is the relation between the area between the parabola $y = x^2 - 1$ and the $x$-axis and these definite integrals?

(a)  $\displaystyle\int_1^2 (x^2 - 1)\,dx$

(b)  $\displaystyle\int_{-1}^1 (x^2 - 1)\,dx$

Solution   (a) The parabola lies above the $x$-axis between $x = 1$ and $x = 2$. (See Figure 5.29.) So,

$$\int_1^2 (x^2 - 1)\,dx = \text{Area} = 1.33.$$

(b) The parabola lies below the $x$-axis between $x = -1$ and $x = 1$. (See Figure 5.30.) So,

$$\int_{-1}^1 (x^2 - 1)\,dx = -\text{Area} = -1.33.$$

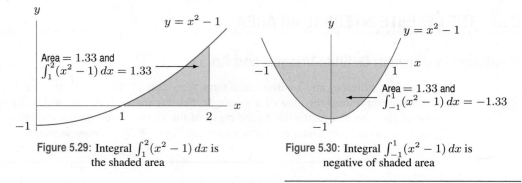

Figure 5.29: Integral $\int_1^2 (x^2 - 1)\, dx$ is
the shaded area

Figure 5.30: Integral $\int_{-1}^1 (x^2 - 1)\, dx$ is
negative of shaded area

Summarizing, assuming $f(x)$ is continuous, we have:

> **When $f(x)$ is positive for some $x$-values and negative for others**, and $a < b$:
>
> $\int_a^b f(x)\, dx$ is the sum of the areas between $a$ and $b$ above the $x$-axis, counted positively, and the areas between $a$ and $b$ below the $x$-axis, counted negatively.

In the following example, we break up the integral. The properties that allow us to do this are discussed in the Focus on Theory section at the end of this chapter.

**Example 2**    Interpret the definite integral $\int_0^4 (x^3 - 7x^2 + 11x)\, dx$ in terms of areas.

**Solution**    Figure 5.31 shows the graph of $f(x) = x^3 - 7x^2 + 11x$ crossing below the $x$-axis at about $x = 2.38$. The integral is the area above the $x$-axis, $A_1$, minus the area below the $x$-axis, $A_2$. Computing the integral with a calculator or computer shows

$$\int_0^4 (x^3 - 7x^2 + 11x)\, dx = 2.67.$$

Breaking the integral into two parts and calculating each one separately gives

$$\int_0^{2.38} (x^3 - 7x^2 + 11x)\, dx = 7.72 \quad \text{and} \quad \int_{2.38}^4 (x^3 - 7x^2 + 11x)\, dx = -5.05,$$

so $A_1 = 7.72$ and $A_2 = 5.05$. Then, as we would expect,

$$\int_0^4 (x^3 - 7x^2 + 11x)\, dx = A_1 - A_2 = 7.72 - 5.05 = 2.67.$$

Figure 5.31: Integral $\int_0^4 (x^3 - 7x^2 + 11x)\, dx = A_1 - A_2$

**Example 3**    Find the total area of the shaded regions in Figure 5.31.

**Solution**    We saw in Example 2 that $A_1 = 7.72$ and $A_2 = 5.05$. Thus we have

$$\text{Total shaded area} = A_1 + A_2 = 7.72 + 5.05 = 12.77.$$

**Example 4**    For each of the functions graphed in Figure 5.32, decide whether $\int_0^5 f(x)\,dx$ is positive, negative or approximately zero.

Figure 5.32: Is $\int_0^5 f(x)dx$ positive, negative or zero?

**Solution**    (a) The graph lies almost entirely below the $x$-axis, so the integral is negative.

(b) The graph lies partly below the $x$-axis and partly above the $x$-axis. However, the area above the $x$-axis is larger than the area below the $x$-axis, so the integral is positive.

(c) The graph lies partly below the $x$-axis and partly above the $x$-axis. Since the areas above and below the $x$-axis appear to be approximately equal in size, the integral is approximately zero.

## Area Between Two Curves

We can use rectangles to approximate the area between two curves. If $g(x) \leq f(x)$, as in Figure 5.33, the height of a rectangle is $f(x) - g(x)$. The area of the rectangle is $(f(x) - g(x))\Delta x$, and we have the following result:

> If $f$ and $g$ are continuous functions, and $g(x) \leq f(x)$ for $a \leq x \leq b$:
>
> $$\text{Area between graphs of } f(x) \text{ and } g(x) \text{ for } a \leq x \leq b = \int_a^b (f(x) - g(x))\,dx.$$

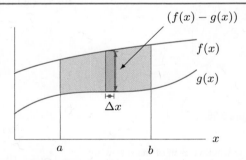

Figure 5.33: Area between two curves $= \int_a^b (f(x) - g(x))\,dx$

**Example 5**    Graphs of $f(x) = 4x - x^2$ and $g(x) = \frac{1}{2}x^{3/2}$ for $x \geq 0$ are shown in Figure 5.34. Use a definite integral to estimate the area enclosed by the graphs of these two functions.

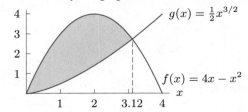

Figure 5.34: Find the area between $f(x) = 4x - x^2$ and $g(x) = \frac{1}{2}x^{3/2}$ using an integral

Solution    The region enclosed by the graphs of the two functions is shaded in Figure 5.34. The two graphs cross at $x = 0$ and at $x \approx 3.12$. Between these values, the graph of $f(x) = 4x - x^2$ lies above the graph of $g(x) = \frac{1}{2}x^{3/2}$. Using a calculator or computer to evaluate the integral, we get

$$\text{Area between graphs} = \int_0^{3.12} \left( (4x - x^2) - \frac{1}{2}x^{3/2} \right) dx = 5.906.$$

## Problems for Section 5.3

**1.** Find the area under the graph of $f(x) = x^2 + 2$ between $x = 0$ and $x = 6$.

**2.** Find the area under $P = 100(0.6)^t$ between $t = 0$ and $t = 8$.

**3.** Find the total area between $y = 4 - x^2$ and the $x$-axis for $0 \leq x \leq 3$.

**4.** Find the area between $y = x+5$ and $y = 2x+1$ between $x = 0$ and $x = 2$.

**5.** Find the area enclosed by $y = 3x$ and $y = x^2$.

**6.** (a) What is the area between the graph of $f(x)$ in Figure 5.35 and the $x$-axis, between $x = 0$ and $x = 5$?
   (b) What is $\int_0^5 f(x)\,dx$?

Area = 7

$f(x)$

Area = 6

**Figure 5.35**

**7.** Using Figure 5.36, decide whether each of the following definite integrals is positive or negative.

   (a) $\int_{-5}^{-4} f(x)\,dx$    (b) $\int_{-4}^{1} f(x)\,dx$

   (c) $\int_{1}^{3} f(x)\,dx$    (d) $\int_{-5}^{3} f(x)\,dx$

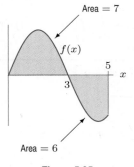

$f(x)$

**Figure 5.36**

**8.** Using Figure 5.36, arrange the following definite integrals in ascending order:

$\int_{-5}^{-3} f(x)\,dx,\ \int_{-5}^{-1} f(x)\,dx,\ \int_{-5}^{1} f(x)\,dx,\ \int_{-5}^{3} f(x)\,dx$.

**9.** (a) Estimate (by counting the squares) the total area shaded in Figure 5.37.
   (b) Using Figure 5.37, estimate $\int_0^8 f(x)\,dx$.
   (c) Why are your answers to parts (a) and (b) different?

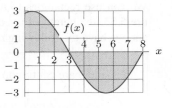

$f(x)$

**Figure 5.37**

**10.** Using Figure 5.38, estimate $\int_{-3}^{5} f(x)\,dx$.

$f(x)$

**Figure 5.38**

**11.** Given $\int_{-1}^{0} f(x)\,dx = 0.25$ and Figure 5.39, estimate:

   (a) $\int_0^1 f(x)\,dx$    (b) $\int_{-1}^1 f(x)\,dx$
   (c) The total shaded area.

$f(x)$

**Figure 5.39**

**12.** Using Figure 5.40, list the following integrals in increasing order (from smallest to largest). Which integrals are negative, which are positive? Give reasons.

I. $\int_a^b f(x)\,dx$    II. $\int_a^c f(x)\,dx$    III. $\int_a^e f(x)\,dx$

IV. $\int_b^e f(x)\,dx$    V. $\int_b^c f(x)\,dx$

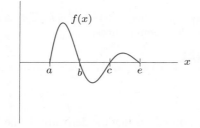

**Figure 5.40**

**13.** Use Figure 5.41 to find the values of

(a) $\int_a^b f(x)\,dx$        (b) $\int_b^c f(x)\,dx$

(c) $\int_a^c f(x)\,dx$        (d) $\int_a^c |f(x)|\,dx$

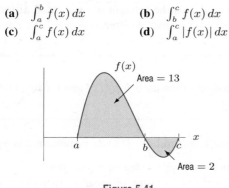

**Figure 5.41**

In Problems 14–17, match the graph with one of the following possible values for the integral $\int_0^5 f(x)\,dx$:

I. $-10.4$      II. $-2.1$      III. $5.2$      IV. $10.4$

**14.**

**15.**

**16.**

**17.**

**18.** (a) Graph $f(x) = x(x+2)(x-1)$.

(b) Find the total area between the graph and the $x$-axis between $x = -2$ and $x = 1$.

(c) Find $\int_{-2}^{1} f(x)\,dx$ and interpret it in terms of areas.

**19.** (a) Using Figure 5.42, find $\int_{-3}^{0} f(x)\,dx$.

(b) If the area of the shaded region is $A$, estimate $\int_{-3}^{4} f(x)\,dx$.

**Figure 5.42**

**20.** Use the following table to estimate the area between $f(x)$ and the $x$-axis on the interval $0 \le x \le 20$.

| $x$    | 0  | 5  | 10 | 15 | 20 |
|--------|----|----|----|----|----|
| $f(x)$ | 15 | 18 | 20 | 16 | 12 |

**21.** Use Figure 5.43 to find the values of

(a) $\int_0^2 f(x)\,dx$        (b) $\int_3^7 f(x)\,dx$

(c) $\int_2^7 f(x)\,dx$        (d) $\int_5^8 f(x)\,dx$

**Figure 5.43**: Graph consists of a semicircle and line segments

In Problems 22–29, use an integral to find the specified area.

**22.** Under $y = 6x^3 - 2$ for $5 \le x \le 10$.

**23.** Under $y = 2\cos(t/10)$ for $1 \le t \le 2$.

**24.** Under $y = 5\ln(2x)$ and above $y = 3$ for $3 \le x \le 5$.

**25.** Between $y = \sin x + 2$ and $y = 0.5$ for $6 \le x \le 10$.

**26.** Between $y = \cos x + 7$ and $y = \ln(x-3)$, $5 \le x \le 7$.

**27.** Above the curve $y = x^4 - 8$ and below the $x$-axis.

**28.** Above the curve $y = -e^x + e^{2(x-1)}$ and below the $x$-axis, for $x \ge 0$.

**29.** Between $y = \cos t$ and $y = \sin t$ for $0 \le t \le \pi$.

For Problems 30–31, compute the definite integral and interpret the result in terms of areas.

**30.** $\displaystyle\int_1^4 \frac{x^2 - 3}{x}\, dx.$

**31.** $\displaystyle\int_1^4 (x - 3\ln x)\, dx.$

**32.** Find the area between the graph of $y = x^2 - 2$ and the $x$-axis, between $x = 0$ and $x = 3$.

**33. (a)** Find the total area between $f(x) = x^3 - x$ and the $x$-axis for $0 \le x \le 3$.

**(b)** Find $\displaystyle\int_0^3 f(x)\, dx.$

**(c)** Are the answers to parts (a) and (b) the same? Explain.

**34.** Compute the definite integral $\int_0^4 \cos\sqrt{x}\, dx$ and interpret the result in terms of areas.

# 5.4  INTERPRETATIONS OF THE DEFINITE INTEGRAL

## The Notation and Units for the Definite Integral

Just as the Leibniz notation $dy/dx$ for the derivative reminds us that the derivative is the limit of a quotient of differences, the notation for the definite integral,

$$\int_a^b f(x)\, dx,$$

reminds us that an integral is a limit of a sum. Since $dx$ can be thought of as a small difference in $x$, the terms being added are products of the form "$f(x)$ times a difference in $x$." We have the following result:

> The unit of measurement for $\displaystyle\int_a^b f(x)\, dx$ is the product of the units for $f(x)$ and the units for $x$.

*Example:* If $x$ and $f(x)$ have the same units, then the integral $\displaystyle\int_a^b f(x)\, dx$ is measured in square units, say cm $\times$ cm $=$ cm$^2$. This is as we expect, since the integral represents an area.

*Example:* If $v = f(t)$ is velocity in meters/second and $t$ is time in seconds, then the integral $\displaystyle\int_a^b f(t)\, dt$ has units of (meters/sec) $\times$ (sec) $=$ meters, as we expect, since the integral represents change in position.

---

**Example 1**    Let $C(t)$ represent the cost per day to heat your home in dollars per day, where $t$ is time measured in days and $t = 0$ corresponds to January 1, 2014. Interpret $\displaystyle\int_0^{90} C(t)\, dt$.

**Solution**    The units for the integral $\int_0^{90} C(t)\, dt$ are (dollars/day) $\times$ (days) $=$ dollars. The integral represents the cost in dollars to heat your house for the first 90 days of 2014, namely the months of January, February, and March.

---

We saw in Section 5.1 that the integral of a rate of change gives total change:

> If $f(t)$ is a rate of change of a quantity, then
>
> $$\int_a^b f(t)\, dt = \text{Total change in quantity between } t = a \text{ and } t = b.$$

The units correspond: If $f(t)$ is a rate of change, with units of quantity/time, then $f(t)\Delta t$ and the definite integral have units of (quantity/time) $\times$ (time) $=$ quantity.

**Example 2**     A bacteria colony initially has a population of 14 million bacteria. Suppose that $t$ hours later the population is growing at a rate of $f(t) = 2^t$ million bacteria per hour.

(a) Give a definite integral that represents the total change in the bacteria population during the time from $t = 0$ to $t = 2$.

(b) Find the population at time $t = 2$.

**Solution**     (a) Since $f(t) = 2^t$ gives the rate of change of population, we have

$$\text{Change in population between } t = 0 \text{ and } t = 2 = \int_0^2 2^t \, dt.$$

(b) Using a calculator, we find $\int_0^2 2^t \, dt = 4.328$. The bacteria population was 14 million at time $t = 0$ and increased 4.328 million between $t = 0$ and $t = 2$. Therefore, at time $t = 2$,

$$\text{Population} = 14 + 4.328 = 18.328 \text{ million bacteria.}$$

**Example 3**     A man starts 50 miles away from his home and takes a trip in his car. He moves on a straight line, and his home lies on this line. His velocity is given in Figure 5.44.

(a) When is the man closest to his home? Approximately how far away is he then?

(b) When is the man farthest from his home? How far away is he then?

Figure 5.44: Velocity of trip starting 50 miles from home

**Solution**     What happens on this trip? The velocity function is positive the first two hours and negative between $t = 2$ and $t = 5$. So the man moves toward his home during the first two hours, then turns around at $t = 2$ and moves away from his home. The distance he travels is represented by the area between the graph of velocity and the $t$-axis; since the area below the axis is greater than the area above the axis, we see that he ends up farther away from home than when he started. Thus he is closest to home at $t = 2$ and farthest from home at $t = 5$. We can estimate how far he went in each direction by estimating areas.

(a) The man starts out 50 miles from home. The distance the man travels during the first two hours is the area under the curve between $t = 0$ and $t = 2$. This area corresponds to about one grid box. Since each grid box has area (30 miles/hour)(1 hour) = 30 miles, the man travels about 30 miles toward home. He is closest to home after 2 hours, and he is about 20 miles away at that time.

(b) Between $t = 2$ and $t = 5$, the man moves away from his home. Since this area is equal to about 3.5 grid boxes, which is $(3.5)(30) = 105$ miles, he has moved 105 miles farther from home. He was already 20 miles from home at $t = 2$, so at $t = 5$ he is about 125 miles from home. He is farthest from home at $t = 5$.

Notice that the man has covered a total distance of $30 + 105 = 135$ miles. However, he went toward his home for 30 miles and away from his home for 105 miles. His *net* change in position is 75 miles.

**Example 4**     The rates of growth of the populations of two species of plants (measured in new plants per year) are shown in Figure 5.45. Assume that the populations of the two species are equal at time $t = 0$.

(a) Which population is larger after one year? After two years?

(b) How much does the population of species 1 increase during the first two years?

Figure 5.45: Population growth rates for two species of plants

Solution    (a) The rate of growth of the population of species 1 is higher than that of species 2 throughout the first year, so the population of species 1 is larger after one year. After two years, the situation is less clear, since the population of species 1 increased faster for the first year and that of species 2 for the second. However, if $r(t)$ is the rate of growth of a population, we have

$$\text{Total change in population during first two years} = \int_0^2 r(t)dt.$$

This integral is the area under the graph of $r(t)$. For $t = 0$ to $t = 2$, the area under the species 1 graph in Figure 5.45 is smaller than the area under the species 2 graph, so the population of species 2 is larger after two years.

(b) The population change for species 1 is the area of the region under the graph of $r(t)$ between $t = 0$ and $t = 2$ in Figure 5.45. The region consists of about 16.5 grid boxes, each of area (750 plants/year)(0.25 year) = 187.5 plants, giving a total of (16.5)(187.5) = 3093.75 plants. The population of species 1 increases by about 3100 plants during the two years.

## Bioavailability of Drugs

In pharmacology, the definite integral is used to measure *bioavailability*; that is, the overall presence of a drug in the bloodstream during the course of a treatment. Unit bioavailability represents 1 unit concentration of the drug in the bloodstream for 1 hour. For example, a concentration of 3 $\mu$g/cm$^3$ in the blood for 2 hours has bioavailability of $3 \cdot 2 = 6$ ($\mu$g/cm$^3$)-hours.

Ordinarily the concentration of a drug in the blood is not constant. Typically, the concentration in the blood increases as the drug is absorbed into the bloodstream, and then decreases as the drug is broken down and excreted.[4] (See Figure 5.46.)

Suppose that we want to calculate the bioavailability of a drug that is in the blood with concentration $C(t)$ $\mu$g/cm$^3$ at time $t$ for the time period $0 \leq t \leq T$. Over a small interval $\Delta t$, we estimate

$$\text{Bioavailability} \approx \text{Concentration} \times \text{Time} = C(t)\Delta t.$$

Summing over all subintervals gives

$$\text{Total bioavailability} \approx \sum C(t)\Delta t.$$

In the limit as $n \to \infty$, where $n$ is the number of intervals of width $\Delta t$, the sum becomes an integral. So for $0 \leq t \leq T$, we have

$$\text{Bioavailability} = \int_0^T C(t)dt.$$

That is, the total bioavailability of a drug is equal to the area under the drug concentration curve.

[4]*Drug Treatment*, Graeme S. Avery (Ed.) (Sydney: Adis Press, 1976).

concentration of drug in blood stream

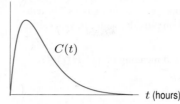

Figure 5.46: Curve showing drug concentration as a function of time

**Example 5**  Blood concentration curves[5] of two drugs are shown in Figure 5.47. Describe the differences and similarities between the two drugs in terms of peak concentration, speed of absorption into the bloodstream, and total bioavailability.

concentration of drug in blood stream

Figure 5.47: Concentration curves of two drugs

**Solution**  Drug $A$ has a peak concentration more than twice as high as that of drug $B$. Because drug $A$ achieves peak concentration sooner than drug $B$, drug $A$ appears to be absorbed more rapidly into the blood stream than drug $B$. Finally, drug $A$ has greater total bioavailability, since the area under the graph of the concentration function for drug $A$ is greater than the area under the graph for drug $B$.

## Problems for Section 5.4

In Problems 1–4, explain in words what the integral represents and give units.

**1.** $\int_1^3 v(t)\,dt$, where $v(t)$ is velocity in meters/sec and $t$ is time in seconds.

**2.** $\int_0^6 a(t)\,dt$, where $a(t)$ is acceleration in km/hr$^2$ and $t$ is time in hours.

**3.** $\int_{2005}^{2011} f(t)\,dt$, where $f(t)$ is the rate at which world population is growing in year $t$, in billion people per year.

**4.** $\int_0^5 s(x)\,dx$, where $s(x)$ is rate of change of salinity (salt concentration) in gm/liter per cm in sea water, and where $x$ is depth below the surface of the water in cm.

**5.** Oil leaks out of a tanker at a rate of $r = f(t)$ gallons per minute, where $t$ is in minutes. Write a definite integral expressing the total quantity of oil which leaks out of the tanker in the first hour.

**6.** Pollution is removed from a lake on day $t$ at a rate of $f(t)$ kg/day.

   **(a)** Explain the meaning of the statement $f(12) = 500$.
   **(b)** If $\int_5^{15} f(t)\,dt = 4000$, give the units of the 5, the 15, and the 4000.
   **(c)** Give the meaning of $\int_5^{15} f(t)\,dt = 4000$.

**7.** Annual coal production in the US (in billion tons per year) is given in the table.[6] Estimate the total amount of coal produced in the US between 1997 and 2009. If $r = f(t)$ is the rate of coal production $t$ years since 1997, write an integral to represent the 1997–2009 coal production.

| Year | 1997 | 1999 | 2001 | 2003 | 2005 | 2007 | 2009 |
|------|------|------|------|------|------|------|------|
| Rate | 1.090 | 1.094 | 1.121 | 1.072 | 1.132 | 1.147 | 1.073 |

---

[5]*Drug Treatment*, Graeme S. Avery (Ed.) (Sydney: Adis Press, 1976).
[6]http://www.eia.doe.gov/cneaf/coal/page/special/tbl1.html. Accessed May 2011.

**8.** The following table gives the US emissions, $H(t)$, of hydrofluorocarbons, or "super greenhouse gasses," in teragrams equivalent of carbon dioxide, with $t$ in years since 2000.[7]

   **(a)** What are the units and meaning of $\int_0^{10} H(t)dt$?
   **(b)** Estimate $\int_0^{10} H(t)dt$.

| Year | 2000 | 2002 | 2004 | 2006 | 2008 | 2010 |
|------|------|------|------|------|------|------|
| $H(t)$ | 7104 | 7022 | 7163 | 7159 | 7048 | 6822 |

**9.** World annual natural gas[8] consumption, $N$, in millions of metric tons of oil equivalent, is approximated by $N = 1770 + 53t$, where $t$ is in years since 1990.

   **(a)** How much natural gas was consumed in 1990? In 2010?
   **(b)** Estimate the total amount of natural gas consumed during the 20-year period from 1990 to 2010.

**10.** Solar photovoltaic (PV) cells are the world's fastest-growing energy source. In year $t$ since 2007, PV cells were manufactured worldwide at a rate of $S = 3.7e^{0.61t}$ gigawatts per year.[9] Estimate the total solar energy-generating capacity of the PV cells manufactured between 2007 and 2011.

Problems 11–14 show the velocity, in cm/sec, of a particle moving along a number line. (Positive velocities represent movement to the right; negative velocities to the left.) Compute the change in position between times $t = 0$ and $t = 5$ seconds.

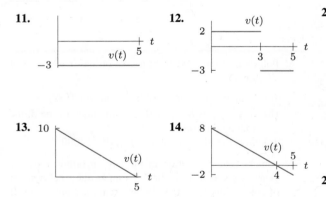

**15.** Your velocity is $v(t) = \ln(t^2+1)$ ft/sec for $t$ in seconds, $0 \le t \le 3$. Find the distance traveled during this time.

**16.** Figure 5.48 shows the length growth rate of a human fetus.

   **(a)** What feature of a graph of length as a function of age corresponds to the maximum in Figure 5.48?
   **(b)** Estimate the length of a baby born in week 40.

**Figure 5.48**

**17.** A forest fire covers 2000 acres at time $t = 0$. The fire is growing at a rate of $8\sqrt{t}$ acres per hour, where $t$ is in hours. How many acres are covered 24 hours later?

**18.** Water is pumped out of a holding tank at a rate of $5 - 5e^{-0.12t}$ liters/minute, where $t$ is in minutes since the pump is started. If the holding tank contains 1000 liters of water when the pump is started, how much water does it hold one hour later?

**19.** With $t$ in seconds, the velocity of an object is $v(t) = 10 + 8t - t^2$ m/sec.

   **(a)** Represent the distance traveled during the first 5 seconds as a definite integral and as an area.
   **(b)** Estimate the distance traveled by the object during the first 5 seconds by estimating the area.
   **(c)** Calculate the distance traveled.

**20.** A bungee jumper leaps off the starting platform at time $t = 0$ and rebounds once during the first 5 seconds. With velocity measured downward, for $t$ in seconds and $0 \le t \le 5$, the jumper's velocity is approximated[10] by $v(t) = -4t^2 + 16t$ meters/sec.

   **(a)** How many meters does the jumper travel during the first five seconds?
   **(b)** Where is the jumper relative to the starting position at the end of the five seconds?
   **(c)** What does $\int_0^5 v(t)\,dt$ represent in terms of the jump?

**21.** After a foreign substance is introduced into the blood, the rate at which antibodies are made is given by

$$r(t) = \frac{t}{t^2 + 1} \text{ thousands of antibodies per minute,}$$

where time, $t$, is in minutes. Assuming there are no antibodies present at time $t = 0$, find the total quantity of antibodies in the blood at the end of 4 minutes.

---

[7]www.epa.gov/climatechange/science/indicators/ghg/us-ghg-emissions.html. Accessed January 2013.
[8]*BP Statistical Review of World Energy 2009*, http://www.bp.com/, accessed September 6, 2009).
[9]www.earth-policy.org/indicators/Temp/solar_power_2011. Accessed February 2013. A gigawatt measures power, the rate of energy generation. In this case, we are considering gigawatts of capacity manufactured per year.
[10]Based on www.itforus.oeiizk.waw.pl/tresc/activ//modules/bj.pdf. Accessed February 12, 2012.

**22.** Figure 5.49 gives your velocity during a trip starting from home. Positive velocities take you away from home and negative velocities take you toward home. Where are you at the end of the 5 hours? When are you farthest from home? How far away are you at that time?

**Figure 5.49**

**23.** A bicyclist pedals along a straight road with velocity, $v$, given in Figure 5.50. She starts 5 miles from a lake; positive velocities take her away from the lake and negative velocities take her toward the lake. When is the cyclist farthest from the lake, and how far away is she then?

**Figure 5.50**

**24.** Figure 5.51 shows the rate of growth of two trees. If the two trees are the same height at time $t = 0$, which tree is taller after 5 years? After 10 years?

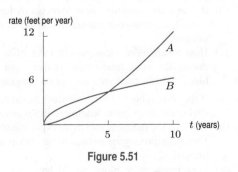

**Figure 5.51**

Problems 25–27 concern the future of the US Social Security Trust Fund, out of which pensions are paid. Figure 5.52 shows the rates (billions of dollars per year) at which income, $I(t)$, from taxes and interest is projected to flow into the fund and at which expenditures, $E(t)$, flow out of the fund. Figure 5.53 shows the value of the fund as a function of time.[11]

**Figure 5.52**

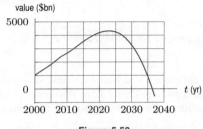

**Figure 5.53**

**25. (a)** Write each of the following areas in Figure 5.52 from 2000 to 2015 as an integral and explain its significance for the fund.
  **(i)** Under the income curve
  **(ii)** Under the expenditure curve
  **(iii)** Between the income and expenditure curves

**(b)** Use Figure 5.53 to estimate the area between the two curves from 2000 to 2015.

**26.** Decide when the value of the fund is projected to be a maximum using

  **(a)** Figure 5.52          **(b)** Figure 5.53

**27.** Express the projected increase in value of the fund from 2000 to 2030 as an integral.

**28.** The rates of consumption of stores of protein and fat in the human body during 8 weeks of starvation are shown in Figure 5.54. Does the body burn more fat or more protein during this period?

**Figure 5.54**

[11]The 2009 OASDI Trustees Report, www.ssa.gov/OACT/TR/2009.

**29.** Figure 5.55 shows the number of sales per month made by two salespeople. Which person has the most total sales after 6 months? After the first year? At approximately what times (if any) have they sold roughly equal total amounts? Approximately how many total sales has each person made at the end of the first year?

**Figure 5.55**

**30.** The birth rate, $B$, in births per hour, of a bacteria population is given in Figure 5.56. The curve marked $D$ gives the death rate, in deaths per hour, of the same population.

(a) Explain what the shape of each of these graphs tells you about the population.
(b) Use the graphs to find the time at which the net rate of increase of the population is at a maximum.
(c) At time $t = 0$ the population has size $N$. Sketch the graph of the total number born by time $t$. Also sketch the graph of the number alive at time $t$. Estimate the time at which the population is a maximum.

**Figure 5.56**

**31.** Height velocity graphs are used by endocrinologists to follow the progress of children with growth deficiencies. Figure 5.57 shows the height velocity curves of an average boy and an average girl between ages 3 and 18.

(a) Which curve is for girls and which is for boys? Explain how you can tell.
(b) About how much does the average boy grow between ages 3 and 10?
(c) The growth spurt associated with adolescence and the onset of puberty occurs between ages 12 and 15 for the average boy and between ages 10 and 12.5 for the average girl. Estimate the height gained by each average child during this growth spurt.
(d) When fully grown, about how much taller is the average man than the average woman? (The average boy and girl are about the same height at age 3.)

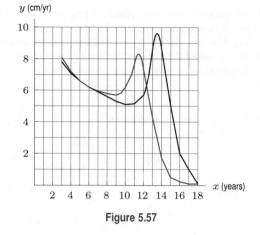

**Figure 5.57**

A healthy human heart pumps about 5 liters of blood per minute. Problems 32–33 refer to Figure 5.58, which shows the response of the heart to bleeding. The pumping rate drops and then returns to normal if the person recovers fully, or drops to zero if the person dies.

**Figure 5.58**

**32.** (a) If the body is bled 2 liters, how much blood is pumped during the three hours leading to death?
(b) If $f(t)$ is the pumping rate in liters per minute at time $t$ hours, express your answer to part (a) as a definite integral.
(c) How much more blood would have been pumped during the same time period if there had been no bleeding? Illustrate your answer on the graph.

**33.** (a) If the body is bled 1 liter, how much blood is pumped during the three hours leading to full recovery?
(b) If $g(t)$ is the pumping rate in liters per minute at time $t$ hours, express your answer to part (a) as a definite integral.
(c) How much more blood would have been pumped during the same time period if there had been no bleeding? Show your answer as an area on the graph.

**34.** The amount of waste a company produces, $W$, in tons per week, is approximated by $W = 3.75e^{-0.008t}$, where $t$ is in weeks since January 1, 2005. Waste removal for the company costs \$15/ton. How much did the company pay for waste removal during the year 2005?

**35.** Figure 5.59 shows plasma concentration curves for two drugs used to slow a rapid heart rate. Compare the two products in terms of level of peak concentration, time until peak concentration, and overall bioavailability.

concentration of drug in plasma

Product B

Product A

hours

**Figure 5.59**

**36.** Figure 5.60 compares the concentration in blood plasma for two pain relievers. Compare the two products in terms of level of peak concentration, time until peak concentration, and overall bioavailability.

concentration of drug in plasma

Product B

Product A

hours

**Figure 5.60**

**37.** Draw plasma concentration curves for two drugs $A$ and $B$ if product $A$ has the highest peak concentration, but product $B$ is absorbed more quickly and has greater overall bioavailability.

**38.** A two-day environmental cleanup started at 9 am on the first day. The number of workers fluctuated as shown in Figure 5.61. If the workers were paid $10 per hour, how much was the total personnel cost of the cleanup?

workers

50
40
30
20
10

8  16  24  32  40  48

hours

**Figure 5.61**

**39.** Suppose in Problem 38 that the workers were paid $10 per hour for work during the time period 9 am to 5 pm and were paid $15 per hour for work during the rest of the day. What would the total personnel costs of the cleanup have been under these conditions?

**40.** At the site of a spill of radioactive iodine, radiation levels were four times the maximum acceptable limit, so an evacuation was ordered. If $R_0$ is the initial radiation level (at $t = 0$) and $t$ is the time in hours, the radiation level $R(t)$, in millirems/hour, is given by

$$R(t) = R_0(0.996)^t.$$

**(a)** How long does it take for the site to reach the acceptable level of radiation of 0.6 millirems/hour?
**(b)** How much total radiation (in millirems) has been emitted by that time?

**41.** If you jump out of an airplane and your parachute fails to open, your downward velocity (in meters per second) $t$ seconds after the jump is approximated by

$$v(t) = 49(1 - (0.8187)^t).$$

**(a)** Write an expression for the distance you fall in $T$ seconds.
**(b)** If you jump from 5000 meters above the ground, estimate, using trial and error, how many seconds you fall before hitting the ground.

**42.** The Montgolfier brothers (Joseph and Etienne) were eighteenth-century pioneers of hot-air ballooning. Had they had the appropriate instruments, they might have left us a record, like that shown in Figure 5.62, of one of their early experiments. The graph shows their vertical velocity, $v$, with upward as positive.

**(a)** Over what intervals was the acceleration positive? Negative?
**(b)** What was the greatest altitude achieved, and at what time?
**(c)** This particular flight ended on top of a hill. How do you know that it did, and what was the height of the hill above the starting point?

$v$ (ft/min)

20
10
0
-10
-20

10  20  30  40  50  60   $t$ (min)

**Figure 5.62**

## 5.5 TOTAL CHANGE AND THE FUNDAMENTAL THEOREM OF CALCULUS

In Section 5.4, we saw that the total change of a quantity can be obtained by integrating its rate of change. Since the change in $F$ between $a$ and $b$ is $F(b) - F(a)$ and the rate of change is $F'(t)$, we have the following result:

---

**The Fundamental Theorem of Calculus**

If $F'(t)$ is continuous for $a \le t \le b$, then

$$\int_a^b F'(t)\, dt = F(b) - F(a).$$

In words:
The definite integral of the derivative of a function gives the total change in the function.

---

In Section 6.3 we see how to use the Fundamental Theorem to compute a definite integral. The Focus on Theory Section gives another version of the Fundamental Theorem.

---

**Example 1**    Figure 5.63 shows $F'(t)$, the rate of change of the value, $F(t)$, of an investment over a 5-month period.

(a) When is the value of the investment increasing in value and when is it decreasing?
(b) Does the investment increase or decrease in value during the 5 months?

Figure 5.63: Did the investment increase or decrease in value over these 5 months?

**Solution**    (a) The investment decreased in value during the first 3 months, since the rate of change of value is negative then. The value rose during the last 2 months.
(b) We want to find the total change in the value of the investment between $t = 0$ and $t = 5$. Since the total change is the integral of the rate of change, $F'(t)$, we are looking for

$$\text{Total change in value} = \int_0^5 F'(t)dt.$$

The integral equals the shaded area above the $t$-axis minus the shaded area below the $t$-axis. Since in Figure 5.63 the area below the axis is greater than the area above the axis, the integral is negative. The total change in value of the investment during this time is negative, so it decreased in value.

## Marginal Cost and Change in Total Cost

Suppose $C(q)$ represents the cost of producing $q$ items. The derivative, $C'(q)$, is the marginal cost. Since marginal cost $C'(q)$ is the rate of change of the cost function with respect to quantity, by the Fundamental Theorem, the integral

$$\int_a^b C'(q)\,dq$$

represents the total change in the cost function between $q = a$ and $q = b$. In other words, the integral gives the amount it costs to increase production from $a$ units to $b$ units.

The cost of producing 0 units is the fixed cost $C(0)$. The area under the marginal cost curve between $q = 0$ and $q = b$ is the total increase in cost between a production of 0 and a production of $b$. This is called the *total variable cost*. Adding this to the fixed cost gives the total cost to produce $b$ units. In summary,

---

If $C'(q)$ is a marginal cost function and $C(0)$ is the fixed cost,

$$\text{Cost to increase production from } a \text{ units to } b \text{ units} = C(b) - C(a) = \int_a^b C'(q)\,dq$$

$$\text{Total variable cost to produce } b \text{ units} = \int_0^b C'(q)\,dq$$

$$\text{Total cost of producing } b \text{ units} = \text{Fixed cost} + \text{Total variable cost}$$

$$= C(0) + \int_0^b C'(q)\,dq$$

---

**Example 2**  A marginal cost curve is given in Figure 5.64. If the fixed cost is $1000, estimate the total cost of producing 250 items.

**Solution**  The total cost of production is Fixed cost + Total variable cost. The total variable cost of producing 250 items is represented by the area under the marginal cost curve. The area in Figure 5.64 between $q = 0$ and $q = 250$ is about 20 grid boxes. Each grid box has area (2 dollars/item)(50 items) = 100 dollars, so

$$\text{Total variable cost} = \int_0^{250} C'(q)\,dq \approx 20(100) = 2000.$$

The total cost to produce 250 items is given by :

$$\text{Total cost} = \text{Fixed cost} + \text{Total variable cost}$$
$$\approx \$1000 + \$2000 = \$3000.$$

Figure 5.64: A marginal cost curve

## Problems for Section 5.5

**1.** A cup of coffee at $90°C$ is put into a $20°C$ room when $t = 0$. The coffee's temperature is changing at a rate of $r(t) = -7(0.9^t)$ $°C$ per minute, with $t$ in minutes. Estimate the coffee's temperature when $t = 10$.

**2.** If the marginal cost function $C'(q)$ is measured in dollars per ton, and $q$ gives the quantity in tons, what are the units of measurement for $\int_{800}^{900} C'(q)\, dq$? What does this integral represent?

**3.** The marginal cost of drilling an oil well depends on the depth at which you are drilling; drilling becomes more expensive, per meter, as you dig deeper into the earth. The fixed costs are 1,000,000 riyals (the riyal is the unit of currency of Saudi Arabia), and, if $x$ is the depth in meters, the marginal costs are

$$C'(x) = 4000 + 10x \quad \text{riyals/meter.}$$

Find the total cost of drilling a 500-meter well.

**4.** The population of Tokyo grew at the rate shown in Figure 5.65. Estimate the change in population between 1970 and 1990.

**Figure 5.65**

**5.** A marginal cost function $C'(q)$ is given in Figure 5.66. If the fixed costs are \$10,000, estimate:

**(a)** The total cost to produce 30 units.
**(b)** The additional cost if the company increases production from 30 units to 40 units.
**(c)** The value of $C'(25)$. Interpret your answer in terms of costs of production.

**Figure 5.66**

**6.** Figure 5.67 shows the rate of change of the quantity of water in a water tower, in liters per day, during the month of April. If the tower had 12,000 liters of water in it on April 1, estimate the quantity of water in the tower on April 30.

**Figure 5.67**

**7.** The total cost in dollars to produce $q$ units of a product is $C(q)$. Fixed costs are \$20,000. The marginal cost is

$$C'(q) = 0.005q^2 - q + 56.$$

**(a)** On a graph of $C'(q)$, illustrate graphically the total variable cost of producing 150 units.
**(b)** Estimate $C(150)$, the total cost to produce 150 units.
**(c)** Find the value of $C'(150)$ and interpret your answer in terms of costs of production.
**(d)** Use parts (b) and (c) to estimate $C(151)$.

**8.** The marginal cost $C'(q)$ (in dollars per unit) of producing $q$ units is given in the following table.

**(a)** If fixed cost is \$10,000, estimate the total cost of producing 400 units.
**(b)** How much would the total cost increase if production were increased one unit, to 401 units?

| $q$ | 0 | 100 | 200 | 300 | 400 | 500 | 600 |
|-----|---|-----|-----|-----|-----|-----|-----|
| $C'(q)$ | 25 | 20 | 18 | 22 | 28 | 35 | 45 |

**9.** The marginal cost function for a company is given by

$$C'(q) = q^2 - 16q + 70 \text{ dollars/unit,}$$

where $q$ is the quantity produced. If $C(0) = 500$, find the total cost of producing 20 units. What is the fixed cost and what is the total variable cost for this quantity?

**10.** The marginal cost function of producing $q$ mountain bikes is

$$C'(q) = \frac{600}{0.3q + 5}.$$

**(a)** If the fixed cost in producing the bicycles is \$2000, find the total cost to produce 30 bicycles.
**(b)** If the bikes are sold for \$200 each, what is the profit (or loss) on the first 30 bicycles?
**(c)** Find the marginal profit on the $31^{st}$ bicycle.

11. The marginal revenue function on sales of $q$ units of a product is $R'(q) = 200 - 12\sqrt{q}$ dollars per unit.

   (a) Graph $R'(q)$.
   (b) Estimate the total revenue if sales are 100 units.
   (c) What is the marginal revenue at 100 units? Use this value and your answer to part (b) to estimate the total revenue if sales are 101 units.

12. Figure 5.68 shows $P'(t)$, the rate of change of the price of stock in a certain company at time $t$.

   (a) At what time during this five-week period was the stock at its highest value? At its lowest value?
   (b) If $P(t)$ represents the price of the stock, arrange the following quantities in increasing order:

   $$P(0), \ P(1), \ P(2), \ P(3), \ P(4), \ P(5).$$

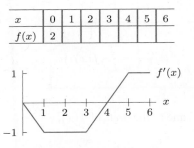

$/share per week

Figure 5.68

13. The net worth, $f(t)$, of a company is growing at a rate of $f'(t) = 2000 - 12t^2$ dollars per year, where $t$ is in years since 2005. How is the net worth of the company expected to change between 2005 and 2015? If the company is worth \$40,000 in 2005, what is it worth in 2015?

14. The graph of a derivative $f'(x)$ is shown in Figure 5.69. Fill in the table of values for $f(x)$ given that $f(0) = 2$.

| $x$ | 0 | 1 | 2 | 3 | 4 | 5 | 6 |
|-----|---|---|---|---|---|---|---|
| $f(x)$ | 2 | | | | | | |

Figure 5.69: Graph of $f'$, not $f$

15. The derivative $f'(x)$ is graphed in Figure 5.70. Fill in the table of values for $f(x)$ given that $f(0) = -10$.

| $x$ | 0 | 1 | 2 | 3 | 4 | 5 | 6 |
|-----|---|---|---|---|---|---|---|
| $f(x)$ | -10 | | | | | | |

Figure 5.70: Graph of $f'$, not $f$

In Problems 16–17, oil is pumped from a well at a rate of $r(t)$ barrels per day, with $t$ in days. Assume $r'(t) < 0$ and $t_0 > 0$.

16. What does the value of $\int_0^{t_0} r(t)\,dt$ tells us about the oil well?

17. Rank in order from least to greatest:

$$\int_0^{2t_0} r(t)\,dt, \quad \int_{t_0}^{2t_0} r(t)\,dt, \quad \int_{2t_0}^{3t_0} r(t)\,dt.$$

In Problems 18–20, let $C(n)$ be a city's cost, in millions of dollars, for plowing the roads, when $n$ inches of snow have fallen. Let $c(n) = C'(n)$. Evaluate the expressions and interpret your answers in terms of the cost of plowing snow, given

$$c'(n) < 0, \quad \int_0^{15} c(n)\,dn = 7.5, \quad c(15) = 0.7,$$
$$c(24) = 0.4, \quad C(15) = 8, \quad C(24) = 13.$$

18. $\displaystyle\int_{15}^{24} c(n)\,dn$

19. $C(0)$

20. $\displaystyle c(15) + \int_{15}^{24} c'(n)\,dn$

Problems 21–23 refer to a May 2, 2010, article:[12]

   "The crisis began around 10 am yesterday when a 10-foot wide pipe in Weston sprang a leak, which worsened throughout the afternoon and eventually cut off Greater Boston from the Quabbin Reservoir, where most of its water supply is stored...Before water was shut off to the ruptured pipe [at 6:40 pm], brown water had been roaring from a massive crater [at a rate of] 8 million gallons an hour rushing into the nearby Charles River."

Let $r(t)$ be the rate in gallons/hr that water flowed from the pipe $t$ hours after it sprang its leak.

21. Which is larger: $\displaystyle\int_0^2 r(t)\,dt$ or $\displaystyle\int_2^4 r(t)\,dt$?

22. Which is larger: $\displaystyle\int_0^4 r(t)\,dt$ or $4r(4)$?

23. Give a reasonable overestimate of $\displaystyle\int_0^8 r(t)\,dt$.

---

[12]"A catastrophic rupture hits region's water system," *The Boston Globe*, May 2, 2010.

# 5.6   AVERAGE VALUE

In this section we show how to interpret the definite integral as the average value of a function.

## The Definite Integral as an Average

We know how to find the average of $n$ numbers: Add them and divide by $n$. But how do we find the average value of a continuously varying function? Let us consider an example. Suppose $f(t)$ is the temperature at time $t$, measured in hours since midnight, and that we want to calculate the average temperature over a 24-hour period. One way to start would be to average the temperatures at $n$ equally spaced times, $t_1, t_2, \ldots, t_n$, during the day.

$$\text{Average temperature} \approx \frac{f(t_1) + f(t_2) + \cdots + f(t_n)}{n}.$$

The larger we make $n$, the better the approximation. We can rewrite this expression as a Riemann sum over the interval $0 \le t \le 24$ if we use the fact that $\Delta t = 24/n$, so $n = 24/\Delta t$:

$$\begin{aligned}
\text{Average temperature} &\approx \frac{f(t_1) + f(t_2) + \cdots + f(t_n)}{24/\Delta t} \\
&= \frac{f(t_1)\Delta t + f(t_2)\Delta t + \cdots + f(t_n)\Delta t}{24} \\
&= \frac{1}{24} \sum_{i=1}^{n} f(t_i)\Delta t.
\end{aligned}$$

As $n \to \infty$, the Riemann sum tends toward an integral, and the approximation gets better. We expect that

$$\begin{aligned}
\text{Average temperature} &= \lim_{n \to \infty} \frac{1}{24} \sum_{i=1}^{n} f(t_i)\Delta t \\
&= \frac{1}{24} \int_0^{24} f(t)\, dt.
\end{aligned}$$

Generalizing for any function $f$, if $a < b$, we have

$$\boxed{\begin{array}{ll} \text{Average value of } f & = \dfrac{1}{b-a} \displaystyle\int_a^b f(x)\, dx. \\ \text{on the interval from } a \text{ to } b & \end{array}}$$

The units of the average value of $f(x)$ are the same as the units of $f(x)$.

## How to Visualize the Average on a Graph

The definition of average value tells us that

$$(\text{Average value of } f) \cdot (b - a) = \int_a^b f(x)\, dx.$$

Let's interpret the integral as the area under the graph of $f$. If $f(x)$ is positive, then the average value of $f$ is the height of a rectangle whose base is $(b - a)$ and whose area is the same as the area between the graph of $f$ and the $x$-axis. (See Figure 5.71.)

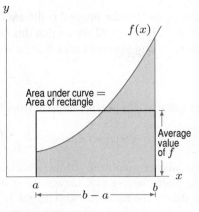

Figure 5.71: Area and average value

**Example 1**    Suppose that $C(t)$ represents the daily cost of heating your house, in dollars per day, where $t$ is time in days and $t = 0$ corresponds to January 1, 2010. Interpret $\dfrac{1}{90 - 0} \displaystyle\int_0^{90} C(t)\, dt$.

Solution    The units for the integral $\int_0^{90} C(t)\, dt$ are (dollars/day)×(days) = dollars. The integral represents the total cost in dollars to heat your house for the first 90 days of 2010, namely the months of January, February, and March. The expression $\frac{1}{90-0} \int_0^{90} C(t)\, dt$ represents the average cost per day to heat your house during the first 90 days of 2010. It is measured in (1/days) × (dollars) = dollars/day, the same units as $C(t)$.

**Example 2**    The population of McAllen, Texas can be modeled by the function
$$P = f(t) = 570(1.037)^t,$$
where $P$ is in thousands of people and $t$ is in years since 2000. Use this function to predict the average population of McAllen between the years 2020 and 2040.

Solution    We want the average value of $f(t)$ between $t = 20$ and $t = 40$. Using a calculator to evaluate the integral, we get
$$\text{Average population} = \frac{1}{40 - 20} \int_{20}^{40} f(t)\, dt = \frac{1}{20}(34{,}656.2) = 1732.81.$$
The average population of McAllen between 2020 and 2040 is predicted to be about 1733 thousand people.

**Example 3**    (a)  For the function $f(x)$ graphed in Figure 5.72, evaluate $\displaystyle\int_0^5 f(x)\, dx$.

(b)  Find the average value of $f(x)$ on the interval $x = 0$ to $x = 5$. Check your answer graphically.

Figure 5.72: Estimate $\int_0^5 f(x)dx$

Area under graph = Area of shaded rectangle

Figure 5.73: Average value of $f(x)$ is 3

Solution    (a) Since $f(x) \geq 0$, the definite integral is the area of the region under the graph of $f(x)$ between $x = 0$ and $x = 5$. Figure 5.72 shows that this region consists of 13 full grid squares and 4 half grid squares, each grid square of area 1, for a total area of 15, so

$$\int_0^5 f(x)\,dx = 15.$$

(b) The average value of $f(x)$ on the interval from 0 to 5 is given by

$$\text{Average value} = \frac{1}{5-0} \int_0^5 f(x)\,dx = \frac{1}{5}(15) = 3.$$

To check the answer graphically, draw a horizontal line at $y = 3$ on the graph of $f(x)$. (See Figure 5.73.) Then observe that, between $x = 0$ and $x = 5$, the area under the graph of $f(x)$ is equal to the area of the rectangle with height 3.

## Problems for Section 5.6

**1.** (a) Use Figure 5.74 to find $\int_0^6 f(x)\,dx$.
   (b) What is the average value of $f$ on the interval $x = 0$ to $x = 6$?

Figure 5.74

**2.** Use Figure 5.75 to estimate the following:

   (a) The integral $\int_0^5 f(x)\,dx$.
   (b) The average value of $f$ between $x = 0$ and $x = 5$ by estimating visually the average height.
   (c) The average value of $f$ between $x = 0$ and $x = 5$ by using your answer to part (a).

Figure 5.75

In Problems 3–4, find the average value of the function over the given interval.

**3.** $g(t) = 1 + t$ over $[0, 2]$

**4.** $g(t) = e^t$ over $[0, 10]$

**5.** (a) What is the average value of $f(x) = \sqrt{1 - x^2}$ over the interval $0 \leq x \leq 1$?
   (b) How can you tell whether this average value is more or less than 0.5 without doing any calculations?

In Problems 6–7, estimate the average value of the function between $x = 0$ and $x = 7$.

**6.**

**7.**

In Problems 8–9, estimate the average value of $f(x)$ from $x = a$ to $x = b$.

**8.** **9.**

**10.** The value, $V$, of a Tiffany lamp, worth $225 in 1975, increases at 15% per year. Its value in dollars $t$ years after 1975 is given by

$$V = 225(1.15)^t.$$

Find the average value of the lamp over the period 1975–2010.

**11.** If $t$ is measured in days since June 1, the inventory $I(t)$ for an item in a warehouse is given by

$$I(t) = 5000(0.9)^t.$$

**(a)** Find the average inventory in the warehouse during the 90 days after June 1.

**(b)** Graph $I(t)$ and illustrate the average graphically.

**12.** The population of the world $t$ years after 2010 is predicted to be $P = 6.9e^{0.012t}$ billion.

**(a)** What population is predicted in 2020?

**(b)** What is the predicted average population between 2010 and 2020?

In Problems 13–14 annual income for ages 25 to 85 is given graphically. People sometimes spend less than their income (to save for retirement) or more than their income (taking out a loan). The process of spreading out spending over a lifetime is called consumption smoothing.

**(a)** Find the average annual income for these years.

**(b)** Assuming that people spend at a constant rate equal to their average income, when are they spending less than they earn, and when are they spending more?

**13.**

annual income
($1000s per year)

**14.**

annual income
($1000s per year)

Problems 15–16 refer to Figure 5.76, which shows human arterial blood pressure during the course of one heartbeat.

arterial pressure
(mm Hg)

**Figure 5.76**

**15. (a)** Estimate the maximum blood pressure, called the systolic pressure.

**(b)** Estimate the minimum blood pressure, called the diastolic pressure.

**(c)** Calculate the average of the systolic and diastolic pressures.

**(d)** Is the average arterial pressure over the entire cycle greater than, less than, or equal to the answer for part (c)?

**16.** Estimate the average arterial blood pressure over one cardiac cycle.

**17.** Figure 5.77 shows the rate, $f(x)$, in thousands of algae per hour, at which a population of algae is growing, where $x$ is in hours.

**(a)** Estimate the average value of the rate over the interval $x = -1$ to $x = 3$.

**(b)** Estimate the total change in the population over the interval $x = -3$ to $x = 3$.

**Figure 5.77**

**18.** The number of hours, $H$, of daylight in Madrid as a function of date is approximated by the formula

$$H = 12 + 2.4\sin\left(0.0172(t - 80)\right),$$

where $t$ is the number of days since the start of the year. Find the average number of hours of daylight in Madrid:

**(a)** in January    **(b)** in June    **(c)** over a year

**(d)** Explain why the relative magnitudes of your answers to parts (a), (b), and (c) are reasonable.

**19.** A bar of metal is cooling from $1000°C$ to room temperature, $20°C$. The temperature, $H$, of the bar $t$ minutes after it starts cooling is given, in $°C$, by

$$H = 20 + 980e^{-0.1t}.$$

**(a)** Find the temperature of the bar at the end of one hour.

**(b)** Find the average value of the temperature over the first hour.

**(c)** Is your answer to part (b) greater or smaller than the average of the temperatures at the beginning and the end of the hour? Explain this in terms of the concavity of the graph of $H$.

**20.** The rate of sales (in sales per month) of a company is given, for $t$ in months since January 1, by

$$r(t) = t^4 - 20t^3 + 118t^2 - 180t + 200.$$

(a) Graph the rate of sales per month during the first year ($t = 0$ to $t = 12$). Does it appear that more sales were made during the first half of the year, or during the second half?

(b) Estimate the total sales during the first 6 months of the year and during the last 6 months of the year.

(c) What are the total sales for the entire year?

(d) Find the average sales per month during the year.

**21.** Throughout much of the 20$^{\text{th}}$ century, the yearly consumption of electricity in the US increased exponentially at a continuous rate of 7% per year. Assume this trend continues and that the electrical energy consumed in 1900 was 1.4 million megawatt-hours.

(a) Write an expression for yearly electricity consumption as a function of time, $t$, in years since 1900.

(b) Find the average yearly electrical consumption throughout the 20$^{\text{th}}$ century.

(c) During what year was electrical consumption closest to the average for the century?

(d) Without doing the calculation for part (c), how could you have predicted which half of the century the answer would be in?

**22.** Using Figure 5.78, list the following numbers from least to greatest:

(a) $f'(1)$

(b) The average value of $f$ on $0 \leq x \leq 4$

(c) $\int_0^1 f(x)dx$

**Figure 5.78**

**23.** Using Figure 5.79, list from least to greatest,

(a) $f'(1)$.

(b) The average value of $f(x)$ on $0 \leq x \leq a$.

(c) The average value of the rate of change of $f(x)$, for $0 \leq x \leq a$.

(d) $\int_0^a f(x)\, dx$.

**Figure 5.79**

# CHAPTER SUMMARY

- **Definite integral as limit of right-hand or left-hand sums**

- **Interpretations of the definite integral**
  Total change from rate of change, change in position given velocity, area, bioavailability, total variable cost.

- **Working with the definite integral**

Estimate definite integral from graph, table of values, or formula.

- **Fundamental Theorem of Calculus**
  Marginal cost and total cost

- **Average value**

# REVIEW PROBLEMS FOR CHAPTER FIVE

**1.** The velocity $v(t)$ in Table 5.8 is decreasing, $2 \leq t \leq 12$. Using $n = 5$ subdivisions to approximate the total distance traveled, find

(a) An upper estimate    (b) A lower estimate

**Table 5.8**

| $t$ | 2 | 4 | 6 | 8 | 10 | 12 |
|---|---|---|---|---|---|---|
| $v(t)$ | 44 | 42 | 41 | 40 | 37 | 35 |

**2.** The velocity $v(t)$ in Table 5.9 is increasing, $0 \leq t \leq 12$.

(a) Find an upper estimate for the total distance traveled using

   (i)  $n = 4$       (ii)  $n = 2$

(b) Which of the two answers in part (a) is more accurate? Why?

(c) Find a lower estimate of the total distance traveled using $n = 4$.

**Table 5.9**

| $t$ | 0 | 3 | 6 | 9 | 12 |
|---|---|---|---|---|---|
| $v(t)$ | 34 | 37 | 38 | 40 | 45 |

**3.** Use the following table to estimate $\int_0^{25} f(x)dx$.

| $x$ | 0 | 5 | 10 | 15 | 20 | 25 |
|---|---|---|---|---|---|---|
| $f(x)$ | 100 | 82 | 69 | 60 | 53 | 49 |

**4.** If $f(t)$ is measured in miles per hour and $t$ is measured in hours, what are the units of $\int_a^b f(t)\, dt$?

**5.** Figure 5.80 shows the velocity of a runner for $0 \le t \le 8$ and the rectangles used to estimate the distance traveled.

  **(a)** Do the rectangles represent a left or a right sum?
  **(b)** Do the rectangles lead to an upper or a lower estimate?
  **(c)** What is the value of $n$?
  **(d)** What is the value of $\Delta t$?
  **(e)** Give an approximate value for the estimate.

**Figure 5.80**

**6.** If $f(t)$ is measured in meters/second$^2$ and $t$ is measured in seconds, what are the units of $\int_a^b f(t)\, dt$?

**7.** If $f(t)$ is measured in dollars per year and $t$ is measured in years, what are the units of $\int_a^b f(t)\, dt$?

**8.** If $f(x)$ is measured in pounds and $x$ is measured in feet, what are the units of $\int_a^b f(x)\, dx$?

**9.** As coal deposits are depleted, it becomes necessary to strip-mine larger areas for each ton of coal. Figure 5.81 shows the number of acres of land per million tons of coal that will be defaced during strip-mining as a function of the number of million tons removed, starting from the present day.

  **(a)** Estimate the total number of acres defaced in extracting the next 4 million tons of coal (measured from the present day). Draw four rectangles under the curve, and compute their area.
  **(b)** Re-estimate the number of acres defaced using rectangles above the curve.
  **(c)** Use your answers to parts (a) and (b) to get a better estimate of the actual number of acres defaced.

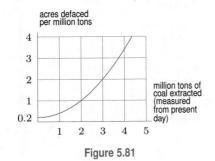

**Figure 5.81**

**10.** Find the area under $y = x^3 + 2$ between $x = 0$ and $x = 2$. Sketch this area.

**11.** Find the area under the graph of $y = 10x(3^{-x})$ between $x = 0$ and $x = 3$. Sketch this area.

For Problems 12–19, use a calculator or computer to evaluate the integral.

**12.** $\displaystyle \int_1^2 2^x\, dx$

**13.** $\displaystyle \int_1^4 (x^2 + x)\, dx$

**14.** $\displaystyle \int_1^5 (3x + 1)^2\, dx$

**15.** $\displaystyle \int_0^1 \sqrt{1 + t^2}\, dt$

**16.** $\displaystyle \int_1^2 (1.03)^t\, dt$

**17.** $\displaystyle \int_2^3 \frac{-1}{(r+1)^2}\, dr$

**18.** $\displaystyle \int_1^3 \frac{z^2 + 1}{z}\, dz$

**19.** $\displaystyle \int_{-3}^3 e^{-t^2}\, dt$

In Problems 20–23, find the given area.

**20.** Between $y = x^2$ and $y = x^3$ for $0 \le x \le 1$.

**21.** Between $y = x^{1/2}$ and $y = x^{1/3}$ for $0 \le x \le 1$.

**22.** Between $y = 3x$ and $y = x^2$.

**23.** Between $y = x$ and $y = \sqrt{x}$.

**24.** Coal gas is produced at a gasworks. Pollutants in the gas are removed by scrubbers, which become less and less efficient as time goes on. The following measurements, made at the start of each month, show the rate at which pollutants are escaping (in tons/month) in the gas:

| Time (months) | 0 | 1 | 2 | 3 | 4 | 5 | 6 |
|---|---|---|---|---|---|---|---|
| Rate pollutants escape | 5 | 7 | 8 | 10 | 13 | 16 | 20 |

  **(a)** Make an overestimate and an underestimate of the total quantity of pollutants that escape during the first month.
  **(b)** Make an overestimate and an underestimate of the total quantity of pollutants that escape during the six months.

**25.** A student is speeding down Route 11 in his fancy red Porsche when his radar system warns him of an obstacle 400 feet ahead. He immediately applies the brakes, starts to slow down, and spots a skunk in the road directly ahead of him. The "black box" in the Porsche records the car's speed every two seconds, producing the following table. The speed decreases throughout the 10 seconds it takes to stop, although not necessarily at a constant rate.

| Time since brakes applied (sec) | 0 | 2 | 4 | 6 | 8 | 10 |
|---|---|---|---|---|---|---|
| Speed (ft/sec) | 100 | 80 | 50 | 25 | 10 | 0 |

  **(a)** What is your best estimate of the total distance the student's car traveled before coming to rest?

(b) Which one of the following statements can you justify from the information given?

  (i) The car stopped before getting to the skunk.

  (ii) The "black box" data is inconclusive. The skunk may or may not have been hit.

  (iii) The skunk was hit by the car.

**26.** The velocity of a particle moving along the $x$-axis is given by $f(t) = 6 - 2t$ cm/sec. Use a graph of $f(t)$ to find the exact change in position of the particle from time $t = 0$ to $t = 4$ seconds.

**27.** A baseball thrown directly upward at 96 ft/sec has velocity $v(t) = 96 - 32t$ ft/sec at time $t$ seconds.

  (a) Graph the velocity from $t = 0$ to $t = 6$.
  (b) When does the baseball reach the peak of its flight? How high does it go?
  (c) How high is the baseball at time $t = 5$?

**28.** A news broadcast in early 1993 said the typical American's annual income is changing at a rate of $r(t) = 40(1.002)^t$ dollars per month, where $t$ is in months from January 1, 1993. How much did the typical American's income change during 1993?

**29.** Two species of plants have the same populations at time $t = 0$ and the growth rates shown in Figure 5.82.

  (a) Which species has a larger population at the end of 5 years? At the end of 10 years?
  (b) Which species do you think has the larger population after 20 years? Explain.

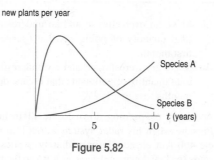

new plants per year

Species A

Species B

$t$ (years)

5      10

**Figure 5.82**

**30.** Figure 5.83 represents your velocity, $v$, on a bicycle trip along a straight road which starts 10 miles from home. Write a paragraph describing your trip: Do you start out going toward or away from home? How long do you continue in that direction and how far are you from home when you turn around? How many times do you change direction? Do you ever get home? Where are you at the end of the four-hour bike ride?

$v$ (mph)

Toward home

Away from home

**Figure 5.83**

**31.** Figure 5.84 shows the weight growth rate of a human fetus.

  (a) What property of a graph of weight as a function of age corresponds to the fact that the function in Figure 5.84 is increasing?
  (b) Estimate the weight of a baby born in week 40.

weight growth rate (kg/week)

age of fetus (wks after last menstruation)

**Figure 5.84**: Rate of increase of fetal weight

**32.** A bicyclist is pedaling along a straight road for one hour with a velocity $v$ shown in Figure 5.85. She starts out five kilometers from the lake and positive velocities take her toward the lake. [Note: The vertical lines on the graph are at 10 minute (1/6 hour) intervals.]

  (a) Does the cyclist ever turn around? If so, at what time(s)?
  (b) When is she going the fastest? How fast is she going then? Toward the lake or away?
  (c) When is she closest to the lake? Approximately how close to the lake does she get?
  (d) When is she farthest from the lake? Approximately how far from the lake is she then?

$v$ (km/hr)

$t$ (minutes)

**Figure 5.85**

In Problems 33–36, decide whether $\int_{-3}^{3} f(x)\,dx$ is positive, negative, or approximately zero.

**33.**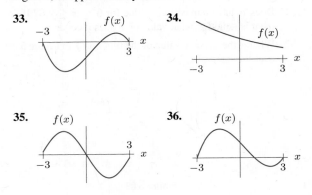

**34.**

**35.**

**36.**

**42.** A car moves along a straight line with velocity, in feet/second, given by

$$v = 6 - 2t \quad \text{for } t \geq 0.$$

(a) With forward being the direction of positive velocity, when is the car moving forward? Backward? Stopped?

(b) Does the car ever return to its starting point? If so, when?

(c) With position measured from its starting point, when is the car farthest forward? Farthest backward?

**43.** The marginal cost function of a product, in dollars per unit, is $C'(q) = q^2 - 50q + 700$. If fixed costs are $500, find the total cost to produce 50 items.

**44.** A warehouse charges its customers $5 per day for every 10 cubic feet of space used for storage. Figure 5.87 records the storage used by one company over a month. How much will the company have to pay?

**37.** Given $\int_{-2}^{0} f(x)\,dx = 4$ and Figure 5.86, estimate:

(a) $\int_{0}^{2} f(x)\,dx$    (b) $\int_{-2}^{2} f(x)\,dx$

(c) The total shaded area.

**Figure 5.86**

**Figure 5.87**

**38.** Use a graph of $y = 2^{-x^2}$ to explain why $\int_{-1}^{1} 2^{-x^2}\,dx$ must be between 0 and 2.

**39.** Without computation, show that $2 \leq \int_{0}^{2} \sqrt{1 + x^3}\,dx \leq 6$.

**40.** The velocity of a car (in miles per hour) is given by $v(t) = 40t - 10t^2$, where $t$ is in hours.

(a) Write a definite integral for the distance the car travels during the first three hours.

(b) Sketch a graph of velocity against time and represent the distance traveled during the first three hours as an area on your graph.

(c) Use a computer or calculator to find this distance.

**41.** The world's oil is being consumed at a continuously increasing rate, $f(t)$ (in billions of barrels per year), where $t$ is in years since the start of 1995.

(a) Write a definite integral which represents the total quantity of oil used between the start of 1995 and the start of 2010.

(b) Suppose $r = 32(1.05)^t$. Using a left-hand sum with five subdivisions, find an approximate value for the total quantity of oil used between the start of 1995 and the start of 2010.

(c) Interpret each of the five terms in the sum from part (b) in terms of oil consumption.

**45.** One of the earliest pollution problems brought to the attention of the Environmental Protection Agency (EPA) was the case of Sioux Lake in eastern South Dakota. For years a small paper plant located nearby had been discharging waste containing carbon tetrachloride (CCl₄) into the waters of the lake. At the time the EPA learned of the situation, the chemical was entering at a rate of 16 cubic yards/year.

The agency immediately ordered the installation of filters designed to slow (and eventually stop) the flow of CCl₄ from the mill. Implementation of this program took exactly three years, during which the flow of pollutant was steady at 16 cubic yards/year. Once the filters were installed, the flow declined. From the time the filters were installed until the time the flow stopped, the rate of flow was well approximated by

$$\text{Rate (in cubic yards/year)} = t^2 - 14t + 49,$$

where $t$ is time measured in years since the EPA learned of the situation (thus, $t \geq 3$).

(a) Draw a graph showing the rate of CCl₄ flow into the lake as a function of time, beginning at the time the EPA first learned of the situation.

**(b)** How many years elapsed between the time the EPA learned of the situation and the time the pollution flow stopped entirely?

**(c)** How much CCl₄ entered the waters during the time shown in the graph in part (a)?

**46. (a)** Graph $x^3 - 5x^2 + 4x$, marking $x = 1, 2, 3, 4, 5$.

**(b)** Use your graph and the area interpretation of the definite integral to decide which of the five numbers

$$I_n = \int_0^n (x^3 - 5x^2 + 4x)\,dx \quad \text{for } n = 1, 2, 3, 4, 5$$

is largest. Which is smallest? How many of the numbers are positive? (Don't calculate the integrals.)

**47.** A mouse moves back and forth in a straight tunnel, attracted to bits of cheddar cheese alternately introduced to and removed from the ends (right and left) of the tunnel. The graph of the mouse's velocity, $v$, is given in Figure 5.88, with positive velocity corresponding to motion toward the right end. Assuming that the mouse starts ($t = 0$) at the center of the tunnel, use the graph to estimate the time(s) at which:

**(a)** The mouse changes direction.

**(b)** The mouse is moving most rapidly to the right; to the left.

**(c)** The mouse is farthest to the right of center; farthest to the left.

**(d)** The mouse's speed (i.e., the magnitude of its velocity) is decreasing.

**(e)** The mouse is at the center of the tunnel.

**Figure 5.88**

**48.** Pollution is being dumped into a lake at a rate which is increasing at a constant rate from 10 kg/year to 50 kg/year until a total of 270 kg has been dumped. Sketch a graph of the rate at which pollution is being dumped in the lake against time. How long does it take until 270 kg has been dumped?

For Problems 49–51, suppose $F(0) = 0$ and $F'(x) = 4 - x^2$.

**49.** Calculate $F(b)$ for $b = 0,\ 0.5,\ 1,\ 1.5,\ 2,\ 2.5$.

**50.** Using a graph of $F'$, decide where $F$ is increasing and where $F$ is decreasing for $0 \leq x \leq 2.5$.

**51.** Does $F$ have a maximum value for $0 \leq x \leq 2.5$? If so, what is it, and at what value of $x$ does it occur?

**52.** What is the average value of the function $f$ in Figure 5.89 over the interval $1 \leq x \leq 6$?

**Figure 5.89**

**53.** Find the average value of $g(t) = e^t$ over the interval $0 \leq t \leq 10$.

**54.** Find the average value of the function $f(x) = 5 + 4x - x^2$ between $x = 0$ and $x = 3$.

**55.** A service station orders 100 cases of motor oil every 6 months. The number of cases of oil remaining $t$ months after the order arrives is modeled by

$$f(t) = 100e^{-0.5t}.$$

**(a)** How many cases are there at the start of the six-month period? How many cases are left at the end of the six-month period?

**(b)** Find the average number of cases in inventory over the six-month period.

**56.** The quantity of a radioactive substance at time $t$ is

$$Q(t) = 4(0.96)^t \text{ grams}.$$

**(a)** Find $Q(10)$ and $Q(20)$.

**(b)** Find the average of $Q(10)$ and $Q(20)$.

**(c)** Find the average value of $Q(t)$ over the interval $10 \leq t \leq 20$.

**(d)** Use the graph of $Q(t)$ to explain the relative sizes of your answers in parts (b) and (c).

In Problems 57–58, estimate the average value of the function $f(x)$ on the interval from $x = a$ to $x = b$.

**59.** The function $f$ in Figure 5.90 is symmetric about the $y$-axis. Consider the average value of $f$ over the following intervals:

I.  $0 \leq x \leq 1$          II.  $0 \leq x \leq 2$

III.  $0 \leq x \leq 5$          IV.  $-2 \leq x \leq 2$

  **(a)** For which interval is the average value of $f$ least?
  **(b)** For which interval is the average value of $f$ greatest?
  **(c)** For which pair of intervals are the average values equal?

**60.** For the function $f$ in Figure 5.90, write an expression involving one or more definite integrals of $f$ that denote:

  **(a)** The average value of $f$ for $0 \leq x \leq 5$.
  **(b)** The average value of $|f|$ for $0 \leq x \leq 5$.

**Figure 5.90**

# STRENGTHEN YOUR UNDERSTANDING

In Problems 1–60, indicate whether the statement is true or false.

**1.** If the velocity is positive, then the total distance traveled is the area under the velocity curve.

**2.** If velocity is constant and positive, then distance traveled during a time interval is the velocity multiplied by the length of the interval.

**3.** If velocity is positive and increasing, using the velocity at the beginning of each subinterval gives an overestimate of the distance traveled.

**4.** A car traveling with increasing velocity (in feet per second) given in the following table travels more than 40 feet between $t = 4$ and $t = 6$ seconds.

| $t$ | 4 | 6 |
|---|---|---|
| $v(t)$ | 10 | 20 |

**5.** A car traveling with increasing velocity (in feet per second) given in the following table travels less than 40 feet between $t = 4$ and $t = 6$ seconds.

**6.** If water flows out of a tank at an increasing rate starting at 20 gallons per minute at the start of a 10-minute period and ending at 50 gallons per minute at the end of the 10-minute period, then at least 200 gallons have flowed out of the tank.

**7.** If water flows out of a tank at an increasing rate starting at 20 gallons per minute at the start of a 10-minute period and ending at 50 gallons per minute at the end of the 10-minute period, then at least 500 gallons have flowed out of the tank.

**8.** At a construction site, money is spent at a continuous, decreasing rate of $r(t)$ dollars per day, where $t$ is in days. If the rates at two particular instants, $t = 3$ and $t = 5$, are given in the table, then at least \$3000 is spent between $t = 3$ and $t = 5$.

| $t$ | 3 | 5 |
|---|---|---|
| $r(t)$ | 1000 | 800 |

**9.** An object traveling with velocity given by $v(t) = 3t$ feet per second travels exactly 150 feet when $0 \leq t \leq 10$ seconds.

**10.** The units of total change and rate of change of a quantity are the same.

**11.** If $f(t)$ is increasing, then the left-hand sum gives an overestimate of $\int_a^b f(t)\, dt$.

**12.** If $f(t)$ is concave up, then the left-hand sum gives an overestimate of $\int_a^b f(t)\, dt$.

**13.** A left-hand sum estimate for $\int_3^5 f(t)\, dt$ is 3000, if $f(t)$ is shown in the following table.

| $t$ | 3 | 5 |
|---|---|---|
| $f(t)$ | 1000 | 800 |

**14.** A right-hand sum estimate for $\int_3^5 f(t)\, dt$ is 1600, if $f(t)$ is shown in the following table.

| $t$ | 3 | 5 |
|---|---|---|
| $f(t)$ | 1000 | 800 |

**15.** If the number of terms in a Riemann sum increases, the quantity $\Delta t$ decreases.

**16.** A 4-term Riemann sum on the interval $4 \leq t \leq 6$ has $\Delta t = 2$.

**17.** The right-hand sum for $\int_a^b f(t)\, dt$ is the total area of rectangles that are above the graph of $f(t)$.

**18.** If $f(t) \geq 0$ then $\int_a^b f(t)\, dt$ is the area between the $t$-axis and the graph of $f(t)$, for $a \leq t \leq b$.

**19.** If $f(t) = t^2$ then the left-hand sum gives an overestimate for $\int_{-2}^{-1} f(t)\, dt$.

**20.** The right-hand sum for $\int_5^{25} t^2\, dt$ using $n = 5$ rectangles has $\Delta t = 5$.

**21.** The integral $\int_0^2 f(x)\, dx$ gives the area between the $x$-axis and the graph of $f(x)$ between $x = 0$ and $x = 2$.

**22.** If $\int_0^2 f(x)\, dx = 0$ then $f(x) = 0$ for all $0 \leq x \leq 2$.

**23.** If $\int_0^2 f(x)\, dx > 0$ then $f(x) > 0$ for all $0 \leq x \leq 2$.

**24.** If $f(x) > 0$ for all $0 \leq x \leq 2$ then $\int_0^2 f(x)\, dx > 0$.

**25.** The integral $\int_{-1}^1 (x^2 - 1)\, dx$ is the negative of the area between the graph of $f(x) = x^2 - 1$ and the $x$-axis for $-1 \leq x \leq 1$.

**26.** If $f(x)$ is both positive and negative when $0 \leq x \leq 2$ then $\int_0^2 f(x)\, dx$ is the sum of the areas between the graph and the $x$-axis for $0 \leq x \leq 2$.

**27.** The integral $\int_0^3 (1 - x)\, dx$ is the area between the graph of $f(x) = 1 - x$ and the $x$-axis between $x = 0$ and $x = 3$.

**28.** The integral $\int_{-1}^2 e^x\, dx$ is the area between the graph of $f(x) = e^x$ and the $x$-axis between $x = -1$ and $x = 2$.

**29.** If $f(x) \geq g(x)$ for all $a \leq x \leq b$ then $\int_a^b f(x) - g(x)\, dx$ gives the area between the graphs of $f(x)$ and $g(x)$ for $a \leq x \leq b$.

**30.** If the graph of $f(x)$ has more area below the $x$-axis than above the $x$-axis when $1 \leq x \leq 10$ then $\int_1^{10} f(x)\, dx$ is negative.

**31.** If flow rate $r(t)$ has units gallons per hour, and $t$ has units in hours, then $\int_0^{100} r(t)\, dt$ has units of gallons.

**32.** If expense rate $s(t)$ has units dollars per day, and $t$ has units in days, then $\int_{20}^{35} s(t)\, dt$ has units of days.

**33.** If acceleration $a(t)$ has units feet/(second)$^2$, and $t$ has units in seconds, then $\int_{2.1}^{7.2} a(t)\, dt$ has units of feet/second.

**34.** If $w(t)$ is the number of workers on a building construction site as a function of $t$, the number of days since the start of construction, then $\int_0^{60} w(t)\, dt$ has units of workers per day.

**35.** If $C(t)$ is the rate, in dollars per day, for electricity to cool and heat a home on day $t$, where $t$ is measured in days since January 1, then $\int_0^{365} C(t)\, dt$ has units of dollars.

**36.** If electricity costs $f(t)$ dollars per day, and $t$ is measured in days, then $\int_0^{30} f(t)\, dt$ gives the total cost of electricity, in dollars, for the 30-day period from $t = 0$ to $t = 30$.

**37.** If $f(t)$ gives the rate of change of water in a reservoir, in gallons per day, and $t$ is measured in days, then $\int_0^{30} f(t)\, dt$ gives the total volume of water, in gallons, in the reservoir on day $t = 30$.

**38.** If $f(t)$ gives the rate of change of water in a reservoir, in gallons per day, and $t$ is measured in days, then $\int_0^{30} f(t)\, dt$ gives the total change in the volume of water, in gallons, in the reservoir during the period $t = 0$ to $t = 30$.

**39.** Bioavailability is the integral of blood concentration as a function of time.

**40.** If the peak concentration of drug $A$ is greater than the peak concentration of drug $B$ then the bioavailability of drug $A$ is greater than the bioavailability of drug $B$.

**41.** The Fundamental Theorem of Calculus says if $F(t)$ is continuous, then $\int_a^b F(t)\, dt = F(b) - F(a)$.

**42.** The Fundamental Theorem of Calculus says if $g'(t)$ is continuous, then $\int_a^b g'(t)\, dt = g(b) - g(a)$.

**43.** The Fundamental Theorem of Calculus says if $F'(t)$ is continuous, then $\int_a^b F'(t)\, dt = F'(b) - F'(a)$.

**44.** If $C(q)$ is the cost to produce $q$ units, then $\int_{100}^{200} C'(q)\, dq$ is the amount it costs to increase production from 100 to 200 units.

**45.** If $C(q)$ is the cost to produce $q$ units, then $\int_0^{1000} C'(q)\, dq$ is the total amount it costs to produce 1000 units.

**46.** If the marginal cost function of a product is $C'(q) = 0.03q + 0.1$ dollars, and the fixed costs are \$1500, then the total cost to produce 1000 items is \$15,100.

**47.** The integral of the marginal cost $C'(q)$ function can be used to find the fixed costs.

**48.** If $\int_0^5 F'(t)\, dt = 0$, then $F$ is constant on the interval between $t = 0$ and $t = 5$.

**49.** If $\int_0^5 F'(t)\, dt < 0$, then $F(0) > F(5)$.

**50.** If $F'(t)$ is constant, then $\int_0^5 F'(t)\, dt = 0$.

**51.** The average value of $f(x)$ on the interval $0 \leq x \leq 10$ is $\int_0^{10} f(x)\, dx$.

**52.** If $f(0) = 0$ and $f(10) = 50$, then the average value of $f$ on the interval $0 \leq x \leq 10$ is between 0 and 50.

**53.** If $f$ is a continuous increasing function and $f(0) = 0$ and $f(10) = 50$, then the average value of $f$ on the interval $0 \leq x \leq 10$ is between 0 and 50.

**54.** The units of the average value of $f$ are the same as the units of $f$.

**55.** The average value of $f$ over the interval $0 \le x \le 20$ is twice the average value of $f$ over the interval $0 \le x \le 10$.

**56.** The average value of $2f(x)$ over the interval $0 \le x \le 10$ is twice the average value of $f(x)$ over the interval $0 \le x \le 10$.

**57.** If the average value of $f$ over the interval $0 \le x \le 10$ is $0$, then $f(x) = 0$ for all $0 \le x \le 10$.

**58.** If $f(x) > g(x) \ge 0$, then the average value of $f(x)$ for $0 \le x \le 10$ is greater than the average value of $g(x)$ for $0 \le x \le 10$.

**59.** The average value of $f$ on the interval $5 \le x \le 7$ is one half of $\int_5^7 f(x)\,dx$.

**60.** The average value of the cost function $C(q)$ for $0 \le q \le 10$ is the same as the average cost for 10 items.

# PROJECTS FOR CHAPTER FIVE

1. **Carbon Dioxide in Pond Water** Biological activity in a pond is reflected in the rate at which carbon dioxide, $CO_2$, is added to or withdrawn from the water. Plants take $CO_2$ out of the water during the day for photosynthesis and put $CO_2$ into the water at night. Animals put $CO_2$ into the water all the time as they breathe. Biologists are interested in how the net rate at which $CO_2$ enters a pond varies during the day. Figure 5.91 shows this rate as a function of time of day.[13] The rate is measured in millimoles (mmol) of $CO_2$ per liter of water per hour; time is measured in hours past dawn. At dawn, there were 2.600 mmol of $CO_2$ per liter of water.

   **(a)** What can be concluded from the fact that the rate is negative during the day and positive at night?

   **(b)** Some scientists have suggested that plants respire (breathe) at a constant rate at night, and that they photosynthesize at a constant rate during the day. Does Figure 5.91 support this view?

   **(c)** When was the $CO_2$ content of the water at its lowest? How low did it go?

   **(d)** How much $CO_2$ was released into the water during the 12 hours of darkness? Compare this quantity with the amount of $CO_2$ withdrawn from the water during the 12 hours of daylight. How can you tell by looking at the graph whether the $CO_2$ in the pond is in equilibrium?

   **(e)** Estimate the $CO_2$ content of the water at three-hour intervals throughout the day. Use your estimates to plot a graph of $CO_2$ content throughout the day.

Figure 5.91: Rate at which $CO_2$ is entering the pond

2. **Flooding in the Grand Canyon**

   The Glen Canyon Dam at the top of the Grand Canyon prevents natural flooding. In 1996, scientists decided an artificial flood was necessary to restore the environmental balance. Water was released through the dam at a controlled rate[14] shown in Figure 5.92. The figure also shows the rate of flow of the last natural flood in 1957.

---

[13]Data from R. J. Beyers, *The Pattern of Photosynthesis and Respiration in Laboratory Microsystems* (Mem. 1st Ital. Idrobiol., 1965).

[14]Adapted from M. Collier, R. Webb, E. Andrews, "Experimental Flooding in Grand Canyon," *Scientific American* (January 1997).

**(a)** At what rate was water passing through the dam in 1996 before the artificial flood?

**(b)** At what rate was water passing down the river in the pre-flood season in 1957?

**(c)** Estimate the maximum rates of discharge for the 1996 and 1957 floods.

**(d)** Approximately how long did the 1996 flood last? How long did the 1957 flood last?

**(e)** Estimate how much additional water passed down the river in 1996 as a result of the artificial flood.

**(f)** Estimate how much additional water passed down the river in 1957 as a result of the flood.

Figure 5.92

### 3. Medical Case Study: Flux of Fluid from a Capillary[15]

The heart pumps blood throughout the body, the arteries are the blood vessels carrying blood away from the heart, and the veins return blood to the heart. Close to the heart, arteries are very large. As they progress toward tissues (such as the brain), the arteries branch repeatedly, getting smaller as they do. The smallest blood vessels are capillaries—microscopic, living tubes that link the smallest arteries to the smallest veins. The capillary is where nutrients and fluids move out of the blood into the adjacent tissues and waste products from the tissues move into the blood. The key to this process is the capillary wall, which is only one cell thick, allowing the unfettered passage of small molecules, such as water, ions, oxygen, glucose, and amino acids, while preventing the passage of large components of the blood (such as large proteins and blood cells).

Precise measurements demonstrate that the flux (rate of flow) of fluid through the capillary wall is not constant over the length of the capillary. Fluids in and around the capillary are subjected to two forces. The *hydrostatic pressure*, resulting from the heart's pumping, pushes fluid out of the capillary into the surrounding tissue. The *oncotic pressure* drives absorption in the other direction. At the start of a capillary, where the capillary branches off the small artery, the hydrostatic pressure is high while the oncotic pressure is low. Along the length of the capillary, the hydrostatic pressure decreases while the oncotic pressure is approximately constant. See Figure 5.93.

For most capillaries there is a net positive value for flow: more fluid flows from the capillaries into the surrounding tissue than the other way around. This presents a major problem for maintaining fluid balance in the body. How is the fluid left in the tissues to get back into circulation? If it cannot, the tissues progressively swell (a condition called edema). Evolution's solution is to provide humans and other mammals with a second set of vessels, the lymphatics, that absorb extra tissue fluid and provide one-way routes back to the bloodstream.

---

[15]From David E. Sloane, M.D.

Along a cylindrical capillary of length $L = 0.1$ cm and radius $r = 0.0004$ cm, the hydrostatic pressure, $p_h$, varies from 35 mm Hg at the artery end to 15 mm Hg at the vein end. (mm Hg, millimeters of mercury, is a unit of pressure.) The oncotic pressure, $p_o$, is approximately 23 mm Hg throughout the length of the capillary.

**(a)** Find a formula for $p_h$ as a function of $x$, the distance in centimeters from the artery end of the capillary, assuming that $p_h$ is a linear function of $x$.

**(b)** Find a formula for $p$, the net outward pressure, as a function of $x$.

**(c)** Write and evaluate an integral for the average outward net pressure in the capillary.

**(d)** The rate of movement, $j$, of fluid volume per capillary wall area across the capillary wall is proportional to the net pressure. We have $j = k \cdot p$ where $k$, the hydraulic conductivity, has value

$$k = 10^{-7} \frac{\text{cm}}{\text{sec} \cdot \text{mm Hg}}.$$

Check that $j$ has units of volume per time per area.

**(e)** Estimate the net volume flow rate (volume per unit time) through the wall of the entire capillary using the average pressure.

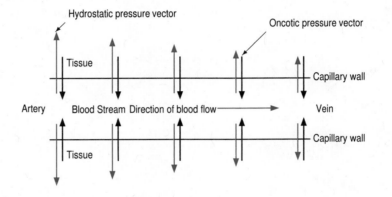

**Figure 5.93**: Vectors representing pressure in and out of capillary

### 4. Medical Case Study: Testing for Kidney Disease[16]

Patients with kidney disease often have protein in their urine. While small amounts of protein are not very worrisome, more than 1 gram of protein excreted in 24 hours warrants active treatment. The most accurate method for measuring urine protein is to have the patient collect all his or her urine in a container for a full 24-hour period. The total mass of protein can then be found by measuring the volume and protein concentration of the urine.

However, this process is not as straightforward as it sounds. Since the urine is collected intermittently throughout the 24-hour period, the first urine voided sits in the container longer than the last urine voided. During this time, the proteins slowly fall to the bottom of the container. Thus, at the end of a 24-hour collection period, there is a higher concentration of protein on the bottom of the container than at the top.

One could try to mix the urine so that the protein concentration is more uniform, but this forms bubbles that trap the protein, leading to an underestimate of the total amount excreted. A better way to determine the total protein is to measure the concentration at the top and at the bottom, and then calculate the average protein concentration.

Suppose a patient voids 2 litres (2000 ml) of urine in 24 hours and collects it in a cylindrical container of diameter 10 cm (note that 1 cm$^3$ = 1 ml). A technician determines that the protein concentration at the top is 0.14 mg/ml, and at the bottom is 0.96 mg/ml. Assume that the concentration of protein varies linearly from the top to the bottom.

---

[16]From David E. Sloane, M.D.

(a) Find a formula for $c$, the protein concentration in mg/ml, as a function of $y$, the distance in centimeters from the base of the cylinder.

(b) Write an integral that gives the average protein concentration in the urine sample.

(c) Estimate the quantity of protein in the sample by multiplying the average protein concentration by the volume of the urine collected. Does this patient require active treatment?

# FOCUS ON THEORY

## THEOREMS ABOUT DEFINITE INTEGRALS

### The Second Fundamental Theorem of Calculus

The Fundamental Theorem of Calculus tells us that if we have a function $F$ whose derivative is a continuous function $f$, then the definite integral of $f$ is given by

$$\int_a^b f(t)\, dt = F(b) - F(a).$$

We now take a different point of view. If $a$ is fixed and the upper limit is $x$, then the value of the integral is a function of $x$. We define a new function $G$ on the interval by

$$G(x) = \int_a^x f(t)\, dt.$$

To visualize $G$, suppose that $f$ is positive and $x > a$. Then $G(x)$ is the area under the graph of $f$ in Figure 5.94. If $f$ is continuous on an interval containing $a$, then it can be shown that $G$ is defined for all $x$ on that interval.

We now consider the derivative of $G$. Using the definition of the derivative,

$$G'(x) = \lim_{h \to 0} \frac{G(x+h) - G(x)}{h}.$$

Suppose $f$ and $h$ are positive. Then we can visualize

$$G(x) = \int_a^x f(t)\, dt$$

and

$$G(x+h) = \int_a^{x+h} f(t)\, dt$$

as areas, which leads to representing

$$G(x+h) - G(x) = \int_x^{x+h} f(t)\, dt$$

as a difference of two areas.

Figure 5.94: Representing $G(x)$ as an area

Figure 5.95: $G(x+h) - G(x)$ is the area of a roughly rectangular region

From Figure 5.95, we see that, if $h$ is small, $G(x + h) - G(x)$ is roughly the area of a rectangle of height $f(x)$ and width $h$ (shaded darker in Figure 5.95), so we have

$$G(x + h) - G(x) \approx f(x)h,$$

hence

$$\frac{G(x + h) - G(x)}{h} \approx f(x).$$

The same result holds when $h$ is negative, suggesting that

$$G'(x) = \lim_{h \to 0} \frac{G(x + h) - G(x)}{h} = f(x).$$

This result is another form of the Fundamental Theorem of Calculus. It is usually stated as follows:

---

### Second Fundamental Theorem of Calculus

If $f$ is a continuous function on an interval, and if $a$ is any number in that interval, then the function $G$ defined on the interval by

$$G(x) = \int_a^x f(t)\, dt$$

has derivative $f$; that is, $G'(x) = f(x)$.

---

## Properties of the Definite Integral

In this chapter, we have used the following properties to break up definite integrals.

---

### Sums and Multiples of Definite Integrals

If $a$, $b$, and $c$ are any numbers and $f$ and $g$ are continuous functions, then

1. $\displaystyle \int_a^c f(x)\, dx + \int_c^b f(x)\, dx = \int_a^b f(x)\, dx.$

2. $\displaystyle \int_a^b (f(x) \pm g(x))\, dx = \int_a^b f(x)\, dx \pm \int_a^b g(x)\, dx.$

3. $\displaystyle \int_a^b cf(x)\, dx = c \int_a^b f(x)\, dx.$

In words:

1. The integral from $a$ to $c$ plus the integral from $c$ to $b$ is the integral from $a$ to $b$.

2. The integral of the sum (or difference) of two functions is the sum (or difference) of their integrals.

3. The integral of a constant times a function is that constant times the integral of the function.

---

These properties can best be visualized by thinking of the integrals as areas or as the limit of the sum of areas of rectangles.

## Problems on the Second Fundamental Theorem of Calculus

For Problems 1–4, find $G'(x)$.

**1.** $G(x) = \displaystyle\int_a^x t^3 \, dt$

**2.** $G(x) = \displaystyle\int_a^x 3^t \, dt$

**3.** $G(x) = \displaystyle\int_a^x t e^t \, dt$

**4.** $G(x) = \displaystyle\int_a^x \ln y \, dy$

**5.** Let $F(b) = \displaystyle\int_0^b 2^x \, dx$.

 **(a)** What is $F(0)$?

 **(b)** Does the value of $F$ increase or decrease as $b$ increases? (Assume $b \geq 0$.)

 **(c)** Estimate $F(1)$, $F(2)$, and $F(3)$.

**6.** For $x = 0$, 0.5, 1.0, 1.5, and 2.0, make a table of values for $I(x) = \int_0^x \sqrt{t^4 + 1} \, dt$.

**7.** Assume that $F'(t) = \sin t \cos t$ and $F(0) = 1$. Find $F(b)$ for $b = 0$, 0.5, 1, 1.5, 2, 2.5, and 3.

In Problems 8–11, find the integral, given that $\int_a^b f(x) \, dx = 8$, $\int_a^b (f(x))^2 \, dx = 12$, $\int_a^b g(t) \, dt = 2$, and $\int_a^b (g(t))^2 \, dt = 3$.

**8.** $\int_a^b (f(x) + g(x)) \, dx$

**9.** $\int_a^b \left((f(x))^2 - (g(x))^2\right) dx$

**10.** $\int_a^b (f(x))^2 \, dx - \left(\int_a^b f(x) \, dx\right)^2$

**11.** $\int_a^b c f(z) \, dz$

# Chapter Six

# ANTIDERIVATIVES AND APPLICATIONS

## Contents

# 6.1 ANALYZING ANTIDERIVATIVES GRAPHICALLY AND NUMERICALLY

## What is an Antiderivative?

If the derivative of $F(x)$ is $f(x)$, that is, if $F'(x) = f(x)$, then we call $F(x)$ an *antiderivative* of $f(x)$. For example, the derivative of $x^2$ is $2x$, so we say that

$$x^2 \text{ is an antiderivative of } 2x.$$

In this section, we see how values of an antiderivative, $F$, are computed using the Fundamental Theorem of Calculus when the derivative, $F'$, and one value of the function, $F(a)$, are known.

**Example 1**    Suppose $F'(t) = (1.8)^t$ and $F(0) = 2$. Find the value of $F(b)$ for $b = 0, 0.1, 0.2, \ldots, 1.0$.

Solution    We apply the Fundamental Theorem with $F'(t) = (1.8)^t$ and $a = 0$ to get values for $F(b)$:

$$F(b) - F(0) = \int_0^b F'(t)\, dt = \int_0^b (1.8)^t\, dt.$$

Since $F(0) = 2$, we have

$$F(b) = 2 + \int_0^b (1.8)^t\, dt.$$

We use a calculator or computer to estimate the definite integral $\int_0^b (1.8)^t\, dt$ for each value of $b$. For example, when $b = 0.1$, we find that $\int_0^b (1.8)^t\, dt = 0.103$. Thus, $F(0.1) = 2.103$. Similar calculations give the values in Table 6.1.

**Table 6.1**    *Approximate values of F*

| $b$ | 0 | 0.1 | 0.2 | 0.3 | 0.4 | 0.5 | 0.6 | 0.7 | 0.8 | 0.9 | 1.0 |
|-----|---|-----|-----|-----|-----|-----|-----|-----|-----|-----|-----|
| $F(b)$ | 2 | 2.103 | 2.212 | 2.328 | 2.451 | 2.581 | 2.719 | 2.866 | 3.021 | 3.186 | 3.361 |

Notice from the table that values of $F(b)$ increase between $b = 0$ and $b = 1$. This is because the derivative $F'(t) = (1.8)^t$ is positive for $t$ between 0 and 1.

## Graphing an Antiderivative

To graph an antiderivative of $F$ from its derivative $F' = f$ we can calculate values of $F$, as in Example 1, or we can use the graph of $f$ and the following results from Section 2.2, page 99.

> Suppose $F$ is an antiderivative of $f$:
> If $f > 0$ on an interval, then $F$ is *increasing* on that interval.
> If $f < 0$ on an interval, then $F$ is *decreasing* on that interval.
> If $f = 0$ on an interval, then $F$ is *constant* on that interval.

**Example 2**    Figure 6.1 shows the derivative $f'(x)$ of a function $f(x)$ and the values of some areas. If $f(0) = 10$, sketch a graph of the function $f(x)$. Give the coordinates of the local maxima and minima.

Figure 6.1: The graph of a derivative $f'$

Solution    Figure 6.1 shows that the derivative $f'$ is positive between 0 and 2, negative between 2 and 5, and positive between 5 and 6. Therefore, the function $f$ is increasing between 0 and 2, decreasing between 2 and 5, and increasing between 5 and 6. (See Figure 6.2.) There is a local maximum at $x = 2$ and a local minimum at $x = 5$.

Notice that we can sketch the general shape of the graph of $f$ in Figure 6.2 without knowing any of the areas in Figure 6.1. The areas are used to make the graph more precise. We are told that $f(0) = 10$, so we plot the point $(0, 10)$ on the graph of $f$ in Figure 6.3. The Fundamental Theorem and Figure 6.1 show that

$$f(2) - f(0) = \int_0^2 f'(x)\,dx = 14.$$

Therefore, the total change in $f$ between $x = 0$ and $x = 2$ is 14. Since $f(0) = 10$, we have

$$f(2) = 10 + 14 = 24.$$

The point $(2, 24)$ is on the graph of $f$. See Figure 6.3.

Figure 6.1 shows that the area between $x = 2$ and $x = 5$ is 20. Since this area lies entirely below the $x$-axis, the Fundamental Theorem gives

$$f(5) - f(2) = \int_2^5 f'(x)\,dx = -20.$$

The total change in $f$ is $-20$ between $x = 2$ and $x = 5$. Since $f(2) = 24$, we have

$$f(5) = 24 - 20 = 4.$$

Thus, the point $(5, 4)$ lies on the graph of $f$. Finally,

$$f(6) = f(5) + \int_5^6 f'(x)\,dx = 4 + 12 = 16,$$

so the point $(6, 16)$ is on the graph of $f$.

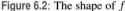

Figure 6.2: The shape of $f$

Figure 6.3: The graph of $f$

## Concavity

If $F$ is an antiderivative of $f$, then $F'' = f'$. Thus, we can determine the concavity of the graph of $F$ from the properties of $f'$ (see Section 2.4, on page 113).

Suppose $F$ is an antiderivative of $f$:
If $f' > 0$ on an interval, then $f$ is increasing and the graph of $F$ is concave up on that interval.
If $f' < 0$ on an interval, then $f$ is decreasing and the graph of $F$ is concave down on that interval.

Thus, inflection points of $F$ occur where $f$ changes from increasing to decreasing or vice versa.

## Problems for Section 6.1

**1.** Suppose $F'(x) = 2x^2 + 5$ and $F(0) = 3$. Find the value of $F(b)$ for $b = 0, 0.1, 0.2, 0.5$, and $1.0$.

**2.** Suppose $G'(t) = (1.12)^t$ and $G(5) = 1$. Find the value of $G(b)$ for $b = 5, 5.1, 5.2, 5.5$, and $6.0$.

**3.** Suppose $f'(t) = (0.82)^t$ and $f(2) = 9$. Find the value of $f(b)$ for $b = 2, 4, 6, 10$, and $20$.

**4.** (a) Using Figure 6.4, estimate $\int_0^7 f(x)dx$.
   (b) If $F$ is an antiderivative of the same function $f$ and $F(0) = 25$, estimate $F(7)$.

Figure 6.4

**5.** Figure 6.5 shows $f$. If $F' = f$ and $F(0) = 0$, find $F(b)$ for $b = 1, 2, 3, 4, 5, 6$.

Figure 6.5

**6.** Figure 6.6 shows the derivative $g'$. If $g(0) = 0$, graph $g$. Give $(x, y)$-coordinates of all local maxima and minima.

Figure 6.6

**7.** The derivative $F'(t)$ is graphed in Figure 6.7. Given that $F(0) = 5$, calculate $F(t)$ for $t = 1, 2, 3, 4, 5$.

Figure 6.7

In Problems 8–13, sketch two functions $F$ such that $F' = f$. In one case let $F(0) = 0$ and in the other, let $F(0) = 1$.

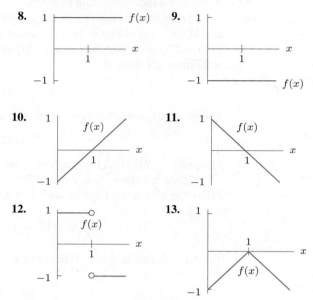

**14.** Figure 6.8 shows the derivative $F'$ of a function $F$. If $F(20) = 150$, estimate the maximum value attained by $F$.

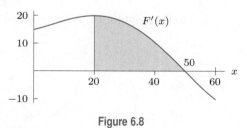

Figure 6.8

**15.** Figure 6.9 shows the rate of change of the concentration of adrenaline, in micrograms per milliliter per minute, in a person's body. Sketch a graph of the concentration of adrenaline, in micrograms per milliliter, in the body as a function of time, in minutes.

Figure 6.9

16. Urologists are physicians who specialize in the health of the bladder. In a common diagnostic test, urologists monitor the emptying of the bladder using a device that produces two graphs. In one of the graphs the flow rate (in milliliters per second) is measured as a function of time (in seconds). In the other graph, the volume emptied from the bladder is measured (in milliliters) as a function of time (in seconds). See Figure 6.10.

(a) Which graph is the flow rate and which is the volume?

(b) Which one of these graphs is an antiderivative of the other?

Figure 6.10

17. Figure 6.11 shows the derivative $F'$ of $F$. Let $F(0) = 0$. Of the four numbers $F(1)$, $F(2)$, $F(3)$, and $F(4)$, which is largest? Which is smallest? How many of these numbers are negative?

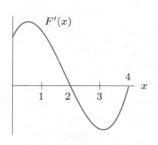

Figure 6.11

Problems 18–19 show the derivative $f'$ of $f$.

(a) Where is $f$ increasing and where is $f$ decreasing? What are the $x$-coordinates of the local maxima and minima of $f$?

(b) Sketch a possible graph for $f$. (You don't need a scale on the vertical axis.)

18.

19.

20. During photosynthesis, plants absorb sunlight and release oxygen. The rate at which a leaf releases oxygen, the rate of photosynthesis, is a function of the age of the leaf. Figure 6.12 shows the rate of photosynthesis for a soybean leaf.[1]

(a) Sketch a graph of the amount of oxygen, $E(t)$, generated by this leaf during the first 20 days of life.

(b) Give the $t$-coordinate of the inflection point in your sketch and interpret what this point tells you about soybean leaves and oxygen.

(c) Give a symbolic expression that represents the total amount of oxygen released by this leaf in its first 10 days of life.

(d) Does the soybean leaf release more oxygen during the first 10 days of its life or during the second 10 days of its life?

Figure 6.12

21. Using Figure 6.13, sketch a graph of an antiderivative $G(t)$ of $g(t)$ satisfying $G(0) = 5$. Label each critical point of $G(t)$ with its coordinates.

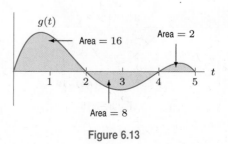

Figure 6.13

[1]Based on: Reich et al., Response of Soybean to Low Concentrations of Ozone: I. Reductions in Leaf and Whole Plant Net Photosynthesis and Leaf Chlorophyll Content, *Journal of Environmental Quality,* 1986, 15(1).

**22.** Use Figure 6.14 and the fact that $F(2) = 3$ to sketch the graph of $F(x)$. Label the values of at least four points.

**Figure 6.14**

**23.** Figure 6.15 shows the derivative $F'$. If $F(0) = 14$, graph $F$. Give $(x, y)$-coordinates of all local maxima and minima.

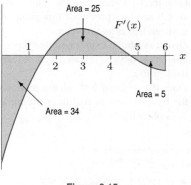

**Figure 6.15**

**24.** Figure 6.16 shows the derivative $F'(t)$. If $F(0) = 3$, find the values of $F(2)$, $F(5)$, $F(6)$. Graph $F(t)$.

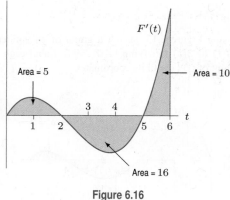

**Figure 6.16**

In Problems 25–26, a graph of $f$ is given. Let $F'(x) = f(x)$.
**(a)** What are the $x$-coordinates of the critical points of $F(x)$?

**(b)** Which critical points are local maxima, which are local minima, and which are neither?

**(c)** Sketch a possible graph of $F(x)$.

**25.**                **26.**

Problems 27–28 concern the graph of $f'$ in Figure 6.17.

**Figure 6.17**: Note: Graph of $f'$, not $f$

**27.** Which is greater, $f(0)$ or $f(1)$?

**28.** List the following in increasing order:
$$\frac{f(4) - f(2)}{2}, \quad f(3) - f(2), \quad f(4) - f(3).$$

For Problems 29–32, show the following quantities on Figure 6.18.

**Figure 6.18**

**29.** A length representing $f(b) - f(a)$.

**30.** A slope representing $\dfrac{f(b) - f(a)}{b - a}$.

**31.** An area representing $F(b) - F(a)$, where $F' = f$.

**32.** A length roughly approximating

$$\frac{F(b) - F(a)}{b - a}, \text{ where } F' = f.$$

## 6.2  ANTIDERIVATIVES AND THE INDEFINITE INTEGRAL

In the previous section we defined an antiderivative of a function $f(x)$ to be a function $F(x)$ whose derivative is $f(x)$. For example, an antiderivative of $2x$ is $F(x) = x^2$. Can you think of another function whose derivative is $2x$? How about $x^2 + 1$? Or $x^2 + 17$? Since, for any constant $C$,

$$\frac{d}{dx}(x^2 + C) = 2x + 0 = 2x,$$

any function of the form $x^2 + C$ is an antiderivative of $2x$. It can be shown that all antiderivatives of $2x$ are of this form, so we say that

$$x^2 + C \text{ is the family of antiderivatives of } 2x.$$

Once we know one antiderivative $F(x)$ for a function $f(x)$ on an interval, then all other antiderivatives of $f(x)$ are of the form $F(x) + C$.

### The Indefinite Integral

We introduce a notation for the family of antiderivatives that looks like a definite integral without the limits. We call $\int f(x)\,dx$ the *indefinite integral* of $f(x)$. If all antiderivatives of $f(x)$ are of the form $F(x) + C$, we write

$$\int f(x)\,dx = F(x) + C.$$

It is important to understand the difference between

$$\int_a^b f(x)\,dx \quad \text{and} \quad \int f(x)\,dx.$$

The first is a number and the second is a family of functions. Because the notation is similar, the word "integration" is frequently used for the process of finding antiderivatives as well as of finding definite integrals. The context usually makes clear which is intended.

---

**Example 1**    (a)  Decide which functions are antiderivatives of $f(x) = 8x^3$

$$F(x) = 24x^2, \qquad G(x) = 8x^4, \qquad H(x) = 2x^4.$$

(b)  Find $\int 8x^3\,dx.$

Solution    (a)  An antiderivative of $8x^3$ is any function whose derivative is $8x^3$. We have:

$$F'(x) = 48x, \qquad G'(x) = 32x^3, \qquad H'(x) = 8x^3.$$

Since $H'(x) = 8x^3$, the function $H(x)$ is an antiderivative of $8x^3$. The two functions $F(x)$ and $G(x)$ are not antiderivatives of $8x^3$.

(b)  Since $H(x) = 2x^4$ is one antiderivative of $f(x)$, all other antiderivatives of $f(x)$ are of the form $H(x) + C$. Thus,

$$\int 8x^3\,dx = 2x^4 + C.$$

---

## Finding Formulas for Antiderivatives

Finding antiderivatives of functions is like taking square roots of numbers: if we pick a number at random, such as 7 or 493, we may have trouble figuring out its square root without a calculator. But if we happen to pick a number such as 25 or 64, which we know is a perfect square, then we can easily guess its square root. Similarly, if we pick a function which we recognize as a derivative, then we can find its antiderivative easily.

For example, noticing that $2x$ is the derivative of $x^2$ tells us that $x^2$ is an antiderivative of $2x$. If we divide by 2, then we guess that

$$\text{An antiderivative of } x \text{ is } \frac{x^2}{2}.$$

To check this statement, take the derivative of $x^2/2$:

$$\frac{d}{dx}\left(\frac{x^2}{2}\right) = \frac{1}{2} \cdot \frac{d}{dx} x^2 = \frac{1}{2} \cdot 2x = x.$$

What about an antiderivative of $x^2$? The derivative of $x^3$ is $3x^2$, so the derivative of $x^3/3$ is $3x^2/3 = x^2$. Thus,

$$\text{An antiderivative of } x^2 \text{ is } \frac{x^3}{3}.$$

Can you see the pattern? It looks like

$$\text{An antiderivative of } x^n \text{ is } \frac{x^{n+1}}{n+1}.$$

(We assume $n \neq -1$, or we would have $x^0/0$, which does not make sense.) It is easy to check this formula by differentiation:

$$\frac{d}{dx}\left(\frac{x^{n+1}}{n+1}\right) = \frac{(n+1)x^n}{n+1} = x^n.$$

Thus, in indefinite integral notation, we see that

$$\int x^n \, dx = \frac{x^{n+1}}{n+1} + C, \quad n \neq -1.$$

Can you think of an antiderivative of the function $f(x) = 5$? We know that the derivative of $5x$ is 5, so $F(x) = 5x$ is an antiderivative of $f(x) = 5$. In general, if $k$ is a constant, the derivative of $kx$ is $k$, so we have the result:

If $k$ is constant,

$$\int k \, dx = kx + C.$$

**Example 2**    Find $\int (3x + x^2) \, dx$.

**Solution**    We know that $x^2/2$ is an antiderivative of $x$ and that $x^3/3$ is an antiderivative of $x^2$, so we expect

$$\int (3x + x^2) \, dx = 3\left(\frac{x^2}{2}\right) + \frac{x^3}{3} + C.$$

Again, we can check by differentiation:

$$\frac{d}{dx}\left(\frac{3}{2}x^2 + \frac{x^3}{3} + C\right) = \frac{3}{2} \cdot 2x + \frac{3x^2}{3} = 3x + x^2.$$

The preceding example illustrates that the sum and constant multiplication rules of differentiation work in reverse:

---

### Properties of Antiderivatives: Sums and Constant Multiples

In indefinite integral notation,

1. $\displaystyle \int [f(x) \pm g(x)]\, dx = \int f(x)\, dx \pm \int g(x)\, dx$

2. $\displaystyle \int cf(x)\, dx = c \int f(x)\, dx.$

In words,

1. An antiderivative of the sum (or difference) of two functions is the sum (or difference) of their antiderivatives.

2. An antiderivative of a constant times a function is the constant times an antiderivative of the function.

---

**Example 3**    Find all antiderivatives of each of the following:    (a) $x^5$    (b) $t^8$    (c) $12x^3$    (d) $q^3 - 6q^2$

**Solution**    (a) $\displaystyle \int x^5\, dx = \frac{x^6}{6} + C.$

(b) $\displaystyle \int t^8\, dt = \frac{t^9}{9} + C.$

(c) $\displaystyle \int 12x^3\, dx = 12\left(\frac{x^4}{4}\right) + C = 3x^4 + C.$

(d) $\displaystyle \int (q^3 - 6q^2)\, dq = \frac{q^4}{4} - 6\left(\frac{q^3}{3}\right) + C = \frac{q^4}{4} - 2q^3 + C.$

To check, differentiate the antiderivative; you should get the original function.

---

What is an antiderivative of $x^n$ when $n = -1$? In other words, what is an antiderivative of $1/x$? Fortunately, we know a function whose derivative is $1/x$, namely, the natural logarithm. Thus, since

$$\frac{d}{dx}(\ln x) = \frac{1}{x},$$

we know that

$$\int \frac{1}{x}\, dx = \ln x + C, \quad \text{for } x > 0.$$

If $x < 0$, then $\ln x$ is not defined, so it can't be an antiderivative of $1/x$. In this case, we can try $\ln(-x)$:

$$\frac{d}{dx}\ln(-x) = (-1)\frac{1}{-x} = \frac{1}{x}$$

so

$$\int \frac{1}{x}\, dx = \ln(-x) + C, \quad \text{for } x < 0.$$

This means $\ln x$ is an antiderivative of $1/x$ if $x > 0$, and $\ln(-x)$ is an antiderivative of $1/x$ if $x < 0$. Since $|x| = x$ when $x > 0$ and $|x| = -x$ when $x < 0$, we can collapse these two formulas into one. On any interval that does not contain 0,

$$\int \frac{1}{x}\, dx = \ln|x| + C.$$

Since the exponential function $e^x$ is its own derivative, it is also one of its own antiderivatives; thus

$$\int e^x \, dx = e^x + C.$$

What about $e^{kx}$? We know that the derivative of $e^{kx}$ is $ke^{kx}$, so, for $k \neq 0$, we have

$$\int e^{kx} \, dx = \frac{1}{k} e^{kx} + C.$$

**Example 4**   Find all antiderivatives of each of the following:   (a)   $8x^3 + \dfrac{1}{x}$    (b)   $12e^{0.2t}$

**Solution**   (a)   $\displaystyle\int \left(8x^3 + \frac{1}{x}\right) dx = 8 \left(\frac{x^4}{4}\right) + \ln |x| + C = 2x^4 + \ln |x| + C.$

(b)   $\displaystyle\int 12e^{0.2t} \, dt = 12 \left(\frac{1}{0.2} e^{0.2t}\right) + C = 60e^{0.2t} + C.$

Differentiate your answers to check them.

### Antiderivatives of Periodic Functions

Antiderivatives of the sine and cosine are easy to guess. Since

$$\frac{d}{dx} \sin x = \cos x \qquad \text{and} \qquad \frac{d}{dx} \cos x = -\sin x,$$

we get

$$\int \cos x \, dx = \sin x + C \qquad \text{and} \qquad \int \sin x \, dx = -\cos x + C.$$

Since the derivative of $\sin(kx)$ is $k \cos(kx)$ and the derivative of $\cos(kx)$ is $-k \sin(kx)$, we have, for $k \neq 0$,

$$\int \cos(kx) \, dx = \frac{1}{k} \sin(kx) + C \qquad \text{and} \qquad \int \sin(kx) \, dx = -\frac{1}{k} \cos(kx) + C.$$

**Example 5**   Find $\displaystyle\int (\sin x + 3\cos(5x)) \, dx.$

**Solution**   We break the antiderivative into two terms:

$$\int (\sin x + 3\cos(5x)) \, dx = \int \sin x \, dx + 3 \int \cos(5x) \, dx = -\cos x + \frac{3}{5} \sin(5x) + C.$$

Check by differentiating:

$$\frac{d}{dx}\left(-\cos x + \frac{3}{5}\sin(5x) + C\right) = \sin x + 3\cos(5x).$$

## Problems for Section 6.2

In Problems 1–6, decide if the function is an antiderivative of $f(x) = 2e^{2x}$.

**1.** $F(x) = e^{2x} + 5$

**2.** $F(x) = e^{2x}$

**3.** $F(x) = 5e^{2x}$

**4.** $F(x) = xe^{2x}$

**5.** $F(x) = 2e^{2x}$

**6.** $F(x) = e^{2x} + \int_0^1 e^{2t}\, dt$

In Problems 7–13, decide whether the expression is a number or a family of functions. (Assume $f(x)$ is a function.)

**7.** $5 + \int 2f(x)\, dx$

**8.** $\int_3^5 2f(x)\, dx$

**9.** $\int 5\, dx$

**10.** $\int f(5)\, dx$

**11.** $\int \frac{1}{x+1}\, dx$

**12.** $\int_1^3 \left(\frac{x}{3} + \frac{3}{x}\right) dx$

**13.** $\int_2^3 f(x)\, dx + \int f(x)\, dx$

In Problems 14–39, find an antiderivative.

**14.** $f(t) = 5t$

**15.** $f(x) = x^2$

**16.** $g(t) = t^2 + t$

**17.** $f(x) = 5$

**18.** $f(x) = x^4$

**19.** $g(t) = t^7 + t^3$

**20.** $f(q) = 5q^2$

**21.** $g(x) = 6x^3 + 4$

**22.** $h(y) = 3y^2 - y^3$

**23.** $k(x) = 10 + 8x^3$

**24.** $p(r) = 2\pi r$

**25.** $f(x) = x + x^5 + x^{-5}$

**26.** $g(z) = \sqrt{z}$

**27.** $p(x) = x^2 - 6x + 17$

**28.** $f(x) = 5x - \sqrt{x}$

**29.** $p(t) = t^3 - \frac{t^2}{2} - t$

**30.** $r(t) = \frac{1}{t^2}$

**31.** $g(z) = \frac{1}{z^3}$

**32.** $f(z) = e^z + 3$

**33.** $f(x) = x^6 - \frac{1}{7x^6}$

**34.** $g(x) = \frac{1}{x} + \frac{1}{x^2} + \frac{1}{x^3}$

**35.** $p(z) = (\sqrt{z})^3$

**36.** $g(t) = e^{-3t}$

**37.** $h(t) = \cos t$

**38.** $g(t) = 5 + \cos t$

**39.** $g(\theta) = \sin\theta - 2\cos\theta$

In Problems 40–43 decide which function is an antiderivative of the other.

**40.** $f(x) = \frac{1}{\sqrt{x}}; g(x) = 2\sqrt{x}$

**41.** $f(x) = -\sin x - \cos x; g(x) = \cos x - \sin x$

**42.** $f(x) = \frac{2}{3}e^{3x}; g(x) = 2e^{3x}$

**43.** $f(x) = 1 - \frac{1}{x^2}; g(x) = \frac{1}{x} + x$

In Problems 44–49, find an antiderivative $F(x)$ with $F'(x) = f(x)$ and $F(0) = 0$. Is there only one possible solution?

**44.** $f(x) = 3$

**45.** $f(x) = 2 + 4x + 5x^2$

**46.** $f(x) = \frac{1}{4}x$

**47.** $f(x) = \sqrt{x}$

**48.** $f(x) = x^2$

**49.** $f(x) = e^x$

In Problems 50–79, find the indefinite integrals.

**50.** $\int (5x + 7)\, dx$

**51.** $\int 9x^2\, dx$

**52.** $\int e^{-0.05t}\, dt$

**53.** $\int \left(1 + \frac{1}{p}\right) dp$

**54.** $\int t^{12}\, dt$

**55.** $\int \left(x^2 + \frac{1}{x^2}\right) dx$

**56.** $\int (t^2 + 5t + 1)\, dt$

**57.** $\int 5e^z\, dz$

**58.** $\int \left(\frac{3}{t} - \frac{2}{t^2}\right) dt$

**59.** $\int (t^3 + 6t^2)\, dt$

**60.** $\int 3\sqrt{w}\, dw$

**61.** $\int (x^2 + 4x - 5)\, dx$

**62.** $\int e^{2t}\, dt$

**63.** $\int \left(x + \frac{1}{\sqrt{x}}\right) dx$

**64.** $\int (x^3 + 5x^2 + 6)\, dx$

**65.** $\int (e^x + 5)\, dx$

**66.** $\int \left(x^2 + \frac{1}{x}\right) dx$

**67.** $\int (x^5 - 12x^3)\, dx$

**68.** $\int e^{3r}\, dr$

**69.** $\int \sin t\, dt$

**70.** $\int 25e^{-0.04q}\, dq$

**71.** $\int 100e^{4x}\, dx$

**72.** $\int \cos\theta\, d\theta$

**73.** $\int \left(\frac{2}{x} + \pi\sin x\right) dx$

**74.** $\int \sin(3x)dx$

**75.** $\int (3\cos x - 7\sin x)\,dx$

**76.** $\int 6\cos(3x)dx$

**77.** $\int (10 + 8\sin(2x))dx$

**78.** $\int (2e^x - 8\cos x)\,dx$

**79.** $\int (12\sin(2x) + 15\cos(5x))dx$

In Problems 80–84 find an antiderivative and use differentiation to check your answer.

**80.** $f(x) = \dfrac{2}{x} + \dfrac{x}{2}$

**81.** $g(x) = x\sqrt{x}$

**82.** $h(x) = \dfrac{x}{\sqrt{x}} + \dfrac{\sqrt{x}}{x}$

**83.** $p(x) = e^{2x} - e^{-2x}$

**84.** $q(x) = 7\sin x - \sin(7x)$

**85.** The marginal revenue function of a monopolistic producer is $MR = 20 - 4q$.

   **(a)** Find the total revenue function.
   **(b)** Find the corresponding demand curve.

**86.** A firm's marginal cost function is $MC = 3q^2 + 4q + 6$. Find the total cost function if the fixed costs are 200.

For Problems 87–90, find an antiderivative $F(x)$ with $F'(x) = f(x)$ and $F(0) = 5$.

**87.** $f(x) = 6x - 5$

**88.** $f(x) = x^2 + 1$

**89.** $f(x) = 8\sin(2x)$

**90.** $f(x) = 6e^{3x}$

**91.** In drilling an oil well, the total cost, $C$, consists of fixed costs (independent of the depth of the well) and marginal costs, which depend on depth; drilling becomes more expensive, per meter, deeper into the earth. Suppose the fixed costs are 1,000,000 riyals (the riyal is the unit of currency of Saudi Arabia), and the marginal costs are

$$C'(x) = 4000 + 10x \text{ riyals/meter,}$$

where $x$ is the depth in meters. Find the total cost of drilling a well $x$ meters deep.

**92.** Over the past fifty years the carbon dioxide level in the atmosphere has increased. Carbon dioxide is believed to drive temperature, so predictions of future carbon dioxide levels are important. If $C(t)$ is carbon dioxide level in parts per million (ppm) and $t$ is time in years since 1950, three possible models are:[2]

   I   $C'(t) = 1.3$
   II  $C'(t) = 0.5 + 0.03t$
   III $C'(t) = 0.5e^{0.02t}$

   **(a)** Given that the carbon dioxide level was 311 ppm in 1950, find $C(t)$ for each model.
   **(b)** Find the carbon dioxide level in 2020 predicted by each model.

## 6.3 USING THE FUNDAMENTAL THEOREM TO FIND DEFINITE INTEGRALS

In the previous section we calculated antiderivatives. In this section we see how antiderivatives are used to calculate definite integrals exactly. This calculation is based on the Fundamental Theorem:

---

**Fundamental Theorem of Calculus**
If $f$ is continuous on the interval $[a, b]$ and $F(x)$ is an antiderivative of $f$, that is if $F'(x) = f(x)$

$$\int_a^b f(x)\,dx = F(b) - F(a).$$

---

So far we have approximated definite integrals using a graph or left- and right-hand sums. The Fundamental Theorem gives us another method of calculating definite integrals. To find $\int_a^b f(x)\,dx$, we first try to find an antiderivative, $F$, of $f(x)$ and then calculate $F(b) - F(a)$. This method of computing definite integrals has an important advantage: it gives an exact answer. However, the method works only when we can find a formula for an antiderivative $F(x)$. We must approximate definite integrals of functions such as $f(x) = e^{-x^2}$ where we can not find a formula for an antiderivative.

---

[2]Based on data from www.esrl.noaa.gov/gmd/ccgg. Accesed March 13, 2013

**Example 1**     Compute $\int_1^3 2x\, dx$ numerically and using the Fundamental Theorem.

**Solution**     Using a calculator, we obtain

$$\int_1^3 2x\, dx = 8.000.$$

The Fundamental Theorem allows us to compute the integral exactly. An antiderivative of $f(x) = 2x$ is $F(x) = x^2$ and we obtain

$$\int_1^3 2x\, dx = F(3) - F(1) = 3^2 - 1^2 = 8.$$

In Example 1 we used the antiderivative $F(x) = x^2$, but $F(x) = x^2 + C$ works just as well for any constant $C$, because the constant cancels out when we subtract $F(a)$ from $F(b)$:

$$\int_1^3 2x\, dx = F(3) - F(1) = (3^2 + C) - (1^2 + C) = 8.$$

It is helpful to introduce a shorthand notation for $F(b) - F(a)$: we write

$$F(x)\Big|_a^b = F(b) - F(a).$$

For example:

$$\int_1^3 2x\, dx = x^2\Big|_1^3 = 3^2 - 1^2 = 8.$$

**Example 2**     Use the Fundamental Theorem to compute the following definite integrals:

(a) $\int_0^2 6x^2\, dx$     (b) $\int_0^2 t^3\, dt$     (c) $\int_1^2 (8x + 5)\, dx$     (d) $\int_0^1 8e^{2t}\, dt$

**Solution**     (a) Since $f(x) = 6x^2$, we take $F(x) = 6(x^3/3) = 2x^3$. So

$$\int_0^2 6x^2\, dx = 6\left(\frac{x^3}{3}\right)\Big|_0^2 = 2x^3\Big|_0^2 = 2 \cdot 2^3 - 2 \cdot 0^3 = 16.$$

(b) Since $f(t) = t^3$, we take $F(t) = t^4/4$, so

$$\int_0^2 t^3\, dt = F(t)\Big|_0^2 = F(2) - F(0) = \frac{2^4}{4} - \frac{0^4}{4} = \frac{16}{4} - 0 = 4.$$

(c) Since $f(x) = 8x + 5$, we take $F(x) = 4x^2 + 5x$, giving

$$\int_1^2 (8x + 5)dx = (4x^2 + 5x)\Big|_1^2 = (4 \cdot 2^2 + 5 \cdot 2) - (4 \cdot 1^2 + 5 \cdot 1)$$
$$= 26 - 9 = 17.$$

(d) Since $f(t) = 8e^{2t}$, we take $F(t) = (8e^{2t})/2 = 4e^{2t}$, so

$$\int_0^1 8e^{2t}dt = 8\left(\frac{1}{2}e^{2t}\right)\Big|_0^1 = 4e^{2t}\Big|_0^1 = 4e^2 - 4e^0 = 25.556.$$

**Example 3**     Write a definite integral to represent the area under the graph of $f(t) = e^{0.5t}$ between $t = 0$ and $t = 4$. Use the Fundamental Theorem to calculate the area.

**Solution**     The function is graphed in Figure 6.19. We have

$$\text{Area} = \int_0^4 e^{0.5t}dt = 2e^{0.5t}\Big|_0^4 = 2e^{0.5(4)} - 2e^{0.5(0)} = 2e^2 - 2 = 12.778.$$

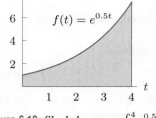

Figure 6.19: Shaded area $= \int_0^4 e^{0.5t}\,dt$

## Improper Integrals

So far, in our discussion of the definite integral $\int_a^b f(x)\,dx$, we have assumed that the interval $a \le x \le b$ is of finite length and the integrand $f$ is continuous. An *improper integral* is a definite integral in which one (or both) of the limits of integration is infinite or the integrand is unbounded. An example of an improper integral is

$$\int_1^\infty \frac{1}{x^2}\,dx.$$

**Example 4**    Interpret and estimate the value of

$$\int_1^\infty \frac{1}{x^2}\,dx.$$

Solution    This integral represents the area under the graph of $\dfrac{1}{x^2}$ from $x = 1$ infinitely far to the right. (See Figure 6.20.)

To estimate the value of the integral, we find the area under the curve between $x = 1$ and $x = b$, where $b$ is large. The larger the value of $b$, the better the estimate. For example for $b = 10, 100, 1000$:

$$\int_1^{10} \frac{1}{x^2}\,dx = 0.9, \qquad \int_1^{100} \frac{1}{x^2}\,dx = 0.99, \qquad \int_1^{1000} \frac{1}{x^2}\,dx = 0.999,$$

These calculations suggest that as the upper limit of integration tends to infinity, the estimates tend to 1.

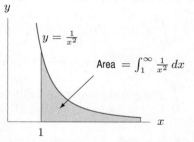

Figure 6.20: Area representation of improper integral

We say that the improper integral $\int_1^\infty \frac{1}{x^2}\,dx$ *converges* to 1. To show that the integral converges to exactly 1 (and not to 1.0001, say), we need to use the Fundamental Theorem of Calculus. (See Problem 29.) It may seem surprising that the region shaded in Figure 6.20 (which has infinite length) can have *finite* area. The area is finite because the values of the function $1/x^2$ shrink to zero very fast as $x \to \infty$. In other examples (where the integrand does not shrink to zero so fast), the area represented by an improper integral may not be finite. In that case, we say the improper integral *diverges*. (See Problem 43.)

## Problems for Section 6.3

Using the Fundamental Theorem, evaluate the definite integrals in Problems 1–20 exactly.

**1.** $\displaystyle\int_0^4 6x \, dx$

**2.** $\displaystyle\int_1^3 5 \, dx$

**3.** $\displaystyle\int_0^3 t^3 \, dt$

**4.** $\displaystyle\int_0^2 (12x^2 + 1) \, dx$

**5.** $\displaystyle\int_0^2 (3t^2 + 4t + 3) \, dt$

**6.** $\displaystyle\int_1^2 \frac{1}{x} \, dx$

**7.** $\displaystyle\int_1^4 \frac{1}{\sqrt{x}} \, dx$

**8.** $\displaystyle\int_0^1 (6q^2 + 4) \, dq$

**9.** $\displaystyle\int_0^5 3x^2 \, dx$

**10.** $\displaystyle\int_0^1 2e^x \, dx$

**11.** $\displaystyle\int_1^2 5t^3 \, dt$

**12.** $\displaystyle\int_1^3 6x^2 \, dx$

**13.** $\displaystyle\int_0^1 (y^2 + y^4) \, dy$

**14.** $\displaystyle\int_1^2 \frac{1}{x^2} \, dx$

**15.** $\displaystyle\int_2^5 (x^3 - \pi x^2) \, dx$

**16.** $\displaystyle\int_0^1 e^{-0.2t} \, dt$

**17.** $\displaystyle\int_{-1}^1 \cos t \, dt$

**18.** $\displaystyle\int_0^{\pi/4} (\sin t + \cos t) \, dt$

**19.** $\displaystyle\int_0^3 e^{0.05t} \, dt$

**20.** $\displaystyle\int_4^9 \sqrt{x} \, dx$

**21.** Find the exact area of the region bounded by the $x$-axis and the graph of $y = x^3 - x$.

**22.** Use the Fundamental Theorem of Calculus to find the average value of $f(x) = e^{0.5x}$ between $x = 0$ and $x = 3$. Show the average value on a graph of $f(x)$.

**23.** Use the Fundamental Theorem to determine the value of $b$ if the area under the graph of $f(x) = x^2$ between $x = 0$ and $x = b$ is equal to 100. Assume $b > 0$.

**24.** Use the Fundamental Theorem to determine the value of $b$ if the area under the graph of $f(x) = 4x$ between $x = 1$ and $x = b$ is equal to 240. Assume $b > 1$.

**25.** If $t$ is in years, and $t = 0$ is January 1, 2005, worldwide energy consumption, $r$, in quadrillion ($10^{15}$) BTUs per year, is modeled by

$$r = 462e^{0.019t}.$$

(a) Write a definite integral for the total energy use between the start of 2005 and the start of 2010.

(b) Use the Fundamental Theorem of Calculus to evaluate the integral. Give units with your answer.

**26.** Oil is leaking out of a ruptured tanker at the rate of $r(t) = 50e^{-0.02t}$ thousand liters per minute.

(a) At what rate, in liters per minute, is oil leaking out at $t = 0$? At $t = 60$?

(b) How many liters leak out during the first hour?

**27.** (a) Between 2000 and 2010, ACME Widgets sold widgets at a continuous rate of $R = R_0 e^{0.125t}$ widgets per year, where $t$ is time in years since January 1, 2000. Suppose they were selling widgets at a rate of 1000 per year on January 1, 2000. How many widgets did they sell between 2000 and 2010? How many did they sell if the rate on January 1, 2000 was 1,000,000 widgets per year?

(b) In the first case (1000 widgets per year on January 1, 2000), how long did it take for half the widgets in the ten-year period to be sold? In the second case (1,000,000 widgets per year on January 1, 2000), when had half the widgets in the ten-year period been sold?

(c) In 2010, ACME advertised that half the widgets it had sold in the previous ten years were still in use. Based on your answer to part (b), how long must a widget last in order to justify this claim?

**28.** Decide if the improper integral $\int_0^\infty e^{-2t} \, dt$ converges, and if so, to what value, by the following method.

(a) Use a computer or calculator to find $\int_0^b e^{-2t} \, dt$ for $b = 3, 5, 7, 10$. What do you observe? Make a guess about the convergence of the improper integral.

(b) Find $\int_0^b e^{-2t} \, dt$ using the Fundamental Theorem. Your answer will contain $b$.

(c) Take a limit as $b \to \infty$. Does your answer confirm your guess?

**29.** In this problem, you will show that the following improper integral converges to 1:

$$\int_1^\infty \frac{1}{x^2} \, dx.$$

(a) Use the Fundamental Theorem to find $\int_1^b 1/x^2 \, dx$. Your answer will contain $b$.

(b) Now take the limit as $b \to \infty$. What does this tell you about the improper integral?

**30.** (a) Graph $f(x) = e^{-x^2}$ and shade the area represented by the improper integral $\int_{-\infty}^\infty e^{-x^2} \, dx$.

(b) Use a calculator or computer to find $\int_{-a}^a e^{-x^2} \, dx$ for $a = 1, a = 2, a = 3, a = 5$.

(c) The improper integral $\int_{-\infty}^\infty e^{-x^2} \, dx$ converges to a finite value. Use your answers from part (b) to estimate that value.

**31.** Graph $y = 1/x^2$ and $y = 1/x^3$ on the same axes. Which do you think is larger: $\int_1^\infty 1/x^2 \, dx$ or $\int_1^\infty 1/x^3 \, dx$? Why?

**32.** At a time $t$ hours after taking a tablet, the rate at which a drug is being eliminated is

$$r(t) = 50 \left( e^{-0.1t} - e^{-0.2t} \right) \text{ mg/hr.}$$

Assuming that all the drug is eventually eliminated, calculate the original dose.

**33.** The rate, $r$, at which people get sick during an epidemic of the flu can be approximated by

$$r = 1000te^{-0.5t},$$

where $r$ is measured in people/day and $t$ is measured in days since the start of the epidemic.

**(a)** Write an improper integral representing the total number of people that get sick.

**(b)** Use a graph of $r$ to represent the improper integral from part (a) as an area.

**34.** An island has a carrying capacity of 1 million rabbits. (That is, no more than 1 million rabbits can be supported by the island.) The rabbit population is two at time $t = 1$ day and grows at a rate of $r(t)$ thousand rabbits/day until the carrying capacity is reached. For each of the following formulas for $r(t)$, is the carrying capacity ever reached? Explain your answer.

**(a)** $r(t) = 1/t^2$  **(b)** $r(t) = t$

**(c)** $r(t) = 1/\sqrt{t}$

# 6.4 APPLICATION: CONSUMER AND PRODUCER SURPLUS

## Supply and Demand Curves

As we saw in Chapter 1, the quantity of a certain item produced and sold can be described by the supply and demand curves of the item. The *supply curve* shows what quantity, $q$, of the item the producers supply at different prices, $p$. The consumers' behavior is reflected in the *demand curve*, which shows what quantity of goods are bought at various prices. See Figure 6.21.

**Figure 6.21:** Supply and demand curves

It is assumed that the market settles at the *equilibrium price* $p^*$ and *equilibrium quantity* $q^*$ where the graphs cross. At equilibrium, a quantity $q^*$ of an item is produced and sold for a price of $p^*$ each.

## Consumer and Producer Surplus

Notice that at equilibrium, a number of consumers have bought the item at a lower price than they would have been willing to pay. (For example, there are some consumers who would have been willing to pay prices up to $p_1$.) Similarly, there are some suppliers who would have been willing to produce the item at a lower price (down to $p_0$, in fact). We define the following terms:

- The **consumer surplus** measures the consumers' gain from trade. It is the total amount gained by consumers by buying the item at the current price rather than at the price they would have been willing to pay.
- The **producer surplus** measures the suppliers' gain from trade. It is the total amount gained by producers by selling at the current price, rather than at the price they would have been willing to accept.

In the absence of price controls, the current price is assumed to be the equilibrium price.

Both consumers and producers are richer for having traded. The consumer and producer surplus measure how much richer they are.

**Figure 6.22**: Calculation of consumer surplus

Suppose that all consumers buy the good at the maximum price they are willing to pay. Subdivide the interval from 0 to $q^*$ into intervals of length $\Delta q$. Figure 6.22 shows that a quantity $\Delta q$ of items are sold at a price of about $p_1$, another $\Delta q$ are sold for a slightly lower price of about $p_2$, the next $\Delta q$ for a price of about $p_3$, and so on. Thus, the consumers' total expenditure is about

$$p_1 \Delta q + p_2 \Delta q + p_3 \Delta q + \cdots = \sum p_i \Delta q.$$

If the demand curve has equation[3] $p = f(q)$, and if all consumers who were willing to pay more than $p^*$ paid as much as they were willing, then as $\Delta q \to 0$, we would have

$$\begin{matrix} \text{Consumer} \\ \text{expenditure} \end{matrix} = \int_0^{q^*} f(q)\, dq = \begin{matrix} \text{Area under demand} \\ \text{curve from 0 to } q^*. \end{matrix}$$

If all goods are sold at the equilibrium price, the consumers' actual expenditure is only $p^* q^*$, which is the area of the rectangle between the $q$-axis and the line $p = p^*$ from $q = 0$ to $q = q^*$. The consumer surplus is the difference between the total consumer expenditure if all consumers pay the maximum they are willing to pay and the actual consumer expenditure if all consumers pay the current price. The consumer surplus is represented by the area in Figure 6.23. Similarly, the producer surplus is represented by the area in Figure 6.24. (See Problems 16 and 17.) Thus:

$$\begin{matrix} \text{Consumer surplus} \\ \text{at price } p^* \end{matrix} = \begin{matrix} \text{Area between demand curve} \\ \text{and horizontal line at } p^*. \end{matrix}$$

$$\begin{matrix} \text{Producer surplus} \\ \text{at price } p^* \end{matrix} = \begin{matrix} \text{Area between supply curve} \\ \text{and horizontal line at } p^*. \end{matrix}$$

[3]Note that here $p$ is written as a function of $q$.

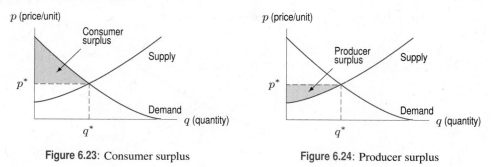

Figure 6.23: Consumer surplus         Figure 6.24: Producer surplus

**Example 1**    The supply and demand curves for a product are given in Figure 6.25.

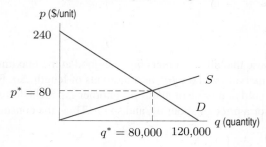

Figure 6.25: Supply and demand curves for a product

(a) What are the equilibrium price and quantity?
(b) At the equilibrium price, calculate and interpret the consumer and producer surplus.

Solution    (a) The equilibrium price is $p^* = \$80$ per unit and the equilibrium quantity is $q^* = 80,000$ units.
(b) The consumer surplus is the area under the demand curve and above the line $p = 80$. (See Figure 6.26.) We have

$$\text{Consumer surplus} = \text{Area of triangle} = \frac{1}{2}\text{Base} \cdot \text{Height} = \frac{1}{2}80,000 \cdot 160 = \$6,400,000.$$

This tells us that consumers gain \$6,400,000 in buying goods at the equilibrium price instead of at the price they would have been willing to pay.

Figure 6.26: Consumer surplus         Figure 6.27: Producer surplus

The producer surplus is the area above the supply curve and below the line $p = 80$. (See Figure 6.27.) We have

$$\text{Producer surplus} = \text{Area of triangle} = \frac{1}{2}\text{Base} \cdot \text{Height} = \frac{1}{2} \cdot 80,000 \cdot 80 = \$3,200,000.$$

So, producers gain \$3,200,000 by supplying goods at the equilibrium price instead of the price at which they would have been willing to provide the goods.

## Wage and Price Controls

In a free market, the price of a product generally moves to the equilibrium price, unless outside forces keep the price artificially high or artificially low. Rent control, for example, keeps prices below market value, whereas cartel pricing or the minimum-wage law raise prices above market value. What happens to consumer and producer surplus at non-equilibrium prices?

**Example 2**    The dairy industry has cartel pricing: the government has set milk prices artificially high. What effect does raising the price to $p^+$ from the equilibrium price have on:

(a)  Consumer surplus?                                    (b)   Producer surplus?

(c)  Total gains from trade (that is, Consumer surplus + Producer surplus)?

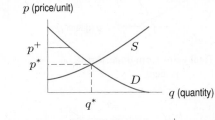

Figure 6.28: What is the effect of the artificially high price, $p^+$, on consumer and producer surplus?
($q^*$ and $p^*$ are equilibrium values)

Solution    (a)  A graph of possible supply and demand curves for the milk industry is given in Figure 6.28. Suppose that the price is fixed at $p^+$, above the equilibrium price. Consumer surplus is the difference between the amount the consumers paid ($p^+$) and the amount they would have been willing to pay (given on the demand curve). This is the area shaded in Figure 6.29. This consumer surplus is less than the consumer surplus at the equilibrium price, shown in Figure 6.30.

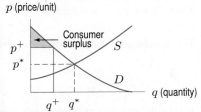

Figure 6.29: Consumer surplus: Artificial price

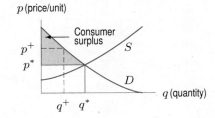

Figure 6.30: Consumer surplus: Equilibrium price

(b)  At a price of $p^+$, the quantity sold, $q^+$, is less than it would have been at the equilibrium price. The producer surplus is represented by the area between $p^+$ and the supply curve at this reduced demand. This area is shaded in Figure 6.31. Compare this producer surplus (at the artificially high price) to the producer surplus in Figure 6.32 (at the equilibrium price). In this case, producer surplus appears to be greater at the artificial price than at the equilibrium price. (However, different supply and demand curves might lead to a different answer.)

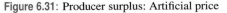

Figure 6.31: Producer surplus: Artificial price

Figure 6.32: Producer surplus: Equilibrium price

(c) The total gains from trade (Consumer surplus + Producer surplus) at the price of $p^+$ is represented by the area shaded in Figure 6.33. The total gains from trade at the equilibrium price of $p^*$ is represented by the area shaded in Figure 6.34. Under artificial price conditions, the total gains from trade decrease. The total financial effect of the artificially high price on all producers and consumers combined is negative.

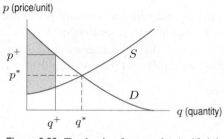

Figure 6.33: Total gains from trade: Artificial price

Figure 6.34: Total gains from trade: Equilibrium price

## Problems for Section 6.4

1. (a) What are the equilibrium price and quantity for the supply and demand curves in Figure 6.35?
   (b) Shade the areas representing the consumer and producer surplus and estimate them.

Figure 6.35

2. The supply and demand curves for a product are given in Figure 6.36. Estimate the equilibrium price and quantity and the consumer and producer surplus. Shade areas representing the consumer surplus and the producer surplus.

Figure 6.36

3. Find the consumer surplus for the demand curve $p = 100 - 3q^2$ when $q^* = 5$ units are sold at the equilibrium price.

4. Given the demand curve $p = 35 - q^2$ and the supply curve $p = 3 + q^2$, find the producer surplus when the market is in equilibrium.

5. Find the consumer surplus for the demand curve $p = 100 - 4q$ when $q^* = 10$ items are sold at the equilibrium price.

6. The demand and supply curves for a product are given as

$$2q - 15p = -120$$

$$3q + 6p = 105$$

   (a) Find the consumer surplus at the equilibrium.
   (b) Find the producer surplus at the equilibrium.

7. The demand curve for a product is given by $q = 100 - 2p$ and the supply curve is given by $q = 3p - 50$.

   (a) Find the consumer surplus at the equilibrium.
   (b) Find the producer surplus at the equilibrium.

8. For a product, the demand curve is $p = 100e^{-0.008q}$ and the supply curve is $p = 4\sqrt{q} + 10$ for $0 \le q \le 500$, where $q$ is quantity and $p$ is price in dollars per unit.

   (a) At a price of $50, what quantity are consumers willing to buy and what quantity are producers willing to supply? Will the market push prices up or down?
   (b) Find the equilibrium price and quantity. Does your answer to part (a) support the observation that market forces tend to push prices closer to the equilibrium price?
   (c) At the equilibrium price, calculate and interpret the consumer and producer surplus.

9. Sketch possible supply and demand curves where the consumer surplus at the equilibrium price is

   **(a)** Greater than the producer surplus.
   **(b)** Less than the producer surplus.

10. Supply and demand curves for a product are in Figure 6.37.

   **(a)** Estimate the equilibrium price and quantity.
   **(b)** Estimate the consumer and producer surplus. Shade them.
   **(c)** What are the total gains from trade for this product?

**Figure 6.37**

11. Supply and demand curves are in Figure 6.37. A price of $40 is artificially imposed.

   **(a)** At the $40 price, estimate the consumer surplus, the producer surplus, and the total gains from trade.
   **(b)** Compare your answers in this problem to your answers in Problem 10. Discuss the effect of price controls on the consumer surplus, producer surplus, and gains from trade in this case.

12. **(a)** Estimate the equilibrium price and quantity for the supply and demand curves in Figure 6.38.
   **(b)** Estimate the consumer and producer surplus.
   **(c)** The price is set artificially low at $p^- = 4$ dollars per unit. Estimate the consumer and producer surplus at this price. Compare your answers to the consumer and producer surplus at the equilibrium price.

**Figure 6.38**

13. Rent controls on apartments are an example of price controls on a commodity. They keep the price artificially low (below the equilibrium price). Sketch a graph of supply and demand curves, and label on it a price $p^-$ below the equilibrium price. What effect does forcing the price down to $p^-$ have on:

   **(a)** The producer surplus?

   **(b)** The consumer surplus?
   **(c)** The total gains from trade (Consumer surplus + Producer surplus)?

14. Supply and demand data are in Tables 6.2 and 6.3.

   **(a)** Which table shows supply and which shows demand?
   **(b)** Estimate the equilibrium price and quantity.
   **(c)** Estimate the consumer and producer surplus.

**Table 6.2**

| $q$ (quantity) | 0 | 100 | 200 | 300 | 400 | 500 | 600 |
|---|---|---|---|---|---|---|---|
| $p$ ($/unit) | 60 | 50 | 41 | 32 | 25 | 20 | 17 |

**Table 6.3**

| $q$ (quantity) | 0 | 100 | 200 | 300 | 400 | 500 | 600 |
|---|---|---|---|---|---|---|---|
| $p$ ($/unit) | 10 | 14 | 18 | 22 | 25 | 28 | 34 |

15. The total gains from trade (consumer surplus + producer surplus) is largest at the equilibrium price. What about the consumer surplus and producer surplus separately?

   **(a)** Suppose a price is artificially high. Can the consumer surplus at the artificial price be larger than the consumer surplus at the equilibrium price? What about the producer surplus? Sketch possible supply and demand curves to illustrate your answers.
   **(b)** Suppose a price is artificially low. Can the consumer surplus at the artificial price be larger than the consumer surplus at the equilibrium price? What about the producer surplus? Sketch possible supply and demand curves to illustrate your answers.

In Problems 16–18, the supply and demand curves have equations $p = S(q)$ and $p = D(q)$, respectively, with equilibrium at $(q^*, p^*)$.

16. Using Riemann sums, explain the economic significance of $\int_0^{q^*} S(q)\, dq$ to the producers.

17. Using Riemann sums, give an interpretation of producer surplus, $\int_0^{q^*} (p^* - S(q))\, dq$ analogous to the interpretation of consumer surplus.

18. Referring to Figures 6.23 and 6.24 on page 308, mark the regions representing the following quantities and explain their economic meaning:

   **(a)** $p^* q^*$               **(b)** $\displaystyle\int_0^{q^*} D(q)\, dq$

   **(c)** $\displaystyle\int_0^{q^*} S(q)\, dq$     **(d)** $\displaystyle\int_0^{q^*} D(q)\, dq - p^* q^*$

   **(e)** $p^* q^* - \displaystyle\int_0^{q^*} S(q)\, dq$  **(f)** $\displaystyle\int_0^{q^*} (D(q) - S(q))\, dq$

# 6.5  APPLICATION: PRESENT AND FUTURE VALUE

In Section 1.7 on page 55, we introduced the present and future value of a single payment. In this section we see how to calculate the present and future value of a continuous stream of payments.

## Income Stream

When we consider payments made to or by an individual, we usually think of *discrete* payments, that is, payments made at specific moments in time. However, we may think of payments made by a company as being *continuous*. The revenues earned by a huge corporation, for example, come in essentially all the time, and therefore they can be represented by a continuous *income stream*. Since the rate at which revenue is earned may vary from time to time, the income stream is described by

$$S(t) \text{ dollars/year.}$$

Notice that $S(t)$ is a *rate* at which payments are made (its units are dollars per year, for example) and that the rate depends on the time, $t$, usually measured in years from the present.

### Present and Future Values of an Income Stream

Just as we can find the present and future values of a single payment, so we can find the present and future values of a stream of payments. As before, the future value represents the total amount of money that you would have if you deposited an income stream into a bank account as you receive it and let it earn interest until that future date. The present value represents the amount of money you would have to deposit today (in an interest-bearing bank account) in order to match what you would get from the income stream by that future date.

When we are working with a continuous income stream, we will assume that interest is compounded continuously. If the interest rate is $r$, the present value, $P$, of a deposit, $B$, made $t$ years in the future is

$$P = Be^{-rt}.$$

Suppose that we want to calculate the present value of the income stream described by a rate of $S(t)$ dollars per year, and that we are interested in the period from now until $M$ years in the future. In order to use what we know about single deposits to calculate the present value of an income stream, we divide the stream into many small deposits, and imagine each deposited at one instant. Dividing the interval $0 \le t \le M$ into subintervals of length $\Delta t$:

Assuming $\Delta t$ is small, the rate, $S(t)$, at which deposits are being made does not vary much within one subinterval. Thus, between $t$ and $t + \Delta t$:

$$\text{Amount paid} \approx \text{Rate of deposits} \times \text{Time}$$
$$\approx (S(t) \text{ dollars/year})(\Delta t \text{ years})$$
$$= S(t)\Delta t \text{ dollars.}$$

The deposit of $S(t)\Delta t$ is made $t$ years in the future. Thus, assuming a continuous interest rate $r$,

$$\begin{array}{c} \text{Present value of money} \\ \text{deposited in interval } t \text{ to } t + \Delta t \end{array} \approx S(t)\Delta t e^{-rt}.$$

Summing over all subintervals gives

$$\text{Total present value} \approx \sum S(t)e^{-rt}\Delta t \text{ dollars.}$$

In the limit as $\Delta t \to 0$, we get the following integral:

$$\text{Present value} = \int_0^M S(t)e^{-rt}dt.$$

As in Section 1.7, the value $M$ years in the future is given by

$$\text{Future value} = \text{Present value} \cdot e^{rM}.$$

**Example 1**   Find the present and future values of a constant income stream of $1000 per year over a period of 20 years, assuming an interest rate of 6% compounded continuously.

**Solution**   Using $S(t) = 1000$ and $r = 0.06$ and a calculator or computer to evaluate the integral, we have

$$\text{Present value} = \int_0^{20} 1000e^{-0.06t}dt = \$11,647.$$

Alternately, using the Fundamental Theorem and the fact that an antiderivative of $1000e^{-0.06t}$ is $\dfrac{1000}{-0.06}e^{-0.06t}$ we have

$$\int_0^{20} 1000e^{-0.06t}dt = \frac{1000}{-0.06}e^{-0.06t}\bigg|_0^{20} = \frac{1000}{-0.06}e^{1.2} - \frac{1000}{-0.06}e^0 = \$11,647.$$

We can get the future value, $B$, from the present value, $P$, using $B = Pe^{rt}$, so

$$\text{Future value} = 11,647e^{0.06(20)} = \$38,669.$$

Notice that since money was deposited at a rate of $1000 a year for 20 years, the total amount deposited was $20,000. The future value is $38,669, so the money has almost doubled because of the interest.

**Example 2**   Suppose you want to have $50,000 in 8 years' time in a bank account earning 2% interest, compounded continuously.

(a)  If you make one lump sum deposit now, how much should you deposit?
(b)  If you deposit money continuously throughout the 8-year period, at what rate should you deposit it?

**Solution**   (a)  If you deposit a lump sum of $P$, then $P$ is the present value of $50,000. So, using $B = Pe^{rt}$ with $B = 50,000$ and $r = 0.02$ and $t = 8$:

$$50000 = Pe^{0.02(8)}$$
$$P = \frac{50000}{e^{0.02(8)}} = 42,607.$$

If you deposit $42,607 into the account now, you will have $50,000 in 8 years' time.

(b)  Suppose you deposit money at a constant rate of $S$ per year. Then

$$\text{Present value of deposits} = \int_0^8 Se^{-0.02t}\,dt$$

Since $S$ is a constant, we can take it out in front of the integral sign and use a calculator to evaluate the integral:

$$\text{Present value} = S\int_0^8 e^{-0.02t}\,dt = S(7.3928).$$

Alternately, using the Fundamental Theorem and the fact that an antiderivative of $e^{-0.02t}$ is $\dfrac{e^{-0.02t}}{-0.02}$ we have

$$S \int_0^8 e^{-0.02t}\,dt = S\frac{e^{-0.02t}}{-0.02}\Big|_0^8 = S\left(\frac{e^{-0.16}}{-0.02} - \frac{e^0}{-0.02}\right) = S(7.3928).$$

But the present value of the continuous deposit must be the same as the present value of the lump sum deposit; that is, $42,607. So

$$42,607 = S(7.3928)$$
$$S = \$5763.$$

To meet your goal of $50,000, you need to deposit money at a continuous rate of $5,763 per year, or about $480 per month.

## Problems for Section 6.5

1. Draw a graph, with time in years on the horizontal axis, of what an income stream might look like for a company that sells sunscreen in the northeast United States.

2. Find the present and future values of an income stream of $12,000 a year for 20 years. The interest rate is 6%, compounded continuously.

3. Find the present and future values of an income stream of $2,000 per year for 15 years, assuming a 5% interest rate compounded continuously.

4. Assuming an interest rate of 3% compounded continuously,

   (a) Find the future value in 10 years of a payment of $10,000 made today.
   (b) Find the future value of an income stream of $1000 per year over 10 years.
   (c) Which is larger, the future value from the lump sum in part (a) or from the income stream in part (b)? Explain why this makes sense financially.

5. Assuming an interest rate of 5% compounded continuously,

   (a) Find the future value in 6 years of a payment of $12,000 made today.
   (b) Find the future value of an income stream of $2000 per year over 6 years.
   (c) Which is larger, the future value from the lump sum in part (a) or from the income stream in part (b)? Explain why this makes sense financially.

6. A person deposits money into an account, which pays 5% interest compounded continuously, at a rate of $1000 per year for 15 years. Calculate:

   (a) The balance in the account at the end of the 15 years.
   (b) The amount of money actually deposited into the account.

   (c) The interest earned during the 15 years.

7. A person deposits money into an account, which pays 6% interest compounded continuously, at a rate of $1000 per year for 30 years. Calculate:

   (a) The balance in the account at the end of the 30 years.
   (b) The amount of money actually deposited into the account.
   (c) The interest earned during the 30 years.

8. (a) Find the present and future value of an income stream of $6000 per year for a period of 10 years if the interest rate, compounded continuously, is 5%.
   (b) How much of the future value is from the income stream? How much is from interest?

9. A small business expects an income stream of $5000 per year for a four-year period.

   (a) Find the present value of the business if the annual interest rate, compounded continuously, is

   (i)   3%                (ii)   10%

   (b) In each case, find the value of the business at the end of the four-year period.

10. The Hershey Company is the largest US producer of chocolate. Between 2005 and 2008, Hershey generated net sales at a rate approximated by $4.8+0.1t$ billion dollars per year, where $t$ is the time in years since January 1, 2005.[4] Assume this rate continues through the year 2010 and that the interest rate is 2% per year compounded continuously.

   (a) Find the value, on January 1, 2005, of Hershey's net sales during the five-year period from from January 1, 2005 to January 1, 2010.
   (b) Find the value, on January 1, 2010, of Hershey's net sales during the same five-year period.

---

[4] 2008 Annual Report, accessed at www.thehersheycompany.com, accessed March 13, 2013.

11. German TV and radio users pay an annual license fee of 200 euros. In 2008, the German poet Friedrich Schiller, who died in 1805, was sent reminders to pay his license fee.[5] (The reminders were sent to an elementary school named after Schiller, despite a teacher pointing out that "the addressee is no longer in a position to listen to the radio or watch television".) Assume the license fee had been charged at a continuous rate of 200 euros per year since 1805 and that the continous interest rate was 3% per year over this period. If Schiller were charged the license fee, with interest, since his death, how much would he have owed by 2008?

12. A recently installed machine earns the company revenue at a continuous rate of $60,000t + 45,000$ dollars per year during the first six months of operation and at the continuous rate of 75,000 dollars per year after the first six months. The cost of the machine is $150,000, the interest rate is 7% per year, compounded continuously, and $t$ is time in years since the machine was installed.

   (a) Find the present value of the revenue earned by the machine during the first year of operation.
   (b) Find how long it will take for the machine to pay for itself; that is, how long it will take for the present value of the revenue to equal the cost of the machine?

13. (a) A bank account earns 10% interest compounded continuously. At what constant, continuous rate must a parent deposit money into such an account in order to save $100,000 in 10 years for a child's college expenses?
   (b) If the parent decides instead to deposit a lump sum now in order to attain the goal of $100,000 in 10 years, how much must be deposited now?

14. Your company needs $500,000 in two years' time for renovations and can earn 9% interest on investments.

   (a) What is the present value of the renovations?
   (b) If your company deposits money continuously at a constant rate throughout the two-year period, at what rate should the money be deposited so that you have the $500,000 when you need it?

15. A company is expected to earn $50,000 a year, at a continuous rate, for 8 years. You can invest the earnings at an interest rate of 7%, compounded continuously. You have the chance to buy the rights to the earnings of the company now for $350,000. Should you buy? Explain.

16. Sales of Version 6.0 of a computer software package start out high and decrease exponentially. At time $t$, in years, the sales are $s(t) = 50,000e^{-t}$ dollars per year. After two years, Version 7.0 of the software is released and replaces Version 6.0. You can invest earnings at an interest rate of 6%, compounded continuously. Calculate the total present value of sales of Version 6.0 over the two-year period.

17. Intel Corporation is a leading manufacturer of integrated circuits. In 2011, Intel generated profits at a continuous rate of 34.6 billion dollars per year based on a total revenue of 54 billion dollars.[6] Assume the interest rate was 6% per year compounded continuously.

   (a) What was the present value of Intel's profits over the 2011 one-year time period?
   (b) What was the value at the end of the year of Intel's profits over the 2011 one-year time period?

18. Harley-Davidson Inc. manufactures motorcycles. During the years following 2003 (the company's 100th anniversary), the company's net revenue can be approximated[7] by $4.6 + 0.4t$ billion dollars per year, where $t$ is time in years since January 1, 2003. Assume this rate holds through January 1, 2014, and assume a continuous interest rate of 3.5% per year.

   (a) What was the net revenue of the Harley-Davidson Company in 2003? What is the projected net revenue in 2013?
   (b) What was the present value, on January 1, 2003, of Harley-Davidson's net revenue for the ten years from January 1, 2003 to January 1, 2013?
   (c) What is the future value, on January 1, 2013, of net revenue for the preceding 10 years?

19. McDonald's Corporation licenses and operates a chain of 31,377 fast-food restaurants throughout the world. Between 2005 and 2008, McDonald's has been generating revenue at continuous rates between 17.9 and 22.8 billion dollars per year.[8] Suppose that McDonald's rate of revenue stays within this range. Use an interest rate of 4.5% per year compounded continuously. Fill in the blanks:

   (a) The present value of McDonald's revenue over a five-year time period is between _____ and _____ billion dollars.
   (b) The present value of McDonald's revenue over a twenty-five-year time period is between _____ and _____ billion dollars.

20. Your company is considering buying new production machinery. You want to know how long it will take for the machinery to pay for itself; that is, you want to find the length of time over which the present value of the profit generated by the new machinery equals the cost of the machinery. The new machinery costs $130,000 and earns profit at the continuous rate of $80,000 per year. Use an interest rate of 8.5% per year compounded continuously.

---

[5] http://news.bbc.co.uk/2/hi/europe/7648021.stm, accessed January 2013.
[6] http://www.intc.com/financials.cfm, accessed May 2012.
[7] 2007 Harley-Davidson Annual Report, accessed from www.harley-davidson.com.
[8] McDonald's Annual Report 2007, www.mcdonalds.com, accessed March 13, 2013.

**21.** An oil company discovered an oil reserve of 100 million barrels. For time $t > 0$, in years, the company's extraction plan is a linear declining function of time as follows:

$$q(t) = a - bt,$$

where $q(t)$ is the rate of extraction of oil in millions of barrels per year at time $t$ and $b = 0.1$ and $a = 10$.

**(a)** How long does it take to exhaust the entire reserve?
**(b)** The oil price is a constant $20 per barrel, the extraction cost per barrel is a constant $10, and the market interest rate is 10% per year, compounded continuously. What is the present value of the company's profit?

**22.** The value of good wine increases with age. Thus, if you are a wine dealer, you have the problem of deciding whether to sell your wine now, at a price of $P a bottle, or to sell it later at a higher price. Suppose you know that the amount a wine-drinker is willing to pay for a bottle of this wine $t$ years from now is $P(1 + 20\sqrt{t})$. Assuming continuous compounding and a prevailing interest rate of 5% per year, when is the best time to sell your wine?

# 6.6  INTEGRATION BY SUBSTITUTION

In Chapter 3, we learned rules to differentiate any function obtained by combining constants, powers of $x$, $\sin x$, $\cos x$, $e^x$, and $\ln x$, using addition, multiplication, division, or composition of functions. Such functions are called *elementary*.

There is a great difference between looking for derivatives and looking for antiderivatives. Every elementary function has elementary derivatives, but many elementary functions do not have elementary antiderivatives. Some examples are $\sqrt{x^3 + 1}$ and $e^{-x^2}$; these are ordinary functions that arise naturally.

In this section, we introduce integration by substitution which reverses the chain rule. According to the chain rule,

$$\frac{d}{dx}(f(g(x))) = f'(\overbrace{g(x)}^{\text{Inside}}) \cdot \underbrace{g'(x)}.$$

Derivative of outside ↗            ↖ Derivative of inside

Thus, any function which is the result of differentiating with the chain rule is the product of two factors: the "derivative of the outside" and the "derivative of the inside." If a function has this form, its antiderivative is $f(g(x)) + C$.

---

**Example 1**   Use the chain rule to find $f'(x)$ and then write the corresponding antidifferentiation formula.

(a)   $f(x) = e^{x^2}$          (b)   $f(x) = \frac{1}{6}(x^2 + 1)^6$          (c)   $f(x) = \ln(x^2 + 4)$

**Solution**   (a) Using the chain rule, we see

$$\frac{d}{dx}\left(e^{x^2}\right) = e^{x^2} \cdot 2x \quad \text{so} \quad \int e^{x^2} \cdot 2x\, dx = e^{x^2} + C.$$

(b) Using the chain rule, we see

$$\frac{d}{dx}\left(\frac{1}{6}(x^2 + 1)^6\right) = (x^2 + 1)^5 \cdot 2x \quad \text{so} \quad \int (x^2 + 1)^5 \cdot 2x\, dx = \frac{1}{6}(x^2 + 1)^6 + C.$$

(c) Using the chain rule, we see

$$\frac{d}{dx}(\ln(x^2 + 4)) = \frac{1}{x^2 + 4} \cdot 2x \quad \text{so} \quad \int \frac{1}{x^2 + 4} \cdot 2x\, dx = \ln(x^2 + 4) + C.$$

---

In Example 1, the derivative of each inside function is $2x$. Notice that the derivative of the inside function is a factor in the integrand in each antidifferentiation formula.

Finding an inside function whose derivative appears as a factor is key to the method of substitution. We formalize this method as follows:

## To Make a Substitution in an Integral

Let $w$ be the "inside function" and $dw = w'(x)\,dx = \dfrac{dw}{dx}\,dx$. Then express the integrand in terms of $w$.

**Example 2**    Make a substitution to find each of the following integrals:

(a) $\displaystyle\int e^{x^2} \cdot 2x\,dx$    (b) $\displaystyle\int (x^2 + 1)^5 \cdot 2x\,dx$    (c) $\displaystyle\int \frac{1}{x^2 + 4} \cdot 2x\,dx$

**Solution**    (a) We look for an inside function whose derivative appears as a factor. In this case, the inside function is $x^2$, with derivative $2x$. We let $w = x^2$. Then $dw = w'(x)\,dx = 2x\,dx$. The original integrand can now be rewritten in terms of $w$:

$$\int e^{x^2} \cdot 2x\,dx = \int e^w\,dw = e^w + C = e^{x^2} + C.$$

By changing the variable to $w$, we simplified the integrand. The final step, after antidifferentiating, is to convert back to the original variable, $x$.

(b) Here, the inside function is $x^2 + 1$, with derivative $2x$. We let $w = x^2 + 1$. Then $dw = w'(x)\,dx = 2x\,dx$. Rewriting the original integral in terms of $w$, we have

$$\int (x^2 + 1)^5 \cdot 2x\,dx = \int w^5\,dw = \frac{1}{6}w^6 + C = \frac{1}{6}(x^2 + 1)^6 + C.$$

Again, by changing the variable to $w$, we simplified the integrand.

(c) The inside function is $x^2 + 4$, so we let $w = x^2 + 4$. Then $dw = w'(x)\,dx = 2x\,dx$. Substituting, we have

$$\int \frac{1}{x^2 + 4} \cdot 2x\,dx = \int \frac{1}{w}\,dw = \ln(w) + C = \ln(x^2 + 4) + C.$$

Notice that the derivative of the inside function must be present in the integral for this method to work. The method works, however, even when the derivative is missing a constant factor, as in the next two examples.

**Example 3**    Find $\displaystyle\int t e^{(t^2 + 1)}\,dt$.

**Solution**    Here the inside function is $t^2 + 1$, with derivative $2t$. Since there is a factor of $t$ in the integrand, we try $w = t^2 + 1$. Then $dw = w'(t)\,dt = 2t\,dt$. Notice, however, that the original integrand has only $t\,dt$, not $2t\,dt$. We therefore write

$$\frac{1}{2}\,dw = t\,dt$$

and then substitute:

$$\int t e^{(t^2+1)}\,dt = \int e^{\overbrace{(t^2 + 1)}^{w}} \cdot \underbrace{t\,dt}_{\frac{1}{2}\,dw} = \int e^w \frac{1}{2}\,dw = \frac{1}{2}\int e^w\,dw = \frac{1}{2}e^w + C = \frac{1}{2}e^{(t^2+1)} + C.$$

Why didn't we put $\frac{1}{2}\int e^w\,dw = \frac{1}{2}e^w + \frac{1}{2}C$ in the preceding example? Since the constant $C$ is arbitrary, it does not really matter whether we add $C$ or $\frac{1}{2}C$. The convention is always to add $C$ to whatever antiderivative we have calculated.

**Example 4**     Find $\int x^3 \sqrt{x^4 + 5}\, dx$.

**Solution**     The inside function is $x^4 + 5$, with derivative $4x^3$. The integrand has a factor of $x^3$, and since the only thing missing is a constant factor, we try

$$w = x^4 + 5.$$

Then

$$dw = w'(x)\, dx = 4x^3\, dx,$$

giving

$$\frac{1}{4} dw = x^3\, dx.$$

Thus,

$$\int x^3 \sqrt{x^4 + 5}\, dx = \int \sqrt{w}\, \frac{1}{4} dw = \frac{1}{4} \int w^{1/2}\, dw = \frac{1}{4} \cdot \frac{w^{3/2}}{3/2} + C = \frac{1}{6}(x^4 + 5)^{3/2} + C.$$

---

**Warning**

We saw in the preceding examples that we can apply the substitution method when a *constant* factor is missing from the derivative of the inside function. However, we may not be able to use substitution if anything other than a constant factor is missing. For example, setting $w = x^4 + 5$ to find

$$\int x^2 \sqrt{x^4 + 5}\, dx$$

does us no good because $x^2\, dx$ is not a constant multiple of $dw = 4x^3\, dx$. In order to use substitution, it helps if the integrand contains the derivative of the inside function, *to within a constant factor.*

---

**Example 5**     Find $\int \dfrac{t^2}{1 + t^3}\, dt$.

**Solution**     Observing that the derivative of $1 + t^3$ is $3t^2$, we take $w = 1 + t^3$, $dw = 3t^2\, dt$, so $\frac{1}{3} dw = t^2\, dt$. Thus,

$$\int \frac{t^2}{1 + t^3}\, dt = \int \frac{\frac{1}{3} dw}{w} = \frac{1}{3} \ln |w| + C = \frac{1}{3} \ln |1 + t^3| + C.$$

Since the numerator is $t^2\, dt$, we might have tried $w = t^3$. This substitution leads to the integral $\frac{1}{3} \int 1/(1+w)\, dw$. To evaluate this integral we would have to make a second substitution $u = 1 + w$. There is often more than one way to do an integral by substitution.

## Using Substitution with Periodic Functions

The method of substitution can be used for integrals involving periodic functions.

**Example 6**     Find $\int 3x^2 \cos(x^3)\, dx$.

**Solution**     We look for an inside function whose derivative appears—in this case $x^3$. We let $w = x^3$. Then $dw = w'(x)\, dx = 3x^2\, dx$. The original integrand can now be completely rewritten in terms of the new variable $w$:

$$\int 3x^2 \cos(x^3)\, dx = \int \cos \underbrace{(x^3)}_{w} \cdot \underbrace{3x^2\, dx}_{dw} = \int \cos w\, dw = \sin w + C = \sin(x^3) + C.$$

By changing the variable to $w$, we have simplified the integrand to $\cos w$, which can be antidifferentiated more easily. The final step, after antidifferentiating, is to convert back to the original variable, $x$.

**Example 7**     Find $\displaystyle\int e^{\cos\theta}\sin\theta\,d\theta$.

Solution     We let $w = \cos\theta$ since its derivative is $-\sin\theta$ and there is a factor of $\sin\theta$ in the integrand. This gives
$$dw = w'(\theta)\,d\theta = -\sin\theta\,d\theta,$$
so
$$-dw = \sin\theta\,d\theta.$$
Thus,
$$\int e^{\cos\theta}\sin\theta\,d\theta = \int e^{w}\,(-dw) = (-1)\int e^{w}\,dw = -e^{w} + C = -e^{\cos\theta} + C.$$

## Definite Integrals by Substitution

The following example shows two ways of computing a definite integral by substitution.

**Example 8**     Compute $\displaystyle\int_{0}^{2} xe^{x^{2}}\,dx$.

Solution     To evaluate this definite integral using the Fundamental Theorem of Calculus, we first need to find an antiderivative of $f(x) = xe^{x^{2}}$. The inside function is $x^{2}$, so we let $w = x^{2}$. Then $dw = 2x\,dx$, so $\frac{1}{2}\,dw = x\,dx$. Thus,
$$\int xe^{x^{2}}\,dx = \int e^{w}\frac{1}{2}\,dw = \frac{1}{2}e^{w} + C = \frac{1}{2}e^{x^{2}} + C.$$
Now we find the definite integral:
$$\int_{0}^{2} xe^{x^{2}}\,dx = \frac{1}{2}e^{x^{2}}\Big|_{0}^{2} = \frac{1}{2}(e^{4} - e^{0}) = \frac{1}{2}(e^{4} - 1).$$

There is another way to look at the same problem. After we established that
$$\int xe^{x^{2}}\,dx = \frac{1}{2}e^{w} + C,$$
our next two steps were to replace $w$ by $x^{2}$, and then $x$ by 2 and 0. We could have directly replaced the original limits of integration, $x = 0$ and $x = 2$, by the corresponding $w$ limits. Since $w = x^{2}$, the $w$ limits are $w = 0^{2} = 0$ (when $x = 0$) and $w = 2^{2} = 4$ (when $x = 2$), so we get
$$\int_{x=0}^{x=2} xe^{x^{2}}\,dx = \frac{1}{2}\int_{w=0}^{w=4} e^{w}\,dw = \frac{1}{2}e^{w}\Big|_{0}^{4} = \frac{1}{2}\left(e^{4} - e^{0}\right) = \frac{1}{2}(e^{4} - 1).$$
As we would expect, both methods give the same answer.

---

### To Use Substitution to Find Definite Integrals

Either
  • Compute the indefinite integral, expressing an antiderivative in terms of the original variable, and then evaluate the result at the original limits,

or
  • Convert the original limits to new limits in terms of the new variable and do not convert the antiderivative back to the original variable.

## Problems for Section 6.6

**1.** **(a)** Find the derivatives of $\sin(x^2 + 1)$ and $\sin(x^3 + 1)$.
   **(b)** Use your answer to part (a) to find antiderivatives of:

       (i)   $x\cos(x^2 + 1)$     (ii)   $x^2 \cos(x^3 + 1)$

   **(c)** Find the general antiderivatives of:

       (i)   $x\sin(x^2 + 1)$     (ii)   $x^2 \sin(x^3 + 1)$

In Problems 2–5 explain how you can tell if substitution can be used to find an antiderivative.

**2.** $\displaystyle \int x(1 - 5x^2)^5\, dx$      **3.** $\displaystyle \int \frac{\sqrt{\ln x}}{x}\, dx$

**4.** $\displaystyle \int \frac{x}{\sqrt{\ln x}}\, dx$      **5.** $\displaystyle \int \sin^9 t \, \cos t \, dt$

Find the integrals in Problems 6–47. Check your answers by differentiation.

**6.** $\displaystyle \int 2x(x^2 + 1)^5\, dx$      **7.** $\displaystyle \int \frac{x}{\sqrt{x^2 + 4}}\, dx$

**8.** $\displaystyle \int (5x - 7)^{10}\, dx$      **9.** $\displaystyle \int x\sqrt{x^2 + 1}\, dx$

**10.** $\displaystyle \int 2q e^{q^2 + 1}\, dq$      **11.** $\displaystyle \int 5e^{5t+2}\, dt$

**12.** $\displaystyle \int x e^{-x^2}\, dx$      **13.** $\displaystyle \int 100 e^{-0.2t}\, dt$

**14.** $\displaystyle \int t^2 (t^3 - 3)^{10}\, dt$      **15.** $\displaystyle \int x\sin(x^2)\, dx$

**16.** $\displaystyle \int x(x^2 - 4)^{7/2}\, dx$      **17.** $\displaystyle \int x(x^2 + 3)^2\, dx$

**18.** $\displaystyle \int \frac{1}{(3x + 1)^2}\, dx$      **19.** $\displaystyle \int \frac{4x^3}{x^4 + 1}\, dx$

**20.** $\displaystyle \int 12x^2 \cos(x^3)\, dx$      **21.** $\displaystyle \int (2t - 7)^{73}\, dt$

**22.** $\displaystyle \int (x^2 + 3)^2\, dx$      **23.** $\displaystyle \int y^2 (1 + y)^2\, dy$

**24.** $\displaystyle \int \sin\theta(\cos\theta + 5)^7\, d\theta$      **25.** $\displaystyle \int \sin^6\theta \cos\theta \, d\theta$

**26.** $\displaystyle \int \sqrt{\cos 3t}\,\sin 3t \, dt$      **27.** $\displaystyle \int \sin(3 - t)\, dt$

**28.** $\displaystyle \int \frac{t}{1 + 3t^2}\, dt$      **29.** $\displaystyle \int x^2 e^{x^3 + 1}\, dx$

**30.** $\displaystyle \int \sin^3\alpha \cos\alpha \, d\alpha$      **31.** $\displaystyle \int x\sin(4x^2)\, dx$

**32.** $\displaystyle \int \sin^2 x \cos x \, dx$      **33.** $\displaystyle \int e^{3x - 4}\, dx$

**34.** $\displaystyle \int \frac{1 + e^x}{\sqrt{x + e^x}}\, dx$      **35.** $\displaystyle \int x e^{3x^2}\, dx$

**36.** $\displaystyle \int x\sqrt{3x^2 + 4}\, dx$      **37.** $\displaystyle \int \frac{e^x - e^{-x}}{e^x + e^{-x}}\, dx$

**38.** $\displaystyle \int \frac{(\ln z)^2}{z}\, dz$      **39.** $\displaystyle \int \frac{y}{y^2 + 4}\, dy$

**40.** $\displaystyle \int \frac{q}{5q^2 + 8}\, dq$      **41.** $\displaystyle \int \frac{e^t + 1}{e^t + t}\, dt$

**42.** $\displaystyle \int \frac{e^{\sqrt{y}}}{\sqrt{y}}\, dy$      **43.** $\displaystyle \int \frac{\cos\sqrt{x}}{\sqrt{x}}\, dx$

**44.** $\displaystyle \int \frac{x + 1}{x^2 + 2x + 19}\, dx$      **45.** $\displaystyle \int \frac{e^t}{e^t + 1}\, dt$

**46.** $\displaystyle \int \sin^6(5\theta) \cos(5\theta)\, d\theta$      **47.** $\displaystyle \int \frac{x\cos(x^2)}{\sqrt{\sin(x^2)}}\, dx$

**48.** If appropriate, evaluate the following integrals by substitution. If substitution is not appropriate, say so, and do not evaluate.

    **(a)** $\displaystyle \int x\sin(x^2)\, dx$      **(b)** $\displaystyle \int x^2 \sin x \, dx$

    **(c)** $\displaystyle \int \frac{x^2}{1 + x^2}\, dx$      **(d)** $\displaystyle \int \frac{x}{(1 + x^2)^2}\, dx$

    **(e)** $\displaystyle \int x^3 e^{x^2}\, dx$      **(f)** $\displaystyle \int \frac{\sin x}{2 + \cos x}\, dx$

**49.** Use substitution to express each of the following integrals as a multiple of $\int_a^b (1/w)\, dw$ for some $a$ and $b$. Then evaluate the integrals.

    **(a)** $\displaystyle \int_0^1 \frac{x}{1 + x^2}\, dx$      **(b)** $\displaystyle \int_0^{\pi/4} \frac{\sin x}{\cos x}\, dx$

Use integration by substitution and the Fundamental Theorem to evaluate the definite integrals in Problems 50–59.

**50.** $\displaystyle \int_0^2 x(x^2 + 1)^2\, dx$      **51.** $\displaystyle \int_0^3 \frac{2x}{x^2 + 1}\, dx$

**52.** $\displaystyle \int_0^{\pi/2} e^{-\cos\theta}\sin\theta \, d\theta$      **53.** $\displaystyle \int_1^4 \frac{e^{\sqrt{x}}}{\sqrt{x}}\, dx$

**54.** $\displaystyle \int_0^3 \frac{1}{\sqrt{t + 1}}\, dt$      **55.** $\displaystyle \int_{-1}^{e-2} \frac{1}{t + 2}\, dt$

**56.** $\displaystyle\int_0^2 \frac{x}{(1+x^2)^2}\, dx$

**57.** $\displaystyle\int_0^1 2te^{-t^2}\, dt$

**58.** $\displaystyle\int_{-1}^2 \sqrt{x+2}\, dx$

**59.** $\displaystyle\int_1^3 \frac{dt}{(t+7)^2}$

In Problems 60–61, find the exact area.

**60.** Under $f(x) = xe^{x^2}$ between $x = 0$ and $x = 2$.

**61.** Under $f(x) = 1/(x+1)$ between $x = 0$ and $x = 2$.

**62.** Find the exact average value of $f(x) = 1/(x+1)$ on the interval $x = 0$ to $x = 2$. Sketch a graph showing the function and the average value.

**63.** Suppose $\int_0^2 g(t)\, dt = 5$. Calculate the following:

 **(a)** $\displaystyle\int_0^4 g(t/2)\, dt$    **(b)** $\displaystyle\int_0^2 g(2-t)\, dt$

**64.** **(a)** Find $\int (x+5)^2\, dx$ in two ways:
  **(i)** By multiplying out
  **(ii)** By substituting $w = x + 5$
 **(b)** Are the results the same? Explain.

**65.** Find $\int 4x(x^2 + 1)\, dx$ using two methods:

 **(a)** Do the multiplication first, and then antidifferentiate.
 **(b)** Use the substitution $w = x^2 + 1$.
 **(c)** Explain how the expressions from parts (a) and (b) are different. Are they both correct?

**66.** **(a)** Find $\int \sin\theta \cos\theta\, d\theta$.
 **(b)** You probably solved part (a) by making the substitution $w = \sin\theta$ or $w = \cos\theta$. (If not, go back and do it that way.) Now find $\int \sin\theta \cos\theta\, d\theta$ by making the *other* substitution.
 **(c)** There is yet another way of finding this integral which involves the trigonometric identities

$$\sin(2\theta) = 2\sin\theta \cos\theta$$
$$\cos(2\theta) = \cos^2\theta - \sin^2\theta.$$

 Find $\int \sin\theta \cos\theta\, d\theta$ using one of these identities and then the substitution $w = 2\theta$.
 **(d)** You should now have three different expressions for the indefinite integral $\int \sin\theta \cos\theta\, d\theta$. Are they really different? Are they all correct? Explain.

# 6.7    INTEGRATION BY PARTS

Now we introduce *integration by parts*, which is a technique for finding integrals based on the product rule. We begin with the product rule:

$$\frac{d}{dx}(uv) = u'v + uv'$$

where $u$ and $v$ are functions of $x$ with derivatives $u'$ and $v'$, respectively. We rewrite this as:

$$uv' = \frac{d}{dx}(uv) - u'v$$

and then integrate both sides:

$$\int uv'\, dx = \int \frac{d}{dx}(uv)\, dx - \int u'v\, dx.$$

Since an antiderivative of $\frac{d}{dx}(uv)$ is just $uv$, we get the following formula:

---

**Integration by Parts**

$$\int uv'\, dx = uv - \int u'v\, dx.$$

---

This technique is useful when the integrand can be viewed as a product and when the integral on the right-hand side is simpler than that on the left.

---

**Example 1**    Use integration by parts to find $\int xe^x\, dx$.

**Solution**    We let $xe^x = (x)\cdot(e^x) = uv'$, and choose $u = x$ and $v' = e^x$. Thus, $u' = 1$ and $v = e^x$, so

$$\int \underbrace{(x)}_{u}\underbrace{(e^x)}_{v'}\, dx = \underbrace{(x)}_{u}\underbrace{(e^x)}_{v} - \int \underbrace{(1)}_{u'}\underbrace{(e^x)}_{v}\, dx = xe^x - e^x + C.$$

Let's look again at Example 1. Notice what would have happened if we took $v = e^x + C_1$. Then

$$\int xe^x \, dx = x(e^x + C_1) - \int (e^x + C_1) \, dx$$
$$= xe^x + C_1 x - e^x - C_1 x + C$$
$$= xe^x - e^x + C,$$

as before. Thus, it is not necessary to include an arbitrary constant in the antiderivative for $v$; any antiderivative will do.

What would have happened if we had picked $u$ and $v'$ the other way around in Example 1? If $u = e^x$ and $v' = x$, then $u' = e^x$ and $v = x^2/2$. The formula for integration by parts then gives

$$\int xe^x \, dx = \frac{x^2}{2}e^x - \int \frac{x^2}{2} \cdot e^x \, dx,$$

which is true but not helpful, since the new integral on the right seems harder than the original one on the left. To use this method, we must choose $u$ and $v'$ to make the integral on the right no harder to find than the integral on the left.

---

### How to Choose $u$ and $v'$

- Whatever you let $v'$ be, you need to be able to find $v$.
- It helps if $u'v$ is simpler (or at least no more complicated) than $uv'$.

---

**Example 2**  Find $\int xe^{3x} \, dx$.

Solution  We let $xe^{3x} = (x) \cdot (e^{3x}) = uv'$, and choose $u = x$ and $v' = e^{3x}$. Thus, $u' = 1$ and $v = \frac{1}{3}e^{3x}$. We have

$$\int \underbrace{(x)}_{u} \underbrace{(e^{3x})}_{v'} \, dx = \underbrace{(x)}_{u} \underbrace{(\tfrac{1}{3}e^{3x})}_{v} - \int \underbrace{(1)}_{u'} \underbrace{(\tfrac{1}{3}e^{3x})}_{v} \, dx = \frac{1}{3}xe^{3x} - \frac{1}{9}e^{3x} + C.$$

There are some examples which don't look like good candidates for integration by parts because they don't appear to involve products, but for which the method works well. Such examples often involve $\ln x$. Here is one:

**Example 3**  Find $\int_2^3 \ln x \, dx$.

Solution  The integrand does not look like a product unless we write $\ln x = (1)(\ln x)$. We might say $u = 1$ so $u' = 0$, which certainly makes things simpler. But if $v' = \ln x$, what is $v$? If we knew, we would not need integration by parts. Let's try the other way: if $u = \ln x$, $u' = 1/x$ and if $v' = 1$, $v = x$, so

$$\int_2^3 \underbrace{(\ln x)}_{u} \underbrace{(1)}_{v'} \, dx = \underbrace{(\ln x)}_{u} \underbrace{(x)}_{v} \Big|_2^3 - \int_2^3 \underbrace{\left(\frac{1}{x}\right)}_{u'} \cdot \underbrace{(x)}_{v} \, dx$$

$$= x \ln x \Big|_2^3 - \int_2^3 1 \, dx = (x \ln x - x) \Big|_2^3$$

$$= 3 \ln 3 - 3 - 2 \ln 2 + 2 = 3 \ln 3 - 2 \ln 2 - 1.$$

Notice that when doing a definite integral by parts, we must remember to put the limits of integration (here 2 and 3) on the $uv$ term (in this case $x \ln x$) as well as on the integral $\int u'v \, dx$.

**Example 4**   Find $\int x^6 \ln x \, dx$.

**Solution**   We can write $x^6 \ln x$ as $uv'$ where $u = \ln x$ and $v' = x^6$. Then $v = \frac{1}{7}x^7$ and $u' = 1/x$, so integration by parts gives us:

$$\int x^6 \ln x \, dx = \int (\ln x) x^6 \, dx = (\ln x)\left(\frac{1}{7}x^7\right) - \int \frac{1}{7}x^7 \cdot \frac{1}{x} \, dx$$

$$= \frac{1}{7}x^7 \ln x - \frac{1}{7}\int x^6 \, dx$$

$$= \frac{1}{7}x^7 \ln x - \frac{1}{49}x^7 + C.$$

In Example 4 we did not choose $v' = \ln x$, because it is not immediately clear what $v$ would be. In fact, we used integration by parts in Example 3 to find the antiderivative of $\ln x$. Also, using $u = \ln x$, as we have done, gives $u'v = x^6/7$, which is simpler to integrate than $uv' = x^6 \ln x$. This example shows that $u$ does not have to be the first factor in the integrand (here $x^6$).

## Problems for Section 6.7

Find the integrals in Problems 1–14.

**1.** $\int te^{5t} \, dt$

**2.** $\int pe^{-0.1p} \, dp$

**3.** $\int y \ln y \, dy$

**4.** $\int (z+1)e^{2z} \, dz$

**5.** $\int q^5 \ln 5q \, dq$

**6.** $\int y\sqrt{y+3} \, dy$

**7.** $\int x^3 \ln x \, dx$

**8.** $\int (t+2)\sqrt{2+3t} \, dt$

**9.** $\int \frac{y}{\sqrt{5-y}} \, dy$

**10.** $\int \frac{z}{e^z} \, dz$

**11.** $\int \frac{t+7}{\sqrt{5-t}} \, dt$

**12.** $\int \frac{\ln x}{x^2} \, dx$

**13.** $\int t \sin t \, dt$

**14.** $\int (\theta+1)\sin(\theta+1) \, d\theta$

**15.** Find $\int_1^2 \ln x \, dx$ numerically. Find $\int_1^2 \ln x \, dx$ using antiderivatives. Check that your answers agree.

Evaluate the integrals in Problems 16–20 both exactly [e.g. $\ln(3\pi)$] and numerically [e.g. $\ln(3\pi) \approx 2.243$].

**16.** $\int_0^{10} ze^{-z} \, dz$

**17.** $\int_1^5 \ln t \, dt$

**18.** $\int_0^5 \ln(1+t) \, dt$

**19.** $\int_1^3 t \ln t \, dt$

**20.** $\int_3^5 x \cos x \, dx$

In Problems 21–22, use integration by parts twice to evaluate the integral.

**21.** $\int (\ln t)^2 \, dt$

**22.** $\int t^2 e^{5t} \, dt$

**23.** For each of the following integrals, indicate whether integration by substitution or integration by parts is more appropriate. Do not evaluate the integrals.

(a) $\int \frac{x^2}{1+x^3} \, dx$    (b) $\int xe^{x^2} \, dx$

(c) $\int x^2 \ln(x^3+1) \, dx$    (d) $\int \frac{1}{\sqrt{3x+1}} \, dx$

(e) $\int x^2 \ln x \, dx$    (f) $\int \ln x \, dx$

In Problems 24–25, find the exact area.

**24.** Under $y = te^{-t}$ for $0 \le t \le 2$.

**25.** Between $y = \ln x$ and $y = \ln(x^2)$ for $1 \le x \le 2$.

**26.** The concentration, $C$, in ng/ml, of a drug in the blood as a function of the time, $t$, in hours since the drug was administered is given by $C = 15te^{-0.2t}$. The area under the concentration curve is a measure of the overall effect of the drug on the body, called the bioavailability. Find the bioavailability of the drug between $t = 0$ and $t = 3$.

**27.** During a surge in the demand for electricity, the rate, $r$, at which energy is used can be approximated by

$$r = te^{-at},$$

where $t$ is the time in hours and $a$ is a positive constant.

(a) Find the total energy, $E$, used in the first $T$ hours. Give your answer as a function of $a$.

(b) What happens to $E$ as $T \to \infty$?

# CHAPTER SUMMARY

- **Computing antiderivatives**
  Powers and polynomials, $e^{kx}$, $\sin(kx)$, $\cos(kx)$

- Integration by substitution

- Integration by parts

- **Using antiderivatives to compute definite integrals analytically**: Fundamental Theorem of Calculus

- **Using definite integrals to analyze antiderivatives numerically and graphically**

- **Improper integrals**

- **Consumer and producer surplus**
  Wage and price controls

- **Present and future value**

# REVIEW PROBLEMS FOR CHAPTER SIX

**1.** Use Figure 6.39 and the fact that $P = 2$ when $t = 0$ to find values of $P$ when $t = 1$, 2, 3, 4 and 5.

**Figure 6.39**

In Problems 2–3, sketch two functions $F$ such that $F' = f$. In one case let $F(0) = 0$ and in the other, let $F(0) = 1$.

**4.** Figure 6.40 shows the derivative $F'(x)$. If $F(0) = 5$, find the value of $F(1)$, $F(3)$, and $F(4)$.

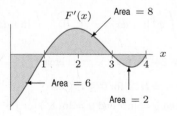

**Figure 6.40**

Problems 5–6 show the derivative $f'$ of $f$.

(a) Where is $f$ increasing and where is $f$ decreasing? What are the $x$-coordinates of the local maxima and minima of $f$?

(b) Sketch a possible graph for $f$. (You don't need a scale on the vertical axis.)

Problems 7–8 give a graph of $f'(x)$. Graph $f(x)$. Mark the points $x_1, \ldots, x_4$ on your graph and label local maxima, local minima and points of inflection.

In Problems 9–18, find an antiderivative.

**9.** $h(t) = 3t^2 + 7t + 1$

**10.** $f(t) = 2t^2 + 3t^3 + 4t^4$

**11.** $f(x) = 6x^2 - 8x + 3$

**12.** $q(y) = y^4 + \dfrac{1}{y}$

**13.** $f(x) = 3x^2 + 5$

**14.** $h(z) = \dfrac{1}{z}$

**15.** $p(y) = \dfrac{1}{y} + y + 1$

**16.** $g(t) = \sin t$

**17.** $f(x) = (2x + 1)^3$

**18.** $g(x) = (x + 1)^3$

In Problems 19–29, find the indefinite integrals.

**19.** $\displaystyle\int (4t + 7)\, dt$

**20.** $\displaystyle\int 3x\, dx$

**21.** $\displaystyle\int (x^3 - x)\, dx$

**22.** $\displaystyle\int (8t + 3)\, dt$

**23.** $\displaystyle\int \left(\dfrac{5}{t^2} + \dfrac{6}{t^3}\right) dt$

**24.** $\displaystyle\int \left(8x^3 + \dfrac{1}{x}\right) dx$

**25.** $\displaystyle\int (4x + 2e^x)\, dx$

**26.** $\displaystyle\int (5\cos x - 3\sin x)\, dx$

**27.** $\displaystyle\int 6x^2\, dx$

**28.** $\displaystyle\int (x + 1)^2\, dx$

**29.** $\displaystyle\int \left(\dfrac{x + 1}{x}\right) dx$

Find the definite integrals in Problems 30–35 using the Fundamental Theorem.

**30.** $\displaystyle\int_1^2 (2x + 3)\, dx$

**31.** $\displaystyle\int_1^2 \frac{1}{t^2}\, dt$

**32.** $\displaystyle\int_{-3}^{-1} \frac{2}{r^3}\, dr$

**33.** $\displaystyle\int_0^1 \sin\theta\, d\theta$

**34.** $\displaystyle\int_0^2 \left(\frac{x^3}{3} + 2x\right) dx$

**35.** $\displaystyle\int_1^2 \frac{1}{2t}\, dt$

**36.** Use the Fundamental Theorem to find the area under $f(x) = x^2$ between $x = 1$ and $x = 4$.

**37.** Write the definite integral for the area under the graph of $f(x) = 6x^2 + 1$ between $x = 0$ and $x = 2$. Use the Fundamental Theorem of Calculus to evaluate it.

**38.** Use the Fundamental Theorem to find the average value of $f(x) = x^2 + 1$ on the interval $x = 0$ to $x = 10$. Illustrate your answer on a graph of $f(x)$.

**39.** Use the Fundamental Theorem to determine the value of $b$ if the area under the graph of $f(x) = 8x$ between $x = 1$ and $x = b$ is equal to 192. Assume $b > 1$.

**40.** Find the exact area below the curve $y = x^3(1 - x)$ and above the $x$-axis.

**41.** Find the exact area enclosed by the curve $y = x^2(1-x)^2$ and the $x$-axis.

**42.** (a) Sketch the area represented by the improper integral $\int_0^\infty xe^{-x}\, dx$.
 (b) Calculate $\int_0^b xe^{-x}\, dx$ for $b = 5, 10, 20$.
 (c) The improper integral in part (a) converges. Use your answers to part (b) to estimate its value.

**43.** Consider the improper integral

$$\int_1^\infty \frac{1}{\sqrt{x}}\, dx.$$

 (a) Use a calculator or computer to find $\int_1^b 1/(\sqrt{x})\, dx$ for $b = 100, 1000, 10,000$. What do you notice?
 (b) Find $\int_1^b 1/(\sqrt{x})\, dx$ using the Fundamental Theorem of Calculus. Your answer will contain $b$.
 (c) Now take the limit as $b \to \infty$. What does this tell you about the improper integral?

**44.** (a) Find $\int_0^b xe^{-x/10}\, dx$ for $b = 10, 50, 100, 200$.
 (b) Assuming that it converges, estimate the value of $\int_0^\infty xe^{-x/10}\, dx$.

**45.** A car moves with velocity, $v$, at time $t$ in hours given by

$$v(t) = \frac{60}{50^t} \quad \text{miles/hour.}$$

 (a) Does the car ever stop?
 (b) Write an integral representing the total distance traveled for $t \ge 0$.
 (c) Do you think the car goes a finite distance for $t \ge 0$? If so, estimate that distance.

**46.** With $t$ in years since 2000, the population, $P$, of the world in billions can be modeled by $P = 6.1e^{0.012t}$.

 (a) What does this model predict for the world population in 2010? In 2020?
 (b) Use the Fundamental Theorem to predict the average population of the world between 2000 and 2010.

**47.** For a product, the supply curve is $p = 5 + 0.02q$ and the demand curve is $p = 30e^{-0.003q}$, where $p$ is the price and $q$ is the quantity sold at that price. Find:

 (a) The equilibrium price and quantity
 (b) The consumer and producer surplus

**48.** Show graphically that the maximum total gains from trade occurs at the equilibrium price. Do this by showing that if outside forces keep the price artificially high or low, the total gains from trade (consumer surplus + producer surplus) are lower than at the equilibrium price.

**49.** In May 1991, *Car and Driver* described a Jaguar that sold for $980,000. At that price only 50 have been sold. It is estimated that 350 could have been sold if the price had been $560,000. Assuming that the demand curve is a straight line, and that $560,000 and 350 are the equilibrium price and quantity, find the consumer surplus at the equilibrium price.

**50.** The demand curve for a product has equation $p = 20e^{-0.002q}$ and the supply curve has equation $p = 0.02q + 1$ for $0 \le q \le 1000$, where $q$ is quantity and $p$ is price in \$/unit.

 (a) Which is higher, the price at which 300 units are supplied or the price at which 300 units are demanded? Find both prices.
 (b) Sketch the supply and demand curves. Find the equilibrium price and quantity.
 (c) Using the equilibrium price and quantity, calculate and interpret the consumer and producer surplus.

**51.** Calculate the present value of a continuous revenue stream of $1000 per year for 5 years at an interest rate of 9% per year compounded continuously.

**52.** At what constant, continuous rate must money be deposited into an account if the account is to contain $20,000 in 5 years? The account earns 6% interest compounded continuously.

**53.** A bond is guaranteed to pay $100 + 10t$ dollars per year for 10 years, where $t$ is in years from the present. Find the present value of this income stream, given an interest rate of 5%, compounded continuously.

**54.** Determine the constant income stream that needs to be invested over a period of 10 years at an interest rate of 5% per year compounded continuously to provide a present value of $5000.

**55.** In 1980, before the unification of Germany in 1990 and the introduction of the Euro, West Germany made a loan of 20 billion Deutsche Marks to the Soviet Union, to be used for the construction of a natural gas pipeline connecting Siberia to Western Russia, and continuing to West Germany (Urengoi–Uschgorod–Berlin). Assume that the deal was as follows: In 1985, upon completion of the pipeline, the Soviet Union would deliver natural gas to West Germany, at a constant rate, for all future times. Assuming a constant price of natural gas of 0.10 Deutsche Mark per cubic meter, and assuming West Germany expects 10% annual interest on its investment (compounded continuously), at what rate does the Soviet Union have to deliver the gas, in billions of cubic meters per year? Keep in mind that delivery of gas could not begin until the pipeline was completed. Thus, West Germany received no return on its investment until after five years had passed. (Note: A more complex deal of this type was actually made between the two countries.)

In Problems 56–58, find an antiderivative $F(x)$ with $F'(x) = f(x)$ and $F(0) = 0$. Is there only one possible solution?

**56.** $f(x) = 2x$

**57.** $f(x) = -7x$

**58.** $\displaystyle\int \frac{2x}{\sqrt{x^2+1}}\,dx$

In Problems 59–68, integrate by substitution.

**59.** $\displaystyle\int t\cos(t^2)\,dt$

**60.** $\displaystyle\int 3x^2(x^3+1)^4\,dx$

**61.** $\displaystyle\int \frac{2x}{x^2+1}\,dx$

**62.** $\displaystyle\int (x+10)^3\,dx$

**63.** $\displaystyle\int x(x^2+9)^6\,dx$

**64.** $\displaystyle\int te^{t^2}\,dt$

**65.** $\displaystyle\int e^{-x}\,dx$

**66.** $\displaystyle\int x^2(1+2x^3)^2\,dx$

**67.** $\displaystyle\int \frac{1}{\sqrt{4-x}}\,dx$

**68.** $\displaystyle\int \frac{dy}{y+5}$

**69.** Estimate $\int_0^{10} f(x)g'(x)\,dx$ if $f(x) = x^2$ and $g$ has the values in the following table.

| $x$ | 0 | 2 | 4 | 6 | 8 | 10 |
|---|---|---|---|---|---|---|
| $g(x)$ | 2.3 | 3.1 | 4.1 | 5.5 | 5.9 | 6.1 |

**70.** Derive the formula (called a reduction formula):

$$\int x^n e^x\,dx = x^n e^x - n\int x^{n-1}e^x\,dx.$$

In Problems 71–73 use integration by parts to evaluate the indefinite integral. Check your answer by differentiating.

**71.** $\displaystyle\int y\sin y\,dy$

**72.** $\displaystyle\int x\cos x\,dx$

**73.** $\displaystyle\int \ln(x^2)\,dx$

## STRENGTHEN YOUR UNDERSTANDING

In Problems 1–70, indicate whether the statement is true or false.

**1.** If a function $f$ is positive on an interval, then its antiderivatives are all increasing on that interval.

**2.** If a function $f$ is increasing on an interval, then its antiderivatives are all concave up on that interval.

**3.** For any function $F$ with continuous derivative, $F(5) = F(0) + \int_0^5 F'(t)\,dt$.

**4.** For any function $F$ with continuous derivative, $F(3) = F(0) + \int_1^3 F'(t)\,dt$.

**5.** If $f'$ is in Figure 6.41, then $f(4) > f(3)$.

**Figure 6.41**

**6.** If $f'$ is in Figure 6.41, then $f(2) > f(1)$.

**7.** If $f'$ is in Figure 6.41, then $f(3) > f(2)$.

**8.** If $f'$ is in Figure 6.41, then $f(5) > f(6)$.

**9.** If $f'$ is in Figure 6.41, then $f(1) > f(0)$.

**10.** If $f'$ is in Figure 6.41, then $f(1) \approx f(3)$.

**11.** $F(t) = \dfrac{t^3}{3} + 5$ is an antiderivative of $f(t) = t^2$.

**12.** $F(x) = \dfrac{x^{-3}}{-3}$ is an antiderivative of $f(x) = x^{-2}$.

**13.** $F(x) = e^{3x}$ is an antiderivative of $f(x) = e^{3x}$.

**14.** $\displaystyle\int t^3\,dt = \dfrac{t^4}{4} + C.$

**15.** $\displaystyle\int \dfrac{1}{\sqrt{z}}\,dz = 2\sqrt{z} + C.$

**16.** $\displaystyle\int e^x\,dx = \dfrac{e^{x+1}}{x+1} + C.$

**17.** $\displaystyle\int \ln|t|\,dt = \dfrac{1}{t} + C.$

**18.** $\int 2^x \, dx = \dfrac{1}{\ln 2} 2^x + C.$

**19.** $\int 5 \cos x \, dx = 5 \sin x + C.$

**20.** If $F(x)$ and $G(x)$ are both antiderivatives of $h(x)$, then $F(x) - G(x)$ is a constant.

**21.** $\int_2^3 \dfrac{1}{x} \, dx = \dfrac{1}{3} - \dfrac{1}{2}.$

**22.** $\int_2^3 \dfrac{1}{x} \, dx = \ln 3 - \ln 2.$

**23.** $\int_1^5 2x \, dx = 5^2 - 1^2.$

**24.** $\int_1^2 3x^2 \, dx = 3(2^2) - 3(1^2).$

**25.** $\int_0^3 t^4 \, dt = \dfrac{t^5}{5} + C.$

**26.** $\int_1^2 e^t \, dt = e^2 - e.$

**27.** The substitution $w = x^2$ converts $\int_0^5 2x e^{x^2} \, dx$ into $\int_0^5 e^w \, dw.$

**28.** The substitution $w = \ln x$ converts $\int_1^e (\ln x)^3/x \, dx$ into $\int_0^1 w^3 \, dw.$

**29.** If $f(x)$ is any function then $\int_{10}^{20} f(x) \, dx = 10 \int_1^2 f(x) \, dx.$

**30.** The integral $\int_1^2 e^{-kx} \, dx$ is positive for any $k \neq 0.$

**31.** The supply curve shows the quantity of an item that a producer supplies at different prices.

**32.** The demand curve shows the quantity of an item that consumers will purchase at various prices.

**33.** The equilibrium price $p^*$ is where the demand curve crosses the $q$-axis.

**34.** Consumer surplus is the total amount gained by consumers by purchasing items at prices higher than they are willing to pay.

**35.** The units of consumer surplus are the same as the units of producer surplus.

**36.** The units of producer surplus are price times quantity.

**37.** Total gains from trade is the difference between consumer and producer surplus.

**38.** The area under the demand curve from 0 to the equilibrium quantity $q^*$ is the amount consumers spend at the equilibrium price $p^*$.

**39.** Consumer surplus at price $p^*$ is the area between the demand curve and the horizontal line at $p^*$.

**40.** Producer surplus at price $p^*$ is the area between the demand curve and the horizontal line at $p^*$.

**41.** Assuming a positive interest rate, the present value of an income stream is always less than its future value.

**42.** The future value of an income stream of $1000 per year for 5 years is more than $5000 if the interest rate is 2%.

**43.** The present value of an income stream of $1000 per year for 5 years is more than $5000 if the interest rate is 2%.

**44.** A single payment at the beginning of the year of $1000 has the same future value as an income stream of $1000 per year if we assume a continuous interest rate of 3% for one year for both.

**45.** If $S(t)$ is an income stream, then $S(t)$ has units of dollars.

**46.** With a continuous interest rate of $r$, the future value of a payment of $3000 today in 5 years is $3000e^{-5r}$.

**47.** With a continuous interest rate of $r$, we would have to deposit $3000e^{-5r}$ today to grow to $3000 in 5 years.

**48.** If an income stream of 2000 dollars per year grows to $11,361 in five years, then the amount of interest earned over the five-year period is $1361.

**49.** The present value of an income stream of 2000 dollars per year that starts now and pays out over 6 years with a continuous interest rate of 2% is $\int_0^6 2000 e^{-2t} \, dt.$

**50.** The future value of an income stream of 2000 dollars per year that starts now and accumulates over 9 years with a positive interest rate is greater than $18,000.

**51.** The substitution $w = q^3 + 3q^2 - q$ converts the integral $\int (q^3 + 3q^2 - q)^{10} \, dq$ into $\int w^{10} \, dw.$

**52.** The substitution $w = \ln x$ converts the integral $\int \dfrac{(\ln x)^2}{x} \, dx$ into $\int w^2 \, dw.$

**53.** The substitution $w = x^2$ converts the integral $\int e^{x^2} \, dx$ into $\int e^w \, dw.$

**54.** The substitution $w = x^2$ converts the integral $\int x e^{x^2} \, dx$ into $\int \dfrac{1}{2} e^w \, dw.$

**55.** The substitution $w = 1 - s$ converts the integral $\int \dfrac{1}{\sqrt{1-s}} \, ds$ into $\int \dfrac{1}{\sqrt{w}} \, dw.$

**56.** The substitution $w = t^2 + 1$ converts the integral $\int \dfrac{t}{\sqrt{t^2 + 1}} \, dt$ into $\int \dfrac{1}{2\sqrt{w}} \, dw.$

**57.** The substitution $w = e^x + e^{-x}$ converts the integral $\int \dfrac{e^x - e^{-x}}{e^x + e^{-x}} \, dx$ into $\int \dfrac{1}{w} \, dw.$

**58.** The substitution $w = q^3$ converts the integral $\int q^2 (q^3 + 5)^{10} \, dq$ into $\int \dfrac{1}{3} w^{10} \, dw.$

**59.** The substitution $w = \sin \alpha$ converts the integral $\int \sin^3 \alpha \cos \alpha \, d\alpha$ into $\int w^3 \, dw.$

**60.** The substitution $w = \cos x$ converts the integral $\int \dfrac{\sin x}{\cos x}\, dx$ into $\int \dfrac{1}{w}\, dw$.

**61.** Setting $u = x^3/3$ and $dv = e^x\, dx$ is a reasonable assignment of the parts for the integral $\int x^2 e^x\, dx$.

**62.** Setting $u = x$ and $dv = \sqrt{3x+1}\, dx$ is a reasonable assignment of the parts for the integral $\int x\sqrt{3x+1}\, dx$.

**63.** If $u = x^2$ and $dv = e^{3x}\, dx$ in integration by parts, then $du = 2x\, dx$ and $v = 3e^{3x}$.

**64.** If $u = x^2$ and $dv = \ln x\, dx$ in integration by parts, then $du = 2x\, dx$ and $v = 1/x$.

**65.** Integration by parts is an appropriate method to use in evaluating $\int x e^{3x^2}\, dx$.

**66.** Integration by parts is an appropriate method to use in evaluating $\int x e^{3x}\, dx$.

**67.** Integration by parts is an appropriate method to use in evaluating $\int \dfrac{x}{\sqrt{5x+1}}\, dx$.

**68.** Integration by parts is an appropriate method to use in evaluating $\int \dfrac{x}{\sqrt{5x^2+1}}\, dx$.

**69.** Integration by parts is an appropriate method to use in evaluating $\int x^2\sqrt{2x^3+9}\, dx$.

**70.** Integration by parts is an appropriate method to use in evaluating $\int x^3 \ln x\, dx$.

## PROJECTS FOR CHAPTER SIX

**1. Quabbin Reservoir** The Quabbin Reservoir in the western part of Massachusetts provides most of Boston's water. The graph in Figure 6.42 represents the flow of water in and out of the Quabbin Reservoir throughout 2007.

   **(a)** Sketch a graph of the quantity of water in the reservoir, as a function of time.

   **(b)** When, in the course of 2007, was the quantity of water in the reservoir largest? Smallest? Mark and label these points on the graph you drew in part (a).

   **(c)** When was the quantity of water increasing most rapidly? Decreasing most rapidly? Mark and label these times on both graphs.

   **(d)** By July 2008 the quantity of water in the reservoir was about the same as in January 2007. Draw plausible graphs for the flow into and the flow out of the reservoir for the first half of 2008.

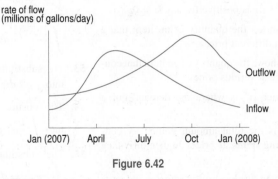

**Figure 6.42**

**2. Distribution of Resources**

   Whether a resource is distributed evenly among members of a population is often an important political or economic question. How can we measure this? How can we decide if the distribution of wealth in this country is becoming more or less equitable over time? How can we measure which country has the most equitable income distribution? This problem describes a way of making such measurements. Suppose the resource is distributed evenly. Then any 20% of the population will have 20% of the resource. Similarly, any 30% will have 30% of the resource and so on. If, however, the resource is not distributed evenly, the poorest $p\%$ of the population (in terms of this resource) will not have $p\%$ of the goods. Suppose $F(x)$ represents the fraction of the resource owned by the poorest fraction $x$ of the population. Thus $F(0.4) = 0.1$ means that the poorest 40% of the population owns 10% of the resource.

   **(a)** What would $F$ be if the resource were distributed evenly?

**(b)** What must be true of any such $F$? What must $F(0)$ and $F(1)$ equal? Is $F$ increasing or decreasing? Is the graph of $F$ concave up or concave down?

**(c)** Gini's index of inequality, $G$, is one way to measure how evenly the resource is distributed. It is defined by

$$G = 2 \int_0^1 (x - F(x)) \, dx.$$

Show graphically what $G$ represents.

**(d)** Graphical representations of Gini's index for two countries are given in Figures 6.43 and 6.44. Which country has the more equitable distribution of wealth? Discuss the distribution of wealth in each of the two countries.

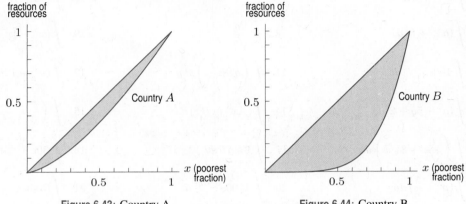

Figure 6.43: Country A                    Figure 6.44: Country B

**(e)** What is the maximum possible value of Gini's index of inequality, $G$? What is the minimum possible value? Sketch graphs in each case. What is the distribution of resources in each case?

## 3. Yield from an Apple Orchard

Figure 6.45 is a graph of the annual yield, $y(t)$, in bushels per year, from an orchard $t$ years after planting. The trees take about 10 years to get established, but for the next 20 years they give a substantial yield. After about 30 years, however, age and disease start to take their toll, and the annual yield falls off.[9]

**(a)** Represent on a sketch of Figure 6.45 the total yield, $F(M)$, up to $M$ years, with $0 \le M \le 60$. Write an expression for $F(M)$ in terms of $y(t)$.

**(b)** Sketch a graph of $F(M)$ against $M$ for $0 \le M \le 60$.

**(c)** Write an expression for the average annual yield, $a(M)$, up to $M$ years.

**(d)** When should the orchard be cut down and replanted? Assume that we want to maximize average revenue per year, and that fruit prices remain constant, so that this is achieved by maximizing average annual yield. Use the graph of $y(t)$ to estimate the time at which the average annual yield is a maximum. Explain your answer geometrically and symbolically.

Figure 6.45

---

[9]From Peter D. Taylor, *Calculus: The Analysis of Functions* (Toronto: Wall & Emerson, Inc., 1992).

# FOCUS ON PRACTICE

For Problems 1–47, evaluate the integrals. Assume $a$, $b$, $A$, $B$, $P_0$, $h$, and $k$ are constants.

1. $\displaystyle\int y(y^2+5)^8 \, dy$

2. $\displaystyle\int (q^3+8q+15) \, dq$

3. $\displaystyle\int (u^4+5) \, du$

4. $\displaystyle\int (x^2+1) \, dx$

5. $\displaystyle\int e^{-3t} \, dt$

6. $\displaystyle\int (6\sqrt{x}) \, dx$

7. $\displaystyle\int (ax^2+b) \, dx$

8. $\displaystyle\int \frac{dq}{\sqrt{q}}$

9. $\displaystyle\int (x^3+4x+8) \, dx$

10. $\displaystyle\int 100e^{-0.5t} \, dt$

11. $\displaystyle\int \left(q+\frac{1}{q^3}\right) \, dq$

12. $\displaystyle\int (w^4-12w^3+6w^2-10) \, dw$

13. $\displaystyle\int (q^2+5q+2) \, dq$

14. $\displaystyle\int (Ax^3+Bx) \, dx$

15. $\displaystyle\int \left(\frac{4}{x}+\frac{5}{x^2}\right) \, dx$

16. $\displaystyle\int \left(\frac{6}{\sqrt{x}}+8\sqrt{x}\right) \, dx$

17. $\displaystyle\int 3\sin\theta \, d\theta$

18. $\displaystyle\int 30e^{-0.2t} \, dt$

19. $\displaystyle\int \left(p^2+\frac{5}{p}\right) \, dp$

20. $\displaystyle\int 1000e^{0.075t} \, dt$

21. $\displaystyle\int (5\sin x+3\cos x) \, dx$

22. $\displaystyle\int (10+5\sin x) \, dx$

23. $\displaystyle\int (Aq+B) \, dq$

24. $\displaystyle\int \frac{5}{w} \, dw$

25. $\displaystyle\int \pi r^2 h \, dr$

26. $\displaystyle\int xe^x \, dx$

27. $\displaystyle\int 15p^2q^4 \, dp$

28. $\displaystyle\int 15p^2q^4 \, dq$

29. $\displaystyle\int (3x^2+6e^{2x}) \, dx$

30. $\displaystyle\int 5e^{2q} \, dq$

31. $\displaystyle\int \left(p^3+\frac{1}{p}\right) \, dp$

32. $\displaystyle\int 12\cos(4x) \, dx$

33. $\displaystyle\int \frac{1}{y+2} \, dy$

34. $\displaystyle\int (6\sqrt{x}+15) \, dx$

35. $\displaystyle\int (x^2+8+e^x) \, dx$

36. $\displaystyle\int (t^2-6t+5) \, dt$

37. $\displaystyle\int \left(\frac{a}{x}+\frac{b}{x^2}\right) \, dx$

38. $\displaystyle\int_0^{10} ze^{-z} \, dz$

39. $\displaystyle\int (e^{2t}+5) \, dt$

40. $\displaystyle\int \cos(4x) \, dx$

41. $\displaystyle\int P_0 e^{kt} \, dt$

42. $\displaystyle\int \sin(3x) \, dx$

43. $\displaystyle\int A\sin(Bt) \, dt$

44. $\displaystyle\int \sqrt{3x+1} \, dx$

45. $\displaystyle\int \frac{e^x}{2+e^x} \, dx$

46. $\displaystyle\int \frac{\cos x}{\sqrt{1+\sin x}} \, dx$

47. $\displaystyle\int x\ln x \, dx$

# Chapter Seven

# PROBABILITY

## Contents

# 7.1 DENSITY FUNCTIONS

Understanding the distribution of various quantities through the population can be important to decision makers. For example, the income distribution gives useful information about the economic structure of a society. In this section we look at the distribution of ages in the US. To allocate funding for education, health care, and social security, the government needs to know how many people are in each age group. We see how to represent such information by a density function.

## US Age Distribution

Table 7.1 *Distribution of ages in the US in 2000*

| Age group | Percentage of total population |
|-----------|-------------------------------|
| 0 − 20 | 29% |
| 20 − 40 | 29% |
| 40 − 60 | 26% |
| 60 − 80 | 13% |
| 80 − 100 | 3% |

Figure 7.1: How ages were distributed in the US in 2000

Suppose we have the data in Table 7.1 showing how the ages of the US population[1] were distributed in 2000. To represent this information graphically we use a type of *histogram*[2] putting a vertical bar above each age group in such a way that the *area* of each bar represents the percentage in that age group. The total area of all the rectangles is $100\% = 1$. We only consider people who are less than 100 years old.[3] For the 0–20 age group, the base of the rectangle is 20, and we want the area to be 29%, so the height must be $29\%/20 = 1.45\%$. We treat ages as though they were continuously distributed. The category 0–20, for example, contains people who are just one day short of their twentieth birthday. Notice that the vertical axis is measured in percent/year. (See Figure 7.1.)

---

**Example 1**    In 2000, estimate what percentage of the US population was:

    (a)    Between 20 and 60 years old?         (b)    Less than 10 years old?

    (c)    Between 75 and 80 years old?       (d)    Between 80 and 85 years old?

Solution    (a)  We add the percentages, so $29\% + 26\% = 55\%$.

    (b)  To find the percentage less than 10 years old, we could assume, for example, that the population was distributed evenly over the 0–20 group. (This means we are assuming that babies were born at a fairly constant rate over the last 20 years, which is probably reasonable.) If we make this assumption, then we can say that the population less than 10 years old was about half that in the 0–20 group, that is, $14.5\%$. Notice that we get the same result by computing the area of the rectangle from 0 to 10. (See Figure 7.2.)

    (c)  To find the population between 75 and 80 years old, since 13% of Americans in 2000 were in the 60-80 group, we might apply the same reasoning and say that $\frac{1}{4}(13\%) = 3.25\%$ of the population was in this age group. This result is represented as an area in Figure 7.2. The assumption that the population was evenly distributed is not a good one here; certainly there were more people between the ages of 60 and 65 than between 75 and 80. Thus, the estimate of 3.25% is certainly too high.

---

[1] www.censusscope.org/us/chart_age.html, accessed May 10, 2005.

[2] There are other types of histograms which have frequency on the vertical axis.

[3] In fact, 0.02% of the population is over 100, but this is too small to be visible on the histogram.

(d) Again using the (faulty) assumption that ages in each group were distributed uniformly, we would find that the percentage between 80 and 85 was $\frac{1}{4}(3\%) = 0.75\%$. (See Figure 7.2.) This estimate is also poor—there were certainly more people in the 80–85 group than, say, the 95–100 group, and so the 0.75% estimate is too low.

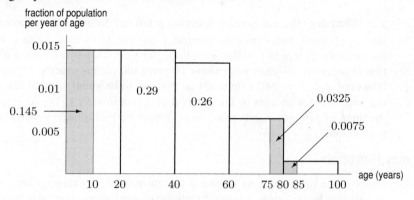

Figure 7.2: Ages in the US in 2000—various subgroups (for Example 1)

### Smoothing Out the Histogram

We could get better estimates if we had smaller age groups (each age group in Figure 7.1 is 20 years, which is quite large) or if the histogram were smoother. Suppose we have the more detailed data in Table 7.2, which leads to the new histogram in Figure 7.3.

As we get more detailed information, the upper silhouette of the histogram becomes smoother, but the area of any of the bars still represents the percentage of the population in that age group. Imagine, in the limit, replacing the upper silhouette of the histogram by a smooth curve in such a way that area under the curve above one age group is the same as the area in the corresponding rectangle. The total area under the whole curve is again 100% = 1. (See Figure 7.3.)

### The Age Density Function

If $t$ is age in years, we define $p(t)$, the age *density function*, to be a function which "smooths out" the age histogram. This function has the property that

$$\begin{matrix} \text{Fraction of population} \\ \text{between ages } a \text{ and } b \end{matrix} = \begin{matrix} \text{Area under} \\ \text{graph of } p \\ \text{between } a \text{ and } b \end{matrix} = \int_a^b p(t)\,dt.$$

Table 7.2  *Ages in the US in 2000 (more detailed)*

| Age group | Percentage of total population |
|-----------|-------------------------------|
| 0 − 10    | 14%                           |
| 10 − 20   | 15%                           |
| 20 − 30   | 14%                           |
| 30 − 40   | 15%                           |
| 40 − 50   | 15%                           |
| 50 − 60   | 11%                           |
| 60 − 70   | 7%                            |
| 70 − 80   | 6%                            |
| 80 − 90   | 2%                            |
| 90 − 100  | 1%                            |

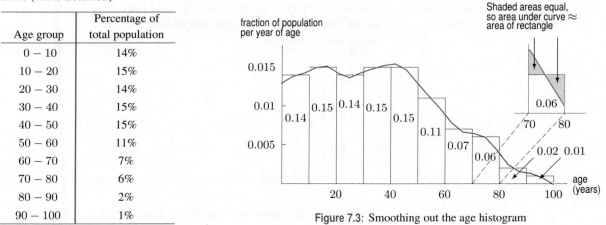

Figure 7.3: Smoothing out the age histogram

If $a$ and $b$ are the smallest and largest possible ages (say, $a = 0$ and $b = 100$), so that the ages of all of the population are between $a$ and $b$, then

$$\int_a^b p(t)dt = \int_0^{100} p(t)dt = 1.$$

**What does the age density function $p$ tell us?** Notice that we have not talked about the meaning of $p(t)$ itself, but *only* of the integral $\int_a^b p(t)\,dt$. Let's look at this in a bit more detail. Suppose, for example, that $p(10) = 0.014 = 1.4\%$ per year. This is *not* telling us that $1.4\%$ of the population is precisely 10 years old (where 10 years old means exactly 10, not $10\frac{1}{2}$, not $10\frac{1}{4}$, not 10.1). However, $p(10) = 0.014$ does tell us that for some small interval $\Delta t$ around 10, the fraction of the population with ages in this interval is approximately $p(10)\,\Delta t = 0.014\,\Delta t$. Notice also that the units of $p(t)$ are % *per year*, so $p(t)$ must be multiplied by years to give a percentage of the population.

## The Density Function

Suppose we are interested in how a certain numerical characteristic, $x$, is distributed through a population. For example, $x$ might be height or age if the population is people, or might be wattage for a population of light bulbs. Then we define a general density function with the following properties:

---

The function, $p(x)$, is a **density function** if

$$\begin{array}{ccc} \text{Fraction of population} & & \text{Area under} \\ \text{for which } x \text{ is} & = & \text{graph of } p & = \int_a^b p(x)dx. \\ \text{between } a \text{ and } b & & \text{between } a \text{ and } b \end{array}$$

$$\int_{-\infty}^{\infty} p(x)\,dx = 1 \quad \text{and} \quad p(x) \geq 0 \quad \text{for all } x.$$

---

The density function must be nonnegative if its integral always gives a fraction of the population. The fraction of the population with $x$ between $-\infty$ and $\infty$ is 1 because the entire population has the characteristic $x$ between $-\infty$ and $\infty$. The function $p$ that was used to smooth out the age histogram satisfies this definition of a density function. Notice that we do not assign a meaning to the value $p(x)$ directly, but rather interpret $p(x)\,\Delta x$ as the fraction of the population with the characteristic in a short interval of length $\Delta x$ around $x$.

---

**Example 2**    Figure 7.4 gives the density function for the amount of time spent waiting at a doctor's office.

(a) What is the longest time anyone has to wait?
(b) Approximately what fraction of patients wait between 1 and 2 hours?
(c) Approximately what fraction of patients wait less than an hour?

fraction of patients per number
of hours spent waiting

Figure 7.4: Distribution of waiting time at a doctor's office

Solution

(a) The density function is zero for all $t > 3$, so no one waits more than 3 hours. The longest time anyone has to wait is 3 hours.

(b) The fraction of patients who wait between 1 and 2 hours is equal to the area under the density curve between $t = 1$ and $t = 2$. We can estimate this area by counting squares: There are about 7.5 squares in this region, each of area $(0.5)(0.1) = 0.05$. The area is approximately $(7.5)(0.05) = 0.375$. Thus about 37.5% of patients wait between 1 and 2 hours.

(c) This fraction is equal to the area under the density function for $t < 1$. There are about 12 squares in this area, and each has area 0.05 as in part (b), so our estimate for the area is $(12)(0.05) = 0.60$. Therefore, about 60% of patients see the doctor in less than an hour.

## Problems for Section 7.1

In Problems 1–4, the distribution of the heights, $x$, in meters, of trees is represented by the density function $p(x)$. In each case, calculate the fraction of trees which are:

(a) Less than 5 meters high

(b) More than 6 meters high

(c) Between 2 and 5 meters high

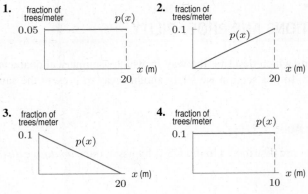

5. The density function $p(t)$ for the length of the larval stage, in days, for a breed of insect is given in Figure 7.5. What fraction of these insects are in the larval stage for between 10 and 12 days? For less than 8 days? For more than 12 days? In which one-day interval is the length of a larval stage most likely to fall?

Figure 7.5

6. Figure 7.6[4] shows the distribution of elevation, in miles, across the earth's surface. Positive elevation denotes land above sea level; negative elevation shows land below sea level (i.e., the ocean floor).

(a) Describe in words the elevation of most of the earth's surface.

(b) Approximately what fraction of the earth's surface is below sea level?

Figure 7.6

7. Let $p(x)$ be the density function for annual family income, where $x$ is in thousands of dollars. What is the meaning of the statement $p(70) = 0.05$?

8. Suppose that $p(x)$ is the density function for heights of American men, in inches. What is the meaning of the statement $p(68) = 0.2$?

In Problems 9–12, calculate the value of $c$ if $p$ is a density function.

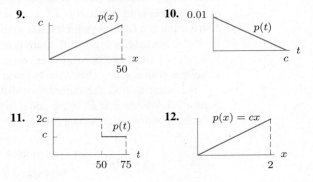

[4]Adapted from *Statistics, 2nd Edition*, by D. Freedman, R. Pisani, R. Purves, and A. Adikhari (New York: Norton, 1991).

**13.** A machine lasts up to 10 years. Figure 7.7 shows the density function, $p(t)$, for the length of time it lasts.

   **(a)** What is the value of $C$?

   **(b)** Is a machine more likely to break in its first year or in its tenth year? In its first or second year?

   **(c)** What fraction of the machines lasts 2 years or less? Between 5 and 7 years? Between 3 and 6 years?

**Figure 7.7**

**14.** Find a density function $p(x)$ such that $p(x) = 0$ when $x \geq 5$ and when $x < 0$, and is decreasing when $0 \leq x \leq 5$.

In Problems 15–17, graph a possible density function representing crop yield (in kilograms) from a field under the given circumstance.

**15.** All yields from 0 to 100 kg are equally likely; the field never yields more than 100 kg.

**16.** High yields are more likely than low. The maximum yield is 200 kg.

**17.** A drought makes low yields most common, and there is no yield greater than 30 kg.

**18.** Which of the following functions makes the most sense as a model for the probability density representing the time (in minutes, starting from $t = 0$) that the next customer walks into a store?

   **(a)** $p(t) = \begin{cases} \cos t & 0 \leq t \leq 2\pi \\ e^{t-2\pi} & t \geq 2\pi \end{cases}$

   **(b)** $p(t) = 3e^{-3t}$ for $t \geq 0$

   **(c)** $p(t) = e^{-3t}$ for $t \geq 0$

   **(d)** $p(t) = 1/4$ for $0 \leq t \leq 4$

## 7.2 CUMULATIVE DISTRIBUTION FUNCTIONS AND PROBABILITY

Section 7.1 introduced density functions which describe the way in which a numerical characteristic is distributed through a population. In this section we study another way to present the same information.

### Cumulative Distribution Function for Ages

An alternative way of showing how ages are distributed in the US is by using the *cumulative distribution function* $P(t)$, defined by

$$P(t) = \begin{array}{c} \text{Fraction of population} \\ \text{of age less than } t \end{array} = \int_0^t p(x)\,dx.$$

Thus, $P$ is the antiderivative of $p$ with $P(0) = 0$, so $P(t)$ is the area under the density curve between 0 and $t$. See the left-hand part of Figure 7.8.

    Notice that the cumulative distribution function is nonnegative and increasing (or at least nondecreasing), since the number of people younger than age $t$ increases as $t$ increases. Another way of seeing this is to notice that $P' = p$, and $p$ is positive (or nonnegative). Thus the cumulative age distribution is a function which starts with $P(0) = 0$ and increases as $t$ increases. We have $P(t) = 0$ for $t < 0$ because, when $t < 0$, there is no one whose age is less than $t$. The limiting value of $P$, as $t \to \infty$, is 1 since as $t$ becomes very large (100 say), everyone is younger than age $t$, so the fraction of people with age less than $t$ tends toward 1.

    We want to find the cumulative distribution function for the age density function shown in Figure 7.3. We see that $P(10)$ is equal to 0.14, since Figure 7.3 shows that 14% of the population is between 0 and 10 years of age. Also,

$$P(20) = \begin{array}{c} \text{Fraction of the population} \\ \text{between 0 and 20 years old} \end{array} = 0.14 + 0.15 = 0.29$$

and similarly

$$P(30) = 0.14 + 0.15 + 0.14 = 0.43.$$

Continuing in this way gives the values for $P(t)$ in Table 7.3. These values were used to graph $P(t)$ in the right-hand part of Figure 7.8.

**Table 7.3** *Cumulative distribution function, $P(t)$, giving fraction of US population of age less than t years*

| $t$ | 0 | 10 | 20 | 30 | 40 | 50 | 60 | 70 | 80 | 90 | 100 |
|---|---|---|---|---|---|---|---|---|---|---|---|
| $P(t)$ | 0 | 0.14 | 0.29 | 0.43 | 0.58 | 0.73 | 0.84 | 0.91 | 0.97 | 0.99 | 1.00 |

**Figure 7.8:** Graph of $p(x)$, the age density function, and its relation to $P(t)$, the cumulative age distribution function

## Cumulative Distribution Function

A **cumulative distribution function**, $P(t)$, of a density function $p$, is defined by

$$P(t) = \int_{-\infty}^{t} p(x)\, dx = \begin{array}{l}\text{Fraction of population having}\\ \text{values of } x \text{ below } t.\end{array}$$

Thus, $P$ is an antiderivative of $p$, that is, $P' = p$.
Any cumulative distribution function has the following properties:
- $P$ is increasing (or nondecreasing).
- $\lim_{t \to \infty} P(t) = 1$  and  $\lim_{t \to -\infty} P(t) = 0.$
- $\begin{array}{l}\text{Fraction of population}\\ \text{having values of } x\\ \text{between } a \text{ and } b\end{array} = \int_{a}^{b} p(x)\, dx = P(b) - P(a).$

**Example 1** The time to conduct a routine maintenance check on a machine has a cumulative distribution function $P(t)$, which gives the fraction of maintenance checks completed in time less than or equal to $t$ minutes. Values of $P(t)$ are given in Table 7.4.

**Table 7.4** *Cumulative distribution function for time to conduct maintenance checks*

| $t$ (minutes) | 0 | 5 | 10 | 15 | 20 | 25 | 30 |
|---|---|---|---|---|---|---|---|
| $P(t)$ (fraction completed) | 0 | 0.03 | 0.08 | 0.21 | 0.38 | 0.80 | 0.98 |

(a) What fraction of maintenance checks are completed in 15 minutes or less?
(b) What fraction of maintenance checks take longer than 30 minutes?
(c) What fraction take between 10 and 15 minutes?
(d) Draw a histogram showing how times for maintenance checks are distributed.
(e) In which of the given 5-minute intervals is the length of a maintenance check most likely to fall?
(f) Give a rough sketch of the density function.
(g) Sketch a graph of the cumulative distribution function.

Solution    (a)  The fraction of maintenance checks completed in 15 minutes is $P(15) = 0.21$, or 21%.
(b)  Since $P(30) = 0.98$, we see that 98% of maintenance checks take 30 minutes or less. Therefore, only 2% take more than 30 minutes.
(c)  Since 8% take 10 minutes or less and 21% take 15 minutes or less, the fraction taking between 10 and 15 minutes is $0.21 - 0.08 = 0.13$, or 13%.
(d)  We begin by making a table showing how the times are distributed. Table 7.4 shows that the fraction of checks completed between 0 and 5 minutes is 0.03, and the fraction completed between 5 and 10 minutes is 0.05, and so on. See Table 7.5.

Table 7.5    *Distribution of time to conduct maintenance checks*

| $t$ (minutes) | $0 - 5$ | $5 - 10$ | $10 - 15$ | $15 - 20$ | $20 - 25$ | $25 - 30$ | $> 30$ |
|---|---|---|---|---|---|---|---|
| Fraction completed | 0.03 | 0.05 | 0.13 | 0.17 | 0.42 | 0.18 | 0.02 |

The histogram in Figure 7.9 is drawn so that the area of each bar is the fraction of checks completed in the corresponding time period. For instance, the first bar has area 0.03 and width 5 minutes, so its height is $0.03/5 = 0.006$.

Figure 7.9: Histogram of times for maintenance checks

(e)  From Figure 7.9, we see that more of the checks take between 20 and 25 minutes to complete, so this is the most likely length of time.
(f)  The density function, $p(t)$, is a smoothed version of the histogram in Figure 7.9. A reasonable sketch is given in Figure 7.10.
(g)  A graph of $P(t)$ is given in Figure 7.11. Since $P(t)$ is a cumulative distribution function, $P(t)$ is approaching 1 as $t$ gets large, but is never larger than 1.

Figure 7.10: Density function for time to conduct maintenance checks

Figure 7.11: Cumulative distribution function for time to conduct maintenance checks

## Probability

Suppose we pick a member of the US population at random. What is the probability that we pick a person who is between, say, the ages of 70 and 80? We saw in Table 7.2 on page 333 that 6% of the population is in this age group. We say that the probability, or chance, that the person is between 70 and 80 is 0.06. Using any age density function $p(t)$, we define probabilities as follows:

$$\begin{array}{ccccc} \text{Probability that a person is} & = & \text{Fraction of population} & = & \displaystyle\int_a^b p(t)\,dt. \\ \text{between ages } a \text{ and } b & & \text{between ages } a \text{ and } b & & \end{array}$$

Since the cumulative distribution gives the fraction of the population younger than age $t$, the cumulative distribution function can also be used to calculate the probability that a randomly selected person is in a given age group.

$$\begin{array}{ccccc} \text{Probability that a person is} & = & \text{Fraction of population} & = & P(t) = \displaystyle\int_0^t p(x)\,dx. \\ \text{younger than age } t & & \text{younger than age } t & & \end{array}$$

In the next example, both a density function and a cumulative distribution function are used to describe the same situation.

**Example 2**  Suppose you want to analyze the fishing industry in a small town. Each day, the boats bring back at least 2 tons of fish, but never more than 8 tons.

(a) Using the density function describing the daily catch in Figure 7.12, find and graph the corresponding cumulative distribution function and explain its meaning.

(b) What is the probability that the catch is between 5 and 7 tons?

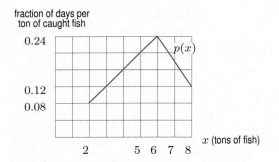

Figure 7.12: Density function of daily catch

**Solution**  (a) The cumulative distribution function $P(t)$ is equal to the fraction of days on which the catch is less than $t$ tons of fish. Since the catch is never less than 2 tons, we have $P(t) = 0$ for $t \le 2$. Since the catch is always less than 8 tons, we have $P(t) = 1$ for $t \ge 8$. For $t$ in the range $2 < t < 8$ we must evaluate the integral

$$P(t) = \int_{-\infty}^t p(x)\,dx = \int_2^t p(x)\,dx.$$

This integral equals the area under the graph of $p(x)$ between $x = 2$ and $x = t$. It can be computed by counting grid squares in Figure 7.12; each square has area 0.04. For example,

$$P(3) = \int_2^3 p(x)\,dx \approx \text{Area of 2.5 squares} = 2.5(0.04) = 0.10.$$

Table 7.6 contains values of $P(t)$; the graph is shown in Figure 7.13.

Table 7.6   *Estimates for $P(t)$ of daily catch*

| $t$ (tons of fish) | $P(t)$ (fraction of fishing days) |
|:---:|:---:|
| 2 | 0 |
| 3 | 0.10 |
| 4 | 0.24 |
| 5 | 0.42 |
| 6 | 0.64 |
| 7 | 0.85 |
| 8 | 1 |

Figure 7.13: Cumulative distribution, $P(t)$, of daily catch

(b) The probability that the catch is between 5 and 7 tons can be found using either the density function $p$ or the cumulative distribution function $P$. When we use the density function, this probability is represented by the shaded area in Figure 7.14, which is about 10.75 squares, so

$$\text{Probability catch is between 5 and 7 tons} = \int_5^7 p(x)\,dx \approx \text{Area of 10.75 squares} = 10.75(0.04) = 0.43.$$

The probability can be found from the cumulative distribution function as follows:

$$\text{Probability catch is between 5 and 7 tons} = P(7) - P(5) = 0.85 - 0.42 = 0.43.$$

Figure 7.14: Shaded area represents the probability the catch is between 5 and 7 tons

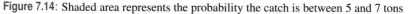

## Problems for Section 7.2

1. (a) Using the density function in Example 2 on page 334, fill in values for the cumulative distribution function $P(t)$ for the length of time people wait in the doctor's office.

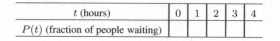

| $t$ (hours) | 0 | 1 | 2 | 3 | 4 |
|:---|:---:|:---:|:---:|:---:|:---:|
| $P(t)$ (fraction of people waiting) | | | | | |

(b) Graph $P(t)$.

2. Show that the area under the fishing density function in Figure 7.12 on page 339 is 1. Why is this to be expected?

3. Figure 7.15 shows a density function and the corresponding cumulative distribution function.[5]

(a) Which curve represents the density function and which represents the cumulative distribution function? Give a reason for your choice.

[5] Adapted from *Calculus*, by David A. Smith and Lawrence C. Moore (Lexington, D.C. Heath, 1994).

**(b)** Put reasonable values on the tick marks on each of the axes.

**Figure 7.15**

4. In an agricultural experiment, the quantity of grain from a given size field is measured. The yield can be anything from 0 kg to 50 kg. For each of the following situations, pick the graph that best represents the:
(i) Probability density function
(ii) Cumulative distribution function.

**(a)** Low yields are more likely than high yields.
**(b)** All yields are equally likely.
**(c)** High yields are more likely than low yields.

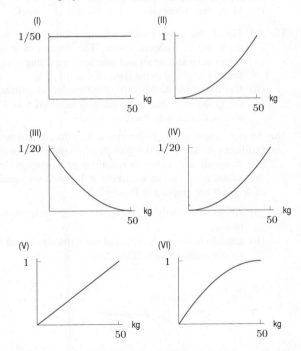

Decide if the function graphed in Problems 5–10 is a probability density function (pdf) or a cumulative distribution function (cdf). Give reasons. Find the value of $c$. Sketch and label the other function. (That is, sketch and label the cdf if the problem shows a pdf, and the pdf if the problem shows a cdf.)

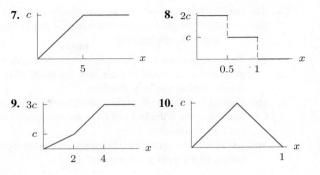

11. A person who travels regularly on the 9:00 am bus from Oakland to San Francisco reports that the bus is almost always a few minutes late but rarely more than five minutes late. The bus is never more than two minutes early, although it is on very rare occasions a little early.

**(a)** Sketch a density function, $p(t)$, where $t$ is the number of minutes that the bus is late. Shade the region under the graph between $t = 2$ minutes and $t = 4$ minutes. Explain what this region represents.

**(b)** Now sketch the cumulative distribution function $P(t)$. What measurement(s) on this graph correspond to the area shaded? What do the inflection point(s) on your graph of $P$ correspond to on the graph of $p$? Interpret the inflection points on the graph of $P$ without referring to the graph of $p$.

12. Suppose $F(x)$ is the cumulative distribution function for heights (in meters) of trees in a forest.

**(a)** Explain in terms of trees the meaning of the statement $F(7) = 0.6$.

**(b)** Which is greater, $F(6)$ or $F(7)$? Justify your answer in terms of trees.

13. Students at the University of California were surveyed and asked their grade point average. (The GPA ranges from 0 to 4, where 2 is just passing.) The distribution of GPAs is shown in Figure 7.16.[6]

**(a)** Roughly what fraction of students are passing?
**(b)** Roughly what fraction of the students have honor grades (GPAs above 3)?
**(c)** Why do you think there is a peak around 2?
**(d)** Sketch the cumulative distribution function.

**Figure 7.16**

---

[6]Adapted from *Statistics*, by Freedman, Pisani, Purves, and Adikhari (New York: Norton, 1991).

**14.** The density function and cumulative distribution function of heights of grass plants in a meadow are in Figures 7.17 and 7.18, respectively.

   **(a)** There are two species of grass in the meadow, a short grass and a tall grass. Explain how the graph of the density function reflects this fact.

   **(b)** Explain how the graph of the cumulative distribution function reflects the fact that there are two species of grass in the meadow.

   **(c)** About what percentage of the grasses in the meadow belong to the short grass species?

*fraction of plants per meter of height*

*height (meter)*

**Figure 7.17**

*fraction of plants*

*height (meter)*

**Figure 7.18**

**15.** A congressional committee is investigating a defense contractor whose projects often incur cost overruns. The data in Table 7.7 show $y$, the fraction of the projects with an overrun of at most $C\%$.

   **(a)** Plot the data with $C$ on the horizontal axis. Is this a density function or a cumulative distribution function? Sketch a curve through these points.

   **(b)** If you think you drew a density function in part (a), sketch the corresponding cumulative distribution function on another set of axes. If you think you drew a cumulative distribution function in part (a), sketch the corresponding density function.

   **(c)** Based on the table, what is the probability that there will be a cost overrun of 50% or more? Between 20% and 50%? Near what percent is the cost overrun most likely to be?

**Table 7.7**  *Fraction, $y$, of overruns that are at most $C\%$*

| $C$ | −20% | −10% | 0% | 10% | 20% | 30% | 40% | 50% |
|-----|------|------|-----|-----|-----|-----|-----|-----|
| $y$ | 0.01 | 0.08 | 0.19 | 0.32 | 0.50 | 0.80 | 0.94 | 0.99 |

For Problems 16–17, let $p(t) = -0.0375t^2 + 0.225t$ be the density function for the shelf life of a brand of banana, with $t$ in weeks and $0 \le t \le 4$. See Figure 7.19.

*fraction of bananas per week of age*

$$p(t) = -0.0375t^2 + 0.225t$$

*t (weeks)*

**Figure 7.19**

**16.** Find the probability that a banana will last

   **(a)** Between 1 and 2 weeks.

   **(b)** More than 3 weeks.        **(c)** More than 4 weeks.

**17. (a)** Sketch the cumulative distribution function for the shelf life of bananas. [Note: The domain of your function should be all real numbers, including to the left of $t = 0$ and to the right of $t = 4$.]

   **(b)** Use the cumulative distribution function to estimate the probability that a banana lasts between 1 and 2 weeks. Check with Problem 16(a).

**18.** An experiment is done to determine the effect of two new fertilizers A and B on the growth of a species of peas. The cumulative distribution functions of the heights of the mature peas without treatment and treated with each of A and B are graphed in Figure 7.20.

   **(a)** About what height are most of the unfertilized plants?

   **(b)** Explain in words the effect of the fertilizers A and B on the mature height of the plants.

*fraction of plants*

*Unfertilized*

*x height (meters)*

**Figure 7.20**

**19.** A group of people have received treatment for cancer. Let $t$ be the survival time, the number of years a person lives after the treatment. The density function giving the distribution of $t$ is $p(t) = Ce^{-Ct}$ for some positive constant $C$. What is the practical meaning of the cumulative distribution function $P(t) = \int_0^t p(x)\,dx$?

**20.** The probability of a transistor failing between $t = a$ months and $t = b$ months is given by $c\int_a^b e^{-ct}dt$, for some constant $c$.

    **(a)** If the probability of failure within the first six months is 10%, what is $c$?

    **(b)** Given the value of $c$ in part (a), what is the probability the transistor fails within the second six months?

**21.** While taking a walk along the road where you live, you accidentally drop your glove, but you don't know

where. The probability density $p(x)$ for having dropped the glove $x$ kilometers from home (along the road) is

$$p(x) = 2e^{-2x} \quad \text{for } x \geq 0.$$

    **(a)** What is the probability that you dropped it within 1 kilometer of home?

    **(b)** At what distance $y$ from home is the probability that you dropped it within $y$ km of home equal to 0.95?

# 7.3 THE MEDIAN AND THE MEAN

It is often useful to be able to give an "average" value for a distribution. Two measures that are in common use are the *median* and the *mean*.

## The Median

A **median** of a quantity $x$ distributed through a population is a value $T$ such that half the population has values of $x$ less than (or equal to) $T$, and half the population has values of $x$ greater than (or equal to) $T$. Thus, if $p$ is the density function, a median $T$ satisfies

$$\int_{-\infty}^{T} p(x)\, dx = 0.5.$$

In other words, half the area under the graph of $p$ lies to the left of $T$. Equivalently, if $P$ is the cumulative distribution function,

$$P(T) = 0.5.$$

**Example 1**    Let $t$ days be the length of time a pair of jeans remains in a shop before it is sold. The density function of $t$ is graphed in Figure 7.21 and given by

$$p(t) = 0.04 - 0.0008t.$$

    **(a)** What is the longest time a pair of jeans remains unsold?

    **(b)** Would you expect the median time till sale to be less than, equal to, or greater than 25 days?

    **(c)** Find the median time required to sell a pair of jeans.

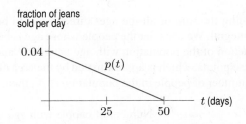

Figure 7.21: Density function for time till sale of a pair of jeans

**Solution**    **(a)** The density function is 0 for all times $t > 50$, so all jeans are sold within 50 days.

    **(b)** The area under the graph of the density function in the interval $0 \leq t \leq 25$ is greater than the area under the graph in the interval $25 \leq t \leq 50$. So more than half the jeans are sold before their $25^{\text{th}}$ day in the shop. The median time till sale is less than 25 days.

(c) Let $P$ be the cumulative distribution function. We want to find the value of $T$ such that

$$P(T) = \int_{-\infty}^{T} p(t)\, dt = \int_{0}^{T} p(t)\, dt = 0.5.$$

Using a calculator to evaluate the integrals, we obtain the values for $P$ in Table 7.8.

**Table 7.8**  *Cumulative distribution for selling time*

| $T$ (days) | 0 | 5 | 10 | 15 | 20 | 25 |
|---|---|---|---|---|---|---|
| $P(T)$ (fraction of jeans sold by day $T$) | 0 | 0.19 | 0.36 | 0.51 | 0.64 | 0.75 |

Since about half the jeans are sold within 15 days, the median time to sale is about 15 days. See Figures 7.22 and 7.23. We could also use the Fundamental Theorem of Calculus to find the median exactly. See Problem 19.

Figure 7.22: Median and density function          Figure 7.23: Median and cumulative distribution function

## The Mean

Another commonly used average value is the *mean*. To find the mean of $N$ numbers, we add the numbers and divide the sum by $N$. For example, the mean of the numbers 1, 2, 7, and 10 is $(1 + 2 + 7 + 10)/4 = 5$. The mean age of the entire US population is therefore defined as

$$\text{Mean age} = \frac{\sum \text{Ages of all people in the US}}{\text{Total number of people in the US}}.$$

Calculating the sum of all the ages directly would be an enormous task; we approximate the sum by an integral. We consider the people whose age is between $t$ and $t + \Delta t$. How many are there?

The fraction of the population with age between $t$ and $t + \Delta t$ is the area under the graph of $p$ between these points, which is approximated by the area of the rectangle, $p(t)\Delta t$. (See Figure 7.24.) If the total number of people in the population is $N$, then

$$\text{Number of people with age between } t \text{ and } t + \Delta t \approx p(t)\Delta t N.$$

The age of each of these people is approximately $t$, so

$$\text{Sum of ages of people between age } t \text{ and } t + \Delta t \approx tp(t)\Delta t N.$$

Figure 7.24: Shaded area is percentage of
population with age between $t$ and $t + \Delta t$

Therefore, adding and factoring out an $N$ gives us

$$\text{Sum of ages of all people} \approx \left( \sum tp(t)\Delta t \right) N.$$

In the limit, as $\Delta t$ shrinks to 0, the sum becomes an integral. Assuming no one is over 100 years old, we have

$$\text{Sum of ages of all people} = \left( \int_0^{100} tp(t)dt \right) N.$$

Since $N$ is the total number of people in the US,

$$\text{Mean age} = \frac{\text{Sum of ages of all people in US}}{N} = \int_0^{100} tp(t)dt.$$

We can give the same argument for any[7] density function $p(x)$.

> If a quantity has density function $p(x)$,
>
> $$\textbf{Mean value of the quantity} = \int_{-\infty}^{\infty} xp(x)\,dx.$$

It can be shown that the mean is the point on the horizontal axis where the region under the graph of the density function, if it were made out of cardboard, would balance.

**Example 2**   Find the mean time for jeans sales, using the density function of Example 1.

**Solution**   The formula for $p$ is $p(t) = 0.04 - 0.0008t$. We compute

$$\text{Mean time} = \int_0^{50} tp(t)\,dt = \int_0^{50} t(0.04 - 0.0008t)\,dt = 16.67 \text{ days.}$$

The mean is represented by the balance point in Figure 7.25. Notice that the mean is different from the median computed in Example 1.

---

[7]Provided all the relevant improper integrals converge.

Figure 7.25: Mean sale time for jeans

## Normal Distributions

How much rain do you expect to fall in your home town this year? If you live in Anchorage, Alaska, the answer is something close to 15 inches (including the snow). Of course, you don't expect exactly 15 inches. Some years there are more than 15 inches, and some years there are less. Most years, however, the amount of rainfall is close to 15 inches; only rarely is it well above or well below 15 inches. What does the density function for the rainfall look like? To answer this question, we look at rainfall data over many years. Records show that the distribution of rainfall is well approximated by a *normal distribution*. The graph of its density function is a bell-shaped curve which peaks at 15 inches and slopes downward approximately symmetrically on either side.

Normal distributions are frequently used to model real phenomena, from grades on an exam to the number of airline passengers on a particular flight. A normal distribution is characterized by its *mean*, $\mu$, and its *standard deviation*, $\sigma$. The mean tells us the location of the central peak. The standard deviation tells us how closely the data is clustered around the mean. A small value of $\sigma$ tells us that the data is close to the mean; a large $\sigma$ tells us the data is spread out. In the following formula for a normal distribution, the factor of $1/(\sigma\sqrt{2\pi})$ makes the area under the graph equal to 1.

---

A **normal distribution** has a density function of the form

$$p(x) = \frac{1}{\sigma\sqrt{2\pi}}e^{-(x-\mu)^2/(2\sigma^2)},$$

where $\mu$ is the mean of the distribution and $\sigma$ is the standard deviation, with $\sigma > 0$.

---

To model the rainfall in Anchorage, we use a normal distribution with $\mu = 15$ and $\sigma = 1$. (See Figure 7.26.)

Figure 7.26: Normal distribution with $\mu = 15$ and $\sigma = 1$

**Example 3**   For Anchorage's rainfall, use the normal distribution with the density function with $\mu = 15$ and $\sigma = 1$ to compute the fraction of the years with rainfall between
(a)   14 and 16 inches,       (b)   13 and 17 inches,       (c)   12 and 18 inches.

**Solution**   (a)   The fraction of the years with annual rainfall between 14 and 16 inches is $\int_{14}^{16} \frac{1}{\sqrt{2\pi}} e^{-(x-15)^2/2}\, dx$.
Since there is no elementary antiderivative for $e^{-(x-15)^2/2}$, we find the integral numerically. Its value is about 0.68.

$$\begin{array}{c}\text{Fraction of years with rainfall} \\ \text{between 14 and 16 inches}\end{array} = \int_{14}^{16} \frac{1}{\sqrt{2\pi}} e^{-(x-15)^2/2}\, dx \approx 0.68.$$

(b)   Finding the integral numerically again:

$$\begin{array}{c}\text{Fraction of years with rainfall} \\ \text{between 13 and 17 inches}\end{array} = \int_{13}^{17} \frac{1}{\sqrt{2\pi}} e^{-(x-15)^2/2}\, dx \approx 0.95.$$

(c)

$$\begin{array}{c}\text{Fraction of years with rainfall} \\ \text{between 12 and 18 inches}\end{array} = \int_{12}^{18} \frac{1}{\sqrt{2\pi}} e^{-(x-15)^2/2}\, dx \approx 0.997.$$

Since 0.95 is so close to 1, we expect that most of the time the rainfall will be between 13 and 17 inches a year.

Among the normal distributions, the one having $\mu = 0$, $\sigma = 1$ is called the *standard normal distribution*. Values of the corresponding cumulative distribution function are published in tables.

# Problems for Section 7.3

1. Estimate the median daily catch for the fishing data given in Example 2 of Section 7.2.

2. (a) Use the cumulative distribution function in Figure 7.27 to estimate the median.
   (b) Describe the density function: For what values is it positive? Increasing? Decreasing? Identify all local maxima and minima values.

**Figure 7.27**

3. A quantity $x$ is distributed with density function $p(x) = 0.5(2-x)$ for $0 \le x \le 2$ and $p(x) = 0$ otherwise. Find the mean and median of $x$.

4. A quantity $x$ has cumulative distribution function $P(x) = x - x^2/4$ for $0 \le x \le 2$ and $P(x) = 0$ for $x < 0$ and $P(x) = 1$ for $x > 2$. Find the mean and median of $x$.

For Problems 5–6, let $p(t) = -0.0375t^2 + 0.225t$ be the density function for the shelf life of a brand of banana which lasts up to 4 weeks. Time, $t$, is measured in weeks and $0 \le t \le 4$.

5. Find the median shelf life of a banana using $p(t)$. Plot the median on a graph of $p(t)$. Does it look like half the area is to the right of the median and half the area is to the left?

6. Find the mean shelf life of a banana using $p(t)$. Plot the mean on a graph of $p(t)$. Does it look like the mean is the place where the density function balances?

7. Suppose that $x$ measures the time (in hours) it takes for a student to complete an exam. All students are done within two hours and the density function for $x$ is

$$p(x) = \begin{cases} x^3/4 & \text{if } 0 < x < 2 \\ 0 & \text{otherwise.} \end{cases}$$

   (a) What proportion of students take between 1.5 and 2.0 hours to finish the exam?
   (b) What is the mean time for students to complete the exam?
   (c) Compute the median of this distribution.

**8.** Let $p(t) = 0.1e^{-0.1t}$ be the density function for the waiting time at a subway stop, with $t$ in minutes, $0 \le t \le 60$.

   **(a)** Graph $p(t)$. Use the graph to estimate visually the median and the mean.

   **(b)** Calculate the median and the mean. Plot both on the graph of $p(t)$.

   **(c)** Interpret the median and mean in terms of waiting time.

**9.** The speeds of cars on a road are approximately normally distributed with a mean $\mu = 58$ km/hr and standard deviation $\sigma = 4$ km/hr.

   **(a)** What is the probability that a randomly selected car is going between 60 and 65 km/hr?

   **(b)** What fraction of all cars are going slower than 52 km/hr?

**10.** The distribution of IQ scores can be modeled by a normal distribution with mean 100 and standard deviation 15.

   **(a)** Write the formula for the density function of IQ scores.

   **(b)** Estimate the fraction of the population with IQ between 115 and 120.

**11.** Let $P(x)$ be the cumulative distribution function for the household income distribution in the US in 2009.[8] Values of $P(x)$ are in the following table:

| Income $x$ (thousand \$) | 20 | 40 | 60 | 75 | 100 |
|---|---|---|---|---|---|
| $P(x)$ (%) | 29.5 | 50.1 | 66.8 | 76.2 | 87.1 |

   **(a)** What percent of the households made between \$40,000 and \$60,000? More than \$100,000?

   **(b)** Approximately what was the median income?

   **(c)** Is the statement "More than one-third of households made between \$40,000 and \$75,000" true or false?

## CHAPTER SUMMARY

- **Density function**
- **Cumulative distribution function**
- **Probability**

- **Median**
- **Mean**
- **Normal distribution**

## REVIEW PROBLEMS FOR CHAPTER SEVEN

In Problems 1–4, given that $p(x)$ is a density function, find the value of $a$.

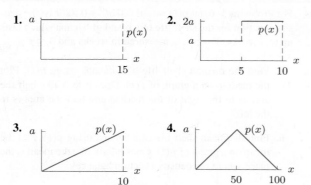

**1.**

**2.**

**3.**

**4.**

**7.** Match the graphs of the density functions (a), (b), and (c) with the graphs of the cumulative distribution functions I, II, and III.

In Problems 5–6, graph a density function representing the given distribution.

**5.** The age at which a person dies in a society with high infant mortality and in which adults usually die between age 40 and age 60.

**6.** The heights of the people in an elementary school.

In Problems 8–10, graph a density function and a cumulative distribution function which could represent the distribution of income through a population with the given characteristics.

**8.** A large middle class.

**9.** Small middle and upper classes and many poor people.

**10.** Small middle class, many poor and many rich people.

---

[8]http://www.census.gov/hhes/www/income/income.html, accessed January 7, 2012.

11. An insect has a life-span of no more than one year. Figure 7.28 shows the density function, $p(t)$, for the life-span.

   (a) Do more insects die in the first month of their life or the twelfth month of their life?
   (b) What fraction of the insects live no more than 6 months?
   (c) What fraction of the insects live more than 9 months?

fraction of population
per month

Figure 7.28

12. A large number of people take a standardized test, receiving scores described by the density function $p$ graphed in Figure 7.29. Does the density function imply that most people receive a score near 50? Explain why or why not.

fraction of students
per test score

Figure 7.29

13. Figure 7.30 shows the distribution of the number of years of education completed by adults in a population. What does the shape of the graph tell you? Estimate the percentage of adults who have completed less than 10 years of education.

% of population
per year of education

Figure 7.30

14. Figure 7.31 shows $P(t)$, the percentage of inventory of an item that has sold by time $t$, where $t$ is in days and day 1 is January 1.

   (a) When did the first item sell? The last item?
   (b) On May 1 (day 121), what percentage of the inventory had been sold?
   (c) Approximately what percentage of the inventory sold during May and June (days 121–181)?
   (d) What percentage of the inventory remained after half of the year had passed (at day 181)?
   (e) Estimate when items went on sale and sold quickly.

% of inventory sold

Figure 7.31

15. The density function for radii $r$ (mm) of spherical raindrops during a storm is constant over the range $0 < r < 5$ and zero elsewhere.

   (a) Find the density function $f(r)$ for the radii.
   (b) Find the cumulative distribution function $F(r)$.

16. Major absorption differences have been reported for different commercial versions of the same drug. One study compared three commercial versions of timed-release theophylline capsules.[9] A theophylline solution was included for comparison. Figure 7.32 shows the cumulative distribution functions $P(t)$, which represent the fraction of the drug absorbed by time $t$. Which curve represents the solution? Compare absorption rates of the four versions of the drug.

fraction of drug
absorbed

Figure 7.32

---

[9] *Progress in Drug Metabolism*, Bridges and Chasseaud (eds.) (New York: Wiley, 1980).

17. In southern Switzerland, most rain falls in the spring and fall; summers and winters are relatively dry. Sketch possible graphs for the density function and the cumulative distribution function of the rain distribution over the course of one year. Put the date on the horizontal axis and fraction of the year's rainfall on the vertical axis.

18. After measuring the duration of many telephone calls, the telephone company found their data was well approximated by the density function $p(x) = 0.4e^{-0.4x}$, where $x$ is the duration of a call, in minutes.

    (a) What percentage of calls last between 1 and 2 minutes?
    (b) What percentage of calls last 1 minute or less?
    (c) What percentage of calls last 3 minutes or more?
    (d) Find the cumulative distribution function.

19. Find the median of the density function given by $p(t) = 0.04 - 0.0008t$ for $0 \le t \le 50$ using the Fundamental Theorem of Calculus.

20. In 1950 an experiment was done observing the time gaps between successive cars on the Arroyo Seco Free-

way. The data[10] show that, if $x$ is time in seconds and $0 \le x \le 40$, the density function of these time gaps is

$$p(x) = 0.122e^{-0.122x}.$$

Find the median and mean time gap. Interpret them in terms of cars on the freeway.

In Problems 21–25, a quantity $x$ is distributed through a population with probability density function $p(x)$ and cumulative distribution function $P(x)$. Decide if each statement is true or false. Give an explanation for your answer.

21. If $p(10) = 1/2$, then half the population has $x < 10$.

22. If $P(10) = 1/2$, then half the population has $x < 10$.

23. If $p(10) = 1/2$, then the fraction of the population lying between $x = 9.98$ and $x = 10.04$ is about $0.03$.

24. If $p(10) = p(20)$, then none of the population has $x$ values lying between 10 and 20.

25. If $P(10) = P(20)$, then none of the population has $x$ values lying between 10 and 20.

## STRENGTHEN YOUR UNDERSTANDING

In Problems 1–30, indicate whether the statement is true or false.

1. If $\int_{-\infty}^{\infty} p(x)\,dx = 1$ then $p(x)$ is a density function.

2. The function given by $p(x) = 0.25$ when $0 \le x \le 4$ and $p(x) = 0$ when $x < 0$ or $x > 4$ is a density function.

3. If $p(x)$ is a density function for the age in years of a population, then $\int_0^{10} p(x)\,dx$ is the fraction of the population with ages between 0 and 10 years.

4. If $p(t)$ is a density function for waiting times in minutes at a bank teller, then $\int_{10}^{15} p(x)\,dx$ is the fraction of the people waiting in line for that teller who wait between 10 and 15 minutes.

5. If $p(x)$ is the density function for age in years of the US population, then $\int_0^{70} p(x)\,dx \approx 0.5$.

6. If $p(x)$ is the density function for age in years of a population, then $p(50)$ is the fraction of the population exactly 50 years old.

7. If $p(x)$ is the density function for age in years of a population, and $p(10) = 0.014$, then about 1.4 percent of the population have ages between 9.5 and 10.5 years.

8. If $p(x)$ is a density function, then $\int_0^{\infty} p(x)\,dx = 0.5$.

9. If $p(x)$ is a density function, then $\int_0^1 p(x)\,dx \le \int_0^2 p(x)\,dx$.

10. If $p(x)$ is a density function, then it could never happen that $\int_0^{100} p(x)\,dx = \int_0^{200} p(x)\,dx$.

11. A cumulative distribution function $P(t)$ can never be decreasing.

12. If $P(t)$ is the cumulative distribution function corresponding to the density function $p(t)$, then $p' = P$.

13. If $P(t)$ is a cumulative distribution function for a population, then $P(30)$ is the fraction of the population with values above 30.

14. If $P(t)$ is a cumulative distribution function for a population, then $P(20) - P(10)$ is the fraction of the population with values between 10 and 20.

15. If $P(t)$ is a cumulative distribution function for a population, then $P(30) - P(10) = P(20)$.

16. If $P(t)$ is a cumulative distribution function for age in years of a population and $P(10) = 0.5$, then one half of the population is less than 10 years old.

17. The units of a density function $p(x)$ and its associated cumulative distribution function $P(x)$ are the same.

18. A cumulative distribution function $P(t)$ satisfies $0 \le P(t) \le 1$ for all $t$.

19. If $P(t)$ is a cumulative distribution function such that $P(10) = 0.05$ and $P(15) = 0.08$, then $P(25) = 0.13$.

20. If $P(t)$ is the cumulative distribution function for a density function $p(x)$, then $P(50) - P(25) = \int_{25}^{50} p(x)\,dx$.

21. If $p(x)$ is the probability density function for a quantity, then the mean value of the quantity is $\int_{-\infty}^{\infty} xp(x)\,dx$.

---

[10]Reported by Daniel Furlough and Frank Barnes.

**22.** If $P(t)$ is the cumulative distribution function for a quantity, then the mean value of the quantity is given by $\int_{-\infty}^{\infty} tP(t)\,dt$.

**23.** If $P(t)$ is the cumulative distribution function for a quantity, then the median value $T$ of the quantity is given by $T = P(0.5)$.

**24.** If $p(x)$ is the density function for a quantity $x$, then the median $T$ satisfies $\int_{-\infty}^{T} p(x)\,dx = 0.5$.

**25.** If $p(x)$ is the density function for a quantity $x$, then the median $T$ satisfies $\int_{T}^{\infty} p(x)\,dx = 0.5$.

**26.** If a quantity has density function $p(x)$, then the mean

value and median are never equal.

**27.** The normal distribution with density function $p(x) = (1/\sqrt{2\pi})e^{-x^2/2}$ has mean $\mu = 0$ and standard deviation $\sigma = 1$.

**28.** The normal distribution with density function $p(x) = (1/\sqrt{2\pi})e^{-(x-5)^2/2}$ has mean $\mu = -5$ and standard deviation $\sigma = 1$.

**29.** The integral $\int_{-\infty}^{\infty} (1/\sqrt{2\pi})e^{-(x-7)^2/2}\,dx$ equals 1.

**30.** The mean value of a quantity $x$ distributed through a population is the value $T$ such that half of the population has values $x$ less than or equal to $T$.

# PROJECTS FOR CHAPTER SEVEN

### 1. Triangular Probability Distribution

Triangular probability distributions, such as the one with density function graphed in Figure 7.33, are used in business to model uncertainty. Such a distribution can be used to model a variable where only three pieces of information are available: a lower bound ($x = a$), a most likely value ($x = c$), and an upper bound ($x = b$).

**Figure 7.33**

Thus, we can write the function $p(x)$ as two linear functions:

$$p(x) = \begin{cases} m_1 x + b_1 & a \le x \le c \\ m_2 x + b_2 & c < x \le b. \end{cases}$$

**(a)** Find the value of $p(c)$ geometrically, using the criterion that the probability that $x$ takes on some value between $a$ and $b$ is 1.

Suppose a new product costs between \$6 and \$10 per unit to produce, with a most likely cost of \$9.

**(b)** Find $p(9)$.

**(c)** Use the fact that $p(6) = p(10) = 0$ and the value of $p(9)$ you found in part (b) to find $m_1$, $m_2$, $b_1$, and $b_2$.

**(d)** What is the probability that the production cost per unit will be less than \$8?

**(e)** What is the median cost?

**(f)** Write a formula for the cumulative probability distribution function $P(x)$ for

    (i) $6 \le x \le 9$,                       (ii) $9 < x \le 10$.

Sketch the graph of $P(x)$.

# Chapter Eight

# FUNCTIONS OF SEVERAL VARIABLES

## Contents

# 8.1 UNDERSTANDING FUNCTIONS OF TWO VARIABLES

In business, science, and politics, outcomes are rarely determined by a single variable. For example, consider an airline's ticket pricing. To avoid flying planes with many empty seats, it sells some tickets at full price and some at a discount. For a particular route, the airline's revenue, $R$, earned in a given time period is determined by the number of full-price tickets, $x$, and the number of discount tickets, $y$, sold. We say that $R$ is a function of $x$ and $y$, and we write

$$R = f(x, y).$$

This is just like the function notation of one-variable calculus. The variable $R$ is the dependent variable and the variables $x$ and $y$ are the independent variables. The letter $f$ stands for the *function* or rule that gives the value, or output, of $R$ corresponding to given values of $x$ and $y$. The collection of all possible inputs, $(x, y)$, is called the *domain* of $f$. We say a function is an *increasing* (*decreasing*) function of one of its variables if it increases (decreases) as that variable increases while the other independent variables are held constant.

A function of two variables can be represented numerically by a table of values, algebraically by a formula, or pictorially by a contour diagram. In this section we give numerical and algebraic examples; contour diagrams are introduced in Section 8.2.

## Functions Given Numerically

The revenue, $R$ (in dollars), from a particular airline route is shown in Table 8.1 as a function of the number of full-price tickets and the number of discount tickets sold.

**Table 8.1**  *Revenue from ticket sales as a function of $x$ and $y$*

|  | Number of full-price tickets, $x$ | | | |
|---|---|---|---|---|
|  | 100 | 200 | 300 | 400 |
| 200 | 75,000 | 110,000 | 145,000 | 180,000 |
| 400 | 115,000 | 150,000 | 185,000 | 220,000 |
| 600 | 155,000 | 190,000 | 225,000 | 260,000 |
| 800 | 195,000 | 230,000 | 265,000 | 300,000 |
| 1000 | 235,000 | 270,000 | 305,000 | 340,000 |

(Number of discount tickets, $y$, labels the rows 200, 400, 600, 800, 1000.)

Values of $x$ are shown across the top, values of $y$ are down the left side, and the corresponding values of $f(x, y)$ are in the table. For example, to find the value of $f(300, 600)$, we look in the column corresponding to $x = 300$ at the row $y = 600$, where we find the number 225,000. Thus,

$$f(300, 600) = 225,000.$$

This means that the revenue from 300 full-price tickets and 600 discount tickets is $225,000. We see in Table 8.1 that $f$ is an increasing function of $x$ and an increasing function of $y$.

Notice how this differs from the table of values of a one-variable function, where one row or one column is enough to list the values of the function. Here many rows and columns are needed because the function has an output for every pair of values of the independent variables.

## Functions Given Algebraically

The function given in Table 8.1 can be represented by a formula. Looking across the rows, we see that each additional 100 full-price tickets sold raises the revenue by $35,000, so each full-price ticket must cost $350. Similarly, looking down a column shows that an additional 200 discount tickets sold increases the revenue by $40,000, so each discount ticket must cost $200. Thus, the revenue function is given by the formula

$$R = 350x + 200y.$$

**Example 1**  Give a formula for the function $M = f(B, t)$ where $M$ is the amount of money in a bank account $t$ years after an initial investment of $B$ dollars, if interest accrues at a rate of 5% per year compounded
(a)  Annually  (b)  Continuously.

Solution    (a) Annual compounding means that $M$ increases by a factor of 1.05 every year, so

$$M = f(B, t) = B(1.05)^t.$$

(b) Continuous compounding means that $M$ grows according to the function $e^{kt}$, with $k = 0.05$, so

$$M = f(B, t) = Be^{0.05t}.$$

**Example 2**    A car rental company charges \$40 a day and 15 cents a mile for its cars.

(a) Write a formula for the cost, $C$, of renting a car as a function of the number of days, $d$, and the number of miles driven, $m$.

(b) If $C = f(d, m)$, find $f(5, 300)$ and interpret it.

Solution    (a) The total cost in dollars of renting a car is 40 times the numbers of days plus 0.15 times the number of miles, so

$$C = 40d + 0.15m.$$

(b) We have

$$f(5, 300) = 40(5) + 0.15(300)$$
$$= 200 + 45$$
$$= 245.$$

We see that $f(5, 300) = 245$. This tells us that if we rent a car for 5 days and drive it 300 miles, it costs us \$245.

## Strategy to Investigate Functions of Two Variables: Vary One Variable at a Time

We can learn a great deal about a function of two variables by letting one variable vary while holding the other fixed. This gives a function of one variable, called a *cross-section* of the original function.

### Concentration of a Drug in the Blood

When a drug is injected into muscle tissue, it diffuses into the bloodstream. The concentration of the drug in the blood increases until it reaches a maximum, and then decreases. The concentration, $C$ (in mg per liter), of the drug in the blood is a function of two variables: $x$, the amount (in mg) of the drug given in the injection, and $t$, the time (in hours) since the injection was administered. We are told that

$$C = f(x, t) = te^{-t(5-x)} \qquad \text{for } 0 \le x \le 4 \text{ and } t \ge 0.$$

**Example 3**    In terms of the drug concentration in the blood, explain the significance of the cross-sections:

(a)  $f(4, t)$                                        (b)  $f(x, 1)$

Solution    (a) Holding $x$ fixed at 4 means that we are considering an injection of 4 mg of the drug; letting $t$ vary means we are watching the effect of this dose as time passes. Thus the function $f(4, t)$ describes the concentration of the drug in the blood resulting from a 4-mg injection as a function of time. Figure 8.1 shows the graph of $f(4, t) = te^{-t}$. Notice that the concentration in the blood from this dose is at a maximum at 1 hour after injection, and that the concentration in the blood eventually approaches zero.

**Figure 8.1**: The function $f(4, t)$ shows the concentration in the blood resulting from a 4-mg injection

**Figure 8.2**: The function $f(x, 1)$ shows the concentration in the blood 1 hour after the injection

(b) Holding $t$ fixed at 1 means that we are focusing on the blood 1 hour after the injection; letting $x$ vary means we are considering the effect of different doses at that instant. Thus, the function $f(x, 1)$ gives the concentration of the drug in the blood 1 hour after injection as a function of the amount injected. Figure 8.2 shows the graph of $f(x, 1) = e^{-(5-x)} = e^{x-5}$. Notice that $f(x, 1)$ is an increasing function of $x$. This makes sense: If we administer more of the drug, the concentration in the bloodstream is higher.

**Example 4**    Continue with $C = f(x, t) = te^{-t(5-x)}$. Graph the cross-sections of $f(a, t)$ for $a = 1, 2, 3$, and 4 on the same axes. Describe how the graph changes for larger values of $a$ and explain what this means in terms of drug concentration in the blood.

**Solution**    The one-variable function $f(a, t)$ represents the effect of an injection of $a$ mg at time $t$. Figure 8.3 shows the graphs of the four functions $f(1, t) = te^{-4t}$, $f(2, t) = te^{-3t}$, $f(3, t) = te^{-2t}$, and $f(4, t) = te^{-t}$ corresponding to injections of 1, 2, 3, and 4 mg of the drug. The general shape of the graph is the same in every case: The concentration in the blood is zero at the time of injection $t = 0$, then increases to a maximum value, and then decreases toward zero again. We see that if a larger dose of the drug is administered, the peak of the graph is later and higher. This makes sense, since a larger dose will take longer to diffuse fully into the bloodstream and will produce a higher concentration when it does.

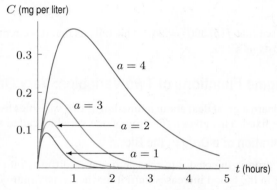

Figure 8.3: Concentration $C = f(a, t)$ of the drug resulting from an $a$-mg injection

## Problems for Section 8.1

Problems 1–2 concern the cost, $C$, of renting a car from a company which charges \$40 a day and 15 cents a mile, so $C = f(d, m) = 40d + 0.15m$, where $d$ is the number of days, and $m$ is the number of miles.

**1.** Make a table of values for $C$, using $d = 1, 2, 3, 4$ and $m = 100, 200, 300, 400$. You should have 16 values in your table.

**2.** (a) Find $f(3, 200)$ and interpret it.
   (b) Explain the significance of $f(3, m)$ in terms of rental car costs. Graph this function, with $C$ as a function of $m$.
   (c) Explain the significance of $f(d, 100)$ in terms of rental car costs. Graph this function, with $C$ as a function of $d$.

**3.** The number, $n$, of new cars sold in a year is a function of the price of new cars, $c$, and the average price of gas, $g$.
   (a) If $c$ is held constant, is $n$ an increasing or decreasing function of $g$? Why?

   (b) If $g$ is held constant, is $n$ an increasing or decreasing function of $c$? Why?

Problems 4–8 refer to Table 8.2, which shows[1] the weekly beef consumption, $C$, (in lbs) of an average household as a function of $p$, the price of beef (in \$/lb) and $I$, annual household income (in \$1000s).

Table 8.2    *Quantity of beef bought (lbs/household/week)*

| | | | $p$ | |
|---|---|---|---|---|
| | | 3.00 | 3.50 | 4.00 | 4.50 |
| | 20 | 2.65 | 2.59 | 2.51 | 2.43 |
| | 40 | 4.14 | 4.05 | 3.94 | 3.88 |
| $I$ | 60 | 5.11 | 5.00 | 4.97 | 4.84 |
| | 80 | 5.35 | 5.29 | 5.19 | 5.07 |
| | 100 | 5.79 | 5.77 | 5.60 | 5.53 |

[1] From Richard G. Lipsey, *An Introduction to Positive Economics*, 3rd Ed. (London: Weidenfeld and Nicolson, 1971).

**4.** Give tables for beef consumption as a function of $p$, with $I$ fixed at $I = 20$ and $I = 100$. Give tables for beef consumption as a function of $I$, with $p$ fixed at $p = 3.00$ and $p = 4.00$. Comment on what you see in the tables.

**5.** How does beef consumption vary as a function of household income if the price of beef is held constant?

**6.** Make a table showing the amount of money, $M$, that the average household spends on beef (in dollars per household per week) as a function of the price of beef and household income.

**7.** Make a table of the proportion, $P$, of household income spent on beef per week as a function of price and income. (Note that $P$ is the fraction of income spent on beef.)

**8.** Express $P$, the proportion of household income spent on beef per week, in terms of the original function $f(I, p)$ which gave consumption as a function of $p$ and $I$.

**9.** The total sales of a product, $S$, can be expressed as a function of the price $p$ charged for the product and the amount, $a$, spent on advertising, so $S = f(p, a)$. Do you expect $f$ to be an increasing or decreasing function of $p$? Do you expect $f$ to be an increasing or decreasing function of $a$? Why?

**10.** Graph the bank-account function $f$ in Example 1 on page 354, holding $B$ fixed at $B = 10, 20, 30$ and letting $t$ vary. Then graph $f$, holding $t$ fixed at $t = 0, 5, 10$ and letting $B$ vary. Explain what you see.

**11.** The heat index is a temperature which tells you how hot it feels as a result of the combination of temperature and humidity. See Table 8.3. Heat exhaustion is likely to occur when the heat index reaches 105°F.

  **(a)** If the temperature is 80°F and the humidity is 50%, how hot does it feel?
  **(b)** At what humidity does 90°F feel like 90°F?
  **(c)** Make a table showing the approximate temperature at which heat exhaustion becomes a danger, as a function of humidity.
  **(d)** Explain why the heat index is sometimes above the actual temperature and sometimes below it.

**12.** Using Table 8.3, graph heat index as a function of humidity with temperature fixed at 70°F and at 100°F. Explain the features of each graph and the difference between them in common-sense terms.

**13.** The monthly payments, $P$ dollars, on a mortgage in which $A$ dollars were borrowed at an annual interest rate of $r\%$ for $t$ years is given by $P = f(A, r, t)$. Is $f$ an increasing or decreasing function of $A$? Of $r$? Of $t$?

**14.** An airport can be cleared of fog by heating the air. The amount of heat required, $H(T, w)$ (in calories per cubic meter of fog), depends on the temperature of the air, $T$ (in °C), and the wetness of the fog, $w$ (in grams per cubic meter of fog). Figure 8.4 shows several graphs of $H$ against $T$ with $w$ fixed.

  **(a)** Estimate $H(20, 0.3)$ and explain what information it gives us.
  **(b)** Make a table of values for $H(T, w)$. Use $T = 0, 10, 20, 30, 40$, and $w = 0.1, 0.2, 0.3, 0.4$.

**Figure 8.4**

In Problems 15–16, the fallout, $V$ (in kilograms per square kilometer), from a volcanic explosion depends on the distance, $d$, from the volcano and the time, $t$, since the explosion:

$$V = f(d, t) = (\sqrt{t})e^{-d}.$$

**15.** On the same axes, graph cross-sections of $f$ with $t = 1$, and $t = 2$. As distance from the volcano increases, how does the fallout change? Look at the relationship between the graphs: how does the fallout change as time passes? Explain your answers in terms of volcanoes.

**16.** On the same axes, graph cross-sections of $f$ with $d = 0$, $d = 1$, and $d = 2$. As time passes since the explosion, how does the fallout change? Look at the relationship between the graphs: how does fallout change as a function of distance? Explain your answers in terms of volcanoes.

**Table 8.3** *Heat index (°F) as a function of humidity (H%) and temperature (T°F)*

|  |  | | | | | $T$ | | | | |
|---|---|---|---|---|---|---|---|---|---|---|
|  |  | 70 | 75 | 80 | 85 | 90 | 95 | 100 | 105 | 110 | 115 |
| $H$ | 0 | 64 | 69 | 73 | 78 | 83 | 87 | 91 | 95 | 99 | 103 |
|  | 10 | 65 | 70 | 75 | 80 | 85 | 90 | 95 | 100 | 105 | 111 |
|  | 20 | 66 | 72 | 77 | 82 | 87 | 93 | 99 | 105 | 112 | 120 |
|  | 30 | 67 | 73 | 78 | 84 | 90 | 96 | 104 | 113 | 123 | 135 |
|  | 40 | 68 | 74 | 79 | 86 | 93 | 101 | 110 | 123 | 137 | 151 |
|  | 50 | 69 | 75 | 81 | 88 | 96 | 107 | 120 | 135 | 150 |  |
|  | 60 | 70 | 76 | 82 | 90 | 100 | 114 | 132 | 149 |  |  |

# 8.2  CONTOUR DIAGRAMS

How can we visualize a function of two variables? Just as a function of one variable can be represented by a graph, a function of two variables can be represented by a surface in space or by a *contour diagram* in the plane. Numerical information is more easily obtained from contour diagrams, so we concentrate on their use.

## Weather Maps

Figure 8.5 shows a weather map from a newspaper. This contour diagram shows the predicted high temperature, $T$, in degrees Fahrenheit (°F), throughout the US on that day. The curves on the map, called *isotherms*, separate the country into zones, according to whether $T$ is in the 60s, 70s, 80s, 90s, or 100s. (*Iso* means same and *therm* means heat.) Notice that the isotherm separating the 80s and 90s zones connects all the points where the temperature is predicted to be exactly 90°F.

If the function $T = f(x, y)$ gives the predicted high temperature (in °F) on this particular day as a function of latitude $x$ and longitude $y$, then the isotherms are graphs of the equations

$$f(x, y) = c$$

where $c$ is a constant. In general, such curves are called *contours*, and a graph showing selected contours of a function is called a contour diagram.

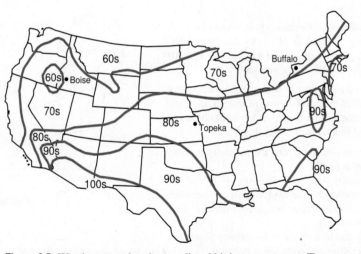

Figure 8.5: Weather map showing predicted high temperatures, $T$, on a summer day

**Example 1**    Estimate the predicted value of $T$ in Boise, Idaho; Topeka, Kansas; and Buffalo, New York.

Solution    Boise and Buffalo are in the 70s region, and Topeka is in the 80s region. Thus, the predicted temperature in Boise and Buffalo is between 70 and 80 while the predicted temperature in Topeka is between 80 and 90.

In fact, we can say more. Although both Boise and Buffalo are in the 70s, Boise is quite close to the $T = 70$ isotherm, whereas Buffalo is quite close to the $T = 80$ isotherm. So we estimate that the temperature will be in the low 70s in Boise and in the high 70s in Buffalo. Topeka is about halfway between the $T = 80$ isotherm and the $T = 90$ isotherm. Thus, we guess that the temperature in Topeka will be in the mid-80s. In fact, the actual high temperatures for that day were 71°F for Boise, 79°F for Buffalo, and 86°F for Topeka.

Figure 8.6: A topographical map showing the region around South Hamilton, NY

## Topographical Maps

Another common example of a contour diagram is a topographical map like that shown in Figure 8.6. Here, the contours separate regions of lower elevation from regions of higher elevation, and give an overall picture of the nature of the terrain. Such topographical maps are frequently colored green at the lower elevations and brown, red, or even white at the higher elevations.

**Example 2**   Explain why the topographical map shown in Figure 8.7 corresponds to the surface of the terrain shown in Figure 8.8.

Figure 8.7: A topographical map

Figure 8.8: Terrain corresponding to the topographical map in Figure 8.7

**Solution**   We see from the topographical map in Figure 8.7 that there are two hills, one with height about 12, and the other with height about 4. Most of the terrain is around height 0, and there is one valley with height about $-4$. This matches the surface of the terrain in Figure 8.8 since there are two hills (one taller than the other) and one valley.

The contours on a topographical map outline the contour or shape of the land. Because every point along the same contour has the same elevation, contours are also called *level curves* or *level sets*. We usually draw contours for equally spaced values of the function. The more closely spaced the contours, the steeper the terrain; the more widely spaced the contours, the flatter the terrain (provided, of course, that the elevation between contours varies by a constant amount). Certain features have distinctive characteristics. A mountain peak is typically surrounded by contours like those in Figure 8.9. A pass in a range of mountains may have contours that look like Figure 8.10. A long valley has parallel contours indicating the rising elevations on both sides of the valley (see Figure 8.11); a long ridge of mountains has the same type of contours, only the elevations decrease on both sides of the ridge. Notice that the elevation numbers on the contours are as important as the curves themselves.

Figure 8.9: Mountain peak

Figure 8.10: Pass between two mountains

Figure 8.11: Long valley

Figure 8.12: Impossible contour lines

There are some things contours cannot do. Two contours corresponding to different elevations cannot cross each other as shown in Figure 8.12. If they did, the point of intersection of the two curves would have two different elevations, which is impossible (assuming the terrain has no over-hangs).

## Using Contour Diagrams

Consider the effect of different weather conditions on US corn production. What would happen if the average temperature were to increase (due to global warming, for example) or if the rainfall were to decrease (due to a drought)? One way of estimating the effect of these climatic changes is to use Figure 8.13. This map is a contour diagram giving the corn production $C = f(R, T)$ in the US as a function of the total rainfall, $R$, in inches, and average temperature, $T$, in degrees Fahrenheit, during the growing season.[2] Suppose at the present time, $R = 15$ inches and $T = 76°$F. Production is measured as a percentage of the present production; thus, the contour through $R = 15, T = 76$ is $C = 100$, that is, $C = f(15, 76) = 100$.

**Example 3**    Use Figure 8.13 to evaluate $f(18, 78)$ and $f(12, 76)$ and explain the answers in terms of corn pro-duction.

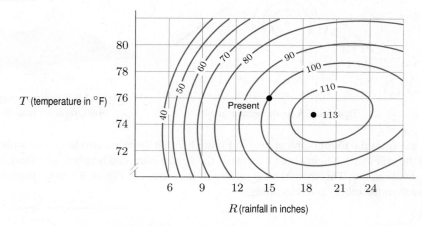

Figure 8.13: Corn production, $C$, as a function of rainfall and temperature

[2] Adapted from S. Beaty and R. Healy, *The Future of American Agriculture*, Scientific American, Vol. 248, No. 2, Febru-ary, 1983.

Solution    The point with $R$-coordinate 18 and $T$-coordinate 78 is on the contour with value $C = 100$, so $f(18, 78) = 100$. This means that if the annual rainfall were 18 inches and the temperature were 78°F, the country would produce about the same amount of corn as at present, although it would be wetter and warmer than it is now. The point with $R$-coordinate 12 and $T$-coordinate 76 is about halfway between the $C = 80$ and $C = 90$ contours, so $f(12, 76) \approx 85$. This means that if the rainfall dropped to 12 inches and the temperature stayed at 76°F, then corn production would drop to about 85% of what it is now.

**Example 4**    Describe how corn production changes as a function of rainfall if temperature is fixed at the present value in Figure 8.13. Describe how corn production changes as a function of temperature if rainfall is held constant at the present value. Give common-sense explanations for your answers.

Solution    To see what happens to corn production if the temperature stays fixed at 76°F but the rainfall changes, look along the horizontal line $T = 76$. Starting from the present and moving left along the line $T = 76$, the values on the contours decrease. In other words, if there is a drought, corn production decreases. Conversely, as rainfall increases, that is, as we move from the present to the right along the line $T = 76$, corn production increases, reaching a maximum of more than 110% when $R = 21$, and then decreases (too much rainfall floods the fields). If, instead, rainfall remains at the present value and temperature increases, we move up the vertical line $R = 15$. Under these circumstances corn production decreases; a 2° increase causes a 10% drop in production. This makes sense since hotter temperatures lead to greater evaporation and hence drier conditions, even with rainfall constant at 15 inches. Similarly, a decrease in temperature leads to a very slight increase in production, reaching a maximum of around 102% when $T = 74$, followed by a decrease (the corn won't grow if it is too cold).

## Cobb-Douglas Production Functions

Suppose you are running a small printing business, and decide to expand because you have more orders than you can handle. How should you expand? Should you start a night shift and hire more workers? Should you buy more expensive but faster computers which will enable the current staff to keep up with the work? Or should you do some combination of the two?

Obviously, the way such a decision is made in practice involves many other considerations—such as whether you could get a suitably trained night shift, or whether there are any faster computers available. Nevertheless, you might model the quantity, $P$, of work produced by your business as a function of two variables: your total number, $N$, of workers, and the total value, $V$, of your equipment. What might the contour diagram of the production function look like?

**Example 5**    Explain why the contour diagram in Figure 8.14 does not model the behavior expected of the production function, whereas the contour diagram in Figure 8.15 does.

Figure 8.14: Incorrect contours for printing production

Figure 8.15: Correct contours for printing production

Solution    Look at  Figure 8.14. Notice that the contour $P = 1$ intersects the $N$- and the $V$- axis, suggesting that it is possible to produce work with no workers or with no equipment; this is unreasonable. However, no contours in Figure 8.15 intersect either the $N$- or the $V$-axis.

In Figure 8.15, fixing $V$ and letting $N$ increase corresponds to moving to the right, crossing contours less and less frequently. Production increases more and more slowly because hiring additional workers does little to boost production if the machines are already used to capacity.

Similarly, if we fix $N$ and let $V$ increase,  Figure 8.15 shows production increasing, but at a decreasing rate. Buying machines without enough people to use them does not increase production much. Thus  Figure 8.15 fits the expected behavior of the production function best.

### The Cobb-Douglas Production Model

In 1928, Cobb and Douglas used a simple formula to model the production of the entire US economy in the first quarter of the $20^{\text{th}}$ century. Using government estimates of $P$, the total yearly production between 1899 and 1922, and of $K$, the total capital investment over the same period, and of $L$, the total labor force, they found that $P$ was well approximated by the function:

$$P = 1.01 L^{0.75} K^{0.25}.$$

This function turned out to model the US economy surprisingly accurately, both for the period on which it was based and for some time afterward. The contour diagram of this function is similar to that in Figure 8.15. In general, production is often modeled by a function of the following form:

---

**Cobb-Douglas Production Function**

$$P = f(N, V) = cN^{\alpha}V^{\beta}$$

where $P$ is the total quantity produced and $c$, $\alpha$, and $\beta$ are positive constants with $0 < \alpha < 1$ and $0 < \beta < 1$.

---

### Contour Diagrams and Tables

Table 8.4 shows the heat index as a function of temperature and humidity. The heat index is a temperature which tells you how hot it feels as a result of the combination of the two. We can also display this function using a contour diagram. Scales for the two independent variables (temperature and humidity) go on the axes. The heat indices shown range from 64 to 151, so we will draw contours at values of 70, 80, 90, 100, 110, 120, 130, 140, and 150. How do we know where the contour for 70 goes? Table 8.4 shows that, when humidity is 0%, a heat index of 70 occurs between $75°F$ and $80°F$, so the contour will go approximately through the point $(76, 0)$. It also goes  through the point $(75, 10)$. Continuing in this way, we can approximate the 70 contour. See Figure 8.16. You can construct all the contours in Figure 8.17 in a similar way.

Table 8.4    *Heat index (°F)*

|            |      | Temperature (°F) |     |     |     |     |     |     |     |     |
|------------|------|------|-----|-----|-----|-----|-----|-----|-----|-----|
|            |      | 70   | 75  | 80  | 85  | 90  | 95  | 100 | 105 | 110 | 115 |
|            | 0    | 64   | 69  | 73  | 78  | 83  | 87  | 91  | 95  | 99  | 103 |
|            | 10   | 65   | 70  | 75  | 80  | 85  | 90  | 95  | 100 | 105 | 111 |
|            | 20   | 66   | 72  | 77  | 82  | 87  | 93  | 99  | 105 | 112 | 120 |
| Humidity (%) | 30 | 67   | 73  | 78  | 84  | 90  | 96  | 104 | 113 | 123 | 135 |
|            | 40   | 68   | 74  | 79  | 86  | 93  | 101 | 110 | 123 | 137 | 151 |
|            | 50   | 69   | 75  | 81  | 88  | 96  | 107 | 120 | 135 | 150 |     |
|            | 60   | 70   | 76  | 82  | 90  | 100 | 114 | 132 | 149 |     |     |

Figure 8.16: The contour for a heat index of 70

Figure 8.17: Contour diagram for the heat index

**Example 6**    Heat exhaustion is likely to occur where the heat index is 105 or higher. On the contour diagram in Figure 8.17, shade in the region where heat exhaustion is likely to occur.

Solution    The shaded region in Figure 8.18 shows the values of temperature and humidity at which the heat index is above 105.

Heat exhaustion is likely here

Figure 8.18: Shaded region shows conditions under which heat exhaustion is likely

## Finding Contours Algebraically

Algebraic equations for the contours of a function $f$ are easy to find if we have a formula for $f(x, y)$. A contour consists of all the points $(x, y)$ where $f(x, y)$ has a constant value, $c$. Its equation is

$$f(x, y) = c.$$

**Example 7**    Draw a contour diagram for the airline revenue function $R = 350x + 200y$. Include contours for $R = 4000, 8000, 12000, 16000$.

Solution    The contour for $R = 4000$ is given by

$$350x + 200y = 4000.$$

This is the equation of a line with intercepts $x = 4000/350 = 11.43$ and $y = 4000/200 = 20$. (See Figure 8.19.) The contour for $R = 8000$ is given by

$$350x + 200y = 8000.$$

This is the equation of a parallel line with intercepts $x = 8000/350 = 22.86$ and $y = 8000/200 = 40$. The contours for $R = 12000$ and $R = 16000$ are parallel lines drawn similarly. (See Figure 8.19.)

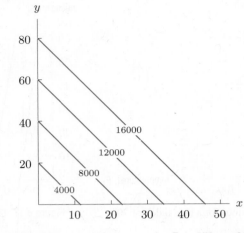

Figure 8.19: A contour diagram for $R = 350x + 200y$

## Problems for Section 8.2

**1.** Figure 8.20 shows contours for the function $z = f(x, y)$. Is $z$ an increasing or a decreasing function of $x$? Is $z$ an increasing or a decreasing function of $y$?

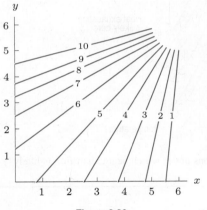

Figure 8.20

**2.** Figure 8.21 is a contour diagram for the sales of a product as a function of the price of the product and the amount spent on advertising. Which axis corresponds to the amount spent on advertising? Explain.

Figure 8.21

**3.** Figure 8.22 shows the contours of the temperature $H$ in a room near a recently opened window. Label the three contours with reasonable values of $H$ if the house is in the following locations.

   **(a)** Minnesota in winter (where winters are harsh).
   **(b)** San Francisco in winter (where winters are mild).
   **(c)** Houston in summer (where summers are hot).
   **(d)** Oregon in summer (where summers are mild).

Figure 8.22

**4.** A topographic map is given in Figure 8.23. How many hills are there? Estimate the $x$- and $y$-coordinates of the tops of the hills. Which hill is the highest? A river runs through the valley; in which direction is it flowing?

Figure 8.23

In Problems 5–12, sketch a contour diagram for the function with at least four labeled contours. Describe in words the contours and how they are spaced.

**5.** $f(x, y) = x + y$      **6.** $f(x, y) = 3x + 3y$

**7.** $f(x, y) = x + y + 1$      **8.** $f(x, y) = 2x - y$

**9.** $f(x, y) = -x - y$      **10.** $f(x, y) = y - x^2$

**11.** $f(x, y) = x^2 + y^2$      **12.** $f(x, y) = xy$

**13.** Draw a contour diagram for $C(d, m) = 40d + 0.15m$. Include contours for $C = 50, 100, 150, 200$.

**14.** Maple syrup production is highest when the nights are cold and the days are warm. Make a possible contour diagram for maple syrup production as a function of the high (daytime) temperature and the low (nighttime) temperature. Label the contours with 10, 20, 30, and 40 (in liters of maple syrup).

**15.** Hiking on a level trail going due east, you decide to leave the trail and climb toward the mountain on your left. The farther you go along the trail before turning off, the gentler the climb. Sketch a possible topographical map showing the elevation contours.

Problems 16–18 refer to the map in Figure 8.5 on page 358.

**16.** Give the range of daily high temperatures for:

**(a)** Pennsylvania      **(b)** North Dakota
**(c)** California

**17.** Sketch a possible graph of the predicted high temperature $T$ on a line north-south through Topeka.

**18.** Sketch possible graphs of the predicted high temperature on a north-south line and an east-west line through Boise.

**19.** A manufacturer sells two products, one at a price of $4000 a unit and the other at a price of $13,000 a unit. A quantity $q_1$ of the first product and $q_2$ of the second product are sold at a total cost of $(4000 + q_1 + q_2)$ to the manufacturer.

**(a)** Express the manufacturer's profit, $\pi$, as a function of $q_1$ and $q_2$.
**(b)** Sketch contours of $\pi$ for $\pi = 10,000$, $\pi = 20,000$, and $\pi = 30,000$ and the break-even curve $\pi = 0$.

**20.** The contour diagram in Figure 8.24 shows your happiness as a function of love and money.

**(a)** Describe in words your happiness as a function of:
  (i) Money, with love fixed.
  (ii) Love, with money fixed.
**(b)** Graph two different cross-sections with love fixed and two different cross-sections with money fixed.

**Figure 8.24**

**21.** Sketch a contour diagram for $z = y - \sin x$. Include at least four labeled contours. Describe the contours in words and how they are spaced.

**22.** Each of the contour diagrams in Figure 8.25 shows population density in a certain region. Choose the contour diagram that best corresponds to each of the following situations. Many different matchings are possible. Pick any reasonable one and justify your choice.

**(a)** The center of the diagram is a city.
**(b)** The center of the diagram is a lake.
**(c)** The center of the diagram is a power plant.

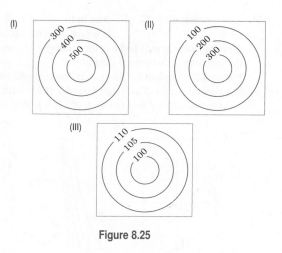

**Figure 8.25**

**23.** Figure 8.26 shows contours of the function giving the species density of breeding birds at each point in the US, Canada, and Mexico.[3] Are the following statements true or false? Explain your answers.

**(a)** Moving from south to north across Canada, the species density increases.

[3]From the undergraduate senior thesis of Professor Robert Cook, Director of Harvard's Arnold Arboretum.

**(b)** In general, peninsulas (for example, Florida, Baja California, the Yucatan) have lower species densities than the areas around them.

**(c)** The species density around Miami is over 100.

**(d)** The greatest rate of change in species density with distance is in Mexico. If this is true, mark the point and direction giving the maximum rate.

Figure 8.26

**24.** The concentration, $C$, of a drug in the blood is given by $C = f(x, t) = te^{-t(5-x)}$, where $x$ is the amount of drug injected (in mg) and $t$ is the number of hours since the injection. The contour diagram of $f(x, t)$ is given in Figure 8.27. Explain the diagram by varying one variable at a time: describe $f$ as a function of $x$ if $t$ is held fixed, and then describe $f$ as a function of $t$ if $x$ is held fixed.

Figure 8.27

**25.** The wind chill tells you how cold it feels as a function of the air temperature and wind speed. Figure 8.28 is a contour diagram of wind chill (°F).

**(a)** If the wind speed is 15 mph, what temperature feels like −20°F?

**(b)** Estimate the wind chill if the temperature is 0°F and the wind speed is 10 mph.

**(c)** Humans are at extreme risk when the wind chill is below −50°F. If the temperature is −20°F, estimate the wind speed at which extreme risk begins.

**(d)** If the wind speed is 15 mph and the temperature drops by 20°F, approximately how much colder do you feel?

Figure 8.28

**26.** In a small printing business, $P = 2N^{0.6}V^{0.4}$, where $N$ is the number of workers, $V$ is the value of the equipment, and $P$ is production, in thousands of pages per day.

**(a)** If this company has a labor force of 300 workers and 200 units worth of equipment, what is production?

**(b)** If the labor force is doubled (to 600 workers), how does production change?

**(c)** If the company purchases enough equipment to double the value of its equipment (to 400 units), how does production change?

**(d)** If both $N$ and $V$ are doubled from the values given in part (a), how does production change?

**27.** Figure 8.29 shows a contour map of a hill with two paths, $A$ and $B$.

**(a)** On which path, $A$ or $B$, will you have to climb more steeply?

**(b)** On which path, $A$ or $B$, will you probably have a better view of the surrounding countryside? (Assume trees do not block your view.)

**(c)** Alongside which path is there more likely to be a stream?

Figure 8.29

**28.** Figure 8.30 shows cardiac output (in liters per minute) in patients suffering from shock as a function of blood pressure in the central veins (in mm Hg) and the time in hours since the onset of shock.[4]

Figure 8.30

(a) In a patient with blood pressure of 4 mm Hg, what is cardiac output when the patient first goes into shock? Estimate cardiac output three hours later. How much time has passed when cardiac output is reduced to 50% of the initial value?

(b) In patients suffering from shock, is cardiac output an increasing or decreasing function of blood pressure?

(c) Is cardiac output an increasing or decreasing function of time, $t$, where $t$ represents the elapsed time since the patient went into shock?

(d) If blood pressure is 3 mm Hg, explain how cardiac output changes as a function of time. In particular, does it change rapidly or slowly during the first two hours of shock? During hours 2 to 4? During the last hour of the study? Explain why this information is useful to a physician treating a patient for shock.

**29.** The cornea is the front surface of the eye. Corneal specialists use a TMS, or Topographical Modeling System, to produce a "map" of the curvature of the eye's surface. A computer analyzes light reflected off the eye and draws level curves joining points of constant curvature. The regions between these curves are colored different colors.

The first two pictures in Figure 8.31 are cross-sections of eyes with constant curvature, the smaller being about 38 units and the larger about 50 units. For contrast, the third eye has varying curvature.

(a) Describe in words how the TMS map of an eye of constant curvature will look.

(b) Draw the TMS map of an eye with the cross-section in Figure 8.32. Assume the eye is circular when viewed from the front, and the cross-section is the same in every direction. Put reasonable numeric labels on your level curves.

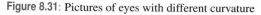

Figure 8.31: Pictures of eyes with different curvature

Figure 8.32

**30.** The power $P$ produced by a windmill is proportional to the square of the diameter $d$ of the windmill and to the cube of the speed $v$ of the wind.[5]

(a) Write a formula for $P$ as a function of $d$ and $v$.

(b) A windmill generates 100 kW of power at a certain wind speed. If a second windmill is built having twice the diameter of the original, what fraction of the original wind speed is needed by the second windmill to produce 100 kW?

(c) Sketch a contour diagram for $P$.

**31.** Antibiotics can be toxic in large doses. If repeated doses of an antibiotic are to be given, the rate at which the medicine is excreted through the kidneys should be monitored by a physician. One measure of kidney function is the glomerular filtration rate, or GFR, which measures the amount of material crossing the outer (or glomerular) membrane of the kidney, in milliliters per minute. A normal GFR is about 125 ml/min. Figure 8.33 gives a contour diagram of the percent, $P$, of a dose of mezlocillin (an antibiotic) excreted, as a function of the patient's GFR and the time, $t$, in hours since the dose was administered. [6]

(a) In a patient with a GFR of 50, approximately how long will it take for 30% of the dose to be excreted?

(b) In a patient with a GFR of 60, approximately what percent of the dose has been excreted after 5 hours?

---

[4] Arthur C. Guyton and John E. Hall, *Textbook of Medical Physiology, Ninth Edition*, p. 288 (Philadelphia: W. B. Saunders, 1996).

[5] From www.ecolo.org/documents/documents_in_english/WindmillFormula.htm, accessed October 9, 2011.

[6] Peter G. Welling and Francis L. S. Tse, *Pharmacokinetics of Cardiovascular, Central Nervous System, and Antimicrobial Drugs*, The Royal Society of Chemistry, 1985, p. 316.

(c) Explain how we can tell from the graph that, for a patient with a fixed GFR, the amount excreted changes very little after 12 hours.

(d) Is the percent excreted an increasing or decreasing function of time? Explain why this makes sense.

(e) Is the percent excreted an increasing or decreasing function of GFR? Explain what this means to a physician giving antibiotics to a patient with kidney disease.

Figure 8.33

32. Each contour diagram (a) and (b) shows satisfaction with quantities of two items $X$ and $Y$ combined. Match (a) and (b) with the items in (I) and (II).

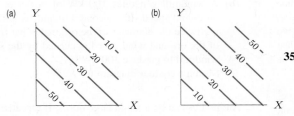

(I)  $X$: Hours worked; $Y$: Time spent commuting
(II) $X$: Hourly wage; $Y$: Time for leisure

33. Each contour diagram (a) and (b) shows satisfaction with quantities of two items $X$ and $Y$ combined. Match (a) and (b) with the items in (I) and (II).

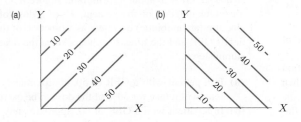

(I)  $X$: Income; $Y$: Leisure time
(II) $X$: Income; $Y$: Hours worked

34. Figure 8.34 shows a contour plot of job satisfaction as a function of the hourly wage and the safety of the workplace. Match the jobs at points $P$, $Q$, and $R$ with the three descriptions.

(a) The job is so unsafe that higher pay alone would not increase my satisfaction very much.

(b) I could trade a little less safety for a little more pay. It would not matter to me.

(c) The job pays so little that improving safety would not make me happier.

Figure 8.34

35. A shopper buys $x$ units of item $A$ and $y$ units of item $B$, obtaining satisfaction $s(x, y)$ from the purchase. (Satisfaction is called *utility* by economists.) The contours $s(x, y) = xy = c$ are called *indifference curves* because they show pairs of purchases that give the shopper the same satisfaction.

(a) A shopper buys 8 units of $A$ and 2 units of $B$. What is the equation of the indifference curve showing the other purchases that give the shopper the same satisfaction? Sketch this curve.

(b) After buying 4 units of item $A$, how many units of $B$ must the shopper buy to obtain the same satisfaction as obtained from buying 8 units of $A$ and 2 units of $B$?

(c) The shopper reduces the purchase of item $A$ by $k$, a fixed number of units, while increasing the purchase of $B$ to maintain satisfaction. In which of the following cases is the increase in $B$ largest?

   • Initial purchase of $A$ is 6 units

   • Initial purchase of $A$ is 8 units

# 8.3  PARTIAL DERIVATIVES

In one-variable calculus we saw how the derivative measures the rate of change of a function. We begin by reviewing this idea.

## Rate of Change of Airline Revenue

In Section 8.1 we saw a two-variable function which gives an airline's revenue, $R$, as a function of the number of full-price tickets, $x$, and the number of discount tickets, $y$, sold:

$$R = f(x, y) = 350x + 200y.$$

If we fix the number of discount tickets at $y = 10$, we have a one-variable function

$$R = f(x, 10) = g(x) = 350x + 2000.$$

The rate of the change of revenue with respect to $x$ is given by the one-variable derivative

$$g'(x) = 350.$$

This tells us that, if $y$ is fixed at 10, then the revenue increases by \$350 for the next additional full-price ticket sold. We call $g'(x)$ the *partial derivative of R with respect to x* at the point $(x, 10)$. If $R = f(x, y)$, we write

$$\frac{\partial R}{\partial x} = f_x(x, 10) = g'(x) = 350.$$

---

**Example 1**    Find the rate of change of revenue, $R$, as $y$ increases with $x$ fixed at $x = 20$.

**Solution**    Substituting $x = 20$ into $R = 350x + 200y$ gives the one-variable function

$$R = h(y) = 350(20) + 200y = 7000 + 200y.$$

The rate of change of $R$ as $y$ increases with $x$ fixed is

$$\frac{\partial R}{\partial y} = f_y(20, y) = h'(y) = 200.$$

---

We call $\partial R/\partial y = f_y(20, y)$ the *partial derivative of R with respect to y* at the point $(20, y)$. The fact that both partial derivatives of $R$ are positive corresponds to the fact that the revenue is increasing as more of either type of ticket is sold.

## Definition of the Partial Derivative

For any function $f(x, y)$ we study the influence of $x$ and $y$ separately on the value $f(x, y)$ by keeping one fixed and letting the other vary. The method of the previous example allows us to calculate the rates of change of $f(x, y)$ with respect to $x$ and $y$. For all points $(a, b)$ at which the limits exist, we make the following definitions:

## Partial Derivatives of $f$ with Respect to $x$ and $y$

The *partial derivative of $f$ with respect to $x$* at $(a, b)$ is the derivative of $f$ with $y$ fixed at $b$:

$$f_x(a, b) = \begin{array}{c} \text{Rate of change of } f \text{ with respect to } x \\ \text{at the point } (a, b) \end{array} = \lim_{h \to 0} \frac{f(a + h, b) - f(a, b)}{h}.$$

The *partial derivative of $f$ with respect to $y$* at $(a, b)$ is the derivative of $f$ with $x$ fixed at $a$:

$$f_y(a, b) = \begin{array}{c} \text{Rate of change of } f \text{ with respect to } y \\ \text{at the point } (a, b) \end{array} = \lim_{h \to 0} \frac{f(a, b + h) - f(a, b)}{h}.$$

If we think of $a$ and $b$ as variables, $a = x$ and $b = y$, we have the **partial derivative functions** $f_x(x, y)$ and $f_y(x, y)$.

Just as with ordinary derivatives, there is an alternative notation:

## Alternative Notation for Partial Derivatives

If $z = f(x, y)$ we can write

$$f_x(x, y) = \frac{\partial z}{\partial x} \qquad \text{and} \qquad f_y(x, y) = \frac{\partial z}{\partial y}$$

$$f_x(a, b) = \left.\frac{\partial z}{\partial x}\right|_{(a,b)} \qquad \text{and} \qquad f_y(a, b) = \left.\frac{\partial z}{\partial y}\right|_{(a,b)}$$

We use the symbol $\partial$ to distinguish partial derivatives from ordinary derivatives. In cases where the independent variables have names different from $x$ and $y$, we adjust the notation accordingly. For example, the partial derivatives of $f(u, v)$ are denoted by $f_u$ and $f_v$.

## Estimating Partial Derivatives from a Table

**Example 2**    An experiment[7] done on rats to measure the toxicity of formaldehyde yielded the data shown in Table 8.5. The values in the table show the percent, $P$, of rats that survived an exposure with concentration $c$ (in parts per million) after $t$ months, so $P = f(t, c)$. Using Table 8.5, estimate $f_t(18, 6)$ and $f_c(18, 6)$. Interpret your answers in terms of formaldehyde toxicity.

**Table 8.5**    *Percent, $P$, of rat population surviving after exposure to formaldehyde vapor*

Time $t$ (months)

|          |     | 0 | 2 | 4 | 6 | 8 | 10 | 12 | 14 | 16 | 18 | 20 | 22 | 24 |
|----------|-----|---|---|---|---|---|----|----|----|----|----|----|----|----|
|          | 0   | 100 | 100 | 100 | 100 | 100 | 100 | 100 | 100 | 100 | 100 | 99 | 97 | 95 |
| Conc. $c$ | 2   | 100 | 100 | 100 | 100 | 100 | 100 | 100 | 100 | 99 | 98 | 97 | 95 | 92 |
| (ppm)    | 6   | 100 | 100 | 100 | 99 | 99 | 98 | 96 | 96 | 95 | 93 | 90 | 86 | 80 |
|          | 15  | 100 | 100 | 100 | 99 | 99 | 99 | 99 | 96 | 93 | 82 | 70 | 58 | 36 |

**Solution**    For $f_t(18, 6)$, we fix $c$ at 6 ppm, and find the rate of change of percent surviving, $P$, with respect to $t$. We have

$$f_t(18, 6) \approx \frac{\Delta P}{\Delta t} = \frac{f(20, 6) - f(18, 6)}{20 - 18} = \frac{90 - 93}{20 - 18} \approx -1.5 \text{ \% per month.}$$

[7]James E. Gibson, *Formaldehyde Toxicity*, p. 125 (Hemisphere Publishing Company, McGraw-Hill, 1983).

This is the rate of change of percent surviving, $P$, *in the time $t$ direction* at the point $(18, 6)$. The fact that it is negative means that $P$ is decreasing as we read across the $c = 6$ row of the table in the direction of increasing $t$ (that is, horizontally from left to right in Table 8.5). For $f_c(18, 6)$, we fix $t$ at 18, and calculate the rate of change of $P$ as we move in the direction of increasing $c$ (that is, from top to bottom in Table 8.5). We have

$$f_c(18, 6) \approx \frac{\Delta P}{\Delta c} = \frac{f(18, 15) - f(18, 6)}{15 - 6} = \frac{82 - 93}{15 - 6} = -1.22\% \text{ per ppm.}$$

The rate of change of $P$ as $c$ increases is about $-1.22\%$ per ppm. This means that as the concentration increases by 1 ppm from 6 ppm, the percent surviving 18 months decreases by about 1.22% per unit increase ppm. The partial derivative is negative because fewer rats survive this long when the concentration of formaldehyde increases. (That is, $P$ goes down as $c$ goes up.)

## Using Partial Derivatives to Estimate Values of the Function

**Example 3**    Use Table 8.5 and partial derivatives to estimate the percent of rats surviving if they are exposed to formaldehyde with a concentration of

(a)   6 ppm for 18.5 months      (b)   18 ppm for 24 months      (c)   9 ppm for 20.5 months

Solution    (a)  Since $t = 18.5$ and $c = 6$, we want to evaluate $P = f(18.5, 6)$. Table 8.5 tells us that $f(18, 6) = 93\%$ and we have just calculated

$$\left.\frac{\partial P}{\partial t}\right|_{(18,6)} = f_t(18, 6) = -1.5\% \text{ per month.}$$

This partial derivative tells us that after 18 months of exposure to formaldehyde at a concentration of 6 ppm, $P$ decreases by 1.5% for every additional month of exposure. Therefore after an additional 0.5 month, we have

$$P \approx 93 - 1.5(0.5) = 92.25\%.$$

(b)  Now we wish to evaluate $f(24, 18)$. The closest entry to this in Table 8.5 is $f(24, 15) = 36$. We keep $t$ fixed at 24 and increase $c$ from 15 to 18. We estimate the rate of change in $P$ as $c$ changes; this is $\partial P / \partial c$. We see from Table 8.5 that

$$\left.\frac{\partial P}{\partial c}\right|_{(24,15)} \approx \frac{\Delta P}{\Delta c} = \frac{36 - 80}{15 - 6} = -4.89\% \text{ per ppm.}$$

The percent surviving 24 months goes down from 36% by about 4.89% for one unit increase in the formaldehyde concentration above 15 ppm. We have:

$$f(24, 18) \approx 36 - 4.89(3) = 21.33\%.$$

We estimate that only about 21% of the rats would survive for 24 months if they were exposed to formaldehyde as strong as 18 ppm. Since this figure is an extrapolation from the available data, we should use it with caution.

(c)  To estimate $f(20.5, 9)$, we use the closest entry $f(20, 6) = 90$. As we move from $(20, 6)$ to $(20.5, 9)$, the percentage, $P$, changes both due to the change in $t$ and due to the change in $c$. We estimate the two partial derivatives at $t = 20$, $c = 6$:

$$\left.\frac{\partial P}{\partial t}\right|_{(20,6)} \approx \frac{\Delta P}{\Delta t} = \frac{86 - 90}{22 - 20} = -2\% \text{ per month,}$$

$$\left.\frac{\partial P}{\partial c}\right|_{(20,6)} \approx \frac{\Delta P}{\Delta c} = \frac{70 - 90}{15 - 6} = -2.22\% \text{ per month.}$$

The change in $P$ due to a change of $\Delta t = 0.5$ month and $\Delta c = 3$ ppm is

$$\Delta P \approx \text{Change due to } \Delta t + \text{Change due to } \Delta c$$
$$= -2(0.5) - 2.22(3)$$
$$= -7.66.$$

So for $t = 20.5$, $c = 9$ we have

$$f(20.5, 9) \approx f(20, 6) - 7.66 = 82.34\%.$$

In Example 3(c), we used the relationship among $\Delta P$, $\Delta t$, and $\Delta c$. In general, the relationship between the change $\Delta f$, in function value $f(x, y)$ and the changes $\Delta x$ and $\Delta y$ is as follows:

---

**Local Linearity**

$$\begin{matrix} \text{Change} \\ \text{in } f \end{matrix} \approx \begin{matrix} \text{Rate of change} \\ \text{in } x\text{-direction} \end{matrix} \cdot \Delta x + \begin{matrix} \text{Rate of change} \\ \text{in } y\text{-direction} \end{matrix} \cdot \Delta y$$

$$\Delta f \approx f_x \cdot \Delta x + f_y \cdot \Delta y$$

---

## Estimating Partial Derivatives from a Contour Diagram

If we move parallel to one of the axes on a contour diagram, the partial derivative is the rate of change of the value of the function on the contours. For example, if the values on the contours are increasing in the direction of positive change, then the partial derivative must be positive.

**Example 4**    Figure 8.35 shows the contour diagram for the temperature $H(x, t)$ (in °F) in a room as a function of distance $x$ (in feet) from a heater and time $t$ (in minutes) after the heater has been turned on. What are the signs of $H_x(10, 20)$ and $H_t(10, 20)$? Estimate these partial derivatives and explain the answers in practical terms.

Figure 8.35: Temperature in a heated room

    The point $(10, 20)$ is on the $H = 80$ contour. As $x$ increases, we move toward the $H = 75$ contour, so $H$ is decreasing and $H_x(10, 20)$ is negative. This makes sense because as we move further from the heater, the temperature drops. On the other hand, as $t$ increases, we move toward the $H = 85$ contour, so $H$ is increasing and $H_t(10, 20)$ is positive. This also makes sense, because it says that as time passes, the room warms up.

To estimate the partial derivatives, use a difference quotient. Looking at the contour diagram, we see there is a point on the $H = 75$ contour about 14 units to the right of $(10, 20)$. Hence, $H$ decreases by 5 when $x$ increases by 14, so the rate of change of $H$ with respect to $x$ is about $\Delta H / \Delta x = -5/14 \approx -0.36$. Thus, we find

$$H_x(10, 20) \approx -0.36°F/ft.$$

This means that near the point 10 feet from the heater, after 20 minutes the temperature drops about 1/3 of a degree for each foot we move away from the heater.

To estimate $H_t(10, 20)$, we look again at the contour diagram and notice that the $H = 85$ contour is about 32 units directly above the point $(10, 20)$. So $H$ increases by 5 when $t$ increases by 32. Hence,

$$H_t(10, 20) \approx \frac{\Delta H}{\Delta t} = \frac{5}{32} \approx 0.16°F/min.$$

This means that after 20 minutes the temperature is going up about 1/6 of a degree in one more minute at the point 10 ft from the heater.

## Using Units to Interpret Partial Derivatives

The units of the independent and dependent variables can often be helpful in explaining the meaning of a partial derivative.

**Example 5**    Suppose that your weight $w$ in pounds is a function $f(c, n)$ of the number $c$ of calories you consume daily and the number $n$ of minutes you exercise daily. Using the units for $w$, $c$ and $n$, interpret in everyday terms the statements

$$\left.\frac{\partial w}{\partial c}\right|_{(2000, 15)} = 0.02 \quad \text{and} \quad \left.\frac{\partial w}{\partial n}\right|_{(2000, 15)} = -0.025.$$

**Solution**    The units of $\partial w / \partial c$ are pounds per calorie. The statement

$$\left.\frac{\partial w}{\partial c}\right|_{(2000, 15)} = 0.02$$

means that if you are presently consuming 2000 calories daily and exercising 15 minutes daily, you will weigh about 0.02 pounds more for one more calorie you consume daily, or about 2 pounds for an extra 100 calories per day. The units of $\partial w / \partial n$ are pounds per minute. The statement

$$\left.\frac{\partial w}{\partial n}\right|_{(2000, 15)} = -0.025$$

means that for the same calorie consumption and number of minutes of exercise, you will weigh about 0.025 pounds less for one extra minute you exercise daily, or about 1 pound less for an extra 40 minutes per day. So if you eat an extra 100 calories each day and exercise about 80 minutes more each day, your weight should remain roughly steady.

## Problems for Section 8.3

1. Using the contour diagram for $f(x, y)$ in Figure 8.36, decide whether each of these partial derivatives is positive, negative, or approximately zero.

   (a)  $f_x(4, 1)$        (b)  $f_y(4, 1)$
   (c)  $f_x(5, 2)$        (d)  $f_y(5, 2)$

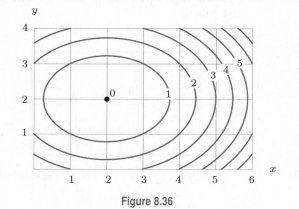

Figure 8.36

2. According to the contour diagram for $f(x, y)$ in Figure 8.36, which is larger: $f_x(3, 1)$ or $f_x(5, 2)$? Explain.

For Problems 3–4 refer to Table 8.4 on page 362 giving the heat index, $I$, in °F, as a function $f(H, T)$ of the relative humidity, $H$, and the temperature, $T$, in °F. The heat index is a temperature which tells you how hot it feels as a result of the combination of humidity and temperature.

3. Estimate $\partial I/\partial H$ and $\partial I/\partial T$ for typical weather conditions in Tucson in summer ($H = 10$, $T = 100$). What do your answers mean in practical terms for the residents of Tucson?

4. Answer the question in Problem 3 for Boston in summer ($H = 50$, $T = 80$).

5. The demand for coffee, $Q$, in pounds sold per week, is a function of the price of coffee, $c$, in dollars per pound and the price of tea, $t$, in dollars per pound, so $Q = f(c, t)$.

   (a) Do you expect $f_c$ to be positive or negative? What about $f_t$? Explain.
   (b) Interpret each of the following statements in terms of the demand for coffee:
   $$f(3, 2) = 780 \quad f_c(3, 2) = -60 \quad f_t(3, 2) = 20$$

6. A drug is injected into a patient's blood vessel. The function $c = f(x, t)$ represents the concentration of the drug at a distance $x$ mm in the direction of the blood flow measured from the point of injection and at time $t$ seconds since the injection. What are the units of the following partial derivatives? What are their practical interpretations? What do you expect their signs to be?

   (a)  $\partial c/\partial x$          (b)  $\partial c/\partial t$

7. The quantity $Q$ (in pounds) of beef that a certain community buys during a week is a function $Q = f(b, c)$ of the prices of beef, $b$, and chicken, $c$, during the week. Do you expect $\partial Q/\partial b$ to be positive or negative? What about $\partial Q/\partial c$?

8. Table 8.6 gives the number of calories burned per minute, $B = f(s, w)$, for someone roller-blading,[8] as a function of the person's weight, $w$, and speed, $s$.

   (a) Is $f_w$ positive or negative? Is $f_s$ positive or negative? What do your answers tell us about the effect of weight and speed on calories burned per minute?
   (b) Estimate $f_w(160, 10)$ and $f_s(160, 10)$. Interpret your answers.

Table 8.6   *Calories burned per minute*

| $w \backslash s$ | 8 mph | 9 mph | 10 mph | 11 mph |
|---|---|---|---|---|
| 120 lbs | 4.2 | 5.8 | 7.4 | 8.9 |
| 140 lbs | 5.1 | 6.7 | 8.3 | 9.9 |
| 160 lbs | 6.1 | 7.7 | 9.2 | 10.8 |
| 180 lbs | 7.0 | 8.6 | 10.2 | 11.7 |
| 200 lbs | 7.9 | 9.5 | 11.1 | 12.6 |

[8]From the August 28, 1994, issue of *Parade Magazine*.

9. Estimate $z_x(1, 0)$ and $z_x(0, 1)$ and $z_y(0, 1)$ from the contour diagram for $z(x, y)$ in Figure 8.37.

Figure 8.37

10. The monthly mortgage payment in dollars, $P$, for a house is a function of three variables:

$$P = f(A, r, N),$$

where $A$ is the amount borrowed in dollars, $r$ is the interest rate, and $N$ is the number of years before the mortgage is paid off.

   (a) $f(92000, 14, 30) = 1090.08$. What does this tell you, in financial terms?
   (b) $\left. \dfrac{\partial P}{\partial r} \right|_{(92000, 14, 30)} = 72.82$. What is the financial significance of the number 72.82?
   (c) Would you expect $\partial P/\partial A$ to be positive or negative? Why?
   (d) Would you expect $\partial P/\partial N$ to be positive or negative? Why?

11. The sales of a product, $S = f(p, a)$, are a function of the price, $p$, of the product (in dollars per unit) and the amount, $a$, spent on advertising (in thousands of dollars).

   (a) Do you expect $f_p$ to be positive or negative? Why?
   (b) Explain the meaning of the statement $f_a(8, 12) = 150$ in terms of sales.

12. Figure 8.13 on page 360 gives a contour diagram of corn production as a function of rainfall, $R$, in inches and temperature, $T$, in °F. Corn production, $C$, is measured as a percentage of the present production, and $C = f(R, T)$. Estimate the following quantities. Give units and interpret your answers in terms of corn production:

   (a)  $f_R(15, 76)$          (b)  $f_T(15, 76)$

**13.** Figure 8.38 shows a contour diagram for the monthly payment $P$ as a function of the interest rate, $r\%$, and the amount, $L$, of a 5-year loan. Estimate $\partial P/\partial r$ and $\partial P/\partial L$ at the point where $r = 8$ and $L = 5000$. Give the units and the financial meaning of your answers.

$L(\$)$

**Figure 8.38**

**14.** Use the diagram from Problem 14 in Section 8.1, to estimate $H_T(T, w)$ for $T = 10, 20, 30$ and $w = 0.1, 0.2, 0.3$. What is the practical meaning of these partial derivatives?

**15.** People commuting to a city can choose to go either by bus or by train. The number of people who choose either method depends in part upon the price of each. Let $f(P_1, P_2)$ be the number of people who take the bus when $P_1$ is the price of a bus ride and $P_2$ is the price of a train ride. What can you say about the signs of $\partial f/\partial P_1$ and $\partial f/\partial P_2$? Explain your answers.

**16.** Suppose that $x$ is the price of one brand of gasoline and $y$ is the price of a competing brand. Then $q_1$, the quantity of the first brand sold in a fixed time period, depends on both $x$ and $y$, so $q_1 = f(x, y)$. Similarly, if $q_2$ is the quantity of the second brand sold during the same period, $q_2 = g(x, y)$. What do you expect the signs of the following quantities to be? Explain.

(a) $\partial q_1/\partial x$ and $\partial q_2/\partial y$
(b) $\partial q_1/\partial y$ and $\partial q_2/\partial x$

**17.** An airline's revenue, $R$, is a function of the number of full-price tickets, $x$, and the number of discount tickets, $y$, sold. Values of $R = f(x, y)$ are in Table 8.1 on page 354.

(a) Evaluate $f(200, 400)$, and interpret your answer.
(b) Is $f_x(200, 400)$ positive or negative? Is $f_y(200, 400)$ positive or negative? Explain.
(c) Estimate the partial derivatives in part (b). Give units and interpret your answers in terms of revenue.

**18.** In Problem 17 the revenue is $150,000 when 200 full-price tickets and 400 discount tickets are sold; that is, $f(200, 400) = 150,000$. Use this fact and the partial derivatives $f_x(200, 400) = 350$ and $f_y(200, 400) = 200$ to estimate the revenue when

(a) $x = 201$ and $y = 400$ (b) $x = 200$ and $y = 405$
(c) $x = 203$ and $y = 406$

**19.** For a function $f(x, y)$, we are given $f(100, 20) = 2750$, and $f_x(100, 20) = 4$, and $f_y(100, 20) = 7$. Estimate $f(105, 21)$.

**20.** For a function $f(r, s)$, we are given $f(50, 100) = 5.67$, and $f_r(50, 100) = 0.60$, and $f_s(50, 100) = -0.15$. Estimate $f(52, 108)$.

**21.** Table 8.5 on page 370 gives the percent of rats surviving, $P$, as a function of time, $t$, in months and concentration of formaldehyde, $c$, in ppm, so $P = f(t, c)$. Use partial derivatives to estimate the percent surviving after 26 months when the concentration is 15.

**22.** The cardiac output, represented by $c$, is the volume of blood flowing through a person's heart per unit time. The systemic vascular resistance (SVR), represented by $s$, is the resistance to blood flowing through veins and arteries. Let $p$ be a person's blood pressure. Then $p$ is a function of $c$ and $s$, so $p = f(c, s)$.

(a) What does $\partial p/\partial c$ represent?

Suppose now that $p = kcs$, where $k$ is a constant.

(b) Sketch the level curves of $p$. What do they represent? Label your axes.
(c) For a person with a weak heart, it is desirable to have the heart pumping against less resistance, while maintaining the same blood pressure. Such a person may be given the drug nitroglycerine to decrease the SVR and the drug Dopamine to increase the cardiac output. Represent this on a graph showing level curves. Put a point $A$ on the graph representing the person's state before drugs are given and a point $B$ for after.
(d) Right after a heart attack, a patient's cardiac output drops, thereby causing the blood pressure to drop. A common mistake made by medical residents is to get the patient's blood pressure back to normal by using drugs to increase the SVR, rather than by increasing the cardiac output. On a graph of the level curves of $p$, put a point $D$ representing the patient before the heart attack, a point $E$ representing the patient right after the heart attack, and a third point $F$ representing the patient after the resident has given the drugs to increase the SVR.

**23.** In each case, give a possible contour diagram for the function $f(x, y)$ if

(a) $f_x > 0$ and $f_y > 0$   (b) $f_x > 0$ and $f_y < 0$
(c) $f_x < 0$ and $f_y > 0$   (d) $f_x < 0$ and $f_y < 0$

**24.** Figure 8.39 shows contours of $f(x, y)$ with values of $f$ on the contours omitted. If $f_x(P) > 0$, find the sign of

(a) $f_y(P)$      (b) $f_y(Q)$      (c) $f_x(Q)$

**25.** Figure 8.40 shows a contour diagram of Dan's happiness with snacks of different numbers of cherries and grapes.

(a) What is the slope of the contours?
(b) What does the slope tell you?

Figure 8.39

Figure 8.40

# 8.4   COMPUTING PARTIAL DERIVATIVES ALGEBRAICALLY

The partial derivative $f_x(x, y)$ is the ordinary derivative of the function $f(x, y)$ with respect to $x$ with $y$ fixed, and the partial derivative $f_y(x, y)$ is the ordinary derivative of $f(x, y)$ with respect to $y$ with $x$ fixed. Thus, we can use all the techniques for differentiation from single-variable calculus to find partial derivatives.

**Example 1**    Let $f(x, y) = x^2 + 5y^2$. Find $f_x(3, 2)$ and $f_y(3, 2)$ algebraically.

**Solution**    We use the fact that $f_x(3, 2)$ is the derivative of $f(x, 2)$ at $x = 3$. To find $f_x$, we fix $y$ at 2:

$$f(x, 2) = x^2 + 5(2^2) = x^2 + 20.$$

Differentiating with respect to $x$ gives

$$f_x(x, 2) = 2x \qquad \text{so} \qquad f_x(3, 2) = 2(3) = 6.$$

Similarly, $f_y(3, 2)$ is the derivative of $f(3, y)$ at $y = 2$. To find $f_y$, we fix $x$ at 3:

$$f(3, y) = 3^2 + 5y^2 = 9 + 5y^2.$$

Differentiating with respect to $y$, we have

$$f_y(3, y) = 10y \qquad \text{so} \quad f_y(3, 2) = 10(2) = 20.$$

**Example 2**    Let $f(x, y) = x^2 + 5y^2$ as in Example 1. Find $f_x$ and $f_y$ as functions of $x$ and $y$.

**Solution**    To find $f_x$, we treat $y$ as a constant. Thus $5y^2$ is a constant and the derivative with respect to $x$ of this term is 0. We have

$$f_x(x, y) = 2x + 0 = 2x.$$

To find $f_y$, we treat $x$ as a constant and so the derivative of $x^2$ with respect to $y$ is zero. We have

$$f_y(x, y) = 0 + 10y = 10y.$$

**Example 3**     Find both partial derivatives of each of the following functions:

(a) $f(x, y) = 3x + e^{-5y}$     (b) $f(x, y) = x^2 y$     (c) $f(u, v) = u^2 e^{2v}$

Solution     (a) To find $f_x$, we treat $y$ as a constant, so the term $e^{-5y}$ is a constant, and the derivative of this term is zero. Likewise, to find $f_y$, we treat $x$ as a constant. We have

$$f_x(x, y) = 3 + 0 = 3 \quad \text{and} \quad f_y(x, y) = 0 + (-5)e^{-5y} = -5e^{-5y}.$$

(b) To find $f_x$, we treat $y$ as a constant, so the function is treated as a constant times $x^2$. The derivative of a constant times $x^2$ is the constant times $2x$, and so we have

$$f_x(x, y) = (2x)y = 2xy \quad \text{Similarly,} \quad f_y(x, y) = (x^2)(1) = x^2.$$

(c) To find $f_u$, we treat $v$ as a constant, and to find $f_v$, we treat $u$ as a constant. We have

$$f_u(u, v) = (2u)(e^{2v}) = 2ue^{2v} \quad \text{and} \quad f_v(u, v) = u^2(2e^{2v}) = 2u^2 e^{2v}.$$

**Example 4**     The concentration $C$ of bacteria in the blood (in millions of bacteria/ml) following the injection of an antibiotic is a function of the dose $x$ (in gm) injected and the time $t$ (in hours) since the injection. Suppose we are told that $C = f(x, t) = te^{-xt}$. Evaluate the following quantities and explain what each one means in practical terms:     (a) $f_x(1, 2)$     (b) $f_t(1, 2)$

Solution     (a) To find $f_x$, we treat $t$ as a constant and differentiate with respect to $x$, giving

$$f_x(x, t) = -t^2 e^{-xt}.$$

Substituting $x = 1, t = 2$ gives

$$f_x(1, 2) = -4e^{-2} \approx -0.54.$$

To see what $f_x(1, 2)$ means, think about the function $f(x, 2)$ of which it is the derivative. The graph of $f(x, 2)$ in Figure 8.41 gives the concentration of bacteria as a function of the dose two hours after the injection. The derivative $f_x(1, 2)$ is the slope of this graph at the point $x = 1$; it is negative because a larger dose reduces the bacteria population. More precisely, the partial derivative $f_x(1, 2)$ gives the rate of change of bacteria concentration with respect to the dose injected, namely a decrease in bacteria concentration of 0.54 million/ml per gram of additional antibiotic injected.

(b) To find $f_t$, treat $x$ as a constant and differentiate using the product rule:

$$f_t(x, t) = 1 \cdot e^{-xt} - xte^{-xt}.$$

Substituting $x = 1, t = 2$ gives

$$f_t(1, 2) = e^{-2} - 2e^{-2} \approx -0.14.$$

To see what $f_t(1, 2)$ means, think about the function $f(1, t)$ of which it is the derivative. The graph of $f(1, t)$ in Figure 8.42 gives the concentration of bacteria at time $t$ if the dose of antibiotic is 1 gm. The derivative $f_t(1, 2)$ is the slope of the graph at the point $t = 2$; it is negative because after 2 hours the concentration of bacteria is decreasing. More precisely, the partial derivative $f_t(1, 2)$ gives the rate at which the bacteria concentration is changing with respect to time, namely a decrease in bacteria concentration of 0.14 million/ml per hour.

Figure 8.41: Bacteria concentration after 2 hours as a function of the quantity of antibiotic injected

Figure 8.42: Bacteria concentration as a function of time if 1 unit of antibiotic is injected

**Example 5**    Let's consider a small printing business where $N$ is the number of workers, $V$ is the value of the equipment (in units of $25,000), and $P$ is the production, measured in thousands of pages per day. Suppose the production function for this company is given by

$$P = f(N, V) = 2N^{0.6}V^{0.4}.$$

(a)  If this company has a labor force of 100 workers and 200 units' worth of equipment, what is the production output of the company?

(b)  Find $f_N(100, 200)$ and $f_V(100, 200)$. Interpret your answers in terms of production.

**Solution**    (a)  We have $N = 100$ and $V = 200$, so

$$\text{Production} = 2(100)^{0.6}(200)^{0.4} = 263.9 \text{ thousand pages per day.}$$

(b)  To find $f_N$, we treat $V$ as a constant and differentiate with respect to $N$:

$$f_N(N, V) = 2(0.6)N^{-0.4}V^{0.4}.$$

Substituting $N = 100, V = 200$ gives

$$f_N(100, 200) = 1.2(100^{-0.4})(200^{0.4}) \approx 1.583 \text{ thousand pages/worker.}$$

This tells us that if we have 200 units of equipment and increase the number of workers by 1 from 100 to 101, the production output will go up by about 1.58 units, or 1580 pages per day.

Similarly, to find $f_V(100, 200)$, we treat $N$ as a constant and differentiate with respect to $V$:

$$f_V(N, V) = 2(0.4)N^{0.6}V^{-0.6}.$$

Substituting $N = 100, V = 200$ gives

$$f_V(100, 200) = 0.8(100^{0.6})(200^{-0.6}) \approx 0.53 \text{ thousand pages/unit of equipment.}$$

This tells us that if we have 100 workers and increase the value of the equipment by 1 unit ($25,000) from 200 units to 201 units, the production goes up by about 0.53 units, or 530 pages per day.

## Second-Order Partial Derivatives

Since the partial derivatives of a function are themselves functions, we can usually differentiate them, giving *second-order partial derivatives*. A function $z = f(x, y)$ has two first-order partial derivatives, $f_x$ and $f_y$, and four second-order partial derivatives.

---

## The Second-Order Partial Derivatives of $z = f(x, y)$

$$\frac{\partial^2 z}{\partial x^2} = f_{xx} = (f_x)_x, \qquad \frac{\partial^2 z}{\partial x \partial y} = f_{yx} = (f_y)_x,$$

$$\frac{\partial^2 z}{\partial y \partial x} = f_{xy} = (f_x)_y, \qquad \frac{\partial^2 z}{\partial y^2} = f_{yy} = (f_y)_y.$$

---

It is usual to omit the parentheses, writing $f_{xy}$ instead of $(f_x)_y$ and $\dfrac{\partial^2 z}{\partial y \partial x}$ instead of $\dfrac{\partial}{\partial y}\left(\dfrac{\partial z}{\partial x}\right)$.

**Example 6**     Use the values of the function $f(x, y)$ in Table 8.7 to estimate $f_{xy}(1, 2)$ and $f_{yx}(1, 2)$.

**Table 8.7**     *Values of $f(x, y)$*

|  |  | $x$ | | |
|---|---|---|---|---|
|  |  | 0.9 | 1.0 | 1.1 |
|  | 1.8 | 4.72 | 5.83 | 7.06 |
| $y$ | 2.0 | 6.48 | 8.00 | 9.60 |
|  | 2.2 | 8.62 | 10.65 | 12.88 |

**Solution**     Since $f_{xy} = (f_x)_y$, we first estimate $f_x$:

$$f_x(1, 2) \approx \frac{f(1.1, 2) - f(1, 2)}{0.1} = \frac{9.60 - 8.00}{0.1} = 16.0,$$

$$f_x(1, 2.2) \approx \frac{f(1.1, 2.2) - f(1, 2.2)}{0.1} = \frac{12.88 - 10.65}{0.1} = 22.3.$$

Thus,

$$f_{xy}(1, 2) \approx \frac{f_x(1, 2.2) - f_x(1, 2)}{0.2} = \frac{22.3 - 16.0}{0.2} = 31.5.$$

Similarly,

$$f_{yx}(1, 2) \approx \frac{f_y(1.1, 2) - f_y(1, 2)}{0.1} \approx \frac{1}{0.1}\left(\frac{f(1.1, 2.2) - f(1.1, 2)}{0.2} - \frac{f(1, 2.2) - f(1, 2)}{0.2}\right)$$

$$= \frac{1}{0.1}\left(\frac{12.88 - 9.60}{0.2} - \frac{10.65 - 8.00}{0.2}\right) = 31.5.$$

Observe that in this example, $f_{xy} = f_{yx}$ at the point $(1, 2)$.

---

**Example 7**     Compute the four second-order partial derivatives of $f(x, y) = xy^2 + 3x^2 e^y$.

**Solution**     From $f_x(x, y) = y^2 + 6xe^y$ we get

$$f_{xx}(x, y) = \frac{\partial}{\partial x}(y^2 + 6xe^y) = 6e^y \quad \text{and} \quad f_{xy}(x, y) = \frac{\partial}{\partial y}(y^2 + 6xe^y) = 2y + 6xe^y.$$

From $f_y(x, y) = 2xy + 3x^2 e^y$ we get

$$f_{yx}(x, y) = \frac{\partial}{\partial x}(2xy + 3x^2 e^y) = 2y + 6xe^y \quad \text{and} \quad f_{yy}(x, y) = \frac{\partial}{\partial y}(2xy + 3x^2 e^y) = 2x + 3x^2 e^y.$$

Observe that $f_{xy} = f_{yx}$ in this example.

## The Mixed Partial Derivatives Are Equal

It is not an accident that the estimates for $f_{xy}(1,2)$ and $f_{yx}(1,2)$ are equal in Example 6, because the same values of the function are used to calculate each one. The fact that $f_{xy} = f_{yx}$ in Example 7 corroborates the following general result:

---

If $f_{xy}$ and $f_{yx}$ are continuous at $(a,b)$, then

$$f_{xy}(a,b) = f_{yx}(a,b).$$

---

Most of the functions we will encounter not only have $f_{xy}$ and $f_{yx}$ continuous, but all their higher-order partial derivatives (such as $f_{xxy}$ or $f_{xyyy}$) will be continuous. We call such functions *smooth*.

## Problems for Section 8.4

Find the partial derivatives in Problems 1–13. The variables are restricted to a domain on which the function is defined.

**1.** $f_x$ and $f_y$ if $f(x,y) = x^2 + 2xy + y^3$

**2.** $f_x$ and $f_y$ if $f(x,y) = 2x^2 + 3y^2$

**3.** $f_x$ and $f_y$ if $f(x,y) = 100x^2 y$

**4.** $f_u$ and $f_v$ if $f(u,v) = u^2 + 5uv + v^2$

**5.** $\dfrac{\partial z}{\partial x}$ if $z = x^2 e^y$

**6.** $\dfrac{\partial Q}{\partial p}$ if $Q = 5a^2 p - 3ap^3$

**7.** $f_t$ if $f(t,a) = 5a^2 t^3$

**8.** $f_x$ and $f_y$ if $f(x,y) = 5x^2 y^3 + 8xy^2 - 3x^2$

**9.** $f_x$ and $f_y$ if $f(x,y) = 10x^2 e^{3y}$

**10.** $z_x$ if $z = x^2 y + 2x^5 y$

**11.** $\dfrac{\partial}{\partial m}\left(\dfrac{1}{2}mv^2\right)$

**12.** $\dfrac{\partial P}{\partial r}$ if $P = 100e^{rt}$

**13.** $\dfrac{\partial A}{\partial h}$ if $A = \frac{1}{2}(a+b)h$

**14.** If $f(x,y) = x^3 + 3y^2$, find $f(1,2)$, $f_x(1,2)$, $f_y(1,2)$.

**15.** If $f(u,v) = 5uv^2$, find $f(3,1)$, $f_u(3,1)$, and $f_v(3,1)$.

**16.** Figure 8.43 is a contour diagram of $f(x,y)$. In each of the following cases, list the marked points in the diagram (there may be none or more than one) at which

   **(a)** $f_x < 0$        **(b)** $f_y > 0$

   **(c)** $f_{xx} > 0$     **(d)** $f_{yy} < 0$

*y*

**Figure 8.43**

**17. (a)** Let $f(x,y) = x^2 + y^2$. Estimate $f_x(2,1)$ and $f_y(2,1)$ using the contour diagram for $f$ in Figure 8.44.

   **(b)** Estimate $f_x(2,1)$ and $f_y(2,1)$ from a table of values for $f$ with $x = 1.9, 2, 2.1$ and $y = 0.9, 1, 1.1$.

   **(c)** Compare your estimates in parts (a) and (b) with the exact values of $f_x(2,1)$ and $f_y(2,1)$ found algebraically.

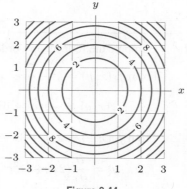

**Figure 8.44**

**18.** The amount of money, $B$, in a bank account earning interest at a continuous rate, $r$, depends on the amount deposited, $P$, and the time, $t$, it has been in the bank, where

$$B = Pe^{rt}.$$

Find $\partial B/\partial t$, $\partial B/\partial r$ and $\partial B/\partial P$ and interpret each in financial terms.

**19.** A company's production output, $P$, is given in tons, and is a function of the number of workers, $N$, and the value of the equipment, $V$, in units of $25,000$. The production function for the company is

$$P = f(N, V) = 5N^{0.75}V^{0.25}.$$

The company currently employs 80 workers, and has equipment worth $750,000$. What are $N$ and $V$? Find the values of $f$, $f_N$, and $f_V$ at these values of $N$ and $V$. Give units and explain what each answer means in terms of production.

**20.** The cost of renting a car from a certain company is $40 per day plus 15 cents per mile, and so we have

$$C = 40d + 0.15m.$$

Find $\partial C/\partial d$ and $\partial C/\partial m$. Give units and explain why your answers make sense.

For Problems 21–32, calculate all four second-order partial derivatives and confirm that the mixed partials are equal.

**21.** $f(x, y) = x^2 y$

**22.** $f(x, y) = xe^y$

**23.** $f(x, y) = x^2 + 2xy + y^2$

**24.** $f(x, y) = \dfrac{2x}{y}, \quad y \neq 0$

**25.** $f = 5 + x^2 y^2$

**26.** $f = e^{xy}$

**27.** $B = 5xe^{-2t}$

**28.** $f(x, t) = t^3 - 4x^2 t$

**29.** $f = 100e^{rt}$

**30.** $Q = 5p_1^2 p_2^{-1}, \quad p_2 \neq 0$

**31.** $V = \pi r^2 h$

**32.** $P = 2KL^2$

**33.** Is there a function $f$ which has the following partial derivatives? If so what is it? Are there any others?

$$f_x(x, y) = 4x^3 y^2 - 3y^4,$$
$$f_y(x, y) = 2x^4 y - 12xy^3.$$

**34.** Show that the Cobb-Douglas function

$$Q = bK^\alpha L^{1-\alpha} \quad \text{where} \quad 0 < \alpha < 1$$

satisfies the equation

$$K\frac{\partial Q}{\partial K} + L\frac{\partial Q}{\partial L} = Q.$$

Problems 35–37 are about the money supply, $M$, which is the total value of all the cash and checking account balances in an economy. It is determined by the value of all the cash, $B$, the ratio, $c$, of cash to checking deposits, and the fraction, $r$, of checking account deposits that banks hold as cash:

$$M = \frac{c+1}{c+r}B.$$

**(a)** Find the partial derivative.

**(b)** Give its sign.

**(c)** Explain the significance of the sign in practical terms.

**35.** $\partial M/\partial B$

**36.** $\partial M/\partial r$

**37.** $\partial M/\partial c$

# 8.5   CRITICAL POINTS AND OPTIMIZATION

To optimize a function means to find the largest or smallest value of the function. If the function represents profit, we may want to find the conditions that maximize profit. On the other hand, if the function represents cost, we may want to find the conditions that minimize cost. In Chapter 4, we saw how to optimize a function of one variable by investigating critical points. In this section, we see how to extend the notions of critical points and local extrema to a function of more than one variable.

## Local and Global Maxima and Minima for Functions of Two Variables

Functions of several variables, like functions of one variable, can have *local* and *global extrema* (that is, local and global maxima and minima). A function has a local extremum at a point where it takes on the largest or smallest value in a small region around the point. Global extrema are the largest or smallest value anywhere. For a function $f$ defined on a domain $R$, we say:

- $f$ has a **local maximum** at $P_0$ if $f(P_0) \geq f(P)$ for all points $P$ near $P_0$
- $f$ has a **local minimum** at $P_0$ if $f(P_0) \leq f(P)$ for all points $P$ near $P_0$
- $f$ has a **global maximum** at $P_0$ if $f(P_0) \geq f(P)$ for all points $P$ in $R$
- $f$ has a **global minimum** at $P_0$ if $f(P_0) \leq f(P)$ for all points $P$ in $R$

**Example 1**    Table 8.8 gives a table of values for a function $f(x, y)$. Estimate the location and value of any global maxima or minima for $0 \le x \le 1$ and $0 \le y \le 20$.

Table 8.8    *Where are the extreme points of this function $f(x, y)$?*

|  |  | \multicolumn{6}{c}{$x$} |
|---|---|---|---|---|---|---|---|
|  |  | 0 | 0.2 | 0.4 | 0.6 | 0.8 | 1.0 |
|  | 0 | 80 | 84 | 82 | 76 | 71 | 65 |
|  | 5 | 86 | 90 | 88 | 73 | 77 | 71 |
| $y$ | 10 | 91 | 95 | 93 | 88 | 82 | 76 |
|  | 15 | 87 | 91 | 89 | 84 | 78 | 72 |
|  | 20 | 82 | 86 | 84 | 79 | 73 | 67 |

**Solution**    The global maximum value of the function appears to be 95 at the point $(0.2, 10)$. Since the table only gives certain values, we cannot be sure that this is exactly the maximum. (The function might have a larger value at, for example, $(0.3, 11)$.) The global minimum value of this function on the points given is 65 at the point $(1, 0)$.

**Example 2**    Figure 8.45 gives a contour diagram for a function $f(x, y)$. Estimate the location and value of any local maxima or minima. Are any of these global maxima or minima on the square shown?

Figure 8.45: Where are the local and global extreme points of this function?

**Solution**    There is a local maximum of above 8 near the point $(6, 5)$, a local maximum of above 6 near the point $(2, 6)$, and a local minimum of below 3 near the point $(3, 2)$. The value above 8 is the global maximum and the value below 3 is the global minimum on the given domain.

In Example 1 and Example 2, we can estimate the location and value of extreme points, but we do not have enough information to find them exactly. This is usually true when we are given a table of values or a contour diagram. To find local or global extrema exactly, we usually need to have a formula for the function.

## Finding a Local Maximum or Minimum Analytically

In one-variable calculus, the local extrema of a function occur at points where the derivative is zero or undefined. How does this generalize to the case of functions of two or more variables? Suppose that a function $f(x, y)$ has a local maximum at a point $(x_0, y_0)$ which is not on the boundary of the domain of $f$. If the partial derivative $f_x(x_0, y_0)$ were defined and positive, then we could increase $f$ by increasing $x$. If $f_x(x_0, y_0) < 0$, then we could increase $f$ by decreasing $x$. Since $f$ has a local maximum at $(x_0, y_0)$, there can be no direction in which $f$ is increasing, so we must have $f_x(x_0, y_0) = 0$. Similarly, if $f_y(x_0, y_0)$ is defined, then $f_y(x_0, y_0) = 0$. The case in which $f(x, y)$ has a local minimum is similar. Therefore, we arrive at the following conclusion:

If a function $f(x, y)$ has a local maximum or minimum at a point $(x_0, y_0)$ not on the boundary of the domain of $f$, then either

$$f_x(x_0, y_0) = 0 \quad \text{and} \quad f_y(x_0, y_0) = 0$$

or (at least) one partial derivative is undefined at the point $(x_0, y_0)$. Points where each of the partial derivatives is either zero or undefined are called **critical points**.

As in the single-variable case, the fact that $(x_0, y_0)$ is a critical point for $f$ does not necessarily mean that $f$ has a maximum or a minimum there.

### How Do We Find Critical Points?

To find critical points of a function $f$, we find the points where both partial derivatives of $f$ are zero or undefined.

**Example 3**    Find and analyze the critical points of $f(x, y) = x^2 - 2x + y^2 - 4y + 5$.

Solution    To find the critical points, we set both partial derivatives equal to zero:

$$f_x(x, y) = 2x - 2 = 0,$$
$$f_y(x, y) = 2y - 4 = 0.$$

Solving these equations gives $x = 1$ and $y = 2$. Hence, $f$ has only one critical point, namely $(1, 2)$. What is the behavior of $f$ near $(1, 2)$? The values of the function in Table 8.9 suggest that the function has a local minimum value of 0 at the point $(1, 2)$.

**Table 8.9**    *Values of $f(x, y)$ near the point $(1, 2)$*

| | | 0.8 | 0.9 | 1.0 | 1.1 | 1.2 |
|---|---|---|---|---|---|---|
| | 1.8 | 0.08 | 0.05 | 0.04 | 0.05 | 0.08 |
| | 1.9 | 0.05 | 0.02 | 0.01 | 0.02 | 0.05 |
| $y$ | 2.0 | 0.04 | 0.01 | 0.00 | 0.01 | 0.04 |
| | 2.1 | 0.05 | 0.02 | 0.01 | 0.02 | 0.05 |
| | 2.2 | 0.08 | 0.05 | 0.04 | 0.05 | 0.08 |

**Example 4**    A manufacturing company produces two products which are sold in two separate markets. The company's economists analyze the two markets and determine that the quantities, $q_1$ and $q_2$, demanded by consumers and the prices, $p_1$ and $p_2$ (in dollars), of each item are related by the equations

$$p_1 = 600 - 0.3q_1 \quad \text{and} \quad p_2 = 500 - 0.2q_2.$$

Thus, if the price for either item increases, the demand for it decreases. The company's total production cost is given by

$$C = 16 + 1.2q_1 + 1.5q_2 + 0.2q_1q_2.$$

If the company wants to maximize its total profits, how much of each product should it produce? What is the maximum profit?[9]

Solution    The total revenue $R$ is the sum of the revenues, $p_1q_1$ and $p_2q_2$, from each market. Substituting for $p_1$ and $p_2$, we get

$$R = p_1q_1 + p_2q_2$$
$$= (600 - 0.3q_1)q_1 + (500 - 0.2q_2)q_2$$
$$= 600q_1 - 0.3q_1^2 + 500q_2 - 0.2q_2^2.$$

[9] Adapted from M. Rosser, *Basic Mathematics for Economists*, p. 316 (New York: Routledge, 1993).

Thus the total profit $\pi$ is given by

$$\pi = R - C$$
$$= 600q_1 - 0.3q_1^2 + 500q_2 - 0.2q_2^2 - (16 + 1.2q_1 + 1.5q_2 + 0.2q_1q_2)$$
$$= -16 + 598.8q_1 - 0.3q_1^2 + 498.5q_2 - 0.2q_2^2 - 0.2q_1q_2.$$

To maximize $\pi$, we compute partial derivatives:

$$\frac{\partial \pi}{\partial q_1} = 598.8 - 0.6q_1 - 0.2q_2,$$

$$\frac{\partial \pi}{\partial q_2} = 498.5 - 0.4q_2 - 0.2q_1.$$

Since the partial derivatives are defined everywhere, the only critical points of $\pi$ are those where the partial derivatives of $\pi$ are both equal to zero. Thus, we solve the equations for $q_1$ and $q_2$,

$$598.8 - 0.6q_1 - 0.2q_2 = 0,$$
$$498.5 - 0.4q_2 - 0.2q_1 = 0,$$

giving

$$q_1 = 699.1 \approx 699 \quad \text{and} \quad q_2 = 896.7 \approx 897.$$

To see whether this is a maximum, we look at a table of values of profit $\pi$ around this point. Table 8.10 suggests that profit is greatest at $(699, 897)$. So the company should produce 699 units of the first product priced at \$390.30 per unit, and 897 units of the second product priced at \$320.60 per unit. The maximum profit is then $\pi(699, 897) = \$432,797$.

Table 8.10    *Does this profit function have a maximum at* $(699, 897)$*?*

| Quantity, $q_2$ | | Quantity, $q_1$ | | |
|---|---|---|---|---|
| | | 698 | 699 | 700 |
| | 896 | 432,796.4 | 432,796.9 | 432,796.8 |
| | 897 | 432,796.7 | 432,797.0 | 432,796.7 |
| | 898 | 432,796.6 | 432,796.7 | 432,796.2 |

## Is a Critical Point a Local Maximum or a Local Minimum?

We can often see whether a critical point is a local maximum or minimum or neither by looking at a table or contour diagram. The following analytic method may also be useful in distinguishing between local maxima and minima.[10] It is analogous to the Second Derivative Test in Chapter 4.

### Second Derivative Test for Functions of Two Variables

Suppose $(x_0, y_0)$ is a critical point where $f_x(x_0, y_0) = f_y(x_0, y_0) = 0$. Let

$$D = f_{xx}(x_0, y_0)f_{yy}(x_0, y_0) - f_{xy}(x_0, y_0)^2.$$

- If $D > 0$ and $f_{xx}(x_0, y_0) > 0$, then $f$ has a local minimum at $(x_0, y_0)$.
- If $D > 0$ and $f_{xx}(x_0, y_0) < 0$, then $f$ has a local maximum at $(x_0, y_0)$.
- If $D < 0$, then we say $f$ has a *saddle point* at $(x_0, y_0)$.
- If $D = 0$, the test is inconclusive.

[10]An explanation of this test can be found, for example, in *Multivariable Calculus* by W. McCallum et al. (New York: John Wiley, 2009).

If $(x_0, y_0)$ is a saddle point of $f$, then it is neither a local maximum nor a local minimum of $f$. Figure 8.46 gives a contour diagram of a function $f$ around a saddle point. As we move in the $y$-direction from the center of the diagram, the value of $f$ decreases; but as we move in the $x$-direction from the center, the value of $f$ increases.

Figure 8.46: A saddle point

**Example 5**    Use the second derivative test to confirm that the critical point $q_1 = 699.1$, $q_2 = 896.7$ gives a local maximum of the profit function $\pi$ of Example 4.

Solution    To see whether or not we have found a maximum point, we compute the second-order partial derivatives:

$$\frac{\partial^2 \pi}{\partial q_1^2} = -0.6, \quad \frac{\partial^2 \pi}{\partial q_2^2} = -0.4, \quad \frac{\partial^2 \pi}{\partial q_1 \partial q_2} = -0.2.$$

Since

$$D = \frac{\partial^2 \pi}{\partial q_1^2}\frac{\partial^2 \pi}{\partial q_2^2} - \left(\frac{\partial^2 \pi}{\partial q_1 \partial q_2}\right)^2 = (-0.6)(-0.4) - (-0.2)^2 = 0.2 > 0,$$

and

$$\frac{\partial^2 \pi}{\partial q_1^2} < 0$$

the second derivative test implies that we have found a local maximum point.

## Problems for Section 8.5

**1.** Figure 8.47 shows contours of $f(x, y)$. List the $x$- and $y$-coordinates and the value of the function at any local maximum and local minimum points, and identify which is which. Are any of these local extrema also global extrema on the region shown? If so, which ones?

**2.** Figure 8.48 shows contours of $f(x, y)$. List $x$- and $y$-coordinates and the value of the function at any local maximum and local minimum points, and identify which is which. Are any of these local extrema also global extrema on the region shown? If so, which ones?

Figure 8.47

Figure 8.48

In Problems 3–5, estimate the position and approximate value of the global maxima and minima on the region shown.

**3.**

**4.**

**5.**

In Problems 6–15, find all the critical points and determine whether each is a local maximum, local minimum, a saddle point, or none of these.

**6.** $f(x, y) = x^2 + 4x + y^2$

**7.** $f(x, y) = x^2 + xy + 3y$

**8.** $f(x, y) = x^2 + y^2 + 6x - 10y + 8$

**9.** $f(x, y) = y^3 - 3xy + 6x$

**10.** $f(x, y) = x^3 + y^2 - 3x^2 + 10y + 6$

**11.** $f(x, y) = x^3 + y^3 - 6y^2 - 3x + 9$

**12.** $f(x, y) = x^3 + y^3 - 3x^2 - 3y + 10$

**13.** $f(x, y) = x^2 - 2xy + 3y^2 - 8y$

**14.** $f(x, y) = x^3 - 3x + y^3 - 3y$

**15.** $f(x, y) = 400 - 3x^2 - 4x + 2xy - 5y^2 + 48y$

**16.** By looking at the weather map in Figure 8.5 on page 358, find the maximum and minimum daily high temperatures in the states of Mississippi, Alabama, Pennsylvania, New York, California, Arizona, and Massachusetts.

**17.** For $f(x, y) = A - (x^2 + Bx + y^2 + Cy)$, what values of $A$, $B$, and $C$ give $f$ a local maximum value of 15 at the point $(-2, 1)$?

**18.** A missile has a guidance device which is sensitive to both temperature, $t°C$, and humidity, $h$. The range in km over which the missile can be controlled is given by

$$\text{Range} = 27{,}800 - 5t^2 - 6ht - 3h^2 + 400t + 300h.$$

What are the optimal atmospheric conditions for controlling the missile?

**19.** The quantity of a product demanded by consumers is a function of its price. The quantity of one product demanded may also depend on the price of other products. For example, if the only chocolate shop in town (a monopoly) sells milk and dark chocolates, the price it sets for each affects the demand of the other. The quantities demanded, $q_1$ and $q_2$, of two products depend on their prices, $p_1$ and $p_2$, as follows:

$$q_1 = 150 - 2p_1 - p_2$$

$$q_2 = 200 - p_1 - 3p_2.$$

**(a)** What does the fact that the coefficients of $p_1$ and $p_2$ are negative tell you? Give an example of two products that might be related this way.

**(b)** If one manufacturer sells both products, how should the prices be set to generate the maximum possible revenue? What is that maximum possible revenue?

**20.** Two products are manufactured in quantities $q_1$ and $q_2$ and sold at prices of $p_1$ and $p_2$, respectively. The cost of producing them is given by

$$C = 2q_1^2 + 2q_2^2 + 10.$$

**(a)** Find the maximum profit that can be made, assuming the prices are fixed.

**(b)** Find the rate of change of that maximum profit as $p_1$ increases.

**21.** A company operates two plants which manufacture the same item and whose total cost functions are

$$C_1 = 8.5 + 0.03q_1^2 \quad \text{and} \quad C_2 = 5.2 + 0.04q_2^2,$$

where $q_1$ and $q_2$ are the quantities produced by each plant. The company is a monopoly. The total quantity demanded, $q = q_1 + q_2$, is related to the price, $p$, by

$$p = 60 - 0.04q.$$

How much should each plant produce in order to maximize the company's profit?[11]

---

[11]Adapted from M. Rosser, *Basic Mathematics for Economists*, p. 318 (New York: Routledge, 1993).

# 8.6  CONSTRAINED OPTIMIZATION

Many real optimization problems are constrained by external circumstances. For example, a city wanting to build a public transportation system has a limited number of tax dollars available. A nation trying to maintain its balance of trade must spend less on imports than it earns on exports. In this section, we see how to find an optimum value under such constraints.

## A Constrained Optimization Problem

Suppose we want to maximize the production of a company under a budget constraint. Suppose production, $f$, is a function of two variables, $x$ and $y$, which are quantities of two raw materials, and

$$f(x, y) = x^{2/3} y^{1/3}.$$

If $x$ and $y$ are purchased at prices of $p_1$ and $p_2$ dollars per unit, what is the maximum production $f$ that can be obtained with a budget of $c$ dollars?

To increase $f$ without regard to the budget, we simply increase $x$ and $y$. However, the budget prevents us from increasing $x$ and $y$ beyond a certain point. Exactly how does the budget constrain us? Suppose that $x$ and $y$ each cost $100 per unit, and suppose that the total budget is $378,000. The amount spent on $x$ and $y$ together is given by $g(x, y) = 100x + 100y$, and since we can't spend more than the budget allows, we must have:

$$g(x, y) = 100x + 100y \leq 378{,}000.$$

The goal is to maximize the function

$$f(x, y) = x^{2/3} y^{1/3}.$$

Since we expect to exhaust the budget, we have

$$100x + 100y = 378{,}000.$$

---

**Example 1**  A company has production function $f(x, y) = x^{2/3} y^{1/3}$ and budget constraint $100x + 100y = 378{,}000$.

(a) If $100,000 is spent on $x$, how much can be spent on $y$? What is the production in this case?

(b) If $200,000 is spent on $x$, how much can be spent on $y$? What is the production in this case?

(c) Which of the two options above is the better choice for the company? Do you think this is the best of all possible options?

Solution

(a) If the company spends $100,000 on $x$, then it has $278,000 left to spend on $y$. In this case, we have $100x = 100{,}000$, so $x = 1000$, and $100y = 278{,}000$, so $y = 2780$. Therefore,

$$\text{Production} = f(1000, 2780) = (1000)^{2/3}(2780)^{1/3} = 1406 \text{ units.}$$

(b) If the company spends $200,000 on $x$, then it has $178,000 left to spend on $y$. Therefore, $x = 2000$ and $y = 1780$, and so

$$\text{Production} = f(2000, 1780) = (2000)^{2/3}(1780)^{1/3} = 1924 \text{ units.}$$

(c) Of these two options, (b) is better since production is larger in this case. This is probably not optimal, since there are many other combinations of $x$ and $y$ that we have not checked.

## Graphical Approach: Maximizing Production Subject to a Budget Constraint

How can we find the maximum value of production? We maximize the *objective function*

$$f(x, y) = x^{2/3}y^{1/3}$$

subject to $x \geq 0$ and $y \geq 0$ and the budget constraint

$$g(x, y) = 100x + 100y = 378,000.$$

The constraint is represented by the line in Figure 8.49. Any point on or below the line represents a pair of values of $x$ and $y$ that we can afford. A point on the line completely exhausts the budget, while a point below the line represents values of $x$ and $y$ which can be bought without using up the budget. Any point above the line represents a pair of values that we cannot afford.

Figure 8.49 also shows some contours of the production function $f$. Since we want to maximize $f$, we want to find the point which lies on the contour with the largest possible $f$ value *and* which lies within the budget. The point we are looking for must lie on the budget constraint because we should spend all the available money. The key observation is this: The maximum occurs at a point $P$ where the budget constraint is tangent to a production contour. (See Figure 8.49.) The reason is that if we are on the constraint line to the left of $P$, moving right on the constraint increases $f$; if we are on the line to the right of $P$, moving left increases $f$. Thus, the maximum value of $f$ on the budget constraint line occurs at the point $P$.

In general, provided $f$ and $g$ are smooth, we have the following result:

---

If $f(x, y)$ has a global maximum or minimum on the constraint $g(x, y) = c$, it occurs at a point where the graph of the constraint is tangent to a contour of $f$, or at an endpoint of the constraint.[12]

---

Figure 8.49: At the optimal point $P$ the budget constraint is tangent to a production contour

## Analytical Approach: The Method of Lagrange Multipliers

Suppose we want to optimize $f(x, y)$ subject to the constraint $g(x, y) = c$. We make the following definition.

---

Suppose $P_0$ is a point satisfying the constraint $g(x, y) = c$.
- $f$ has a **local maximum** at $P_0$ **subject to the constraint** if $f(P_0) \geq f(P)$ for all points $P$ near $P_0$ satisfying the constraint.
- $f$ has a **global maximum** at $P_0$ **subject to the constraint** if $f(P_0) \geq f(P)$ for all points $P$ satisfying the constraint.

Local and global minima are defined similarly.

---

[12]If the constraint has endpoints.

It can be shown[13] that the constraint is tangent to a contour of $f$ at the point which satisfies the equations laid out in the following method.

---

**Method of Lagrange Multipliers** To optimize $f(x, y)$ subject to the constraint $g(x, y) = c$, solve the following system of three equations:

$$f_x(x, y) = \lambda g_x(x, y),$$
$$f_y(x, y) = \lambda g_y(x, y),$$
$$g(x, y) = c,$$

for the three unknowns $x, y$, and $\lambda$; the number $\lambda$ is called the *Lagrange multiplier*. If $f$ has a constrained global maximum or minimum, then it occurs at one of the solutions $(x_0, y_0)$ to this system or at an endpoint of the constraint.

---

**Example 2**     Maximize $f(x, y) = x^{2/3}y^{1/3}$ subject to $100x + 100y = 378{,}000$ and $x \geq 0$, $y \geq 0$.

Solution       Differentiating gives

$$f_x(x, y) = \frac{2}{3}x^{-1/3}y^{1/3} \qquad \text{and} \qquad f_y(x, y) = \frac{1}{3}x^{2/3}y^{-2/3}$$

and

$$g_x(x, y) = 100 \qquad \text{and} \qquad g_y(x, y) = 100,$$

leading to the equations

$$\frac{2}{3}x^{-1/3}y^{1/3} = \lambda(100)$$

$$\frac{1}{3}x^{2/3}y^{-2/3} = \lambda(100)$$

$$100x + 100y = 378{,}000.$$

The first two equations show that we must have

$$\frac{2}{3}x^{-1/3}y^{1/3} = \frac{1}{3}x^{2/3}y^{-2/3}.$$

Using the fact that $x^{-1/3} = 1/x^{1/3}$, we can rewrite this as

$$\frac{2y^{1/3}}{3x^{1/3}} = \frac{x^{2/3}}{3y^{2/3}}.$$

Multiplying through by the denominators gives

$$2y^{1/3}(3y^{2/3}) = x^{2/3}(3x^{1/3}),$$

and simplifying using $y^{1/3} \cdot y^{2/3} = y^1$ gives

$$6y = 3x$$
$$2y = x.$$

---
[13] See W. McCallum et al., *Multivariable Calculus* (New York: John Wiley, 2009).

Since we must also satisfy the constraint $100x + 100y = 378{,}000$, we substitute $x = 2y$ and get

$$100(2y) + 100y = 378{,}000$$
$$300y = 378{,}000$$
$$y = 1260.$$

Since $x = 2y$, we have $x = 2520$. The optimum value occurs at $x = 2520$ and $y = 1260$. For these values,

$$f(2520, 1260) = (2520)^{2/3}(1260)^{1/3} \approx 2000.1.$$

The endpoints of the constraint are the points $(3780, 0)$ and $(0, 3780)$. Since

$$f(3780, 0) = f(0, 3780) = 0,$$

we see that the maximum value of $f$ is approximately 2000 and that it occurs at $x = 2520$ and $y = 1260$.

## The Meaning of $\lambda$

In the previous example, we never found (or needed) the value of $\lambda$. However, $\lambda$ does have a practical interpretation. In the production problem we maximized

$$f(x, y) = x^{2/3}y^{1/3}$$

subject to the constraint

$$g(x, y) = 100x + 100y = 378{,}000.$$

We solved the equations

$$\frac{2}{3}x^{-1/3}y^{1/3} = 100\lambda,$$
$$\frac{1}{3}x^{2/3}y^{-2/3} = 100\lambda,$$
$$100x + 100y = 378{,}000,$$

to get $x = 2520, y = 1260$. Continuing to find $\lambda$ gives us

$$\lambda \approx 0.0053.$$

Suppose now we do another, apparently unrelated calculation. Suppose our budget is increased by \$1000, from \$378,000 to \$379,000. The new budget constraint is

$$100x + 100y = 379{,}000.$$

The corresponding solution is at $x = 2527, y = 1263$ and the new maximum value (instead of $f = 2000.1$) is

$$f = (2527)^{2/3}(1263)^{1/3} \approx 2005.4.$$

The additional \$1000 in the budget increased the production level $f$ by 5.3 units. Notice that production increased by $5.3/1000 = 0.0053$ units per dollar, which is our value of $\lambda$. The value of $\lambda$ represents the extra production achieved by increasing the budget by one dollar—in other words, the extra "bang" you get for an extra "buck" of budget.

Solving for $\lambda$ in either of the equations $f_x = \lambda g_x$ or $f_y = \lambda g_y$ suggests that the Lagrange multiplier is given by the ratio of the changes:

$$\lambda \approx \frac{\Delta f}{\Delta g} = \frac{\text{Change in optimum value of } f}{\text{Change in } g}.$$

These results suggest the following interpretations of the Lagrange multiplier $\lambda$:

- The value of $\lambda$ is approximately the change in the optimum value of $f$ when the value of the constraint is increased by 1 unit.
- The value of $\lambda$ represents the rate of change of the optimum value of $f$ as the constraint increases.

**Example 3**    The quantity of goods produced according to the function $f(x, y) = x^{2/3}y^{1/3}$ is maximized subject to the budget constraint $100x + 100y = 378{,}000$. Suppose the budget is increased to allow a small increase in production. What price must the product sell for if it is to be worth the increased budget?

**Solution**    We know that $\lambda = 0.0053$. Therefore, increasing the budget by \$1 increases production by about $0.0053$ unit. In order to make the increase in budget profitable, the extra goods produced must sell for more than \$1. If the price is $p$ in dollars, we must have $0.0053p > 1$. Thus, we need $p > 1/0.0053 \approx \$189$.

**Example 4**    If $x$ and $y$ are the amounts of raw materials used, the quantity, $Q$, of a product manufactured is

$$Q = xy.$$

Assume that $x$ costs \$20 per unit, $y$ costs \$10 per unit, and the production budget is \$10,000.

(a) How many units of $x$ and $y$ should be purchased in order to maximize production? How many units are produced at that point?

(b) Find the value of $\lambda$ and interpret it.

**Solution**    (a) We maximize $f(x, y) = xy$ subject to the constraint $g(x, y) = 20x + 10y = 10{,}000$ and $x \geq 0$, $y \geq 0$. We have the following partial derivatives:

$$f_x = y, \qquad f_y = x, \qquad \text{and} \qquad g_x = 20, \qquad g_y = 10.$$

The method of Lagrange multipliers gives the following equations:

$$y = 20\lambda$$
$$x = 10\lambda$$
$$20x + 10y = 10{,}000.$$

Substituting values of $x$ and $y$ from the first two equations into the third gives

$$20(10\lambda) + 10(20\lambda) = 10{,}000$$
$$400\lambda = 10{,}000$$
$$\lambda = 25.$$

Substituting $\lambda = 25$ in the first two equations above gives $x = 250$ and $y = 500$.
    The endpoints of the constraint are the point $(500, 0)$ and $(0, 1000)$. Since

$$f(500, 0) = 0 \quad \text{and} \quad f(0, 1000) = 0,$$

the maximum value of the production function is

$$f(250, 500) = 250 \cdot 500 = 125{,}000 \text{ units.}$$

The company should purchase 250 units of $x$ and 500 units of $y$, giving 125,000 units of products.

(b) We have $\lambda = 25$. This tells us that if the budget is increased by \$1, we expect production to go up by about 25 units. If the budget goes up by \$1000, maximum production will increase about 25,000 to a total of roughly 150,000 units.

## The Lagrangian Function

Constrained optimization problems are frequently solved using a *Lagrangian function*, $\mathcal{L}$. For example, to optimize the function $f(x, y)$ subject to the constraint $g(x, y) = c$, we use the Lagrangian function

$$\mathcal{L}(x, y, \lambda) = f(x, y) - \lambda(g(x, y) - c).$$

To see why the function $\mathcal{L}$ is useful, compute the partial derivatives of $\mathcal{L}$:

$$\frac{\partial \mathcal{L}}{\partial x} = \frac{\partial f}{\partial x} - \lambda \frac{\partial g}{\partial x},$$

$$\frac{\partial \mathcal{L}}{\partial y} = \frac{\partial f}{\partial y} - \lambda \frac{\partial g}{\partial y},$$

$$\frac{\partial \mathcal{L}}{\partial \lambda} = -(g(x, y) - c).$$

Notice that if $(x_0, y_0)$ gives a maximum or minimum value of $f(x, y)$ subject to the constraint $g(x, y) = c$ and $\lambda_0$ is the corresponding Lagrange multiplier, then at the point $(x_0, y_0, \lambda_0)$, we have

$$\frac{\partial \mathcal{L}}{\partial x} = 0 \quad \text{and} \quad \frac{\partial \mathcal{L}}{\partial y} = 0 \quad \text{and} \quad \frac{\partial \mathcal{L}}{\partial \lambda} = 0.$$

In other words, $(x_0, y_0, \lambda_0)$ is a critical point for the unconstrained problem of optimization of the Lagrangian, $\mathcal{L}(x, y, \lambda)$.

We can therefore attack constrained optimization problems in two steps. First, write down the Lagrangian function $\mathcal{L}$. Second, find the critical points of $\mathcal{L}$.

## Problems for Section 8.6

In Problems 1–10, use Lagrange multipliers to find the maximum or minimum values of $f(x, y)$ subject to the constraint.

1. $f(x, y) = x + y, \quad x^2 + y^2 = 1$

2. $f(x, y) = x^2 + 4xy, \quad x + y = 100$

3. $f(x, y) = xy, \quad 5x + 2y = 100$

4. $f(x, y) = x^2 + 3y^2 + 100, \quad 8x + 6y = 88$

5. $f(x, y) = 5xy, \quad x + 3y = 24$

6. $f(x, y) = 3x - 2y, \quad x^2 + 2y^2 = 44$

7. $f(x, y) = x^2 + y, \quad x^2 - y^2 = 1$

8. $f(x, y) = xy, \quad 4x^2 + y^2 = 8$

9. $f(x, y) = x^2 + y^2, \quad 4x - 2y = 15$

10. $f(x, y) = x^2 + y^2, \quad x^4 + y^4 = 2$

11. Figure 8.50 shows contours labeled with values of $f(x, y)$ and a constraint $g(x, y) = c$. Mark the approximate points at which:

   (a) $f$ has a maximum
   (b) $f$ has a maximum on the constraint $g = c$.

$g = c$

**Figure 8.50**

12. Figure 8.51 shows contours of $f(x, y)$ and the constraint $g(x, y) = c$. Approximately what values of $x$ and $y$ maximize $f(x, y)$ subject to the constraint? What is the approximate value of $f$ at this maximum?

**Figure 8.51**

**13.** The quantity, $Q$, of a good produced depends on the quantities $x_1$ and $x_2$ of two raw materials used:

$$Q = x_1^{0.3} x_2^{0.7}.$$

A unit of $x_1$ costs \$10, and a unit of $x_2$ costs \$25. We want to maximize production with a budget of \$50 thousand for raw materials.

**(a)** What is the objective function?
**(b)** What is the constraint?

**14.** The quantity, $Q$, of a certain product manufactured depends on the quantity of labor, $L$, and of capital, $K$, used according to the function

$$Q = 900 L^{1/2} K^{2/3}.$$

Labor costs \$100 per unit and capital costs \$200 per unit. What combination of labor and capital should be used to produce 36,000 units of the goods at minimum cost? What is that minimum cost?

**15.** The Cobb-Douglas production function for a product is

$$P = 5 L^{0.8} K^{0.2},$$

where $P$ is the quantity produced, $L$ is the size of the labor force, and $K$ is the amount of total equipment. Each unit of labor costs \$300, each unit of equipment costs \$100, and the total budget is \$15,000.

**(a)** Make a table of $L$ and $K$ values which exhaust the budget. Find the production level, $P$, for each.
**(b)** Use the method of Lagrange multipliers to find the optimal way to spend the budget.

**16.** A firm manufactures a commodity at two different factories. The total cost of manufacturing depends on the quantities, $q_1$ and $q_2$, supplied by each factory, and is expressed by the *joint cost function*,

$$C = f(q_1, q_2) = 2q_1^2 + q_1 q_2 + q_2^2 + 500.$$

The company's objective is to produce 200 units, while minimizing production costs. How many units should be supplied by each factory?

**17.** The quantity, $Q$, of a product manufactured by a company is given by

$$Q = a K^{0.6} L^{0.4},$$

where $a$ is a positive constant, $K$ is the quantity of capital and $L$ is the quantity of labor used. Capital costs are \$20 per unit, labor costs are \$10 per unit, and the company wants costs for capital and labor combined to be no higher than \$150. Suppose you are asked to consult for the company, and learn that 5 units each of capital and labor are being used.

**(a)** What do you advise? Should the company use more or less labor? More or less capital? If so, by how much?
**(b)** Write a one-sentence summary that could be used to sell your advice to the board of directors.

**18.** For a cost function, $f(x, y)$, the minimum cost for a production of 50 is given by $f(33, 87) = 1200$, with $\lambda = 15$. Estimate the cost if the production quota is:

**(a)**  Raised to 51       **(b)**  Lowered to 49

**19.** A company has the production function $P(x, y)$, which gives the number of units that can be produced for given values of $x$ and $y$; the cost function $C(x, y)$ gives the cost of production for given values of $x$ and $y$.

**(a)** If the company wishes to maximize production at a cost of \$50,000, what is the objective function $f$? What is the constraint equation? What is the meaning of $\lambda$ in this situation?
**(b)** If instead the company wishes to minimize the costs at a fixed production level of 2000 units, what is the objective function $f$? What is the constraint equation? What is the meaning of $\lambda$ in this situation?

**20.** You have set aside 20 hours to work on two class projects. You want to maximize your grade (measured in points), which depends on how you divide your time between the two projects.

**(a)** What is the objective function for this optimization problem and what are its units?
**(b)** What is the constraint?
**(c)** Suppose you solve the problem by the method of Lagrange multipliers. What are the units for $\lambda$?
**(d)** What is the practical meaning of the statement $\lambda = 5$?

**21.** A steel manufacturer can produce $P(K, L)$ tons of steel using $K$ units of capital and $L$ units of labor, with production costs $C(K, L)$ dollars. With a budget of \$600,000, the maximum production is 2,500,000 tons, using \$400,000 of capital and \$200,000 of labor. The Lagrange multiplier is $\lambda = 3.17$.

**(a)** What is the objective function?
**(b)** What is the constraint?
**(c)** What are the units for $\lambda$?
**(d)** What is the practical meaning of the statement $\lambda = 3.17$?

**22.** The quantity, $q$, of a product manufactured depends on the number of workers, $W$, and the amount of capital invested, $K$, and is given by the Cobb-Douglas function

$$q = 6W^{3/4}K^{1/4}.$$

In addition, labor costs are $10 per worker and capital costs are $20 per unit and the budget is $3000.

**(a)** What are the optimum number of workers and the optimum number of units of capital?

**(b)** Recompute the optimum values of $W$ and $K$ when the budget is increased by $1. Check that increasing the budget by $1 allows the production of $\lambda$ extra units of the product, where $\lambda$ is the Lagrange multiplier.

**23.** The terminal velocity (meters/second) that a two-stage rocket achieves is a function of the amount of fuel $x_1$ and $x_2$ (measured in liters) loaded into the two stages. You wish to minimize the total quantity of fuel required to achieve a specified terminal velocity, $v_0$.

**(a)** What is the objective function and what are its units?

**(b)** What is the constraint?

**(c)** Suppose you solve the problem by the method of Lagrange multipliers. What are the units for $\lambda$?

**(d)** What is the practical meaning of the statement $\lambda = 8$ when the terminal velocity of the rocket is 50 meters/second?

**24.** Each person tries to balance his or her time between leisure and work. The tradeoff is that as you work less your income falls. Therefore each person has *indifference curves* which connect the number of hours of leisure, $l$, and income, $s$. If, for example, you are indifferent between 0 hours of leisure and an income of $1125 a week on the one hand, and 10 hours of leisure and an income of $750 a week on the other hand, then the points $l = 0$,

$s = 1125$, and $l = 10$, $s = 750$ both lie on the same indifference curve. Table 8.11 gives information on three indifference curves, I, II, and III.

**Table 8.11**

| Weekly income | | | Weekly leisure hours | | |
|---|---|---|---|---|---|
| I | II | III | I | II | III |
| 1125 | 1250 | 1375 | 0 | 20 | 40 |
| 750 | 875 | 1000 | 10 | 30 | 50 |
| 500 | 625 | 750 | 20 | 40 | 60 |
| 375 | 500 | 625 | 30 | 50 | 70 |
| 250 | 375 | 500 | 50 | 70 | 90 |

**(a)** Graph the three indifference curves.

**(b)** You have 100 hours a week available for work and leisure combined, and you earn $10/hour. Write an equation in terms of $l$ and $s$ which represents this constraint.

**(c)** On the same axes, graph this constraint.

**(d)** Estimate from the graph what combination of leisure hours and income you would choose under these circumstances. Give the corresponding number of hours per week you would work.

**25.** If $x_1$ and $x_2$ are the number of items of two goods bought, a customer's utility is

$$U(x_1, x_2) = 2x_1x_2 + 3x_1.$$

The unit cost is $1 for the first good and $3 for the second. Use Lagrange multipliers to find the maximum value of $U$ if the consumer's disposable income is $100. Estimate the new optimal utility if the consumer's disposable income increases by $6.

# CHAPTER SUMMARY

- **Functions of two variables**
  Represented by: tables, graphs, formulas, cross-sections (one variable fixed), contours (function value fixed).

- **Partial derivatives**
  Definition as a difference quotient, interpreting using units, estimating from a contour diagram or a table, computing from a formula, second-order partial derivatives.

- **Optimization**
  Critical points, local and global maxima and minima.

- **Constrained optimization**
  Geometric interpretation of Lagrange multiplier method, solving Lagrange multiplier problems algebraically, interpreting $\lambda$, Lagrangian function.

# REVIEW PROBLEMS FOR CHAPTER EIGHT

**1.** Use Table 8.12. Is $f$ an increasing or decreasing function of $x$? Is $f$ an increasing or decreasing function of $y$?

**Table 8.12**    *Values of a function $f(x, y)$*

| | | | | $y$ | | |
|---|---|---|---|---|---|---|
| | | 0 | 1 | 2 | 3 | 4 | 5 |
| | 0 | 102 | 107 | 114 | 123 | 135 | 150 |
| | 20 | 96 | 101 | 108 | 117 | 129 | 144 |
| $x$ | 40 | 90 | 95 | 102 | 111 | 123 | 138 |
| | 60 | 85 | 90 | 97 | 106 | 118 | 133 |
| | 80 | 81 | 86 | 93 | 102 | 114 | 129 |

**2.** The balance, $B$, in dollars, in a bank account depends on the amount deposited, $A$ dollars, the annual interest rate, $r\%$, and the time, $t$, in months since the deposit, so $B = f(A, r, t)$.

   **(a)** Is $f$ an increasing or decreasing function of $A$? Of $r$? Of $t$?

   **(b)** Interpret the statement $f(1250, 1, 25) \approx 1276$. Give units.

In Problems 3–4, make a contour plot for the function in the region $-2 < x < 2$ and $-2 < y < 2$. What is the equation and the shape of the contours?

**3.** $z = 3x - 5y + 1$      **4.** $z = 2x^2 + y^2$

**5.** Table 8.13 shows the wind-chill factor as a function of wind speed and temperature. Draw a possible contour diagram for this function. Include contours at wind chills of $20°$, $0°$, and $-20°$.

**6.** The temperature adjusted for wind chill is a temperature which tells you how cold it feels, as a result of the combination of wind and temperature.[14] See Table 8.13.

**Table 8.13**  *Temperature adjusted for wind chill (°F) as a function of wind speed and temperature*

| | | Temperature (°F) | | | | | | | |
|---|---|---|---|---|---|---|---|---|---|
| | | 35 | 30 | 25 | 20 | 15 | 10 | 5 | 0 |
| Wind Speed (mph) | 5 | 31 | 25 | 19 | 13 | 7 | 1 | -5 | -11 |
| | 10 | 27 | 21 | 15 | 9 | 3 | -4 | -10 | -16 |
| | 15 | 25 | 19 | 13 | 6 | 0 | -7 | -13 | -19 |
| | 20 | 24 | 17 | 11 | 4 | -2 | -9 | -15 | -22 |
| | 25 | 23 | 16 | 9 | 3 | -4 | -11 | -17 | -24 |

   **(a)** If the temperature is $0°F$ and the wind speed is 15 mph, how cold does it feel?

   **(b)** If the temperature is $35°F$, what wind speed makes it feel like $24°F$?

   **(c)** If the temperature is $25°F$, what wind speed makes it feel like $12°F$?

   **(d)** If the wind is blowing at 20 mph, what temperature feels like $0°F$?

In Problems 7–8, use Table 8.13 to make tables with the given properties.

**7.** The temperature adjusted for wind chill as a function of wind speed for temperatures of $20°F$ and $0°F$.

**8.** The temperature adjusted for wind chill as a function of temperature for wind speeds of 5 mph and 20 mph.

[14]Data from www.nws.noaa.gov/om/windchill, accessed May 30, 2004.

**9.** Figure 8.52 is a contour diagram for the demand for orange juice as a function of the price of orange juice and the price of apple juice. Which axis corresponds to orange juice? Which to apple juice? Explain.

**Figure 8.52**

**10.** Match the following descriptions of a company's success with the contour diagrams of success as a function of money and work in Figure 8.53.

   **(a)** Our success is measured in dollars, plain and simple. More hard work won't hurt, but it also won't help.

   **(b)** No matter how much money or hard work we put into the company, we just can't make a go of it.

   **(c)** Although we are not always totally successful, it seems that the amount of money invested does not matter. As long as we put hard work into the company, our success increases.

   **(d)** The company's success is based on both hard work and investment.

**Figure 8.53**

**11.** Each of the contour diagrams in Figure 8.54 shows population density in a certain region of a city. Choose the contour diagram that best corresponds to each of the following situations. Many different matchings are possible. Pick a reasonable one and justify your choice.

   **(a)** The middle contour is a highway.
   **(b)** The middle contour is an open sewage canal.
   **(c)** The middle contour is a railroad line.

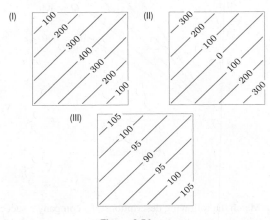

**Figure 8.54**

**12.** Figure 8.55 shows contour diagrams of temperature in °C in a room at three different times. Describe the heat flow in the room. What could be causing this?

**Figure 8.55**

**13.** Figure 8.56 is a contour diagram of the monthly payment on a 5-year car loan as a function of the interest rate and the amount you borrow. The interest rate is 8% and you borrow $6000 for a used car.

   **(a)** What is your monthly payment?
   **(b)** If interest rates drop to 6%, how much more can you borrow without increasing your monthly payment?

   **(c)** Make a table of how much you can borrow, without increasing your monthly payment, as a function of the interest rate.

**Figure 8.56**

**14.** Match tables (a)–(d) with the contour diagrams (I)–(IV) in Figure 8.57.

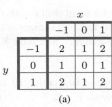

|   | $x$ | | |
|---|---|---|---|
|   | −1 | 0 | 1 |
| −1 | 2 | 1 | 2 |
| $y$  0 | 1 | 0 | 1 |
| 1 | 2 | 1 | 2 |

(a)

|   | $x$ | | |
|---|---|---|---|
|   | −1 | 0 | 1 |
| −1 | 0 | 1 | 0 |
| $y$  0 | 1 | 2 | 1 |
| 1 | 0 | 1 | 0 |

(b)

|   | $x$ | | |
|---|---|---|---|
|   | −1 | 0 | 0 |
| −1 | 2 | 0 | 2 |
| $y$  0 | 2 | 0 | 2 |
| 1 | 2 | 0 | 2 |

(c)

|   | $x$ | | |
|---|---|---|---|
|   | −1 | 0 | 1 |
| −1 | 2 | 2 | 2 |
| $y$  0 | 0 | 0 | 0 |
| 1 | 2 | 2 | 2 |

(d)

**Figure 8.57**

15. Figure 8.58 gives contour diagrams for different Cobb-Douglas production functions $F(L, K)$. Match each contour diagram with the correct statement.

   (A) Tripling each input triples output.

   (B) Quadrupling each input doubles output.

   (C) Doubling each input almost triples output.

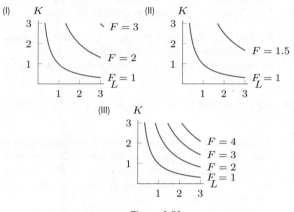

Figure 8.58

16. Figure 8.59 is a contour diagram for $z = f(x, y)$. Is $f_x$ positive or negative? Is $f_y$ positive or negative? Estimate $f(2, 1)$, $f_x(2, 1)$, and $f_y(2, 1)$.

Figure 8.59

17. You borrow $\$A$ at an interest rate of $r\%$ (per month) and pay it off over $t$ months by making monthly payments of $P = g(A, r, t)$ dollars. In financial terms, what do the following statements tell you?

   (a) $g(8000, 1, 24) = 376.59$

   (b) $\left.\dfrac{\partial g}{\partial A}\right|_{(8000,1,24)} = 0.047$

   (c) $\left.\dfrac{\partial g}{\partial r}\right|_{(8000,1,24)} = 44.83$

For Problems 18–20, refer to Table 8.13 on page 395 giving the temperature adjusted for wind chill, $C$, in $°$F, as a function $f(w, T)$ of the wind speed, $w$, in mph, and the temperature, $T$, in $°$F. The temperature adjusted for wind chill tells you how cold it feels, as a result of the combination of wind and temperature.

18. Estimate $f_w(10, 25)$. What does your answer mean in practical terms?

19. Estimate $f_T(5, 20)$. What does your answer mean in practical terms?

20. From Table 8.13 you can see that when the temperature is $20°$F, the temperature adjusted for wind-chill drops by an average of about $0.8°$F with every 1 mph increase in wind speed from 5 mph to 10 mph. Which partial derivative is this telling you about?

21. In the 1940s the quantity, $q$, of beer sold each year in Britain was found to depend on $I$ (the aggregate personal income, adjusted for taxes and inflation), $p_1$ (the average price of beer), and $p_2$ (the average price of all other goods and services). Would you expect $\partial q/\partial I$, $\partial q/\partial p_1$, $\partial q/\partial p_2$ to be positive or negative? Give reasons for your answers.

22. The average price of large cars getting low gas mileage ("gas guzzlers") is $x$ and the average price of a gallon of gasoline is $y$. The number, $q_1$, of gas guzzlers bought in a year, depends on both $x$ and $y$, so $q_1 = f(x, y)$. Similarly, if $q_2$ is the number of gallons of gas bought to fill gas guzzlers in a year, then $q_2 = g(x, y)$.

   (a) What do you expect the signs of $\partial q_1/\partial x$ and $\partial q_2/\partial y$ to be? Explain.

   (b) What do you expect the signs of $\partial q_1/\partial y$ and $\partial q_2/\partial x$ to be? Explain.

23. Figure 8.60 shows the density of the fox population $P$ (in foxes per square kilometer) for southern England. Draw two different graphs of the fox population as a function of kilometers north, with kilometers east fixed at two different values, and draw two different graphs of the fox population as a function of kilometers east, with kilometers north fixed at two different values.

Figure 8.60

**24.** Figure 8.60 gives a contour diagram for the number $n$ of foxes per square kilometer in southwestern England. Estimate $\partial n/\partial x$ and $\partial n/\partial y$ at the points $A$, $B$, and $C$, where $x$ is kilometers east and $y$ is kilometers north.

Find the partial derivatives in Problems 25–30. The variables are restricted to a domain on which the function is defined.

**25.** $f_x$ and $f_y$ if $f(x,y) = x^2 + xy + y^2$

**26.** $P_a$ and $P_b$ if $P = a^2 - 2ab^2$

**27.** $\dfrac{\partial Q}{\partial p_1}$ and $\dfrac{\partial Q}{\partial p_2}$ if $Q = 50p_1p_2 - p_2^2$

**28.** $\dfrac{\partial f}{\partial x}$ and $\dfrac{\partial f}{\partial t}$ if $f = 5xe^{-2t}$

**29.** $\dfrac{\partial P}{\partial K}$ and $\dfrac{\partial P}{\partial L}$ if $P = 10K^{0.7}L^{0.3}$

**30.** $f_x$ and $f_y$ if $f(x,y) = \sqrt{x^2 + y^2}$

**31.** A manufacturing company produces two items in quantities $q_1$ and $q_2$, respectively. Total production costs are given by

$$\text{Cost} = f(q_1, q_2) = 16 + 1.2q_1 + 1.5q_2 + 0.2q_1q_2.$$

Find $f(500, 1000)$, $f_{q_1}(500, 1000)$, and $f_{q_2}(500, 1000)$. Give units with your answers and interpret each of your answers in terms of production cost.

**32.** The Cobb-Douglas production function for a product is given by

$$Q = 25K^{0.75}L^{0.25},$$

where $Q$ is the quantity produced for a capital investment of $K$ dollars and a labor investment of $L$.

   **(a)** Find $Q_K$ and $Q_L$.

   **(b)** Find the values of $Q$, $Q_K$ and $Q_L$ given that $K = 60$ and $L = 100$.

   **(c)** Interpret each of the values you found in part (b) in terms of production.

**33.** You are an anthropologist observing a native ritual. Sixteen people arrange themselves with their backs to you along a bench; all but the three on the far left side are seated. The first person on the far left is standing with her hands at her side, the second is standing with his hands raised and the third is standing with her hands at her side. At some unseen signal, the first one sits down, and everyone else copies what his neighbor to the left was doing one second earlier. Every second that passes, this behavior is repeated until all are once again seated.

   **(a)** Draw graphs at several different times showing how the height depends upon the distance along the bench.

   **(b)** Graph the location of the raised hands as a function of time.

   **(c)** What US ritual is most closely related to what you have observed?

**34.** You are in a stadium doing the wave. This is a ritual in which members of the audience stand up and down in such a way as to create a wave that moves around the stadium. Normally a single wave travels all the way around the stadium, but we assume there is a continuous sequence of waves. Let $h(x,t) = 5 + \cos(0.5x - t)$ be the function describing this stadium wave. The value of $h(x,t)$ gives the height (in feet) of the head of the spectator in seat $x$ at time $t$ seconds. Evaluate $h_x(2,5)$ and $h_t(2,5)$ and interpret each in terms of the wave.

**35.** Find all critical points of $f(x,y) = x^3 - 3x + y^2$. Make a table of values to determine if each critical point is a local minimum, a local maximum, a saddle point, or none of these.

**36.** Find all critical points of $f(x,y) = x^2 + 3y^2 - 4x + 6y + 10$.

**37.** A company sells two products which are partial substitutes for each other, such as coffee and tea. If the price of one product rises, then the demand for the other product rises. The quantities demanded, $q_1$ and $q_2$, are given as a function of the prices, $p_1$ and $p_2$, by

$$q_1 = 517 - 3.5p_1 + 0.8p_2, \quad q_2 = 770 - 4.4p_2 + 1.4p_1.$$

   **(a)** Write total sales revenue as a function of $p_1$ and $p_2$.

   **(b)** What prices should the company charge in order to maximize the total sales revenue?[15]

Figure 8.61 shows contours of $f$. In Problems 38–40 give an approximate maximum or minimum value of $f$ for $0 \le x \le 300$, $0 \le y \le 300$ subject to the given constraint.

**Figure 8.61**

**38.** Minimum, constraint is $y = 100$

**39.** Maximum, constraint is $y = 100$

**40.** Maximum, constraint is $y = x$

---

[15]Adapted from M. Rosser, *Basic Mathematics for Economists*, p. 318 (New York: Routledge, 1993).

**41.** The quantity, $Q$, of a good produced depends on the quantities $x_1$ and $x_2$ of two raw materials used:

$$Q = x_1^{0.6} x_2^{0.4}.$$

A unit of $x_1$ costs \$127 and a unit of $x_2$ costs \$92. We want to minimize the cost, $C$, of producing 500 units of the good.

    **(a)** What is the objective function?
    **(b)** What is the constraint?
    **(c)** Explain what the Lagrange multiplier, $\lambda = 219$, tells us about production.

**42.** Figure 8.62 shows level curves for production $f(x, y)$ as a function of the quantities $x$ and $y$ of two raw materials utilized. The cost of the materials is $15x + 20y$ thousand dollars. What is the maximum production possible with a budget of 300 thousand dollars? How much of each raw material should be purchased to achieve this maximum?

**Figure 8.62**

**43.** An automobile manufacturing plant currently employs 1500 workers and has capital investment of 15 million dollars per month. The production function is

$$Q = x^{0.4} y^{0.6},$$

where $Q$ is the number of cars produced per month, $x$ is the number of workers and $y$ is capital investment. Each

worker's salary is \$5000 per month and each unit of capital costs \$4000 per month.

    **(a)** How many cars is the factory currently assembling each month?
    **(b)** Due to the sluggish economy, the factory decides to decrease production to 2000 cars per month. The factory wants to minimize the cost of producing these 2000 cars. How many workers will need to be laid off? By what amount should monthly investment be decreased?
    **(c)** Give the value of the Lagrange multiplier, $\lambda$, and interpret it in terms of the car factory.

**44.** A company manufactures $x$ units of one item and $y$ units of another. The total cost in dollars, $C$, of producing these two items is approximated by the function

$$C = 5x^2 + 2xy + 3y^2 + 800.$$

    **(a)** If the production quota for the total number of items (both types combined) is 39, find the minimum production cost.
    **(b)** Estimate the additional production cost or savings if the production quota is raised to 40 or lowered to 38.

**45.** A monopolistic producer of two goods A and B has a joint total cost function

$$C = 10q_1 + q_1 q_2 + 10q_2,$$

where $q_1$ and $q_2$ denote the quantities of A and B respectively. The demand curves for the corresponding prices $p_1$ and $p_2$ are

$$p_1 = 50 - q_1 + q_2$$
$$p_2 = 30 + 2q_1 - q_2.$$

    **(a)** Find the maximum profit if the firm produces a total of 15.
    **(b)** Estimate the new optimal profit if the production quota increases by one unit.

# STRENGTHEN YOUR UNDERSTANDING

In Problems 1–60, indicate whether the statement is true or false.

  **1.** If $Q = f(x, t)$ gives the quantity $Q$ of pollutants, in ppm (parts per million), at a distance $x$ kilometers from a waste incinerator at time $t$ hours after incineration ends, we have $f(1.5, 6) = 4.1$. The units for 1.5 are ppm.

  **2.** If $Q = f(x, t)$ gives the quantity $Q$ of pollutants, in ppm (parts per million), at a distance $x$ kilometers from a waste incinerator at time $t$ hours after incineration ends, we have $f(1.5, 6) = 4.1$. The units for 6 are hours.

  **3.** If $Q = f(x, t)$ gives the quantity $Q$ of pollutants, in ppm (parts per million), at a distance $x$ kilometers from a

waste incinerator at time $t$ hours after incineration ends, we have $f(1.5, 6) = 4.1$. The units for 4.1 are kilometers.

  **4.** If $Q = f(x, t)$ gives the quantity $Q$ of pollutants, in ppm (parts per million), at a distance $x$ kilometers from a waste incinerator at time $t$ hours after incineration ends, then $Q$ is most likely an increasing function of $x$.

  **5.** If $Q = f(x, t)$ gives the quantity $Q$ of pollutants, in ppm (parts per million), at a distance $x$ kilometers from a waste incinerator at time $t$ hours after incineration ends, in the statement $f(2, 3) = 5$, the units of the 2 are km.

6. If $f(x, y)$ is a function of two variables, then $f$ is an increasing function of $x$ if $f$ increases when both $x$ increases and $y$ increases.

7. A function $f(x, y)$ can be both an increasing function of $x$ and a decreasing function of $y$.

8. The function $f(x, y) = x^2 - y$ is a decreasing function of $y$.

9. If $f(x, y) = e^{xy} - y^2$, then the cross-section $x = 1$ is $f(1, y) = e^y - 1$.

10. If $f(x, y) = e^{xy} - y^2$, then the cross-section $y = 0$ is $f(x, 0) = 0$.

11. The function $f(x, y) = y + 3x - 1$ has contours which are lines.

12. The function $f(x, y) = x^2 - y$ has contours which are parabolas.

13. For a given function $f(x, y)$ the two contours $f(x, y) = 1$ and $f(x, y) = 2$ can never intersect.

14. Contours of the function $g(x, y) = 3x + 2y$ are parallel lines.

15. The function $P = 3N^{1/2}V^{1/2}$ is a Cobb-Douglas production function.

16. The function $P = 10N^3V^2$ is a Cobb-Douglas production function.

17. The function $f(x, y)$ has the same value at all points along a specific contour.

18. A contour can consist of a single point.

19. Contours of a Cobb-Douglas production function are decreasing, concave up.

20. Every point in the domain of $g(x, y)$ has a contour that contains it.

21. The partial derivative $f_x(a, b)$ is the rate of change of the function $f$ with respect to $x$ at the point $(a, b)$ with $y$ fixed at $b$.

22. If $P = f(m, t)$ gives the price $P$ (in dollars) of a used car as a function of its mileage $m$ (in miles) and its age $t$ (in years), then $\partial P / \partial m$ has units miles per year.

23. If $P = f(m, t)$ gives the price $P$ (in dollars) of a used car as a function of its mileage $m$ (in miles) and its age $t$ (in years), then $\partial P / \partial m$ is most likely to be negative.

24. If $W = f(c, t)$ gives the weight $W$ (in pounds) of a person as a function of their daily food intake $c$ (in calories) and daily aerobic exercise time $t$ (in hours), then $\partial W / \partial c$ has units pounds per calorie.

25. If $W = f(c, t)$ gives the weight $W$ (in pounds) of a person as a function of their daily food intake $c$ (in calories) and daily aerobic exercise time $t$ (in hours), then $\partial W / \partial c$ is most likely to be negative.

26. If $W = f(c, t)$ gives the weight $W$ (in pounds) of a person as a function of their daily food intake $c$ (in calories) and daily aerobic exercise time $t$ (in hours), then $\partial W / \partial c$ and $\partial W / \partial t$ most likely have opposite signs.

27. For a function $z = f(x, y)$, assume $f(1, 2) = 10$ and $f(1.1, 2) = 10.5$ and $f(1, 2.1) = 10.8$ and $f(1.1, 2.1) = 11.3$. Then $f_x(1, 2) \approx 5$.

28. For a function $z = f(x, y)$, assume $f(1, 2) = 10$ and $f(1.1, 2) = 10.5$ and $f(1, 2.1) = 10.8$ and $f(1.1, 2.1) = 11.3$. Then $f_y(1, 2) \approx 13$.

29. For a function $z = f(x, y)$, assume $f(5, 3) = 7$ and $f(5.1, 3) = 7.9$ and $f(5, 3.1) = 6.4$ and $f(5.1, 3.1) = 7.3$. Then $f_x(5, 3) \approx 9$.

30. For a function $z = f(x, y)$, assume $f(5, 3) = 7$ and $f(5.1, 3) = 7.9$ and $f(5, 3.1) = 6.4$ and $f(5.1, 3.1) = 7.3$. Then $f_y(5, 3) \approx 6$.

31. If $f(x, y) = x^2y + 3x$ then $f_x(x, y) = 2xy + 3$.

32. If $f(x, y) = x^2y + 3x$ then $f_y(1, 2) = 4$.

33. If $g(u, v) = ue^v$ then $g_u(0, 0) = 1$.

34. There exists a function $f$ with $f_x(x, y) = f_y(x, y)$.

35. The function $Q(x, y) = x^3y^2$ is decreasing in the $y$ direction near $(1, 2)$.

36. If $P = 2N^{0.6}V^{0.4}$ then $\dfrac{\partial P}{\partial V} = 0.8N^{0.6}V^{-0.6}$.

37. For all functions $f$ it is always true that $f_{xx} = f_{yy}$ if $f_{xx}$ and $f_{yy}$ are continuous.

38. If $f(x, y) = 3x^2e^{2y}$ then $f_y(1, 0) < f_x(1, 0)$.

39. If $z = p(A, B) = (1/2)(A^2 - B)$ then $\dfrac{\partial z}{\partial A} = A$.

40. If $z = V(r, h) = \pi r^2 h$ then $\dfrac{\partial^2 z}{\partial r \partial h} = 2\pi$.

41. If $f$ is a function with $f_x(1, 2) = 0$ then $(1, 2)$ is a critical point of $f$.

42. The point $(1, 1)$ is a critical point of $f(x, y) = x^2 + y^2$.

43. The point $(3, 2)$ is a critical point of $g(u, v) = (u-3)^2 + (v - 2)^2$.

44. The function $f(x, y) = xe^y$ has no critical points.

45. If $(0, 0)$ is a critical point of $f$ then $f$ has either a local maximum or local minimum at $(0, 0)$.

46. If $D > 0$ and $f_{xx} > 0$ in the second derivative test at the point $(a, b)$ then $f$ has a local minimum at $(a, b)$.

47. To use the second derivative test on a function $f$ at a point $(a, b)$, we must have $f_x(a, b) = 0$ and $f_y(a, b) = 0$.

48. The function $f(x, y) = x^2 - y^2$ has a local minimum at $(0, 0)$.

49. The function $f(x, y) = 3xy$ has a neither a local maximum or minimum at $(0, 0)$.

50. A local minimum of $f$ can also be a global minimum of $f$.

51. If $f$ has a local maximum at $P_0$ subject to the constraint $g(x, y) = c$ then $P_0$ is a critical point of $f$.

**52.** If $f$ has a local maximum at $P_0$ subject to the constraint $g(x, y) = c$ then $P_0$ satisfies the equation $g(x, y) = c$.

**53.** If we wish to maximize production given a fixed budget, then the production function is the constraint equation.

**54.** If we wish to minimize costs given a fixed production level, then the production equation is the constraint equation.

**55.** The minimum value of $f(x, y) = x^2 + y^2$ subject to the constraint $x - y = 0$ is $f(0, 0) = 0$.

**56.** The minimum value of $f(x, y) = x^2 + y^2$ subject to the constraint $2x + 3y = 12$ is $f(0, 0) = 0$.

**57.** If the minimum cost is \$50,000 given a fixed production level of 8,000 tons with $\lambda = 120$, then we expect production of 8,001 tons to cost about \$50,120.

**58.** If the maximum production level is 50,000 tons given a fixed budget of \$80,000 with $\lambda = 120$, then we expect production of 50,001 tons to cost about \$80,120.

**59.** The second derivative test can be used to classify a point found by the Lagrange multiplier method as constrained maximum or minimum.

**60.** If the quantity $Q$ of a good produced depends only on the quantities $x$ and $y$ of two raw materials used to manufacture the good, and there is a total of \$50,000 to spend on the two raw materials, then a budget constraint for $Q$ is $x + y = 50000$.

# PROJECTS FOR CHAPTER EIGHT

**1. A Heater in a Room**

Figure 8.63 shows the contours of the temperature along one wall of a heated room through one winter day, with time indicated as on a 24-hour clock. The room has a heater located at the leftmost corner of the wall and one window in the wall. The heater is controlled by a thermostat about 2 feet from the window.

**(a)** Where is the window?  **(b)** When is the window open?

**(c)** When is the heat on?

**(d)** Draw graphs of the temperature along the wall of the room at 6 am, at 11 am, at 3 pm (15 hours) and at 5 pm (17 hours).

**(e)** Draw a graph of the temperature as a function of time at the heater, at the window and midway between them.

**(f)** The temperature at the window at 5 pm (17 hours) is less than at 11 am. Why do you think this might be?

**(g)** To what temperature do you think the thermostat is set? How do you know?

**(h)** Where is the thermostat?

Figure 8.63:

2. **Optimizing Relative Prices for Adults and Children**

Some items are sold at a discount to senior citizens or children. The reason is that these groups are more sensitive to price, so a discount has greater impact on their purchasing decisions. The seller faces an optimization problem: How large a discount to offer in order to maximize profits? Suppose a theater can sell $q_c$ child tickets and $q_a$ adult tickets at prices $p_c$ and $p_a$, according to the demand functions:

$$q_c = r p_c^{-4} \qquad \text{and} \qquad q_a = s p_a^{-2},$$

and has operating costs proportional to the total number of tickets sold. What should be the relative price of children's and adults' tickets?

3. **Maximizing Production and Minimizing Cost: "Duality"**

A company's production function is $P = 270 x_1^{1/3} x_2^{2/3}$ for quantities $x_1$ and $x_2$ of two raw materials, costing \$4 per unit and \$27 per unit, respectively.

(a) How much of each raw material should be used to maximize production if the budget for raw materials is \$324? What is the maximum production achieved, $P_0$?

(b) What is the minimum cost at which a production level of $P_0$ can be achieved? How much of each raw material is used at this minimum?

(c) Comment on the relationship between your answers to parts (a) and (b).

# FOCUS ON THEORY

## DERIVING THE FORMULA FOR A REGRESSION LINE

Suppose we want to find the "best fitting" line for some experimental data. In Appendix A, we use a computer or calculator to find the formula for this line. In this section, we derive this formula.

We decide which line fits the data best by using the following criterion. The data is plotted in the plane. The distance from a line to the data points is measured by adding the squares of the vertical distances from each point to the line. The smaller this sum of squares is, the better the line fits the data. The line with the minimum sum of square distances is called the *least-squares line*, or the *regression line*. If the data is nearly linear, the least-squares line will be a good fit; otherwise it may not be. (See Figure 8.64.)

Data almost linear: line fits well        Data not very linear: line does not fit well

**Figure 8.64**: Fitting lines to data points

**Example 1**    Find a least-squares line for the following data points: $(1, 1)$, $(2, 1)$, and $(3, 3)$.

Solution    Suppose the line has equation $y = b + mx$. If we find $b$ and $m$ then we have found the line. So, for this problem, $b$ and $m$ are the two variables. We want to minimize the function $f(b, m)$ that gives the sum of the three squared vertical distances from the points to the line in Figure 8.65.

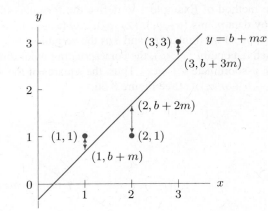

**Figure 8.65**: The least-squares line minimizes the sum of the squares of these vertical distances

The vertical distance from the point $(1, 1)$ to the line is the difference in the $y$-coordinates $1 - (b + m)$; similarly for the other points. Thus, the sum of squares is

$$f(b, m) = (1 - (b + m))^2 + (1 - (b + 2m))^2 + (3 - (b + 3m))^2.$$

To minimize $f$ we look for critical points. First we differentiate $f$ with respect to $b$:

$$f_b(b, m) = -2(1 - (b + m)) - 2(1 - (b + 2m)) - 2(3 - (b + 3m))$$
$$= -2 + 2b + 2m - 2 + 2b + 4m - 6 + 2b + 6m$$
$$= -10 + 6b + 12m.$$

Now we differentiate with respect to $m$:

$$f_m(b, m) = 2(1 - (b + m))(-1) + 2(1 - (b + 2m))(-2) + 2(3 - (b + 3m))(-3)$$
$$= -2 + 2b + 2m - 4 + 4b + 8m - 18 + 6b + 18m$$
$$= -24 + 12b + 28m.$$

The equations $f_b = 0$ and $f_m = 0$ give a system of two linear equations in two unknowns:

$$-10 + 6b + 12m = 0,$$
$$-24 + 12b + 28m = 0.$$

The solution to this pair of equations is the critical point $b = -1/3$ and $m = 1$. Since

$$D = f_{bb}f_{mm} - (f_{mb})^2 = (6)(28) - 12^2 = 24 \quad \text{and} \quad f_{bb} = 6 > 0,$$

we have found a local minimum. This local minimum is also the global minimum of $f$. Thus, the least-squares line is

$$y = x - \frac{1}{3}.$$

As a check, notice that the line $y = x$ passes through the points $(1, 1)$ and $(3, 3)$. It is reasonable that introducing the point $(2, 1)$ moves the $y$-intercept down from 0 to $-1/3$.

## Derivation of the Formulas for the Regression Line

We use the method of Example 1 to derive the formulas for the least-squares line $y = b + mx$ generated by data points $(x_1, y_1)$, $(x_2, y_2)$, ..., $(x_n, y_n)$. Notice that we are looking for the slope and $y$-intercept, so we think of $m$ and $b$ as the variables.

For each data point $(x_i, y_i)$, the corresponding point directly above the line or below it on the line has the $y$-coordinate $b + mx_i$. Thus, the squares of the vertical distances from the point to the line is $(y_i - (b + mx_i))^2$. (See Figure 8.66.)

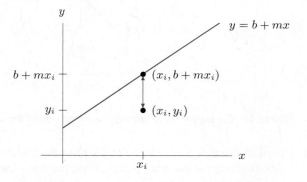

**Figure 8.66**: The vertical distance from a point to the line

We find the sum of the $n$ squared distances from points to the line, and think of the sum as a function of $m$ and $b$:

$$f(b, m) = \sum_{i=1}^{n} (y_i - (b + mx_i))^2.$$

To minimize this function, we first find the two partial derivatives, $f_b$ and $f_m$. We use the chain rule and the properties of sums.

$$f_b(b, m) = \frac{\partial}{\partial b} \left( \sum_{i=1}^{n} (y_i - (b + mx_i))^2 \right) = \sum_{i=1}^{n} \frac{\partial}{\partial b} (y_i - (b + mx_i))^2$$

$$= \sum_{i=1}^{n} 2(y_i - (b + mx_i)) \cdot \frac{\partial}{\partial b} (y_i - (b + mx_i))$$

$$= \sum_{i=1}^{n} 2(y_i - (b + mx_i)) \cdot (-1)$$

$$= -2 \sum_{i=1}^{n} (y_i - (b + mx_i))$$

$$f_m(b, m) = \frac{\partial}{\partial m} \left( \sum_{i=1}^{n} (y_i - (b + mx_i))^2 \right) = \sum_{i=1}^{n} \frac{\partial}{\partial m} (y_i - (b + mx_i))^2$$

$$= \sum_{i=1}^{n} 2(y_i - (b + mx_i)) \cdot \frac{\partial}{\partial m} (y_i - (b + mx_i))$$

$$= \sum_{i=1}^{n} 2(y_i - (b + mx_i)) \cdot (-x_i)$$

$$= -2 \sum_{i=1}^{n} (y_i - (b + mx_i)) \cdot x_i$$

We now set the partial derivatives equal to zero and solve for $m$ and $b$. This is easier than it looks: we simplify the appearance of the equations by temporarily substituting other symbols for the sums: write $SY$ for $\sum y_i$, $SX$ for $\sum x_i$, $SXY$ for $\sum y_i x_i$ and $SXX$ for $\sum x_i^2$. Remember, the $x_i$ and $y_i$ are all constants. We get a pair of simultaneous linear equations in $m$ and $b$; solving for $m$ and $b$ gives us formulas in terms of $SX$, $SY$, $SXY$, and $SXX$. We separate $f_b(b, m)$ into three sums as shown:

$$f_b(b, m) = -2 \left( \sum_{i=1}^{n} y_i - b \sum_{i=1}^{n} 1 - m \sum_{i=1}^{n} x_i \right).$$

Similarly, we can separate $f_m(b, m)$ after multiplying through by $x_i$:

$$f_m(b, m) = -2 \left( \sum_{i=1}^{n} y_i x_i - b \sum_{i=1}^{n} x_i - m \sum_{i=1}^{n} x_i^2 \right).$$

Rewriting the sums as suggested and setting $\frac{\partial f}{\partial b}$ and $\frac{\partial f}{\partial m}$ equal to zero, we have:

$$0 = SY - bn - mSX$$
$$0 = SYX - bSX - mSXX$$

Solving this pair of simultaneous equations, we get the result:

$$b = ((SXX) \cdot (SY) - (SX) \cdot (SYX)) / (n(SXX) - (SX)^2)$$
$$m = (n(SYX) - (SX) \cdot (SY)) / (n(SXX) - (SX)^2)$$

Writing these expressions with summation notation, we arrive at the following result:

> The least-squares line for data points $(x_1, y_1)$, $(x_2, y_2)$, $\cdots$, $(x_n, y_n)$ is the line $y = b + mx$ where
>
> $$b = \left( \sum_{i=1}^{n} x_i^2 \sum_{i=1}^{n} y_i - \sum_{i=1}^{n} x_i \sum_{i=1}^{n} y_i x_i \right) \Big/ \left( n \sum_{i=1}^{n} x_i^2 - \left( \sum_{i=1}^{n} x_i \right)^2 \right)$$
>
> $$m = \left( n \sum_{i=1}^{n} y_i x_i - \sum_{i=1}^{n} x_i \sum_{i=1}^{n} y_i \right) \Big/ \left( n \sum_{i=1}^{n} x_i^2 - \left( \sum_{i=1}^{n} x_i \right)^2 \right).$$

**Example 2**    Use these formulas to find the best fitting line for the data point $(1, 5)$, $(2, 4)$, $(4, 3)$.

Solution    We compute the sums needed in the formulas:

$$\sum_{i=1}^{3} x_i = 1 + 2 + 4 = 7$$

$$\sum_{i=1}^{3} y_i = 5 + 4 + 3 = 12$$

$$\sum_{i=1}^{3} x_i^2 = 1^2 + 2^2 + 4^2 = 1 + 4 + 16 = 21$$

$$\sum_{i=1}^{3} y_i x_i = (5)(1) + (4)(2) + (3)(4) = 5 + 8 + 12 = 25.$$

Since $n = 3$, we have:

$$b = \left( \sum_{i=1}^{3} x_i^2 \sum_{i=1}^{3} y_i - \sum_{i=1}^{3} x_i \sum_{i=1}^{3} y_i x_i \right) \Big/ \left( 3 \sum_{i=1}^{3} x_i^2 - \left( \sum_{i=1}^{3} x_i \right)^2 \right)$$
$$= ((21)(12) - (7)(25)) \, / \, (3(21) - (7^2))$$
$$= 77/14 = 5.5$$

and

$$m = \left( 3 \sum_{i=1}^{3} y_i x_i - \sum_{i=1}^{3} x_i \sum_{i=1}^{3} y_i \right) \Big/ \left( 3 \sum_{i=1}^{3} x_i^2 - \left( \sum_{i=1}^{3} x_i \right)^2 \right)$$
$$= (3(25) - (7)(12)) \, / \, (3(21) - (7^2))$$
$$= -9/14 = -0.64.$$

The least-squares line for these three points is

$$y = 5.5 - 0.64x.$$

To check this equation, plot the line and the three points together.

Many calculators have the formulas for the least-squares line built in, so that when you enter the data, out come the values of $b$ and $m$. At the same time, you get the *correlation coefficient*, which measures how close the data points actually come to fitting the least-squares line.

# Problems on Deriving the Formula for Regression Lines

In Problems 1–2, use the method of Example 1 to find the least-squares line. Check by graphing the points with the line.

**1.** $(-1, 2), (0, -1), (1, 1)$    **2.** $(0, 2), (1, 4), (2, 5)$

In Problems 3–5, use the formulas for $b$ and $m$ to check that you get the same result as in the problem or example specified.

**3.** $(-1, 2), (0, -1), (1, 1)$. See Problem 1.

**4.** $(0, 2), (1, 4), (2, 5)$. See Problem 2.

**5.** $(1, 1), (2, 1), (3, 3)$. See Example 1.

In Problems 6–7, we transform nonlinear data so that it looks more linear. For example, suppose the data points $(x, y)$ fit the exponential equation,

$$y = Ce^{ax},$$

where $a$ and $C$ are constants. Taking the natural log of both sides, we get

$$\ln y = ax + \ln C.$$

Thus, $\ln y$ is a linear function of $x$. To find $a$ and $C$, we can use least squares for the graph of $\ln y$ against $x$.

**6.** The population of the US was about 180 million in 1960, grew to 206 million in 1970, and 226 million in 1980.

 **(a)** Assuming that the population was growing exponentially, use logarithms and the method of least squares to estimate the population in 1990.

 **(b)** According to the national census, the 1990 population was 249 million. What does this say about the assumption of exponential growth?

 **(c)** Predict the population in the year 2010.

**7.** A biological rule of thumb states that as the area $A$ of an island increases tenfold, the number of animal species, $N$, living on it doubles. The table contains data for islands in the West Indies. Assume that $N$ is a power function of $A$.

 **(a)** Use the biological rule of thumb to find

   (i)  $N$ as a function of $A$

   (ii) $\ln N$ as a function of $\ln A$

 **(b)** Using the data given, tabulate $\ln N$ against $\ln A$ and find the line of best fit. Does your answer agree with the biological rule of thumb?

| Island | Area (sq km) | Number of species |
|--------|--------------|-------------------|
| Redonda | 3 | 5 |
| Saba | 20 | 9 |
| Montserrat | 192 | 15 |
| Puerto Rico | 8858 | 75 |
| Jamaica | 10854 | 70 |
| Hispaniola | 75571 | 130 |
| Cuba | 113715 | 125 |

# Chapter Nine

# MATHEMATICAL MODELING USING DIFFERENTIAL EQUATIONS

## Contents

# 9.1    MATHEMATICAL MODELING: SETTING UP A DIFFERENTIAL EQUATION

Sometimes we do not know a function, but we have information about its rate of change, or its derivative. Then we may be able to write a new type of equation, called a *differential equation*, from which we can get information about the original function. For example, we may use what we know about the derivative of a population function (its rate of change) to predict the population in the future.

In this section, we use a verbal description to write a differential equation.

## Marine Harvesting

We begin by investigating the effect of fishing on a fish population. Suppose that, left alone, a fish population increases at a continuous rate of 20% per year. Suppose that fish are also being harvested (caught) by fishermen at a constant rate of 10 million fish per year. How does the fish population change over time?

Notice that we have been given information about the rate of change, or derivative, of the fish population. Combined with information about the initial population, we can use this to predict the population in the future. We know that

$$\begin{array}{ccc} \text{Rate of change} \\ \text{of fish population} \end{array} = \begin{array}{c} \text{Rate of increase} \\ \text{due to breeding} \end{array} - \begin{array}{c} \text{Rate fish removed} \\ \text{due to harvesting} \end{array}.$$

Suppose the fish population, in millions, is $P$ and its derivative is $dP/dt$, where $t$ is time in years. If left alone, the fish population increases at a continuous rate of 20% per year, so we have

$$\text{Rate of increase due to breeding} = 20\% \cdot \text{Current population}$$
$$= 0.20P \text{ million fish/year}.$$

In addition,

$$\text{Rate fish removed due to harvesting} = 10 \text{ million fish/year}.$$

Since the rate of change of the fish population is $dP/dt$, we have

$$\frac{dP}{dt} = 0.20P - 10.$$

This is a differential equation that models how the fish population changes. The unknown quantity in the equation is the function giving $P$ in terms of $t$.

## Net Worth of a Company

A company earns revenue (income) and also makes payroll payments. Assume that revenue is earned continuously, that payroll payments are made continuously, and that the only factors affecting net worth are revenue and payroll. The company's revenue is earned at a continuous annual rate of 5% times its net worth. At the same time, the company's payroll obligations are paid out at a constant rate of 200 million dollars a year.

We use this information to write a differential equation to model the net worth of the company, $W$, in millions of dollars, as a function of time, $t$, in years. We know that

$$\begin{array}{ccc} \text{Rate at which} \\ \text{net worth is changing} \end{array} = \begin{array}{c} \text{Rate revenue} \\ \text{is earned} \end{array} - \begin{array}{c} \text{Rate payroll payments} \\ \text{are made} \end{array}.$$

Since the company's revenue is earned at a rate of 5% of its net worth, we have

$$\text{Rate revenue is earned} = 5\% \cdot \text{Net worth} = 0.05W \text{ million dollars/year}.$$

Since payroll payments are made at a rate of 200 million dollars a year, we have

$$\text{Rate payroll payments are made} = 200 \text{ million dollars/year}.$$

Putting these two together, since the rate at which net worth is changing is $dW/dt$, we have

$$\frac{dW}{dt} = 0.05W - 200.$$

This is a differential equation that models how the net worth of the company changes. The unknown quantity in the equation is the function giving net worth $W$ as a function of time $t$.

## Pollution in a Lake

If clean water flows into a polluted lake and a stream takes water out, the level of pollution in the lake will decrease (assuming no new pollutants are added).

**Example 1**   The quantity of pollutant in the lake decreases at a rate proportional to the quantity present. Write a differential equation to model the quantity of pollutant in the lake. Is the constant of proportionality positive or negative? Use the differential equation to explain why the graph of the quantity of pollutant against time is decreasing and concave up, as in Figure 9.1.

Figure 9.1: Quantity of pollutant in a lake

Solution   Let $Q$ denote the quantity of pollutant present in the lake at time $t$. The rate of change of $Q$ is proportional to $Q$, so $dQ/dt$ is proportional to $Q$. Thus, the differential equation is

$$\frac{dQ}{dt} = kQ.$$

Since no new pollutants are being added to the lake, the quantity $Q$ is decreasing over time, so $dQ/dt$ is negative. Thus, the constant of proportionality $k$ is negative.

Why does the differential equation $dQ/dt = kQ$, with $k$ negative, give us the graph shown in Figure 9.1? Since $k$ is negative and $Q$ is positive, we know $kQ$ is negative. Thus, $dQ/dt$ is negative, so the graph of $Q$ against $t$ is decreasing as in Figure 9.1. Why is it concave up? Since $Q$ is getting smaller and $k$ is fixed, as $t$ increases, the product $kQ$ is getting smaller in magnitude, and so the derivative $dQ/dt$ is getting smaller in magnitude. Thus, the graph of $Q$ is more horizontal as $t$ increases. Therefore, the graph is concave up. See Figure 9.1.

## The Quantity of a Drug in the Body

In the previous example, the rate at which pollutants leave a lake is proportional to the quantity of pollutants in the lake. This model works for any contaminants flowing in or out of a fluid system with complete mixing. Another example is the quantity of a drug in a person's body.

**Example 2**   A patient having major surgery is given the antibiotic vancomycin intravenously at a rate of 85 mg per hour. The rate at which the drug is excreted from the body is proportional to the quantity present, with proportionality constant 0.1 if time is in hours.

(a) Write a differential equation for the quantity, $Q$ in mg, of vancomycin in the body after $t$ hours.
(b) When $Q = 100$ mg, is $Q$ increasing or decreasing?

Solution   (a) The quantity of vancomycin, $Q$, is increasing at a constant rate of 85 mg/hour and is decreasing at a rate of 0.1 times $Q$. The administration of 85 mg/hour makes a positive contribution to the rate of change $dQ/dt$. The excretion at a rate of $0.1Q$ makes a negative contribution to $dQ/dt$.

Putting these together, we have

$$\text{Rate of change of a quantity} = \text{Rate in} - \text{Rate out},$$

so

$$\frac{dQ}{dt} = 85 - 0.1Q.$$

(b) When $Q = 100$ mg, the rate of change of $Q$ is positive

$$\frac{dQ}{dt} = 85 - 0.1(100) = 75 \text{ mg/hour},$$

so $Q$ is increasing at that moment.

## The Logistic Model

A population in a confined space grows proportionally to the product of the current population, $P$, and the difference between the *carrying capacity*, $L$, and the current population. (The carrying capacity is the maximum population the environment can sustain.) We use this information to write a differential equation for the population $P$.

The rate of change of $P$ is proportional to the product of $P$ and $L - P$, so

$$\frac{dP}{dt} = kP(L - P), \qquad \text{where } k \text{ is the positive constant of proportionality.}$$

This is called a *logistic differential equation*. What does it tell us about the graph of $P$? The derivative $dP/dt$ is the product of $k$ and $P$ and $L - P$, so when $P$ is small, the derivative $dP/dt$ is small and the population grows slowly. As $P$ increases, the derivative $dP/dt$ increases and the population grows more rapidly. However, as $P$ approaches the carrying capacity $L$, the term $L - P$ is small, and $dP/dt$ is again small and the population grows more slowly. The *logistic growth curve* in Figure 9.2 satisfies these conditions.

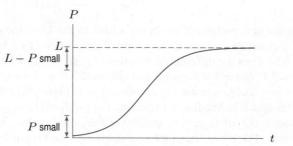

Figure 9.2: The logistic growth curve is a solution to $dP/dt = kP(L - P)$

## Problems for Section 9.1

1. Match the graphs in Figure 9.3 with the following descriptions.

   (a) The temperature of a glass of ice water left on the kitchen table.
   (b) The amount of money in an interest-bearing bank account into which \$50 is deposited.
   (c) The speed of a constantly decelerating car.
   (d) The temperature of a piece of steel heated in a furnace and left outside to cool.

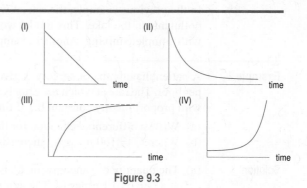

Figure 9.3

**2.** The graphs in Figure 9.4 represent the temperature, $H(°C)$, of four eggs as a function of time, $t$, in minutes. Match three of the graphs with the descriptions (a)–(c). Write a similar description for the fourth graph, including an interpretation of any intercepts and asymptotes.

  **(a)** An egg is taken out of the refrigerator (just above $0°C$) and put into boiling water.

  **(b)** Twenty minutes after the egg in part (a) is taken out of the fridge and put into boiling water, the same thing is done with another egg.

  **(c)** An egg is taken out of the refrigerator at the same time as the egg in part (a) and left to sit on the kitchen table.

**Figure 9.4**

**3.** A population of insects grows at a rate proportional to the size of the population. Write a differential equation for the size of the population, $P$, as a function of time, $t$. Is the constant of proportionality positive or negative?

**4.** Money in a bank account earns interest at a continuous annual rate of 5% times the current balance. Write a differential equation for the balance, $B$, in the account as a function of time, $t$, in years.

**5.** Radioactive substances decay at a rate proportional to the quantity present. Write a differential equation for the quantity, $Q$, of a radioactive substance present at time $t$. Is the constant of proportionality positive or negative?

**6.** A bank account that initially contains $25,000 earns interest at a continuous rate of 4% per year. Withdrawals are made out of the account at a constant rate of $2000 per year. Write a differential equation for the balance, $B$, in the account as a function of the number of years, $t$.

**7.** A pollutant spilled on the ground decays at a rate of 8% a day. In addition, cleanup crews remove the pollutant at a rate of 30 gallons a day. Write a differential equation for the amount of pollutant, $P$, in gallons, left after $t$ days.

**8.** Morphine is administered to a patient intravenously at a rate of 2.5 mg per hour. About 34.7% of the morphine is metabolized and leaves the body each hour. Write a differential equation for the amount of morphine, $M$, in milligrams, in the body as a function of time, $t$, in hours.

**9.** Alcohol is metabolized and excreted from the body at a rate of about one ounce of alcohol every hour. If some alcohol is consumed, write a differential equation for the amount of alcohol, $A$ (in ounces), remaining in the body as a function of $t$, the number of hours since the alcohol was consumed.

**10.** Toxins in pesticides can get into the food chain and accumulate in the body. A person consumes 10 micrograms a day of a toxin, ingested throughout the day. The toxin leaves the body at a continuous rate of 3% every day. Write a differential equation for the amount of toxin, $A$, in micrograms, in the person's body as a function of the number of days, $t$.

**11.** A cup of coffee contains about 100 mg of caffeine. Caffeine is metabolized and leaves the body at a continuous rate of about 17% every hour.

  **(a)** Write a differential equation for the amount, $A$, of caffeine in the body as a function of the number of hours, $t$, since the coffee was consumed.

  **(b)** Use the differential equation to find $dA/dt$ at the start of the first hour (right after the coffee is consumed). Use your answer to estimate the change in the amount of caffeine during the first hour.

**12.** A person deposits money into an account at a continuous rate of $6000 a year, and the account earns interest at a continuous rate of 7% per year.

  **(a)** Write a differential equation for the balance in the account, $B$, in dollars, as a function of years, $t$.

  **(b)** Use the differential equation to calculate $dB/dt$ if $B = 10,000$ and if $B = 100,000$. Interpret your answers.

**13.** A quantity $W$ satisfies the differential equation

$$\frac{dW}{dt} = 5W - 20.$$

  **(a)** Is $W$ increasing or decreasing at $W = 10$? $W = 2$?

  **(b)** For what values of $W$ is the rate of change of $W$ equal to zero?

**14.** A quantity $y$ satisfies the differential equation

$$\frac{dy}{dt} = -0.5y.$$

Under what conditions is $y$ increasing? Decreasing?

**15.** An early model of the growth of the Wikipedia assumed that every day a constant number, $B$, of articles are added by dedicated Wikipedians and that other articles are created by the general public at a rate proportional to the number of articles already there. Express this model as a differential equation for $N(t)$, the total number of Wikipedia articles $t$ days after it started on January 15, 2001.

**16.** A country's infrastructure is its transportation and communication systems, power plants, and other public institutions. The Solow model asserts that the value of national infrastructure $K$ increases due to investment and decreases due to capital depreciation. The rate of increase due to investment is proportional to national income, $Y$. The rate of decrease due to depreciation is proportional to the value of existing infrastructure. Write a differential equation for $K$.

# 9.2 SOLUTIONS OF DIFFERENTIAL EQUATIONS

What does it mean to "solve" a differential equation? A differential equation is an equation involving the derivative of an unknown function. The unknown is not a number but a function. A *solution* to a differential equation is any function that satisfies the differential equation.

In this section, we see how to solve a differential equation numerically and how to check whether or not a function is a solution to a differential equation. In the next section, we see how to visualize a solution.

## Another Look at Marine Harvesting

Let's take another look at the fish population discussed in Section 9.1. Left alone, the population increases at a continuous rate of 20% per year. The fish are being harvested at a constant rate of 10 million fish per year. If $P$ is the fish population, in millions, in year $t$, then we have

$$\frac{dP}{dt} = 0.20P - 10.$$

Solving this differential equation means finding a function giving $P$ in terms of $t$. Combined with information about the initial population, we can use the equation to predict the population at any time in the future.

### Solving the Differential Equation Numerically

We can approximate the solution to this differential equation by observing that the change in $P$ is approximately $dP/dt \cdot \Delta t$ when $\Delta t$ is small.

**Example 1**  Suppose at time $t = 0$, the fish population is 60 million. Find approximate values for $P(t)$ for $t = 1, 2, 3, 4, 5$.

**Solution**  We can substitute $P = 60$ into the differential equation to compute the derivative, $dP/dt$:

$$\text{At time } t = 0, \qquad \frac{dP}{dt} = 0.20P - 10 = 0.20(60) - 10 = 12 - 10 = 2.$$

Since at $t = 0$, the fish population is changing at a rate of 2 million fish a year, at the end of the first year, the fish population will have increased by about 2 million fish. So:

$$\text{At } t = 1, \qquad \text{we estimate} \quad P = 60 + 2 = 62.$$

We use this new value of $P$ to estimate $dP/dt$ during the second year:

$$\text{At time } t = 1, \qquad \frac{dP}{dt} = 0.20P - 10 = 12.4 - 10 = 2.4.$$

During the second year, the fish population increased by about 2.4 million fish, so:

$$\text{At } t = 2, \qquad \text{we estimate} \quad P = 62 + 2.4 = 64.4.$$

We use this value of $P$ to estimate the rate of change during the third year, and so on. Continuing in this fashion, we compute the approximate values of $P$ in Table 9.1. This table gives approximate numerical values for $P$ at future times.

**Table 9.1**  *Approximate values of the fish population as a function of time*

| $t$ (years)      | 0  | 1  | 2    | 3     | 4     | 5     | ... |
|------------------|----|----|------|-------|-------|-------|-----|
| $P$ (millions)   | 60 | 62 | 64.4 | 67.28 | 70.74 | 74.89 | ... |

## A Formula for the Solution to the Differential Equation

A function $P = f(t)$ which satisfies the differential equation

$$\frac{dP}{dt} = 0.20P - 10$$

is called a *solution* of the differential equation. Table 9.1 shows approximate numerical values of a solution. It is sometimes (but not always) possible to find a formula for the solution. In this particular case, there is a formula; it is

$$P = 50 + Ce^{0.20t}, \qquad \text{where } C \text{ is any constant.}$$

We check that this is a solution to the differential equation by substituting it into the left and right sides of the differential equation separately. We find

$$\text{Left side} = \frac{dP}{dt} = 0.20Ce^{0.20t}$$
$$\text{Right side} = 0.20P - 10 = 0.20(50 + Ce^{0.20t}) - 10$$
$$= 10 + 0.20Ce^{0.20t} - 10$$
$$= 0.20Ce^{0.20t}.$$

Since we get the same expression on both sides, we say that $P = 50 + Ce^{0.20t}$ is a solution of this differential equation. Any choice of $C$ works, so the solutions form a family of functions with parameter $C$. Several members of the family of solutions are graphed in Figure 9.5.

## Finding the Arbitrary Constant: Initial Conditions

To find a value for the constant $C$—in other words, to select a single solution from the family of solutions—we need an additional piece of information, usually the initial population. In this case, we know that $P = 60$ when $t = 0$, so substituting into

$$P = 50 + Ce^{0.20t}$$

gives

$$60 = 50 + Ce^{0.20(0)}$$
$$60 = 50 + C \cdot 1$$
$$C = 10.$$

The function $P = 50 + 10e^{0.20t}$ satisfies the differential equation *and* the initial condition that $P = 60$ when $t = 0$.

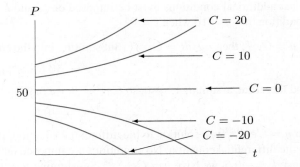

Figure 9.5: Solution curves for $dP/dt = 0.20P - 10$: Members of the family $P = 50 + Ce^{0.20t}$

## General Solutions and Particular Solutions

For the differential equation $dP/dt = 0.20P - 10$, it can be shown that every solution is of the form $P = 50 + Ce^{0.20t}$ for some value of $C$. We say that the *general solution* of the differential equation $dP/dt = 0.20P - 10$ is the family of functions $P = 50 + Ce^{0.20t}$. The solution $P = 50 + 10e^{0.20t}$ that satisfies the differential equation together with the initial condition that $P = 60$ when $t = 0$ is called a *particular solution*. The differential equation and the initial condition together are called an *initial-value problem*.

**Example 2**    (a) Check that $P = Ce^{2t}$ is a solution to the differential equation
$$\frac{dP}{dt} = 2P.$$
(b) Find the particular solution satisfying the initial condition $P = 100$ when $t = 0$.

**Solution**    (a) Since $P = Ce^{2t}$ where $C$ is a constant, we find expressions for each side:
$$\text{Left side} = \frac{dP}{dt} = Ce^{2t} \cdot 2 = 2Ce^{2t}$$
$$\text{Right side} = 2P = 2Ce^{2t}.$$
Since the two expressions are equal, $P = Ce^{2t}$ is a solution to the differential equation.

(b) We substitute $P = 100$ and $t = 0$ into the general solution $P = Ce^{2t}$, and solve for $C$:
$$100 = Ce^{2(0)}$$
$$100 = C \cdot 1$$
$$100 = C.$$
The particular solution for this initial-value problem is $P = 100e^{2t}$.

**Example 3**    Decide whether or not $y = e^{-2x}$ is a solution of the differential equation $y' - 2y = 0$.

**Solution**    Note that $y' = dy/dx$. Differentiating $y = e^{-2x}$ gives $y' = -2e^{-2x}$. Substituting, we have
$$y' - 2y = -2e^{-2x} - 2e^{-2x} = -4e^{-2x} \neq 0,$$
and so $y = e^{-2x}$ is not a solution to this differential equation.

**Example 4**    (a) What conditions must be imposed on the constants $C$ and $k$ if $y = Ce^{kt}$ is a solution to the differential equation
$$\frac{dy}{dt} = -0.5y?$$
(b) What additional conditions must be imposed on $C$ and $k$ if $y = Ce^{kt}$ also satisfies the initial condition that $y = 10$ when $t = 0$?

**Solution**    (a) If $y = Ce^{kt}$, then $dy/dt = Cke^{kt}$. Substituting into the equation $dy/dt = -0.5y$ gives
$$Cke^{kt} = -0.5(Ce^{kt}),$$
and therefore, assuming $C \neq 0$, so $Ce^{kt} \neq 0$, we have
$$k = -0.5.$$
So $y = Ce^{-0.5t}$ is a solution to the differential equation. If $C = 0$, then $Ce^{kt} = 0$ is a solution to the differential equation. No conditions are imposed on $C$.

(b) Since $k = -0.5$, we have $y = Ce^{-0.5t}$. Substituting $y = 10$ when $t = 0$ gives
$$10 = Ce^0$$

so

$$10 = C.$$

So $y = 10e^{-0.5t}$ is a solution to the differential equation together with the initial condition.

---

## Problems for Section 9.2

1. Decide whether or not each of the following is a solution to the differential equation $xy' - 2y = 0$.
   (a) $y = x^2$        (b) $y = x^3$

2. Check that $y = t^4$ is a solution to the differential equation $t\dfrac{dy}{dt} = 4y$.

3. Find the general solution to the differential equation
$$\frac{dy}{dt} = 2t.$$

In Problems 4–12, use the fact that the derivative gives the slope of a curve to decide which of the graphs (A)–(F) in Figure 9.6 could represent a solution to the differential equation.

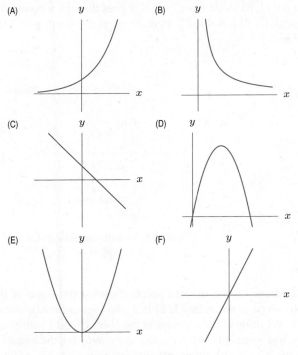

Figure 9.6

4. $\dfrac{dy}{dx} = -1$    5. $\dfrac{dy}{dx} = 0.1$    6. $\dfrac{dy}{dx} = -y^2$

7. $\dfrac{dy}{dx} = 2x$    8. $\dfrac{dy}{dx} = 2$    9. $\dfrac{dy}{dx} = y$

10. $\dfrac{dy}{dx} = -\dfrac{1}{x^2}$    11. $\dfrac{dy}{dx} = 1 - x$    12. $\dfrac{dy}{dx} = 2y$

13. Fill in the missing values in Table 9.2 given that $dy/dt = 4 - y$. Assume the rate of growth, given by $dy/dt$, is approximately constant over each unit time interval.

Table 9.2

| $t$ | 0 | 1 | 2 | 3 | 4 |
|-----|---|---|---|---|---|
| $y$ | 8 |   |   |   |   |

14. Fill in the missing values in Table 9.3 given that $dy/dt = 0.5t$. Assume the rate of growth, given by $dy/dt$, is approximately constant over each unit time interval.

Table 9.3

| $t$ | 0 | 1 | 2 | 3 | 4 |
|-----|---|---|---|---|---|
| $y$ | 8 |   |   |   |   |

15. Fill in the missing values in Table 9.4 given that $dy/dt = 0.5y$. Assume the rate of growth, given by $dy/dt$, is approximately constant over each unit time interval.

Table 9.4

| $t$ | 0 | 1 | 2 | 3 | 4 |
|-----|---|---|---|---|---|
| $y$ | 8 |   |   |   |   |

16. For a certain quantity $y$, assume that $dy/dt = \sqrt{y}$. Fill in the value of $y$ in Table 9.5. Assume that the rate of growth, $dy/dt$, is approximately constant over each unit time interval.

Table 9.5

| $t$ | 0 | 1 | 2 | 3 | 4 |
|-----|-----|---|---|---|---|
| $y$ | 100 |   |   |   |   |

17. If the initial population of fish is 70 million, use the differential equation $dP/dt = 0.2P - 10$ to estimate the fish population after 1, 2, 3 years.

18. Show that, for any constant $P_0$, the function $P = P_0 e^t$ satisfies the equation

$$\frac{dP}{dt} = P.$$

**19.** Suppose $Q = Ce^{kt}$ satisfies the differential equation

$$\frac{dQ}{dt} = -0.03Q.$$

What (if anything) does this tell you about the values of $C$ and $k$?

**20.** Is there a value of $n$ which makes $y = x^n$ a solution to the equation $13x(dy/dx) = y$? If so, what value?

**21.** Find the values of $k$ for which $y = x^2 + k$ is a solution to the differential equation $2y - xy' = 10$.

**22.** Match solutions and differential equations. (Note: Each equation may have more than one solution, or no solution.)

(a) $\dfrac{dy}{dx} = \dfrac{y}{x}$      (I) $y = x^3$

(b) $\dfrac{dy}{dx} = 3\dfrac{y}{x}$      (II) $y = 3x$

(c) $\dfrac{dy}{dx} = 3x$      (III) $y = e^{3x}$

(d) $\dfrac{dy}{dx} = y$      (IV) $y = 3e^x$

(e) $\dfrac{dy}{dx} = 3y$      (V) $y = x$

# 9.3  SLOPE FIELDS

In this section, we see how to visualize a differential equation and its solutions. Let's start with the equation

$$\frac{dy}{dx} = y.$$

Any solution to this differential equation has the property that at any point in the plane, the slope of its graph is equal to its $y$ coordinate. (That's what the equation $dy/dx = y$ is telling us!) This means that if the solution goes through the point $(0, 1)$, its slope there is 1; if it goes through a point with $y = 4$ its slope is 4. A solution going through $(0, 2)$ has slope 2 there; at the point where $y = 8$ the slope of this solution is 8. (See Figure 9.7.)

Figure 9.7: Solutions to $\frac{dy}{dx} = y$

Figure 9.8: Visualizing the slope of $y$, if $\frac{dy}{dx} = y$

In Figure 9.8 a small line segment is drawn at the marked points showing the slope of the solution curve there. Since $dy/dx = y$, the slope at the point $(1, 2)$ is 2 (the $y$-coordinate), and so we draw a line segment there with slope 2. We draw a line segment at the point $(0, -1)$ with slope $-1$, and so on. If we draw many of these line segments, we have the *slope field* for the equation $dy/dx = y$ shown in Figure 9.9. Above the $x$-axis, the slopes are positive (because $y$ is positive there), and the slopes increase as we move upward (as $y$ increases). Below the $x$-axis, the slopes are negative, and get more so as we move downward. Notice that on any horizontal line (where $y$ is constant) the slopes are constant. In the slope field you can see the ghost of the solution curve lurking. Start anywhere on the plane and move so that the slope lines are tangent to your path; you will trace out one of the solution curves. Try penciling in some solution curves on Figure 9.9, some above the $x$-axis and some below. The curves you draw should have the shape of exponential functions. By substituting $y = Ce^x$ into the differential equation, you can check that each curve in the family of exponentials, $y = Ce^x$, is a solution to this differential equation.

Figure 9.9: Slope field for $\frac{dy}{dx} = y$

In most problems, we are interested in getting the solution curves from the slope field. Think of the slope field as a set of signposts pointing in the direction you should go at each point. Imagine starting anywhere in the plane: look at the slope field at that point and start to move in that direction. After a small step, look at the slope field again, and alter your direction if necessary. Continue to move across the plane in the direction the slope field points, and you'll trace out a solution curve. Notice that the solution curve is not necessarily the graph of a function, and even if it is, we may not have a formula for the function. Geometrically, solving a differential equation means finding the family of solution curves.

**Example 1**  Figure 9.10 shows the slope field of the differential equation $\dfrac{dy}{dx} = 2x$.

(a) What do you notice about the slope field?

(b) Compare the solution curves in Figure 9.11 with the formula $y = x^2 + C$ for the solutions to this differential equation.

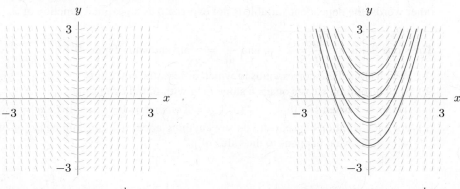

Figure 9.10: Slope field for $\frac{dy}{dx} = 2x$        Figure 9.11: Some solutions to $\frac{dy}{dx} = 2x$

**Solution**  (a) In Figure 9.10, notice that on any vertical line (where $x$ is constant) the slopes are all the same. This is because in this differential equation $dy/dx$ depends on $x$ only. (In the previous example, $dy/dx = y$, the slopes depended on $y$ only.)

(b) The solution curves in Figure 9.11 look like parabolas. It is easy to check by substitution that

$$y = x^2 + C \qquad \text{is a solution to} \qquad \frac{dy}{dx} = 2x,$$

so the parabolas $y = x^2 + C$ are solution curves; they can also be obtained by using antiderivatives.

**Example 2**    Using the slope field, guess the equation of the solution curves of the differential equation

$$\frac{dy}{dx} = -\frac{x}{y}.$$

**Solution**    The slope field is shown in Figure 9.12. Notice that on the $y$-axis, where $x$ is 0, the slope is 0. On the $x$-axis, where $y$ is 0, the line segments are vertical and the slope is undefined. At the origin the slope is undefined and there is no line segment.

What do the solution curves of this differential equation look like? The slope field suggests they are circles centered at the origin. We guess that the general solution to this differential equation is

$$x^2 + y^2 = r^2.$$

This solution is derived in the Focus on Theory section at the end of the chapter.

Figure 9.12: Slope field for $\frac{dy}{dx} = -\frac{x}{y}$

The previous example shows that the solutions to differential equations may sometimes be expressed as *implicit functions*. Implicit functions are ones which have not been "solved" for $y$; in other words, the dependent variable is not expressed as an explicit function of $x$.

**Example 3**    The slope fields for $\dfrac{dy}{dt} = 2 - y$ and $\dfrac{dy}{dt} = \dfrac{t}{y}$ are shown in Figure 9.13.

(a) Which slope field corresponds to which differential equation?
(b) Sketch solution curves on each slope field with initial conditions
   (i)   $y = 1$ when $t = 0$        (ii)   $y = 3$ when $t = 0$        (iii)   $y = 0$ when $t = 1$
(c) For each solution curve, can you say anything about the long-run behavior of $y$? In particular, as $t \to \infty$, what happens to the value of $y$?

(I)

(II)

Figure 9.13: Slope fields for $\dfrac{dy}{dt} = 2 - y$ and $\dfrac{dy}{dt} = \dfrac{t}{y}$: Which is which?

**Solution**

(a) Consider the slopes at different points for the two differential equations. In particular, look at the line $y = 2$ in Figure 9.13. The equation $dy/dt = 2 - y$ has slope 0 all along this line, whereas the line $dy/dt = t/2$ has slope $t/2$. Since slope field (I) looks horizontal at $y = 2$, slope field (I) corresponds to $dy/dt = 2 - y$ and slope field (II) corresponds to $dy/dt = t/y$.

(b) The initial conditions (i) and (ii) give the value of $y$ when $t$ is 0, that is, the $y$-intercept. To draw the solution curve satisfying the condition (i), draw the solution curve with $y$-intercept 1. For (ii), draw the solution curve with $y$-intercept 3. For (iii), the solution goes through the point $(1, 0)$, so draw the solution curve passing through this point. See Figures 9.14 and 9.15.

(c) For $dy/dt = 2 - y$, all solution curves have $y = 2$ as a horizontal asymptote, so $y \to 2$ as $t \to \infty$. For $dy/dt = t/y$ with initial conditions $(0, 1)$ and $(0, 3)$, we see that $y \to \infty$ as $t \to \infty$. The graph has asymptotes which appear to be diagonal lines. In fact, they are $y = t$ and $y = -t$, so $y \to \pm\infty$ as $t \to \infty$.

Figure 9.14: Solution curves for $\dfrac{dy}{dt} = 2 - y$

Figure 9.15: Solution curves for $\dfrac{dy}{dt} = \dfrac{t}{y}$

## Existence and Uniqueness of Solutions

Since differential equations are used to model many real situations, the question of whether a solution exists and is unique can have great practical importance. If we know how the velocity of a satellite is changing, can we know its velocity for all future time? If we know the initial population of a city, and we know how the population is changing, can we predict the population in the future? Common sense says yes: if we know the initial value of some quantity and we know exactly how it is changing, we should be able to figure out the future value of the quantity.

In the language of differential equations, an initial-value problem (that is, a differential equation and an initial condition) representing a real situation almost always has a unique solution. One way to see this is by looking at the slope field. Imagine starting at the point representing the initial condition. Through that point there will usually be a line segment pointing in the direction the solution curve must go. By following the line segments in the slope field, we trace out the solution curve. Several examples with different starting points are shown in Figure 9.16. In general, at each point there is one line segment and therefore only one direction for the solution curve to go. Thus the solution curve *exists* and is *unique* provided we are given an initial point.

It can be shown that if the slope field is continuous as we move from point to point in the plane, we can be sure that the solution curve exists around every point. Ensuring that each point has only one solution curve through it requires a slightly stronger condition.

Figure 9.16: There is one and only one solution curve through each point in the plane for this slope field

## Problems for Section 9.3

**1.** Sketch three solution curves for each of the slope fields in Figure 9.17.

**Figure 9.17**

**2.** Sketch the slope field for $dy/dx = y^2$ at the points marked in Figure 9.18.

**Figure 9.18**            **Figure 9.19**

**3.** Sketch the slope field for $dy/dx = x/y$ at the points marked in Figure 9.19.

**4.** Figure 9.20 is a slope field for $dy/dx = y - 10$.

(a) Draw the solution curve for each of the following initial conditions:

  (i)   $y = 8$ when $x = 0$   (ii)   $y = 12$ when $x = 0$
  (iii)   $y = 10$ when $x = 0$

(b) Since $dy/dx = y - 10$, when $y = 10$, we have $dy/dx = 10 - 10 = 0$. Explain why this matches your answer to part (iii).

**Figure 9.20:** Slope field for $dy/dx = y - 10$

**5.** Figure 9.21 is the slope field for the equation $y' = x + y$.

(a) Sketch the solutions that pass through the points

  (i)   $(0, 0)$     (ii)   $(-3, 1)$     (iii)   $(-1, 0)$

(b) From your sketch, guess the equation of the solution passing through $(-1, 0)$.

(c) Check your solution to part (b) by substituting it into the differential equation.

**Figure 9.21:** Slope field for $y' = x + y$

**6. (a)** For $dy/dx = x^2 - y^2$, find the slope at the following points:

$$(1, 0), \quad (0, 1), \quad (1, 1), \quad (2, 1), \quad (1, 2), \quad (2, 2)$$

(b) Sketch the slope field at these points.

**7.** Match the slope fields in Figure 9.22 with their differential equations:

(a)  $y' = 1 + y^2$  (b)  $y' = x$     (c)  $y' = \sin x$
(d)  $y' = y$        (e)  $y' = x - y$  (f)  $y' = 4 - y$

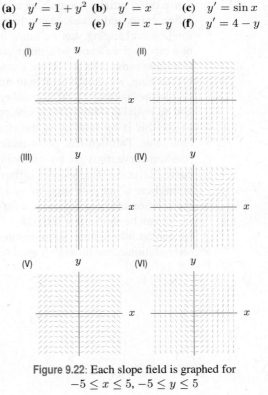

**Figure 9.22:** Each slope field is graphed for $-5 \leq x \leq 5, -5 \leq y \leq 5$

8. Match the slope fields in Figure 9.23 with their differential equations. Explain your reasoning.

(a) $y' = -y$   (b) $y' = y$   (c) $y' = x$

(d) $y' = 1/y$   (e) $y' = y^2$

Figure 9.23: Each slope field is graphed for $-5 \leq x \leq 5, -5 \leq y \leq 5$

9. Which one of the following differential equations best fits the slope field shown in Figure 9.24? Explain.

I.   $dP/dt = P - 1$    II.  $dP/dt = P(P - 1)$

III.  $dP/dt = 3P(1 - P)$  IV.  $dP/dt = 1/3P(1-P)$

Figure 9.24

10. (a) Consider the slope field for $dy/dx = xy$. What is the slope of the line segment at the point $(2, 1)$? At $(0, 2)$? At $(-1, 1)$? At $(2, -2)$?

(b) Sketch part of the slope field by drawing line segments with the slopes calculated in part (a).

For Problems 11–16, consider a solution curve for each of the slope fields in Problem 7. Write one or two sentences describing qualitatively the long-run behavior of $y$. For example, as $x$ increases, does $y \to \infty$, or does $y$ remain finite? You may get different limiting behavior for different starting points. In each case, your answer should discuss how the limiting behavior depends on the starting point.

11. Slope field (I)        12. Slope field (IV)

13. Slope field (III)      14. Slope field (V)

15. Slope field (II)       16. Slope field (VI)

17. The Gompertz equation, which models growth of animal tumors, is $y' = -ay \ln(y/b)$, where $a$ and $b$ are positive constants. Use Figures 9.25 and 9.26 to write a paragraph describing the similarities and/or differences between solutions to the Gompertz equation with $a = 1$ and $b = 2$ and solutions to the equation $y' = y(2 - y)$.

Figure 9.25: Slope field for $y' = -y \ln(y/2)$

Figure 9.26: Slope field for $y' = y(2 - y)$

# 9.4 EXPONENTIAL GROWTH AND DECAY

What is a solution to the differential equation

$$\frac{dy}{dt} = y?$$

A solution is a function that is its own derivative. The function $y = e^t$ has this property, so $y = e^t$ is a solution. In fact, any multiple of $e^t$ also has this property. The family of functions $y = Ce^t$ is the general solution to this differential equation. If $k$ is a constant, the differential equation

$$\frac{dy}{dt} = ky,$$

is similar. This differential equation says that the rate of change of $y$ is proportional to $y$. The constant $k$ is the constant of proportionality. By substituting $y = Ce^{kt}$ into the differential equation, you can check that $y = Ce^{kt}$ is a solution. For another derivation of the solution, see the Focus on Theory section at the end of the chapter. We have the following result:

---

The general solution to the differential equation $\dfrac{dy}{dt} = ky$ is

$$y = Ce^{kt} \qquad \text{for any constant C.}$$

- This is exponential growth for $k > 0$, and exponential decay for $k < 0$.
- The constant $C$ is the value of $y$ when $t$ is 0.

---

Graphs of solution curves for some $k > 0$ are in Figure 9.27. For $k < 0$, the graphs are reflected about the $y$-axis. See Figure 9.28.

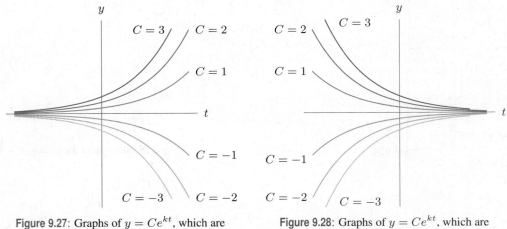

**Figure 9.27:** Graphs of $y = Ce^{kt}$, which are solutions to $\dfrac{dy}{dt} = ky$ for some fixed $k > 0$

**Figure 9.28:** Graphs of $y = Ce^{kt}$, which are solutions to $\dfrac{dy}{dt} = ky$ for some fixed $k < 0$

**Example 1**  (a) Find the general solution to each of the following differential equations:

(i) $\dfrac{dy}{dt} = 0.05y$    (ii) $\dfrac{dP}{dt} = -0.3P$    (iii) $\dfrac{dw}{dz} = 2z$    (iv) $\dfrac{dw}{dz} = 2w$

(b) For differential equation (i), find the particular solution satisfying $y = 50$ when $t = 0$.

**Solution**  (a) The differential equations given in (i), (ii), and (iv) are all examples of exponential growth or decay, since each is in the form

$$\text{Derivative} = \text{Constant} \cdot \text{Dependent variable.}$$

Notice that differential equation (iii) is not in this form. Example 1 on page 419 showed that the solution to (iii) is $w = z^2 + C$. The general solutions are

(i) $y = Ce^{0.05t}$    (ii) $P = Ce^{-0.3t}$    (iii) $w = z^2 + C$    (iv) $w = Ce^{2z}$

(b) The general solution to (i) is $y = Ce^{0.05t}$. Substituting $y = 50$ and $t = 0$ gives

$$50 = Ce^{0.05(0)}$$
$$50 = C \cdot 1.$$

So $C = 50$, and the particular solution to this initial-value problem is $y = 50e^{0.05t}$.

## Population Growth

Consider the population $P$ of a region where there is no immigration or emigration. The rate at which the population is growing is often proportional to the size of the population. This means larger populations grow faster, as we expect since there are more people to have babies. If the population has a continuous growth rate of 2% per unit time, then we know

$$\text{Rate of growth of population} = 2\% \text{ of current population,}$$

so

$$\frac{dP}{dt} = 0.02P.$$

This equation is of the form $dP/dt = kP$ for $k = 0.02$ and has the general solution $P = Ce^{0.02t}$. If the initial population at time $t = 0$ is $P_0$, then $P_0 = Ce^{0.02(0)} = C$. So $C = P_0$ and we have

$$P = P_0 e^{0.02t}.$$

## Continuously Compounded Interest

In Chapter 1 we introduced continuous compounding as the limiting case in which interest was added more and more often. Here we approach continuous compounding from a different point of view. We imagine interest being accrued at a rate proportional to the balance at that moment. Thus, the larger the balance, the faster interest is earned and the faster the balance grows.

**Example 2**  A bank account earns interest continuously at a rate of 5% of the current balance per year. Assume that the initial deposit is $1000 and that no other deposits or withdrawals are made.

(a) Write a differential equation satisfied by the balance in the account.
(b) Solve the differential equation and graph the solution.

Solution    (a) We are looking for $B$, the balance in the account in dollars, as a function of $t$, time in years. Interest is being added continuously to the account at a rate of 5% of the balance at that moment, so

Rate at which balance is increasing $= 5\%$ of current balance.

Thus, a differential equation that describes the process is

$$\frac{dB}{dt} = 0.05B.$$

Notice that it does not involve the $1000, the initial condition, because the initial deposit does not affect the process by which interest is earned.

(b) Since $B_0 = 1000$ is the initial value of $B$, the solution to this differential equation is

$$B = B_0 e^{0.05t} = 1000 e^{0.05t}.$$

This function is graphed in Figure 9.29.

Figure 9.29: Bank balance against time

You may wonder how we can represent an amount of money by a differential equation, since money can only take on discrete values (you can't have fractions of a cent). In fact, the differential equation is only an approximation, but for large amounts of money, it is a pretty good approximation.

## Pollution in the Great Lakes

In the 1960s pollution in the Great Lakes became an issue of public concern. We will set up a model for how long it would take the lakes to flush themselves clean, assuming no further pollutants were being dumped in the lake.

Let $Q$ be the total quantity of pollutant in a lake of volume $V$ at time $t$. Suppose that clean water is flowing into the lake at a constant rate $r$ and that water flows out at the same rate. Assume that the pollutant is evenly spread throughout the lake, and that the clean water coming into the lake immediately mixes with the rest of the water.

How does $Q$ vary with time? First, notice that since pollutants are being taken out of the lake but not added, $Q$ decreases, and the water leaving the lake becomes less polluted, so the rate at which the pollutants leave decreases. This tells us that $Q$ is decreasing and concave up. In addition, the pollutants will never be completely removed from the lake though the quantity remaining will become arbitrarily small. In other words, $Q$ is asymptotic to the $t$-axis. (See Figure 9.30.)

### Setting Up a Differential Equation for the Pollution

To understand how $Q$ changes with time, we write a differential equation for $Q$. We know that

$$\begin{pmatrix} \text{Rate } Q \\ \text{changes} \end{pmatrix} = -\begin{pmatrix} \text{Rate pollutants} \\ \text{leave in outflow} \end{pmatrix}$$

where the negative sign represents the fact that $Q$ is decreasing. At time $t$, the concentration of pollutants is $Q/V$ and water containing this concentration is leaving at rate $r$. Thus,

$$\begin{matrix} \text{Rate pollutants} \\ \text{leave in outflow} \end{matrix} = \begin{matrix} \text{Rate of} \\ \text{outflow} \end{matrix} \times \text{Concentration} = r \cdot \frac{Q}{V}.$$

So the differential equation is

$$\frac{dQ}{dt} = -\frac{r}{V}Q$$

and its general solution is

$$Q = Q_0 e^{-rt/V}.$$

Table 9.6 contains values of $r$ and $V$ for four of the Great Lakes.[1] We use this data to calculate how long it would take for certain fractions of the pollution to be removed from Lake Erie.

$Q$ (quantity of pollutant)

$t$ (time)

Figure 9.30: Pollutant in lake versus time

Table 9.6    *Volume and outflow in Great Lakes*

|  | $V$ (km$^3$) | $r$ (km$^3$/year) |
|---|---|---|
| Superior | 12,200 | 65.2 |
| Michigan | 4900 | 158 |
| Erie | 460 | 175 |
| Ontario | 1600 | 209 |

**Example 3**    How long will it take for 90% of the pollution to be removed from Lake Erie? For 99% to be removed?

Solution    For Lake Erie, $r/V = 175/460 = 0.38$, so at time $t$ we have

$$Q = Q_0 e^{-0.38t}.$$

When 90% of the pollution has been removed, 10% remains, so $Q = 0.1Q_0$. Substituting gives

$$0.1Q_0 = Q_0 e^{-0.38t}.$$

Canceling $Q_0$ and solving for $t$ gives

$$t = \frac{-\ln(0.1)}{0.38} \approx 6 \text{ years}.$$

Similarly, when 99% of the pollution has been removed, $Q = 0.01Q_0$, so we solve

$$0.01Q_0 = Q_0 e^{-0.38t},$$

giving

$$t = \frac{-\ln(0.01)}{0.38} \approx 12 \text{ years}.$$

---

[1]Data from William E. Boyce and Richard C. DiPrima, *Elementary Differential Equations* (New York: Wiley, 1977).

## The Quantity of a Drug in the Body

As we saw in Section 9.1, the rate at which a drug leaves a patient's body is proportional to the quantity of the drug left in the body. If we let $Q$ represent the quantity of drug left, then

$$\frac{dQ}{dt} = -kQ.$$

The negative sign indicates the quantity of drug in the body is decreasing. The solution to this differential equation is $Q = Q_0 e^{-kt}$; the quantity decreases exponentially. The constant $k$ depends on the drug and $Q_0$ is the amount of drug in the body at time zero. Sometimes physicians convey information about the relative decay rate with a *half life*, which is the time it takes for $Q$ to decrease by a factor of $1/2$.

---

**Example 4**    Valproic acid is a drug used to control epilepsy; its half-life in the human body is about 15 hours.

(a) Use the half-life to find the constant $k$ in the differential equation $dQ/dt = -kQ$, where $Q$ represents the quantity of drug in the body $t$ hours after the drug is administered.

(b) At what time will 10% of the original dose remain?

Solution    (a) Since the half-life is 15 hours, we know that the quantity remaining $Q = 0.5Q_0$ when $t = 15$. We substitute into the solution to the differential equation, $Q = Q_0 e^{-kt}$, and solve for $k$:

$$Q = Q_0 e^{-kt}$$
$$0.5Q_0 = Q_0 e^{-k(15)}$$
$$0.5 = e^{-15k} \qquad \text{(Divide through by } Q_0\text{)}$$
$$\ln 0.5 = -15k \qquad \text{(Take the natural logarithm of both sides)}$$
$$k = \frac{-\ln 0.5}{15} = 0.0462. \qquad \text{(Solve for } k\text{)}$$

(b) To find the time when 10% of the original dose remains in the body, we substitute $0.10Q_0$ for the quantity remaining, $Q$, and solve for the time, $t$.

$$0.10Q_0 = Q_0 e^{-0.0462t}$$
$$0.10 = e^{-0.0462t}$$
$$\ln 0.10 = -0.0462t$$
$$t = \frac{\ln 0.10}{-0.0462} = 49.84.$$

There will be 10% of the drug still in the body at $t = 49.84$, or after about 50 hours.

---

## Problems for Section 9.4

Find solutions to the differential equations in Problems 1–6, subject to the given initial condition.

**1.** $\dfrac{dP}{dt} = 0.02P, \quad P(0) = 20$

**2.** $\dfrac{dw}{dr} = 3w, \quad w = 30$ when $r = 0$

**3.** $\dfrac{dy}{dx} = -0.14y, \quad y = 5.6$ when $x = 0$

**4.** $\dfrac{dQ}{dt} = \dfrac{Q}{5}, \quad Q = 50$ when $t = 0$

**5.** $\dfrac{dp}{dq} = -0.1p, \quad p = 100$ when $q = 5$

**6.** $\dfrac{dy}{dx} + \dfrac{y}{3} = 0, \quad y(0) = 10$

**7.** A deposit of $5000 is made to a bank account paying 1.5% annual interest, compounded continuously.

(a) Write a differential equation for the balance in the account, $B$, as a function of time, $t$, in years.
(b) Solve the differential equation.
(c) How much money is in the account in 10 years?

8. Money in a bank account grows continuously at an annual rate of $r$ (when the interest rate is 5%, $r = 0.05$, and so on). Suppose $2000 is put into the account in 2010.

   (a) Write a differential equation satisfied by $M$, the amount of money in the account at time $t$, measured in years since 2010.
   (b) Solve the differential equation.
   (c) Sketch the solution until the year 2040 for interest rates of 5% and 10%.

9. A bank account that earns 10% interest compounded continuously has an initial balance of zero. Money is deposited into the account at a continuous rate of $1000 per year.

   (a) Write a differential equation that describes the rate of change of the balance $B = f(t)$.
   (b) Solve the differential equation.

10. The amount of ozone, $Q$, in the atmosphere is decreasing at a rate proportional to the amount of ozone present. If time $t$ is measured in years, the constant of proportionality is $-0.0025$. Write a differential equation for $Q$ as a function of $t$, and give the general solution for the differential equation. If this rate continues, approximately what percent of the ozone in the atmosphere now will decay in the next 20 years?

11. Using the model in the text and the data in Table 9.6 on page 427, find how long it would take for 90% of the pollution to be removed from Lake Michigan and from Lake Ontario, assuming no new pollutants are added. Explain how you can tell which lake will take longer to be purified just by looking at the data in the table.

12. Use the model in the text and the data in Table 9.6 on page 427 to determine which of the Great Lakes would require the longest time and which would require the shortest time for 80% of the pollution to be removed, assuming no new pollutants are being added. Find the ratio of these two times.

13. The rate at which a drug leaves the bloodstream and passes into the urine is proportional to the quantity of the drug in the blood at that time. If an initial dose of $Q_0$ is injected directly into the blood, 20% is left in the blood after 3 hours.

   (a) Write and solve a differential equation for the quantity, $Q$, of the drug in the blood after $t$ hours.

(b) How much of this drug is in a patient's body after 6 hours if the patient is given 100 mg initially?

14. In some chemical reactions, the rate at which the amount of a substance changes with time is proportional to the amount present. For example, this is the case as $\delta$-glucono-lactone changes into gluconic acid.

   (a) Write a differential equation satisfied by $y$, the quantity of $\delta$-glucono-lactone present at time $t$.
   (b) If 100 grams of $\delta$-glucono-lactone is reduced to 54.9 grams in one hour, how many grams will remain after 10 hours?

15. Oil is pumped continuously from a well at a rate proportional to the amount of oil left in the well. Initially there were 1 million barrels of oil in the well; six years later 500,000 barrels remain.

   (a) At what rate was the amount of oil in the well decreasing when there were 600,000 barrels remaining?
   (b) When will there be 50,000 barrels remaining?

16. Hydrocodone bitartrate is used as a cough suppressant. After the drug is fully absorbed, the quantity of drug in the body decreases at a rate proportional to the amount left in the body. The half-life of hydrocodone bitartrate in the body is 3.8 hours and the dose is 10 mg.

   (a) Write a differential equation for the quantity, $Q$, of hydrocodone bitartrate in the body at time $t$, in hours since the drug was fully absorbed.
   (b) Solve the differential equation given in part (a).
   (c) Use the half-life to find the constant of proportionality, $k$.
   (d) How much of the 10-mg dose is still in the body after 12 hours?

17. The amount of land in use for growing crops increases as the world's population increases. Suppose $A(t)$ represents the total number of hectares of land in use in year $t$. (A hectare is about $2\frac{1}{2}$ acres.)

   (a) Explain why it is plausible that $A(t)$ satisfies the equation $A'(t) = kA(t)$. What assumptions are you making about the world's population and its relation to the amount of land used?
   (b) In 1966 about 4.55 billion hectares of land were in use; in 1996 the figure was 4.93 billion hectares.[2] If the total amount of land available for growing crops is thought to be 6 billion hectares, when does this model predict it will be exhausted? (Let $t = 0$ in 1966.)

---

[2]http://www.farmingsolutions.org/facts/factscontent_det.asp, accessed June 6, 2011.

# 9.5 APPLICATIONS AND MODELING

In the last section, we considered several situations modeled by the differential equation

$$\frac{dy}{dt} = ky.$$

In this section, we consider situations where the rate of change of $y$ is a linear function of $y$ of the form

$$\frac{dy}{dt} = k(y - A), \qquad \text{where } k \text{ and } A \text{ are constants.}$$

## The Quantity of a Drug in the Body

A patient is given the drug warfarin, an anticoagulant, intravenously at the rate of 0.5 mg/hour. Warfarin is metabolized and leaves the body at the rate of about 2% per hour. A differential equation for the quantity, $Q$ (in mg), of warfarin in the body after $t$ hours is given by

$$\text{Rate of change} = \text{Rate in} - \text{Rate out}$$
$$\frac{dQ}{dt} = 0.5 - 0.02Q.$$

What does this tell us about the quantity of warfarin in the body for different initial values of $Q$?

If $Q$ is small, then $0.02Q$ is also small and the rate the drug is excreted is less than the rate at which the drug is entering the body. Since the rate in is greater than the rate out, the rate of change is positive and the quantity of drug in the body is increasing. If $Q$ is large enough that $0.02Q$ is greater than 0.5, then $0.5 - 0.02Q$ is negative, so $dQ/dt$ is negative and the quantity is decreasing.

For small $Q$, the quantity will increase until the rate in equals the rate out. For large $Q$, the quantity will decrease until the rate in equals the rate out. What is the value of $Q$ at which the rate in exactly matches the rate out? We have

$$\text{Rate in} = \text{Rate out}$$
$$0.5 = 0.02Q$$
$$Q = 25.$$

If the amount of warfarin in the body is initially 25 mg, then the amount being excreted exactly matches the amount being added. The quantity of drug $Q$ will stay constant at 25 mg. Notice also that when $Q = 25$, the derivative $dQ/dt$ is zero, since

$$\frac{dQ}{dt} = 0.5 - 0.02(25) = 0.5 - 0.5 = 0.$$

If the initial quantity is 25, then the solution is the horizontal line $Q = 25$. This solution is called an *equilibrium solution*.

The slope field for this differential equation is shown in Figure 9.31, with solution curves drawn for $Q_0 = 20$, $Q_0 = 25$, and $Q_0 = 30$. In each case, we see that the quantity of drug in the body is approaching the equilibrium solution of 25 mg. The solution curve with $Q_0 = 30$ should remind you of an exponential decay function. It is, in fact, an exponential decay function that has been shifted up 25 units.

Figure 9.31: Slope field for $dQ/dt = 0.5 - 0.02Q$

## Solving the Differential Equation $dy/dt = k(y - A)$

The drug concentration in the previous example satisfies a differential equation of the form

$$\frac{dy}{dt} = k(y - A).$$

Let us find the general solution to this equation. Since $A$ is a constant, $dA/dt = 0$ so that we have

$$\frac{d}{dt}(y - A) = \frac{dy}{dt} - \frac{dA}{dt} = \frac{dy}{dt} - 0 = k(y - A).$$

Thus $y - A$ satisfies an exponential differential equation, so $y - A$ must be of the form

$$y - A = Ce^{kt}.$$

For an alternative derivation of the solution, see the Focus on Theory section at the end of the chapter.

---

The general solution to the differential equation

$$\frac{dy}{dt} = k(y - A)$$

is

$$y = A + Ce^{kt}, \qquad \text{for any constant } C.$$

---

*Warning*: Notice that, for differential equations of this form, the arbitrary constant $C$ is *not* the initial value of the variable, but rather the initial value of $y - A$.

---

**Example 1**   Give the solution to each of the following differential equations:

(a)  $\dfrac{dy}{dt} = 0.02(y - 50)$              (b)  $\dfrac{dP}{dt} = 5(P - 10), \quad P = 8$ when $t = 0$

(c)  $\dfrac{dy}{dt} = 3y - 300$                    (d)  $\dfrac{dW}{dt} = 500 - 0.1W$

Solution

(a) The general solution is $y = 50 + Ce^{0.02t}$.

(b) The general solution is $P = 10 + Ce^{5t}$. Use the initial condition to solve for $C$:

$$8 = 10 + C(e^0)$$
$$8 = 10 + C.$$

So $C = -2$, and the particular solution is $P = 10 - 2e^{5t}$.

(c) First rewrite the right-hand side of the equation in the form $k(y - A)$ by factoring out a 3:

$$\frac{dy}{dt} = 3(y - 100).$$

The general solution to this differential equation is $y = 100 + Ce^{3t}$.

(d) We begin by factoring out the coefficient of $W$:

$$\frac{dW}{dt} = 500 - 0.1W = -0.1\left(W - \frac{500}{0.1}\right) = -0.1(W - 5000).$$

The general solution to this differential equation is $W = 5000 + Ce^{-0.1t}$.

---

**Example 2**

At the start of this section, we gave the following differential equation for the quantity of warfarin in the body:

$$\frac{dQ}{dt} = 0.5 - 0.02Q.$$

Write the general solution to this differential equation. Find particular solutions for $Q_0 = 20$, $Q_0 = 25$, and $Q_0 = 30$.

Solution

We first rewrite the differential equation in the form $dQ/dt = k(Q - A)$ by factoring out $-0.02$:

$$\frac{dQ}{dt} = 0.5 - 0.02Q = -0.02(Q - 25).$$

The general solution to this differential equation is

$$Q = 25 + Ce^{-0.02t}.$$

To find the particular solution when $Q_0 = 20$, we use the initial condition to solve for $C$:

$$20 = 25 + C(e^0)$$
$$C = -5.$$

The particular solution when $Q_0 = 20$ is $Q = 25 - 5e^{-0.02t}$.

When $Q_0 = 25$, we have $C = 0$ and the particular solution is the horizontal line $Q = 25$. When $Q_0 = 30$, we have $C = 5$ and the particular solution is $Q = 25 + 5e^{-0.02t}$. These three solutions are the three we saw earlier in Figure 9.31.

---

**Example 3**

A company's revenue is earned at a continuous annual rate of 5% of its net worth. At the same time, the company's payroll obligations are paid out at a constant rate of 200 million dollars a year. We saw in Section 9.1 that the differential equation governing the net worth, $W$ (in millions of dollars), of this company in year $t$ is given by

$$\text{Rate of change of } W \ = \ \text{Rate in} \ - \ \text{Rate out}$$
$$\frac{dW}{dt} = 0.05W - 200.$$

(a) Solve the differential equation, assuming an initial net worth of $W_0$ million dollars.

(b) Sketch the solution for $W_0 = 3000, 4000$ and $5000$. For which of these values of $W_0$ does the company go bankrupt? In which year?

Solution    (a) Factor out 0.05 to get

$$\frac{dW}{dt} = 0.05(W - 4000).$$

The general solution is

$$W = 4000 + Ce^{0.05t}.$$

To find $C$ we use the initial condition that $W = W_0$ when $t = 0$.

$$W_0 = 4000 + Ce^0$$
$$W_0 - 4000 = C$$

Substituting this value for $C$ into $W = 4000 + Ce^{0.05t}$ gives

$$W = 4000 + (W_0 - 4000)e^{0.05t}.$$

(b) If $W_0 = 4000$, then $W = 4000$, the equilibrium solution.
If $W_0 = 5000$, then $W = 4000 + 1000e^{0.05t}$.
If $W_0 = 3000$, then $W = 4000 - 1000e^{0.05t}$. The graphs of these functions are in Figure 9.32. Notice that if the net worth starts with $W_0$ near, but not equal to, \$4000 million, then $W$ moves further away. We see that if $W_0 = 3000$, the value of $W$ goes to 0, and the company goes bankrupt. Solving $W = 0$ gives $t \approx 27.7$, so the company goes bankrupt in its twenty-eighth year.

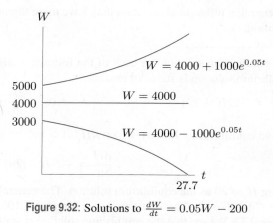

Figure 9.32: Solutions to $\frac{dW}{dt} = 0.05W - 200$

## Equilibrium Solutions

Figure 9.31 shows the quantity of warfarin in the body for several different initial quantities. All these curves are solutions to the differential equation

$$\frac{dQ}{dt} = 0.5 - 0.02Q = -0.02(Q - 25),$$

and all the solutions have the form

$$Q = 25 + Ce^{-0.02t}$$

for some $C$. Notice that $Q \to 25$ as $t \to \infty$ for all solutions because $e^{-0.02t} \to 0$ as $t \to \infty$. In other words, in the long run, the quantity approaches the *equilibrium solution* of $Q = 25$ no matter what the initial quantity.

Notice that the equilibrium solution can be found directly from the differential equation by solving $dQ/dt = 0$:

$$\frac{dQ}{dt} = -0.02(Q - 25) = 0,$$

giving $Q = 25$. Because $Q$ always gets closer and closer to the equilibrium value of 25 as $t \to \infty$, we call $Q = 25$ a *stable* equilibrium for $Q$.

A different situation is shown in Figure 9.32 with the solutions to the differential equation $dW/dt = 0.05W - 200$. We find the equilibrium by looking at the solution curves or by setting $dW/dt = 0$:

$$\frac{dW}{dt} = 0.05W - 200 = 0.05(W - 4000) = 0,$$

giving $W = 4000$ as the equilibrium solution. This equilibrium solution is called *unstable* because if $W$ starts near, but not equal to, 4000, the net worth $W$ moves further away from 4000 as $t \to \infty$.

---

- An **equilibrium solution** is constant for all values of the independent variable. The graph is a horizontal line. Equilibrium solutions can be identified by setting the derivative of the function to zero.
- An equilibrium solution is **stable** if a small change in the initial conditions gives a solution which tends toward the equilibrium as the independent variable tends to positive infinity.
- An equilibrium solution is **unstable** if a small change in the initial conditions gives a solution curve which veers away from the equilibrium as the independent variable tends to positive infinity.

---

In general, a differential equation may have more than one equilibrium solution or no equilibrium solution.

---

**Example 4**    Find the equilibrium solution for each of the following differential equations. Determine whether the equilibrium solution is stable or unstable.

(a)  $\dfrac{dH}{dt} = -2(H - 20)$        (b)  $\dfrac{dB}{dt} = 2(B - 10)$

**Solution**    (a)  To find equilibrium solutions, we set $dH/dt = 0$:

$$\frac{dH}{dt} = -2(H - 20) = 0,$$

giving $H = 20$ as the equilibrium solution. The general solution to this differential equation is $H = 20 + Ce^{-2t}$. The solution curves for $H_0 = 10$, $H_0 = 20$, and $H_0 = 30$ are shown in Figure 9.33. We see that the equilibrium solution is stable.

Figure 9.33: $H = 20$ is stable equilibrium          Figure 9.34: $B = 10$ is unstable equilibrium

(b)  To find equilibrium solutions, we set $dB/dt = 0$:

$$\frac{dB}{dt} = 2(B - 10) = 0,$$

giving $B = 10$ as the equilibrium solution. The general solution to this differential equation is $B = 10 + Ce^{2t}$. The solution curves for $B_0 = 9$, $B_0 = 10$, and $B_0 = 11$ are shown in Figure 9.34. We see that the equilibrium solution is unstable.

## Newton's Law of Heating and Cooling

Newton proposed that the temperature of a hot object decreases at a rate proportional to the difference between its temperature and that of its surroundings. Similarly, a cold object heats up at a rate proportional to the temperature difference between the object and its surroundings.

For example, a hot cup of coffee standing on a table cools at a rate proportional to the temperature difference between the coffee and the surrounding air. As the coffee cools, the rate at which it cools decreases because the temperature difference between the coffee and the air decreases. In the long run, the rate of cooling tends to zero and the temperature of the coffee approaches room temperature. Figure 9.35 shows the temperature of two cups of coffee against time, one starting at a higher temperature than the other, but both tending toward room temperature in the long run.

Figure 9.35: Temperature of coffee versus time

Let $H$ be the temperature at time $t$ of a cup of coffee in a $70°F$ room. Newton's Law says that the rate of change of $H$ is proportional to the temperature difference between the coffee and the room:

Rate of change of temperature $=$ Constant $\cdot$ Temperature difference.

The rate of change of temperature is $dH/dt$. The temperature difference between the coffee and the room is $(H - 70)$, so

$$\frac{dH}{dt} = \text{Constant} \cdot (H - 70).$$

What about the sign of the constant? If the coffee starts out hotter than $70°$ (that is, $H - 70 > 0$), then the temperature of the coffee decreases (i.e., $dH/dt < 0$) and so the constant must be negative:

$$\frac{dH}{dt} = -k(H - 70) \qquad k > 0.$$

What can we learn from this differential equation? Suppose we take $k = 1$. The slope field for this differential equation in Figure 9.36 shows several solution curves. Notice that, as we expect, the temperature of the coffee is approaching the temperature of the room. The general solution to this differential equation is

$$H = 70 + Ce^{-t},$$

where $C$ is an arbitrary constant.

Figure 9.36: Slope field for $\dfrac{dH}{dt} = -(H - 70)$

**Example 5**    The body of a murder victim is found at noon in a room with a constant temperature of $20°C$. At noon the temperature of the body is $35°C$; two hours later the temperature of the body is $33°C$.

(a) Find the temperature, $H$, of the body as a function of $t$, the time in hours since it was found.
(b) Graph $H$ against $t$. What happens to the temperature in the long run?
(c) At the time of the murder, the victim's body had the normal body temperature, $37°C$. When did the murder occur?

**Solution**    (a) Newton's Law of Cooling says that

$$\text{Rate of change of temperature} = \text{Constant} \cdot \text{Temperature difference}.$$

Since the temperature difference is $H - 20$, we have for some constant $k$

$$\frac{dH}{dt} = -k(H - 20).$$

The general solution is

$$H = 20 + Ce^{-kt}.$$

To determine $C$, we use the fact that $H = 35$ at $t = 0$:

$$35 = 20 + Ce^0$$
$$35 = 20 + C.$$

So $C = 15$ and we have

$$H = 20 + 15e^{-kt}.$$

To find $k$, we use the fact that $H = 33$ when $t = 2$:

$$33 = 20 + 15e^{-k(2)}.$$

We isolate the exponential and solve for $k$:

$$13 = 15e^{-2k}$$
$$\frac{13}{15} = e^{-2k}$$
$$\ln\left(\frac{13}{15}\right) = -2k$$
$$k = -\frac{\ln(13/15)}{2} = 0.072.$$

Therefore, the temperature, $H$, of the body as a function of time, $t$, is given by

$$H = 20 + 15e^{-0.072t}.$$

(b) The graph of $H = 20 + 15e^{-0.072t}$ has a vertical intercept of $H = 35$, the initial temperature. The temperature decays exponentially with a horizontal asymptote of $H = 20$. (See Figure 9.37.) "In the long run" means as $t \to \infty$. The graph shows that $H \to 20$ as $t \to \infty$.

**Figure 9.37**: Temperature of dead body

(c)  We want to know when the temperature was $37°C$. We substitute $H = 37$ and solve for $t$:

$$37 = 20 + 15e^{-0.072t}$$
$$\frac{17}{15} = e^{-0.072t}.$$

Taking natural logs on both sides gives

$$\ln\left(\frac{17}{15}\right) = -0.072t$$

so

$$t = -\frac{\ln(17/15)}{0.072} = -1.74 \text{ hours.}$$

The murder occurred about 1.74 hours before noon, that is, about 10:15 am.

## Problems for Section 9.5

Find particular solutions in Problems 1–8.

**1.** $\dfrac{dy}{dt} = 0.5(y - 200)$,   $y = 50$ when $t = 0$

**2.** $\dfrac{dP}{dt} = P + 4$,   $P = 100$ when $t = 0$

**3.** $\dfrac{dH}{dt} = 3(H - 75)$,   $H = 0$ when $t = 0$

**4.** $\dfrac{dm}{dt} = 0.1m + 200$,   $m(0) = 1000$

**5.** $\dfrac{dB}{dt} = 4B - 100$,   $B = 20$ when $t = 0$

**6.** $\dfrac{dQ}{dt} = 0.3Q - 120$,   $Q = 50$ when $t = 0$

**7.** $\dfrac{dB}{dt} + 2B = 50$,   $B(1) = 100$

**8.** $\dfrac{dB}{dt} + 0.1B - 10 = 0$    $B(2) = 3$

**9.** Check that $y = A + Ce^{kt}$ is a solution to the differential equation

$$\frac{dy}{dt} = k(y - A).$$

**10.** A bank account earns 5% annual interest, compounded continuously. Money is deposited in a continuous cash flow at a rate of $1200 per year into the account.

   (a) Write a differential equation that describes the rate at which the balance $B = f(t)$ is changing.
   (b) Solve the differential equation given an initial balance $B_0 = 0$.
   (c) Find the balance after 5 years.

**11.** Money in an account earns interest at a continuous rate of 8% per year, and payments are made continuously out of the account at the rate of $5000 a year. The account initially contains $50,000. Write a differential equation for

the amount of money in the account, $B$, in $t$ years. Solve the differential equation. Does the account ever run out of money? If so, when?

**12.** A company earns 2% per month on its assets, paid continuously, and its expenses are paid out continuously at a rate of $80,000 per month.

   (a) Write a differential equation for the value, $V$, of the company as a function of time, $t$, in months.
   (b) What is the equilibrium solution for the differential equation? What is the significance of this value for the company?
   (c) Solve the differential equation found in part (a).
   (d) If the company has assets worth $3 million at time $t = 0$, what are its assets worth one year later?

**13.** A bank account earns 7% annual interest compounded continuously. You deposit $10,000 in the account, and withdraw money continuously from the account at a rate of $1000 per year.

   (a) Write a differential equation for the balance, $B$, in the account after $t$ years.
   (b) What is the equilibrium solution to the differential equation? (This is the amount that must be deposited now for the balance to stay the same over the years.)
   (c) Find the solution to the differential equation.
   (d) How much is in the account after 5 years?
   (e) Graph the solution. What happens to the balance in the long run?

**14.** One theory on the speed an employee learns a new task claims that the more the employee already knows, the more slowly he or she learns. Suppose that the rate at which a person learns is equal to the percentage of the task not yet learned. If $y$ is the percentage learned by time $t$, the percentage not yet learned by that time is $100 - y$, so we can model this situation with the differential equation

$$\frac{dy}{dt} = 100 - y.$$

(a) Find the general solution to this differential equation.

(b) Sketch several solutions.

(c) Find the particular solution if the employee starts learning at time $t = 0$ (so $y = 0$ when $t = 0$).

15. A patient is given the drug theophylline intravenously at a rate of 43.2 mg/hour to relieve acute asthma. The rate at which the drug leaves the patient's body is proportional to the quantity there, with proportionality constant 0.082 if time, $t$, is in hours. The patient's body contains none of the drug initially.

(a) Describe in words how you expect the quantity of theophylline in the patient to vary with time.

(b) Write a differential equation satisfied by the quantity of theophylline in the body, $Q(t)$.

(c) Solve the differential equation and graph the solution. What happens to the quantity in the long run?

16. A chain smoker smokes five cigarettes every hour. From each cigarette, 0.4 mg of nicotine is absorbed into the person's bloodstream. Nicotine leaves the body at a rate proportional to the amount present, with constant of proportionality $-0.346$ if $t$ is in hours.

(a) Write a differential equation for the level of nicotine in the body, $N$, in mg, as a function of time, $t$, in hours.

(b) Solve the differential equation from part (a). Initially there is no nicotine in the blood.

(c) The person wakes up at 7 am and begins smoking. How much nicotine is in the blood when the person goes to sleep at 11 pm (16 hours later)?

17. As you know, when a course ends, students start to forget the material they have learned. One model (called the Ebbinghaus model) assumes that the rate at which a student forgets material is proportional to the difference between the material currently remembered and some positive constant, $a$.

(a) Let $y = f(t)$ be the fraction of the original material remembered $t$ weeks after the course has ended. Set up a differential equation for $y$. Your equation will contain two constants; the constant $a$ is less than $y$ for all $t$.

(b) Solve the differential equation.

(c) Describe the practical meaning (in terms of the amount remembered) of the constants in the solution $y = f(t)$.

18. (a) Find the equilibrium solution of the equation

$$\frac{dy}{dt} = 0.5y - 250.$$

(b) Find the general solution of this equation.

(c) Graph several solutions with different initial values.

(d) Is the equilibrium solution stable or unstable?

19. (a) What are the equilibrium solutions for the differential equation

$$\frac{dy}{dt} = 0.2(y - 3)(y + 2)?$$

(b) Use a graphing calculator or computer to sketch a slope field for this differential equation. Use the slope field to determine whether each equilibrium solution is stable or unstable.

20. Figure 9.38 gives the slope field for a differential equation. Estimate all equilibrium solutions and indicate whether each is stable or unstable.

Figure 9.38

21. A yam is put in a 200°C oven and heats up according to the differential equation

$$\frac{dH}{dt} = -k(H - 200), \quad \text{for } k \text{ a positive constant.}$$

(a) If the yam is at 20°C when it is put in the oven, solve the differential equation.

(b) Find $k$ using the fact that after 30 minutes the temperature of the yam is 120°C.

22. At 1:00 pm one winter afternoon, there is a power failure at your house in Wisconsin, and your heat does not work without electricity. When the power goes out, it is 68°F in your house. At 10:00 pm, it is 57°F in the house, and you notice that it is 10°F outside.

(a) Assuming that the temperature, $T$, in your home obeys Newton's Law of Cooling, write the differential equation satisfied by $T$.

(b) Solve the differential equation to estimate the temperature in the house when you get up at 7:00 am the next morning. Should you worry about your water pipes freezing?

(c) What assumption did you make in part (a) about the temperature outside? Given this (probably incorrect) assumption, would you revise your estimate up or down? Why?

**23.** A detective finds a murder victim at 9 am. The temperature of the body is measured at $90.3°$F. One hour later, the temperature of the body is $89.0°$F. The temperature of the room has been maintained at a constant $68°$F.

  **(a)** Assuming the temperature, $T$, of the body obeys Newton's Law of Cooling, write a differential equation for $T$.

  **(b)** Solve the differential equation to estimate the time the murder occurred.

**24.** A drug is administered intravenously at a constant rate of $r$ mg/hour and is excreted at a rate proportional to the quantity present, with constant of proportionality $\alpha > 0$.

  **(a)** Solve a differential equation for the quantity, $Q$, in milligrams, of the drug in the body at time $t$ hours. Assume there is no drug in the body initially. Your answer will contain $r$ and $\alpha$. Graph $Q$ against $t$. What is $Q_\infty$, the limiting long-run value of $Q$?

  **(b)** What effect does doubling $r$ have on $Q_\infty$? What effect does doubling $r$ have on the time to reach half the limiting value, $\frac{1}{2}Q_\infty$ ?

  **(c)** What effect does doubling $\alpha$ have on $Q_\infty$? On the time to reach $\frac{1}{2}Q_\infty$?

**25.** Some people write the solution of the initial value problem

$$\frac{dy}{dt} = k(y - A) \qquad y = y_0 \text{ at } t = 0$$

in the form

$$\frac{y - A}{y_0 - A} = e^{kt}.$$

Show that this formula gives the correct solution for $y$, assuming $y_0 \neq A$.

# 9.6 MODELING THE INTERACTION OF TWO POPULATIONS

So far we have used a differential equation to model the growth of a single quantity. We now consider the growth of two interacting populations, a situation which requires a system of two differential equations. Examples include two species competing for food, one species preying on another, or two species helping each other (symbiosis).

## A Predator-Prey Model: Robins and Worms

We model a predator-prey system using what are called the Lotka-Volterra equations. Let's look at a simplified and idealized case in which robins are the predators and worms the prey.[3] Suppose there are $r$ thousand robins and $w$ million worms. If there were no robins, the worms would increase exponentially according to the equation

$$\frac{dw}{dt} = aw \qquad \text{where } a \text{ is a positive constant.}$$

If there were no worms, the robins would have no food and so their population would decrease according to the equation[4]

$$\frac{dr}{dt} = -br \qquad \text{where } b \text{ is a positive constant.}$$

Now imagine the effect of the two populations on one another. Clearly, the presence of the robins is bad for the worms, so

$$\frac{dw}{dt} = aw - \text{Effect of robins on worms.}$$

On the other hand, the robins do better with the worms around, so

$$\frac{dr}{dt} = -br + \text{Effect of worms on robins.}$$

How exactly do the two populations interact? Let's assume the effect of one population on the other is proportional to the number of "encounters." (An encounter is when a robin eats a worm.)

---

[3] Based on work by Thomas A. McMahon.

[4] This assumption unrealistically predicts that the robin population will decay exponentially, rather than die out in finite time.

The number of encounters is likely to be proportional to the product of the populations because if one population is held fixed, the number of encounters should be directly proportional to the other population. So we assume

$$\frac{dw}{dt} = aw - cwr \qquad \text{and} \qquad \frac{dr}{dt} = -br + kwr,$$

where $c$ and $k$ are positive constants.

To analyze this system of equations, let's look at the specific example with $a = b = c = k = 1$:

$$\frac{dw}{dt} = w - wr \qquad \text{and} \qquad \frac{dr}{dt} = -r + wr.$$

## The Phase Plane

To see the growth of the populations, we want graphs of $r$ and $w$ against $t$. However, it is easier to obtain a graph of $r$ against $w$ first. If we plot a point $(w, r)$ representing the number of worms and robins at any moment, then, as the populations change, the point moves. The $wr$-plane on which the point moves is called the *phase plane* and the path of the point is called the *phase trajectory*.

To find the phase trajectory, we need a differential equation relating $w$ and $r$ directly. We have the two differential equations

$$\frac{dw}{dt} = w - wr \qquad \text{and} \qquad \frac{dr}{dt} = -r + wr.$$

Thinking of $r$ as a function of $w$ and $w$ as a function of $t$, the chain rule gives

$$\frac{dr}{dt} = \frac{dr}{dw} \cdot \frac{dw}{dt}.$$

This tells us that

$$\frac{dr}{dw} = \frac{dr/dt}{dw/dt},$$

so we have

$$\frac{dr}{dw} = \frac{-r + wr}{w - wr}.$$

Figure 9.39 shows the slope field of this differential equation in the phase plane.

**Figure 9.39:** Slope field for $\dfrac{dr}{dw} = \dfrac{-r + wr}{w - wr}$

## The Slope Field and Equilibrium Points

We can get an idea of what solutions of this equation look like from the slope field. At the point $(1, 1)$ there is no slope drawn because $dr/dw$ is undefined there since the rates of change of both populations with respect to time are zero:

$$\frac{dw}{dt} = 1 - 1 \cdot 1 = 0, \qquad \text{and} \qquad \frac{dr}{dt} = -1 + 1 \cdot 1 = 0.$$

In terms of worms and robins, this means that if at some moment $w = 1$ and $r = 1$ (that is, there are 1 million worms and 1 thousand robins), then $w$ and $r$ remain constant forever. The point $w = 1$, $r = 1$ is therefore an equilibrium solution. The origin is also an equilibrium point, since if $w = 0$ and $r = 0$, then $w$ and $r$ remain constant. The slope field suggests that there are no other equilibrium points. We check this by solving

$$\frac{dw}{dt} = w - wr = 0 \qquad \text{and} \qquad \frac{dr}{dt} = -r + rw = 0,$$

which yields only $w = 0$, $r = 0$ and $w = 1$, $r = 1$ as solutions.

## Trajectories in the $wr$-Phase Plane

Let's look at the trajectories in the phase plane. A point on a curve represents a pair of populations $(w, r)$ existing at the same time $t$ (though $t$ is not shown on the graph). A short time later, the pair of populations is represented by a nearby point. As time passes, the point traces out a trajectory. It can be shown that the trajectory is a closed curve. See Figure 9.40.

In which direction does the point move on the trajectory? Look at the original pair of differential equations. They tell us how $w$ and $r$ change with time. Imagine, for example, that we are at the point $P_0$ in Figure 9.41, where $w = 2.2$ and $r = 1$; then

$$\frac{dr}{dt} = -r + wr = -1 + (2.2)(1) = 1.2 > 0.$$

Therefore, $r$ is increasing, so the point is moving in the direction shown by the arrow in Figure 9.41.

Figure 9.40: Solution curve is closed          Figure 9.41: A trajectory

---

**Example 1**   Suppose that at time $t = 0$, there are 2.2 million worms and 1 thousand robins. Describe how the robin and worm populations change over time.

Solution   The trajectory through the point $P_0$ where $w = 2.2$ and $r = 1$ is shown on the slope field in Figure 9.40 and by itself in Figure 9.41.

Initially there are lots of worms so the robin population does well. The robin population is increasing and the worm population is decreasing until there are about 2.2 thousand robins and 1 million worms (point $P_1$ in Figure 9.41). At this point, there are too few worms to sustain the robin population; it begins to decrease and the worm population continues to fall as well. The robin population falls dramatically until there are about 1 thousand robins and 0.4 million worms (point $P_2$ in Figure 9.41). With so few robins, the worm population starts to recover, but the robin population is still decreasing. The worm population increases until there are about 0.4 thousand robins and 1 million worms ($P_3$ in Figure 9.41). Now there are lots of worms for the small population of robins so both populations increase. The populations return to the starting values (since the trajectory forms a closed curve) and the cycle starts over.

Problem 17 at the end of the section shows how to calculate approximate coordinates of points on the curve.

## The Populations as Functions of Time

The shape of a trajectory tells us how the populations vary with time. We use this information to graph each population against time, as in Figure 9.42. The fact that the trajectory is a closed curve means that both populations oscillate periodically. Both populations have the same period, and the worms (the prey) are at their maximum a quarter of a cycle before the robins.

Figure 9.42: Populations of robins (in thousands) and worms (in millions) over time

## Lynxes and Hares

A predator-prey system for which there are long-term data is the Canadian lynx and the hare. Both animals were of interest to fur trappers and the records of the Hudson Bay Company shed some light on their populations through much of the 20$^{\text{th}}$ century. These records show that both populations oscillated up and down, quite regularly, with a period of about ten years. This is the behavior predicted by Lotka-Volterra equations.

# Other Forms of Species Interaction

The methods of this section can be used to model other types of interactions between two species, such as competition and symbiosis.

**Example 2**    Describe the interactions between two populations $x$ and $y$ modeled by the following systems of differential equations.

(a) $\dfrac{dx}{dt} = 0.2x - 0.5xy$

  $\dfrac{dy}{dt} = 0.6y - 0.8xy$

(b) $\dfrac{dx}{dt} = -2x + 5xy$

  $\dfrac{dy}{dt} = -y + 0.2xy$

(c) $\dfrac{dx}{dt} = 0.5x$

  $\dfrac{dy}{dt} = -1.6y + 2xy$

(d) $\dfrac{dx}{dt} = 0.3x - 1.2xy$

  $\dfrac{dy}{dt} = -0.7y + 2.5xy$

Solution      (a) If we ignore the interaction terms with $xy$, we have $dx/dt = 0.2x$ and $dy/dt = 0.6y$, so both populations grow exponentially. Since both interaction terms are negative, each species inhibits the other's growth, such as when deer and elk compete for food.

       (b) If we ignore the interaction terms, the populations of both species decrease exponentially. However, both interaction terms are positive, meaning each species benefits from the other, so the relationship is symbiotic. An example is the pollination of plants by insects.

       (c) Ignoring interaction, $x$ grows and $y$ decays. But the interaction term means that $y$ benefits from $x$, in the way birds that build nests benefit from trees.

       (d) Without the interaction, $x$ grows and $y$ decays. The interaction terms show that $y$ hurts $x$ while $x$ benefits $y$. This is a predator-prey model where $y$ is the predator and $x$ is the prey.

## Problems for Section 9.6

Problems 1–3 give the rates of growth of two populations, $x$ and $y$, measured in thousands.

(a) Describe in words what happens to the population of each species in the absence of the other.

(b) Describe in words how the species interact with one another. Give reasons why the populations might behave as described by the equations. Suggest species that might interact in that way.

**1.** $\dfrac{dx}{dt} = 0.2x$

$\dfrac{dy}{dt} = 0.4xy - 0.1y$

**2.** $\dfrac{dx}{dt} = 0.01x - 0.05xy$

$\dfrac{dy}{dt} = -0.2y + 0.08xy$

**3.** $\dfrac{dx}{dt} = 0.01x - 0.05xy$

$\dfrac{dy}{dt} = 0.2y - 0.08xy$

**4.** The following system of differential equations represents the interaction between two populations, $x$ and $y$.

$$\frac{dx}{dt} = -3x + 2xy$$

$$\frac{dy}{dt} = -y + 5xy$$

(a) Describe how the species interact. How would each species do in the absence of the other? Are they helpful or harmful to each other?

(b) If $x = 2$ and $y = 1$, does $x$ increase or decrease? Does $y$ increase or decrease? Justify your answers.

(c) Write a differential equation involving $dy/dx$.

(d) Use a computer or calculator to draw the slope field for the differential equation in part (c).

(e) Draw the trajectory starting at point $x = 2$, $y = 1$ on your slope field, and describe how the populations change as time increases.

Create a system of differential equations to model the situations in Problems 5–7. You may assume that all constants of proportionality are 1.

**5.** The concentrations of two chemicals are denoted by $x$ and $y$, respectively. Alone, each decays at a rate proportional to its concentration. Together, they interact to form a third substance. As the third substance is created, the concentrations of the initial two populations get smaller.

**6.** Two businesses are in competition with each other. Both businesses would do well without the other one, but each hurts the other's business. The values of the two businesses are given by $x$ and $y$.

**7.** A population of fleas is represented by $x$, and a population of dogs is represented by $y$. The fleas need the dogs in order to survive. The dog population, however, is unaffected by the fleas.

**8.** Two companies, $A$ and $B$, are in competition with each other. Let $x$ represent the net worth (in millions of dollars) of Company $A$, and $y$ represent the net worth (in millions of dollars) of Company $B$. Four trajectories are given in Figure 9.43. For each trajectory: Describe the initial conditions. Describe what happens initially: Do the companies gain or lose money early on? What happens in the long run?

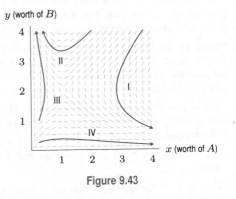

Figure 9.43

For Problems 9–19, let $w$ be the number of worms (in millions) and $r$ the number of robins (in thousands) living on an island. Suppose $w$ and $r$ satisfy the following differential equations, which correspond to the slope field in Figure 9.44.

$$\frac{dw}{dt} = w - wr, \qquad \frac{dr}{dt} = -r + wr.$$

*r* (predator)

Figure 9.44: $\frac{dr}{dw} = \frac{r(w-1)}{w(1-r)}$

*w* (prey)

9. Explain why these differential equations are a reasonable model for interaction between the two populations. Why have the signs been chosen this way?

10. Solve these differential equations in the two special cases when there are no robins and when there are no worms living on the island.

11. Describe and explain the symmetry you observe in the slope field. What consequences does this symmetry have for the solution curves?

12. Assume $w = 2$ and $r = 2$ when $t = 0$. Do the numbers of robins and worms increase or decrease at first? What happens in the long run?

13. For the case discussed in Problem 12, estimate the maximum and the minimum values of the robin population. How many worms are there at the time when the robin population reaches its maximum?

14. On the same axes, graph $w$ and $r$ (the worm and the robin populations) against time. Use initial values of 1.5 for $w$ and 1 for $r$. You may do this without units for $t$.

15. People on the island like robins so much that they decide to import 200 robins all the way from England, to increase the initial population from $r = 2$ to $r = 2.2$ when $t = 0$. Does this make sense? Why or why not?

16. Assume that $w = 3$ and $r = 1$ when $t = 0$. Do the numbers of robins and worms increase or decrease initially? What happens in the long run?

17. At $t = 0$ there are 2.2 million worms and 1 thousand robins.

   (a) Use the differential equations to calculate the derivatives $dw/dt$ and $dr/dt$ at $t = 0$.

   (b) Use the initial values and your answer to part (a) to estimate the number of robins and worms at $t = 0.1$.

   (c) Using the method of part (a) and (b), estimate the number of robins and worms at $t = 0.2$ and $0.3$.

18. (a) Assume that there are 3 million worms and 2 thousand robins. Locate the point corresponding to this situation on the slope field given in Figure 9.44. Draw the trajectory through this point.

   (b) In which direction does the point move along this trajectory? Put an arrow on the trajectory and justify your answer using the differential equations for $dr/dt$ and $dw/dt$ given in this section.

   (c) How large does the robin population get? What is the size of the worm population when the robin population is at its largest?

   (d) How large does the worm population get? What is the size of the robin population when the worm population is at its largest?

19. Repeat Problem 18 if initially there are 0.5 million worms and 3 thousand robins.

20. For each system of differential equations in Example 2, determine whether $x$ increases or decreases and whether $y$ increases or decreases when $x = 2$ and $y = 2$.

For Problems 21–25, suppose $x$ and $y$ are the populations of two different species. Describe in words how each population changes with time.

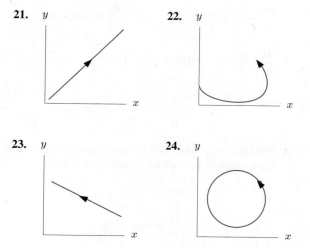

21. *y*

22. *y*

23. *y*

24. *y*

25. A kidney removes toxin from the blood. If a kidney does not function, the toxin can be removed by dialysis. This problem explores a model for $Q_1(t)$, the quantity of toxin in the body outside the blood, and $Q_2(t)$, the quantity of toxin in the blood, where $t$ is the time after dialysis started.

   (a) The quantity $Q_1$ changes for three reasons. First, toxin is created outside the blood at a constant rate, say $A$. Second, toxin flows into the blood at a rate proportional to the quantity outside the blood. Third, toxin flows out of the blood at a rate proportional to the quantity in the blood. Write a differential equation for $Q_1$.

(b) The quantity $Q_2$ changes for three reasons. First, dialysis removes toxin from the blood at a rate proportional to the toxin in the blood. Second and third, the same flows into and out of the blood that change

$Q_1$ also change $Q_2$. Write a differential equation for $Q_2$.

26. For each system of equations in Example 2, write a differential equation involving $dy/dx$. Use a computer or calculator to draw the slope field for $x, y > 0$. Then draw the trajectory through the point $x = 3, y = 1$.

# 9.7   MODELING THE SPREAD OF A DISEASE

Differential equations can be used to predict when an outbreak of a disease becomes so severe that it is called an *epidemic*[5] and to decide what level of vaccination is necessary to prevent an epidemic. Let's consider a specific example.

## Flu in a British Boarding School

In January 1978, 763 students returned to a boys' boarding school after their winter vacation. A week later, one boy developed the flu, followed immediately by two more. By the end of the month, nearly half the boys were sick. Most of the school had been affected by the time the epidemic was over in mid-February.[6]

Being able to predict how many people will get sick, and when, is an important step toward controlling an epidemic. This is one of the responsibilities of Britain's Communicable Disease Surveillance Centre and the US's Center for Disease Control and Prevention.

## The $S$-$I$-$R$ model

We apply one of the most commonly used models for an epidemic, called the $S$-$I$-$R$ model, to the boarding school flu example. Imagine the population of the school divided into three groups:

$S$ = the number of *susceptibles*, the people who are not yet sick
   but who could become sick

$I$ = the number of *infecteds*, the people who are currently sick

$R$ = the number of *recovered*, or *removed*, the people who have
   been sick and can no longer infect others or be reinfected.

In this model, the number of susceptibles decreases with time, as people become infected. We assume that the rate people become infected is proportional to the number of contacts between susceptible and infected people. We expect the number of contacts between the two groups to be proportional to both $S$ and $I$. (If $S$ doubles, we expect the number of contacts to double; similarly, if $I$ doubles, we expect the number of contacts to double.) Thus, we assume that the number of contacts is proportional to the product, $SI$. In other words, we assume that for some constant $a > 0$,

$$\frac{dS}{dt} = -\left( \begin{array}{c} \text{Rate susceptibles} \\ \text{get sick} \end{array} \right) = -aSI.$$

(The negative sign is used because $S$ is decreasing.)

---

[5] Exactly when a disease should be called an epidemic is not always clear. The medical profession generally classifies a disease an epidemic when the frequency is higher than usually expected—leaving open the question of what is usually expected. See, for example, *Epidemiology in Medicine* by C. H. Hennekens and J. Buring (Boston: Little, Brown, 1987).

[6] Data from the Communicable Disease Surveillance Centre (UK); reported in "Influenza in a Boarding School," *British Medical Journal* March 4, 1978, and by J. D. Murray in *Mathematical Biology* (New York: Springer Verlag, 1990).

The number of infecteds is changing in two ways: newly sick people are added to the infected group and others are removed. The newly sick people are exactly those people leaving the susceptible group and so accrue at a rate of $aSI$ (with a positive sign this time). People leave the infected group either because they recover (or die), or because they are physically removed from the rest of the group and can no longer infect others. We assume that people are removed at a rate proportional to the number sick, or $bI$, where $b$ is a positive constant. Thus,

$$\frac{dI}{dt} = \text{Rate susceptibles get sick} - \text{Rate infecteds get removed} = aSI - bI.$$

Assuming that those who have recovered from the disease are no longer susceptible, the recovered group increases at the rate of $bI$, so

$$\frac{dR}{dt} = bI.$$

We are assuming that having the flu confers immunity on a person, that is, that the person cannot get the flu again. (This is true for a given strain of flu, at least in the short run.)

We can use the fact that the total population $S+I+R$ is not changing. (The total population, the total number of boys in the school, did not change during the epidemic; see Problem 2 on page 448.) Thus, once we know $S$ and $I$, we can calculate $R$. So we restrict our attention to the two equations

$$\frac{dS}{dt} = -aSI$$
$$\frac{dI}{dt} = aSI - bI.$$

### The Constants $a$ and $b$

The constant $a$ measures how infectious the disease is—that is, how quickly it is transmitted from the infecteds to the susceptibles. In the case of the flu, we know from medical accounts that the epidemic started with one sick boy, with two more becoming sick about a day later. Thus, when $I = 1$ and $S = 762$, we have $dS/dt \approx -2$, enabling us to roughly[7] approximate $a$:

$$a = -\frac{dS/dt}{SI} = \frac{2}{762 \cdot 1} = 0.0026.$$

The constant $b$ represents the rate at which infected people are removed from the infected population. In this case of the flu, boys were generally taken to the infirmary within one or two days of becoming sick. Assuming half the infected population was removed each day, we take $b \approx 0.5$. Thus, our equations are:

$$\frac{dS}{dt} = -0.0026SI$$
$$\frac{dI}{dt} = 0.0026SI - 0.5I.$$

## The Phase Plane

As in Section 9.6, we look at trajectories in the phase plane. Thinking of $I$ as a function of $S$, and $S$ as a function of $t$, we use the chain rule to get

$$\frac{dI}{dt} = \frac{dI}{dS} \cdot \frac{dS}{dt},$$

so

$$\frac{dI}{dS} = \frac{dI/dt}{dS/dt}.$$

Substituting for $dI/dt$ and $dS/dt$, we get

$$\frac{dI}{dS} = \frac{0.0026SI - 0.5I}{-0.0026SI}.$$

[7]The values of $a$ and $b$ are close to those obtained by J. D. Murray in *Mathematical Biology* (New York: Springer Verlag, 1990).

Assuming $I$ is not zero, this equation simplifies to approximately

$$\frac{dI}{dS} = -1 + \frac{192}{S}.$$

The slope field of this differential equation is shown in Figure 9.45. The trajectory with initial condition $S_0 = 762$, $I_0 = 1$ is shown in Figure 9.46. Time is represented by the arrow showing the direction that a point moves on the trajectory. The disease starts at the point $S_0 = 762$, $I_0 = 1$. At first, more people become infected and fewer are susceptible. In other words, $S$ decreases and $I$ increases. Later, $I$ decreases as $S$ continues to decrease.

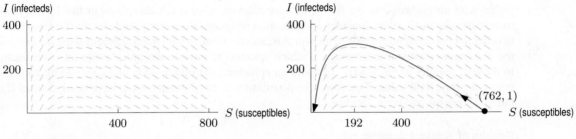

Figure 9.45: Slope field for $dI/dS = -1 + 192/S$        Figure 9.46: Trajectory for $S_0 = 762$, $I_0 = 1$

### What does the $SI$-Phase Plane Tell Us?

To learn how the disease progresses, look at the shape of the curve in Figure 9.46. The value of $I$ first increases, then decreases to zero. This peak value of $I$ occurs when $S \approx 200$. We can determine exactly when the peak value occurs by solving

$$\frac{dI}{dS} = -1 + \frac{192}{S} = 0,$$

which gives

$$S = 192.$$

Notice that the peak value for $I$ always occurs at the same value of $S$, namely $S = 192$. The graph shows that if a trajectory starts with $S_0 > 192$, then $I$ first increases and then decreases to zero. On the other hand, if $S_0 < 192$, there is no peak, since $I$ decreases right away.

For this example, the value $S = 192$ is called a *threshold population*. If $S_0$ is around or below 192, there is no epidemic. If $S_0$ is significantly greater than 192, an epidemic occurs.[8]

The phase diagram makes clear that the maximum value of $I$ is about 300, which is the maximum number infected at any one time. In addition, the point at which the trajectory crosses the $S$-axis represents the time when the epidemic has passed (since $I = 0$). Thus, the $S$-intercept shows how many boys never get the flu and, hence, how many do get sick.

---

**Example 1**    In the boarding school model, if $S = 400$ and $I = 250$, use Figure 9.46 to decide the signs of $dI/dt$ and $dS/dt$. Confirm your answers using the differential equations.

Solution    Since $S = 400$ is greater than the peak value of $S = 192$, we expect that the infected population is still increasing, so $dI/dt > 0$. The susceptible population is always decreasing (until the disease dies out), so $dS/dt < 0$. Checking the differential equations when $S = 400$ and $I = 250$, we see $dS/dt = -0.0026SI = -260$ and $dI/dt = 0.0026SI - 0.5I = 135$.

---

[8]Here we are using J. D. Murray's definition of an epidemic as an outbreak in which the number of infecteds increases from the initial value, $I_0$. See *Mathematical Biology* (New York: Springer Verlag, 1990).

## Threshold Value

For the general SIR model, we have the following result:

$$\text{Threshold population} = \frac{b}{a}.$$

If $S_0$, the initial number of susceptibles, is above $b/a$, there is an epidemic; if $S_0$ is below $b/a$, there is no epidemic. See Problem 11.

### How Many People Should Be Vaccinated?

Faced with an outbreak of the flu or, as happened on several US campuses in the 1980s, of the measles, many institutions consider a vaccination program. How many students must be vaccinated in order to control an outbreak? To answer this, we can think of vaccination as removing people from the $S$ category (without increasing $I$), which amounts to moving the initial point on the trajectory to the left, parallel to the $S$-axis. To avoid an epidemic, the initial value of $S_0$ should be around or below the threshold value. Therefore, the boarding-school epidemic would have been avoided if all but 192 students had been vaccinated.

### Graphs of $S$ and $I$ Against $t$

On the trajectory in Figure 9.46, the number of susceptible people decreases throughout the epidemic. This makes sense since people are getting sick and then well again, and thus are no longer susceptible to infection. The trajectory also shows that the number of infected people increases and then decreases. Graphs of $S$ and $I$ against time, $t$, are shown in Figure 9.47.

To get the scale on the time axis, we would need to use numerical methods. It turns out that the number of infecteds peaked after about 6 days and then dropped. The epidemic ran its course in about 20 days.

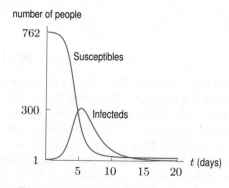

Figure 9.47: Progress of the flu over time

## Problems for Section 9.7

1. Let $I$ be the number of infected people and $S$ be the number of susceptible people in an outbreak of a disease. Explain why it is reasonable to model the interaction between these two groups by the differential equations

$$\frac{dS}{dt} = -aSI$$

$$\frac{dI}{dt} = aSI - bI \quad \text{where } a, b \text{ are positive constants.}$$

Why have the signs been chosen this way? Why is the constant $a$ the same in both equations?

2. Show that if $S$, $I$, and $R$ satisfy the differential equations in Problem 1, the total population, $S + I + R$, is constant.

3. Explain how you can tell from the graph of the trajectory shown in Figure 9.46 that most people at the British boarding school eventually got sick.

4. (a) In a school of 150 students, one of the students has the flu initially. What is $I_0$? What is $S_0$?

**(b)** Use these values of $I_0$ and $S_0$ and the equation

$$\frac{dI}{dt} = 0.0026SI - 0.5I$$

to determine whether the number of infected people initially increases or decreases. What does this tell you about the spread of the disease?

**5.** Repeat Problem 4 for a school with 350 students.

**6. (a)** On the slope field for $dI/dS$ in Figure 9.45 trajectory through the point where $I = 1$ and $S = 400$.

   **(b)** How many susceptible people are there when the number of infected people is at its maximum?

**7.** Use Figure 9.47 to estimate the maximum number of infecteds. What does this represent? When does it occur?

**8.** Compare the diseases modeled by each of the following differential equations with the flu model in this section. Match each set of differential equations with one of the following statements. Write a system of differential equations corresponding to each of the unmatched statements.

(I) $\dfrac{dS}{dt} = -0.04SI$     (II) $\dfrac{dS}{dt} = -0.002SI$

   $\dfrac{dI}{dt} = 0.04SI - 0.2I$     $\dfrac{dI}{dt} = 0.002SI - 0.3I$

(III) $\dfrac{dS}{dt} = -0.03SI$

   $\dfrac{dI}{dt} = 0.03SI$

   **(a)** More infectious; infecteds removed more slowly.
   **(b)** More infectious; infecteds removed more quickly.
   **(c)** Less infectious; infecteds removed more slowly.
   **(d)** Less infectious; infecteds removed more quickly.
   **(e)** Infecteds never removed.

**9.** For the equations (I) in Problem 8, what is the threshold value of $S$?

**10.** For the equations (II) in Problem 8, suppose $S_0 = 100$. Does the disease spread initially? What if $S_0 = 200$?

**11.** Let $S$ and $I$ satisfy the differential equations in Problem 1. Assume $I \neq 0$.

   **(a)** If $dI/dt = 0$, find $S$.
   **(b)** Show that $I$ increases if $S$ is greater than the value you found in part (a). Show that $I$ decreases if $S$ is less than the value you found in part (a).
   **(c)** Explain how you know that your answer to part (a) is the threshold value.

**12.** During World War I, a particularly lethal form of flu killed about 40 million people around the world.[9] The epidemic started in an army camp of 45,000 soldiers outside of Boston, where the first soldier fell sick on September 7, 1918. With time, $t$, in days since September 7, values of the constants in the SIR model,

$$\frac{dS}{dt} = -aSI$$
$$\frac{dI}{dt} = aSI - bI,$$

are estimated to be $a = 0.000267$, $b = 9.865$.

   **(a)** What are the initial values, $S_0$ and $I_0$?
   **(b)** Explain how you know that this model predicts an epidemic in this case.
   **(c)** Find the differential equation for $dI/dS$. Sketch its slope field and estimate the total number of soldiers infected over the course of the disease.
   **(d)** Solve the differential equation for $dI/dS$ analytically. Use the solution to solve approximately for the number of soldiers affected over the course of the disease.

# CHAPTER SUMMARY

- **Differential equations terminology**
  Family of solutions, particular solution, initial conditions, stable/unstable equilibrium solutions
- **Estimating values of a solution**
- **Slope fields**
  Visualizing the solution to a differential equation
- **Solving differential equations analytically**

Solutions to $dy/dt = ky$, and $dy/dt = k(y - A)$
- **Modeling with differential equations**
  Growth and decay, pollution in a lake, quantity of drug in the body, Newton's law of heating and cooling, net worth of a company
- **Systems of differential equations**
  Interaction of two species or businesses, predator-prey model, spread of a disease

---

[9] "Capturing a Killer Flu Virus," J. Taukenberger, A. Reid, T. Fanning, in *Scientific American*, Vol. 292, No. 1, January 2005.

## REVIEW PROBLEMS FOR CHAPTER NINE

1. Match the graphs in Figure 9.48 with the following descriptions.

    (a) The population of a new species introduced onto a tropical island.
    (b) The temperature of a metal ingot placed in a furnace and then removed.
    (c) The speed of a car traveling at uniform speed and then braking uniformly.
    (d) The mass of carbon-14 in a historical specimen.
    (e) The concentration of tree pollen in the air over the course of a year.

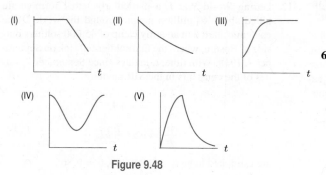

**Figure 9.48**

2. (a) Determine which of the following functions is a solution to the differential equation

$$x\frac{dy}{dx} = 3y.$$

    (i)  $y = Cx^2$        (ii)  $y = Cx^3$
    (iii)  $y = x^3 + C$

    (b) For any function which is a solution, find $C$ if $y = 40$ when $x = 2$.

3. Is $y = x^3$ a solution to the differential equation $xy' - 3y = 0$? Justify your answer.

4. For a certain quantity $y$, assume that $dy/dt = -0.20y$. Fill in the values of $y$ in Table 9.7. Assume that the rate of growth given by $dy/dt$ is approximately constant over each unit time interval.

**Table 9.7**

| $t$ | 0 | 1 | 2 | 3 | 4 |
|-----|-----|---|---|---|---|
| $y$ | 125 | | | | |

5. Slope fields for $dy/dx = 1 + x$ and $dy/dx = 1 + y$ are in Figures 9.49 and 9.50.

    (a) Which slope field corresponds to which equation?
    (b) On each slope field, draw the solution curve through the origin.

(c) For each slope field, list all equilibrium solutions and indicate whether each is stable or unstable.

**Figure 9.49**        **Figure 9.50**

6. (a) Sketch the slope field for the equation $y' = x - y$ in Figure 9.51 at the points indicated.
    (b) Check that $y = x - 1$ is the solution to the differential equation passing through the point $(1, 0)$.

**Figure 9.51**

7. Which one of the following differential equations best fits the slope field shown in Figure 9.52? Explain.

   I.   $y' = 1 + y$          II.  $y' = 2 - y$
   III.  $y' = (1 + y)(2 - y)$   IV.  $y' = 1 + x$
   V.   $y' = xy$

**Figure 9.52**

8. Match each of the slope field segments in (I)–(VI) with one or more of the differential equations in (a)–(f).

(a) $y' = e^{-x^2}$

(b) $y' = \cos y$

(c) $y' = \cos(4 - y)$

(d) $y' = y(4 - y)$

(e) $y' = y(3 - y)$

(f) $y' = x(3 - x)$

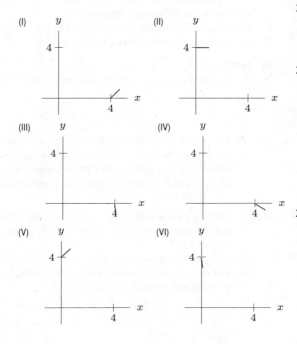

9. A deposit is made to a bank account paying an annual interest rate of 7% compounded continuously. No other deposits or withdrawals are made to the account.

(a) Write a differential equation satisfied by $B$, the balance in the account after $t$ years.

(b) Solve the differential equation given in part (a).

(c) If the initial deposit is $5000, give the particular solution satisfying this initial condition.

(d) How much is in the account after 10 years?

10. Radioactive iodine decays at a continuous rate of about 9% per day. Write a differential equation to model this behavior. Find the general solution.

Solve the differential equations in Problems 11–20.

11. $\dfrac{dP}{dt} = t$

12. $\dfrac{dy}{dt} = 5y$

13. $\dfrac{dy}{dt} = 5t$

14. $\dfrac{dP}{dt} = 0.03P$

15. $\dfrac{dA}{dt} = -0.07A$

16. $\dfrac{1}{Q}\dfrac{dQ}{dt} = 2$

---

[10]*The New York Times*, October 18, 1988.

17. $\dfrac{dP}{dt} = 10 - 2P$

18. $\dfrac{dy}{dt} = 100 - y$

19. $\dfrac{dy}{dx} = 0.2y - 8$

20. $\dfrac{dH}{dt} = 0.5H + 10$

21. Write a differential equation whose solution is the temperature as a function of time of a bottle of orange juice taken out of a $40°$F refrigerator and left in a $65°$F room. Solve the equation and graph the solution.

22. The rate of growth of a tumor is proportional to the size of the tumor.

(a) Write a differential equation satisfied by $S$, the size of the tumor, in mm, as a function of time, $t$.

(b) Find the general solution to the differential equation.

(c) If the tumor is 5 mm at time $t = 0$, what does that tell you about the solution?

(d) If, in addition, the tumor is 8 mm at time $t = 3$, what does that tell you about the solution?

23. The radioactive isotope carbon-14 is present in small quantities in all life forms, and it is constantly replenished until the organism dies, after which it decays to stable carbon-12 at a rate proportional to the amount of carbon-14 present, with a half-life of 5730 years. Suppose $C(t)$ is the amount of carbon-14 present at time $t$.

(a) Find the value of the constant $k$ in the differential equation $C' = -kC$.

(b) In 1988 three teams of scientists found that the Shroud of Turin, which was reputed to be the burial cloth of Jesus, contained 91% of the amount of carbon-14 contained in freshly made cloth of the same material.[10] How old is the Shroud of Turin, according to these data?

24. A bank account earns 5% annual interest compounded continuously. Continuous payments are made out of the account at a rate of $12,000 per year for 20 years.

(a) Write a differential equation describing the balance $B = f(t)$, where $t$ is in years.

(b) Solve the differential equation given an initial balance of $B_0$.

(c) What should the initial balance be such that the account has zero balance after precisely 20 years?

25. Warfarin is a drug used as an anticoagulant. After administration of the drug is stopped, the quantity remaining in a patient's body decreases at a rate proportional to the quantity remaining. The half-life of warfarin in the body is 37 hours.

(a) Sketch the quantity, $Q$, of warfarin in a patient's body as a function of the time, $t$, since stopping administration of the drug. Mark the 37 hours on your graph.

**(b)** Write a differential equation satisfied by $Q$.

**(c)** How many days does it take for the drug level in the body to be reduced to 25% of the original level?

**26.** Dead leaves accumulate on the ground in a forest at a rate of 3 grams per square centimeter per year. At the same time, these leaves decompose at a continuous rate of 75% per year. Write a differential equation for the total quantity of dead leaves (per square centimeter) at time $t$. Sketch a solution showing that the quantity of dead leaves tends toward an equilibrium level. What is that equilibrium level?

**27.** Morphine is often used as a pain-relieving drug. The half-life of morphine in the body is 2 hours. Suppose morphine is administered to a patient intravenously at a rate of 2.5 mg per hour, and the rate at which the morphine is eliminated is proportional to the amount present.

**(a)** Use the half-life to show that, to three decimal places, the constant of proportionality for the rate at which morphine leaves the body (in mg/hour) is $k = -0.347$.

**(b)** Write a differential equation for the quantity, $Q$, of morphine in the blood after $t$ hours.

**(c)** Use the differential equation to find the equilibrium solution. (This is the long-term amount of morphine in the body, once the system has stabilized.)

**28.** **(a)** Find all equilibrium solutions for the equation

$$\frac{dy}{dx} = 0.5y(y - 4)(2 + y).$$

**(b)** With a calculator or computer, draw a slope field for this differential equation. Use it to determine whether each equilibrium solution is stable or unstable.

**29.** According to a simple physiological model, an athletic adult male needs 20 Calories per day per pound of body weight to maintain his weight. If he consumes more or fewer Calories than those required to maintain his weight, his weight changes at a rate proportional to the difference between the number of Calories consumed and the number needed to maintain his current weight; the constant of proportionality is $1/3500$ pounds per Calorie.

Suppose that a particular person has a constant caloric intake of $I$ Calories per day. Let $W(t)$ be the person's weight in pounds at time $t$ (measured in days).

**(a)** What differential equation has solution $W(t)$?

**(b)** Find the equilibrium solution of the differential equation. Based on the context, do you expect the equilibrium to be stable or unstable?

**(c)** Solve this differential equation.

**(d)** Graph $W(t)$ if the person starts out weighing 160 pounds and consumes 3000 Calories a day.

**30.** **(a)** Graph $f(y) = y - y^2$.

**(b)** Sketch the slope field of the differential equation

$$\frac{dy}{dx} = y - y^2.$$

**(c)** Describe how the two graphs are related. In particular, explain how you can determine the equilibrium solutions to the differential equation from the graph of $f(y)$ and how you can tell if the equilibrium solutions are stable.

**31.** **(a)** What are the equilibrium solutions to the differential equation $y' = f(y)$, where $f(y)$ is graphed in Figure 9.53?

**(b)** Sketch the slope field for $y' = f(y)$.

**(c)** For each of the following initial conditions, sketch the solution curve on your slope field:

(i)   $y(0) = 0$   (ii)   $y(0) = 1$   (iii)   $y(0) = 6$
(iv)   $y(0) = 8$   (v)   $y(0) = 10$   (vi)   $y(0) = 16$
(vii)   $y(0) = 17$

**(d)** Which of the equilibrium solutions are stable? Which are unstable?

**Figure 9.53**

# STRENGTHEN YOUR UNDERSTANDING

In Problems 1–50, indicate whether the statement is true or false.

**1.** If a quantity $Q$ is increasing at a constant rate of 8 grams per hour and $Q$ is in grams and $t$ is in hours, then the quantity satisfies the differential equation $dQ/dt = 8$.

**2.** If a population $P$ is decreasing at a continuous rate of 5% per year with $t$ in years, then the population satisfies the differential equation $dP/dt = -5$.

**3.** If a population $P$ is decreasing at a continuous rate of 5%

per year with $t$ in years, then the population satisfies the differential equation $dP/dt = 0.05P$.

**4.** If the balance $B$ in a bank account earns 3% interest a year compounded continuously, and there are no other deposits to or withdrawals from the account, then the balance satisfies the differential equation $dB/dt = 0.03B$, where $t$ is in years.

**5.** If the rate at which an investment $I$ (in dollars) grows as a function of time $t$ (in years) is proportional to the size of the investment, then $dI/dt = kI$.

**6.** If fish in a population are harvested at a rate of 200 tons of fish per year and the fish population would stay stable without the harvesting, then the size of the fish population $P$ in tons satisfies the differential equation $dP/dt = -200P$ where $t$ is in years.

**7.** If the balance, $B$, in a bank account is earning interest at a rate of 5 percent per year, compounded continuously, and payments are being made out of the account at a rate of 8000 dollars per year, then the balance $B$ satisfies the differential equation $dB/dt = 0.05B - 8000$ where $B$ is in dollars and $t$ is in years.

**8.** If the rate at which the quantity $Q$ of pollutants (in tons) in a lake decreases as a function of time (in years) is proportional to $Q$, and if new pollutants are being dumped into the lake at a rate of 200 tons per year, then $dQ/dt = kQ - 200$.

**9.** If a drug is entering a patient's body through an intravenous line at a continuous rate of 12 mg per hour and if the drug is being metabolized at a continuous rate of 6.3% per hour, then the quantity, $Q$, in mg, of the drug in the body at time $t$ hours satisfies the differential equation $dQ/dt = 12 - 0.063Q$.

**10.** A deposit of \$10,000 is made into a bank account and the account earns interest at a rate of 3.2% per year, compounded continuously. The balance, $B$, in the account in $t$ years satisfies the differential equation $dB/dt = 10,000 + 0.032B$.

**11.** The differential equation $dP/dt = 3P(10 - P)$ has $P = 10$ as a solution.

**12.** The differential equation $dP/dt = 3P(10 - P)$ has $P = 0$ as a solution.

**13.** The differential equation $dP/dt = 3P(10 - P)$ has $P = 5$ as a solution.

**14.** If $y = Ce^{0.05t}$ is the general solution to a differential equation, then $y = 40e^{0.05t}$ is the particular solution satisfying the initial condition $y(0) = 40$.

**15.** If $y = 25 + Ce^{0.05t}$ is the general solution to a differential equation, then $y = 25 + 40e^{0.05t}$ is the particular solution satisfying the initial condition $y(0) = 40$.

**16.** If $y = 25 + Ce^{0.05t}$ is the general solution to a differential equation, then $y = 25 + 15e^{0.05t}$ is the particular solution satisfying the initial condition $y(0) = 40$.

**17.** If $y(0) = 100$ and $y' = 0.2y$, then $y(1) \approx 20$. Assume the rate of growth is approximately constant over unit intervals.

**18.** If $y(0) = 100$ and $y' = 0.2y$, then $y(1) \approx 120$. Assume the rate of growth is approximately constant over unit intervals.

**19.** If $dQ/dt = 5Q - 200$ then when $Q = 10$, the quantity $Q$ will be decreasing.

**20.** If $dQ/dt = 5Q - 200$ there is a solution of the form $Q(t) = C$ for some constant $C$.

**21.** The slope field of the differential equation $dy/dx = 2x$ has slope 5 at the point $(3, 5)$.

**22.** The slope field of the differential equation $dy/dx = 2x$ has slope 6 at the point $(3, 5)$.

**23.** The slope field of the differential equation $dy/dx = 3xy$ has slope $-6$ at the point $(1, -2)$.

**24.** The slope field of the differential equation $dy/dx = 3xy$ has slope 6 at the point $(2, 2)$.

**25.** The slope field of the differential equation $dy/dx = 3xy$ has slope 18 at the point $(3, 2)$.

**26.** The slope field of the differential equation $dy/dx = 2x$ has positive slopes when $y > 0$.

**27.** The slope field of the differential equation $dy/dx = 2y$ has slope 2 at the points $(a, 1)$ for all $a$.

**28.** The slope field of the differential equation $dy/dx = 5(x-3)(y-2)$ has horizontal line segments when $x = 3$.

**29.** The slope field of the differential equation $dP/dt = 12 - 4P$ has positive slopes when $P > 3$.

**30.** The lines in a slope field for a differential equation are tangent to solutions of the differential equation.

**31.** The general solution of the differential equation $dy/dt = ky$ is $y = ke^{Ct}$.

**32.** The general solution of the differential equation $dQ/dt = 0.25Q$ is $Q = Ce^{0.25t}$.

**33.** The general solution of the differential equation $dw/dr = 0.3r$ is $w = Ce^{0.3r}$.

**34.** The function $H = 57e^{0.5t}$ is one solution to the differential equation $dH/dt = 0.5t$.

**35.** There is exactly one solution of the differential equation $dy/dt = 3y$ which has $y(0) = 5$.

**36.** The particular solution of $dy/dt = -2y$ satisfying $y = 3$ when $t = 0$ is $y = Ce^{-2t}$.

**37.** The balance $B$ in a bank account that earns interest continuously at a rate of 3% per year on an initial deposit of \$5000 has differential equation $dB/dt = 5000B$.

**38.** If $Q(t)$ is the quantity of a drug in a patient's bloodstream at time $t$, and the rate at which the drug leaves the bloodstream is proportional to the quantity in the bloodstream, then $dQ/dt = -kQ$ where $k$ is some negative constant.

**39.** A quantity, $Q$, of dead leaves decomposes at a rate proportional to the quantity present. We can model this with the differential equation $Q = Ce^{kt}$, where $k$ is negative and $t$ represents time.

**40.** A quantity, $Q$, of dead leaves decomposes at a rate proportional to the quantity present. We can model this with the differential equation $dQ/dt = kQ$, where $k$ is negative and $t$ represents time.

**41.** The general solution to the differential equation $dy/dt = 0.3(y - 75)$ is $y = 75 + Ce^{0.3t}$.

**42.** The general solution to the differential equation $dP/dt = 2P - 100$ is $P = 100 + Ce^{2t}$.

**43.** The general solution to the differential equation $dQ/dt = 0.5(Q + 20)$ is $Q = 20 + Ce^{0.5t}$.

**44.** The general solution to the differential equation $dW/dt = 600 - 3W$ is $W = 200 + Ce^{-3t}$.

**45.** The solution to the differential equation $dA/dt = 0.25(A - 40)$ with initial condition $A(0) = 50$ is $A = 40 + 50e^{0.25t}$.

**46.** The solution to the differential equation $dQ/dt = 50 - 2Q$ with initial condition $Q(0) = 100$ is $Q = 25 + 75e^{-2t}$.

**47.** The balance, $B$, in a bank account earns 4% interest per year, compounded continuously, and payments are made out of the account at a rate of \$12,000 per year. If $t$ is in years, the differential equation to model this situation is $B = 12,000 + Ce^{0.04t}$.

**48.** A drug enters a patient's body intravenously at a continuous rate of 12 mg per hour, and the drug is metabolized at a continuous rate of 18% per hour. If $A$ gives the quantity of drug in the body at hour $t$, then the differential equation to model this situation is $dA/dt = 12 - 0.18A$.

**49.** An equilibrium solution for the differential equation $dH/dt = -0.037(H - 225)$ is $H = 225$.

**50.** The graph of an equilibrium solution for a differential equation is a horizontal line.

In Problems 51–60, indicate whether the statement is true or false. Assume $x$ and $y$ represent the sizes of populations of two interacting species $X$ and $Y$ with system of differential equations as given.

**51.** Assume $dx/dt = ax + bxy$ and $dy/dt = cy + dxy$. If $X$ would do fine if $Y$ did not exist, then $b$ must be positive.

**52.** Assume $dx/dt = ax + bxy$ and $dy/dt = cy + dxy$. If species $X$ eats species $Y$, then $c$ must be negative.

**53.** Assume $dx/dt = ax + bxy$ and $dy/dt = cy + dxy$. If species $X$ eats species $Y$, then $d$ must be negative.

**54.** Assume $dx/dt = ax + bxy$ and $dy/dt = cy + dxy$. If species $X$ cannot survive without species $Y$ and does fine with species $Y$, then $a$ must be negative and $b$ must be positive.

**55.** If $dx/dt = 0.02x - 0.15xy$ and $dy/dt = 0.05y - 0.18xy$, then both populations need the other to survive.

**56.** If $dx/dt = 0.02x - 0.15xy$ and $dy/dt = 0.05y - 0.18xy$, then both populations would do fine if the other population did not exist.

**57.** If $dx/dt = 0.02x - 0.15xy$ and $dy/dt = 0.05y - 0.18xy$, then the two populations have a negative impact on each other.

**58.** If $dx/dt = -0.12x + 0.07xy$ and $dy/dt = -0.10y + 0.25xy$, then the two populations need each other to survive..

**59.** Assume $dx/dt = -3x + xy$ and $dy/dt = 2y - 5xy$. If $x = 1$ and $y = 2$, then both populations will decrease in size.

**60.** Assume $dx/dt = -3x + xy$ and $dy/dt = 2y - 5xy$. If $x = 2$ and $y = 5$, then both populations will decrease in size.

In Problems 61–70, indicate whether the statement is true or false. The problems refer to the $S - I - R$ model, in which the variable $S$ represents the number of people susceptible to becoming sick, the variable $I$ represents the number of people currently infected, and $R$ represents the rest of the population. We have

$$\frac{dS}{dt} = -aSI$$
$$\frac{dI}{dt} = aSI - bI.$$

**61.** The derivative $dS/dt$ is negative because people are dying from the epidemic.

**62.** The parameter $a$ in $dS/dt = -aSI$ is the same as the parameter $a$ in $dI/dt = aSI - bI$ because people are moving from one group to the other.

**63.** The term $-bI$ in $dI/dt = aSI - bI$ is negative because people are moving back to the susceptible group.

**64.** The term $-bI$ in $dI/dt = aSI - bI$ is negative because people are either recovering or dying or being separated from the rest of the population and are no longer in either the $S$ group or the $I$ group.

**65.** If Type I flu is much more contagious than Type II flu, then the parameter $b$ will be larger for Type I flu.

**66.** If Type I flu is much more contagious than Type II flu, then the parameter $a$ will be larger for Type I flu.

**67.** If Type I flu lasts 10 days and Type II flu lasts 3 days, then the parameter $b$ will be larger for Type I flu.

**68.** If Type I flu lasts 10 days and Type II flu lasts 3 days, then the parameter $b$ will be smaller for Type I flu.

**69.** If $a = 0.001$ and $b = 0.3$ and if current numbers are $S = 500$ and $I = 100$, then the number of sick people will increase.

**70.** If $a = 0.001$ and $b = 0.3$ and if current numbers are $S = 100$ and $I = 500$, then the number of sick people will increase.

# PROJECTS FOR CHAPTER NINE

1. **Harvesting and Logistic Growth** In this project, we look at the effects of *harvesting* a population which is growing logistically. Harvesting could be, for example, fishing or logging. An important question is what level of harvesting leads to a *sustainable yield*. In other words, how much can be harvested without having the population depleted in the long run?

   **(a)** When there is no fishing, a population of fish is governed by the differential equation

   $$\frac{dN}{dt} = 2N - 0.01N^2,$$

   where $N$ is the number of fish at time $t$ in years. Sketch a graph of $dN/dt$ against $N$. Mark on your graph the equilibrium values of $N$.

   Notice on your graph that if $N$ is between 0 and 200, then $dN/dt$ is positive and $N$ increases. If $N$ is greater than 200, then $dN/dt$ is negative and $N$ decreases. Check this by sketching a slope field for this differential equation. Use the slope field to sketch solutions showing $N$ against $t$ for various initial values. Describe what you see.

   **(b)** Fish are now removed by fishermen at a continuous rate of 75 fish/year. Let $P$ be the number of fish at time $t$ with harvesting. Explain why $P$ satisfies the differential equation

   $$\frac{dP}{dt} = 2P - 0.01P^2 - 75.$$

   **(c)** Sketch $dP/dt$ against $P$. Find and label the intercepts.

   **(d)** Sketch the slope field for the differential equation for $P$.

   **(e)** Recall that if $dP/dt$ is positive for some values of $P$, then $P$ increases for these values, and if $dP/dt$ is negative for some values of $P$, then $P$ decreases for these values. The value of $P$, however, never goes past an equilibrium value. Use this information and the graph from part (c) to answer the following questions:

   (i) What are the equilibrium values of $P$?

   (ii) For what initial values of $P$ does $P$ increase? At what value does $P$ level off?

   (iii) For what initial values of $P$ does $P$ decrease?

   **(f)** Use the slope field in part (d) to sketch graphs of $P$ against $t$, with the initial values:

   (i)   $P(0) = 40$          (ii)   $P(0) = 50$          (iii)   $P(0) = 60$
   (iv)   $P(0) = 150$        (v)    $P(0) = 170$

   **(g)** Using the graphs you drew, decide what the equilibrium values of the populations are and whether or not they are stable.

   **(h)** We now look at the effect of different levels of fishing on a fish population. If fishing takes place at a continuous rate of $H$ fish/year, the fish population $P$ satisfies the differential equation

   $$\frac{dP}{dt} = 2P - 0.01P^2 - H.$$

   (i) For each of the values $H = 75, 100, 200$, plot $dP/dt$ against $P$.

   (ii) For which of the three values of $H$ that you considered in part (i) is there an initial condition such that the fish population does not die out eventually?

   (iii) Looking at your answer to part (ii), decide for what values of $H$ there is an initial value for $P$ such that the population does not die out eventually.

   (iv) Recommend a policy to ensure long-term survival of the fish population.

2. **Population Genetics**
   Population genetics is the study of hereditary traits in a population. A specific hereditary trait has two possibilities, one dominant, such as brown eyes, and one recessive, such as blue

eyes.[11] Let $b$ denote the gene responsible for the recessive trait and $B$ denote the gene responsible for the dominant trait. Each member of the population has a pair of these genes—either $BB$ (dominant individuals), $bb$ (recessive individuals), or $Bb$ (hybrid individuals). The *gene frequency* of the $b$ gene is the total number of $b$ genes in the population divided by the total number of all genes ($b$ and $B$) controlling this trait. The gene frequency is essentially constant when there are no mutations or outside influences on the population. In this project, we consider the effect of mutations on the gene frequency.

Let $q$ denote the gene frequency of the $b$ gene. Then $q$ is between 0 and 1 (since it is a fraction of a whole) and, since $b$ and $B$ are the only genes influencing this trait, the gene frequency of the $B$ gene is $1 - q$. Let time $t$ be measured in generations. Every generation, a fraction $k_1$ of the $b$ genes mutate to become $B$ genes, and a fraction $k_2$ of the $B$ genes mutate to become $b$ genes.

**(a)** Explain why the gene frequency $q$ satisfies the differential equation:

$$\frac{dq}{dt} = -k_1 q + k_2 (1 - q).$$

**(b)** If $k_1 = 0.0001$ and $k_2 = 0.0004$, simplify the differential equation for $q$ and solve it. The initial value is $q_0$. Sketch the solutions with $q_0 = 0.1$ and $q_0 = 0.9$. What is the equilibrium value of $q$? Explain how you can tell that the gene frequency gets closer to the equilibrium value as generations pass. Explain how you can tell that the equilibrium value is completely determined by the relative mutation rates.

**(c)** Repeat part (b) if $k_1 = 0.00003$ and $k_2 = 0.00001$.

### 3. The Spread of SARS

In the spring of 2003, SARS (Severe Acute Respiratory Syndrome) spread rapidly in several Asian countries and Canada. Predicting the course of the disease—how many people would be infected, how long it would last—was important to officials trying to minimize the impact of the disease. This project analyzes the spread of SARS through interaction between infected and susceptible people.

The variables are $S$, the number of susceptibles, $I$, the number of infecteds who can infect others, and $R$, the number removed (this group includes those in quarantine and those who die, as well as those who have recovered and acquired immunity). Time, $t$, is in days since March 17, 2003, the date the World Health Organization (WHO) started to publish daily SARS reports. On March 17, Hong Kong reported 95 cases. In this model

$$\frac{dS}{dt} = -aSI$$

$$\frac{dI}{dt} = aSI - bI,$$

and $S + I + R = 6.8$ million, the population of Hong Kong in 2003.[12] Estimates based on WHO data give $a = 1.25 \cdot 10^{-8}$.

**(a)** What are $S_0$ and $I_0$, the initial values of $S$ and $I$?

**(b)** During March 2003, the value of $b$ was about 0.06. Using a calculator or computer, sketch the slope field for this system of differential equations and the solution trajectory corresponding to the initial conditions. (Use $0 \leq S \leq 7 \cdot 10^6, 0 \leq I \leq 0.4 \cdot 10^6$.)

**(c)** What does your graph tell you about the total number of people infected over the course of the disease if $b = 0.06$? What is the threshold value? What does this value tell you?

**(d)** During April, as public health officials worked to get the disease under control, people who had been in contact with the disease were quarantined. Explain why quarantining has the effect of raising the value of $b$.

---

[11] Adapted from C. C. Li, *Population Genetics* (Chicago: University of Chicago Press, 1995).
[12] www.census.gov, International Data Base (IDB), accessed June 8, 2004.

(e) Using the April value, $b = 0.24$, sketch the slope field. (Use the same value of $a$ and the same window.)

(f) What is the threshold value for $b = 0.24$? What does this tell you? Comment on the quarantine policy.

(g) Comment on the effectiveness of each of the following policies intended to prevent an epidemic and protect a city from an outbreak of SARS in a nearby region.

      I Close off the city from contact with the infected region. Shut down roads, airports, trains, and other forms of direct contact.

      II Institute a quarantine policy. Isolate anyone who has been in contact with a SARS patient or anyone who shows symptoms of SARS.

# FOCUS ON THEORY

## SEPARATION OF VARIABLES

We have seen how to sketch solution curves of a differential equation using a slope field. Now we see how to solve certain differential equations analytically, finding an equation for the solution curve.

First, we look at a familiar example, the differential equation

$$\frac{dy}{dx} = -\frac{x}{y},$$

whose solution curves are the circles

$$x^2 + y^2 = C.$$

We can check that these circles are solutions by differentiation; the question now is how they were obtained. The method of *separation of variables* works by putting all the $x$s on one side of the equation and all the $y$s on the other, giving

$$y \, dy = -x \, dx.$$

We then integrate each side separately:

$$\int y \, dy = -\int x \, dx,$$

$$\frac{y^2}{2} = -\frac{x^2}{2} + k.$$

This gives the circles we were expecting:

$$x^2 + y^2 = C \qquad \text{where } C = 2k.$$

You might worry about whether it is legitimate to separate the $dx$ and the $dy$. The reason it can be done is explained at the end of this section.

## The Exponential Growth and Decay Equations

We use separation of variables to derive the general solution of the equation

$$\frac{dy}{dt} = ky.$$

Separating variables, we have

$$\frac{1}{y} dy = k \, dt,$$

and integrating,

$$\int \frac{1}{y} \, dy = \int k \, dt,$$

gives

$$\ln|y| = kt + C \quad \text{for some constant } C.$$

Solving for $|y|$ leads to

$$|y| = e^{kt+C} = e^{kt} e^C = Ae^{kt}$$

where $A = e^C$, so $A$ is positive. Thus,

$$y = (\pm A)e^{kt} = Be^{kt}$$

where $B = \pm A$, so $B$ is any nonzero constant. Even though there's no $C$ leading to $B = 0$, we can have $B = 0$ because $y = 0$ is a solution to the differential equation. We lost this solution when we divided through by $y$ at the first step. Thus we have derived the solution used earlier in the chapter:

$$y = Be^{kt} \quad \text{for any constant } B.$$

**Example 1**    Find all solutions of

$$\frac{dy}{dt} = k(y - A).$$

Solution    We separate variables and integrate:

$$\int \frac{1}{y - A}\, dy = \int k\, dt.$$

This gives

$$\ln |y - A| = kt + D,$$

where $D$ is a constant of integration. Solving for $y$ leads to

$$|y - A| = e^{kt+D} = e^{kt}e^D = Be^{kt}$$

or

$$y - A = (\pm B)e^{kt} = Ce^{kt}$$
$$y = A + Ce^{kt}.$$

Also, $C = 0$ gives a solution. This is the same result we used earlier.

**Example 2**    Find and sketch the solution to

$$\frac{dP}{dt} = 2P - 2Pt \qquad \text{satisfying } P = 5 \text{ when } t = 0.$$

Solution    Factoring the right-hand side gives

$$\frac{dP}{dt} = P(2 - 2t).$$

Separating variables, we get

$$\int \frac{dP}{P} = \int (2 - 2t)\, dt,$$

so

$$\ln |P| = 2t - t^2 + C.$$

Solving for $P$ leads to

$$|P| = e^{2t-t^2+C} = e^C e^{2t-t^2} = Ae^{2t-t^2}$$

with $A = e^C$, so $A > 0$. In addition, $A = 0$ gives a solution. Thus the general solution to the differential equation is

$$P = Be^{2t-t^2} \quad \text{for any } B.$$

To find the value of $B$, substitute $P = 5$ and $t = 0$ into the general solution, giving

$$5 = Be^{2\cdot 0 - 0^2} = B$$

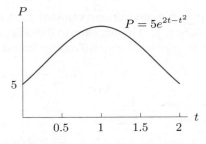

**Figure 9.54**: Bell-shaped solution curve

so

$$P = 5e^{2t-t^2}.$$

The graph of this function is in Figure 9.54. Since the solution can be rewritten as

$$P = 5e^{1-1+2t-t^2} = 5e^1 e^{-1+2t-t^2} = (5e)e^{-(t-1)^2},$$

the graph has the same shape as the graph of $y = e^{-t^2}$, the bell-shaped curve of statistics. Here the maximum, normally at $t = 0$, is shifted one unit to the right to $t = 1$.

## Justification for Separation of Variables

Suppose a differential equation can be written in the form

$$\frac{dy}{dx} = g(x)f(y).$$

Provided $f(y) \neq 0$, we write $f(y) = 1/h(y)$ so the right-hand side can be thought of as a fraction,

$$\frac{dy}{dx} = \frac{g(x)}{h(y)}.$$

If we multiply through by $h(y)$ we get

$$h(y)\frac{dy}{dx} = g(x).$$

Thinking of $y$ as a function of $x$, so $y = y(x)$, and $dy/dx = y'(x)$, we can rewrite the equation as

$$h(y(x)) \cdot y'(x) = g(x).$$

Now integrate both sides with respect to $x$:

$$\int h(y(x)) \cdot y'(x)\, dx = \int g(x)\, dx.$$

The form of the integral on the left suggests that we use the substitution $y = y(x)$. Since $dy = y'(x)\, dx$, we get

$$\int h(y)\, dy = \int g(x)\, dx.$$

If we can find antiderivatives of $h$ and $g$, then this gives the equation of the solution curve.

Note that transforming the original differential equation,

$$\frac{dy}{dx} = \frac{g(x)}{h(y)},$$

into

$$\int h(y)\, dy = \int g(x)\, dx$$

looks as though we have treated $dy/dx$ as a fraction, cross-multiplied and then integrated. Although that's not exactly what we have done, you may find this a helpful way of remembering the method. In fact, the $dy/dx$ notation was introduced by Leibniz to allow shortcuts like this (more specifically, to make the chain rule look like cancellation).

## Problems on Separation of Variables

In Problems 1–12, use separation of variables to find the solutions to the differential equations subject to the given initial conditions.

**1.** $\dfrac{dP}{dt} = -2P, \quad P(0) = 1$

**2.** $\dfrac{dL}{dp} = \dfrac{L}{2}, \quad L(0) = 100$

**3.** $P\dfrac{dP}{dt} = 1, \quad P(0) = 1$

**4.** $\dfrac{dm}{ds} = m, \quad m(1) = 2$

**5.** $2\dfrac{du}{dt} = u^2, \quad u(0) = 1$

**6.** $\dfrac{dz}{dy} = zy, \quad z = 1$ when $y = 0$

**7.** $\dfrac{dR}{dy} + R = 1, \quad R(1) = 0.1$

**8.** $\dfrac{dy}{dt} = \dfrac{y}{3+t}, \quad y(0) = 1$

**9.** $\dfrac{dz}{dt} = te^z, \quad$ through the origin

**10.** $\dfrac{dy}{dx} = \dfrac{5y}{x}, \quad y = 3$ where $x = 1$

**11.** $\dfrac{dy}{dt} = y^2(1+t), \quad y = 2$ when $t = 1$

**12.** $\dfrac{dz}{dt} = z + zt^2, \quad z = 5$ when $t = 0$

**13.** Determine which of the following differential equations are separable. Do not solve the equations.

(a) $y' = y$
(b) $y' = x + y$
(c) $y' = xy$
(d) $y' = \sin(x+y)$

(e) $y' - xy = 0$
(f) $y' = y/x$
(g) $y' = \ln(xy)$
(h) $y' = (\sin x)(\cos y)$
(i) $y' = (\sin x)(\cos xy)$
(j) $y' = x/y$
(k) $y' = 2x$
(l) $y' = (x+y)/(x+2y)$

Use separation of variables to solve the differential equations in Problems 14–19. Assume $a$, $b$, and $k$ are nonzero constants.

**14.** $\dfrac{dP}{dt} = P - a$

**15.** $\dfrac{dQ}{dt} = b - Q$

**16.** $\dfrac{dP}{dt} = k(P - a)$

**17.** $\dfrac{dR}{dt} = aR + b$

**18.** $\dfrac{dP}{dt} - aP = b$

**19.** $\dfrac{dy}{dt} = ky^2(1+t^2)$

**20.** (a) Find the general solution to the differential equation modeling how a person learns:

$$\frac{dy}{dt} = 100 - y.$$

(b) Plot the slope field of this differential equation and sketch solutions with $y(0) = 25$ and $y(0) = 110$.

(c) For each of the initial conditions in part (b), find the particular solution and add to your sketch.

(d) Which of these two particular solutions could represent how a person learns?

**21.** (a) Sketch the slope field for the differential equation $dy/dx = xy$.

(b) Sketch several solution curves.

(c) Solve the differential equation analytically.

## Chapter Ten

# GEOMETRIC SERIES

## Contents

# 10.1  GEOMETRIC SERIES

## Repeated Drug Dosage

Malaria is a parasitic infection transmitted by mosquito bites, mainly in tropical areas of the world. The disease has existed since ancient times, and currently there are hundreds of millions of cases each year, with millions of deaths. In the 1640s, the Jesuits in Peru introduced the bark of the cinchona tree to the West as the first treatment for malaria. The drug quinine is the active ingredient in the bark, and it is still used today.

Suppose a person is given a 50-mg dose of quinine at the same time every day for the treatment of malaria. After the first dose, the person has 50 mg of quinine in the body. What about after the second dose? Each day, the person's body metabolizes some of the quinine so that, after one day, 23% of the original amount remains. After the second dose, the amount of quinine in the body is the amount from the second dose (50 mg) plus the remnants of the first dose (that is, $50 \cdot 0.23 = 11.5$ mg) for a total of 61.5 mg.

Let $Q_n$ represent the quantity, in mg, of quinine in the body right after the $n^{\text{th}}$ dose. Then

$$Q_1 = \text{First dose} = 50.$$
$$Q_2 = \text{Second dose + Remnants of first dose} = 50 + 50(0.23) = 61.5.$$
$$Q_3 = \text{Third dose + Remnants of previous doses} = 50 + 61.5(0.23) = 64.145.$$

Notice that we can multiply out the expression for $Q_3$ to show the contributions of the first and second dose separately:

$$Q_3 = 50 + 61.5(0.23) = 50 + (50 + 50(0.23))(0.23)$$
$$Q_3 = 50 + 50(0.23) + 50(0.23)^2,$$

so we have

$$Q_3 = \text{Third dose + Remnants of second dose + Remnants of first dose.}$$

The multiplied-out form of $Q_3$ enables us to guess formulas for later values of $Q_n$:

$$Q_4 = 50 + 50(0.23) + 50(0.23)^2 + 50(0.23)^3 = 64.753.$$
$$Q_5 = 50 + 50(0.23) + 50(0.23)^2 + 50(0.23)^3 + 50(0.23)^4 = 64.893.$$
$$Q_6 = 50 + 50(0.23) + 50(0.23)^2 + 50(0.23)^3 + 50(0.23)^4 + 50(0.23)^5 = 64.925.$$

$$\vdots$$

$$Q_{10} = 50 + 50(0.23) + 50(0.23)^2 + \cdots + 50(0.23)^8 + 50(0.23)^9 = 64.935.$$

The values of $Q_6$ and $Q_{10}$ suggest that the quantity is stabilizing at around 64.9 mg. See Figure 10.1.

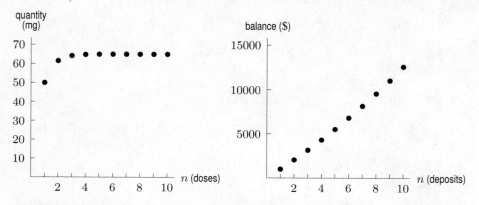

Figure 10.1: Quantity of quinine levels off    Figure 10.2: Bank balance grows without bound

## Repeated Deposits into a Savings Account

People who save money often do so by putting a fixed amount aside regularly. Suppose $1000 is deposited every year in a savings account earning 5% interest a year, compounded annually. Let $B_n$ represent the balance, in dollars, in the account right after the $n^{\text{th}}$ deposit. Then

$B_1 = $ First deposit $= 1000.$

$B_2 = $ Second deposit + Amount from first deposit $= 1000 + 1000(1.05) = 2050.$

$B_3 = $ Third deposit + Amount from previous deposits $= 1000 + 2050(1.05) = 3152.5.$

As before, we multiply out the expression for $B_3$ to show the contributions of the first and second deposits separately:

$$B_3 = 1000 + 2050(1.05) = 1000 + (1000 + 1000(1.05))(1.05)$$
$$B_3 = 1000 + 1000(1.05) + 1000(1.05)^2$$
$$B_3 = \text{Third deposit} + \text{Amount from second deposit} + \text{Amount from first deposit}.$$

The multiplied-out formula for $B_3$ enables us to guess formulas for $B_6$ and $B_{10}$. Evaluating gives

$$B_6 = 1000 + 1000(1.05) + 1000(1.05)^2 + 1000(1.05)^3 + 1000(1.05)^4 + 1000(1.05)^5 = 6801.91.$$

$$B_{10} = 1000 + 1000(1.05) + 1000(1.05)^2 + \cdots + 1000(1.05)^8 + 1000(1.05)^9 = 12{,}577.89.$$

Notice that the balance is growing without bound. See Figure 10.2.

## Finite Geometric Series

In the two previous examples, we encountered sums of the form $a + ar + ar^2 + ar^3 + \cdots + ar^8 + ar^9$. Such a sum is called a *finite geometric series*. A geometric series is a sum in which each term is a constant multiple of the preceding one. The first term is $a$, and the constant multiplier, or common ratio, of successive terms is $r$.

---

A **finite geometric series** with $n$ terms has (for $n$ a positive integer) the form

$$a + ar + ar^2 + ar^3 + \cdots + ar^{n-2} + ar^{n-1}.$$

---

### Sum of a Finite Geometric Series

In the quinine example, suppose we want to find $Q_{40}$, the quantity of quinine in the body after 40 doses:
$$Q_{40} = 50 + 50(0.23) + 50(0.23)^2 + \cdots + 50(0.23)^{38} + 50(0.23)^{39}.$$

To calculate $Q_{40}$, we could add these 40 terms. Fortunately, there is a better way.

We write $S_n$ for the sum of the first $n$ terms of the series, that is, up to the term $ar^{n-1}$:

$$S_n = a + ar + ar^2 + ar^3 + \cdots + ar^{n-2} + ar^{n-1}.$$

Multiplying both sides by $r$ gives

$$rS_n = ar + ar^2 + ar^3 + ar^4 + \cdots + ar^{n-1} + ar^n.$$

Now subtract $rS_n$ from $S_n$, so all the terms except two on the right cancel, giving

$$S_n - rS_n = a - ar^n,$$

so

$$(1 - r)S_n = a(1 - r^n).$$

Provided $r \neq 1$, we can solve for $S_n$. The result is called a *closed form* for $S_n$.

> The **sum of a finite geometric series** is given by
>
> $$S_n = a + ar + ar^2 + ar^3 + \cdots + ar^{n-1} = \frac{a(1-r^n)}{1-r}, \quad \text{provided } r \neq 1.$$

Note that the value of $n$ in the formula is the number of terms in the sum $S_n$.

**Example 1**  In the quinine example, calculate and interpret $Q_{40}$ and $Q_{100}$.

Solution    We saw earlier that

$$Q_{40} = 50 + 50(0.23) + 50(0.23)^2 + \cdots + 50(0.23)^{39}.$$

This is a finite geometric series with $a = 50$ and $r = 0.23$. Using the formula for the sum with $n = 40$, we have

$$Q_{40} = \frac{50(1-(0.23)^{40})}{1-0.23} = 64.935.$$

The amount of quinine in the body right after the $40^{\text{th}}$ dose is 64.935 mg.
   Similarly, using $n = 100$, we have

$$Q_{100} = \frac{50(1-(0.23)^{100})}{1-0.23} = 64.935.$$

Right after the $100^{\text{th}}$ dose, the amount of quinine in the body is still 64.935 mg. To three decimal places, the amount appears to have stabilized.

**Example 2**  In the bank deposit example, calculate and interpret $B_{40}$ and $B_{100}$.

Solution    We have

$$B_{40} = 1000 + 1000(1.05) + 1000(1.05)^2 + \cdots + 1000(1.05)^{39}.$$

This is a finite geometric series with $a = 1000$ and $r = 1.05$. The formula for the sum with $n = 40$ gives

$$B_{40} = \frac{1000(1-(1.05)^{40})}{1-1.05} = 120{,}799.77.$$

The balance in the account right after the $40^{\text{th}}$ deposit is \$120,799.77.
   Similarly, using $n = 100$, we have

$$B_{100} = \frac{1000(1-(1.05)^{100})}{1-1.05} = 2{,}610{,}025.16.$$

Right after the $100^{\text{th}}$ deposit, the balance in the account is \$2,610,025.16. Compound interest has increased the \$100,000 investment to over \$2 million.

## Infinite Geometric Series

Suppose a finite geometric series has $n$ terms in it. What happens as $n \to \infty$? We get an infinite geometric series that goes on forever.

> An **infinite geometric series** has the form
>
> $$a + ar + ar^2 + ar^3 + \cdots + ar^{n-1} + ar^n + \cdots.$$

The "$\cdots$" at the end of the series tells us that the series goes on forever—it has an infinite number of terms.

## Sum of an Infinite Geometric Series

Given an infinite geometric series

$$a + ar + ar^2 + ar^3 + \cdots,$$

we call the sum of the first $n$ terms a *partial sum*, written $S_n$. To calculate $S_n$, we use the formula

$$S_n = \frac{a(1 - r^n)}{1 - r}.$$

What happens to $S_n$ as $n \to \infty$? It depends on the value of $r$. If $|r| < 1$, that is, $-1 < r < 1$, then $r^n \to 0$ as $n \to \infty$, so as $n \to \infty$,

$$S_n = \frac{a(1 - r^n)}{1 - r} \to \frac{a(1 - 0)}{1 - r} = \frac{a}{1 - r}.$$

Thus, provided $|r| < 1$, as $n \to \infty$ the partial sums $S_n$ approach a limit of $a/(1 - r)$. When this happens, we define the sum of the infinite geometric series to be that limit and say the series *converges* to $a/(1 - r)$.

---

For $|r| < 1$, the **sum of the infinite geometric series** is given by

$$S = a + ar + ar^2 + ar^3 + \cdots + ar^{n-1} + ar^n + \cdots = \frac{a}{1 - r}.$$

---

If, on the other hand, $|r| > 1$, then $r^n$ and the partial sums have no limit as $n \to \infty$ (if $a \neq 0$). In this case, we say the series *diverges*. If $r > 1$, the terms in the series become larger and larger in magnitude, and the partial sums diverge to $+\infty$ if $a > 0$, or to $-\infty$ if $a < 0$. If $r < -1$, the terms become larger in magnitude, the partial sums oscillate as $n \to \infty$, and the series diverges.

What happens if $r = 1$? The series is

$$a + a + a + a + \cdots,$$

so if $a \neq 0$, the partial sums grow without bound, and the series does not converge. If $r = -1$, the series is

$$a - a + a - a + a - \cdots,$$

and, if $a \neq 0$, the partial sums oscillate between $a$ and $0$, and the series does not converge.

---

**Example 3**    For each of the following infinite series, find the first three partial sums and the sum (if it exists):

(a)  $10 + 10(0.75) + 10(0.75)^2 + \cdots$
(b)  $250 + 250(1.2) + 250(1.2)^2 + \cdots$

Solution    (a) This is an infinite geometric series with $a = 10$ and $r = 0.75$. The first three partial sums are:

$$S_1 = 10.$$
$$S_2 = 10 + 10(0.75) = 10 + 7.5 = 17.5.$$
$$S_3 = 10 + 10(0.75) + 10(0.75)^2 = 10 + 7.5 + 5.625 = 23.125.$$

Since $|r| < 1$, the series converges and the sum is

$$S = \frac{a}{1 - r} = \frac{10}{1 - 0.75} = 40.$$

If we find partial sums for larger and larger $n$, they get closer and closer to 40. (See Problem 23.)
(b) This is an infinite geometric series with $a = 250$ and $r = 1.2$. The first three partial sums are:

$$S_1 = 250.$$
$$S_2 = 250 + 250(1.2) = 250 + 300 = 550.$$
$$S_3 = 250 + 250(1.2) + 250(1.2)^2 = 250 + 300 + 360 = 910.$$

Since $r > 1$, the series diverges, and the partial sums grow without bound. (See Problem 22.)

**Example 4**    Suppose 50-mg doses of quinine are taken daily forever. Find the long-run quantities of quinine in the body right after and right before a dose is given.

**Solution**    Since quinine is given forever, from Example 1 we know that the long-run quantity of quinine, right after a dose, is given by

$$Q = 50 + 50(0.23) + 50(0.23)^2 + \cdots.$$

This is an infinite geometric series with $a = 50$ and $r = 0.23$. Since $-1 < r < 1$, the series converges to a finite sum given by

$$Q = \frac{a}{1-r} = \frac{50}{1-0.23} = 64.935.$$

The long-run quantity of quinine in the body right after a dose is 64.935 mg. The quantity levels off to this value in Figure 10.1.

What is the long-run quantity of quinine right before a dose? Since a dose is 50 mg, the quantity of quinine in the body right before a dose is $64.935 - 50 = 14.935$ mg. Thus, in the long run, the quinine level oscillates between 15 mg and 65 mg.

**Example 5**    Suppose that $1000 a year is deposited forever into the bank account in Example 2. Does the balance in the account stabilize at a fixed amount? Explain.

**Solution**    Since the deposits are made forever, the account balance right after a deposit is represented by

$$B = 1000 + 1000(1.05) + 1000(1.05)^2 + \cdots.$$

This is an infinite geometric series with $a = 1000$ and $r = 1.05$. Since $r$ is larger than 1, the series diverges. This makes sense, since if you keep depositing $1000 in an account, your balance grows without bound, even if you don't earn interest. This matches Figure 10.2 and Example 2.

Sometimes the terms of the geometric series may need to be rewritten before the values of $a$ and $r$ can be identified.

**Example 6**    Find the sum of the geometric series.
(a) $1 + 0.1 + 0.01 + 0.001 + \cdots$
(b) $4 + 2 + 1 + \dfrac{1}{2} + \dfrac{1}{4} + \cdots + \dfrac{1}{128}$

**Solution**    (a) The infinite series $1 + 0.1 + 0.01 + 0.001 + \cdots$ can be rewritten as

$$1 + 1(0.1) + 1(0.1)^2 + 1(0.1)^3 + \cdots.$$

The series is geometric with $a = 1$ and $r = 0.1$ and the sum is $S = \dfrac{1}{1 - 0.1} = 1.111\ldots$.

(b) The finite series $4 + 2 + 1 + \dfrac{1}{2} + \dfrac{1}{4} + \cdots + \dfrac{1}{128}$ can be rewritten as

$$4 + 4\left(\frac{1}{2}\right) + 4\left(\frac{1}{2}\right)^2 + 4\left(\frac{1}{2}\right)^3 + 4\left(\frac{1}{2}\right)^4 + \cdots + 4\left(\frac{1}{2}\right)^9.$$

With $a = 4$ and $r = 1/2$ we have

$$S_{10} = \frac{4(1 - (1/2)^{10})}{1 - (1/2)} = 7.992.$$

## Problems for Section 10.1

1. Find the sum of the following series in two ways: by adding terms and by using the geometric series formula.

$$3 + 3 \cdot 2 + 3 \cdot 2^2$$

2. Find the sum of the following series in two ways: by adding terms and by using the geometric series formula.

$$50 + 50(0.9) + 50(0.9)^2 + 50(0.9)^3$$

In Problems 3–9, decide which of the following are geometric series. For those which are, give the first term and the ratio between successive terms. For those which are not, explain why not.

3. $5 - 10 + 20 - 40 + 80 - \cdots$

4. $1 + \dfrac{1}{2} + \dfrac{1}{3} + \dfrac{1}{4} + \dfrac{1}{5} + \cdots$

5. $2 + 1 + \dfrac{1}{2} + \dfrac{1}{4} + \dfrac{1}{8} + \cdots$

6. $1 - \dfrac{1}{2} + \dfrac{1}{4} - \dfrac{1}{8} + \dfrac{1}{16} + \cdots$

7. $1 + 2z + (2z)^2 + (2z)^3 + \cdots$

8. $1 + x + 2x^2 + 3x^3 + 4x^4 + \cdots$

9. $y^2 + y^3 + y^4 + y^5 + \cdots$

In Problems 10–21, find the sum, if it exists.

10. $5 + 5 \cdot 3 + 5 \cdot 3^2 + \cdots + 5 \cdot 3^{12}$

11. $100 + 100(0.85) + 100(0.85)^2 + \cdots + 100(0.85)^{10}$

12. $1000 + 1000(1.05) + 1000(1.05)^2 + \cdots$

13. $75 + 75(0.22) + 75(0.22)^2 + \cdots$

14. $20 + 20(1.45) + 20(1.45)^2 + \cdots + 20(1.45)^{14}$

15. $500(0.4) + 500(0.4)^2 + 500(0.4)^3 + \cdots$

16. $31500 + 6300 + 1260 + 252 + \cdots$

17. $3 + \dfrac{3}{2} + \dfrac{3}{4} + \dfrac{3}{8} + \cdots + \dfrac{3}{2^{10}}$

18. $1000 + 1500 + 2250 + 3375 + 5062.5 + \cdots$

19. $200 + 100 + 50 + 25 + 12.5 + \cdots$

20. $65 + \dfrac{65}{1.02} + \dfrac{65}{(1.02)^2} + \cdots + \dfrac{65}{(1.02)^{18}}$

21. $-2 + 1 - \dfrac{1}{2} + \dfrac{1}{4} - \dfrac{1}{8} + \dfrac{1}{16} - \cdots$

22. In Example 3(b) on page 467, we found partial sums for the geometric series with $a = 250$ and $r = 1.2$. Find the partial sums $S_n$ for $n = 5, 10, 15, 20$. As $n$ gets larger, do the partial sums appear to grow without bound, as expected if $r > 1$?

23. In Example 3(a), we found partial sums of the geometric series with $a = 10$ and $r = 0.75$ and showed that the sum of this series is 40. Find the partial sums $S_n$ for $n = 5, 10, 15, 20$. As $n$ gets larger, do the partial sums appear to be approaching 40?

24. A repeating decimal can always be expressed as a fraction. This problem shows how writing a repeating decimal as a geometric series enables you to find the fraction.

   (a) Write the repeating decimal 0.232323... as a geometric series using the fact that $0.232323\ldots = 0.23 + 0.0023 + 0.000023 + \cdots$.

   (b) Use the formula for the sum of a geometric series to show that $0.232323\ldots = 23/99$.

25. Every month, $500 is deposited into an account earning 0.1% interest a month, compounded monthly.

   (a) How much is in the account right after the $6^{\text{th}}$ deposit? Right before the $6^{\text{th}}$ deposit?

   (b) How much is in the account right after the $12^{\text{th}}$ deposit? Right before the $12^{\text{th}}$ deposit?

26. Each year, a family deposits $5000 into an account paying 1.25% interest per year, compounded annually. How much is in the account right after the $25^{\text{th}}$ deposit?

27. A smoker inhales 0.4 mg of nicotine from a cigarette. After one hour, 71% of the nicotine remains in the body. If a person smokes one cigarette every hour beginning at 7 am, how much nicotine is in the body right after the 11 pm cigarette?

28. Each morning, a patient receives a 25 mg injection of an anti-inflammatory drug, and 40% of the drug remains in the body after 24 hours. Find the quantity in the body:

   (a) Right after the $3^{\text{rd}}$ injection.
   (b) Right after the $6^{\text{th}}$ injection.
   (c) In the long run, right after an injection.

29. In Example 4 on page 468, we saw that if 50 mg of quinine is given every 24 hours, the long-run quantity of quinine in the body is about 65 mg right after a dose and about 15 mg right before a dose. The concentration of quinine in the body is measured in milligrams of quinine per kilogram of body weight. To be effective, the average concentration of quinine in the body must be at least 0.4 mg/kg. Concentrations above 3.0 mg/kg are not safe.

   (a) Estimate the average quantity of quinine in the body in the long run by averaging the long-run quantities of quinine in the body right after a dose and right before a dose.

   (b) Find the average concentration for a person weighing 70 kilograms. Is this treatment safe and effective for such a person?

   (c) For what range of weights would this treatment produce a long-run average concentration that is

   (i)  Too low?          (ii)  Unsafe?

**30.** A ball is dropped from a height of 10 feet and bounces. Each bounce is $\frac{3}{4}$ of the height of the bounce before. Thus, after the ball hits the floor for the first time, the ball rises to a height of $10(\frac{3}{4}) = 7.5$ feet, and after it hits the floor for the second time, it rises to a height of $7.5(\frac{3}{4}) = 10(\frac{3}{4})^2 = 5.625$ feet.

(a) Find an expression for the height to which the ball

rises after it hits the floor for the $n^{\text{th}}$ time.

(b) Find an expression for the total vertical distance the ball has traveled when it hits the floor for the first, second, third, and fourth times.

(c) Find an expression for the total vertical distance the ball has traveled when it hits the floor for the $n^{\text{th}}$ time. Express your answer in closed form.

# 10.2 APPLICATIONS TO BUSINESS AND ECONOMICS

## Annuities

An *annuity* is a sequence of equal payments made at regular intervals. We can use the sum of a geometric series to calculate the total value of an annuity.

**Example 1** An annuity pays $5000 every year into an account that earns 7% interest per year, compounded annually. What is the balance in the account right after the $10^{\text{th}}$ deposit?

Solution The $10^{\text{th}}$ deposit contributes $5000 to the balance. The previous deposit has earned interest for a year, so it contributes $5000(1.07)$. The deposit the year before that has earned interest for two years, so it contributes $5000(1.07)^2$. Continuing, we see that

$$\text{Balance after } 10^{\text{th}} \text{ deposit } = 5000 + 5000(1.07) + 5000(1.07)^2 + \cdots + 5000(1.07)^9.$$

This sum is a finite geometric series with $a = 5000$ and $r = 1.07$. We use the formula for the sum with $n = 10$:

$$\text{Balance after } 10^{\text{th}} \text{ deposit } = \frac{a(1 - r^n)}{1 - r} = \frac{5000(1 - (1.07)^{10})}{1 - 1.07} = 69{,}082.24 \text{ dollars.}$$

The balance in the account right after the $10^{\text{th}}$ deposit is $69,082.24.

## Present Value of an Annuity

The *present value of an annuity* is the amount of money that must be deposited today to make a series of fixed payments in the future. How can we compute this present value? We begin by considering a single payment. Suppose a payment of $1000 is to be made three years in the future from an account paying interest at a rate of 8% per year, compounded annually. The present value is the amount $P$ such that

$$P(1.08)^3 = 1000,$$

so we have

$$\text{Present value} = P = 1000(1.08)^{-3}.$$

To find the present value of four payments of $1000 at the same 8% interest, one made now, one in one year's time, one in two years, and one in three years, we add their present values:

$$\text{Present value of four payments } = 1000 + 1000(1.08)^{-1} + 1000(1.08)^{-2} + 1000(1.08)^{-3}.$$

This pattern allows us to find the present value of any annuity, as in the following example.

**Example 2** An account earns 8% interest per year, compounded annually. Twenty payments of $10,000 each, made once a year starting now, are to be made out of the account. How much must be deposited in the account now to cover these payments? In other words, what is the present value of this annuity?

Solution The present value of the payment to be made immediately is $10,000. The present value of next year's payment is $10{,}000(1.08)^{-1}$. Since the $20^{\text{th}}$ payment is made 19 years in the future, the present value of the $20^{\text{th}}$ payment is $10{,}000(1.08)^{-19}$. The present value, $P$, of the entire annuity, in dollars, is the sum

$$P = 10{,}000 + 10{,}000(1.08)^{-1} + 10{,}000(1.08)^{-2} + \cdots + 10{,}000(1.08)^{-19}.$$

Rewriting $(1.08)^{-2} = \left((1.08)^{-1}\right)^2$ and $(1.08)^{-3} = \left((1.08)^{-1}\right)^3$, and so on, shows that $P$ is the sum of the finite geometric series

$$P = 10{,}000 + 10{,}000(1.08)^{-1} + 10{,}000((1.08)^{-1})^2 + \cdots + 10{,}000((1.08)^{-1})^{19}.$$

We use the formula for the sum with $a = 10{,}000$ and $r = (1.08)^{-1}$ and $n = 20$, giving

$$\text{Present value } = P = \frac{a(1 - r^n)}{1 - r} = \frac{10{,}000(1 - ((1.08)^{-1})^{20})}{1 - (1.08)^{-1}} = 106{,}035.99.$$

Thus, \$106,035.99 must be deposited now to cover the payments for this annuity. Notice that the annuity pays out a total of $20 \cdot \$10{,}000 = \$200{,}000$, so the present value is considerably less than the amount eventually paid out.

**Example 3**    The annuity in Example 2 now makes annual payments of \$10,000 in perpetuity (that is, forever), rather than just twenty times. What is the present value of this annuity?

Solution    Since the payments are made forever, the present value is given by the infinite sum:

$$\text{Present value } = 10{,}000 + 10{,}000(1.08)^{-1} + 10{,}000((1.08)^{-1})^2 + 10{,}000((1.08)^{-1})^3 + \cdots.$$

This is an infinite geometric series with $a = 10{,}000$ and $r = (1.08)^{-1} = 0.925926$. Since $-1 < r < 1$, this series converges to a finite sum. We have

$$\text{Present value } = \frac{a}{1 - r} = \frac{10{,}000}{1 - (1.08)^{-1}} = 135{,}000.$$

The present value of this annuity in perpetuity is \$135,000. Notice that the amount needed to make annual payments forever is only about \$29,000 more than the amount needed to make 20 annual payments. This is the power of compound interest.

## The Multiplier Effect

A government decides to give a tax rebate to stimulate the economy. What is the total effect of the rebate on spending? Each individual who receives a tax rebate spends some proportion of the additional income, and this money becomes additional income for a second individual, who spends a proportion of it, providing additional income for a third individual, and so on. The total effect of the rebate on the economy is much larger than the size of the rebate itself; this is called the *multiplier effect*.

**Example 4**    A government gives tax rebates totaling 3 billion dollars. Everyone who receives money spends 75% of it and saves the other 25%. Find the total additional spending resulting from this tax rebate.

Solution    The additional spending refers to all the additional money spent by consumers as a result of this tax rebate. The recipients of the 3 billion dollars spend 75% of what they receive, that is $3(0.75) = 2.25$ billion dollars. The recipients of this 2.25 billion dollars spend 75% of that, or $2.25(0.75) = 1.6875$ billion dollars. The recipients of this money spend 75% of this amount, and so on. Thus,

$$\text{Total additional spending} = 2.25 + 2.25(0.75) + 2.25(0.75)^2 + 2.25(0.75)^3 + \cdots \text{ billion dollars.}$$

(Notice that the initial amount spent was 2.25, not 3 billion dollars.) This is an infinite geometric series with $a = 2.25$ and $r = 0.75$. Since $-1 < r < 1$, this series converges to a finite sum:

$$\text{Total additional spending} = \frac{a}{1 - r} = \frac{2.25}{1 - 0.75} = 9 \text{ billion dollars.}$$

Thus, a 3 billion dollar tax rebate generates 9 billion dollars of additional spending.

## Market Stabilization

Each year, a manufacturer produces a fixed number of units of a product and each year a fixed percentage of these units (regardless of age) fail or go out of use. The total number of units in use in the long run is called the *market stabilization point*.

---

**Example 5**    The US Mint produces about 7.4 billion pennies a year and about 5% of them are removed from circulation each year.[1] Approximately how many pennies are in circulation?

**Solution**    We can estimate the number of pennies in circulation using geometric series if we assume (for example) that the yearly production takes place at the start of the year and that the 5% are removed at the end of the year. In any year, 7.4 billion pennies are produced, and $7.4(0.95)$ billion pennies remain from the previous year's production (since 5% went out of circulation). There are $7.4(0.95)^2$ billion pennies remaining from those produced two years before, and so on. If $N$ is the number of pennies in circulation, in billions, then

$$N = 7.4 + 7.4(0.95) + 7.4(0.95)^2 + \cdots.$$

This is an infinite geometric series with $a = 7.4$ and $r = 0.95$. Since $-1 < r < 1$, the series converges and its sum is given by

$$N = \frac{a}{1-r} = \frac{7.4}{1-0.95} = 148.$$

Thus, the market has stabilized with about 148 billion pennies in circulation today. Of the 148 billion pennies in circulation, 5% or $(148)(0.05) = 7.4$ billion are removed each year, which exactly equals the number produced each year.

---

## Problems for Section 10.2

**1.** A yearly deposit of $1000 is made into a bank account that pays 2% interest per year, compounded annually. What is the balance in the account right after the $20^{\text{th}}$ deposit? How much of the balance comes from the annual deposits and how much comes from interest?

**2.** Annual deposits of $2000 are made into an account paying 2.5% interest per year, compounded continuously. What is the balance in the account right after and right before the $5^{\text{th}}$ deposit?

**3.** An annuity makes annual payments of $50,000, starting now, from an account paying 3.65% interest per year, compounded annually. Find the present value of the annuity if it makes

    **(a)** Ten payments    **(b)** Payments in perpetuity

**4.** Twenty annual payments of $5000 each, with the first payment one year from now, are to be made from an account earning 2% per year, compounded annually. How much must be deposited now to cover the payments?

**5.** What is the present value of an annuity that pays $20,000 each year, forever, starting today, from an account that pays 1% interest per year, compounded annually?

**6.** An annuity earning 0.25% per month, compounded monthly, is to make 36 monthly payments of $1000 each, starting now. What is the present value of this annuity?

**7.** A donor sets up an endowment to fund an annual scholarship of $10,000. The endowment earns 3% interest per year, compounded annually. Find the amount that must be deposited now if the endowment is to fund one award each year, with one award now and continuing

    **(a)** Until twenty awards have been made
    **(b)** Forever

**8.** An employee accepts a job with a starting salary of $30,000 and a cost-of-living increase of 2% every year for the next 10 years. What is the employee's salary at the start of the $11^{\text{th}}$ year? What are her total earnings during the first 10 years?

**9.** An employer pays you 1 penny the first day you work and doubles your wages each day after that. Find your total earnings after working 7 days a week for

    **(a)** One week        **(b)** Two weeks
    **(c)** Three weeks    **(d)** Four weeks

---

[1] From www.usmint.gov.

**10.** Find the market stabilization point for a product if 10,000 new units of the product are manufactured at the start of each year and 25% of the total number of units in use fail at the end of each year.

**11.** Every year, a company sells 1000 units of a product while 20% of the total number in use fail. Assume sales are at the start of the year and failures are at the end of the year.

    **(a)** Find the market stabilization point for this product.

    **(b)** If the stabilization point is approached very slowly, the number of units in use may not get close to this value because market conditions change first. Make a table for $S_n$, the number of units in use right after the $n^{\text{th}}$ annual sale, for $n = 5, 10, 15, 20$, to see how rapidly this market approaches the stabilization point.

**12.** Since 2007, the Bureau of Engraving and Printing has produced about 11 million new \$1 bills a day; worn bills are removed by Federal Reserve banks. There are about 9.2 billion dollar bills currently in circulation. Assuming that a fixed percentage of \$1 bills are removed from circulation each day, use a geometric series to estimate this percentage.[2]

Problems 13–15 are about *bonds*, which are issued by a government to raise money. An individual who buys a \$1000 bond gives the government \$1000 and in return receives a fixed sum of money, called the *coupon*, every six months or every year for the life of the bond. At the time of the last coupon, the individual also gets back the \$1000, or *principal*.

**13.** What is the present value of a \$1000 bond which pays \$50 a year for 10 years, starting one year from now? Assume the interest rate is 4% per year, compounded annually.

**14.** What is the present value of a \$1000 bond which pays \$50 a year for 10 years, starting one year from now? Assume the interest rate is 6% per year, compounded annually.

**15.** **(a)** What is the present value of a \$1000 bond which pays \$50 a year for 10 years, starting one year from now? Assume the interest rate is 5% per year, compounded annually.

    **(b)** Since \$50 is 5% of \$1000, this bond is called a 5% bond. What does your answer to part (a) tell you about the relationship between the principal and the present value of this bond if the interest rate is 5%?

    **(c)** If the interest rate is more than 5% per year, compounded annually, which is larger: the principal or the present value of the bond? Why is the bond then described as *trading at a discount*?

    **(d)** If the interest rate is less than 5% per year, compounded annually, why is the bond described as *trading at a premium*?

**16.** To stimulate the economy in 2002, the government gave a tax rebate totaling 40 billion dollars. Find the total additional spending resulting from this tax rebate if everyone who receives money spends

    **(a)** 80% of it         **(b)** 90% of it

**17.** To stimulate the economy in 2008, the government gave a tax rebate totaling 100 billion dollars. Find the total additional spending resulting from this tax rebate if everyone who receives money spends

    **(a)** 80% of it         **(b)** 90% of it

**18.** In April 2009, economists predicted that each dollar in tax cuts would generate \$3 in economic growth. What spending rate was assumed in arriving at this estimated multiplier effect?

**19.** This problem illustrates how banks create credit and can thereby lend out more money than has been deposited. Suppose that initially \$100 is deposited in a bank. Experience has shown bankers that on average only 8% of the money deposited is withdrawn by the owner at any time. Consequently, bankers feel free to lend out 92% of their deposits. Thus \$92 of the original \$100 is loaned out to other customers (to start a business, for example). This \$92 becomes someone else's income and, sooner or later, is redeposited in the bank. Thus 92% of \$92, or $\$92(0.92) = \$84.64$, is loaned out again and eventually redeposited. Of the \$84.64, the bank again loans out 92%, and so on.

    **(a)** Find the total amount of money deposited in the bank as a result of these transactions.

    **(b)** The total amount of money deposited divided by the original deposit is called the *credit multiplier*. Calculate the credit multiplier for this example and explain what this number tells us.

**20.** A person who deposits money in a bank account starts a long process described by the reserve-deposit ratio, $r$. For every dollar deposited, the bank keeps $r$ dollars and lends $1 - r$ dollars to someone else, who deposits the loan in a bank account. The same fraction of the second deposit is loaned out, to be deposited in turn, and so on. If the initial deposit is $N$ dollars, find the total value of the bank accounts generated by this deposit:

    **(a)** After the second deposit
    **(b)** After the third deposit
    **(c)** If the process continues forever

---

[2] www.dallasnews.com/sharedcontent/dws/bus/stories/DN-obsoletedollarbill_22bus.State.Edition1.c8a2b4.html, accessed May 25, 2009.

# 10.3 APPLICATIONS TO THE NATURAL SCIENCES

## Steady-State Drug Levels

A patient is given a drug at regular intervals. In Section 10.1, we saw that in the long run, the quantity of drug in the body varies between a maximum level right after a dose and a minimum level right before a dose. At this *steady state*, the quantity eliminated between doses is equal to one dose. (See Problem 19.)

**Example 1**    A child with an ear infection is given a 200-mg ampicillin tablet once every 4 hours. About 12% of the drug in the body at the start of a four-hour period is still there at the end of that period. What is the quantity of ampicillin in the body

(a) Right after taking the $3^{\text{rd}}$ tablet?             (b)  Right after taking the $6^{\text{th}}$ tablet?

(c) At the steady state, right after and right before taking a tablet?

Solution    Let $Q_n$ be the quantity of ampicillin, in mg, in the body right after taking the $n^{\text{th}}$ tablet. Then

$$Q_n = 200 + 200(0.12) + 200(0.12)^2 + \cdots + 200(0.12)^{n-1}.$$

(a) Using the formula for the sum of a finite geometric series with $a = 200$, $r = 0.12$, and $n = 3$, we have

$$Q_3 = \frac{a(1 - r^n)}{1 - r} = \frac{200(1 - (0.12)^3)}{1 - 0.12} = 226.88 \text{ mg.}$$

(b) Using $n = 6$, we have

$$Q_6 = \frac{a(1 - r^n)}{1 - r} = \frac{200(1 - (0.12)^6)}{1 - 0.12} = 227.2720 \text{ mg.}$$

(c) At the steady state, the quantity $Q$ in mg, right after a tablet is taken is the sum of the infinite geometric series

$$Q = 200 + 200(0.12) + 200(0.12)^2 + 200(0.12)^3 + \cdots .$$

Since $r = 0.12$ and $-1 < r < 1$, the series converges to a finite sum. At the steady state

$$\text{Quantity right after a dose } = Q = \frac{a}{1 - r} = \frac{200}{1 - 0.12} = 227.2727 \text{ mg.}$$

The quantity of ampicillin in the body right before a dose is exactly 200 mg less than the quantity right after the dose, so at the steady state

$$\text{Quantity before dose } = \text{Quantity after dose} - \text{Size of one dose}$$
$$= 227.2727 - 200$$
$$= 27.2727 \text{ mg.}$$

Problem 4 shows how this relationship can be used to calculate $Q$, the long-run quantity of ampicillin right after a dose.

**Example 2**    Valproic acid, a drug used to control epilepsy, has a half-life of 15 hours in the body. If $D$ mg of valproic acid is taken every 12 hours, at the steady state, what quantity of the drug is in the body right after taking a tablet?

Solution    After a dose $D$ of valproic acid, the quantity, $Q$, in the body decays exponentially, so $Q = Db^t$, where $t$ is time in hours. The half-life is 15 hours, so

$$0.5D = Db^{15}$$
$$0.5 = b^{15}$$
$$b = (0.5)^{1/15}.$$

Right before the next dose at $t = 12$, we have

Fraction of drug remaining after 12 hours $= b^{12} = ((0.5)^{1/15})^{12} = (0.5)^{12/15} = (0.5)^{0.8}.$

Since $D$ mg of valproic acid is given every 12 hours, in the long run

Quantity right after dose $= D + D(0.5)^{0.8} + D\left((0.5)^{0.8}\right)^2 + \cdots.$

This is an infinite geometric series with $r = (0.5)^{0.8} = 0.57435$. Since $-1 < r < 1$, the series converges and its sum is

Quantity right after dose $= \dfrac{D}{1 - (0.5)^{0.8}} = 2.35D.$

Thus, in the long run, the quantity of the drug right after taking a dose is about 2.35 times the dose.

## Accumulation of Toxins in the Body

Toxins found in pesticides can get into the food chain and accumulate in people's bodies through the food they eat. We use a geometric series to calculate the total accumulation of toxin in the body.

**Example 3**    Every day, a person consumes 5 micrograms ($\mu$g) of a toxin, which leaves the body at a continuous rate of 2% per day. In the long run, how much toxin is in the body at the end of the day?

Solution    Since the toxin leaves the body at a continuous rate of 2% every day, the 5 $\mu$g amount consumed one day earlier has decayed to $5e^{-0.02}$, the 5 $\mu$g consumed two days earlier has decayed to $5e^{-0.02(2)} = 5(e^{-0.02})^2$, and so on. We assume that the 5 $\mu$g consumed during the day has not yet decayed. In the long run, at the end of each day we have, in micrograms,

Total accumulation of toxin $= 5 + 5(e^{-0.02}) + 5(e^{-0.02})^2 + 5(e^{-0.02})^3 + \cdots.$

This is an infinite geometric series with $a = 5$ and $r = e^{-0.02} = 0.9802$. Since $-1 < r < 1$, the series converges and its sum is

Total accumulation of toxin $= \dfrac{a}{1 - r} = \dfrac{5}{1 - e^{-0.02}} = 252.5$ micrograms.

In the long run, there are 252.5 micrograms of toxin in the body at the end of the day.

## Depletion of Natural Resources

Geometric series can be used to estimate how long a natural resource (such as oil) will last, assuming that usage levels increase at a constant percentage rate.

**Example 4**    At the end of 2008, world oil reserves were about 1950 billion barrels.[3] During 2008, about 29.3 billion barrels of oil were consumed.[4] Over the past decade, oil consumption has been increasing at about 1% per year.[5] Assuming yearly oil consumption increases at this rate in the future, how long will the reserves last?

**Solution**    Under these assumptions, the oil used in 2009, in billions of barrels, is predicted to be $29.3(1.01)$. In 2010, we predict $29.3(1.01)^2$ billion barrels to be used, and $29.3(1.01)^3$ the next year, and so on. Thus, starting with 2009, the total quantity of oil used in $n$ years, $Q_n$, is

$$Q_n = 29.3(1.01) + 29.3(1.01)^2 + 29.3(1.01)^3 + \cdots + 29.3(1.01)^n \text{ billions of barrels.}$$

This is a finite geometric series with $n$ terms where $a = 29.3(1.01)$ and $r = 1.01$. (Notice that the last term can be written $29.3(1.01)(1.01)^{n-1}$.) The sum is

$$Q_n = \frac{a(1 - r^n)}{1 - r} = 29.3(1.01)\left(\frac{1 - (1.01)^n}{1 - 1.01}\right) = 2959((1.01)^n - 1) \text{ billions of barrels.}$$

We want to find the value of $n$ for which $Q_n$ reaches the total reserves, 1950. Solving gives

$$2959((1.01)^n - 1) = 1950$$
$$(1.01)^n - 1 = \frac{1950}{2959} = 0.6590$$
$$(1.01)^n = 1.6590.$$

Taking logarithms and using $\ln(A^p) = p \ln A$, we have

$$n \ln(1.01) = \ln(1.6590)$$
$$n = \frac{\ln(1.6590)}{\ln(1.01)} = 50.9 \text{ years.}$$

Thus, if present consumption patterns are maintained, the world's oil supply will be exhausted in about 51 years. However, if consumption patterns change, the length of time until the reserves run out can be very different. Problem 3 concerns predictions using a 2.5% yearly increase and a 5.5% yearly decrease, the maximum and minimum figures for the past decade.

## Geometric Series and Differential Equations

In this section, we used geometric series to model drug levels; in Chapter 9, we used differential equations to model drug levels. How do we know whether to use a geometric series or a differential equation? The answer depends on whether the drug is given in *discrete* doses (such as a tablet each morning) or *continuously* (such as intravenously).

**Example 5**    A patient receives 25 mg of a drug each day, and the drug is metabolized and eliminated at a continuous rate of 10% per day. Find the quantity of drug in the patient's body in the long run:

(a) Using a geometric series, assuming the 25-mg dose of the drug is administered in a single injection each morning. (Find the quantity both before and after an injection is given.)
(b) Using a differential equation, assuming the 25-mg dose of the drug is administered continuously throughout the day, using an intravenous drip.

---

[3] www.theoildrum.com/node/5395, accessed March 13, 2013.
[4] *CIA World Factbook 2008.*
[5] www.eia.doe.gov/emeu/international/oilcomsumption.html, accessed March 13, 2013.

Solution    (a) A 25-mg injection is given each day. Since the drug is metabolized at a continuous rate of 10% per day, the quantity remaining a day later is $25e^{-0.1}$ mg. The quantity remaining two days later is $25(e^{-0.1})^2$ mg. In the long run,

$$\text{Quantity after injection } = 25 + 25(e^{-0.1}) + 25(e^{-0.1})^2 + 25(e^{-0.1})^3 + \cdots \text{ mg.}$$

We use the formula for the sum of an infinite geometric series with $a = 25$ and $r = e^{-0.1}$:

$$\text{Quantity after injection } = \frac{a}{1 - r} = \frac{25}{1 - e^{-0.1}} = 262.7 \text{ mg.}$$

Since each injection is 25 mg, in the long run

$$\text{Quantity before injection } = 262.7 - 25 = 237.7 \text{ mg.}$$

(b) The drug is entering the body at the continuous rate of 25 mg per day and leaving at the continuous rate of 0.1 times the current level in the body. Thus, if $Q$ is the quantity of drug in the body after $t$ days, then

$$\frac{dQ}{dt} = \text{Rate in} - \text{Rate out} = 25 - 0.1Q.$$

In Chapter 9, we saw that $Q$ tends toward the equilibrium solution which occurs when $dQ/dt = 0$. Then

$$\frac{dQ}{dt} = 25 - 0.1Q = 0$$
$$Q = 250 \text{ mg.}$$

When the drug is given continuously, the quantity of the drug in the body levels off at 250 mg.

## Problems for Section 10.3

1. Every morning, a patient receives a 50-mg injection of a drug. At the end of a 24-hour period, 60% of the drug remains in the body. What quantity of drug is in the body

   (a) Right after the $3^{\text{rd}}$ injection?
   (b) Right after the $7^{\text{th}}$ injection?
   (c) Right after an injection, at the steady state?

2. In 2010, world oil consumption was 87.4 million barrels per day,[6] an increase of 3.1% from 2009. Assuming that consumption continues to decrease at the same percentage rate, make a table showing yearly consumption between 2010 and 2017, inclusive. Find the total quantity of oil consumed during this decade.

3. As in Example 4, assume that oil reserves at the end of 2008 were 1950 billion barrels and that consumption in 2008 was 29.3 billion barrels. What happens in the long run if oil consumption

   (a) Decreases by 5.5% per year
   (b) Increases by 2.5% per year

4. This problem gives another way of finding, $Q$, the long-run ampicillin quantity right after a dose in Example 1. (See page 474.) In the four hours after a dose, 200 mg of ampicillin must be excreted, as the next 200-mg tablet elevates the ampicillin quantity back to $Q$ mg. Use this information to solve for $Q$.

5. A dose of 120 mg is taken by a patient at the same time every day. In one day, 30% of the drug is excreted.

   (a) At the steady state, find the quantity of drug in the body right after a dose.
   (b) Check that at the steady state, the quantity excreted in one day is equal to the dose.

6. A person with chronic pain takes a 30 mg tablet of morphine every 4 hours. The half-life of morphine is 2 hours.

   (a) How much morphine is in the body right after and right before taking the $6^{\text{th}}$ tablet?
   (b) At the steady state, find the quantity of morphine in the body right after and right before taking a tablet.

---

[6] *Statistical Review of World Energy 2010*, www.bp.com.

7. At the same time every day, a patient takes 50 mg of the antidepressant fluoxetine, whose half-life is 3 days.

   (a) What fraction of the dose remains in the body after a 24-hour period?
   (b) What is the quantity of fluoxetine in the body right after taking the $7^{th}$ dose?
   (c) In the long run, what is the quantity of fluoxetine in the body right after a dose?

8. (a) An allergy drug with a half-life of 18 weeks is given in 100-mg doses once a week. At the steady state, find the quantity of the drug in the body right after a dose.
   (b) The drug does not become effective until the quantity in the body right after a dose reaches 2000 mg. How many weeks after the first dose does the drug become effective?

9. Each day at lunch a person consumes 8 micrograms of a toxin found in a pesticide; the toxin is metabolized at a continuous rate of 0.5% per day. In the long run, how much of this toxin accumulates in the person's body? Give the quantities right after and right before lunch.

10. A cigarette puts 1.2 mg of nicotine into the body. Nicotine leaves the body at a continuous rate of 34.65% per hour, but more than 60 mg can be lethal. If a person smokes a cigarette with each of the following frequencies, find the long-run quantity of nicotine in the body right after a cigarette. Does the nicotine reach the lethal level?

    (a)  Every hour          (b)  Every half hour
    (c)  Every 15 minutes    (d)  Every 6 minutes
    (e)  Every 3 minutes

11. At the end of 2008, the total reserve of a mineral was 350,000 $m^3$. In the year 2009, about 5000 $m^3$ was used. Each year, consumption of the mineral is expected to increase by 8%. Under these assumptions, in how many years will all reserves of the mineral be depleted?

12. At the end of 2007, natural gas reserves were 180 trillion $m^3$; during 2007, about 3 trillion $m^3$ of natural gas were consumed.[7] Estimate how long natural gas reserves will last if consumption increases at 2% per year.

13. Over the past decade, natural gas consumption has been increasing at between 0% and 5% a year. Using the data

from Problem 12, estimate how long the natural gas reserves will last assuming the rate of increase is

    (a)  0%                  (b)  5%

14. We use 1500 kg of a mineral this year and consumption of the mineral is increasing annually by 4%. The total reserves of the mineral are estimated to be 120,000 kg. Approximately when will the reserves run out?

Problems 15–17 concern how long reserves of the mineral in Problem 11 last if usage patterns change. For example, as reserves get lower, substitutes may be developed.

15. How long will the reserves last if the annual increase in usage is 4%?

16. How long will the reserves last if the annual usage stays constant at 5000 $m^3$ per year?

17. How long will the reserves last if the usage decreases each year by 4%?

18. (a) A dose $D$ of a drug is administered at intervals equal to the half-life. (That is, the second dose is given when half the first dose remains.) At the steady state, find the quantity of drug in the body right after a dose.
    (b) If the quantity of a drug in the body after a dose is 300 mg at the steady state and if the interval between doses equals the half-life, what is the dose?

19. A dose, $D$, of a drug is taken at regular time intervals, and a fraction $r$ remains after one time interval. Show that at the steady state, the quantity of the drug excreted between doses equals the dose.

20. Cephalexin is an antibiotic with a half-life in the body of 0.9 hours, taken in tablets of 250 mg every six hours.

    (a) What percentage of the cephalexin in the body at the start of a six-hour period is still there at the end (assuming no tablets are taken during that time)?
    (b) Write an expression for $Q_1, Q_2, Q_3, Q_4$, where $Q_n$ mg is the amount of cephalexin in the body right after the $n^{th}$ tablet is taken.
    (c) Express $Q_3, Q_4$ in closed form and evaluate them.
    (d) Write an expression for $Q_n$ and put it in closed form.
    (e) If the patient keeps taking the tablets, use your answer to part (d) to find the quantity of cephalexin in the body in the long run, right after taking a tablet.

## CHAPTER SUMMARY

- **Geometric series**
  Finite and infinite.
- **Sums of geometric series**
  Partial sums, convergence of infinite series.
- **Applications to business and economics**

  Annuities, present value, multiplier effect, market stabilization.

- **Applications to life sciences**
  Repeated drug doses, accumulation of toxins, depletion of natural resources.

[7]www.worldenergyoutlook.org/docs/weo2008/weo2008_es_english.pdf

# REVIEW PROBLEMS FOR CHAPTER TEN

In Problems 1–8, find the sum, if it exists.

1. $2 + 2^2 + 2^3 + \cdots + 2^{10}$

2. $20 + 20(1.4) + 20(1.4)^2 + \cdots + 20(1.4)^8$

3. $1000 + 1000(1.08) + 1000(1.08)^2 + 1000(1.08)^3 + \cdots$

4. $500 + 500(0.6) + 500(0.6)^2 + \cdots + 500(0.6)^{15}$

5. $30 + 30(0.85) + 30(0.85)^2 + 30(0.85)^3 + \cdots$

6. $25 + 25(0.2) + 25(0.2)^2 + 25(0.2)^3 + \cdots$

7. $1 + \dfrac{1}{2} + \dfrac{1}{2^2} + \cdots + \dfrac{1}{2^8}$

8. $1 + \dfrac{1}{3} + \dfrac{1}{3^2} + \dfrac{1}{3^3} + \cdots$

9. Around January 1, 1993, Barbra Streisand signed a contract with Sony Corporation for $2 million a year for 10 years. Suppose the first payment was made on the day of signing and that all other payments were made on the first day of the year. Suppose also that all payments were made into a bank account earning 4% a year, compounded annually.

    (a) How much money was in the account
        (i) On the night of December 31, 1999?
        (ii) On the day the last payment was made?
    (b) What was the present value of the contract on the day it was signed?

10. A drug is given in daily doses of 100 mg. After 24 hours, 82% of the previous day's dose remains in the body. What is the long-run quantity of drug in the body, right after and right before a dose is given?

11. A used car costs $15,000. The repair contract costs $500 at the end of the first year and increases by 20% at the end of each subsequent year. Find the total cost of owning the car for ten years. Include the payment at the end of the tenth year.

12. A deposit of $100,000 is made into an account paying 8% interest per year, compounded annually. Annual payments of $10,000 each, starting right after the deposit, are made out of the account. How many payments can be made before the account runs out of money?

13. This problem shows how to estimate the cumulative effect of a tax cut on a country's economy. Suppose the government proposes a tax cut totaling $100 million. We assume that all the people who have extra money spend 80% of it and save 20%. Thus, of the extra income generated by the tax cut, $100(0.8)$ million $= \$80$ million is spent and becomes extra income to someone else. These people also spend 80% of their additional income, or $80(0.8)$ million, and so on. Calculate the total additional spending created by such a tax cut.

14. To stimulate the economy, the government gives a tax rebate totaling 5 billion dollars. Find the total additional spending resulting from this tax rebate if everyone who receives money spends

    (a) 80% of it          (b) 90% of it

15. A government gives a tax rebate of $N$ dollars to stimulate the economy. Everyone who receives money spends a fixed fraction, $k$, of the money received, with $0 < k < 1$.

    (a) Find a formula (in terms of $N$ and $k$) for the total additional spending resulting from the tax rebate.
    (b) If $k = 0.85$, what is the total additional spending as a multiple of the size, $N$, of the tax rebate?

16. Before World War I, the British government issued what are called *consols*, which pay the owner or his heirs a fixed amount of money every year forever. (Cartoonists of the time described aristocrats living off such payments as "pickled in consols.") What should a person expect to pay for consols which pay £10 a year forever? Assume the first payment is one year from the date of purchase and that interest remains 4% per year, compounded annually. (£ denotes pounds, the British unit of currency.)

17. Figure 10.3 shows the quantity of the drug atenolol in the blood as a function of time, with the first dose at time $t = 0$. Atenolol is taken in 50 mg doses once a day to lower blood pressure.

    (a) If the half-life of atenolol in the blood is 6.3 hours, what percentage of the atenolol present at the start of a 24-hour period is still there at the end?
    (b) Find expressions for the quantities $Q_0, Q_1, Q_2, Q_3,$ ..., and $Q_n$ shown in Figure 10.3. Write the expression for $Q_n$ in closed form.
    (c) Find expressions for the quantities $P_1, P_2, P_3, \ldots,$ and $P_n$ shown in Figure 10.3. Write the expression for $P_n$ in closed form.

Figure 10.3

18. One way of valuing a company is to calculate the present value of all its future earnings. A farm expects to sell $1000 worth of Christmas trees once a year forever, with the first sale in the immediate future. What is the present value of this Christmas tree business? The interest rate is 1% per year, compounded continuously.

## STRENGTHEN YOUR UNDERSTANDING

In Problems 1–30, indicate whether the statement is true or false.

1. The sum $1 + 2 + 4 + 8 + 16 + 32$ is a finite geometric series with 6 terms.

2. The sum $1 + 2 + 4 + 8 + 16 + 32 + \cdots + 2^{10}$ is a finite geometric series with 10 terms.

3. The sum $1 + 3 + 5 + 7 + 9 + 11$ is a finite geometric series with 6 terms.

4. The sum $1 - 2 + 4 - 8 + 16 - 32$ is a finite geometric series with 6 terms.

5. The sum of $1 + (1/3) + (1/9) + \cdots + (1/3)^{10}$ is $(1 - (1/3)^{11})/(1 - (1/3))$.

6. The sum of $3 \cdot 1 + 3 \cdot 2 + 3 \cdot 4 + \cdots + 3(2^{20})$ is $3(1 - 2^{20})/(1 - 2)$.

7. The sum of the infinite geometric series $3 + 3^2 + 3^3 + \cdots + 3^n + \cdots$ is $3/(1 - 3)$.

8. The sum of the infinite geometric series $(1/2) + (1/2)^2 + (1/2)^3 + \cdots + (1/2)^n + \cdots$ is $1/(1 - (1/2))$.

9. The sum of the infinite geometric series $(1/3) + (1/3)^2 + (1/3)^3 + \cdots + (1/3)^n + \cdots$ is $1/2$.

10. The sum of the infinite geometric series $5(1/2) + 5(1/2)^2 + 5(1/2)^3 + \cdots + 5(1/2)^n + \cdots$ is 5.

11. An annuity is a sequence of equal payments or deposits made at regular intervals.

12. The present value of an annuity is the amount of money deposited today to make a series of fixed payments in the future.

13. The present value of an annuity that makes payments of $6000 per year for 10 years is less than $60,000, assuming an annual interest rate of 3%.

14. The present value of a series of constant annual payments made forever is infinite.

15. If annual deposits of $3000 are made at the beginning of each year into an account paying 2% interest per year, compounded annually, then the account balance after the fourth deposit is $3000(1.02)^4 + 3000(1.02)^3 + 3000(1.02)^2 + 3000(1.02)$ dollars.

16. If annual deposits of $3000 are made at the beginning of each year into an account paying 2% interest per year, compounded annually, then the account balance after the tenth deposit is $3000(1 - (1.02)^{10})/(1 - 1.02)$ dollars.

17. A deposit of $735,000 into an account earning 5% compounded annually is sufficient to generate annual payments of $35,000 in perpetuity, starting now.

18. The present value of a payment 5 years in the future of $2000, assuming annual interest rate of 3%, is $2000(1.03)^5$ dollars.

19. The present value of 3 annual payments of $600, starting now, assuming annual interest rate of 4%, is $600 + 600(1.04)^{-1} + 600(1.04)^{-2}$ dollars.

20. The present value of 10 annual payments of $600, starting now, assuming annual interest rate of 4%, is $600(1 - (1.04)^{-10})/(1 - (1.04)^{-1})$ dollars.

21. If a person consumes a 25-mg tablet of a drug four times throughout the day, at the end of the day the person will have 100 mg of the drug in the body.

22. If the quantity of a drug in the body has reached the steady-state level for a person taking a drug at regular intervals, then the quantity of drug in the person's body stays constant.

23. A person consuming 3 micrograms of a toxin with breakfast each day, of which 5% leaves the body each day, has $3/(1-0.05)$ micrograms of toxin in the body right after breakfast, in the long run.

24. If a country used 10 billion barrels of oil last year, and oil consumption increases at 2% annually, then over the next 5 years, the total oil consumption will be $10(1.02)(1 - (1.02)^5)/(1 - 1.02)$ billion barrels.

25. In a person taking a constant dose $D$ mg of medication everyday, the steady-state level is the same before and after each daily dose.

26. In a person taking a constant dose $D$ mg of medication every day, at the steady-state level the quantity of the drug eliminated daily is equal to the daily dose $D$.

27. If a drug is administered intravenously, then a geometric series is a better model than a differential equation for the quantity of drug in the bloodstream.

28. If a certain drug has a half-life of three hours in the body, then nine hours after a dosage of 160 mg, the quantity in the body drops to 20 mg.

29. If a 50-mg injection of a drug is given once every day, and the drug is metabolized at a continuous rate of 5% per day, then the long-term steady-state quantity in the body after injection is $50/(1 - e^{0.05})$.

30. If a drug is administered intravenously at a rate of 50 mg per day, and the drug is metabolized at a continuous rate of 5% per day, then the long-term steady-state quantity in the body is 1000 mg.

# PROJECTS FOR CHAPTER TEN

**1. Do You Have Any Common Ancestors?**

In this project, we estimate the number of ancestors you have and determine whether you have any common ancestors. (A common ancestor is one who appears on two sides of your family tree. For example, if your great-grandmother on your mother's mother's side is also your grandmother on your father's side, then she would be a common ancestor.)

**(a)** In general, each person has 2 biological parents, 4 biological grandparents, 8 biological great-grandparents, and so on. Write a formula for the number of ancestors you have, going back $n$ generations.

**(b)** How long is one generation? Estimate the age of typical parents when a baby is born. This is the length of time for a generation. How many generations are included if we go back 100 years? 500 years? 1000 years? 2000 years?

**(c)** Use your answers to parts (a) and (b) to estimate the number of ancestors you have if we go back 100 years, 500 years, 1000 years, or 2000 years.

**(d)** In parts (a) and (c), we counted every ancestor separately, so we assumed that you have no common ancestors. Use the fact that the population of the world was about 6 billion people in 1999 and was about 200 million people in the year 1 AD to determine whether this is a reasonable assumption. Explain your reasoning.

**2. Harrod-Hicks Model of an Expanding National Economy**

In an expanding national economy, the Harrod-Hicks model relates the national income in one year to the national income in the preceding year. If $f(n)$ is the national income in year $n$, then the model predicts, for some constants $k$ and $h$ with $k > 1$ and $h > 0$, that

$$f(n+1) = kf(n) - h.$$

**(a)** Let $C = f(0)$. Write $f(1)$, $f(2)$, and $f(3)$ in terms of $k$, $h$, and $C$.

**(b)** Show that

$$f(1) = kC - h,$$
$$f(2) = k^2C - (1 + k)h,$$
$$f(3) = k^3C - (1 + k + k^2)h.$$

Use these formulas to guess a formula for $f(n)$.

**(c)** Use the formula for the sum of a finite geometric series to rewrite the formula for $f(n)$ in closed form.

**3. Probability of Winning in Sports**

In certain sports, winning a game requires a lead of two points. That is, if the score is tied you have to score two points in a row to win.

**(a)** For some sports (e.g. tennis), a point is scored every play. Suppose your probability of scoring the next point is always $p$. Then, your opponent's probability of scoring the next point is always $1 - p$.

  (i) What is the probability that you win the next two points?

  (ii) What is the probability that you and your opponent split the next two points, that is, that neither of you wins both points?

  (iii) What is the probability that you split the next two points but you win the two after that?

  (iv) What is the probability that you either win the next two points or split the next two and then win the next two after that?

  (v) Give a formula for your probability $w$ of winning a tied game.

  (vi) Compute your probability of winning a tied game when $p = 0.5$; when $p = 0.6$; when $p = 0.7$; when $p = 0.4$. Comment on your answers.

**(b)** In other sports (e.g. volleyball prior to 1999), you can score a point only if it is your turn, with turns alternating until a point is scored. Suppose your probability of scoring a point when it is your turn is $p$, and your opponent's probability of scoring a point when it is her turn is $q$.

   (i) Find a formula for the probability $S$ that you are the first to score the next point, assuming it is currently your turn.

   (ii) Suppose that if you score a point, the next turn is yours. Using your answers to part (a) and your formula for $S$, compute the probability of winning a tied game (if you need two points in a row to win).

- Assume $p = 0.5$ and $q = 0.5$ and it is your turn.
- Assume $p = 0.6$ and $q = 0.5$ and it is your turn.

**4. Medical Case Study: Drug Desensitization Schedule**[8]

Some patients have allergic reactions to critical medications for which there are no effective alternatives. In some such cases, the drug can be given safely by a process known as drug desensitization. Desensitization starts by administering a very small amount of the needed medication intravenously, and then progressively increasing the concentration or the rate that the drug is infused until the full dose is achieved.

An example of a drug desensitization regimen is shown in Table 10.1. Three solutions of the drug at different concentrations (full strength, 10-fold diluted, and 100-fold diluted) are prepared. The procedure starts with a low rate of infusion of the most dilute solution and progresses in 15-minute steps until the highest infusion rate of the most concentrated solution is reached. At the last stage, the infusion runs until the target dose is reached.

**(a)** For a target dose of 500 mg of a drug and a full strength solution of 2 mg/ml, make a spreadsheet that enables you to fill out the first 11 steps in Table 10.1, each of which runs for 15 minutes.

**(b)** How much of the drug is administered in the 12th step? How long does this step last? Fill in the last row of the table.

**(c)** Show how a geometric series can be used to calculate the total drug administered in the first 11 steps.

**(d)** How long does it take from the beginning of step 1 for the patient to receive the target dose?

Table 10.1

| Step | Solution | Concentration (mg/ml) | Rate (ml/hr) | Time (min) | Volume infused per step (ml) | Dose administered per step (mg) | Cumulative dose (mg) | Ratio of dose administered in this step to dose administered in previous step |
|---|---|---|---|---|---|---|---|---|
| 1 | 100-fold dilution | | 2.5 | | | | | |
| 2 | 100-fold dilution | | 5.0 | | | | | |
| 3 | 100-fold dilution | | 10.0 | | | | | |
| 4 | 100-fold dilution | | 20.0 | | | | | |
| 5 | 10-fold dilution | | 4.0 | | | | | |
| 6 | 10-fold dilution | | 8.0 | | | | | |
| 7 | 10-fold dilution | | 16.0 | | | | | |
| 8 | 10-fold dilution | | 32.0 | | | | | |
| 9 | undiluted | | 6.4 | | | | | |
| 10 | undiluted | | 12.8 | | | | | |
| 11 | undiluted | | 25.6 | | | | | |
| 12 | undiluted | | 51.2 | | | | | |

[8]From David E. Sloane, M.D.

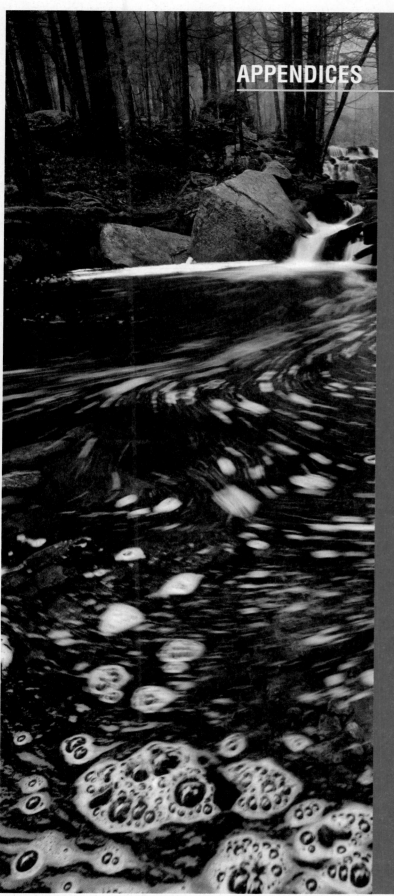
©Patrick Zephyr/Patrick Zephyr Nature Photography

# APPENDICES

# A   FITTING FORMULAS TO DATA

In this section we see how the formulas that are used in a mathematical model can be developed. Some of the formulas we use are exact. However, many formulas we use are approximations, often constructed from data.

## Fitting a Linear Function to Data

A company wants to understand the relationship between the amount spent on advertising, $a$, and total sales, $S$. The data they collect might look like that found in Table A.1.

**Table A.1**   *Advertising and sales: Linear relationship*

| $a$ (advertising in \$1000s) | 3 | 4 | 5 | 6 |
|---|---|---|---|---|
| $S$ (sales in \$1000s) | 100 | 120 | 140 | 160 |

The data in Table A.1 are linear, so a formula fits it exactly. The slope of the line is 20, and we can determine that the vertical intercept is 40, so the line is

$$S = 40 + 20a.$$

Now suppose that the company collected the data in Table A.2. This time the data are not linear. In general, it is difficult to find a formula to fit data exactly. We must be satisfied with a formula that is a good approximation to the data.

**Table A.2**   *Advertising and sales: Nonlinear relationship*

| $a$ (advertising in \$1000s) | 3 | 4 | 5 | 6 |
|---|---|---|---|---|
| $S$ (sales in \$1000s) | 105 | 117 | 141 | 152 |

Figure A.1 shows the data in Table A.2. Since the relationship is nearly, though not exactly, linear, it is well approximated by a line. Figure A.2 shows the line $S = 40 + 20a$ and the data.

Figure A.1: The sales data from Table A.2

Figure A.2: The line $S = 40 + 20a$ and the data from Table A.2

## The Regression Line

Is there a line that fits the data better than the one in Figure A.2? If so, how do we find it? The process of fitting a line to a set of data is called *linear regression* and the line of best fit is called the *regression line*. (Later in the section, we discuss what "best fit" means.) Many calculators and computer programs calculate the regression line from the data points. Alternatively, the regression line can be estimated by plotting the points on paper and fitting a line "by eye." In Chapter 8, we derive the formulas for the regression line. For the data in Table A.2, the regression line is

$$S = 54.5 + 16.5a.$$

This line is graphed with the data in Figure A.3.

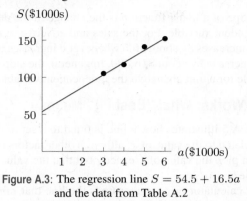

Figure A.3: The regression line $S = 54.5 + 16.5a$
and the data from Table A.2

## Using the Regression Line to Make Predictions

We can use the formula for sales as a function of advertising to make predictions. For example, to predict total sales if $3500 is spent on advertising, substitute $a = 3.5$ into the regression line:

$$S = 54.5 + 16.5(3.5) = 112.25.$$

The regression line predicts sales of $112,250. To see that this is reasonable, compare it to the entries in Table A.2. When $a = 3$, we have $S = 105$, and when $a = 4$, we have $S = 117$. Predicted sales of $S = 112.25$ when $a = 3.5$ makes sense because it falls between 105 and 117. See Figure A.4. Of course, if we spent $3500 on advertising, sales would probably not be exactly $112,250. The regression equation allows us to make predictions, but does not provide exact results.

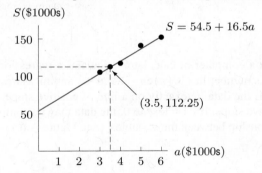

Figure A.4: Predicting sales when spending $3,500 on advertising

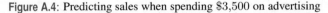

**Example 1**    Predict total sales given advertising expenditures of $4800 and $10,000.

Solution    When $4800 is spent on advertising, $a = 4.8$, so

$$S = 54.5 + 16.5(4.8) = 133.7.$$

Sales are predicted to be $133,700. When $10,000 is spent on advertising, $a = 10$, so

$$S = 54.5 + 16.5(10) = 219.5.$$

Sales are predicted to be $219,500.

Consider the two predictions made in Example 1 at $a = 4.8$ and $a = 10$. We have more confidence in the accuracy of the prediction when $a = 4.8$, because we are *interpolating* within an interval we already know something about. The prediction for $a = 10$ is less reliable, because we are *extrapolating* outside the interval defined by the data values in Table A.2. In general, interpolation is safer than extrapolation.

### Interpreting the Slope of the Regression Line

The slope of a linear function is the change in the dependent variable divided by the change in the independent variable. For the sales and advertising regression line, the slope is 16.5. This tells us that $S$ increases by about 16.5 whenever $a$ increases by 1. If advertising expenses increase by \$1000, sales increase by about \$16,500. In general, the slope tells us the expected change in the dependent variable for a unit change in the independent variable.

## How Regression Works: What "Best Fit" Means

Figure A.5 illustrates how a line is fitted to a set of data. We assume that the value of $y$ is in some way related to the value of $x$, although other factors could influence $y$ as well. Thus, we assume that we can pick the value of $x$ exactly but that the value of $y$ may be only partially determined by this $x$-value.

A calculator or computer finds the line that minimizes the sum of the squares of the vertical distances between the data points and the line. See Figure A.5. The regression line is also called a *least-squares line*, or the *line of best fit*.

Figure A.5: Data and the corresponding
least-squares regression line

## Correlation

When a computer or calculator calculates a regression line, it also gives a *correlation coefficient*, $r$. This number lies between $-1$ and $+1$ and measures how well the regression line fits the data. If $r = 1$, the data lie exactly on a line of positive slope. If $r = -1$, the data lie exactly on a line of negative slope. If $r$ is close to 0, the data may be completely scattered, or there may be a nonlinear relationship between the variables. (See Figure A.6.)

Figure A.6: Various data sets and correlation coefficients

**Example 2**    The correlation coefficient for the sales data in Table A.2 is $r \approx 0.99$. The fact that $r$ is positive tells us that the regression line has positive slope. The fact that $r$ is close to 1 tells us that the regression line fits the data well.

### The Difference Between Relation, Correlation, and Causation

It is important to understand that a high correlation (either positive or negative) between two quantities does *not* imply causation. For example, there is a high correlation between children's reading level and shoe size.[1] However, large feet do not cause a child to read better (or vice versa). Larger feet and improved reading ability are both a consequence of growing older.

Notice also that a correlation of 0 does not imply that there is no relationship between $x$ and $y$. For example, in Figure A.6(d) there is a relationship between $x$ and $y$-values, while Figure A.6(c) exhibits no apparent relationship. Both data sets have a correlation coefficient of $r \approx 0$. Thus, a correlation of $r = 0$ usually implies there is no linear relationship between $x$ and $y$, but this does not mean there is no relationship at all.

## Regression When the Relationship Is Not Linear

Table A.3 shows the population of the US (in millions) from 1790 to 1860. These points are plotted in Figure A.7. Do the data look linear? Not really. It appears to make more sense to fit an exponential function than a linear function to this data. Finding the exponential function of best fit is called *exponential regression.* One algorithm used by a calculator or computer gives the exponential function that fits the data as

$$P = 3.9(1.03)^t,$$

where $P$ is the US population in millions and $t$ is years since 1790. Other algorithms may give different answers. See Figure A.8.

Since the base of this exponential function is 1.03, the US population was increasing at the rate of about 3% per year between 1790 and 1860. Is it reasonable to expect the population to continue to increase at this rate? It turns out that this exponential model does not fit the population of the US well beyond 1860. In Section 4.7, we see another function that is used to model the US population.

**Table A.3**   *US Population in millions, 1790–1860*

| Year | 1790 | 1800 | 1810 | 1820 | 1830 | 1840 | 1850 | 1860 |
|---|---|---|---|---|---|---|---|---|
| Population | 3.9 | 5.3 | 7.2 | 9.6 | 12.9 | 17.1 | 23.1 | 31.4 |

**Figure A.7**: US Population 1790–1860

**Figure A.8**: US population and an exponential regression function

Calculators and computers can do linear regression, exponential regression, logarithmic regression, quadratic regression, and more. To fit a formula to a set of data, the first step is to graph the data and identify the appropriate family of functions.

---

[1]From *Statistics*, 2nd ed., by David Freedman, Robert Pisani, Roger Purves, Ani Adhikari, p. 142 (New York: W.W.Norton, 1991).

**Example 3**    The average fuel efficiency (miles per gallon of gasoline) of US automobiles declined until the 1960s and then started to rise as manufacturers made cars more fuel efficient.[2] See Table A.4.

(a) Plot the data. What family of functions should be used to model the data: linear, exponential, logarithmic, power function, or a polynomial? If a polynomial, state the degree and whether the leading coefficient is positive or negative.

(b) Use quadratic regression to fit a quadratic polynomial to the data; graph it with the data.

**Table A.4**   *What function fits these data?*

| Year | 1940 | 1950 | 1960 | 1970 | 1980 | 1986 |
|------|------|------|------|------|------|------|
| Average miles per gallon | 14.8 | 13.9 | 13.4 | 13.5 | 15.5 | 18.3 |

**Solution**    (a) The data are shown in Figure A.9, with time $t$ in years since 1940. Miles per gallon decreases and then increases, so a good function to model the data is a quadratic (degree 2) polynomial. Since the parabola opens up, the leading coefficient is positive.

(b) If $f(t)$ is average miles per gallon, one algorithm for quadratic regression tells us that the quadratic polynomial that fits the data is

$$f(t) = 0.00617t^2 - 0.225t + 15.10.$$

In Figure A.10, we see that this quadratic does fit the data reasonably well.

$f(t) = 0.00617t^2 - 0.225t + 15.10$

**Figure A.9**: Data showing fuel efficiency of US automobiles over time

**Figure A.10**: Data and best quadratic polynomial, found using regression

# Problems for Appendix A

1. Table A.5 gives the gross world product, $G$, which measures global output of goods and services.[3] If $t$ is in years since 1950, the regression line for these data is

$$G = 3.543 + 0.734t.$$

(a) Plot the data and the regression line on the same axes. Does the line fit the data well?

(b) Interpret the slope of the line in terms of gross world product.

(c) Use the regression line to estimate gross world product in 2005 and in 2020. Comment on your confidence in the two predictions.

**Table A.5**   *G, in trillions of 1999 dollars*

| Year | 1950 | 1960 | 1970 | 1980 | 1990 | 2000 |
|------|------|------|------|------|------|------|
| $G$ | 6.4 | 10.0 | 16.3 | 23.6 | 31.9 | 43.2 |

2. Table A.6 shows worldwide cigarette production as a function of $t$, the number of years since 1950.[4]

(a) Find the regression line for this data.

(b) Use the regression line to estimate world cigarette production in the year 2010.

(c) Interpret the slope of the line in terms of cigarette production.

(d) Plot the data and the regression line on the same axes. Does the line fit the data well?

**Table A.6**   *Cigarette production, P, in billions*

| $t$ | 0 | 10 | 20 | 30 | 40 | 50 |
|-----|-----|------|------|------|------|------|
| $P$ | 1686 | 2150 | 3112 | 4388 | 5419 | 5564 |

[2]C. Schaufele and N. Zumoff, *Earth Algebra, Preliminary Version*, p. 91 (New York: Harper Collins, 1993).
[3]The Worldwatch Institute, *Vital Signs* 2001, p. 57 (New York: W.W. Norton, 2001).
[4]The Worldwatch Institute, *Vital Signs* 2001, p. 77 (New York: W.W. Norton, 2001).

**3.** Table A.7 shows the US Gross National Product (GNP).[5]

(a) Plot GNP against years since 1970. Does a line fit the data well?

(b) Find the regression line and graph it with the data.

(c) Use the regression line to estimate the GNP in 1985 and in 2020. Which estimate do you have more confidence in? Why?

**Table A.7**   *GNP in 2003 dollars*

| Year | 1970 | 1980 | 1990 | 2000 |
|---|---|---|---|---|
| GNP (billions) | 1045 | 2824 | 5838 | 9856 |

**4.** The acidity of a solution is measured by its pH, with lower pH values indicating more acidity. A study of acid rain was undertaken in Colorado between 1975 and 1978, in which the acidity of rain was measured for 150 consecutive weeks.[6] The data followed a generally linear pattern. If $P$ is the pH and $t$ is the number of weeks into the study, the regression line was determined to be

$$P = 5.43 - 0.0053t.$$

(a) Is the pH level increasing or decreasing over the period of the study? What does this tell you about the level of acidity in the rain?

(b) According to the line, what was the pH at the beginning of the study? At the end of the study ($t = 150$)?

(c) What is the slope of the regression line? Explain what this slope is telling you about the pH.

**5.** In a 1977 study[7] of 21 of the best American female runners, researchers measured the average stride rate, $S$, at different speeds, $v$. The data are given in Table A.8.

(a) Find the regression line for these data, using stride rate as the dependent variable.

(b) Plot the regression line and the data on the same axes. Does the line fit the data well?

(c) Use the regression line to predict the stride rate when the speed is 18 ft/sec and when the speed is 10 ft/sec. Which prediction do you have more confidence in? Why?

**6.** Table A.9 shows the atmospheric concentration of carbon dioxide, $CO_2$ (in parts per million, ppm), at the Mauna Loa Observatory in Hawaii.[8]

(a) Find the average rate of change of the concentration of carbon dioxide between 1980 and 2000. Give units and interpret your answer in terms of carbon dioxide.

(b) Plot the data, and find the regression line for carbon dioxide concentration against years since 1980. Use the regression line to predict the concentration of carbon dioxide in the atmosphere in the year 2020.

**Table A.9**

| Year | 1980 | 1985 | 1990 | 1995 | 2000 |
|---|---|---|---|---|---|
| $CO_2$ | 349.6 | 346.7 | 354.4 | 360.8 | 368.9 |

**7.** In Problem 6, carbon dioxide concentration was modeled as a linear function of time. However, if we include data for carbon dioxide concentration from as far back as 1900, the data appear to be more exponential than linear. (They looked linear in Problem 6 because we were only looking at a small piece of the graph.) If $C$ is the $CO_2$ concentration in ppm and $t$ is in years since 1900, an exponential regression function to fit the data is

$$C = 272.27(1.0026)^t.$$

(a) What is the annual percent growth rate during this period? Interpret this rate in terms of $CO_2$ concentration.

(b) What $CO_2$ concentration is given by the model for 1900? For 1980? Compare the 1980 estimate to the actual value in Table A.9.

**8.** (a) Fit an exponential function to the population data in Table A.10. Plot the data and the exponential function on the same axes.

(b) At approximately what percentage rate was the population growing between 1960 and 2000?

(c) If the population continues to grow at the same percentage rate, what population is projected for 2020?

**Table A.8**   *Stride rate, $S$, in steps/sec, and speed, $v$, in ft/sec*

| $v$ | 15.86 | 16.88 | 17.50 | 18.62 | 19.97 | 21.06 | 22.11 |
|---|---|---|---|---|---|---|---|
| $S$ | 3.05 | 3.12 | 3.17 | 3.25 | 3.36 | 3.46 | 3.55 |

**Table A.10**   *US Population 1960-2000*

| $t$, years since 1960 | 0 | 10 | 20 | 30 | 40 |
|---|---|---|---|---|---|
| population (m) | 179.3 | 203.3 | 226.5 | 248.7 | 281.4 |

---

[5]*The World Almanac and Book of Facts 2005*, p. 111 (New York).

[6]William M. Lewis and Michael C. Grant, "Acid Precipitation in the Western United States," *Science* 207 (1980), pp. 176-177.

[7]R.C. Nelson, C.M. Brooks, and N.L. Pike, "Biomechanical Comparison of Male and Female Distance Runners." *The Marathon: Physiological, Medical, Epidemiological, and Psychological Studies*, ed. P. Milvy, pp. 793–807 (New York: New York Academy of Sciences, 1977).

[8]www.cmdl.noaa.gov/ccgg/iadv, accessed on February 20, 2005.

**9.** Table A.11 shows the public debt, $D$, of the US[9] in billions of dollars, $t$ years after 1998.

(a) Plot the public debt against the number of years since 1998.
(b) Does the data look more linear or more exponential?
(c) Fit an exponential function to the data and graph it with the data.
(d) What annual percentage growth rate does the exponential model show?
(e) Do you expect this model to give accurate predictions beyond 2004? Explain.

**Table A.11**

| $t$ | 0 | 1 | 2 | 3 | 4 | 5 | 6 |
|---|---|---|---|---|---|---|---|
| $D$ | 5526 | 5656 | 5674 | 5808 | 6228 | 6783 | 7379 |

**10.** A company collects the data in Table A.12. Find the regression line and interpret its slope. Sketch the data and the line. What is the correlation coefficient? Why is the value you get reasonable?

**Table A.12**    *Cost to produce various quantities of a product*

| $q$ (quantity in units) | 25 | 50 | 75 | 100 | 125 |
|---|---|---|---|---|---|
| $C$ (cost in dollars) | 500 | 625 | 689 | 742 | 893 |

**11.** Match the $r$ values with scatter plots in Figure A.11.

$$r = -0.98, \quad r = -0.5, \quad r = -0.25,$$

$$r = 0, \quad r = 0.7, \quad r = 1.$$

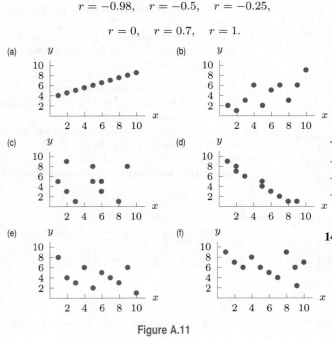

**Figure A.11**

**12.** Table A.13 shows the number of cars, $N$, in millions in the US[10] $t$ years after 1940.

(a) Plot the data, with number of passenger cars as the dependent variable.
(b) Does a linear or exponential model appear to fit the data better?
(c) Use a linear model first: Find the regression line for these data. Graph it with the data. Use the regression line to predict the number of passenger cars in the year 2010 ($t = 70$).
(d) Interpret the slope of the regression line found in part (c) in terms of passenger cars.
(e) Now use an exponential model: Find the exponential regression function for these data. Graph it with the data. Use the exponential function to predict the number of passenger cars in the year 2010 ($t = 70$). Compare your prediction with the prediction obtained from the linear model.
(f) What annual percent growth rate in number of US passenger cars does your exponential model show?

**Table A.13**    *Number of passenger cars, in millions*

| $t$ | 0 | 10 | 20 | 30 | 40 | 50 | 60 |
|---|---|---|---|---|---|---|---|
| $N$ | 27.5 | 40.3 | 61.7 | 89.2 | 121.6 | 133.7 | 133.6 |

**13.** Table A.14 gives the population of the world in billions.

(a) Plot these data. Does a linear or exponential model seem to fit the data best?
(b) Find an exponential regression function.
(c) What annual percent growth rate does the exponential function show?
(d) Predict the population of the world in the year 2020 and in the year 2050. Comment on the relative confidence you have in these two estimates.

**Table A.14**    *World population in billions*

| Year (since 1950) | 0 | 10 | 20 | 30 | 40 | 50 | 58 |
|---|---|---|---|---|---|---|---|
| Population (bn) | 2.6 | 3.0 | 3.7 | 4.5 | 5.3 | 6.1 | 6.7 |

**14.** In 1969, all field goal attempts in the National Football League and American Football League were analyzed. See Table A.15. (The data has been summarized: all attempts between 10 and 19 yards from the goal post are listed as 14.5 yards out, etc. )

(a) Graph the data, with success rate as the dependent variable. Discuss whether a linear or an exponential model fits best.

---

[9]*The World Almanac and Book of Facts 2005*, p. 119 (New York).
[10]*The World Almanac and Book of Facts 2005*, p. 237 (New York).

**(b)** Find the linear regression function; graph it with the data. Interpret the slope of the regression line in terms of football.

**(c)** Find the exponential regression function; graph it with the data. What success rate does this function predict from a distance of 50 yards?

**(d)** Using the graphs in parts (b) and (c), decide which model seems to fit the data best.

**Table A.15**  *Successful fraction of field goal attempts*

| Distance from goal, $x$ yards | 14.5 | 24.5 | 34.5 | 44.5 | 52.0 |
|---|---|---|---|---|---|
| Fraction successful, $Y$ | 0.90 | 0.75 | 0.54 | 0.29 | 0.15 |

**15.** Table A.16 shows the number of Japanese cars imported into the US.[11]

**(a)** Plot the number of Japanese cars imported against the number of years since 1964.

**(b)** Does the data look more linear or more exponential?

**(c)** Fit an exponential function to the data and graph it with the data.

**(d)** What annual percentage growth rate does the exponential model show?

**(e)** Do you expect this model to give accurate predictions beyond 1971? Explain.

**Table A.16**  *Imported Japanese cars, 1964–1971*

| Year since 1964 | 0 | 1 | 2 | 3 | 4 | 5 | 6 | 7 |
|---|---|---|---|---|---|---|---|---|
| Cars (thousands) | 16 | 24 | 56 | 70 | 170 | 260 | 381 | 704 |

**16.** Figure A.12 shows oil production in the Middle East.[12] If you were to model this function with a polynomial, what degree would you choose? Would the leading coefficient be positive or negative?

**Figure A.12**

**17.** After the oil crisis in 1973, the average fuel efficiency, $E$, of cars increased until the early 1990s, when it started to decrease again.

**(a)** Plot the data [13] in Table A.17, using $t$ in years since 1975. If you were to fit a quadratic polynomial to the data, what would be the sign of the leading coefficient?

**(b)** Fit a quadratic polynomial and plot it with the data.

**Table A.17**

| Year | 1975 | 1980 | 1985 | 1990 | 1995 | 2000 |
|---|---|---|---|---|---|---|
| $E$, mpg | 13.1 | 19.2 | 21.3 | 21.5 | 21.1 | 20.7 |

**18.** Table A.18 gives the area of rain forest destroyed for agriculture and development.[14]

**(a)** Plot these data.

**(b)** Are the data increasing or decreasing? Concave up or concave down? In each case, interpret your answer in terms of rain forest.

**(c)** Use a calculator or computer to fit a logarithmic function to this data. Plot this function on the axes in part (a).

**(d)** Use the curve you found in part (c) to predict the area of rain forest destroyed in 2010.

**Table A.18**  *Destruction of rain forest*

| $x$ (year) | 1960 | 1970 | 1980 | 1988 |
|---|---|---|---|---|
| $y$ (million hectares) | 2.21 | 3.79 | 4.92 | 5.77 |

In Problems 19–21, tables of data are given.[15]

**(a)** Use a plot of the data to decide whether a linear, exponential, logarithmic, or quadratic function fits the data best.

**(b)** Use regression to find a formula for the function you chose in part (a). If the function is linear or exponential, interpret the rate of change or percent rate of change.

**(c)** Use your function to predict the value of the function in the year 2015.

**(d)** Plot your function on the same axes as the data, and comment on the fit.

---

[11] *The World Almanac 1995.*

[12] Lester R. Brown, et al., *Vital Signs*, p. 49 (New York: W. W. Norton and Co., 1994).

[13] *The World Almanac and Book of Facts* (New York, 2005).

[14] C. Schaufele and N. Zumoff, *Earth Algebra, Preliminary Version*, p. 131 (New York: Harper Collins, 1993).

[15] The Worldwatch Institute, *Vital Signs 2007–2008* (New York: W.W. Norton & Company, 2007).

**19.**

*World solar power, S, in megawatts; t in years since 1990*

| t | 0 | 1 | 2 | 3 | 4 | 5 | 6 | 7 |
|---|---|---|---|---|---|---|---|---|
| S | 47 | 55 | 58 | 60 | 69 | 78 | 89 | 126 |

| t | 8 | 9 | 10 | 11 | 12 | 13 | 14 | 15 |
|---|---|---|---|---|---|---|---|---|
| S | 153 | 201 | 277 | 386 | 547 | 748 | 1194 | 1782 |

**20.**

*Nuclear warheads, N, in thousands; t in years since 1960*

| t | 0 | 5 | 10 | 15 | 20 | 25 | 30 | 35 | 40 | 45 |
|---|---|---|---|---|---|---|---|---|---|---|
| N | 22 | 38 | 39 | 48 | 55 | 65 | 59 | 40 | 33 | 28 |

**21.**

*Carbon dioxide, C, in ppm; t in years since 1970*

| t | 0 | 5 | 10 | 15 | 20 | 25 | 30 | 35 |
|---|---|---|---|---|---|---|---|---|
| C | 326 | 331 | 339 | 346 | 354 | 361 | 369 | 380 |

**22.** For each graph in Figure A.13, decide whether the best fit for the data appears to be a linear function, an exponential function, or a polynomial.

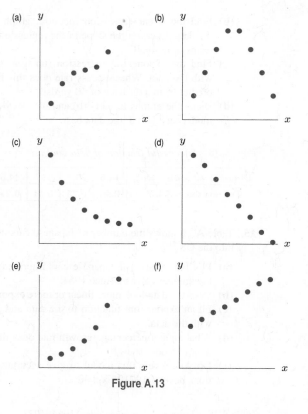

Figure A.13

# B   COMPOUND INTEREST AND THE NUMBER $e$

If you have some money, you may decide to invest it to earn interest. The interest can be paid in many different ways—for example, once a year or many times a year. If the interest is paid more frequently than once per year and the interest is not withdrawn, there is a benefit to the investor since the interest earns interest. This effect is called *compounding*. You may have noticed banks offering accounts that differ both in interest rates and in compounding methods. Some offer interest compounded annually, some quarterly, and others daily. Some even offer continuous compounding.

What is the difference between a bank account advertising 8% compounded annually (once per year) and one offering 8% compounded quarterly (four times per year)? In both cases 8% is an annual rate of interest. The expression 8% *compounded annually* means that at the end of each year, 8% of the current balance is added. This is equivalent to multiplying the current balance by 1.08. Thus, if $100 is deposited, the balance, $B$, in dollars, will be

$$B = 100(1.08) \quad \text{after one year,}$$
$$B = 100(1.08)^2 \quad \text{after two years,}$$
$$B = 100(1.08)^t \quad \text{after } t \text{ years.}$$

The expression 8% *compounded quarterly* means that interest is added four times per year (every three months) and that $\frac{8}{4} = 2\%$ of the current balance is added each time. Thus, if $100 is deposited, at the end of one year, four compoundings have taken place and the account will contain $100(1.02)^4$. Thus, the balance will be

$$B = 100(1.02)^4 \quad \text{after one year,}$$
$$B = 100(1.02)^8 \quad \text{after two years,}$$
$$B = 100(1.02)^{4t} \quad \text{after } t \text{ years.}$$

Note that 8% is *not* the rate used for each three-month period; the annual rate is divided into four 2% payments. Calculating the total balance after one year under each method shows that

$$\text{Annual compounding:} \quad B = 100(1.08) = 108.00,$$
$$\text{Quarterly compounding:} \quad B = 100(1.02)^4 = 108.24.$$

Thus, more money is earned from quarterly compounding, because the interest earns interest as the year goes by. In general, the more often interest is compounded, the more money will be earned (although the increase may not be very large).

We can measure the effect of compounding by introducing the notion of *effective annual rate*. Since $100 invested at 8% compounded quarterly grows to $108.24 by the end of one year, we say that the effective annual rate in this case is 8.24%. We now have two interest rates that describe the same investment: the 8% compounded quarterly and the 8.24% effective annual rate. We call the 8% the *nominal rate* (nominal means "in name only"). However, it is the effective rate that tells you exactly how much interest the investment really pays. Thus, to compare two bank accounts, simply compare the effective annual rate. The next time you walk by a bank, look at the advertisements, which should (by law) include both the nominal rate and the effective annual rate.

## Using the Effective Annual Yield

**Example 1**   Which is better: Bank X paying a 7% annual rate compounded monthly or Bank Y offering a 6.9% annual rate compounded daily?

Solution   We find the effective annual rate for each bank.

Bank X: There are 12 interest payments in a year, each payment being $0.07/12 = 0.005833$ times the current balance. If the initial deposit were $100, then the balance $B$ would be

$$B = 100(1.005833) \quad \text{after one month,}$$
$$B = 100(1.005833)^2 \quad \text{after two months,}$$
$$B = 100(1.005833)^t \quad \text{after } t \text{ months.}$$

To find the effective annual rate, we look at one year, or 12 months, giving $B = 100(1.005833)^{12}$ $= 100(1.072286)$, so the effective annual rate $\approx 7.23\%$.

Bank Y: There are 365 interest payments in a year (assuming it is not a leap year), each being $0.069/365 = 0.000189$ times the current balance. Then the balance is

$$B = 100(1.000189) \quad \text{after one day,}$$
$$B = 100(1.000189)^2 \quad \text{after two days,}$$
$$B = 100(1.000189)^t \quad \text{after } t \text{ days.}$$

so at the end of one year we have multiplied the initial deposit by

$$(1.000189)^{365} = 1.071413$$

so the effective annual rate for Bank Y $\approx 7.14\%$.

Comparing effective annual rates for the banks, we see that Bank X is offering a better investment, by a small margin.

**Example 2**   If $1000 is invested in each bank in Example 1, write an expression for the balance in each bank after $t$ years.

Solution   For Bank X, the effective annual rate $\approx 7.23\%$, so after $t$ years the balance, in dollars, will be

$$B = 100 \left(1 + \frac{0.07}{12}\right)^{12t} = 1000(1.005833)^{12t} = 1000(1.0723)^t.$$

For Bank Y, the effective annual rate $\approx 7.14\%$, so after $t$ years the balance, in dollars, will be

$$B = 1000\left(1 + \frac{0.069}{365}\right)^{365t} = 1000(1.0714)^t.$$

(Again, we are ignoring leap years.)

---

> If interest at an annual rate of $r$ is compounded $n$ times a year, then $r/n$ times the current balance is added $n$ times a year. Therefore, with an initial deposit of $P$, the balance $t$ years later is
>
> $$B = P\left(1 + \frac{r}{n}\right)^{nt}.$$
>
> Note that $r$ is the nominal rate; for example, $r = 0.05$ when the annual rate is $5\%$.

## Increasing the Frequency of Compounding: Continuous Compounding

Let us look at the effect of increasing the frequency of compounding. How much effect does it have?

---

**Example 3**  Find the effective annual rate for a $7\%$ annual rate compounded
(a)   1000 times a year.      (b)   10,000 times a year.

**Solution**  (a)  In one year, a deposit is multiplied by

$$\left(1 + \frac{0.07}{1000}\right)^{1000} \approx 1.0725056,$$

giving an effective annual rate of about $7.25056\%$.
(b)  In one year, a deposit is multiplied by

$$\left(1 + \frac{0.07}{10,000}\right)^{10,000} \approx 1.0725079,$$

giving an effective annual yield of about $7.25079\%$.

---

Notice that there's not a great deal of difference—$7.25056\%$ versus $7.25079\%$—between compounding 1000 times each year (about three times per day) and 10,000 times each year (about 30 times per day). What happens if we compound more often still? Every minute? Every second? Surprisingly, the effective annual rate does not increase indefinitely, but tends to a finite value. The benefit of increasing the frequency of compounding becomes negligible beyond a certain point.

For example, computing the effective annual rate on a $7\%$ investment compounded $n$ times per year for values of $n$ larger than 100,000 gives

$$\left(1 + \frac{0.07}{n}\right)^{n} \approx 1.0725082.$$

So the effective annual rate is about $7.25082\%$. Even if you take $n = 1{,}000{,}000$ or $n = 10^{10}$, the effective annual rate does not change appreciably. The value $7.25082\%$ is an upper bound that is approached as the frequency of compounding increases.

When the effective annual rate is at this upper bound, we say that the interest is being *compounded continuously*. (The word *continuously* is used because the upper bound is approached by compounding more and more frequently.) Thus, when a $7\%$ nominal annual rate is compounded so frequently that the effective annual rate is $7.25082\%$, we say that the $7\%$ is compounded *continuously*. This represents the most one can get from a $7\%$ nominal rate.

### Where Does the Number $e$ Fit In?

It turns out that $e$ is intimately connected to continuous compounding. To see this, use a calculator to check that $e^{0.07} \approx 1.0725082$, which is the same number we obtained by compounding 7% a large number of times. So you have discovered that for very large $n$

$$\left(1 + \frac{0.07}{n}\right)^n \approx e^{0.07}.$$

As $n$ gets larger, the approximation gets better and better, and we write

$$\lim_{n \to \infty} \left(1 + \frac{0.07}{n}\right)^n = e^{0.07},$$

meaning that as $n$ increases, the value of $(1 + 0.07/n)^n$ approaches $e^{0.07}$.

If $P$ is deposited at an annual rate of 7% compounded continuously, the balance, $B$, after $t$ years, is given by

$$B = P(e^{0.07})^t = Pe^{0.07t}.$$

---

If interest on an initial deposit of $P$ is *compounded continuously* at an annual rate $r$, the balance $t$ years later can be calculated using the formula

$$B = Pe^{rt}.$$

---

In working with compound interest, it is important to be clear whether interest rates are nominal rates or effective rates, as well as whether compounding is continuous or not.

---

**Example 4**    Find the effective annual rate of a 6% annual rate, compounded continuously.

Solution     In one year, an investment of $P$ becomes $Pe^{0.06}$. Using a calculator, we see that

$$Pe^{0.06} = P(1.0618365).$$

So the effective annual rate is about 6.18%.

---

**Example 5**    You invest money in a certificate of deposit (CD) for your child's education, and you want it to be worth $120,000 in 10 years. How much should you invest if the CD pays interest at a 9% annual rate compounded quarterly? Continuously?

Solution     Suppose you invest $P$ initially. A 9% annual rate compounded quarterly has an effective annual rate given by $(1 + 0.09/4)^4 = 1.0930833$, or 9.30833%. So after 10 years you have

$$P(1.0930833)^{10} = 120,000.$$

Therefore, you should invest

$$P = \frac{120,000}{(1.0930833)^{10}} = \frac{120,000}{2.4351885} = 49,277.50.$$

On the other hand, if the CD pays 9% per year, compounded continuously, after 10 years you have

$$Pe^{(0.09)10} = 120,000.$$

So you would need to invest

$$P = \frac{120,000}{e^{(0.09)10}} = \frac{120,000}{2.4596031} = 48,788.36.$$

Notice that to achieve the same result, continuous compounding requires a smaller initial investment than quarterly compounding. This is to be expected since the effective annual rate is higher for continuous than for quarterly compounding.

## Problems for Appendix B

**1.** A department store issues its own credit card, with an interest rate of 2% per month. Explain why this is not the same as an annual rate of 24%. What is the effective annual rate?

**2.** A deposit of $10,000 is made into an account paying a nominal yearly interest rate of 8%. Determine the amount in the account in 10 years if the interest is compounded:

   **(a)** Annually   **(b)** Monthly   **(c)** Weekly

   **(d)** Daily      **(e)** Continuously

**3.** A deposit of $50,000 is made into an account paying a nominal yearly interest rate of 6%. Determine the amount in the account in 20 years if the interest is compounded:

   **(a)** Annually   **(b)** Monthly   **(c)** Weekly

   **(d)** Daily      **(e)** Continuously

**4.** Use a graph of $y = (1 + 0.07/x)^x$ to estimate the number that $(1 + 0.07/x)^x$ approaches as $x \to \infty$. Confirm that the value you get is approximately $e^{0.07}$.

**5.** **(a)** Find $(1 + 0.04/n)^n$ for $n = 10,000$, and $100,000$, and $1,000,000$. Use the results to predict the effective annual rate of a 4% annual rate compounded continuously.

   **(b)** Confirm your answer by computing $e^{0.04}$.

**6.** Find the effective annual rate of a 6% annual rate, compounded continuously.

**7.** What nominal annual interest rate has an effective annual rate of 5% under continuous compounding?

**8.** What is the effective annual rate, under continuous compounding, for a nominal annual interest rate of 8%?

**9.** **(a)** Find the effective annual rate for a 5% annual interest rate compounded $n$ times/year if

   **(i)** $n = 1000$      **(ii)** $n = 10,000$
   **(iii)** $n = 100,000$

   **(b)** Look at the sequence of answers in part (a), and predict the effective annual rate for a 5% annual rate compounded continuously.

   **(c)** Compute $e^{0.05}$. How does this confirm your answer to part (b)?

**10.** A bank account is earning interest at 6% per year compounded continuously.

   **(a)** By what percentage has the bank balance in the account increased over one year? (This is the effective annual rate.)

   **(b)** How long does it take the balance to double?

   **(c)** For a continuous interest rate $r$, find a formula for the doubling time in terms of $r$.

**11.** Explain how you can match the interest rates (a)–(e) with the effective annual rates I–V without calculation.

   **(a)** 5.5% annual rate, compounded continuously.
   **(b)** 5.5% annual rate, compounded quarterly.
   **(c)** 5.5% annual rate, compounded weekly.
   **(d)** 5% annual rate, compounded yearly.
   **(e)** 5% annual rate, compounded twice a year.

   I.  5%      II.  5.06%      III.  5.61%

   IV.  5.651%    V.  5.654%

Countries with very high inflation rates often publish monthly rather than yearly inflation figures, because monthly figures are less alarming. Problems 12–13 involve such high rates, which are called *hyperinflation*.

**12.** In 1989, US inflation was 4.6% a year. In 1989 Argentina had an inflation rate of about 33% a month.

   **(a)** What is the yearly equivalent of Argentina's 33% monthly rate?

   **(b)** What is the monthly equivalent of the US 4.6% yearly rate?

**13.** Between December 1988 and December 1989, Brazil's inflation rate was 1290% a year. (This means that between 1988 and 1989, prices increased by a factor of $1 + 12.90 = 13.90$.)

   **(a)** What would an article which cost 1000 cruzados (the Brazilian currency unit) in 1988 cost in 1989?

   **(b)** What was Brazil's monthly inflation rate during this period?

# C  SPREADSHEET PROJECTS

The following projects require the use of a spreadsheet. They can all be done using only the ideas in Chapter 1. In addition, Project 9 (Verhulst: The Logistic Model) and Project 10 (The Spread of Information) give another perspective on material in Chapters 4 and 9. Project 4 (Comparing Home Mortgages) uses a geometric series but can be done before Chapter 10.

## 1. MALTHUS: POPULATION OUTSTRIPS FOOD SUPPLY

In this project, we compare exponential and linear growth. We see the eventual dominance of exponential functions over linear functions.

One of the most famous models of population growth was made by Thomas Malthus in the early 19th century. Malthus believed that while human population increased exponentially, its means of subsistence increased linearly. The gloomy conclusion that Malthus drew from this observation was that the population of the earth would inevitably outstrip its means of subsistence, resulting in an inadequate supply of food. (Malthus went on to note that this state of affairs could only be averted by war, famine, epidemic disease, wide-scale sexual restraint, or other such drastic checks on population growth.)

The following table shows part of a spreadsheet showing such as a scenario.[16] The starting population is 1 million, while the available food feeds 2 million people. The population grows at an annual rate of 3% per year and the food production increases by 100,000 per year. These population and food growth rates are in cells on the right of the spreadsheet. The fourth column contains the ratio of available food per person in the population. The spreadsheet includes a safety ratio—so long as the food-to-population ratio is above this figure of 1.5, the fifth column displays "Yes"; whenever the ratio drops below this figure the fifth column displays "No" (as it does by the end of the 21st century).

We see that at first there is plenty of food—the ratio of food to population is 2, which means that there is twice as much food as is necessary to feed the population. For the first few years the ratio increases, but at a certain point it starts to decrease, and eventually the ratio drops below one.

| Year | Population | Food supply | Ratio | Above safety ratio? | |
|------|-----------|-------------|-------|---------------------|---|
| 1999 | 1000000 | 2000000 | 2.00 | Yes | Annual pop growth rate 3.00% |
| 2000 | 1030000 | 2100000 | 2.04 | Yes | |
| 2001 | 1060900 | 2200000 | 2.07 | Yes | |
| 2002 | 1092727 | 2300000 | 2.10 | Yes | Annual food growth rate 100,000 |
| 2003 | 1125509 | 2400000 | 2.13 | Yes | |
| 2004 | 1159274 | 2500000 | 2.16 | Yes | |
| 2005 | 1194052 | 2600000 | 2.18 | Yes | Safety ratio 1.5 |
| 2006 | 1229874 | 2700000 | 2.20 | Yes | |
| 2007 | 1266770 | 2800000 | 2.21 | Yes | |
| 2008 | 1304773 | 2900000 | 2.22 | Yes | |
| ⋮ | ⋮ | ⋮ | ⋮ | ⋮ | |
| 2098 | 18658866 | 11900000 | 0.64 | No | |
| 2099 | 19218632 | 12000000 | 0.62 | No | |
| 2100 | 19795191 | 12100000 | 0.61 | No | |

---

[16]From Graeme Bird.

1. Set up your spreadsheet to look like the one shown in the table, extending it to the year 2100. Virtually every cell must contain a formula — the exceptions being the six cells containing "1999," "1,000,000," "2,000,000," "3.00%," "100,000," and "1.5."

2. (a) About what year is the food-to-population ratio the highest?
   (b) In which year does this ratio reach 1?

3. There are at least two ways to improve upon the current situation: we can lower the population growth rate, or we can increase the food supply.

   (a) What would the population growth rate have to be lowered to, in order to have the food-to-population ratio not reach 1 until the year 2100? (Keep the food supply increasing at 100,000 per year.)

   (b) What would the food supply rate have to be increased to, in order to achieve this same goal, of the ratio not reaching 1 until the year 2100? (Keep the population growth rate at its original 3%.)

4. Using the original scenario, create each of the following charts (both line and column). Extend the charts to the year 2100, so that the point where the population outstrips the food supply is clearly evident.

   (a) Showing population and food, with the years on the horizontal axis.
   (b) Showing only the ratio, with the years on the horizontal axis.

## 2. CREDIT CARD DEBT

You have a credit card on which you owe $2000. Your credit card company charges a monthly interest rate of 1.5% and requires a minimum monthly payment of 2.5% of your current balance. (This payment scheme is similar to ones used by many credit card companies, but see Question 8.) [Note: For Questions 1–2, you will not need a spreadsheet, although you will need a calculator.]

1. If the monthly interest rate is 1.5%, what is the effective annual interest rate?

2. As a rule, the minimum monthly payment required exceeds the interest accrued in a month. (For example, here the minimum monthly payment of 2.5% exceeds the monthly interest charges of 1.5%.) Explain why this should be the case. What would happen to the card balance if the minimum required payment was less than the accrued interest?

Suppose that you decide to pay off your $2000 credit card debt by making only the minimum required payment every month. Assume that you make no further charges to the card, since you're trying to pay it off.

3. Since 2.5% of $2000 is $50, your first monthly payment is $50. Before you do any spreadsheet calculations, guess how long it will take to bring your total balance down from $2000 to less than $50, assuming that you make only the minimum required payment every month. A rough guess is fine; use common sense and explain your reasoning.

4. Over time, your monthly payments, which start at $50, will decrease. Explain why this happens. Does the fact that your monthly payments decrease affect the answer you gave to Question 3?

5. Although you only owe the credit card company $2000, you will end up paying quite a bit more than $2000, due to interest charges. Make your best guess (before making any specific calculations) as to how much, roughly, you will end up having paid the credit card company for your initial $2000 debt.

Set up a spreadsheet showing the number of months since you began paying off your debt, your current balance, the interest due that month, and the payment you make, each in a separate column. Each quantity should be calculated by a formula.

*Example:* To figure out what formulas you need, recall that your initial balance is $2000, the monthly interest charged is 1.5%, and the minimum required payment is 2.5%. Thus, at the beginning of Month 1, your balance is $2000, since you have paid off nothing yet. Therefore, at the end of Month 1, the interest that you owe is 1.5% of the $2000 balance, or $30. Your minimum payment is 2.5% of the $2000 balance, or $50. Thus, at the beginning of Month 2, your new balance is the old balance of $2000 plus the $30 in interest minus the $50 payment, or $1980. Notice that the figures for Month 2 depend on the figures for Month 1; similarly, the figures for Month 3 depend on Month 2 figures, and so on. Follow this procedure to figure out what formulas you need in each column of your spreadsheet.

Once you have set up a working spreadsheet, answer the following questions.

6. How good was your guess in Question 3? Using your spreadsheet, find out how many months it takes to bring your balance down to less than $50. Was your guess close, or were you surprised by how long it really takes?

7. How good was your guess in Question 5? Using your spreadsheet, figure out exactly how much you pay the credit card company to bring your balance down to less than $50. How does this figure compare to the original debt of $2000?

8. Use your spreadsheet to find out how long it takes to bring your balance down to $0. Or can't you tell? Does there ever come a point when you have exactly paid off your debt? [Hint: Eventually, the minimum monthly payments and the interest charges become unrealistic. In what way are they unrealistic? How do real credit card companies avoid this problem?]

9. Now let's try experimenting with the numbers and see what happens. In each of the following cases, make the appropriate changes to your spreadsheet. Assume that as soon as your balance is under $50, you pay it off in a lump sum.

    (a) If every month you pay $1 more than the minimum required payment, how long does it take to bring your debt down to less than $50? How much do you end up paying to your creditors in total? How much money do you save by using this payment scheme instead of the one in Question 5?

    (b) Your first monthly payment is $50. If you paid $50 every month, instead of the minimum required payment, how long does it take to bring your debt down to less than $50? How much money do you save by using this payment scheme instead of the one in Question 5?

    (c) Recently, many credit card companies have made offers similar to the following: if you transfer your debt from a competitor's card to their card, they will charge you a lower interest rate. Suppose you find a credit card company willing to make this transaction, and that their monthly interest rate is 1%, not 1.5%. Leaving all the other original assumptions unchanged, how long does it take to bring your debt down to less than $50, and how much do you pay your creditors in total? How much money do you save compared to what you would have paid your original card company?

10. Comparing the scheme used in Questions 3–5 with each of the schemes in Question 9, what conclusions can you reach about paying off a credit card debt?

## 3. CHOOSING A BANK LOAN

A local bank offers the following loan packages. Use a spreadsheet to decide which option is the best. The packages are as follows:

- A loan of $2000, at an annual rate of 9%, payable in 24 monthly installments.
- A loan of $2000, at an annual rate of 10%, payable in 36 monthly installments.
- A loan of $2000, at an annual rate of 9.25%, payable in 52 biweekly installments.

Interest is compounded with the same frequency as payments are made. Notice that the first and last loans have two-year payoff periods; the middle loan is for three years.

1. Use a spreadsheet to decide which loan is cheapest in terms of total payoff to the bank. (See the following hint.)

2. Use a spreadsheet to decide which loan is easiest to afford in terms of lowest monthly payment. (See the following hint.)

*Hint:* The difficult part of Questions 1 and 2 is figuring out your monthly (or biweekly) payments. There are formulas that give the payment based on the period and amount of the loan and the interest charged, but instead of using them, we will use a spreadsheet. The idea is that you can make an educated guess as to what the payment ought to be, and then use a spreadsheet to check your answer. By looking at the spreadsheet, you can decide whether your guess was too high or too low, and thus improve upon your original guess. It's surprising how quickly you can zero in on the required monthly payment, down to the nearest penny, by this guess-and-check method.

For example, consider the first loan, the two-year $2000 loan at 9%. Set up a spreadsheet with the initial balance of $2000, the interest for the first month, which is $(9\%/12) \cdot \$2000 = \$15$, and a guess at the monthly payment. There are lots of ways to make a guess at the monthly payment. One way is to say that if you were to borrow $2000 for 2 years at 9%, you would owe about $\$2000(1.09)^2 = \$2376$. (Never mind the monthly compounding—this is just a rough approximation.) To pay off this amount in 24 equal monthly payments would require $\$2376/24 = \$99$. So, we guess a monthly payment of $100. Using this guess, the second month's balance will be

$$(\$2000) + (\$15 \text{ in interest for month 1}) - (\text{Payment of } \$100) = \$1915.$$

Thus, the next month's interest will be $(9\%/12) \cdot \$1915$, and the next month's payment should be the same as the first month's payment, or $100. Continue this process until 24 months' (two years') worth of payments have been made. You will see that the final balance is negative, meaning you paid the bank more than you really owed. This means that $100 is too high a monthly payment to pay off your $2000 loan. (We could have predicted that this was the case when we made our estimate above. Do you see why?) So, since $100 is too high, you might guess that an $80 monthly payment would be right. If you do, you'll see that you'd still owe the bank some money after 24 months had passed. This tells you that $80 is too low a monthly payment, and that the actual payment is somewhere between $80 and $100. This procedure can be repeated until the exact monthly payment is reached.

## 4. COMPARING HOME MORTGAGES

To do this project, first go to any bank and ask for a fact sheet of their most recent *mortgage loan rates*. Banks are happy to provide them.

Obtain rates for a thirty-year loan, a fifteen-year loan, a thirty-year biweekly loan, and a twenty-year loan (if available) for $100,000 with zero points. (Note: Some loans include points. A point is an additional fee paid to the lender at the time of the loan equal to 1% of the amount borrowed. Typically, you get lower interest rates by paying a point or two. We will only consider loans with zero points.)

The following formula can be used to determine your payment, $x$:

$$x = \frac{Pr^n(r-1)}{r^n - 1},$$

where $P$ is the amount of the loan—in this case $100,000—and $n$ is the number of payments. For a thirty-year loan with monthly payments, $n = 360$; for a thirty-year biweekly loan, $n = 780$ (there are 26 payments every year). Finally, $r$ is the interest rate per period plus 1. (For example, if the interest rate is 2%, then $r = 1.02$.) In Question 4, you will derive this formula for $x$ using the following formula for the sum of a geometric series:[17]

$$1 + r + r^2 + \cdots + r^{n-2} + r^{n-1} = \frac{1 - r^n}{1 - r}.$$

---

[17]Geometric series are discussed in detail in Chapter 10.

1. Using the information given, as well as the fact sheet you got from the bank, determine which loan (30-year, 30-year biweekly, 20-year or 15-year) is best if you intend to live in your house for the full term of the loan. Assume the best mortgage is the one that ends up costing you the least overall. (The situation in real life can be more complicated when points and taxes are considered.) Although it's possible to work this problem without a spreadsheet, you might want to set one up anyway.

2. Banks usually require that the monthly payments not exceed some stated fraction of the applicant's monthly income. For this reason, it is generally easier to qualify for loans with smaller monthly payments. Thus, it may be that the "best loan"—the one you found in Question 1— is not the "easiest" loan to qualify for. Which of the loans on your fact sheet has the lowest monthly payment? The highest?

3. Suppose that you expect to sell your house for $145,000 in five years. In this case, which loan should you take? [Hint: The goal here is to maximize profit. Figure out how much money you have paid to the bank after five years, and your remaining debt at that time. When you sell your house, the remaining debt is paid to the bank immediately, so your total profit is (Selling price of house)−(Loan payoff to bank)−(Amount paid to bank during first five years).]

4. Derive the formula for the monthly payment, $x$. [Hint: Set up a geometric series in terms of $x$ and $r$ to give your loan balance after $n$ months. The loan balance equals 0 when you have paid off your loan; use this fact to solve for $x$. Simplify the resulting expression (by summing a geometric series) to get the formula given for $x$.]

## 5. PRESENT VALUE OF LOTTERY WINNINGS

On Thursday, February 24th, 1993, Bruce Hegarty of Dennis Port, MA, received the first installment of the $26,680,940 prize he won in the Mass Millions state lottery. Mr. Hegarty was scheduled to receive 19 more such installments on a yearly basis. Each check written by the Lottery Commission is for one twentieth of the total prize, or $1,334,047. Why doesn't the Lottery Commission pay all of Mr. Hegarty's prize up front, instead of making him wait for twenty years?

1. Compute the present value of the money paid out by the Lottery Commission, assuming annual discount rates (interest rates) of 5%, 10% and 15%. In each case, what percent does the present value represent of the face value of the prize, $26,680,940?

2. What discount rate would result in a present value of the payments worth only half the face value of the prize?

3. Graph the present value of the payments against the discount rate, ranging from a rate of 0% up to 15%. Describe the graph. What does it tell you about why the Lottery Commission does not pay the prize money up front?

## 6. COMPARING INVESTMENTS

Consider two investment projects. Project $A$ is built in one year at an initial cost of $10,000. It then yields the following decreasing stream of benefits over a five-year period: $5000, $4000, $3000, $2000, $1000. Project $B$ is built in two years. Initial costs are $10,000 in the first year and $5000 in the second year. It then yields yearly profits of $6000 for the next four years. Which of these investment projects is preferable?

1. Compute the present values of both projects assuming an annual discount rate (interest rate) of 4%. Which project seems preferable? [Hint: Treat expenditures as negative and income as positive.]

2. Compute the present values of both projects assuming an annual discount rate of 16%. Which project seems preferable now?

3. Describe in complete sentences why one of the investment projects is favored by a low discount rate, whereas the other is favored by a high discount rate.

4. The discount rate at which the present value of a project becomes zero is known as the *internal rate of return*. What is the internal rate of return of project $A$? Of project $B$? [Hint: Guess different discount rates until you find the one that brings the present value down to $0.]

5. Make a chart of the present value of the two investments against discount rates ranging from 0% to 30%. What features of this chart correspond to the internal rates of return of the two projects?

## 7. INVESTING FOR THE FUTURE: TUITION PAYMENTS

Parents of two teenagers, ages 13 and 17, deposit a sum of money into an account earning interest at the rate of 7% per year compounded annually. The deposit will be used for a series of eight annual college tuition payments of $10,000 each. Payments out of the account will begin one year after the initial deposit.

1. Use a spreadsheet to model the savings account that the parents opened. At the end of every year, the account earns 7% interest, and then there is a $10,000 withdrawal. Determine what initial deposit provides just enough money to make the eight yearly payments of $10,000. Do this by guessing different values, and seeing which value leaves you with nothing exactly nine years later.

2. Having answered Question 1, use a spreadsheet to compute the present value of eight yearly payments of $10,000 each, beginning one year in the future, at a discount rate of 7%.

3. Compare your answer to Question 1 with your answer to Question 2. Is this a coincidence? Discuss.

4. Suppose the parents have only $50,000 to deposit into the savings account. What annual interest rate must the account earn if the eight payments of $10,000 are to be made? [Hint: Compute the present value of the payments for various discount rates.]

## 8. NEW OR USED?

You are deciding whether to buy a new or used car (of the same make) and how many years to keep the car. You want to minimize your total costs, which consist of two parts: the loss in value of the car and the repairs. A new car costs $20,000 and loses 20% of its value each year. Repairs are $400 the first year and increase by 25% each subsequent year.

1. Set up a spreadsheet that gives, for each year, the value of the car, its loss in value, its repair costs, and the total cost for that year. The first two lines look like this, rounded to the nearest dollar:

| Year | Value | Loss | Repair | Cost |
|------|-------|------|--------|------|
| 1 | 20,000 | 4000 | 400 | 4400 |
| 2 | 16,000 | 3200 | 500 | 3700 |
| ⋮ | ⋮ | ⋮ | ⋮ | ⋮ |

2. Which year has the lowest cost?

3. You intend to keep your car 5 years. Compare your total costs for a new car and for a two-year-old car.

4. How old a car should you buy if you plan to keep it for 5 years?

5. Add two columns to your spreadsheet showing the average yearly cost for second-hand cars of different ages kept for 4 years and 5 years. Which is the best buy?

6. A new car costs $30,000 and loses 25% of its value each year; repairs start at $500 and increase at 10% per year. If you buy a seven-year-old car, should you keep it for 4 or 5 years? What is the average yearly cost in each case?

7. A car costs $30,000 when new. You buy a four-year-old car and keep it for 5 years; repairs are as in Problem 6. Find the rate at which it loses value if the average yearly cost is $2300.

# 9. VERHULST: THE LOGISTIC MODEL

The relative growth rate of a population, $P$, over a time interval, $\Delta t$, is given by

$$\text{Relative growth rate} = \frac{1}{P} \cdot \frac{\Delta P}{\Delta t}.$$

In exponential growth, the relative growth rate is a constant. Although exponential growth is often used to model populations, this model predicts that a population will increase without limit, which is unrealistic. In the 1830s, a Belgian mathematician, P. F. Verhulst, suggested the *logistic model*, in which the relative growth rate of a population decreases to 0 linearly as the population increases. Verhulst's model predicts that the population size eventually levels off to a value known as the *carrying capacity*.

To see how Verhulst's logistic model works, assume that a pair of breeding rabbits is introduced onto a small island with no rabbits. At the outset the rabbit population doubles every month. This means that initially the relative growth rate is 100% per month. Eventually, though, as the population grows, the relative growth rate drops down to 0% per month. Suppose that the growth rate reaches 0 when the population reaches 10,000 rabbits. (Thus, 10,000 is the carrying capacity of the island.) Using spreadsheets, we will model the rabbit population over time.

1. Let $P$ be the population and $r$ be the relative growth rate per month. Verhulst assumed that the relative growth rate decreases linearly as population increases. This means that $r$ goes from 100% to 0% as $P$ goes from 0 to 10,000 rabbits. Explain why the following formula for $r$ corresponds to Verhulst's assumptions: $r = 0.0001(10,000 - P)$.

2. Use a spreadsheet to model the monthly rabbit population on the island for the first two years (24 months). Graph the rabbit population over time. Describe the behavior of the rabbit population. [Hint: Start with two rabbits, and compute the growth rate using the formula in Question 1. Then, for each month, update the rabbit population as well as the relative growth rate.]

3. Draw a graph comparing your logistic model of the rabbit population to a population growing exponentially at a constant relative growth rate of 100% per month. Both models should start out with two rabbits. Describe the similarities and the differences between the two charts. What advantages does the logistic model have over the exponential model? (You'll have to be careful when setting the chart parameters; otherwise, all you'll be able to see is the exponential population, which climbs so quickly that the logistic one will not be visible at all.)

4. The key to the logistic model is that the relative growth rate is decreasing linearly as the population increases. However, this does not mean that the relative growth rate is decreasing linearly over time. Make a chart of the relative growth rate against time for the first two years. Describe the behavior of the relative growth rate over time.

5. (a) Different assumptions about the growing rabbit population lead to different logistic curves. In Question 1, we assumed that the relative growth rate was 100% initially, dropping to 0% when the population reached 10,000. This led to the formula $r = 0.0001(10000 - P)$. Now assume that the initial relative growth rate is 10% (instead of 100%). What is the new formula relating $r$ and $P$? (The carrying capacity is still 10,000, so $r = 10\%$ when $P = 0$, and $r$ decreases to 0% as $P$ increases to 10,000.)

(b) Using your new formula for the relative growth rate, $r$, let's see how different initial populations of rabbits lead to different logistic curves. Model the following scenarios, over a 5-year (60-month) period: a population starting at 100 rabbits, a population starting at 5,000 rabbits, a population starting at 12,500 rabbits, and a population starting at 17,500 rabbits. Place all of your data on the same chart. What happens to the rabbit population when it starts out above the island's rabbit carrying capacity? Why does this make sense?

## 10. THE SPREAD OF INFORMATION: A COMPARISON OF TWO MODELS

The spread of information through a population is important to policy makers. For example, agricultural ministries use mathematical models to understand the spread of technical innovations or new seed types through their countries.

In this project, you will compare two different models—one of them logistic —for the spread of information. In both cases, assume that the population is 10,000 and that initially only 100 people have the information. Let $N$ be the number of people who have the information at time $t$.

**Model 1:** If the information is spread by mass media (TV, radio, newspapers), the absolute rate, $\Delta N/\Delta t$, at which the information is spread is assumed to be proportional to the number of people *not* having the information at that time. If $t$ is in days, the constant of proportionality is 10%. For example, on the first day, the number of people not having the information is $10,000 - 100 = 9900$. Since 10% of 9900 is 990, the rate of spread of information is 990 people per day on the first day. This means that on the second day, the number of people not having the information is 8910 and that the rate of spread is 10% of 8910, or 891 people per day, and so on.

**Model 2:** If instead the information is spread by word of mouth, the absolute rate at which information is spread is assumed to be proportional to the product of the number of people who know and the number of people who do not know. If $t$ is in days, the constant of proportionality is 0.002%. For example, on the first day, the product of the number of people who know and the number of people who do not know is $100 \cdot 9900 = 990,000$. Since 0.002% of 990,000 is about 20, the rate of spread of information is 20 people per day on the first day. This means that on the second day, the product of the number of people who know and the number who do not know is $120 \cdot 9880 = 1,188,600$, giving a rate of spread of 0.002% of 1,188,600 or about 24 people per day, and so on.

1. Using spreadsheets, compare the spread of information throughout the population using both models. Make a chart comparing both models' predictions of the number of people over time who have the information. Describe the similarities and differences between the two models. Why is Model 1 used when mass media are present? Why is Model 2 used when mass media are absent?

2. Which of the two models is logistic? How can you tell? What type of growth does the other model exhibit? How can you tell?

3. By definition, a population exhibits logistic growth if its relative rate of change is a decreasing linear function of the current population. Explain why Model 2 leads to logistic growth although it was defined in terms of absolute growth rates.

4. The solutions from our spreadsheets are only approximations. Discuss why this is the case. [Hint: There's more going on here than rounding error.]

## 11. THE FLU IN WORLD WAR I

During World War I, a particularly lethal form of flu killed about 40 million people around the world.[18] The epidemic started in an army camp of 45,000 soldiers outside of Boston, where the first soldier fell sick on September 7, 1918. In this problem you will make a spreadsheet for the $SIR$

---

[18]"Capturing a Killer Flu Virus," J. Taukenberger, A. Reid, T. Fanning, in *Scientific American*, Vol. 292, No. 1, Jan. 2005.

model of the 1918 flu outbreak. Starting from the initial values $S_0$ and $I_0$, for any increment in time $\Delta t$, the changes in the number of susceptibles and infecteds are approximated by

$$\Delta S \approx -aSI\Delta t$$
$$\Delta I \approx aSI\Delta t - bI\Delta t.$$

1. Choosing $\Delta t = 0.1$, $a = 0.0003$, $b = 10$, make a spreadsheet whose first few lines look like this:

| $t$ | $S$ | $I$ | $\Delta S$ | $\Delta I$ |
|---|---|---|---|---|
| 0 | 44999 | 1 | $-1.3500$ | 0.3500 |
| 0.1 | 44997.65 | 1.3500 | $-1.82240$ | 0.4724 |
| 0.2 | 44995.828 | 1.8224 | $\ldots$ | $\ldots$ |

2. How many soldiers got sick on the fifth day? How many were susceptible on this day?

3. Alter the spreadsheet so that it accepts any values of $\Delta t, a, b$ input by the user.

4. Using the values $a = 0.000267$, $b = 9.865$ for the 1918 epidemic, decrease the value of $\Delta t$ until a stable estimate is reached for the number of soldiers sick on September 16th. How many soldiers had been infected by this date?

5. Approximately how long did it take for the 1918 epidemic to run its course?

# ANSWERS TO ODD NUMBERED PROBLEMS

## Section 1.1

1 (a) (IV)
   (b) (II)
   (c) (III)

3 Increasing

CO₂

time

5 Decreasing

noise level

distance

7 Argentina produced 14 million
  metric tons of wheat in 2010

9 (a) 8; 7
   (b) 10

11 $f(5) = 25$

13 $f(5) = 2$

15 (a) 2
   (b) 11
   (c) 3 and $-3$
   (d) No

17 $f(0)$ meters

19 $f(0) = f(1) + 0.001$

23 Greatest number of species at
   intermediate number of snails; yes

25 (a) $1000
   (b) About $2200
   (c) About 20 years

27 heart
   rate

administration
of drug

time

29 concentration

Peak
concen-
tration

Time of
peak concentration

time

## Section 1.2

35 driving speed

time

37 distance from exit

time

1 $y = (1/2)x + 2$

3 $y = (1/2)x + 2$

5 Slope: $-12/7$
  Vertical intercept: $2/7$

7 Slope: 2
  Vertical intercept: $-2/3$

9 (a) $l_1$
   (b) $l_3$
   (c) $l_2$
   (d) $l_4$

11 (a) $P = 30{,}700 + 850t$
   (b) 39,200 people
   (c) In 2026

13 (a) 300 miles
   (b) 50 mph
   (c) $D = 300 + 50t$

15 (a) $y = -2x + 27$
   (b) $s = 2t + 32$

17 (a) 1.8 billion dollars/year
   (b) 19.1 billion dollars
   (c) 37.1 billion dollars
   (d) 2013

19 (a) About 480 million tons
   (b) About 10 million tons/year
   (c) $M = 480 + 10t$

21 (a) $P = 1241 + 26.9t$
   (b) 26.9 million tons per year
   (c) 1241 million tons in 1975
   (d) 2317 million tons
   (e) In the year 2021

23 (b) $P = 100 - 0.5d$
   (c) $-0.5\%/\text{ft}$
   (d) 100%; 200 ft

25 (a) $N = 36.67 - 0.2424l$
   (b) $-0.2424$ species per degree latitude
       36.67 species at the equator
   (c) number of species

40
30
20
10

10 20 30 40 50  $l°S$

27 (c)

29 Female 6 years older than male

31 Yes

33 (a) 3.5% annual increase in production when
       unemployment rate constant
   (b) Decreases 2.5%
   (c) Increases 1.75%

## Section 1.3

1 Concave down

3 Concave up

5 Decreasing
  Concave up

7 (a) $D$ to $E$, $H$ to $I$
   (b) $A$ to $B$, $E$ to $F$
   (c) $C$ to $D$, $G$ to $H$
   (d) $B$ to $C$, $F$ to $G$

9 $-3$

20
Slope $= -3$
10
$f(x)$
$-2$  $-1$  1  $x$

11 (a) $-$134 million dollars
   (b) $-$67 million dollars per year
   (c) Yes, 2009-2010

13 (a) 155,000 people/year
   (b) 0.07, 0.08, 0.41, 0.06
   (c) 155,000 people/year

15 1 meter/sec

17 (a) 0.077 billion people per year
       0.980 million cars per year
       207.7 million subscribers per year
   (b)    (i) Population

         (ii) Cell phone subscribers

19 2 meters/sec

21 (a) Approximately $-11.86$ million pounds/year
   (b) Yes, between 2003 and 2004, and any year
       between 2005 and 2009

23 1490 thousand people/year
   912.9 thousand people/year
   1879 thousand people/year

25 (a) $-$35 billion dollars
   (b) $-$7 billion dollars per year
   (c) Yes; 2006–2007, 2007–2008

27 (a) Negative
   (b) $-0.087$ mg/hour

29 15.468, 57.654, 135.899,
   146.353, 158.549 people/min

31 (a) About $-11$ cm/sec
   (b) About $-5.5$ (cm/sec)/kg

33 (a)    (i) $f(1985) = 13$

         (ii) $f(1990) = 99$
   (b) $(f(1990) - f(1985))/(1990 - 1985) =$
       17.2 billionaires/yr
   (c) $f(t) = 17.2t - 34{,}129$

35 (a) Concave up; no
   (b) About 2.6 m/sec

37 Decreasing, concave down

39 Increases by 25%

41 Decreases by 83.3%

508

43  Change in 1931

45  The small class

47 (a)  100%
   (b)  −50%
   (c)  0.1%

49  Increase by 2.2%

51 (a)

| $t$ | 0 | 0.25 | 0.5 | 0.75 |
|-----|---|------|-----|------|
| % | 4.0 | 3.4 | −5.8 | −3.1 |

   (b)  Yes, last two quarters

53 (a)  2005–2007
   (b)  2004–2007

55 (a)  25%
   (b)  12%
   (c)  0.48

## Section 1.4

1

(c) (ii) loses money
(a) Fixed costs
(c) (i) makes profit
(b) Break-even quantity
$R$
$C$

3 (a)  About \$75; \$7.50 per unit
  (b)  About \$150

5  Fixed cost: \$5.7 million
   Variable cost: \$2000 per unit

7 (a)  Price \$12, sell 60
  (b)  Decreasing

9  5500: Quantity demanded at price 0
   100: Drop in quantity demanded if price increases \$1

11  $C(q) = 500 + 6q$, $R(q) = 12q$, $\pi(q) = 6q - 500$

13  $C(q) = 5000 + 15q$, $R(q) = 60q$, $\pi(q) = 45q - 5000$

15 (a)  $C(q) = 5000 + 30q$
        $R(q) = 50q$
   (b)  \$30/unit, \$50/unit
   (c)

$p$ (\$)
25000
20000
15000
10000
5000
(250, 12,500)
$R(q)$
$C(q)$
100  300  500  $q$

   (d)  250 chairs and \$12,500

17 (a)  First price list:
        $C_1(q) = 100 + 0.03q$ dollars
        Second price list:
        $C_2(q) = 200 + 0.02q$ dollars
   (b)  First price list
   (c)  10,000

19 (a)  When there are more than 1000 customers

(b)
\$
22,000
15,000
10,000
5000
$R$
$C$
1000  2000  $q$

21 (a)  $C(q) = 650,000 + 20q$
        $R(q) = 70q$
        $\pi(q) = 50q - 650,000$
   (b)  \$20/pair, \$70/pair, \$50/pair
   (c)  More than 13,000 pairs

23 (a)  $V(t) = -2000t + 50,000$
   (b)
\$
50,000
10,000
20  25  $t$ (years)

   (c)  (0 years, \$50,000) and (25 years, \$0)

25 (a)  Roughly 360 scoops
   (b)  Roughly 120 scoops

27 (a)  First: demand curve;
        Second: supply curve
   (b)  Roughly 14
   (c)  Roughly 24
   (d)  Lower
   (e)  Any price less than or equal to \$143
   (f)  Any price greater than or equal to \$110

29 (a)  $C = 5q + 7000$
        $R = 12q$
   (b)  $q = 1520$, $\pi(12) = \$3640$
   (c)  $C = 17,000 - 200p$
        $R = 2000p - 40p^2$
        $\pi(p) = -40p^2 + 2200p - 17,000$
   (d)  At \$27.50 per shirt the profit is \$13,250

31 (a)  $q = 820 - 20p$
   (b)  $p = 41 - 0.05q$

33
$P$
4000
3000
2000
1000
8000  10,000  $Q$

35 (a)  $25,000r + 100m = 500,000$
   (b)  $m = 5000 - 250r$
   (c)  $r = 20 - \frac{1}{250}m$

37 (a)

$p$
Supply
$p_0$
Demand
$q_0$ 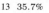 $q$

(b)  Equilibrium price will increase;
     equilibrium quantity will decrease
(c)  Equilibrium price and quantity will decrease

39  $q = 90 - 5p$

41  Pre-tax: $p = \$190$, $q = 70$ units
    Post-tax: $p = \$194$, $q = 68$ units

43 (a)  Demand: $q = 100 - 2.1p$
        Supply: $q = 3p - 50$
   (b)  $p = \$29.41$
        $q = 38.23$ units
   (c)  Producer pays \$0.59
        Consumer pays \$0.88
        Total tax \$1.47
   (d)  \$56.20

## Section 1.5

1 (a)  (i), 12%
  (b)  (ii), 1000
  (c)  Yes, (iv)

3 (a)  II
  (b)  I
  (c)  III
  (d)  V

5  $y = 30(0.94)^t$

7 (a)  $P = 1000 + 50t$
  (b)  $P = 1000(1.05)^t$

9 (a)  $Q = 30 - 2t$

$Q$ (grams)
30
$Q = 30 - 2t$
15  $t$ (days)

(b)  $Q = 30(0.88)^t$

$Q$ (grams)
30
$Q = 30(0.88)^t$
15  $t$ (days)

11 (a)  $A = 50(0.94)^t$
   (b)  11.33 mg
   (c)
$A$ (mg)
50
5
20  40  $t$ (hours)

   (d)  About 37 hours

13  35.7%

15 (a)

| $x$ | 0 | 1 | 2 | 3 |
|-----|---|---|---|---|
| $e^x$ | 1 | 2.72 | 7.39 | 20.09 |

(b)

(c)

| $x$ | 0 | 1 | 2 | 3 |
|---|---|---|---|---|
| $e^{-x}$ | 1 | 0.37 | 0.14 | 0.05 |

(d)

17 $g(t) = 5.50(0.8)^t$

19 Table D

21 (a) $a = 0.9$ and $P_0 = 27.435$
   (b) Initial quantity 27.435,
      decaying 10% per unit time

23 (a) $a = 1.265$ and $P_0 = 454.05$
   (b) Initial quantity 454.05,
      growing 26.5% per unit time

25 1.7%

27 (a) $y = 2700 + 486t$
      486 zebra mussels per year
   (b) $y = 2700(1.18)^t$
      18% per year

29 (a) $h(x) = 31 - 3x$
   (b) $g(x) = 36(1.5)^x$

31 (a) Exponential
   (b) $P = 161.0(1.058)^t$
   (c) 5.8% per year

33 (a) \$3486.78
   (b) Approx 11 years (or 21 years from
      initial investment)

35 (a) $w = 1108.773(1.12557)^t$
   (b) 12.557% per year
   (c) No; recent growth rate higher

37 (a) 261 million gallons, 358 million gallons
   (b)

consumption of
biodiesel (mn gal)

39 (a) 16 trillion BTUs, 32 trillion BTUs
   (b) consumption of hydro.
      power (trillion BTU)

   (c) 2007, 13 trillion BTUs

41 (a) Increased: 2006, 2008; decreased: none
   (b) Yes

## Section 1.6

1 $t = (\ln 10)/(\ln 2) \approx 3.3219$

3 $t = (\ln 2)/(\ln 1.02) \approx 35.003$

5 $t = \ln 10 \approx 2.3026$

7 $t = (\ln 5)/(\ln 3) \approx 1.465$

9 $t = (\ln 100)/3 \approx 1.535$

11 $t = 30.54$

13 $t = (\ln B - \ln P)/r$

15 $t = (\ln 7 - \ln 5)/(\ln 2 - \ln 3) \approx -0.8298$

17 5; 7%

19 15; $-6\%$ (continuous)

21 $P = 15(1.2840)^t$; growth

23 $P = P_0(1.2214)^t$; growth

25 $P = 15e^{0.4055t}$; growth

27 $P = 174e^{-0.1054t}$

29 (a) $k = 0.168$ and $P_0 = 84.575$
   (b) Initial quantity 84.575,
      growing 16.8% per unit time

31 (a) 6%
   (b) $P = 100(1.0618)^t$, 6.18%

33 8.33%

35 (a) $D$
   (b) $C$
   (c) $B$

37 (a) $P = 5.4(1.034)^t$
   (b) $P = 5.4e^{0.0334t}$
   (c) Annual = 3.4%
      Continuous = 3.3%

39 $P = 7e^{0.01143t}$

41 (a) $S = 6.1e^{0.042t}$
   (b) 7.21 billion dollars
   (c) Midway through 2017

43 (a) $P = 50,000e^{0.045t}$
   (b) 78,416
   (c) 15.403 years

45 27 meters

47 2023

## Section 1.7

1 $A$: continuous
   $B$: annual
   \$20

3 (a) \$1534.69
   (b) \$1552.71

5 \$10,976.23

7 About 11.6 years

9 Just over 6 hours

11 347 days

13 (a) $A = 100e^{-0.17t}$
   (b) $t \approx 4$ hours

   (c) $t = 4.077$ hours

15 (a) 47.6%
   (b) 23.7%

17 8.45%

19 (a) $P(t) = (0.975)^t$
   (b)

   (c) About 27 years
   (d) About 8%

21 (a) About 4 years
   (b) About 4 years

23 About 173 hours

25 96.336 years

27 (a) 2023
   (b) 338.65 million people

29 It is a fake

31 (a) 0.00664
   (b) $t = 2.167$; March 2, 2013

33 \$12,712.49

35 \$6549.85

37 (a) Choice 1
   (b) Yes. Above 25%

39 (a) 8.75 years
   (b) About 9.01 years

41 (a) Option 1
   (b) \$2102.54, \$2051.27, \$2000
   (c) \$2000, \$1951.23, \$1902.46

43 (a) Option 1
   (b) Option 1: \$10.929 million;
      Option 2: \$10.530 million

45 Buy

## Section 1.8

1 (a) $15x + 9$
   (b) $15x - 1$
   (c) $25x - 6$

3 (a) $3e^{2x}$
   (b) $e^{6x}$
   (c) $9x$

5 (a) $h^2 + 6h + 11$
   (b) 11
   (c) $h^2 + 6h$

7 (a) 4
   (b) 2
   (c) $(x + 1)^2$
   (d) $x^2 + 1$
   (e) $t^2(t + 1)$

9 (a) $e$
   (b) $e^2$
   (c) $e^{x^2}$
   (d) $e^{2x}$
   (e) $e^t t^2$

11 (a) 5
   (b) 2
   (c) 3
   (d) 4
   (e) 5
   (f) 2

13 (a)

| $x$ | $f(x) + 3$ |
|---|---|
| 0 | 13 |
| 1 | 9 |
| 2 | 6 |
| 3 | 7 |
| 4 | 10 |
| 5 | 14 |

(b)

| $x$ | $f(x - 2)$ |
|---|---|
| 2 | 10 |
| 3 | 6 |
| 4 | 3 |
| 5 | 4 |
| 6 | 7 |
| 7 | 11 |

(c)

| $x$ | $5g(x)$ |
|---|---|
| 0 | 10 |
| 1 | 15 |
| 2 | 25 |
| 3 | 40 |
| 4 | 60 |
| 5 | 75 |

(d)

| $x$ | $-f(x) + 2$ |
|---|---|
| 0 | -8 |
| 1 | -4 |
| 2 | -1 |
| 3 | -2 |
| 4 | -5 |
| 5 | -9 |

(e)

| $x$ | $g(x - 3)$ |
|---|---|
| 3 | 2 |
| 4 | 3 |
| 5 | 5 |
| 6 | 8 |
| 7 | 12 |
| 8 | 15 |

(f)

| $x$ | $f(x) + g(x)$ |
|---|---|
| 0 | 12 |
| 1 | 9 |
| 2 | 8 |
| 3 | 12 |
| 4 | 19 |
| 5 | 26 |

15 (a) $y = 2^u$, $u = 3x - 1$
(b) $P = \sqrt{u}$, $u = 5t^2 + 10$
(c) $w = 2\ln u$, $u = 3r + 4$

17 $2zh + h^2$

19 $4hz$
21 6
23 3
25 4
27 1.1
29 About 0
31 $2(y - 1)^3 - (y - 1)^2$
33 About 18
35 Cannot be done

37

39

41

43 (a)

45 (a)

(b)

(c)

(d)

(e)

(b)

(c)

(d)

(e)

(f)

47

49

51

53 (a) $y = 2x^2 + 1$

(b) $y = 2(x^2 + 1)$
(c) No

55 $g(2r)$ ft$^3$

57 $f^{-1}(g^{-1}(10{,}000))$ min

## Section 1.9

1 $y = (1/5)x$

3 $y = 8x^{-1}$

5 Not a power function.

7 $y = 9x^{10}$

9 Not a power function

11 $y = 125x^3$

13 $S = kh^2$

15 $v = d/t$

17 (a) $y = (x - 2)^3 + 1$
 (b) $y = -(x + 3)^2 - 2$

19 $N = kA^{1/4}$, with $k > 0$,
 Increasing, concave down

species of lizard

area

21 (a) $C = kW^{0.75}$
 (b)
 (c) Horse: 5,716 calories
 Rabbit: 218 calories
 (d) Mouse

23 $N = k/L^2$; small

25 (a) $T = kB^{1/4}$
 (b) $k = 17.4$
 (c) 50.3 seconds

27 (a) $N = kP^{0.77}$
 (b) A has 5.888 times more than B
 (c) Town

29 (a) $q = -8p + 700$
 (b) $R = -8p^2 + 700p$
 (c) At roughly \$44 per unit, revenue $\approx$ \$15,300

## Section 1.10

1 Amplitude = 3; Period = $2\pi$

3 Amplitude = 3; Period = $\pi$

5 Amplitude = 1; Period = $\pi$

7 (b) Max: 2nd quarter; Min: 4th quarter
 (c) Period = 4 quarters or 1 year; amplitude = 5
 million barrels

9 (a) 5
 (b) 8
 (c) $f(x) = 5\cos((\pi/4)x)$

11 Period = 25, amplitude = 0.45
 $f(15) = 2.0$, $f(75) = 1.4$, $f(135) = 2.3$

13 Yes; About 28 days; day 12; days 17–21

15 (a) bird species

(b) 9 species, 12 months
 (c) $N = 19 + 9\cos(\pi t/6)$

17 $x = 50 - 40\sin(2t)$

19 $f(x) = 2\sin(x/4)$

21 $f(x) = (\sin x) + 2$

23 $f(x) = \sin(2(\pi/5)x)$

25 $f(x) = 2\cos(5x)$

27 $f(x) = 3\sin(\pi x/9)$

29 Depth = $7 + 1.5\sin(\pi t/3)$

31 (a) Period is 12; amplitude is 4
 (b) $g(34) = 11$; $g(60) = 14$

## Chapter 1 Review

1　Pop 12 million in 2005

5　contamination

depth below
ground (meters)
3　6　9　12

7 (a)　(I)
　(b)　(IV)
　(c)　(II) and (III)
　(d)　Bread in (III) heats up faster

9　$y = 8/3 - x/3$

11　$x = -1$

13　$y = 14x - 45$

15 (a)　$S = 113 - 0.94t$
　(b)　During 2038

17　8 mm/sec

19　4 mm/sec

21　$-1/2$ mm/sec

23 (b)　200 bushels
　(c)　80 lbs
　(d)　About $0 \le Y \le 550$
　(e)　Decreasing
　(f)　Concave down

25 (a)　$k(t)$
　(b)　$h(t)$
　(c)　$g(t)$

27 (b)　Lung cancer: 1.1 (answers may vary)
　(c)　Stomach cancer: $-0.5$ (answers may vary)

29 (a)　(i)　Positive
　　　(ii)　Positive
　　　(iii)　Negative
　　　(iv)　Positive
　(b)　(i)　$0 \le t \le 5$
　　　(ii)　$0 \le t \le 20$
　(c)　About 25 m$^3$/week

31　More than 875 students

33　Graph (a): supply
　　Graph (b): demand

35　$y = (-3/7)x + 3$

37　$y = e^{0.4621x}$ or $y = (1.5874)^x$

39　$y = 3e^{0.2197t}$
　　or $y = 3(1.2457)^t$

41　$f(x)$ is neither,
　　$g(x) = 30.8 - 3.2x$ is linear,
　　$h(x) = 15,000(0.6)^x$ is exponential

43　$P = 40,000,000(1.2)^{t/10}$
　　57,600,000 in 2020
　　Doubling time $= 38.02$ years

45　$(\ln(2/5))/(\ln 1.04) = -23.4$

47　$\ln(0.4)/3 = -0.305$

49 (a)　15%
　(b)　$P = 10(1.162)^t$
　(c)　16.2%
　(d)　Graphs are the same since functions are equal

51 (a)　15,678.7 years
　(b)　5728.489, or about 5730 years

53　7.925 hours

55　$3.68e^{0.2899t}$
　　28.99%

57　Yes

59 (a)　$\ln(2x + 3)$
　(b)　$2 \ln x + 3$
　(c)　$4x + 9$

61 (a)　$10x^2 + 3$
　(b)　$20x^2 + 60x + 45$
　(c)　$4x + 9$

63

65

67

69

71

73

75　$y = -(x + 3)^2 + 2$

77　No

79　$2\pi/3; 7$

81　$2; 0.1$

83 (a)　Period about 12 months;
　　　Amplitude about 4500 cases
　(b)　About 2000 cases and 2000 cases

85　$f(x) = 2\sin(x/4) + 2$

## Ch. 1 Understanding

1　False

3　True

5　True

7　True

9　False

11　True

13　True

15　True

17　False

19　False

21　False

23　False

25 True
27 False
29 True
31 True
33 True
35 False
37 True
39 False
41 False
43 True
45 False
47 True
49 False
51 True
53 True
55 False
57 True
59 True
61 True
63 True
65 True
67 False
69 False
71 True
73 True
75 False
77 True
79 True
81 False
83 True
85 False
87 False
89 False
91 False
93 True
95 True
97 True
99 True
101 False
103 False
105 True

## Section 2.1

1 (a) Negative
  (b) $f'(1960)$

3 (a) 2.5 ft/sec
  (b) 6.5 ft/sec
  (c) 4.5 ft/sec

5 (a) Between $x = 0$ and $x = 3$
  (b) At $x = 1$
  (c) Thousands of dollars/kilogram

7 (a) 0.080 billion people/yr
  (b) About 0.088 billion people/yr

9 $g'(1) \approx 5.549$

11 Positive: $A$ and $D$
   Negative: $C$ and $F$
   Most positive: $A$
   Most negative: $F$

13 $f'(1) \approx 3.3$; greater

15 (a) 0.401 percent/year
   (b) 0.15–0.38 percent/year

(c) Between 0.10 and 0.36 percent/year

17 (4, 25); (4.2, 25.3); (3.9, 24.85)

19

21 $f'(1) \approx 1.0005$;
   $f'(2) \approx 1.6934$;
   $f$ is concave up between 1 and 2

23 (a) Negative or zero;
      Positive;
      Positive
   (b)  (i) $-0.2$ hr/yr, 0 hr/yr
       (ii) $0.27/yr, $0.47/yr
      (iii) $8.90/yr, $16.18/yr

## Section 2.2

1

3

5

7 About 1.0, 0.3, $-0.5$, $-1$

9 (a) $x_3$
  (b) $x_4$
  (c) $x_5$
  (d) $x_3$

11 $R'(0) \approx 9.531$

13

15

17

19 IV
21 VI
23 5.2
25

Other answers possible

27 (a) $f'(1) \approx 0.95$
       $f'(2) \approx 0.49$
       $f'(3) \approx 0.33$
       $f'(4) \approx 0.25$
       $f'(5) \approx 0.20$
   (b) $1/x$

29 (a) (III)
   (b) (III)
   (c) (III), (IV)
   (d) (II), (IV)

## Section 2.3

1 $dD/dt$; feet per minute

3 $dN/dD$; gallons per mile

5 (a) ml; minutes
  (b) ml; minutes/ml

7 (a) 12 pounds, 5 dollars
  (b) Positive
  (c) 12 pounds, 0.4 dollars/pound, extra pound costs about 40 cents

9 (a) Liters per centimeter
  (b) About 0.042 liters per centimeter
  (c) Cannot expand much more

11 (a) Negative
   (b) °F/min

13 (a) °C/km

(b) Air temp decreases about 6.5° for a 1 km increase in altitude

15 (a) Negative until 2008, then positive
   (b) Between 2008 and 2009
   (c) About 160 metric tons/year
   (d) About 2610 metric tons,
       About 3410 metric tons

17 (a) Costs $1300 for 200 gallons
   (b) Costs about $6 for 201$^{st}$ gallon

19 (a) Positive
   (b) Child weighs 45 pounds at 8 years
   (c) lbs/year
   (d) At 8 years of age, child weighs about 4 pounds more after the next year
   (e) Decrease

21 (a) Shells thinner with more PCB
   (b) 200 ppm PCB corresponds 0.28 mm shell
       1 ppm increase PCB corresponds 0.0005 mm decrease shell

23 $f(21) \approx 65$
   $f(19) \approx 71$
   $f(25) \approx 53$

25 (a) $g'(36)$
   (b) Grows more rapidly at week 36 than at week 20

27 (a) about 0.09 kg/week
   (b) about 0.2 kg/week
   (c) about 0.08 kg/week

29 (a) Dose for 140 lbs is 120 mg
       Dose increases by 3mg/lb
   (b) About 135 mg

31 (a) 20 minutes,
       0.36 mg,
       $-0.002$ mg/minute
   (b) $f(21) \approx 0.358$
       $f(30) \approx 0.34$

33 (a) About $-4$ (cm/sec)/kg
   (b) About $-0.20$cm/sec
   (c) $v'(2) \approx 4$

35 Dollars/percent; positive

37 Used at constant rate for 4 weeks

39 Switch from fat to protein

41 (a), (b)

concentration of enzymes

Normal level

time

$f' > 0 \quad f' < 0$

43 (b) $f'(100) = 2$: Yes
       $f'(100) = 0.5$: No

45 (a) $f(t)$ volume of ice sheet $t$ years after 2011
   (b) $-224 < f'(0) < -82$

47 $f(4) = 200$ million users;
   $f'(4) \approx 12.5$ million users/month;
   Increasing at about 6.25%/month

49 0.20

51 (a) Weighs 5.67 kg at 2 1/2 months
   (b) Weight increasing 13% per month at 2 1/2 months

53 (a) About 6.1% per month
   (b) About 5.9% per month
   (c) About 5.9% per month

## Section 2.4

1 (a) Negative
  (b) Negative

3 (a)

(b)

(c)

(d)

5 $f'(x) = 0$
  $f''(x) = 0$

7 $f'(x) < 0$
  $f''(x) > 0$

9 $f'(x) < 0$
  $f''(x) < 0$

11 Derivative:
     Pos. about $-2.3 < t < -0.5$
     Neg. about $-0.5 < t < 4$
   Second derivative:
     Pos. about $0.5 < t < 4$
     Neg. about $-2.3 < t < 0.5$

13 $s'(t)$: positive
   $s''(t)$: positive or zero

15 A positive second derivative indicates a successful campaign
   A negative second derivative indicates an unsuccessful campaign

17 (a) Positive; negative
   (b) Neither; positive
   (c) Number of cars increasing at about 600,000 million cars per year in 2005

19

21 (b)

23 22 only possible value

25 (a)

(b) $dN/dt$ is positive.
    $d^2N/dt^2$ is negative.

27 (a) $dP/dt > 0, d^2P/dt^2 > 0$
   (b) $dP/dt < 0, d^2P/dt^2 > 0$
       (but $dP/dt$ is close to zero)

29 (a) $a'(t) > 0, m'(t) > 0$
       $a''(t) > 0, m''(t) > 0$
   (b) $2 < a'(t) < 4; 2 < m'(t) < 10$
   (c) (i) Between 200 mm and 400 mm
       (ii) 100 years

31 (a)

| $\Delta t$ | 0–2 | 2–4 | 4–6 | 6–8 | 8–10 |
|---|---|---|---|---|---|
| $\Delta P/\Delta t$ | 9.7 | 21.1 | 51.8 | 88.1 | 81.3 |

| $\Delta t$ | 10–12 | 12–14 | 14–16 | 16–18 |
|---|---|---|---|---|
| $\Delta P/\Delta t$ | 40.8 | 23.0 | 7.6 | 2.9 |

(b) Positive $0 < t < 8$; negative $8 < t < 18$

## Section 2.5

1 About $3 per item

3 About $16.67 (answers may vary)

5 About $0.42 (answers may vary)

7 $C'(2000) \approx \$0.37$/ton
  The marginal cost is smallest on the interval $2500 \le q \le 3000$.

9 (a) About $2408
  (b) About $2192

11 (a) About $4348
   (b) $11 profit
   (c) No, company will lose money

13 (a) $1.8 million
   (b) About $28,000 increase
   (c) About $35,000 decrease
   (d) About $4000 increase
       About $5000 decrease

15 (a) Fixed costs
   (b) Decreases slowly, then increases

17

| $q$ | 1 | 2 | 3 | 4 | 5 |
|---|---|---|---|---|---|
| $MC(q)$ | 40 | 60 | 80 | 100 | 120 |
| $MR(q)$ | 120 | 110 | 80 | 40 | 30 |

## Chapter 2 Review

1 (a) (i) 6.3 m/sec
      (ii) 6.03 m/sec
      (iii) 6.003 m/sec
   (b) 6 m/sec

3 (a) Negative
   (b) $f'(1) = -3$

5 (a) Positive at $C$ and $G$
Negative at $A$ and $E$. Zero at $B$, $D$, and $F$
(b) Largest at $G$
Most negative at $A$

7 (a) (i) $-1.00801$ m/sec
(ii) $-0.8504$ m/sec
(iii) $-0.834$ m/sec
(b) $-0.83$ m/sec

9 $f'(2) \approx 40.268$

11

13

15

17

19

21 (a) About 3
(b) Positive: $0 < x < 4$
Negative: $4 < x < 12$

23 kilograms/meter

25 (a) Positive
(b) °F/min

27 about 6 cm/yr

29 Wind stronger at 15.1 km than at 15 km

31 About 1.389 billion people in 2020;
growing at about 5.5 million people per year

33 (a) $f'(t) > 0$: depth increasing
$f'(t) < 0$: depth decreasing
(b) Depth increasing 20 cm/min
(c) 12 meters/hr

35 $B$

39 (a) Negative
(b) Degrees/min

41 Dollars/year; negative

43 (a)

(b)

(c)

(d)

45 (a) Minutes/kilometer
(b) Minutes/kilometer$^2$

47 (a) $x_4, x_5$
(b) $x_3, x_4$
(c) $x_3, x_4$
(d) $x_2, x_3$
(e) $x_1, x_2, x_5$
(f) $x_1, x_4, x_5$

49 (a) $t_3, t_4, t_5$
(b) $t_2, t_3$
(c) $t_1, t_2, t_5$
(d) $t_1, t_4, t_5$
(e) $t_3, t_4$

51 (a)

(b) Student C's

## Ch. 2 Understanding

1 True
3 True
5 False
7 False
9 False
11 True
13 False
15 True
17 False
19 True
21 True
23 True
25 True
27 True
29 True
31 False
33 False
35 True
37 True

39 True
41 True
43 True
45 False
47 True
49 False
51 True
53 True
55 True

## Theory: Limits, Derivatives

1

3 (a) $0/0$, undefined
(b) $6.487, 5.127, 5.013, 5.001$
(c) $\approx 5$

5 (a) $0/0$, undefined
(b) $0.953, 0.995, 0.9995, 0.99995$
(c) $\approx 1$

7 1.6

9 1.9

11 0

13 No; yes

15 No; yes

17 (a) Yes
(b) Yes
(c) No
(d) No

19 2

21 2

23 Yes

25 Yes

27 No

29 Not continuous

31 Continuous

33 Not continuous

## Section 3.1

1 3

3 $-12x^{-13}$

5 $24t^2$

7 5

9 $3q^2$

11 $18x^2 + 8x - 2$

13 $24t^2 - 8t + 12$

15 $-12x^3 - 12x^2 - 6$

17 $6.1z^{-7.1}$

19 $(1/2)x^{-1/2}$

21 $-(3/2)x^{-5/2}$

23 $2t$

25 $2z - \frac{1}{2}z^{-2}$

27 $-3t^{-2} - 8t^{-3}$

29 $(1/2)\theta^{-1/2} + \theta^{-2}$

31 $2ax + b$

33 $2at - 2b/t^3$

35 $(8\pi rb)/3$

37 $a/c$

39 (a) $P'(1)$ : Positive;
$P'(3)$: Zero;
$P'(4)$: Negative

(b) $P'(1) = 4$, $P'(3) = 0$, $P'(4) = -2$

41 (a) $2t - 4$
(b) $f'(1) = -2$, $f'(2) = 0$

43 Height $= 625$ cm,
Changing (eroding) at $-30$ cm/year

45 69.6% per year

47 4800 mussels after 4 months, increasing by
2400 mussels per month

49 $f'(t) = 6t^2 - 8t + 3$
$f''(t) = 12t - 8$

51 $y = -4 - x$

53 $y = -2t + 16$

55 (a) $C(w) = 42w^{0.75}$;
$C'(w) = 31.5w^{-0.25}$
(b) (i) 236.2 calories a day;
17.7 calories/pound
(ii) 1328 calories a day;
10 calories/pound
(iii) 7,469 calories a day;
5.6 calories/pound

57 (a) $dA/dr = 2\pi r$
(b) Circumference of a circle

61 (a) $R(p) = 300p - 3p^2$
(b) \$240 per dollar price increase when price is
\$10
(c) Positive for $p < 50$, negative for $p > 50$

63 (a) 770 bushels per acre
(b) 40 bushels per acre per pound of fertilizer
(c) Use more fertilizer

65 (a) $dC/dq = 0.24q^2 + 75$
(b) $C(50) = \$14{,}750$;
$C'(50) = \$675$ per item

67 (a) $R(q) = bq + mq^2$
(b) $R'(q) = b + 2mq$

## Section 3.2

1 $9t^2 + 2e^t$

3 $3x^2 + 3^x \ln 3$

5 $5 \cdot 5^t \ln 5 + 6 \cdot 6^t \ln 6$

7 $4(\ln 10)10^x - 3x^2$

9 $5(\ln 2)(2^x) - 5$

11 $0.7e^{0.7t}$

13 $-0.2e^{-0.2t}$

15 $24e^{0.12t}$

17 $12.41(\ln 0.94)(0.94)^t$

19 $Ae^t$

21 $(\ln 10)10^x - 10/x^2$

23 $-1/p$

25 $2q - 2/q$

27 $Ae^t + B/t$

29 $15/(15t + 12)$

31 $-7$

33 $-4/t$

35 $f'(-1) \approx -0.736$
$f'(0) = -2$
$f'(1) \approx -5.437$

37 $y = -2t + 1$

39 (a) 13,394 fish
(b) 8037 fish/month

41 $f(2) = 6065$, $f'(2) = -1516$

43 $f(5) = \$563.30$;
$f'(5) = \$70$ per week;
Relative rate $= 12.4\%$ per week

45 $-544$ people/year

47 $c = -1/\ln 2$

49 $C(50) \approx 1365$, $C'(50) \approx 18.27$

51 About \$2864; \$0.60

53 (a) $P = 1.166(1.015)^t$
(b) $\frac{dP}{dt} = 1.166(1.015)^t(\ln 1.015)$
$\frac{dP}{dt}\big|_{t=0} = 0.017$ billion people per year
$\frac{dP}{dt}\big|_{t=25} = 0.025$ billion people per year

55 $g(x) = x^2/2 + x + 1$

## Section 3.3

1 $99(x + 1)^{98}$

3 $200t(t^2 + 1)^{99}$

5 $15(5r - 6)^2$

7 $-6x + 6e^{3x}$

9 $30e^{5x} - 2xe^{-x^2}$

11 $-6te^{-3t^2}$

13 $5/(5t + 1)$

15 $2t/(t^2 + 1)$

17 $e^x/(e^x + 1)$

19 $1/(x \ln x)$

21 $3/(3t + 2)$

23 $5 + 1/(x + 2)$

25 $0.5/(x(1 + \ln x)^{0.5})$

27 $1/(4\sqrt{x}\sqrt{2 + \sqrt{x}})$

29 49.7% per year

31 1.5

33 $2/t$

35 (a) $P(1 + r/100)^t \ln(1 + r/100)$
(b) $Pt(1 + r/100)^{t-1}/100$

37 $v(t) = 10e^{t/2}$

39 Approx 0.8

41 Approx $-0.4$

43 $1/2$

45 $-1$

47 0.5

49 (a) $g'(1) = 3/4$
(b) $h'(1) = 3/2$

## Section 3.4

1 $5x^4 + 10x$

3 $-2te^{-2t} + e^{-2t}$

5 $2t(3t + 1)^3 + 9t^2(3t + 1)^2$

7 $\ln x + 1$

9 $(t^3 - 4t^2 - 14t + 1)e^t$

11 $-3qe^{-q} + 3e^{-q}$

13 $1 - 3/x^2$

15 $e^{-t^2}(1 - 2t^2)$

17 $2p/(2p + 1) + \ln(2p + 1)$

19 $2we^{w^2}(5w^2 + 8)$

21 $9(te^{3t} + e^{5t})^8(e^{3t} + 3te^{3t} + 5e^{5t})$

23 $-2/(1 + t)^2$

25 $(15 + 10y + y^2)/(5 + y)^2$

27 $(ak - bc)/(cx + k)^2$

29 $ae^{-bx} - abxe^{-bx}$

31 $(1 - 2\alpha)e^{-2\alpha}e^{\alpha e^{-2\alpha}}$

33 $f'(x) = 12x + 1$ and
$f''(x) = 12$

35 $y = 0$

37 (a) $f'(15) > 0$, $f'(45) < 0$

(b) $f(30) \approx 181$ mg/ml, $f'(30) \approx -1.2$
mg/ml/min

39 Revenue $R(10) \approx 22{,}466$.
   $R'(10) \approx \$449$/dollar.

41 $1/t$

43 $(fg)'/(fg) = (f'/f) + (g'/g)$

47 (a) $0.555 = 55.5\%$
  (b) Initially not in search area; unrealistic
  (c) $I(1 - I)/(1 - (1 - I)E)^2$; positive;
    $O$ increases

## Section 3.5

1  $-\sin t$

3  $A \cos t$

5  $5 \cos x - 5$

7  $5 \cos(5t)$

9  $-10 \sin(5t)$

11  $AB \cos(Bt)$

13  $12 \cos(2t) - 4 \sin(4t)$

15  $2 \sin(3x) + 6x \cos(3x)$

17  $((2te^{t^2} + 1) \sin(2t) -$
    $(e^{t^2} + t)2 \cos(2t))/\sin^2(2t)$

19  $(\theta \cos \theta - \sin \theta)/\theta^2$

21  $y = -x + \pi$

23  At $x = 0$:
   $y = x, \sin(\pi/6) \approx 0.524$
   At $x = \pi/3$:
   $y = x/2 + (3\sqrt{3} - \pi)/6$,
   $\sin(\pi/6) \approx 0.604$

25 (a) 5 sec
  (b) $A'(1) = 239$ cc$^3$/second

27 (a) $v(t) = 2\pi \cos(2\pi t)$
  (b)

29 (a) $D(40) = 9.4$ hours daylight; $D'(40) =$
   0.05 hours/day
  (b) $D(172) = 16$ hours daylight; $D'(172) =$
   0 hours/day

## Chapter 3 Review

1  $24t^3$

3  $2e^{2t}$

5  $0.08e^{0.08q}$

7  $e^{3x}(1 + 3x)$

9  $6(1 + 3t)e^{(1+3t)^2}$

11  $5 + 3.6e^{1.2t}$

13  $90(5x - 1)^2$

15  $10e^x(1 + e^x)^9$

17  $x(2 \ln x + 1)$

19  $8t + 7 \cos t$

21  $(-e^{-t} - 1)/(e^{-t} - t)$

23  $(50x - 25x^2)/(e^x)$

25  $2x \cos x - x^2 \sin x$

27  $e$

29  $(e^x - 2 - e^{-x})/(1 - e^{-x})^2$

31  $xe^x + e^x$

33  $-3x^2 \sin(x^3)$

35  $(t^2 + 6t + 13)/(t + 3)^2$

37  $((\ln 3)3^x)/3 - (33x^{-3/2})/2$

39  $-7ke^{-kt}$

41  $f'(0) = 0, f'(1) = 2$,
   $f'(2) = 4, f'(-1) = -2$

43  $y = 2x - 1$

45  81.6 m/yr

47  $(-1, 7)$ and $(7, -209)$

49  $Q(t) = (1 + \ln 2)t - 2 \approx 1.69t - 2$

51 (a) $177°$F
  (b) $74°F$; room temperature
  (c) $C(5) = 161°$F;
    $C'(5) = -2.88°$F/minute
  (d) Less

53 (a) $-0.000121e^{-0.000121t}$
  (b)

$dQ/dt$

55  Increasing for $a > 1$,
   decreasing for $a < 1$

57 (a) $Y(0) = 105°$
  (b) $350°$
  (c) After about 42 minutes
  (d) About 1.67 degrees/minute

59  $y = x$ and $y = \ln(x + 1)$ look the same
   (like the line $y = x$);
   $y = \sqrt{x}$ and $y = \sqrt{2x - x^2}$ look like
   the line $x = 0$;
   $y = x^2, y = x^3 + \frac{1}{2}x^2, y = x^3$, and
   $y = \frac{1}{2}\ln(x^2 + 1)$ all look like the line $y = 0$

61 (a) 2
  (b) 15
  (c) 11
  (d) $-1/4$

63 (a) $CD - D^2$
  (b) $D < C$

65  Approx 0.6

67  Approx 1.6

69  Approx $-8.8$

71  For $x < 0$ or $2 < x < 3$

75  $y = 2x$ and $y = -6x$

77 (a) 0.04 gal/mile; 0.06 gal/mile
  (b) 25 mpg; 16.67 mpg
  (d) 1.4 gallons
  (e) 2.8 gal/hour; 1.8 gal/hour

79  $331.3 + 0.606T$ m/sec

## Ch. 3 Understanding

1  True
3  False
5  False
7  True
9  True
11  False
13  True
15  True
17  False
19  False
21  False
23  True
25  True
27  False
29  True
31  False
33  True
35  False
37  True
39  False
41  True
43  True
45  False
47  False
49  True

## Practice: Differentiation

1  $2t + 4t^3$

3  $15x^2 + 14x - 3$

5  $-2/x^3 + 5/(2\sqrt{x})$

7  $10e^{2x} - 2 \cdot 3^x(\ln 3)$

9  $2pe^{p^2} + 10p$

11  $2x\sqrt{x^2 + 1} + x^3/\sqrt{x^2 + 1}$

13  $16/(2t + 1)$

15  $2^x(\ln 2) + 2x$

17  $6(2q + 1)^2$

19  $bke^{kt}$

21  $2x \ln(2x + 1) + 2x^2/(2x + 1)$

23  $10 \cos(2x)$

25  $15 \cos(5t)$

27  $2e^x + 3 \cos x$

29 $17 + 12x^{-1/2}$

31 $20x^3 - 2/x^3$

33 $1, x \neq -1$

35 $-3\cos(2 - 3x)$

37 $6/(5r + 2)^2$

39 $ae^{ax}/(e^{ax} + b)$

41 $5(w^4 - 2w)^4(4w^3 - 2)$

43 $(\cos x - \sin x)/(\sin x + \cos x)$

45 $6/w^4 + 3/(2\sqrt{w})$

47 $(2t - ct^2)e^{-ct}$

49 $(\cos\theta)e^{\sin\theta}$

51 $3x^2/a + 2ax/b - c$

53 $2r(r + 1)/(2r + 1)^2$

55 $2e^t + 2te^t + 1/(2t^{3/2})$

57 $x^2 \ln x$

59 $6x\left(x^2 + 5\right)^2\left(3x^3 - 2\right)\left(6x^3 + 15x - 2\right)$

61 $(2abr - ar^4)/(b + r^3)^2$

63 $20w/(a^2 - w^2)^3$

## Section 4.1

1 One

3 Four

5 (a)

(b)

7 After 18 hours

9 Local max: $(-1.4, 6.7)$
  Local min: $(1.4, -4.7)$

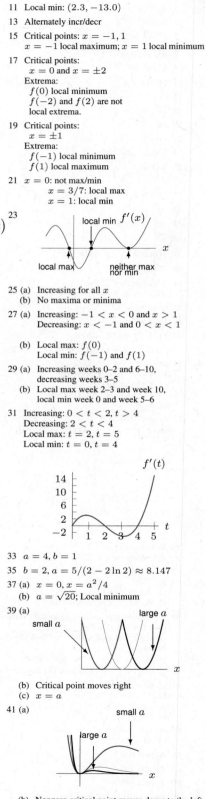

11 Local min: $(2.3, -13.0)$

13 Alternately incr/decr

15 Critical points: $x = -1, 1$
   $x = -1$ local maximum; $x = 1$ local minimum

17 Critical points:
   $x = 0$ and $x = \pm 2$
   Extrema:
   $f(0)$ local minimum
   $f(-2)$ and $f(2)$ are not
   local extrema.

19 Critical points:
   $x = \pm 1$
   Extrema:
   $f(-1)$ local minimum
   $f(1)$ local maximum

21 $x = 0$: not max/min
   $x = 3/7$: local max
   $x = 1$: local min

23

25 (a) Increasing for all $x$
   (b) No maxima or minima

27 (a) Increasing: $-1 < x < 0$ and $x > 1$
       Decreasing: $x < -1$ and $0 < x < 1$

   (b) Local max: $f(0)$
       Local min: $f(-1)$ and $f(1)$

29 (a) Increasing weeks 0–2 and 6–10,
       decreasing weeks 3–5
   (b) Local max week 2–3 and week 10,
       local min week 0 and week 5–6

31 Increasing: $0 < t < 2, t > 4$
   Decreasing: $2 < t < 4$
   Local max: $t = 2, t = 5$
   Local min: $t = 0, t = 4$

33 $a = 4, b = 1$

35 $b = 2, a = 5/(2 - 2\ln 2) \approx 8.147$

37 (a) $x = 0, x = a^2/4$
   (b) $a = \sqrt{20}$; Local minimum

39 (a)

   (b) Critical point moves right
   (c) $x = a$

41 (a)

   (b) Nonzero critical point moves down to the left
   (c) $x = 0, 2/a$

## Section 4.2

1 Two

3 Three

5

7 $y$

9 (a) 6 pm
   (b) Noon; another between noon and 6 pm

11 $x = -1, 1/2$

13 Critical points: $x = -1$,
   local max; $x = 1$, local min
   Inflection point: $x = 0$

15 Critical points: $x = -2$,
   local max; $x = 1$, local min
   Inflection point: $x = -1/2$

17 Critical points:
   $x = 0$ (neither) and $x = 1$ (local max)
   Inflection points: $x = 0$ and $x = 2/3$

19 Critical points: $x = 0$ (not an extrema) and
   $x = 3$ (local minimum)
   Inflection points: $x = 0$ and $x = 2$

21 Critical points:
   $x = -1$ (local maximum)
   $x = 0$ (not an extrema)
   $x = 1$ (local minimum)
   Inflection points:
   $x = 0$ and $x = \pm 1/\sqrt{2}$

23 (a) Critical points: $x = 0, x = \sqrt{a}$,
       $x = -\sqrt{a}$
       Inflection points: $x = \sqrt{a/3}$,
       $x = -\sqrt{a/3}$
   (b) $a = 4, b = 21$

(c) $x = \sqrt{4/3}$, $x = -\sqrt{4/3}$

25

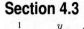

inflection points of $ff''(x)$

27

$y' < 0$ everywhere
$y'' = 0$   $y'' = 0$   $y'' = 0$

$y'' > 0$   $y'' < 0$   $y'' > 0$   $y'' < 0$

$y = f(x)$

$x_1$   $x_2$   $x_3$

29

$y$

$y = f(x)$

$y' = 2$   $y' > 0$
$y'' = 0$   $y'' > 0$

$x_1$

31 (a) cm/week
   (b) Growing at 1.6 cm/wk in week 24

33 (a) Week 14
   (b) Point of fastest growth

35 (a)   depth of water

$d(t)$

slope $= K$

$t$

   (b)   depth of water

$d(t)$

$t$

37 (a) Concavity changes at $y_1$ and $y_3$

$y_3$   $f(t)$

$y_2$

$y_1$

$t_1$   $t_2$   $t_3$

---

(b) $f(t)$ grows most quickly where vase is skinniest and most slowly where vase is widest. Ratio is about 16 : 1

39  $y = (2 + 2e)/(1 + e^{1-t})$

# Section 4.3

1

$y$

8
6
4
2

Global and local max

Local min

Global and local min

1   2   3   4   5   $x$

3 (a) (IV)
  (b) (I)
  (c) (III)
  (d) (II)

5

$y$

3   8   $x$

7

$y$

3   8   $x$

9 (a) Local minima at $x = -1$,
   $x \approx 0.91$, $x = 4$
   Local maxima at $x \approx -0.46$, $x \approx 3.73$
   $f(0.91)$ is global minimum
   $f(3.73)$ is global maximum
  (b) Local minima at $x = -3$, $x \approx 0.91$
   Local maxima at $x \approx -0.46$, $x = 2$
   $f(-3)$ is global minimum
   $f(2)$ is global maximum

11

$y$

3   10   $x$

13

$y$

3   8   10   $x$

15 (a) $t \approx 50$ days
   (b) Throughout interval
      $t \approx 50$ days

---

17 (a) $f'(x) = 6x^2 - 18x + 12$,
      $f''(x) = 12x - 18$.
   (b) $x = 1, 2$
   (c) $x = 3/2$
   (d) Local minimum: $x = -0.5, 2$
      Local maximum: $x = 1, 3$
      Global minimum: $x = -0.5$
      Global maximum: $x = 3$
   (e)

$y$

10

5

$f(x) = 2x^3 - 9x^2 + 12x + 1$

$-1$   1   2   3   $x$

$-5$

$-10$

19 (a) $f'(x) = 1 + \cos x$,
      $f''(x) = -\sin x$.
   (b) $x = \pi$
   (c) $x = 0, \pi, 2\pi$
   (d) Global, local minimum: $x = 0$
      Global, local maximum: $x = 2\pi$
   (e)

6
5
4
3
2
1

$f(x) = x + \sin x$

$\pi$   $2\pi$   $x$

21  $x = -b/2a$,
   Max if $a < 0$, min if $a > 0$

23  2500

25  1536

27  Global max $= -1$ at $x = 2$
   No global min

29  Global max $= 1/e$ at $t = 1$
   No global min

31  Global max $= 1/2$ at $t = 1$
   Global min $= -1/2$ at $t = -1$

33  $w = -(5p)/(6q)$

35  40 feet by 80 feet

37 (a) $y = \begin{cases} 400x & x \le 200 \\ 600x - x^2 & x > 200 \end{cases}$

$y$ (kg)

100,000

50,000

200   400   600   $x$ (trees)

   (b) 300 trees/km$^2$

39  306 children

41 (a) $H = 1/b$, $S = ae^{-1}/b$
   (b) $a$: Increases
      $b$: Decreases

43 (a) 10
   (b) 9

45 (a) 120 mm Hg, 80 mm Hg
   (b) 0.8 sec
   (c)

$p$ (mm Hg)   0.8 sec

120   Maximum
100
80   Minimum

1   2   $t$ (sec)

47 (a)  $0 \le y \le a$

(b)  $y = 0$

## Section 4.4

1  $5.5 < q < 12.5$ positive;
  $0 < q < 5.5$ and $q > 12.5$ negative;
  Maximum at $q \approx 9.5$

3  Global maximum of \$6875 at $q = 75$

5 (a)

7 (a)  \$9
  (b)  $-\$3$
  (c)  $C'(78) = R'(78)$

9 (a)  Increase production
  (b)  $q = 8000$

11 (a)  Increase
  (b)  Decrease
  (c)  Decrease

13  $q = 4000$

15  Above 2000

17  \$0.20/item

19 (a)  \$10; \$30,000; \$50,000
  (b)  $R(q) = 70q - 0.02q^2$
  (c)  1750
  (d)  \$35
  (e)  \$61,250

21  \$14

23 (a)  $10,000 + 2q$
  (b)  $q = 37,820 - 5544p$
  (c)  $\pi = -0.00018q^2 + 4.822q - 10,000$
  (d)  13,394 items, \$22,294

25  \$8378.54

27 (a)  Ordering: $a/q$
    Storage: $bq$
  (b)  $\sqrt{a/b}$

29 (a)  $q/r$ months
  (b)  $(ra/q) + rb$ dollars
  (c)  $C = (ra/q) + rb + kq/2$ dollars
  (d)  $q = \sqrt{2ra/k}$

31  $L = [\beta pcK^\alpha /w]^{1/(1-\beta)}$

## Section 4.5

1 (a)  No
  (b)  Yes

3 (a)  (i) About \$8 per unit
    (ii) About \$4 per unit
  (b)  About 30 units

5  $MC = \$20$; $a(q) = \$25$

7 (a)  $q = 6$

(b)  $q = 6$

9 (a)  $C(q) = 0.01q^3 - 0.6q^2 + 13q$
  (b)  \$1
  (c)  $q = 30, a(30) = 4$
  (d)  Marginal cost is 4

11 (a)

$N(x) = 100 + 20x$

  (b)  (i)  $N'(x) = 20$
    (ii)  $N(x)/x = (100/x) + 20$

15 (b)  $q = [Fa/(K(1 - a))]^a$

## Section 4.6

1 (a)  1.5% decrease
  (b)  1.5% increase

5  Elastic

7  Elastic

9  $E = 2/3$; inelastic

11 (a)  $E \approx 0.470$, inelastic
  (c)  About $P = 1.25$ and 1.50

15  \$12.91

27  1% more time gives 1.3% more sales

## Section 4.7

1 (a)  40 billion

(b)

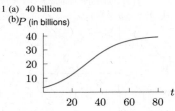

(c)  2020; 2095

3 (a)

(b)  60,000

5 (a)  and  (b)

(c)  $P'$ maximum

7 (a)  About 0.252
  (c)  1975
  (d)  1975

11 (a)  5000
  (b)  499
  (c)  $P(t) = 5000/(1 + 499e^{-1.78t})$

$$P(t) = \frac{5000}{1+499e^{-1.78t}}$$

  (d)  About 3.5 weeks; 2500

13 (b)  $f'(10) < 11$
    $f'(20) < 11$

15 (a)  $C$: largest
    $B$: smallest
  (b)  $A$: largest
    $B$: smallest
  (c)  $C$: safest

17  10 mg to 18 mg

## Section 4.8

1 (a)

$C = 12.4te^{-0.2t}$

  (b)  5 hrs, 22.8 ng/ml
  (c)  1 to 14.4 hrs
  (d)  At least 20.8 hrs

3 (a)  After about 6 hours
  (b)  After about 5 hours

9  $a = 49.3$; $b = 0.769$

13 (b)  Min effective $\approx 0.2$   Max safe $\approx 1.0$
  (c)  Min effective $\approx 1.2$   Max safe $\approx 2.0$

## Chapter 4 Review

1

3  Critical points: $x = 2$, $x = 4$
  Inflection point: $x = 3$

5  Critical points: $x = 0$, $x = -12$
   Inflection points: $x = -9$

7  Critical point: $x = -1/3$
   Inflection point: $x = -2/3$

9  (a)  $f(1)$ local minimum;
        $f(0.1)$, $f(2)$ local maxima
   (b)  $f(0.1)$ global maximum
        $f(1)$ global minimum

11  Local maximum, minimum, or neither
    Price relatively constant around July 1

13

$f$ has a          $f$ has crit. pt.
local min.         Neither max or min

15  $A$: local max
    $B$: local min
    $C$: neither

$f'(x)$

17  (a)  $5x^4 + 1$; positive
    (b)  One

19  Domain: All real numbers except $x = b$;
    Critical points: $x = 0$, $x = 2b$

21  (a)

$f'(x)$

    (b)  $x_1$, $x_3$, and $x_5$
    (c)  $x_2$ and $x_4$

23  $A$ has $a = 1$, $B$ has $a = 2$, $C$ has $a = 5$

25

depth of water
Time at which water reaches corner of vase
time

27  (a)  Yes, at 2000 rabbits

population of rabbits
years since 1774

    (b)  1787, 1000 rabbits
    (c)  1787, 1000 rabbits

29  Intercepts: $(0,0)$, $(1.77, 0)$,
    $(2.51, 0)$
    Critical Points: $(0,0)$, $(1.25, 1)$,
    $(2.17, -1)$, $(2.80, 1)$
    Inflection Points: $(0.81, 0.61)$,
    $(1.81, -0.13)$, $(2.52, 0.07)$

31  (a)

$a = 1$
$a = 20$

    (b)  $-2 < a < 2$

33  (a)  $D = C$
    (b)  $D = C/2$

35  (a)  $V = Ax/4 - x^3/2$
    (b)

$V = \frac{A}{4}x - \frac{1}{2}x^3$

    (c)  $(A/6)^{3/2}$

37  Max area $= 1/\left(2e^3\right)$  at  $x = 1$

39  $1/\sqrt{2}$

41  (a)  $(9/4, \pm\sqrt{7}/4)$
    (b)  $(3, 0)$

43  (a)  $q = 400$
    (b)  \$5 per unit
    (c)  \$700.

45  $q = 1000$ or $q = 4500$

47  (a)  No
    (b)  Yes

49  (a)  \$0
    (b)  \$96.56
    (c)  Raise the price by \$5

51  (a)  $\pi(q)$ max when
        $R(q) > C(q)$ and $R$ and $Q$ are
        farthest apart

\$
$C(q)$
$R(q)$
maximum $\pi(q)$
$q$
$q_0$

    (b)  $C'(q_0) = R'(q_0) = p$
    (c)
\$
$C'(q)$
$p$
$q$
$q_0$

53

Cost
375,000
Quantity
15,000

55  $C'(2)$

57  $(C(75) - C(50))/25$

59  $C(3)/3$

61  $E = 0.05$, demand is inelastic

63  50 m by 50 m

65  Max: 0.552; Min: 0.358

67  (a)  $1/(2e)$
    (b)  $(\ln 2) + 1$

69  (a)  $x = \mu$
    (b)  Yes; $x = \mu \pm \sigma$

75  (a)

load
(number of worms)
Number of worms
8
4
time
$P$          $O$

    (b)  7 worms
    (c)  increases

## Ch. 4 Understanding

1   False
3   False
5   False
7   False
9   False
11  True
13  True
15  False
17  True
19  False
21  True
23  False
25  False
27  False
29  True
31  True
33  False
35  False
37  False
39  True
41  True
43  False
45  False
47  True

522

49  False
51  False
53  False
55  False
57  False
59  True
61  True
63  False
65  True
67  True
69  True
71  False
73  False
75  False
77  True
79  False

## Section 5.1

1 (a)  160 miles
  (b)  velocity
       (miles/hour)

  (c)  velocity
       (miles/hour)

Area = Distance traveled

3 (a)  Right sum
  (b)  Lower estimate
  (c)  5
  (d)  $\Delta t = 3$
  (e)  Lower estimate $\approx$ 160.5

5  352.5 feet

7  Between 140 and 150 meters

9  669.5 bn barrels

11  250 meters

13 (a)  About 420 kg
   (b)  336 and 504 kg

15  220 fish

17 (a)  Car $A$
   (b)  Car $A$
   (c)  Car $B$

19 (b)  $6151

21 (a)  3400 million people
   (b)  3530 million people; differs by 130 mn

23  No

25  About 0.009 miles or 48 feet

27 (a)  663 ft
   (b)  Upper estimate
   (c)  489 ft

---

  (d)  Lower estimate
  (e)  576 ft

29 (a)  72; 328

$f(t) = t^2 + 1$

  (b)  120; 248

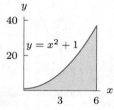
$f(t) = t^2 + 1$

  (c)  148; 212

$f(t) = t^2 + 1$

31 (a)  4; 0, 4, 8, 12, 16; 25, 23, 22, 20, 17
   (b)  360; 328
   (c)  8; 0, 8, 16; 25, 22, 17
   (d)  376; 312

## Section 5.2

1 (a)  Right
  (b)  Upper
  (c)  3
  (d)  2

3  27

5 (a)  0.808
  (b)  0.681

7  17,000, $n = 4$, $\Delta x = 10$

9  16.1, $n = 5$, $\Delta t = 0.2$

11  About 60

13  About 20

15  8.5

17  13

19  2.350

21  About 0.865

23  6.111

25  0

27 (a)  3.6

$f(x) = \sqrt{x}$

---

  (b)  3.4641

29 (a)  2

$f(x) = x^x$

  (b)  2.05045

31 (a)  78

$y = x^2 + 1$

  (b)  46; underestimate

$y = x^2 + 1$

  (c)  118; overestimate

$y = x^2 + 1$

## Section 5.3

1  84

3  7.667

5  $\int_0^3 (3x - x^2)\, dx = 4.5$

7  (a)  Negative
   (b)  Positive
   (c)  Negative
   (d)  Positive

9  (a)  About 16.5
   (b)  About $-3.5$

11 (a)  About $-0.25$
   (b)  About 0
   (c)  About 0.5

13 (a)  13
   (b)  $-2$
   (c)  11
   (d)  15

15  II

17  III

19 (a)  $-2$
   (b)  $-A/2$

21 (a)  1
   (b)  $2\pi$
   (c)  $2\pi - 1/2$
   (d)  $\pi - 3/2$

23  1.977

25  7.799

27  21.527

29  2.828

31  $-0.136$

33 (a)  16.25
   (b)  15.75
   (c)  No

## Section 5.4

1  Change in position; meters

3  Change in world pop; bn people

5  Total amount $= \int_0^{60} f(t)\, dt.$

7  13.295 billion tons
   $\int_0^{12} f(t)\, dt$

9  (a)  1770 million metric tons; 2830 million
         metric tons
   (b)  46,000 million metric tons

11  15 cm to the left

13  25 cm to the right

15  3.406 ft

17  2627 acres

19 (a)  $\int_0^5 (10 + 8t - t^2)\, dt$
   (b)  100
   (c)  108.33

21  1417 antibodies

23  $t = 1$
    About 16.667 miles

25 (a)  (i)  $\int_{2000}^{2015} I(t)\, dt$; Total income from
              2000 to 2015
       (ii)  $\int_{2000}^{2015} E(t)\, dt$; Total expenditures
              from 2000 to 2015
      (iii)  $\int_{2000}^{2015} I(t) - E(t)\, dt$; Change in
              value from 2000 to 2015
   (b)  About 2500 billion dollars

27  $\int_{2000}^{2030} I(t) - E(t)\, dt$

29  6 months: $A$ more
    First year: $B$ more
    Same: roughly 9 months
    $A$ roughly 170 sales
    $B$ roughly 250 sales

31 (a)  Boys: black curve; girls: colored curve
   (b)  About 43 cm
   (c)  Boys: about 23 cm; girls: about 18 cm
   (d)  About 13 cm taller

33 (a)  About 750 liters
   (b)  $\int_0^3 60g(t)\, dt$
   (c)  About 150 liters

35  Product B has a greater peak concentration
    Product A peaks sooner
    Product B has a greater overall bioavailability
    Product A should be used

37

39  About $13,800

41 (a)  $\int_0^T 49(1 - (0.8187)^t)\, dt$
        (meters)
   (b)  $T \approx 107$ seconds

## Section 5.5

1  $45.8°C.$

3  4,250,000 riyals

5  (a)  About $10,550
   (b)  About $150
   (c)  About 10

7  (a)

   (b)  $22,775
   (c)  $C'(150) = 18.5$
   (d)  $C(151) \approx $22,793.50$

9  Fixed cost is $500
   Variable cost is $866.67
   Total cost is $1,366.67

11 (a)

(b)  $12,000
(c)  Marginal revenue is $80/unit
     Total revenue is $12,080

13  $16,000,   $56,000

17  $\int_{2t_0}^{3t_0} r(t)\, dt$   $<$   $\int_{t_0}^{2t_0} r(t)\, dt$   $<$
    $\int_0^{2t_0} r(t)\, dt$

19  0.5; cost of preparing is $0.5 million

21  $\int_0^2 r(t)\, dt < \int_2^4 r(t)\, dt$

23  $\int_0^8 r(t)\, dt < 64$ million

## Section 5.6

1  (a)  20
   (b)  10/3

3  2

5  (a)  0.79

7  8

9  About 17

11 (a)  527.25
   (b)

13 (a)  $26,667 per year
   (b)  Less 25–65; more 65–85

15 (a)  120 mm Hg
   (b)  80 mm Hg
   (c)  100 mm Hg
   (d)  Less

17 (a)  0.375 thousand/hour
   (b)  1.75 thousands

19 (a)  $22°C$
   (b)  $183°C$
   (c)  Smaller

21 (a)  $E(t) = 1.4e^{0.07t}$
   (b)  $\approx 219$
        million megawatt-hours
   (c)  1972
   (d)  Graph $E(t)$ and estimate $t$ such that
        $E(t) = 219$

23  $(a) < (c) < (b) < (d)$

## Chapter 5 Review

1  (a)  408
   (b)  390

3  1692.5

5  (a)  Right sum
   (b)  Upper estimate
   (c)  4
   (d)  $\Delta t = 2$
   (e)  Upper estimate $\approx 122.6$

7  Dollars

9  (a)  About 3.6 acres
   (b)  About 6.9 acres
   (c)  About 5.25 acres

11  About 7

13  28.5

15  1.15

17  −0.083

19  About 1.772

21  0.0833

23  About 0.1667

25 (a)  430 ft
   (b)  (ii)

27 (a)

(b)  3 sec, 144 feet
(c)  80 feet

29 (a)  Species B for both
   (b)  Species A

31 (a)  Concave up
   (b)  About 3.1 kg

33  Negative

35  Approximately zero

37 (a)  −4
   (b)  0
   (c)  8

41 (a)  $\int_0^{15} f(t)\,dt$
   (b)  657.11 billion barrels
   (c)  Lower estimate of 3 years' consumption

43  About $14,667

45 (a)  CCl₄ dumped

(b)  7 years
(c)  69.3 cubic yards

47 (a)  About times 17, 23, 27 seconds
   (b)  Right: $t = 10$ seconds
        Left: $t = 40$ seconds
   (c)  Right: $t = 17$ seconds
        Left: $t = 40$ seconds
   (d)  $t = 10$ to 17 seconds,
        20 to 23 seconds, and
        24 to 27 seconds
   (e)  At $t = 0$ and about $t = 35$

49  $F(0) = 0$, $F(0.5) = 1.958$,
    $F(1) = 3.667$,
    $F(1.5) = 4.875$,
    $F(2) = 5.333$,
    $F(2.5) = 4.792$

51  Maximum at
    $x = 2$ and $F(2) = 5.333$.

53  2202.55

55 (a)  100 cases; 5 cases
   (b)  32 cases

57  About 8.5

59 (a)  III
   (b)  I
   (c)  II and IV

# Ch. 5 Understanding

1  True
3  False
5  True
7  False
9  True
11  False
13  False
15  True
17  False
19  True
21  False
23  False
25  True
27  False
29  True
31  True
33  True
35  True
37  False
39  True
41  False
43  False
45  False
47  False
49  True
51  False
53  True
55  False
57  False
59  True

# Theory: Second Fund. Thm.

1  $x^3$

3  $xe^x$

5 (a)  0
  (b)  $F$ increases
  (c)  $F(1) \approx 1.4$, $F(2) \approx 4.3$, $F(3) \approx 10.1$

9  9

11  $8c$

# Section 6.1

1

| $b$ | 0 | 0.1 | 0.2 | 0.5 | 1.0 |
|-----|---|-----|-----|-----|-----|
| $F(b)$ | 3 | 3.501 | 4.005 | 5.583 | 6.667 |

3

| $b$ | 2 | 4 | 6 | 10 | 20 |
|-----|---|---|---|----|----|
| $f(b)$ | 9 | 10.110 | 10.856 | 11.696 | 12.293 |

5  $F(0) = 0$
   $F(1) = 1$
   $F(2) = 1.5$
   $F(3) = 1$
   $F(4) = 0$
   $F(5) = -1$
   $F(6) = -1.5$

7  3.5, 2, 1.5, 2, 2.5

9

11

13

15

adrenaline concentration (μg/ml)

17  Largest: $F(2)$
    Smallest: $F(4)$
    None negative

19 (a)  Increasing for $x < -1$, $x > 1$,
        Decreasing for $-1 < x < 1$,
        Local maximum at $x = -1$,
        Local minimum at $x = 1$
   (b)

21  Critical points: $(0, 5)$, $(2, 21)$, $(4, 13)$, $(5, 15)$

23  Min: $(1.5, -20)$, max: $(4.67, 5)$

25 (a)  $x = 1, x = 3$
   (b)  Local min at $x = 1$, local max at $x = 3$
   (c)
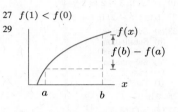

27  $f(1) < f(0)$

29

31

## Section 6.2

1  Yes
3  No
5  No
7  Family functions
9  Family functions
11  Family functions
13  Family functions
15  $x^3/3$
17  $5x$
19  $(t^8/8) + (t^4/4)$
21  $3x^4/2 + 4x$
23  $10x + 2x^4$
25  $F(x) = (x^2/2) + (x^6/6) - (x^{-4}/4) + C$
27  $(x^3/3) - 3x^2 + 17x$
29  $t^4/4 - t^3/6 - t^2/2$
31  $-1/(2z^2)$
33  $F(x) = x^7/7 + x^{-5}/35 + C$
35  $2z^{5/2}/5$
37  $\sin t$
39  $G(\theta) = -\cos\theta - 2\sin\theta + C$
41  $g(x)$
43  $g(x)$
45  $F(x) = 2x + 2x^2 + (5/3)x^3$
   (only possibility)
47  $F(x) = (2/3)x^{3/2}$
   (only possibility)
49  $e^x - 1$ (only possibility)
51  $3x^3 + C$
53  $p + \ln|p| + C$
55  $x^3/3 - 1/x + C$
57  $5e^z + C$
59  $t^4/4 + 2t^3 + C$
61  $x^3/3 + 2x^2 - 5x + C$

63  $x^2/2 + 2x^{1/2} + C$
65  $e^x + 5x + C$
67  $x^6/6 - 3x^4 + C$
69  $-\cos t + C$
71  $25e^{4x} + C$
73  $2\ln|x| - \pi\cos x + C$
75  $3\sin x + 7\cos x + C$
77  $10x - 4\cos(2x) + C$
79  $-6\cos(2x) + 3\sin(5x) + C$
81  $(2/5)x^{5/2}$
83  $(e^{2x} + e^{-2x})/2$
85 (a)  $20q - 2q^2$
   (b)  $p = 20 - 2q$
87  $F(x) = 3x^2 - 5x + 5$
89  $F(x) = -4\cos(2x) + 9$
91  $C(x) =$
   $5x^2 + 4000x + 1,000,000$

## Section 6.3

1  48
3  81/4
5  22
7  2
9  125
11  75/4
13  8/15
15  $609/4 - 39\pi \approx 29.728$
17  $\sin 1 - \sin(-1) = 2\sin 1$
19  $20(e^{0.15} - 1)$
21  1/2
23  $(300)^{1/3} = 6.694$
25 (a)  $\int_0^5 462e^{0.019t}\,dt$
   (b)  About 2423 quadrillion BTUs
27 (a)  First case: 19,923
      Second case: 1.99 billion
   (b)  In both cases, 6.47 yrs
   (c)  3.5 yrs
29 (a)  $-(1/b) + 1$
   (b)  Converges to 1
31  $\int_1^\infty (1/x^2)\,dx$

33 (a)  $\int_0^\infty 1000te^{-0.5t}\,dt$
   (b)  $r$

## Section 6.4

1 (a)  $p^* = \$30, q^* = 6000$
   (b)  Consumer surplus $= \$210,000$;
      Producer surplus $\approx \$70,000$

3  250
5  200
7 (a)  \$400
   (b)  \$266.7
9 (a)

(b)

11 (a)  About \$2250, \$2625, \$4875
   (b)  Consumer surplus: less
      Producer surplus: greater
      Total gains: less
13 (a)  Less
   (b)  Cannot tell
   (c)  Less
15 (a)  No, yes

Large producer surplus

$p$ ($/unit)

$q$ (quantity)

Small producer surplus

$p$ ($/unit)

$q$ (quantity)

(b) Yes, no

$p$ ($/unit)

Producer surplus

$q$ (quantity)

Large consumer surplus

$p$ ($/unit)

$q$ (quantity)

Small consumer surplus

$p$ ($/unit)

$q$ (quantity)

## Section 6.5

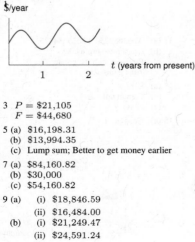

$/year

$t$ (years from present)

3  $P = \$21,105$
   $F = \$44,680$

5 (a)  $16,198.31
  (b)  $13,994.35
  (c)  Lump sum; Better to get money earlier

7 (a)  $84,160.82
  (b)  $30,000
  (c)  $54,160.82

9 (a)  (i)  $18,846.59
    (ii)  $16,484.00
  (b)  (i)  $21,249.47
    (ii)  $24,591.24

11  2,936,142.74 euros

13 (a)  $5820 per year
  (b)  $36,787.94

15  No; present value $= \$306,279$

17 (a)  $33.58 billion
  (b)  $35.66 billion

19 (a)  80.1 and 102.1 billion dollars
  (b)  268.6 and 342.2 billion dollars

21 (a)  10.6 years
  (b)  624.9 million dollars

## Section 6.6

1 (a)  $2x\cos(x^2+1)$;
   $3x^2\cos(x^3+1)$
  (b)  (i)  $\frac{1}{2}\sin(x^2+1)+C$
    (ii)  $\frac{1}{3}\sin(x^3+1)+C$
  (c)  (i)  $-\frac{1}{2}\cos(x^2+1)+C$
    (ii)  $-\frac{1}{3}\cos(x^3+1)+C$

3  Yes

5  Yes

7  $\sqrt{x^2+4}+C$

9  $\frac{1}{3}(x^2+1)^{3/2}+C$

11  $e^{5t+2}+C$

13  $-500e^{-0.2t}+C$

15  $-\frac{1}{2}\cos(x^2)+C$

17  $(1/6)(x^2+3)^3+C$

19  $\ln(x^4+1)+C$

21  $(1/148)(2t-7)^{74}+C$

23  $(1/5)y^5+(1/2)y^4+(1/3)y^3+C$

25  $(1/7)\sin^7\theta+C$

27  $\cos(3-t)+C$

29  $(1/3)e^{x^3+1}+C$

31  $-\frac{1}{8}\cos(4x^2)+C$

33  $\frac{1}{3}e^{3x-4}+C$

35  $\frac{1}{6}e^{3x^2}+C$

37  $\ln(e^x+e^{-x})+C$

39  $(1/2)\ln(y^2+4)+C$

41  $\ln|e^t+t|+C$

43  $2\sin\sqrt{x}+C$

45  $\ln(e^t+1)+C$

47  $\sqrt{\sin(x^2)}+C$

49 (a)  $(\ln 2)/2$
  (b)  $(\ln 2)/2$

51  $\ln 10$

53  $2e(e-1)$

55  1

57  $1-e^{-1}$

59  $1/40$

61  $\ln 3$

63 (a)  10
  (b)  5

65 (a)  $x^4+2x^2+C$
  (b)  $(x^2+1)^2+C$
  (c)  Both correct but differ by a constant

## Section 6.7

1  $\frac{1}{5}te^{5t}-\frac{1}{25}e^{5t}+C$

3  $(1/2)y^2\ln y-(1/4)y^2+C$

5  $(1/6)q^6\ln 5q-(1/36)q^6+C$

7  $(x^4/4)\ln x-(x^4/16)+C$

9  $-2y(5-y)^{1/2}$
   $-(4/3)(5-y)^{3/2}+C$

11  $-2t(5-t)^{1/2}-(4/3)(5-t)^{3/2}$
   $-14(5-t)^{1/2}+C$

13  $-t\cos t+\sin t+C$

15  $0.386, 2\ln 2-1$

17  $5\ln 5-4\approx 4.047$

19  $(9/2)\ln 3-2\approx 2.944$

21  $t(\ln t)^2-2t\ln t+2t+C$

23 (a)  Substitution
  (b)  Substitution
  (c)  Substitution
  (d)  Substitution
  (e)  Parts
  (f)  Parts

25  $2\ln 2-1$

27 (a)  $-(1/a)Te^{-aT}+(1/a^2)(1-e^{-aT})$
  (b)  $\lim_{T\to\infty}E=1/a^2$

## Chapter 6 Review

1  $1, 0, -1/2, 0, 1$

3

$F(0)=1$

$x$

$F(0)=0$

5 (a)  Increasing for $x<-2$, $x>2$
   Decreasing for $-2<x<2$
   Local maximum at $x=-2$
   Local minimum at $x=2$
  (b)

$f(x)$

$x$

7

Point of inflection

$f(x)$

$x$

$x_1$ $x_2$ $x_3$ $x_4$

9  $t^3+(7t^2/2)+t$

11  $2x^3-4x^2+3x$

13  $x^3+5x$

15  $P(y)=\ln|y|+y^2/2+y+C$

17  $(2x+1)^4/8+C$

19  $2t^2+7t+C$

21  $(x^4/4)-(x^2/2)+C$

23  $-5/t-3/t^2+C$

25  $2x^2+2e^x+C$

27  $2x^3+C$

29  $x+\ln|x|+C$

31  $1/2$

33  $1-\cos 1\approx 0.460$

35  $(\ln 2)/2\approx 0.35$

37 $\int_0^2 (6x^2 + 1)\, dx = 18$

39 $b = 7$

41 1/30

43 (a) 18, 61.2, 198
  (b) $2\sqrt{b} - 2$
  (c) Does not converge

45 (a) No
  (b) $\int_0^\infty (60/50^t)\, dt$
  (c) Yes; 15.34 miles

47 (a) $p^* = \$11.43, q^* = 322$ units
  (b) Consumer surplus = \$2513.52;
      Producer surplus = \$1033.62

49 \$85,750,000

51 \$4026.35

53 \$1,147.75

55 33 billion m$^3$/year

57 $F(x) = -7x^2/2$
  (only possibility)

59 $0.5 \sin(t^2) + C$

61 $\ln(x^2 + 1) + C$

63 $\frac{1}{14}(x^2 + 9)^7 + C$

65 $-e^{-x} + C$

67 $-2\sqrt{4 - x} + C$

69 Approximately 77

71 $-y \cos y + \sin y + C$

73 $2x \ln x - 2x + C$

## Ch. 6 Understanding

1 True
3 True
5 True
7 True
9 False
11 True
13 False
15 True
17 False
19 True
21 False
23 True
25 False
27 False
29 False
31 True
33 False
35 True
37 False
39 True
41 True
43 False
45 False
47 True
49 False
51 False
53 False
55 False
57 True
59 True
61 False

63 False
65 False
67 True
69 False

## Chap. 6: Practice

1 $(1/18)(y^2 + 5)^9 + C$
3 $u^5/5 + 5u + C$
5 $-e^{-3t}/3 + C$
7 $ax^3/3 + bx + C$
9 $(x^4/4) + 2x^2 + 8x + C$
11 $q^2/2 - 1/(2q^2) + C$
13 $q^3/3 + 5q^2/2 + 2q + C$
15 $4 \ln |x| - 5/x + C$
17 $-3 \cos \theta + C$
19 $p^3/3 + 5 \ln |p| + C$
21 $-5 \cos x + 3 \sin x + C$
23 $Aq^2/2 + Bq + C$
25 $\pi h r^3/3 + C$
27 $5p^3 q^4 + C$
29 $x^3 + 3e^{2x} + C$
31 $p^4/4 + \ln |p| + C$
33 $\ln |y + 2| + C$
35 $x^3/3 + 8x + e^x + C$
37 $a \ln |x| - b/x + C$
39 $\frac{1}{2} e^{2t} + 5t + C$
41 $P_0 e^{kt}/k + C$
43 $-(A/B) \cos(Bt) + C$
45 $\ln(2 + e^x) + C$
47 $(1/2)x^2 \ln x - (1/4)x^2 + C$

## Section 7.1

1 (a) 0.25
  (b) 0.7
  (c) 0.15

3 (a) 0.4375
  (b) 0.49
  (c) 0.2475

5 10–12: About 27%
  < 8: About 12%
  > 12: About 45%
  12–13 days

7 For small $\Delta x$ around 70, fraction of families
  with incomes in that interval about $0.05\Delta x$

9 0.04

11 0.008

13 (a) 0.19
  (b) Tenth; both same
  (c) 0.02, 0.38, 0.21

15

17

## Section 7.2

1 (a)

| $t$ | 0 | 1 | 2 | 3 | 4 | $\cdots$ |
|---|---|---|---|---|---|---|
| $P(t)$ | 0 | 0.60 | 0.975 | 1 | 1 | $\cdots$ |

(b) fraction of patients

3 (a) Cumulative distribution
      increasing
  (b) Vertical 0.2,
      horizontal 2

5 pdf; 1/4

7 cdf; 1

9 cdf; 1/3

11 (a)

(b)

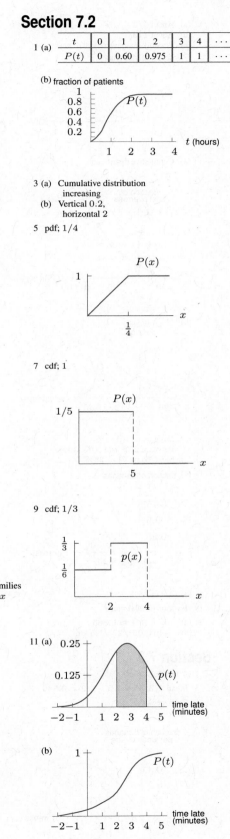

13 (a)  About 2/3
(b)  About 1/3
(c)  Possibly many work just to pass
(d) fraction of students

15 (a)  Cumulative distribution

fraction of
cost overruns

(b)  probability
density

(c)  More than 50%: 1%
Between 20% and 50%: 49%
Most likely: $C \approx 28\%$

17 (a) fraction of bananas

$P(t)$

(b)  About 25%
19  Fraction dead at time $t$
21 (a)  $-e^{-2} + 1 \approx 0.865$
(b)  $-(\ln 0.05)/2 \approx 1.5$ km

## Section 7.3

1  About 5.35 tons
3  Mean 2/3; Median $2 - \sqrt{2} = 0.586$
5  2.48 weeks

fraction of bananas
per week of age

7 (a)  0.684 : 1
(b)  1.6 hours
(c)  1.682 hours
9 (a)  0.2685
(b)  0.067
11 (a)  16.7%; 12.9%
(b)  About \$39,900
(c)  False

## Chapter 7 Review

1  1/15
3  1/5
5 fraction dying
per year

$x$ (years)

7  (a)-(II), (b)-(I), (c)-(III)
9     % of population
per dollar of income

income

% of population having
at least this income

income

11 (a)  Twelfth
(b)  1/4
(c)  7/16
13  About 30%
15 (a)  $f(r) = \begin{cases} 0 & \text{if } r \leq 0 \\ 0.2 & \text{if } 0 < r < 5 \\ 0 & \text{if } r \geq 5 \end{cases}$
(b)  $F(r) = \begin{cases} 0 & \text{if } r \leq 0 \\ 0.2r & \text{if } 0 < r < 5 \\ 1 & \text{if } r \geq 5 \end{cases}$
(c)  $g(v) = \begin{cases} 0 & \text{if } v \leq 0 \\ 0.0413v^{-2/3} & \text{if } 0 < v < 523.6 \\ 0 & \text{if } v \geq 523.6 \end{cases}$
17  Density function

0.14

Mar  Jun  Sep  Dec

Cumulative distribution function

1

Mar  Jun  Sep  Dec

19  14.6 days
21  False
23  True
25  True

## Ch. 7 Understanding

1  False
3  True
5  False
7  True
9  True
11  True
13  False
15  False
17  False
19  False
21  True
23  False
25  True
27  True
29  True

## Section 8.1

3 (a)  Decreasing
(b)  Decreasing
5  Increasing function
9  Decreasing function of $p$
Increasing function of $a$
11 (a)  $81°F$
(b)  30%
13  Incr of $A$ and $r$
Decr of $t$
15

$V$

$t = 2$

$t = 1$

$d$

## Section 8.2

1  Decreasing function of $x$
Increasing function of $y$
3  Answers in $°C$:
(a)

10
0
−10

(b)

15
10
5

(c)

30
35
40

(d)

5 Contours evenly spaced parallel lines

7 Contours evenly spaced parallel lines

9 Contours evenly spaced parallel lines

11

13

15 Elevation in meters

17 predicted high temperature

19 (a) $\pi = 3q_1 + 12q_2 - 4$
(thousand dollars)

21 Contours evenly spaced

23 (a) False
(b) True
(c) False
(d) True

25 (a) About $0°F$
(b) About $-16°F$
(c) About 23 mph
(d) About $25°F$

27 (a) $A$
(b) $B$
(c) $A$

29

31 (a) 4 hours
(b) 40%
(c) Contours approx horizontal
(d) Increasing
(e) Increasing

33 (a) is (II)
(b) is (I)

35 (a) $s(x, y) = xy = 16$

(b) 4
(c) 6

# Section 8.3

1 (a) Positive
(b) Negative
(c) Positive
(d) Zero

3 $\frac{\partial I}{\partial H}\big|_{(10,100)} \approx 0.4$
$\frac{\partial I}{\partial T}\big|_{(10,100)} \approx 1$

5 (a) $f_c$ is negative
$f_t$ is positive

7 $\partial Q/\partial b < 0$
$\partial Q/\partial c > 0$

9 $z_x(1, 0) \approx 2$
$z_x(0, 1) \approx 0$
$z_y(0, 1) \approx 10$

11 (a) Negative

13 2.9; 0.02

15 $\partial f/\partial P_1 < 0$
$\partial f/\partial P_2 > 0$

19 2777

21 14 %

23 (a)

530

(b)

(c)

(d)

25 (a) $-2$ Grapes/Cherry
(b) No change in happiness when replacing 2 grapes with one cherry

## Section 8.4

1 $f_x = 2x + 2y$
$f_y = 2x + 3y^2$

3 $200xy; 100x^2$

5 $2xe^y$

7 $15a^2t^2$

9 $f_x = 20xe^{3y}$,
$f_y = 30x^2e^{3y}$.

11 $(1/2)v^2$

13 $(a+b)/2$

15 $15; 5; 30$

17 (a) $3.3, 2.5$
(b) $4.1, 2.1$
(c) $4, 2$

19 $80; 30; 313$ tons
$2.9$ tons per worker
$2.6$ tons per $\$25,000$

21 $f_{xx} = 2y, f_{xy} = 2x$,
$f_{yy} = 0, f_{yx} = 2x$

23 $f_{xx} = 2, f_{xy} = 2$,
$f_{yy} = 2, f_{yx} = 2$

25 $f_{xx} = 2y^2, f_{xy} = 4xy$,
$f_{yy} = 2x^2, f_{yx} = 4xy$

27 $B_{xx} = 0, B_{tt} = 20xe^{-2t}$,
$B_{xt} = B_{tx} = -10e^{-2t}$

29 $f_{rr} = 100t^2e^{rt}, f_{tt} = 100r^2e^{rt}$,
$f_{tr} = f_{rt} = 100(rt+1)e^{rt}$

31 $V_{rr} = 2\pi h, V_{hh} = 0$,
$V_{rh} = V_{hr} = 2\pi r$

33 $f(x, y) = x^4y^2 - 3xy^4 + C$

35 (a) $(c+1)/(c+r)$
(b) Positive

37 (a) $(r-1)B/(c+r)^2$
(b) Negative

## Section 8.5

1 $f(2, 10) \approx 0.5$ local and global min
$f(6, 4) \approx 9.5$ local max
$f(6.5, 16) \approx 10$ local and global max
$f(9, 10) \approx 4$ local min

3 Max: $11$ at $(5.1, 4.9)$
Min: $-1$ at $(1, 3.9)$

5 Max: $1$ at $(\pi/2, 0); (\pi/2, 2\pi)$
Min: $-1$ at $(\pi/2, \pi)$

7 Saddle pt: $(-3, 6)$

9 Saddle pt: $(4, 2)$

11 Local max: $(-1, 0)$
Saddle pts: $(1, 0), (-1, 4)$
Local min: $(1, 4)$

13 Local min: $(2, 2)$

15 Local max: $(1, 5)$

17 $A = 10, B = 4, C = -2$

19 (b) $p_1 = p_2 = 25$
Max revenue is $4375$

21 $q_1 = 300, q_2 = 225$.

## Section 8.6

1 Min $= -\sqrt{2}$, max $= \sqrt{2}$

3 $f(10, 25) = 250$

5 $f(12, 4) = 240$

7 Min $= \frac{3}{4}$, no max

9 Min $= 11.25$; no max

11 (a) Point $F$
(b) Point $D$

13 (a) $Q = x_1^{0.3}x_2^{0.7}$
(b) $10x_1 + 25x_2 = 50,000$

15 (b) $L = 40, K = 30$

17 (a) Reduce $K$ by $1/2$ unit,
increase $L$ by $1$ unit.

19 (a) $P(x, y); C(x, y) = 50,000$

(b) $C(x, y); P(x, y) = 2000$

21 (a) $P(K, L)$
(b) $C(K, L) = 600,000$
(c) Tons/dollar
(d) Extra dollar produces approximately extra $3.17$ tons

23 (a) Quantity of fuel, $x_1 + x_2$

(b) Terminal velocity (as function of $x_1$ and $x_2$)
$= v_0$
(c) Liters per meter/sec
(d) $51$ meters/sec requires about $8$ more liters than $50$ meters/sec

25 $1820.04$; about $209$

## Chapter 8 Review

1 Decreasing function of $x$
Increasing function of $y$

3 Lines with slope $3/5$, evenly spaced

9 $x$-axis: apple juice
$y$-axis: orange juice

13 (a) About $\$122$
(b) About $\$350$

15 (A) I
(B) II
(C) III

17 (a) Payment $\$376.59$/mo at $1\%$ for $24$ mos
(b) $4.7¢$ extra/mo for $\$1$ increase
(c) Approx $\$44.83$ increase for $1\%$ interest increase

19 $f_T(5, 20) \approx 1.2°\text{F}/°\text{F}$

21 $\partial q/\partial I > 0$
$\partial q/\partial p_1 < 0$
$\partial q/\partial p_2 > 0$

25 $f_x = 2x + y, f_y = 2y + x$

27 $\dfrac{\partial Q}{\partial p_1} = 50p_2$,
$\dfrac{\partial Q}{\partial p_2} = 50p_1 - 2p_2$

29 $\dfrac{\partial P}{\partial K} = 7K^{-0.3}L^{0.3}$,
$\dfrac{\partial P}{\partial L} = 3K^{0.7}L^{-0.7}$

31 $\$102,116$
Additional $\$201.20$ per unit
Additional $\$101.50$ per unit

33 (a) 

height(ft)

$t = 1$

height(ft)

$t = 5$

height(ft)

$t = 14$

(b) location

time

(c) The "wave" at a sports arena

35 Local min: $(1, 0)$
Saddle pt: $(-1, 0)$

37 (a) $517p_1 - 3.5p_1^2 + 770p_2 - 4.4p_2^2 + 2.2p_1p_2$
(b) $p_1 = 110, p_2 = 115$

39 43

41 (a) $C = 127x_1 + 92x_2$
(b) $x_1^{0.6}x_2^{0.4} = 500$
(c) 1 unit decrease in production gives approx $219 reduction in cost

43 (a) 2599

(b) 129; $4,712,958

(c) $8572.54 per car

45 (a) 475 units
(b) 505 units

## Ch. 8 Understanding

1 False
3 False
5 True
7 True
9 False
11 True
13 True
15 True
17 True
19 True

21 True
23 True
25 False
27 True
29 True
31 True
33 True
35 False
37 False
39 True
41 False
43 True
45 False
47 True
49 True
51 False
53 False
55 True
57 True
59 False

## Theory: Least Squares

1 $y = 2/3 - (1/2)x$
3 $y = 2/3 - (1/2)x$
5 $y = x - 1/3$
7 (a) (i) Power function
(ii) Linear function
(b) $\ln N = 1.20 + 0.32 \ln A$
Agrees with biological rule

## Section 9.1

1 (a) (III)
(b) (IV)
(c) (I)
(d) (II)

3 $dP/dt = kP, k > 0$
5 $dQ/dt = kQ, k < 0$
7 $dP/dt = -0.08P - 30$
9 $dA/dt = -1$
11 (a) $dA/dt = -0.17A$
(b) $-17$ mg
13 (a) Increasing, decreasing
(b) $W = 4$
15 $dN/dt = B + kN$

## Section 9.2

1 (a) Yes
(b) No
3 $y = t^2 + C$
5 F
7 E
9 A
11 D
13 4, 4, 4, 4
15 12, 18, 27, 40.5
17 74, 78.8, 84.56 million
19 $k = -0.03$ and $C$ is any number, or $C = 0$ and $k$ is any number
21 $k = 5$

## Section 9.3

1 Other answers possible

3

5 (a)

(b) $y = -x - 1$
7 (a) III
(b) VI
(c) V
(d) I
(e) IV
(f) II
9 III: $dP/dt = 3P(1 - P)$
11 For starting points $y > 0$:
$y \to \infty$ as $x \to \infty$
For starting points $y = 0$:
$y = 0$ for all $x$
For starting points $y < 0$:
$y \to -\infty$ as $x \to \infty$
13 As $x \to \infty$, $y \to \infty$
15 $y \to 4$ as $x \to \infty$

## Section 9.4

1 $P = 20e^{0.02t}$
3 $y = 5.6e^{-0.14x}$
5 $p = 164.87e^{-0.1q}$

7 (a) $dB/dt = 0.015B$
   (b) $B = 5000e^{0.015t}$
   (c) \$5809.17

9 (a) $dB/dt = 0.10B + 1000$
   (b) $B = 10{,}000e^{0.1t} - 10{,}000$

11 Michigan: 72 years
   Ontario: 18 years

13 (a) $dQ/dt = -0.5365Q$
   $Q = Q_0 e^{-0.5365t}$
   (b) 4 mg

15 (a) 69,300 barrels/year
   (b) 25.9 years

17 (b) 2070

## Section 9.5

1 $y = 200 - 150e^{0.5t}$

3 $H = 75 - 75e^{3t}$

5 $B = 25 - 5e^{4t}$

7 $B = 25 + 75e^{2-2t}$

11 $dB/dt = 0.08B - 5000$,
   $B = 62{,}500 - 12{,}500e^{0.08t}$,
   Yes, in 20.1 years

13 (a) $dB/dt = 0.07B - 1000$
   (b) $B \approx \$14{,}285.71$
   (c) $B = 14{,}285.71 - (4285.71)e^{0.07t}$
   (d) $B(5) \approx \$8204$
   (e) Balance is \$0 in long run

$B$ (\$)

10,000
8000
6000
4000
2000

4  8  12  16   $t$ (years)

15 (b) $dQ/dt = 43.2 - 0.082Q$
   (c) $Q = 526.8 - 526.8e^{-0.082t}$
   $Q \to 526.8$ mg as $t \to \infty$

$Q$ (mg)

526.8

$Q = 526.8(1 - e^{-0.082t})$

20  40  60   $t$

17 (a) $dy/dt = -k(y - a)$
   (b) $y = (1 - a)e^{-kt} + a$
   (c) $a$: fraction remembered in the long run
   $k$: relative rate material is forgotten

19 (a) $y = 3$ and $y = -2$
   (b) $y = 3$ is unstable
   $y = -2$ is stable

21 (a) $H = 200 - 180e^{-kt}$
   (b) $k \approx 0.027$ (if $t$ is in minutes)

23 (a) $dT/dt = -k(T - 68)$
   (b) $T = 68 + 22.3e^{-0.06t}$;
   3:45 am.

## Section 9.6

1 (a) $x \to \infty$ exponentially
   $y \to 0$ exponentially

(b) $y$ is helped by the presence of $x$

3 (a) $x$ population grows exponentially
   $y$ population grows exponentially
   (b) Competitor relationship

5 $dx/dt = -x - xy$,
   $dy/dt = -y - xy$

7 $dx/dt = -x + xy$,
   $dy/dt = y$

11 Symmetric about the line $r = w$;
   solutions closed curves

13 Robins:
   Max $\approx 2500$
   Min $\approx 500$
   When robins are at a max,
   the worm population is about 1 million

17 (a) $dw/dt = 0$
   $dr/dt = 1.2$
   (b) $w \approx 2.2, r \approx 1.1$
   (c) At $t = 0.2$:
   $w \approx 2.2, r \approx 1.3$
   At $t = 0.3$
   $w \approx 2.1, r \approx 1.4$

19 (a) $r$ (predator)

4

3

2

1

1  2  3  4   $w$ (prey)

(b) Down and left
(c) $r = 3.3, w = 1$
(d) $w = 3.3, r = 1$

21 $x$ and $y$ increase, about same rate

23 $x$ decreases quickly while $y$ increases more slowly

25 (a) $dQ_1/dt = A - k_1Q_1 + k_2Q_2$
   (b) $dQ_2/dt = -k_3Q_2 + k_1Q_1 - k_2Q_2$

## Section 9.7

5 (a) $I_0 = 1, S_0 = 349$
   (b) Increases; spreads

7 About 300 boys;
   $t \approx 6$ days

9 5

11 (a) $b/a$

## Chapter 9 Review

1 (a) (III)
   (b) (V)
   (c) (I)
   (d) (II)
   (e) (IV)

3 Yes

5 (a) I is $y' = 1 + y$;
   II is $y' = 1 + x$

(b) I

$y$

2

1

-2  -1       1  2   $x$

-1

-2

II

$y$

2

1

-2  -1       1  2   $x$

-1

-2

(c) I: $y' = -1$, unstable;
   II: None

7 III: $y' = (1 + y)(2 - y)$

9 (a) $dB/dt = 0.07B$
   (b) $B = B_0 e^{0.07t}$
   (c) $B = 5000e^{0.07t}$
   (d) $B(10) \approx \$10{,}068.76$

11 $P = (1/2)t^2 + C$

13 $y = (5/2)t^2 + C$

15 $A = Ce^{-0.07t}$

17 $P = Ce^{-2t} + 5$

19 $y = Ce^{0.2x} + 40$

21 $dS/dt = -k(S - 65), k > 0$
   $S = 65 - 25e^{-kt}$

$S$ (°F)

65°
40°

$t$

23 (a) $k \approx 0.000121$
   (b) 779.4 years

25 (a)

$Q$

$Q_0$

$\frac{1}{2}Q_0$        $Q = Q_0 e^{-0.0187t}$

37   $t$

(b) $dQ/dt = -0.0187Q$
(c) 3 days

27 (b) $dQ/dt = -0.347Q + 2.5$
   (c) $Q = 7.2$ mg

29 (a) $dW/dt = (1/3500)(I - 20W)$
   (b) $W = I/20$, stable
   (c) $W = I/20 + (W_0 - I/20)e^{-(1/175)t}$
   (d)

$W$

160
150

100 days   $t$

**31** (a) $y = 1, y = 8, y = 16$
(d) Stable: $y = 1$
Unstable: $y = 8, y = 16$

## Ch. 9 Understanding

1 True
3 False
5 True
7 True
9 True
11 True
13 False
15 False
17 False
19 True
21 False
23 True
25 True
27 True
29 False
31 False
33 False
35 True
37 False
39 False
41 True
43 False
45 False
47 False
49 True
51 False
53 True
55 False
57 True
59 True
61 False
63 False
65 False
67 False
69 True

## Theory: Separation of Vars

1 $P = e^{-2t}$
3 $P = \sqrt{2t + 1}$
5 $u = 1/(1 - (1/2)t)$
7 $R = 1 - 0.9e^{1-y}$
9 $z = -\ln(1 - t^2/2)$
11 $y = -2/(t^2 + 2t - 4)$

13 (a) Yes (b) No (c) Yes
(d) No (e) Yes (f) Yes
(g) No (h) Yes (i) No
(j) Yes (k) Yes (l) No

15 $Q = b - Ae^{-t}$
17 $R = -(b/a) + Ae^{at}$
19 $y = -1/\left(k(t + t^3/3) + C\right)$

**21** (a)

(b)

(c) $y(x) = Ae^{x^2/2}$

## Section 10.1

1 21
3 Yes, $a = 5$, ratio $= -2$
5 Yes, $a = 2$, ratio $= 1/2$
7 Yes, $a = 1$, ratio $= 2z$
9 Yes, $a = y^2$, ratio $= y$
11 555.10
13 96.154
15 333.33
17 $3(2^{11} - 1)/2^{10}$
19 400
21 $-4/3$
23 30.51, 37.75,
39.47, 39.87, Yes
25 (a) $3007.51, $2507.51
(b) $6033.11, $5533.11
27 1.375 mg
29 (a) 40 mg
(b) 0.57 mg/kg, Yes
(c) (i) Greater than 100 kg
(ii) Less than 13.3 kg

## Section 10.2

1 Balance = $24,297.37,
$20,000 from deposits,
$4297.37 from interest
3 (a) $427,767.74
(b) $1,419,863.01
5 $2.02 million
7 (a) $153,237.99
(b) $343,333.33
9 (a) $1.27
(b) $163.83
(c) $20,971.51
(d) $2,684,354.55
11 (a) 5000 units
(b) $S_5 = 3362, S_{10} = 4463$,
$S_{15} = 4824, S_{20} = 4942$

13 $1081.11
15 (a) $1000
(b) When the interest rate is 5%, the present value equals the principal
(c) The principal
(d) Because the present value is more than the principal
17 (a) $400 billion
(b) $900 billion
19 (a) $1250
(b) 12.50

## Section 10.3

1 (a) 98 mg
(b) 121.5 mg
(c) 125 mg
3 (a) Oil supply never runs out
(b) Oil supply exhausted in 39.1 years
5 (a) 400 mg
(b) $400(0.30) = 120$ mg
7 (a) 0.7937
(b) 194.27 mg
(c) 242.37 mg
9 1604.0 micrograms
1596.0 micrograms
11 24.5 years
13 (a) 60 years
(b) 27.7 years
15 About 34 years
17 Lasts forever

## Chapter 10 Review

1 2046
3 Does not exist
5 200
7 1.9961
9 (a) (i) $16.43 million
(ii) $24.01 million
(b) $16.87 million
11 $27,979.34
13 $400 million
15 (a) $N(k/(1 - k))$
(b) $5.667N$
17 (a) $\approx 7\%$
(b) $Q_n = 50(1 - (0.07)^{n+1})/(1 - 0.07)$
(c) $P_n = 0.07(50)(1-(0.07)^n)/(1-0.07)$

## Ch. 10 Understanding

1 True
3 False
5 True
7 False
9 True
11 True
13 True
15 False
17 True
19 True
21 False
23 False
25 False
27 False
29 False

534

# Appendix A

1 (a)

G
50
40
30
20
10
10 20 30 40 50  t

(b)  Increasing at a rate of $734 billion/year
(c)  $43.9 trillion, $54.9 trillion,
     More confidence in the 2005 prediction

3 (a)
G (GNP)
10,000
8000
6000
4000
2000
10 20 30  t (years since 1970)

Yes

(b)
G (GNP)  $G = 473.7 + 294.47t$
10000
8000
6000
4000
2000
10 20 30  t (years since 1970)

$G = 294.47t + 473.7$

(c)  For 1985: 4891
     For 2020: 15,197
     More confidence in 1985

5 (a)  $S = 0.08v + 1.77$
(b)
S
3.6
3.4
3.2
3.0
16 18 20 22  v

Yes

(c)  At $v = 18$ ft/sec, $S = 3.21$
     At $v = 10$ ft/sec, $S = 2.57$
     $v = 18$ better

7 (a)  $0.0026 = 0.26\%$
(b)  For 1900, 272.27
     For 1980, 335.1

9 (a)
D (debt in $ bn)
8000
7000
6000
5000
1 2 3 4 5 6  yrs since 1998

(b)  Exponential

(c)  $D = 5309(1.048)^t$, answers may vary

D (debt in $ bn)
8000
7000
6000
5000
$D = 5309(1.048)^t$
1 2 3 4 5 6  yrs since 1998

(d)  About 4.8%
(e)  No

11 (a)  $r = 1$
(b)  $r = 0.7$
(c)  $r = 0$
(d)  $r = -0.98$
(e)  $r = -0.25$
(f)  $r = -0.5$

13 (a)  Exponential

W
6
4
2
20 40 60  t

(b)  $2.6(1.0165)^t$; answers may vary
(c)  1.65%
(d)  At year 2020, 8.175 billion
     At year 2050, 13.357 billion
     2020 prediction more accurate

15 (a)
number of cars (thousands)
600
400
200
1 2 3 4 5 6 7  years since 1964

(b)  Exponential
(c)  $C = 15.9 \cdot (1.725)^t$, answers may vary

C (number of cars, thousands)
600
400
200
$C = 15.9 \cdot (1.725)^t$
1 2 3 4 5 6 7  t (years since 1964)

(d)  About 73%

(e)  No

17 (a)  Negative
(b)  $f(t) = -0.03t^2 + 1.01t + 13.82$

E (mpg)
20
15
10
10 20  t (years since 1975)

19 (a)  Exponential
(b)  $S = 29.96(1.30)^t$, answers may vary
     Increasing 30%/yr
(c)  21,141 megawatts
(d)
S
2000
1000
5 10 15  t

21 (a)  Linear
(b)  $C = 320 + 1.5t$
     Increasing at 1.5 ppm/yr
(c)  387.5 ppm
(d)
C
400
375
350
325
10 20 30 40  t

# Appendix B

1  27%

3 (a)  $160,356.77
(b)  $165,510.22
(c)  $165,891.05
(d)  $165,989.48
(e)  $166,005.85

5 (a)  1.0408107
     1.0408108
     1.0408108
     4% compounded continuously
     $\approx 4.08108\%$
(b)  $e^{0.04} \approx 1.048108$

7  4.88%

9 (a)  (i)  5.126978...%
     (ii)  5.127096...%
     (iii)  5.127108...%
(b)  5.127%
(c)  $e^{0.05} = 1.05127109...$

11  (a) = V, (b) = III, (c) = IV,
    (d) = I, (e) = II

13 (a)  13,900 cruzados
(b)  24.52%

# PRETEST

The pretest in this section covers skills that are used in this book. Doing it at the start of a course will help you identify areas in algebra where reviewing early on will help you succeed.

## Problems for a Pretest

**1.** What is the equation of the line in Figure P.1?

**Figure P.1**

**2.** What is the value of $a$ in Figure P.2?

**Figure P.2**

**3.** Find $a_1$ and $a_2$ from Figure P.3.

**Figure P.3**

**4.** Match each of the four lines in Figure P.4 with one of the slopes $0, 1, 2, -1, -2$.

**Figure P.4**

**5.** Solve for $P_0$:

$$P = P_0 \left(1 + \frac{r}{n}\right)^t.$$

**6.** Solve for $r$:

$$P = \left(1 + \frac{r}{n}\right)^t.$$

**7.** If $f(t) = 4t + (t+3)^2$, find $f(0)$.

**8.** If $f(x) = 4x + 28$, solve $f(x) = 0$.

**9.** Which of the following is equivalent to $16 - x^2 + 6x$?

   **(a)** $7 + (3 - x)^2$
   **(b)** $16 - (x - 3)^2$
   **(c)** $25 - (x - 3)^2$
   **(d)** $52 - (x - 6)^2$
   **(e)** $25 - (x + 3)^2$
   **(f)** None of the above

**10.** What are the coordinates of the point $Q$ in Figure P.5?

**11.** What are the coordinates of the point $P$ in Figure P.5?

**Figure P.5**

**12.** Find $|-10| + |10|$.

**13.** Which of the following is equivalent to $\dfrac{T}{E} + E$?

   **(a)** $\dfrac{E^2 + T}{E}$

   **(b)** $\dfrac{E}{E^2 + T}$

   **(c)** $E + T$

   **(d)** $\dfrac{T + E}{E + 1}$

   **(e)** $\dfrac{T + E}{E}$

**14.** Which of the following is equivalent to $\dfrac{1}{y} + \dfrac{1}{u}$?

   **(a)** $\dfrac{1}{uy}$

   **(b)** $\dfrac{1}{u + y}$

   **(c)** $\dfrac{u + y}{uy}$

   **(d)** $\dfrac{u}{y}$

   **(e)** $\dfrac{2}{y + u}$

15. Which of the following is equivalent to $x^{-1}y + y^{-1}x$?

 (a) $\dfrac{xy}{x^2 + y^2}$

 (b) $\dfrac{x^2 + y^2}{xy}$

 (c) $\dfrac{xy}{x + y}$

 (d) $\dfrac{x + y}{xy}$

 (e) $\dfrac{y + x}{x + y}$

16. If $\dfrac{\sqrt[3]{t}}{t} = t^a$, what is $a$?

17. Simplify $(x^2 x^5)^4$.

18. Simplify $W^{2/3} W^{3/2}$.

19. Expand and collect like terms: $-5u\left(\dfrac{3}{u} - 2v\right)$.

20. Solve $3p + 4 = 9$ for $p$.

21. Solve $2x + a = 5(1 - x)$ for $x$.

22. Solve $2\sqrt{w} - 3 = 9$ for $w$.

23. Solve $\dfrac{2}{3} = \dfrac{5}{n}$ for $n$.

24. Solve $Cq + Dq = A$ for $q$.

25. With $m = 2, x_0 = 3, y_0 = 10$, solve $y - y_0 = m(x - x_0)$ for $x$.

26. Find the value of $x$ when $y = 0$ if $-2x + 9y - 9 = 0$.

27. Find the value of $s$ when $t = s + 1$ if $3s - 8t = 7$.

28. Factor $12x^2 - 6a^2x$.

29. Factor $C^2 a^3 b - Cab^3$.

30. Which of the following is the factored form of $x^2 + 2x - 15$?

 (a) $(x + 1)^2 - 16$
 (b) $(x - 3)(x + 5)$
 (c) $x(x + 2) - 15$
 (d) $(x + 2)(x - 15)$
 (e) None of the above

31. What are the zeroes of $(x - 2)(x + 1)(2x - 5)$?

32. What is the $y$-intercept of $y = (x - 2)(x + 1)(2x - 5)$?

33. If $W^2 - 2W - 8 = 4(W - 2)$, find all possible values of $W$.

34. If $s = d^2 + d + 1$ and $d = g + 1$ express $s$ in terms of $g$.

35. If $\theta = x^2 - 1$ express $(\theta + 1)^2$ in terms of $x$.

36. If $b = -2z$ express $b^2 - 2b$ in terms of $z$.

37. The graph of the equation $a^x = y$ passes through the point $(-3, \frac{1}{8})$. What is $a$?

38. If $s = 2$ and $t = 0$ is a solution to $as^5 = s^7 + t$, what is $a$?

39. Using Table P.1, what value of $w$ gives $q = 7$?

Table P.1

| $w$ | $-4$ | $-1$ | 1 | 6 | 10 |
|-----|------|------|---|----|----|
| $q$ | 4 | 2 | 7 | $-2$ | 2 |

40. Using Table P.2, what is the temperature at 6 pm?

Table P.2

| Time (hours after midnight) | 0 | 6 | 12 | 18 |
|------------------------------|---|---|----|----|
| Temperature (°F) | 36 | 48 | 65 | 55 |

41. For some constant $k$, let $M = kN$. If $M = 0.84$ when $N = 12$, what is $M$ when $N = 6$?

42. What is the area of the shaded rectangle in Figure P.6?

Figure P.6

43. What is the area of the shaded triangle in Figure P.6?

44. A price increases by a factor of 1.042. By what percent has the price increased?

45. A car, initially valued at $21,000 is now worth 32% less. What is the car's current value?

46. An item priced at $45 is on sale for 25% off. The customer pays the sale price plus 8% sales tax. How much does the customer pay?

## Problems on Trigonometry (Optional)

**1.** What is the vertical intercept of $y = \cos x$?

**2.** What are the zeroes of $y = \sin x$ between $x = 0$ and $x = 2\pi$ (inclusive)?

**3.** How many degrees is $3\pi$ radians?

**4.** What are the coordinates of the highest point on the sine graph in Figure P.7?

Figure P.7

# INDEX